To Adrienne —
God bless you!
Steve Ray
CATHOLICCONVERT.COM

ST. JOHN'S GOSPEL
A Bible Study Guide and Commentary

STEPHEN K. RAY

ST. JOHN'S GOSPEL

A Bible Study Guide and Commentary

IGNATIUS PRESS   SAN FRANCISCO

Nihil Obstat: The Reverend Monsignor Sylvester L. Fedewa
                Westphalia, Michigan

Imprimatur: + Carl F. Mengeling
                Bishop of Lansing

The nihil obstat and imprimatur are official declarations that a book or
pamplet is free of doctrinal or moral error. No implication is contained
therein that those who have granted the nihil obstat or imprimatur
agree with the contents, opinions, or statements expressed.

Cover art by Carl Bloch
The Samaritan Woman with Jesus by the Well
Det National Historiske Museum
Hilleroed, Denmark
Hope Gallery, Provo, Utah

Cover design by Riz Boncan Marsella

DEDICATION

To my wife, Janet,
who is my constant companion and best friend
in the study and teaching of the Bible
in our home and in the
Catholic Church

and

To Charles and Frances Ray—my dad and mom—
who taught me to love, study, and obey
the Sacred Scriptures
(2 Timothy 3:14–17)

To Ricardo Cardinal Vidal,
my friend and Archbishop of Cebu, the Philippines,
for his hospitality and for reading
and approving the manuscript for this book

To my friend Mark Brumley, whose countless hours
of tireless reading and editing helped
make this book a reality

Ignorance of Scripture is ignorance of Christ.

—ST. JEROME

*Now Jesus did many other signs in the presence of the disciples,
which are not written in this book; but these are written that you may believe
that Jesus is the Christ, the Son of God, and that believing
you may have life in his name.*

—JOHN 20:30–31

CONTENTS

ABBREVIATIONS

ANF   *The Ante-Nicene Fathers*. Edited by Alexander Roberts and James Donaldson. 10 vols. Grand Rapids, Mich.: Wm. B. Eerdmans, 1985.

CCC   *Catechism of the Catholic Church*. 2d ed. Vatican City: Libreria Editrice Vaticana, 2000.

JB   Jerusalem Bible.

Knox   Ronald A. Knox, trans. *The New Testament of Our Lord and Saviour Jesus Christ*. New York: Sheed & Ward, 1954.

KJV   King James Version of the Bible.

NASB   New American Standard Bible.

NIV   New International Version of the Bible.

NPNF1   *Nicene and Post-Nicene Fathers*. 1st series. Edited by Philip Schaff. 14 vols. Grand Rapids, Mich.: Wm. B. Eerdmans, 1980.

NPNF2   *Nicene and Post-Nicene Fathers*. 2d series. Edited by Philip Schaff and Henry Wace. 14 vols. Grand Rapids, Mich.: Wm. B. Eerdmans, 1982.

RSV   Revised Standard Version of the Bible.

INTRODUCTION

The Bible is a rich vein of gold in a vast mine shaft. The gold is pure and lovely, and there for the taking. Christians are invited to dig deeply, and many have become enriched beyond words with the result of their labor. The mining tools are inexpensive, the fellow miners anxious to help, and the rewards magnificent.

The Gospel of John is one of the richest veins. Of all literature, in all the world, through all of time, the Gospel of St. John rises to the top. It is not without reason that in art St. John is often portrayed with an eagle. The eagle represents the lofty heights of inspired writing to which St. John soars. He is called the "theologian" and the "philosopher". More than that, he reveals the very heart of God. Meditating on the sacred text of his Gospel draws us inexorably into a great cosmic love affair with God himself.

Even though the Catholic Church has been the custodian of the Bible from the beginning and has encouraged the faithful to know and cherish it, Catholics have often neglected to study the Bible in their daily lives. They have shown great reverence for the biblical text in worship and song. It is held aloft in the entrance procession that begins our Mass. Theologians and other scholars have analyzed every jot and tittle, and the Mass celebrates the inspired words throughout the elegant liturgy. But, in general, Catholics have not pursued a personal study of the Bible as passionately as many Evangelical Protestants have. However, as the Spirit of God breathes anew on his Church at the beginning of the third millennium, there is a growing desire on the part of Catholics to study and know the Bible in all of its richness. This book is a response to that desire and to the breath of God upon his Church.

What do we need to mine the depths of God's written word? Along with a few good translations of the Bible and the time and desire to study, a helpful tool for every miner's backpack is a good Bible study guide. That is what this book is intended to be. This book will provide a blueprint and instructions for mining. We will provide some background material to the Gospel of St. John and some simple principles for biblical interpretation. The heart of the study will provide detailed questions and guidance to guarantee the student/miner a rich experience.

Moreover, this book is designed to be more than a study guide; it can also be used as a scriptural commentary, a study of Church teaching, a manual of Catholic apologetics, an introduction to the Fathers of the Church, and a study of history and culture during the time of Christ. Most importantly, it is hoped that this book will enhance and deepen your spiritual life—your daily walk with Jesus in the heart of his Church.

For Catholics involved in "ecumenical" or "nondenominational" Bible studies, this book provides supplemental material often neglected or overlooked in such a setting. It will help you explain the Catholic faith and why we believe as we do. And it will help demonstrate not only why Catholic teaching is biblical but also how it captures the fullness of the Christian faith and how it is in continuity with historic Christianity—the Christianity of the apostles and the Fathers of the Church.

Bible study is not only a privilege of the Christian, it is above all an *obligation*. As the *Catechism of the Catholic Church* states, quoting one of the Church's great biblical scholars, St. Jerome, "The Church 'forcefully and specifically exhorts all the Christian faithful . . . to learn "the surpassing knowledge of Jesus Christ," by frequent reading of the divine Scriptures. "Ignorance of the Scriptures is ignorance of Christ." ' " [1]

Simple Guidelines for Studying the Bible

To study and interpret the Bible correctly, certain rules and guidelines need to be understood and practiced. The technical term for biblical interpretation is *hermeneutics* (from the Greek *hermeneuein*, which simply means "to interpret"). To interpret the Bible properly, we must bear in mind that the Bible is a book of many different types of literature. There are seventy-three separate documents that make up the Bible—forty-six in the Old Testament and twenty-seven in the New Testament.

Though the Bible is more than literature, it is not less than that for being more. Some passages are history, others are poetry or epic; still others are didactic, prophetic, instructional, philosophical, apocalyptic, biographical, or even Jewish folk wisdom. The spectrum of literary types includes just about every known genre and style. As with any

---

[1] CCC 133, quoting *DV* 25; cf. Phil 3:8 and St. Jerome, *Commentariorum in Isaiam libri xviii* prol.: PL 24, 17b.

written document, the Bible needs to be interpreted in its context, both textually and historically. Our goal must be to discover the intent and purpose of the given biblical author and how the audience was inclined to understand and receive his work.

Catholic and Protestant Approaches

Catholics and Protestants differ significantly in their approaches to the Bible, even though they also agree upon much. Since the days of the apostles, the Church's sacred tradition has always been an essential and welcome component in the interpretation of holy Scripture. The Catholic view was (and is) that one holy, catholic, and apostolic Church is the home of the Bible, because the Church is "the pillar and bulwark [foundation] of the truth" (1 Tim 3:15). But Martin Luther took a new approach and, to put it simply, rejected all authority as binding on the Christian except the text of the Bible. He rejected sacred tradition and the teaching office of the Church as not being authoritative and ended up with the Bible alone—*sola Scriptura*.

Luther's new methodology was not only unbiblical, unhistorical, and unworkable, it helped bring about the confusion and chaos we see in Christendom today: thousands upon thousands of competing and separate denominations all claiming to have a corner on the truth. The confusion could be likened to a United States inhabited only by individuals who decided to interpret and apply the Constitution for themselves, without a government—the legislature, courts, and president all having been rejected. In no time, our land would be divided into thousands of warring city-states, each claiming the proper interpretation of the Constitution and the right to rule.

"Bible Christians", following the innovation of *sola Scriptura*, tend to approach their study of the Bible with the following tenets in mind:

1. There is no infallible authority outside the Bible alone.

2. There is no official interpretation or interpreter of the Bible.

3. The Bible is perspicuous (easy to understand).

4. Any individual can read the Bible and interpret it for himself.

Catholics, on the other hand, following the age-old teaching and practice of the Church from earliest times, and from the Jews before them, use a different set of interpretive principles to direct their study of the Bible:

1. The authority of the apostles and the Church preceded the New Testament writings, and the tradition of the Church is an equally infallible authority flowing from the same divine wellspring (2 Thess 2:15; CCC 80–83).

2. The authoritative interpretation of the Bible is the prerogative of the Catholic Church through the living Magisterium (CCC 85–88).

3. The Bible is not always easy to understand (2 Pet 3:15–16) and needs to be considered within its historical and contextual framework—within the community to which it belongs.

4. Individuals can and must interpret the Bible within the framework of the Church's authoritative teaching, not based on their "own [private] interpretation" (2 Pet 1:20–21).

These basic differences can leave Catholic and Protestant readers worlds apart, even though they read the same book and accept it as an authoritative revelation from God. Their respective methodologies set them in different camps and insure very different results in Bible study. As a convert to the Catholic Church and one who has lived and taught the Bible in both camps, I can personally attest to the different approaches and results.

Misconceptions among Catholics

Two misconceptions about the Bible have sometimes plagued Catholics. First, some Catholics have thought they were not supposed to read the Bible, lest they misinterpret it and end up confused. Second, some have thought that studying the Bible is for Protestants. "Well, isn't the Bible hard to understand? Aren't Catholics forbidden to read the Bible?" some Catholics ask. "Shouldn't we leave Scripture study to priests and religious? If laymen study the Bible, don't they interpret it incorrectly and go off the deep end?"

A parish priest recently visiting our home lamented, "Oh, if I could only get my parishioners over the deep-seated fear that if they study the Bible they will somehow become Fundamentalist Protestants!" This sounds strange to those of us who have converted to the Catholic Church from Protestantism: it was the love and study of the Bible that brought us *into* the Catholic Church. Yet, this fear prevents many Catholics from dusting off the family Bible and making a go at personal study.

Perhaps the following illustration will help answer the concerns of some Catholics. Imagine children running and tussling in the grass of a playground. The playground is unsupervised, with a sharp cliff dropping a thousand feet on one side and a bog of quicksand on the other side. With anguish you observe the number of children rapidly diminish, as they fall prey to the dangers around them.

Now imagine the same children carefully supervised and surrounded by a secure, chain-link fence. To be in danger now, a child would have to disregard all the rules and protective measures. You relax, a sigh of relief passes your lips, and you begin to chuckle at the children's antics.

Our imagined playground illustrates the situation nicely. *Are* there real dangers associated with studying the Bible? Do pitfalls lie to the left and right? Yes, of course. Survey the landscape of Christian history, and you will see well-meaning individuals and groups strewn in every direction. Over thirty thousand competing denominations² —all studying the same Bible and arriving at just as many divergent conclusions—demonstrate this quite adequately. The division brought about by the "Bible-only" theology is evident (cf. 2 Pet 3:15–17). Yet, many people have loved the Bible deeply, read it studiously, and have benefited from it. They have grown to love Jesus and the Catholic Church with ever deepening ardor. What differentiates the two results? Why do some stumble and fall by the wayside, while others "play" with joyful abandon—almost carefree in their study of Scriptures—and, seemingly, with no fear of falling?

The *fence* and the *supervision* make all the difference. They provide a barrier between the children and destruction. They allow the child to frolic carefree. The *fence* is the basic understanding of how to study the Bible, and the *supervision* is the tradition and teaching of the Catholic Church. These two things—readily available to anyone who desires them—make the difference. The dangers are real, but the protections and guidance are just as real. Those who follow the simple guidelines and avoid falling over the cliff or into quicksand will study the Scriptures with great benefit, deep joy, and pleasure.

The basic principles of biblical interpretation are carefully laid out in the *Catechism of the Catholic Church*, paragraphs 109–19. The student of Scripture should become familiar with these age-old principles. In

---

² According to the *World Christian Encyclopedia*, in the year 1970 there were 26,350 Christian denominations. By the year 2000, the number had risen to 33,820 denominations and paradenominations (David. B. Barrett, *World Christian Encyclopedia* [New York: Oxford Univ. Press, 1982], 1:10).

addition, one should read a given passage in context—the immediate context of the passage itself, that of the particular biblical book in which the text appears, and that of the whole Bible and salvation history. Scripture helps interpret other parts of Scripture. Furthermore, we need to understand the historical background and cultural circumstances of Scripture as much as possible. We will provide much of that information for you as you study *St. John's Gospel.*

The Four Simple Steps: Observe, Inquire, Interpret, and Apply

A simple formula will help both the beginning student and the veteran keep on track in studying the Bible. Remember these four words: *Observe, Inquire, Interpret,* and *Apply.* Let us look at each one carefully.

Observe: Read the passage in context. It is always best to read the whole biblical book in which the passage is found. An epistle of Paul can be read in one sitting—even some of the longer books of the Bible can be read in an hour or two. Notice the book's flow and the progression of thought or argument. Try to follow the author and read the passage in the larger context, not just the verse or two in question.

Remember that the chapter and verse divisions of the Bible were not part of the original text. They were added centuries later.[3] The Bible was not intended to be a book of proof texts—a random collection of numbered sayings. Though the chapter and verse divisions are helpful in finding our way around the Bible, we must remember that they are artificial divisions.

Inquire: Ask questions—a whole lot of questions. Do not be embarrassed. There are no dumb questions when searching the Scriptures. Employ the six honest helpers to assist you: Who, What, Where, When, Why, and How. Keep a note pad at your side and write down your questions. This study guide will provide sample questions to direct you along the path.

Ask yourself how a particular New Testament passage relates to the Old Testament. Are there any words used repeatedly? How might they lead us to understand a key theme? Who are the main characters? What

---

[3] It was probably Stephen Langton (d. 1228), archbishop of Canterbury, who worked out the present chapter divisions. The verse divisions of the New Testament appeared first in a Greek New Testament published in 1551 by Robert Étienne (Stephanus), a Paris printer. In 1555, he published an edition of the Latin Vulgate, which was the first Bible to have the present chapters and verses. The first English Bible with such divisions was the Geneva edition of 1560.

is unique about them? Who were the original readers, and how would they have understood this passage? Remember that the Bible is largely a Jewish book—St. Luke was probably the only non-Jewish writer—and it must be read with this in mind. Were the recipients of a particular text struggling with special problems? What is the problem or situation being addressed? Where was the author writing from and where were his readers located? What figures of speech or anecdotes does the author use? Are rhetorical questions or sarcasm used? What deeper meanings may be suggested? Ask as many questions as possible!

Interpret: Research other books you may have on hand, such as Bible commentaries, Bible dictionaries, history books, encyclopedias, and Bible atlases. Discover as much background material and history as you can. Finding answers to the many questions you ask will help you interpret the passage. What is the literal meaning of the text? Is there a deeper meaning than meets the eye? (We will frequently discover deeper meanings in St. John's Gospel.) Decide what the intent of the author was and what the passage is trying to get across. Remember to interpret poetry as poetry, history as history, epistles as letters, and so on.

Compare Scripture with Scripture. It is helpful if you have a Bible with some good cross references and footnotes that can lead you to similar passages. These other passages can enlighten you and expand your understanding of the verses you are studying. Also, consider how the Church has interpreted a passage throughout history. For example, what did the Fathers of the Church teach regarding this passage?

The *Catechism of the Catholic Church* is a marvelous gift of God and a valuable resource for Bible study. Check the scriptural index in the back of the *Catechism* to see if a particular verse is referred to. That can help with the proper interpretation of a text. Again, this study guide will provide much of this information for you.

Write your comments and answers to the questions you pose to yourself in your notebook. Keep track of the truths you discover. Record the insights that the Holy Spirit brings to your mind and heart. Draw conclusions as you interpret, and look through a few commentaries to see if others have discovered the same things. It is always wise to second-guess yourself by comparing your findings with those of other Scripture students and scholars. Always challenge your conclusions by holding them up to the light of Catholic teaching.

Apply: The ultimate goal of all biblical study is, of course, to change our lives and bring us to a closer union with God. Our minds should be enlightened and instructed, our hearts cleansed and made desirous of

God, our spirits renewed and lifted, and our walk with God deepened in faith, hope, and love (Rom 15:4; 1 Cor 10:11). Pray about what you have learned. Ask God to apply the particular passage you study to every aspect of your life (2 Tim 3:16–17) and to probe every dark corner and shed light throughout. Let the sacred Scriptures resonate through your whole being. Ask the Holy Spirit of God, the primary author of the text, to fill every corner of your being with his holy light, to convict of sin, righteousness, and judgment (Jn 16:8).

Which Translation to Use?

There is no definitive answer to this question, though for this study we primarily use the trusted *Revised Standard Version, Catholic Edition*, published by Ignatius Press. It is a reliable Catholic translation. However, a student of the Scriptures should have several good translations from which to read. Translations vary widely, from very literal translations to paraphrases of the text. There is a sliding scale between these two poles. *Literal* translations may be harder to read and therefore less understandable; *dynamic* texts may be easier to read but tend to stray from the literal meaning of the text, and denominational biases are more likely to intrude into the translation.

Of course, being able to read Hebrew and Greek [4] would be marvelous, but that is not an option for most of us. We must depend upon competent scholars and translations to communicate the message of the Scriptures. In addition to Ignatius Press' edition of the *Revised Standard Version, Catholic Edition* already mentioned, there are also the *Jerusalem Bible*, the *New American Bible,* and the older *Douay-Rheims*. The *New American Bible* comes in many popular study editions with notes, maps, and other helpful study materials.

Catholic study Bibles are becoming more common and should be of great benefit. Try to find such a study Bible with cross-references, maps, outlines, concordances, and other helpful tools.

Catholic Bibles include the seven Deuterocanonical books not found in most Protestant Bibles: Judith, Tobit, Wisdom, Sirach, Baruch, and First and Second Maccabees. As inspired texts, these books belong to the canon of Scripture, and your Bible should include them (CCC 120).

---

[4] Most of the Old Testament was written in Hebrew, although part of Daniel is in Aramaic and some of the Deuterocanonical books were apparently originally written in Greek. The New Testament was written in Greek, although some scholars have argued that Matthew's Gospel may have been originally written in Hebrew or Aramaic.

Various Protestant versions can also be helpful, including the *New American Standard Bible*, the *King James Version* and its latest revision, the *New King James Version*, the *New English Bible*, and the *Amplified Bible*, to mention a few. The *Jewish New Testament* by David Stern is an interesting and helpful translation that brings out the Jewishness of the New Testament. He also wrote the extremely helpful *Jewish New Testament Commentary*.

The *New International Version*, though widely acclaimed among Evangelicals and easy to read, tends to take liberties with the meaning of the original text, including a substantial Protestant bias in translation.[5] The *King James Version*, though beautifully written, has become outdated, with more accurate translations taking its place.

Additional Resources

We will be referring to a wide range of sources—Catholic, secular, Jewish, and non-Catholic Christian—to provide background material, theological insights, and historical information. From within the Catholic Church, we will learn from the Fathers, Church documents, commentaries, the writings of saints and Doctors of the Church, and modern theologians and Bible scholars. Even more frequently, we will refer to the *Catechism*. An eclectic and wide-ranging investigation is a necessary ingredient of scholarship, Bible study, and honest inquiry.

It should be abundantly clear that the use of any material from a particular tradition or author is in *no way* an endorsement of everything within that particular tradition or everything proposed or denied by a particular author. We are gleaning helpful information from many sources. Everyone will not agree with everything our sources have written or taught. A particular theologian or commentary on Scripture may provide invaluable historical or textual insights and yet fall short of the fullness of Catholic teaching in other areas. As mature Catholics, we must learn to be discerning and to glean what is good from our sources, while discarding what lacks the fullness of truth. All truth is God's truth, and it can be found in many sources.

As the Pontifical Biblical Commission has said,

---

[5] An example of this can be seen where the Greek word for "tradition", *paradosis* (παράδοσις), is translated in the NIV as "teaching", instead of "tradition". This can be seen in I Corinthians 11:2 and 2 Thessalonians 2:15 and 3:6. The Greek word for teaching is *didache* (διδαχή).

Through the adoption of the same methods and analogous hermeneutical points of view, exegetes of various Christian confessions have arrived at a remarkable level of agreement in the interpretation of Scripture, as is shown by the text and notes of a number of ecumenical translations of the Bible, as well as by other publications.

Indeed, it is clear that on some points differences in the interpretation of Scripture are often stimulating and can be shown to be complementary and enriching. Such is the case when these differences express values belonging to the particular tradition of various Christian communities and so convey a sense of the manifold aspects of the Mystery of Christ.

Since the Bible is the common basis of the rule of faith, the ecumenical imperative urgently summons all Christians to a re-reading of the inspired text, in docility to the Holy Spirit, in charity, sincerity and humility; it calls upon all to meditate on these texts and to live them in such a way as to achieve conversion of heart and sanctity of life. These two qualities, when united with prayer for the unity of Christians, constitute the soul of the entire ecumenical movement (cf. *Unitatis Redintegratio*, 8). To achieve this goal, it is necessary to make the acquiring of a Bible something within the reach of as many Christians as possible, to encourage ecumenical translations—since having a common text greatly assists reading and understanding together—and also ecumenical prayer groups, in order to contribute, by an authentic and living witness, to the achievement of unity within diversity (cf. Rom 12:4–5).[6]

We will happily glean insights from the biblical and theological contributions of our Protestant brethren. As the *Catechism of the Catholic Church* reminds us,

"Furthermore, many elements of sanctification and of truth" [*LG* 8 § 2] are found outside the visible confines of the Catholic Church: "the written Word of God; the life of grace; faith, hope, and charity, with the other interior gifts of the Holy Spirit, as well as visible elements" [*UR* 3 § 2; cf. *LG* 15]. Christ's Spirit uses these Churches and ecclesial communities as means of salvation, whose

---

[6] Joseph A. Fitzmyer, *The Biblical Commission's Document: "The Interpretation of the Bible in the Church"*, Subsidia biblica, 18 (Rome: Pontoficio Istituto Biblico, 1995), 187–88.

power derives from the fullness of grace and truth that Christ has entrusted to the Catholic Church. All these blessings come from Christ and lead to him [cf. *UR* 3], and are in themselves calls to "Catholic unity" (*LG* 8).[7]

How to Use This Study Guide

The best way to start any worthwhile project is to set some priorities. You should consider how important studying the Sacred Scriptures is to you and how much time you should set aside each week for study. Plan a special time each day or each week for this purpose. Maybe you will prefer to use this study guide with a group, such as your family, your fellow seminarians, your parish study group, an RCIA class, or a few close friends. Whatever the circumstances, it is important to develop a plan and a schedule—and then stick to it. You will find yourself anxiously looking forward to these special study times. There is no chore involved here; this is an adventure—fun, pure and simple.

The Bible

We have already discussed translations. It is best to start with a few different versions to help you get the "flavor" of a certain passage and see various nuances of meaning. There are a variety of "parallel Bibles" that have several translations side-by-side in parallel columns. Make sure to have at least one good Catholic Bible.

Using the Catechism of the Catholic Church

A copy of the *Catechism of the Catholic Church* is essential to this study. You will notice throughout this book the letters "CCC". These letters stand for "*Catechism of the Catholic Church*", and they refer you to a paragraph number within the *Catechism*. The *Catechism* will help illuminate many passages in St. John's Gospel and will also provide the protection of interpreting the Scripture in harmony with the tried and true teaching of historic Christianity—the tradition of the Catholic Church. This will give the novice a sense of security while providing the "old hand" with confirmation and backup material. We are blessed by God to have such a marvelous gift as the *Catechism*.

---

[7] CCC 819.

A Notebook

Prepare a notebook to use alongside this study guide. Keep good notes. Answer the study guide questions in your own words, and write out additional questions you come up with on your own. Keep track of insights, discoveries, and applications that the Lord brings to your mind. Keep a detailed journal, because we all know how fast we forget things if we do not write them down.

Prayer

Pray before you begin. A good prayer to recite before Bible study comes down through the centuries from Origen (ca. 185–254), one of the great students of Scripture. He prayed,

> Lord, inspire us to read your Scriptures and to meditate upon them day and night. We beg you to give us real understanding of what we need, that we in turn may put its precepts into practice. Yet we know that understanding and good intentions are worthless, unless rooted in your graceful love. So we ask that the words of Scriptures may also be not just signs on a page, but channels of grace into our hearts.[8]

Sharing and Involvement

Share what you learn with others. When you meet family, friends, and fellow parishioners, share your discoveries. Let your enthusiasm spread and infect others. Invite them to study with you, or offer to start a study group. You will be surprised how many people will share your excitement and ask how they can study the Bible as well.

Our study is divided into chapters. Each chapter is broken down into major themes. We take a passage-by-passage approach, with questions to direct readers to discover the answers for themselves. The questions are interspersed with historical, geographical, patristic, and other pertinent information. In this way, this book can be used as a commentary, with a do-it-yourself approach to finding the answers, or simply as a study guide to deep research of the Fourth Gospel.

---

[8] James Watkins, comp., *Manual of Prayers* (Rome: Pontifical North American College, 1998), 87.

We are now ready to begin our study of John's Gospel. Before turning to John 1:1, however, we should know a bit about the author of the book and the history surrounding it.

Who Wrote the Gospel of St. John?

The Bible itself never identifies the author of the Fourth Gospel by name. In most Bibles, the Gospel is preceded by a heading such as "The Gospel according to John", but this was added many years later, by someone other than the author. This has led some scholars to speculate about the identity of the author. Proposals have ranged from Lazarus to Paul, from Matthias to John Mark. Some scholars have suggested a presbyter named John or, more likely, the community of John who wrote in "his name".

We need not delve into all the arguments here. The Gospel itself is divinely inspired; the title of the Gospel is not. But that does not leave us without any information about authorship. Internal evidence shows that the author is clearly a Palestinian Jew, fully acquainted with life in Israel before the destruction of Jerusalem. He writes as an eyewitness, with amazing detail, a point that even some Jewish historians have admitted. The writer obviously had an intimate place among Jesus' followers.

That said, the internal evidence provides only a little more information. We find references to the disciple "whom Jesus loved" (Jn 13:23) and the nondescript mention of "the disciple". It can be assumed from these references and their context that they refer to the Apostle John, an obvious eyewitness, who in his modesty declines to use his own name and only infrequently quotes his own words (only in Jn 13:25; 21:7; 21:20). But it is the unanimous consent of apostolic tradition that provides certainty as to John's authorship. It is Catholic history and tradition that provide such assurance.

According to the Fathers of the Church, the Fourth Gospel was written by the Apostle John. St. Irenaeus (ca. 120–ca. 200), the bishop of Lyons, writes, "John, the disciple of the Lord, who also had leaned upon His breast, did himself publish a Gospel during his residence at Ephesus in Asia." [9]

Eusebius (ca. 260–ca. 340), referring to earlier sources, writes,

---

[9] Irenaeus, *Against Heresies* 3, 1, 1 in Alexander Roberts and James Donaldson, eds., *The Ante-Nicene Fathers* (hereafter abbreviated ANF) (Grand Rapids, Mich.: Wm. B. Eerdmans, 1985), 1:414.

When Mark and Luke had already published their Gospels, they
say that John, who had employed all his time in proclaiming the
Gospel orally, finally proceeded to write for the following reason.
The three Gospels already mentioned having come into the hands
of all and into his own too, they say that he accepted them and
bore witness to their truthfulness; but that there was lacking in
them an account of the deeds done by Christ at the beginning of
his ministry. . . . They say, therefore, that the apostle John, being
asked to do it for this reason, gave in his Gospel an account of
the period which had been omitted by the earlier evangelists, and
of the deeds done by the Saviour during that period; that is, of
those which were done before the imprisonment of the Baptist.[10]

Eusebius, quoting the earlier Clement of Alexandria (ca. 150–
ca. 215), provides further information on the writing of the Fourth
Gospel:

As Peter had preached the Word publicly at Rome, and declared
the Gospel by the Spirit, many who were present requested that
Mark, who had followed him for a long time and remembered
his sayings, should write them out. And having composed the
Gospel he gave it to those who had requested it. When Peter
learned of this, he neither directly forbade nor encouraged it. But,
last of all, John, perceiving that the external facts had been made
plain in the Gospel, being urged by his friends, and inspired by
the Spirit, composed a spiritual Gospel. This is the account of
Clement.[11]

There are multiple witnesses to St. John's final days. Polycrates (second century) writes (as preserved in Eusebius):

For in Asia also great lights have fallen asleep, which shall rise again
on the last day, at the coming of the Lord, when he shall come
with glory from heaven and shall seek out all the saints. Among
these are Philip, one of the twelve apostles, who sleeps in Hier-
apolis, and his two aged virgin daughters, and another daughter,
who lived in the Holy Spirit and now rests at Ephesus; and moreover John, who was both a witness and a teacher, who reclined

---

[10] Eusebius, *History of the Church* 3, 24, in Philip Schaff and Henry Wace, eds., *Nicene and
Post-Nicene Fathers*, 2d series (hereafter abbreviated NPNF2) (Grand Rapids, Mich.: Wm. B.
Eerdmans, 1982), 1:153.
[11] Ibid., 6, 14, in NPNF2 1:261.

upon the bosom of the Lord, and being a priest wore the sacerdotal plate. He also sleeps at Ephesus.[12]

The ruins of the Church of St. John, built over his grave, still bear
witness to the apostolate and death of John in Ephesus.

We learn from St. Irenaeus that those who knew the disciple of our
Lord, John, said he remained in Ephesus until the time of Trajan.[13]
Interestingly enough, Emperor Trajan reigned from 98–117. Thus, St.
John would have lived and written his Gospel at the turn of the century.
Irenaeus also writes, "The Church in Ephesus, founded by Paul, and
having John remaining among them permanently until the times of
Trajan, is a true witness of the tradition of the apostles."[14] Other Fathers
confirm St. Irenaeus' testimony.

We can conclude, then, that the Fourth Gospel was written by the
Apostle John, about the year 100, from the ancient city of Ephesus.

The Apostle John

Thus, the Apostle John was the author of the Fourth Gospel. But who
was John? As we begin our exciting study of his Gospel, we should
know something about him—as a man, a disciple, an apostle, and as the
writer of this theological, literary, and philosophical masterpiece. What
do Scripture and the earliest Christian tradition tell us?

John was a young fisherman who was intrigued by the message of a
prophet shouting the truth of God from the hills and rocks in the Judean
wilderness. John the Baptist came on the scene preaching repentance in
preparation for the imminent kingdom of God. John, an inquisitive
Jewish teenager, became a disciple of the Baptist. One day, while mending nets on his father Zebedee's fishing boat, this young disciple, along
with his brother James, was called by Jesus to follow him. They immediately left their father and their boat and trotted off behind this new rabbi
(Mt 4:21–22).

John was a loyal disciple of Jesus for the three years they traversed the
dusty paths and rocky fields of Israel, from Galilee to Jerusalem and back
again. The disciples ministered to the poor in the villages and outlying
areas and watched Jesus preach and argue with the religious leaders in

---

[12] Ibid., 3, 31, in NPNF2 1:162–63.
[13] Irenaeus, *Against Heresies* 2, 22, 5, in ANF 1:392.
[14] Ibid., 3, 3, 4, in ANF 1:416.

Jerusalem. John witnessed the miracles; he heard the authoritative teaching; he may have witnessed the dove descend on Jesus at his baptism and may have heard the Father's words from heaven (Jn 1:29–34). He was at the table when our Lord instituted the Eucharist; in fact, he was the one who laid his head on Jesus' breast during the meal (Jn 13:1, 23–25). He received the Holy Spirit with the breath of Jesus (Jn 20:21–23); he had his feet washed by the Lord himself (Jn 13:5). He was one of Jesus' three favorite disciples, along with Peter and James, and tradition and internal evidence of the Gospel of John inform us that it is John who is referred to several times as "the one Jesus loved" (Jn 13:23; 20:2; 21:7, 20). He was a close friend and an eager disciple. Jesus nicknamed him and his brother, James, Boanerges—sons of thunder (Mk 3:17).

John was invited to pray with Jesus in the Garden of Gethsemane but repeatedly fell asleep (Mk 14:32–42). He was there when Judas betrayed the Lord, and then John followed Jesus into the courtyard close to the trial, since he had an acquaintance with the high priest (Jn 18:15). At the crucifixion, he is the only disciple who stayed at the foot of the Cross, while the other disciples scattered (Mk 14:50; Jn 19:26). Jesus committed his Mother to the care of John and John to the care of his Mother with the immortal words, "Woman, behold, your son! . . . Behold, your mother!" (Jn 19:26). John took Mary into his home and later moved to Ephesus, where, as tradition tells us, they both lived for many years.

John was a witness to the Resurrection, being one of the first to peer into the empty tomb (Jn 20:1–10). He conversed with the risen Lord and for forty days saw the proofs of his Resurrection and was further taught concerning the kingdom of God (Mt 28:16–20; Acts 1:1–8). He was the first to recognize the Lord through the morning mist (Jn 21:7) and helped bring the miraculous catch to the shore. He saw the Lord rise into the clouds at the Ascension (Acts 1:9–11) and saw him again, in his glorious stature in the heavenly realms, as described in the book of Revelation. He also saw the heavenly apparition of the Blessed Virgin crowned in glory (Rev 12:1ff.).

Thus, John embarked on the adventure of the early Church. He accompanied Peter in several miracles and trials; and he did jail time for the Name of Jesus. His life beyond the first chapters of Acts is sketchy, though we see him in Jerusalem—respected as a "pillar" of the Church by St. Paul—at the Council in Jerusalem around the year 49 (Acts 15). Along with Peter and the other apostles and elders, John was present at this first Council of the Church, when binding legislation was imposed on believers based upon Peter's doctrinal determination. John took part in these proceedings.

History informs us that St. John spent the last years of his life in Ephesus. During the persecution of Christians by either Nero (reigned 54–68) or Domitian (reigned 81–96)—scholarly opinion is divided on the subject—John was exiled to the island of Patmos. There he fell on his face "as though dead" before the revelation of Jesus and, according to tradition, wrote the book of Revelation (Rev 1:1–10, 19). He is also said to have composed three short epistles, and later, at the end of his life, as an old man, he wrote the Gospel of St. John, the subject of this study.

The Beloved Disciple is a treasure of the Church and a saint to be emulated. "The eagle soars high in the sky and has an amazing power of vision. There is a just reason for calling St. John 'the Divine' and for using the eagle as his symbol." [15] Soon we will be carried high upon his back as he soars above the world and surveys the mystery of Christ. "Because Jesus is God, he is the divine mystery that can never be exhausted. John, himself a mystic, tries to help us to see just a little bit of that mystery." [16]

John's Audience and Purpose in Writing

We have seen that the best evidence supports the conclusion that the Fourth Gospel was written by the Apostle John, and we have learned a bit about him. But what do we know of his audience and his purpose in writing?

It has been said that St. Matthew wrote to show Jesus as the King to the Jews, St. Mark to present him as a servant to the Romans, St. Luke to point Jesus out as a man to the Greeks, and St. John to disclose him as God to the world. It appears that St. John wrote to both Jews and Gentiles—to all mankind. That Gentiles were at least partially a target audience seems the case because John translates Hebrew words and events that any Jew would understand (for example, Jn 4:9; 9:6–7; 19:31). It can also be supposed that John had fellow Christians in mind, writing to encourage and build their faith. He was the "net mender" (Mk 1:19) and was concerned with mending and strengthening the Church.

---

[15] Kenneth Baker, *Inside the Bible: An Introduction to Each Book of the Bible* (San Francisco: Ignatius Press, 1998), 257.

[16] Ibid.

John made no secret of his reason for writing the Gospel: "Now Jesus did many other signs in the presence of the disciples, which are not written in this book; but these are written that you may believe that Jesus is the Christ, the Son of God, and that believing you may have life in his name" (20:30–31).

Another reason John wrote was to fight a dangerous enemy—Gnosticism. The Gnostics said that matter is evil and spirit is good. John put the lie to their error by presenting the truth of the Incarnation—God taking on flesh, spirit, and matter in a holy union. Yet the battle continued to rage through the following centuries and, in fact, has raised its ugly head again in our generation.

> Gnosticism was perhaps the most dangerous heresy ever to appear in the Church's history. The Fathers of the Church of the second and third centuries (Irenaeus, Tertullian, Origen among them) fought violently against it. They instinctively felt that it was a life and death struggle. In John's view, was the message of Christ a Gnostic revelation or not? According to the Gnostics the revelation is "secret" and limited to the good, the pure, the spiritual. The Gnostics are those who pass the secret on by word of mouth. The rest are the unfortunate "uninformed" who stay outside. This is not the case in John's Gospel. Jesus says: "I have spoken openly to the world." It is true that the world is rated negatively, but that is only because the world itself refuses to accept the revelation that Christ brings.[17]

John also crossed swords with the Judaizers, who insisted on circumcision and compliance with all the ceremonial aspects of the Jewish law for Gentiles before they could become Christians. No, said John. One is justified by faith in Christ, not by slavishly following every detail of Judaistic laws and traditions. One enters the kingdom of God through "water and the Spirit", not through circumcision and dietary laws.

John also offered hope to the Greeks and Romans, whose religions were already demonstrating their bankruptcy, leaving them searching for meaning to their lives.

Finally, John wrote to everyone, for every age to come, pulling back the curtain of time to give a glimpse into the eternal. He demonstrated the love of the one God and his gracious and free provision of eternal life

---

[17] Ignace de la Potterie, *The Hour of Jesus: The Passion and the Resurrection of Jesus according to John*, trans. Gregory Murray (New York: Alba House, 1989), 49–50.

through his Son, Jesus Christ. John unabashedly announced to the pagan and Jewish worlds that Jesus was not only the Messiah—the Anointed One of God—but he was also the I AM of the Exodus (Ex 3:14) and the Old Covenant. He was *the* prophet who was to come (Deut 18:15–18) and the Suffering Servant of Isaiah 53. To the Greek, John sought to show that Jesus was the *Logos*, understood as the cosmic principle of the universe; to the Jew, that he was the *Logos*, understood as the powerful Word of God who had dwelled with God before the world was made. John called the Gentile to believe in the Creator of the universe revealed in Jesus Christ, and the Jew to believe in his Messiah, the Son of God sent from heaven—the Lamb of God, the ultimate sacrifice for sins.

We now approach this marvelous story with great respect and excitement, for this Gospel unveils cosmic secrets and reveals the very heart of God. But, as we will see, there are deep waters rushing below the surface of this eyewitness narrative. We will enjoy wading at the surface, but we will also dive deep into this rushing revelation of God.

"We know that in John's gospel there are often two meanings," writes William Barclay, "one which lies on the surface, and a deeper one which lies beneath." Then, commenting on Peter's catch of the 153 fishes at Christ's Resurrection appearance by the Sea of Tiberius (21:1–14), Barclay notes, "In the Fourth Gospel everything is meaningful." It may be, he continues, that the precise number of this large catch was recalled because it had to be counted and divided. "But when we remember John's way of putting hidden meanings in his gospel for those who have eyes to see, we must think that there is more to it than that." [18]

No doubt there is more—much more. John is never satisfied to give only one level of meaning to the words and deeds of Jesus. As Father Kenneth Baker observes, "The Gospel of St. John is a treasure hidden just under the surface. The deeper you dig, the more treasure you find. The book is full of symbolism—Jesus is the source of light and life and truth." [19]

As we embark on our treasure hunt, we should be ready to dig deep and load up on all the wealth John's Gospel has waiting for us. With our Bibles, *Catechisms*, notebooks, and a sense of adventure, we open the pages of sacred Scripture and ask the Holy Spirit of God to enlighten our hearts and minds as we study together in the heart of his one, holy, catholic, and apostolic Church.

---

[18] William Barclay, *The Gospel of John* (Philadelphia: Westminster Press, 1975), 2:280, 283.
[19] Baker, *Inside the Bible*, 256.

JOHN 1 a

THE "OVERTURE": THE WORD BECOMES FLESH

1. St. John's Gospel is like an exquisite symphony, with many "musical themes" cascading throughout the Gospel. Look up the definition of the musical term "overture". How does the prologue, the first eighteen verses, provide the "overture" to the whole Gospel? All of the Gospel's main themes are introduced in the prologue; the prologue summarizes the Gospel in a nutshell. Consequently, it is helpful to memorize the first eighteen verses.

» Comments on the "Overture": "The prologue gives in a nutshell the content of the gospel in relation to the evangelist's purpose of revealing the true identity of a mission of Jesus to the audience. It may be likened to the infancy narratives in Matthew and Luke in that it deals with Jesus' origins and announces the nature of his mission." [1]

An overture is "instrumental music composed as a musical introduction to an opera, oratorio, or suite". [2] "Mozart's operatic overtures to *Don Giovanni* and *The Magic Flute* were among the first designed to summarize and anticipate the high lights of the ensuing operas. . . . The overtures of the French 'grand opéras' are usually a medley of the most important melodies of the opera." [3]

"The Prologue serves somewhat like an overture to a formal musical composition. It may well have been written after the main body of the Gospel. (This is true of most prologues.) In its short span of eighteen verses, it states briefly what the whole of the Gospel will spell out over twenty-one chapters. It has both structure and content. The structure has been partially determined by the presentation of 'wisdom personified' in the Old Testament books. There, as in Wis 9:9–12 or Prov 8:22–36, wisdom is first with God, then shares in creation, will come to earth, and there gift humankind. This same progression is found in our prologue. The other factor that has determined the structure is the Hebrew

---

[1] William R. Farmer, ed., *The International Bible Commentary* (Collegeville, Minn.: Liturgical Press, 1998), 1459.

[2] Patrick Kavanaugh, *Music of the Great Composers* (Grand Rapids, Mich.: Zondervan Pub. House, 1996), 262.

[3] Willi Apel and Ralph T. Daniel, *The Harvard Brief Dictionary of Music* (New York: Pocket Books, 1960), 212.

1. THE WORD WITH GOD
   (vv. 1–2)

1. THE SON AT THE FATHER'S SIDE
   (v. 18)

2. ROLE IN CREATION
   (v. 3)

2. ROLE IN RE-CREATION
   (v. 17)

3. GIFT TO MANKIND
   (vv. 4–5)

3. GIFT TO MANKIND
   (v. 16)

4. TESTIMONY OF JOHN
   (vv. 6–8)

4. TESTIMONY OF JOHN
   (v. 15)

5. THE WORD ENTERS THE WORLD
   (vv. 9–11)

5. THE INCARNATION
   (v. 14)

6. THROUGH THE WORD WE BECOME
   CHILDREN OF GOD
   (vv. 12–13)

Used with permission of Liturgical Press, Collegeville, Minn. (adapted slightly)

fondness for parallelism—notions being repeated in order—and for inverse parallelism, that is repeated in inverse order. Visually, John's poetic prologue unfolds as follows [see diagram above]. The movement of the prologue swings like the arm of a mighty pendulum, each point of which on the left side will be matched by an equivalent on the right [with the most important point at the junction point of both sides]." [4]

2. Most scholars agree that the opening verses of St. John's Gospel are taken from an ancient Christian hymn of the first century. Notice its poetic rhythm, and see if you can discover the extent and form of the hymn.

» COMMENTS ON THE TEXT: "The prologue is a magnificent hymn in praise of Christ. We do not know whether St John composed it when writing his Gospel, or whether he based it on some existing liturgical hymn; but there is no trace of any such text in other early Christian documents." [5]

In several places, the New Testament incorporates ancient Christian hymns into its text. For example, hymns can be found in Philippians 2:5–11; Colossians 1:15–20; 1 Timothy 3:16; and 2 Timothy 2:11–13 (CCC 461, 2667). Imagine how these hymns might have been used in the early Church. [6]

---

[4] Neal M. Flanagan, O.S.M., "John", in *The Collegeville Bible Commentary: New Testament*, ed. Robert J. Karris, O.F.M. (Collegeville, Minn.: Liturgical Press, 1992), 981–82.

[5] José María Casciaro, *The Navarre Bible: The Gospel of Saint John* (Dublin: Four Courts Press, 1992), 43.

[6] For more on hymns embedded in the New Testament text, see Robert J. Karris, O.F.M., *A Symphony of New Testament Hymns* (Collegeville, Minn.: Liturgical Press, 1996).

John 1:1–2
In the Beginning Was the Word

3. John begins with the words "In the beginning". What do these words bring to mind? What do they suggest about John's purpose in writing and the content of his Gospel? Compare these opening words with Genesis 1:1 and 1 John 1:1. How are they alike and different? What is the time period to which each refers?

» OLD TESTAMENT NOTES: "The prologue is very reminiscent of the first chapter of Genesis, on a number of scores: 1) the opening words are the same: 'In the beginning . . .'; in the Gospel they refer to absolute beginning, that is, eternity, whereas in Genesis they mean the beginning of creation and time; 2) there is a parallelism in the role of the Word: in Genesis, God creates things by his word ('And God said . . .'); in the Gospel we are told that they were made through the Word of God; 3) in Genesis, God's work of creation reaches its peak when he creates man in his own image and likeness; in the Gospel, the work of the Incarnate Word culminates when man is raised—by a new creation, as it were—to the dignity of being a son of God." [7]

"The term, then, denotes *duration* thus; *In the beginning* of every thing else that had a beginning—thus are excluded the Father and Holy Ghost, who had no beginning; or, when everything else began to be; before any time, actual or imaginary *'the Word* WAS.' He must, therefore, have no beginning; since, He was, when everything else began; and, consequently, must be Eternal. The *existence* of the Word before all creation is here *directly* proved." [8]

4. St. Matthew and St. Luke both provide human genealogies for Jesus. What kind of "genealogy" does St. John provide, and what does it tell us about Jesus (Jn 1:1–3)? What does the word "was" mean in the first verse?

» WORD STUDY: "It is impossible not to comment on the word 'was', for in the Greek language it represents that part of the verb (the imperfect tense) which refers, not to an isolated past event, but to a continuous condition. The evangelist has not yet reached the point of writing about what can in any sense be called 'history', but is concerned with what are the essential and universal conditions of history. Of these the Word's being with God 'in the beginning' is paramount." [9]

---

[7] Casciaro, *John*, 43.

[8] John MacEvilly, *An Exposition of the Gospel of St. John* (New York: Benziger Bros., 1889), 6.

[9] John Marsh, *The Gospel of St John* (Baltimore, Md.: Penguin Books, 1968), 102.

The Greek tense means that Christ dwells in a continuous, timeless existence. What does the Baptist mean "He existed before me" in John 1:30, since John the Baptist was born six months before Jesus?

5. The Greek word for "Word" is *logos* (λόγος). Why do you think John uses this word to describe Jesus Christ (Rev 19:13–15; Heb 1:1–3; 4:12–13; CCC 65, 102)? How would using this term enable the Gospel to be understood in both Jewish and Gentile cultures? Notice how John keeps the reader in suspense: he does not reveal who or what this Logos is until verse 14, and he does not attach a name to the Logos until verse 17.

» THEOLOGICAL NOTE: Greeks saw the Logos as the core of the universe. "In [Greek] thinking *logos* meant divine utterance, emanation, mediation. In the O[ld] T[estament] [Jewish thought] the word of God is God's manifestation, the revelation of himself, whether in creation, in deeds of power and of grace, or in prophecy. All these strains of thought are taken up by J[oh]n, who shows that Christ, the Incarnate Word, is the ultimate and complete revelation of God." [10] "The term 'logos' was familiar in some Greek philosophical schools, where it denoted the principle of reason or order immanent in the universe, the principle which imposes form on the material world and constitutes the rational soul in man. It is not in Greek philosophical usage, however, that the background of John's thought and language should be sought.... The true background to John's thought and language is found not in Greek philosophy but in Hebrew revelation." [11] Compare Psalm 33:6; 107:20; Wisdom 18:14–15; Isaiah 55:11.

6. In verse 1, what does John tell us about the nature or essence of the Logos—what *is* the Logos (CCC 240–42)? How does the "crescendo" of John's Gospel use "Doubting Thomas" to testify to this reality (Jn 20:28)? How does Thomas' declaration help "frame" the Gospel— beginning and end—and what does it tell us of John's purpose in writing? How does Thomas' statement explain and personalize the first verse of John's Gospel, and how does this first verse anticipate Thomas' exclamation?

7. The Jehovah's Witnesses' *New World Translation* of the Bible renders John 1:1 incorrectly as "In the beginning the Word was, and the Word

---

[10] Raymond Brown, Joseph Fitzmyer, and Roland Murphy, eds., *The Jerome Biblical Commentary* (Englewood Cliffs, N.J.: Prentice-Hall, 1968), 2:422.

[11] F. F. Bruce, *The Gospel of John* (Grand Rapids, Mich.: William B. Eerdmans, 1983), 29.

was with God, and the Word was a god." [12]   What does this spurious translation make of the Logos? Why do you think the Jehovah's Witnesses translated the passage in this way? How does the added article "a", which is not in the original Greek, skew the whole thought and import of John's thesis? Are the Jehovah's Witnesses claiming the existence of more than one God?

» GREEK WORD STUDY: In the Greek, there is no article "a" before the word "God" at the end of the John 1:1. Thus, the meaning is literally: "The Word was divine" or "The Word was, as to his essence, absolute deity": " 'And the Word was God'. These words testify to the divine nature of the Word. In the Greek (*kai theos en ho logos*), no article is used before the word 'God'. John eliminates the article in order to prevent identification of the Word with the Father, to whom the title '*ho theos*' (the God) properly belongs." [13]

John 1:1 means that the Word shared the very nature and being of God, or as the NEB translates the phrase, "what God was, the Word was." John wants us to read the whole Gospel in light of this verse. Realizing that Jesus shares the very nature of God (Col 1:19; 2:9) is the linchpin to understanding John's narrative.

8. Many heretical movements throughout history (for example, Arians, Nestorians, Jehovah's Witnesses, and Mormons) have denied the deity and the two natures of Christ: his full deity and full humanity. How can a Catholic use this first chapter of John's Gospel to support these beliefs as taught by the Church? How might the Jews of the time, who believed "God is one" (Deut 6:4) and invisible (Ex 33:20–23), have understood John's claim that Jesus was divine?

» HISTORICAL NOTE: The Church struggled with the Arian heresy in the third and fourth centuries. The Arians denied the divinity of Christ, claiming he was a created being—*like* God but *not* God. The Council of Nicaea (we recite the Nicene Creed each Sunday at Mass) condemned Arianism in 325. The Nicene Creed states that Christ "is one in being [one substance] with the Father". Jehovah's Witnesses and other groups merely rehash an old heresy rejected and refuted by the Church Fathers and the Church councils of the early centuries.

---

[12] New World Bible Translation Committee, *The Kingdom Interlinear Translation of the Greek Scriptures* (Brooklyn, N.Y.: Watchtower Bible and Tract Society, 1969), 417.

[13] Peter Ellis, *The Genius of John: A Composition-Critical Commentary on the Fourth Gospel* (Collegeville, Minn.: Liturgical Press, 1984), 21.

John 1:3–5

All Things Came into Being through Him

9. Who created the heavens and the earth (Gen 1:1–2)? How did God create (1 Cor 8:6; Col 1:16; Heb 1:2; CCC 291)? If "all things" were created through the Logos ("all things were made through him, and without him was not anything made that was made"), could the Logos have been created?

10. What does John mean when he says that in the Logos was "life" (Jn 5:26; 11:25; 14:6; 1 Jn 5:20; CCC 425)? What does he mean by "the life was the light of men"? The meaning of this seemingly obscure phrase is developed elsewhere in the Gospel. (See Jn 8:12; 9:5; 11:9–10; 12:46; 13:29–30, where John uses a dramatic example of darkness away from Christ.) Psalm 36:9 states, "For with thee is the fountain of life; in thy light do we see light." How does this shed light on John's comments? Also, consider other New Testament passages referring to "light" (Acts 26:18; 2 Cor 4:3–6; Eph 5:13–14; 1 Thess 5:5; 1 Tim 6:15–16; 1 Pet 2:9; 1 Jn 1:5–7; Rev 22:5).

» COMMENT ON THE TEXT: Light is not only necessary for life, as in photosynthesis in plants, and necessary for seeing, it can also have a bleaching, cleansing, and healing effect (Jn 3:20–21; Eph 5:11–14). "Ultraviolet radiation also has positive effects on the human body, however. It stimulates the production of vitamin D in the skin and can be used as a therapeutic agent for such diseases as psoriasis. Because of its bactericidal capabilities at wavelengths of 260–280 nm, ultraviolet radiation is useful as both a research tool and a sterilizing technique." [14] Ultraviolet light's microbiological cleansing effect is interesting when compared to the light of Christ, which exposes sin and has a cleansing, "antibiotic" effect on men as they step into and remain in the light (Eph 5:11–14; 1 Jn 1:6–7; Jn 3:20–21).

Without light our eyes would be worthless, for it is light that brings vision through the optic nerve. Light is essential to life. John is concerned here with spiritual illumination and the cleansing from sin that results in eternal life. Notice the emphasis on life and light in relationship to the Genesis creation story where God declared, "Let there be light."

11. In verse 5, when John says that the "light shines in the darkness", how is he drawing our attention to the story of creation in Genesis (Gen 1:1–

---

[14] "Ultraviolet Radiation", in Encyclopedia Britannica CD 2000 Deluxe Edition (Chicago: Encyclopedia Britannica, 2000).

2)? What was the first thing created in the natural creation? What was the first thing brought into the world at the beginning of the second creation (Jn 1:4–5)—the new mankind, the Church? How has Jesus come to begin a new creation, to bring light out of darkness (CCC 298, 1691)?

» THEOLOGY OF LIGHT: "In Genesis 1 light was the first of God's creatures, because the ancient world believed that light was the principle of life, which put to flight darkness or nonexistence. John 1:4 moves from creation into the sphere of the moral authority of the Word. Verse 5 speaks of the struggle between the light and the darkness, not in the cosmic sense but in the ethical sense. The light 'shines' (present tense), but the darkness 'did not overcome' it (past tense). This light that is God (cf. 1 John 1:5), the light of truth, may be ignored, even suppressed, but it can never be put out. Darkness is the absence of light; it ceases to exist when light appears. No matter how thick the darkness, once there is a glimmer of light, the light cannot but be seen. Hence the saying 'it is better to light one candle than to curse the darkness.' The victory of the light over darkness recalls Paul's injunction, 'do not be overcome by evil, but overcome evil with good' (Rom 12:21). Believers are to serve as light in the world, not to be overcome by the darkness of sin and evil. In this way they too share in the victory of the Word/Light over the darkness. (See also Matt 5:14–16.)" [15]

» THEOLOGY OF LIFE: "Life is not mere existence—even inanimate things exist; life for J[oh]n signifies some kind of sharing in the being of God. This statement prepares for vv. 14ff., which bring out that the supernatural life of man is a sharing in the divine life of the Holy Trinity. Further, since life always has this fullness of meaning in J[oh]n, we should understand that this is 'what came to be' in the Word: The life that men receive from the Word, they receive as God's gift through the One who has manifested him (cf. 3:35f.; 5:26f.; 6:57). . . . J[oh]n agrees with Col 1:15–20 in seeing in the work of creation the model and exemplar of the second creation of salvation. '[*T*]*he life was the light of men*: The life of which John speaks, as truly a sharing in the life of God, must be a life of ultimate understanding, the revelation of God. The rabbis spoke similarly of the Torah as light. . . . John will later apply to Jesus the Word other designations that they used of Torah, such as water (4:10) and bread (6:35)." [16]

» THEOLOGY OF ART: God has brought two great works of art into existence: the created order (including the physical universe) and the creation of the new humanity, the Church. There is a Greek word, used twice in the New Testament, that refers to each of these works of art respectively. The word is *poiēma* (ποίημα) from which we get our English word "poem". A poem is a work of art

---

[15] Farmer, *International Bible Commentary*, 1460.

[16] Brown, Fitzmyer, and Murphy, *Jerome Biblical Commentary*, 2:422.

and implies an artist. In Romans 1:20 (NASB) we read, "For since the creation of the world His invisible attributes, His eternal power and divine nature, have been clearly seen, being understood through *what has been made*, so that they are without excuse." The four words I have italicized come from the one Greek word *poiēma*. Through God's work of art, his "poem" of creation, all men should know of him and his existence. To deny God's existence in the face of the evidence, then, is to be without excuse before God—it is to suppress the truth (Rom 1:18).

The second and only other time the word *poiēma* is used in the New Testament is in Ephesians 2:10, which states, "For we are his *workmanship*, created in Christ Jesus for good works, which God prepared beforehand, that we should walk in them." In this passage, the emphasized word is *poiēma* in the Greek and refers to us—the Church—the new creation. God has written two marvelous "poems", works of art, and the art gloriously testifies of its Creator—not only to his existence, but to his power, creativity, mercy, holiness, personality, and love.

Imagine a group of art lovers viewing an exhibit put on by a particular artist. His works are on prominent display throughout the gallery, with his signature clearly at the bottom of each painting. He is there to greet and answer questions. How would the artist respond if the viewers ignored him altogether and questioned where the paintings came from and who could possibly have made them? "Maybe they got here by chance", one might say. "Maybe they just appeared after many billions of years of mutations and cosmic progression", another might add. What would be the response of the artist?

12. Read John 1:5 in several different Bible versions. If you compare translations, you can see how some translations refer to how the darkness did not *overcome* the light (NAB; RSV) and others refer to how the darkness did not *comprehend* the light (KJV, NASB). John uses a word with a double meaning (overcome/comprehend) to give greater depth to his statement, since both aspects are true. How did the light penetrate the darkness (2 Cor 4:6)? Why could the darkness not *overcome* or *comprehend* the light?

John 1:6–13
True Light and Children of God

13. Who came to witness to the Word, and who sent the witness (Jn 1:6, 15, 19ff.; Mt 3:1)? To discover more about this witness, read Luke 1:1–80.

14. John has so far discussed the Word in eternity; now he presents him in history. Thus, we now step out of eternity and into time. What is John the Baptist sent to do (vv. 7–8; Jn 5:33)? How does he fulfill his task (Jn 1:29–34)? Should the Jews have been prepared for John the Baptist's arrival (Mt 3:1–3; Is 40:3; Mt 11:10)? Do some think the Baptist is the Messiah—the true light (Jn 1:19–23)?

15. The Greek word used here for "witness" is *marturia* (μαρτυρία). What English word is associated with *marturia*? How does John become a *martyr* of the light (Mt 14:1–12)? Explain what Jesus thinks of John the Baptist (Mt 11:7–14).

16. Where does the true light manifest itself (v. 9; 1 Jn 2:8)? What does it mean that the true light enlightens every man (CCC 1216; Heb 6:4; 10:32; 2 Cor 4:3–6)?

» THEOLOGICAL NOTE: Does this phrase, "the true light that enlightens every man", mean that every individual is enlightened or only that every group of people is enlightened? John appears to mean that the true light enlightens every *group* of people or every *nation*, rather than each and every *individual* person. The Jews knew of no greater light than the law. But the law had been given only to them. The true light, on the other hand, "enlightens every man", not just the Jewish people. J. B. Lightfoot writes, "Christ, shining forth in the light of the Gospel, is a light that 'lightens all the world'. The light of the law shone only upon the Jews; but this light spreads wider, even over the face of the whole earth." [17]

17. The world was made through the Word (Jesus the Logos), and he had been present with and shepherded the sons of Abraham for nearly two thousand years (Ex 29:45–46; Lk 13:34–35), yet they did not recognize him when he arrived as the promised Messiah. He was like an alien from another dimension visiting our planet—the ultimate science fiction theme. Think of this in cosmic terms and dimensions of space and time. Though he was one of us, he was different from us (Jn 1:10–11; 8:23; 17:14–16; 18:36).

18. John relates in verses 10–11 how poorly Jesus was received by "the world" and by "his own". Notice the double meaning of "world" (cf. Jn

---

[17] J. B. Lightfoot, *Commentary on the New Testament from the Talmud and Hebraica* (Peabody, Mass.: Hendrickson Pub., 1995), 3:239.

3:16). Coming to "his own" literally means that he came home, or came to his own family—the human family. Notice the repetition of the words "world" and "own". How are these two differentiated—what groups of men are referred to (CCC 530; Rom 11:13–15; Ps 147:19–20)? How should the Creator of the universe (all men) and the King of the Jews expect to be received by his people? Read the parable in Matthew 21:33–46 and consider how the son of the landowner was received. This is a parable about Israel's reception of the Messiah, the Son of God. Since the children of Israel were not ready for the "time of [their] visitation", what was the result (Lk 19:41–44)?

» FROM THE FATHERS: "In a well known passage Augustine speaks of having read in the writings of the Platonists something equivalent to the teaching of the Prologue [of John] up to this point. 'But I did not read in those books that He came unto His own, and His own received Him not' (*Confessions*, vii. 9). Here is the distinctively Christian note, that which sets the gospel apart from the writings of the philosophers." [18]

19. According to verses 12–13, how is one born of God? Other passages of the New Testament refer to "new birth" (Jn 3:3–5 and 1 Pet 1:3, 23; cf. CCC 1228, 2769). Note that the expression "born again" in John 3:3–5 (*gennēthēi anōthen*) is different in Greek from the expression "new birth" used in 1 Peter 1:3, 23 (*anagennēsas*). What three physical elements are *not* included in this new birth (v. 13; CCC 505)? How do we know if one is born of God (1 Jn 2:29; 3:9; 5:4, 18)?

» THEOLOGICAL NOTE: John informs his readers that those who "receive" the Logos (as opposed to "his own", who rejected him) are given the "right to become children of God"—that is, to be "born of God". John then tells us what does *not* bring about this sonship. There are several points to note here. First, the word "blood" is plural (bloods) and refers to the ancient idea that procreation was brought about by the man planting a seed in the woman's womb, or, more specifically, that there was a mixing of fluids—"bloods"—which brought about the birth of a child. Second, the "will of the flesh" roughly means the result of carnal, fleshly passions, as in sexual impulses. Third, the phrase "nor of the will of man" refers, not to man in general, but to the male sex, which is usually considered the initiator of sexual acts and procreation. The Greek word is not *anthropos* (man), but *aner* (male).

Birth into the family of God, then, is not the result of natural processes or

---

[18] Leon Morris, *The Gospel according to John*, The New International Commentary on the New Testament (Grand Rapids, Mich.: Wm. B. Eerdmans Pub., 1971), 96.

physical desires. Furthermore, Jesus, born of the Holy Spirit, is the model of our spiritual birth through Mary, who is a type of the Church.

20. In verse 12, we are told that those who "receive" and "believe" in him are given the power to become children of God. The word "power" (*exousia*) does not refer to physical strength (which would be the Greek word *dunamis*, from which we get our English word "dynamite"), but to legal clout, right, or authority.

Whose children are we prior to believing in Christ (Jn 8:44; 1 Jn 3:8–10; CCC 407)? Did the Jews of Jesus' time consider themselves God's children? According to Scripture and history, could they claim God as their Father (Deut 32:6; Is 63:16; 64:8)? How does John explain something deeper and more profound (cf. Jn 3:3–5)? Who actually had a claim as the father of the rebellious Jewish leaders, according to Jesus (Jn 8:41–44)?

John leaves us with a cliff-hanger: How are we actually born of God? John does not tell us here. He will, however, explain this fully in his account of Jesus' discussion with Nicodemus (Jn 3). The "overture" contains the basic theme; the details are developed later.

21. In verse 12, what does it mean to "receive" and "believe"? (See Jn 3:36; notice that *disobey* is the opposite of *believe* here.) How is obedience an integral part of belief?

» COMMENT ON THE TEXT: "Receiving the Word means accepting him through faith, for it is through faith that Christ dwells in our hearts (cf. Eph 3:17). Believing in his name means believing in his Person, in Jesus as the Christ, the Son of God. In other words, 'those who believe in his name are those who fully hold the name of Christ, not in any way lessening his divinity or his humanity' (St Thomas Aquinas, *Commentary on St John*, 80)."[19]

» THEOLOGICAL NOTE ON THE WORD "BELIEVE": In the New Testament, "believe" is often used as a synecdoche. A synecdoche is a part that represents the whole (as in "head of cattle", where the word "head" is a synecdoche for the whole). When you order a hot dog, the waiter does not just serve you a plain hot dog; he also brings a bun, condiments, a plate, and so on. "Hot dog" can be a synecdoche for the whole meal. "Believe" and "receive" are synecdoches, words that represent all that is included and necessary to "be saved" and follow Christ. Mere belief—mental assent—is not enough (cf. Jas 2:18–26). Belief includes faith, obedience, following Christ, taking up our cross, confessing his

---

[19] Casciaro, *John*, 46.

Name, repentance, baptism, and so on. The idea of being saved by "faith only"—when understood as not including the elements just mentioned—is an unbiblical misunderstanding of biblical language.

John 1:14–18
The Incarnation—the Word Became Flesh

22. In verse 14, the mystery of the Logos is finally revealed. Who or what is the Logos (CCC 423)? Remember John 1:1: the "Word was with God" (forever existent), and "the Word was God." John 1:14 picks up from verse 1 and makes a startling announcement: "The Word became flesh." What does the word "incarnation" mean (CCC 461–64)? Is the word "incarnation" found in the Bible, or is it a term developed by the Church to explain God taking on human flesh (CCC 461)?

» WORD STUDY: The Latin word "incarnate" comes from two smaller words: the prefix *in* simply means "in"; the root word *carne* means "flesh". Compare "incarnation" with the words "carnivore" (an animal that eats flesh), "carnival" ("fleshly" entertainment), "carnage" (a massive slaughter or a pile of corpses), and "carnal" (fleshly). "Incarnation" simply means "being in flesh". The Word—that which is eternal—became flesh—that which is temporal—so that God could become man. What is the result (1 Pet 1:4; CCC 460)?

» JEWISH UNDERSTANDING: "It is not that a man named Yeshua [Jesus], who grew up in Natzeret, one day decided he was God. Rather, the Word, who 'was with God' and 'was God,' gave up the 'glory [he] had with [the Father] before the world existed' (17:5) and 'emptied himself, in that he took the form of a slave by becoming like human beings are' (Pp 2:7). In other words, God sent 'his own Son as a human being with a nature like our own sinful one' (Ro 8:3), so that 'in every respect he was tempted just as we are, the only difference being that he did not sin' (MJ 4:15). It is God the Word, then, who decided to become man, not the other way round. . . .

"Non-Messianic Judaism has generally taken a defensive theological position against Christianity and its concept of incarnation. Thus the *Rambam's* thirteen-point creed has as its third article:

'I believe with perfect faith that the Creator, blessed be his name, is not a body, that he is free from all material properties, and that he has no form whatsoever.'

"Maimonides clearly did not mean to contradict the [Old Testament's] own descriptions of God as having physical features such as a back, a face (v. 18) and an outstretched arm; rather, he meant to exclude incarnation. In the light of the New Testament a Messianic Jew can simply pronounce him wrong. However, for the sake of retaining a traditional Jewish formulation, he can preserve the words but reinterpret them against Maimonides' purpose. For example, a New Testament believer can agree that God's nature is not physical or material, but he would insist that the article does not exclude the incarnation of the Word as Yeshua if it is understood as an occasional, rather than essential, attribute of God, an event necessitated because sin occurred in human history." [20]

23. Imagine for a moment the Creator of the universe becoming an absolutely dependant and helpless infant. Imagine the divine condescension and humiliation (Phil 2:5–11; CCC 461). The one who created Mary's womb is formed in Mary's womb; he who created matter now becomes matter! And imagine him knowing that he will undergo the "curse of sin" on the Cross, something he did not create but despised and loathed. What does Jesus "become" for our sake (2 Cor 5:21; CCC 602)?

» ST. AUGUSTINE COMMENTS: "My mouth will utter the praise of the Lord, / of the Lord through whom all things have been made / And who has been made [man] amidst all things; / Who is the Revealer of His Father, Creator of His mother; / who is the Son of God from His Father without a mother, / The Son of Man through His mother without a father. / . . . He is the word of God before all ages, / and the Word made flesh at the destined time. / Maker of the sun, He is made [man] beneath the sun. . . . / Creator of heaven and earth, / under the heavens He was born upon earth. / Wise beyond all speech, as a speechless child He is wise. / Filling the whole world, He lies in a manger. / Ruling the stars, he nurses at His mother's breast. / He is great in the form of God / and small in the form of a servant, / so much so that His greatness / is not diminished by His smallness, / nor his smallness concealed by His greatness." [21]

» COMMENT ON THE TEXT: "Here we come to the sentence for the sake of which John wrote his gospel. He has thought and talked about the word of God, that powerful, creative, dynamic word which was the agent of creation, that guiding, directing, controlling word which puts order into the universe and mind into man. These were ideas which were known and familiar to both Jew and Greek. Now he says the most startling and incredible thing that he could

---

[20] David H. Stern, *Jewish New Testament Commentary* (Clarksville, Md.: Jewish New Testament Pubs., 1992), 155–56.

[21] St. Augustine, *Sermo in Natale IV* [a poetic version], in Johann Moser, ed., *O Holy Night: Masterworks of Christmas Poetry* (Manchester, N.H.: Sophia Institute Press, 1995), 96–97.

have said. He says quite simply: 'This word which created the world, this reason which controls the order of the world, has become a person and with our own eyes we saw him. . . .' John declares that the word actually came to earth in the form of a man and was seen by human eyes. He says: 'If you want to see what this creating word, this controlling reason, is like, look at Jesus of Nazareth.'

"This is where John parted with all thought which had gone before him. This was the entirely new thing which John brought to the Greek world for which he was writing. Augustine afterwards said that in his pre-Christian days he had read and studied the great pagan philosophers and had read many things, but he had never read that the word became flesh.

"To a Greek this was the impossible thing. The one thing that no Greek would ever have dreamed of was that God could take a body. To the Greek the body was an evil, a prison-house in which the soul was shackled, a tomb in which the spirit was confined. Plutarch, the wise old Greek, did not even believe that God could control the happenings of this world directly; he had to do it by deputies and intermediaries, for as Plutarch saw it, it was nothing less than blasphemy to involve God in the affairs of the world. Philo could never have said it. He said: 'The life of God has not descended to us; nor has it come as far as the necessities of the body. . . .'

"Here was the shatteringly new thing—that God could and would become a human person, that God could enter into this life that we live, that eternity could appear in time, that somehow the Creator could appear in creation in such a way that men's eyes could actually see him." [22]

24. According to verse 14, what two things did the Logos do? Explain what it means to say that the Logos "dwelt" or "had his dwelling" among us. Where had he dwelt before and in what form? The Greek word for "dwelt" literally means: "to pitch a tent" or to "tabernacle among us". How did the Old Testament describe the pitching of God's tent, which contained the Ark of the Covenant (1 Chron 15:1ff.)? What do you think John means by saying the Word "pitched his tent among us" (Ex 33:7ff.; Num 9:15–23; CCC 697)? In the Old Covenant, where did God dwell (Ex 40:38; Num 7:89; Lk 2:49)?

25. In Old Testament times, God dwelt with his people in several ways (Ex 29:42–46). How are these similar to and different from the Incarnation (Ex 25:8; 40:34–35; 2 Chron 7:1–3; CCC 593, 771, 1183, 1197)? What was "overshadowed" with the glory of God at the inception of the Old Covenant (Ex 40:34–35; CCC 697)? What or who was over-

---

[22] William Barclay, *The Gospel of John* (Philadelphia: Westminster Press, 1975), 1:63–64.

shadowed by the Spirit of God at the inception of the New Covenant (Lk 1:35; CCC 437, 484–86; and especially 697)? The Greek word for "overshadow" in the New Testament (Lk 1:35) and the Old Testament Septuagint (Ex 40:35) is the same. Where did the Divine Person of the Logos dwell before his birth? In what form did God dwell after the birth (Col 1:19; 2:9; CCC 484, 515)?

» COMMENT ON THE TEXT: "The verb 'to overshadow', then, and the metaphors 'shadow' and 'cloud' have a characteristic meaning in biblical language, connoting the 'presence of God' in the meeting tent (Ex 40:34–35) and in the Temple of Yahweh where the Ark was kept (1 Kings 8:10–11). Mary also, 'overshadowed' by 'the power of the Most High', is transformed into a true 'tabernacle' of the Most High, into a sanctuary of the living presence of God who also makes Himself her Son."[23]

26. How is the word "glory" related to the Old Testament tabernacle and Jesus (Ex 40:34–38)? How was God's *shekinah* glory manifested in the Temple (1 Kings 8:10–12)? How does this "glory" relate to the Church (CCC 865)? How was this glory revealed in Christ (for example, Jn 2:11)? How does this demonstrate that Jesus is the new Tabernacle, the new presence of God on the earth (Rev 21:3)? How is Mary related to this glory (CCC 2676)? In a biblical context, where are Mary, "the Woman", and the Tabernacle very closely associated (Rev 11:16–12:1; cf. CCC 1138)?

» OLD TESTAMENT BACKGROUND: "When the Prologue proclaims that the Word made his dwelling among men, we are being told that the flesh of Jesus Christ is the new localization of God's presence on earth, and that Jesus is the replacement of the ancient Tabernacle. The Gospel will present Jesus as the replacement of the Temple (2:19–22). . . . In rabbinic theology *shekinah* was a technical term for God's presence dwelling among His people. . . . [T]he use of *shekinah* as a surrogate for Yahweh in His dealings with men was a way of preserving God's transcendence. . . . [W]hat we are primarily interested in is the constant connection of the glory of God with His presence in the Tabernacle and the Temple. When Moses went up Mount Sinai (Exod xxiv 15–16), we are told that a cloud covered the mountain and the glory of God settled there while God told Moses how to build the Tabernacle. When the Tabernacle was erected, the cloud covered it and the glory of God filled it (Exod xl 34). The same phenomenon is reported when Solomon's Temple was dedicated (I Kings viii

---

[23] Stefano M. Manelli, *All Generations Shall Call Me Blessed* (New Bedford, Mass.: Academy of the Immaculate, 1989), 141–42.

10–11). . . . Thus, it is quite appropriate that, after the description of how the word set up a Tabernacle among men in the flesh of Jesus, the Prologue should mention that his *glory* became visible. . . . The great exhibition of the enduring covenant love of God in the O[ld] T[estament] took place at Sinai, the same setting where the Tabernacle became the dwelling for God's glory. So now the supreme exhibition of God's love is the incarnate Word, Jesus Christ, the new Tabernacle of divine glory. If our interpretation of 'love in place of love' is correct, the hymn comes to an end with the triumphant proclamation of a new covenant replacing the Sinai covenant." [24]

27. According to verse 14, what does it mean that Jesus is "the only Son from the Father", or the "Only-begotten from the Father"? Does it mean that Jesus was "created" by God or had a beginning (CCC 465, 242)?

» THEOLOGICAL NOTE: "We believe in one Lord, Jesus Christ, the only Son of God, eternally begotten of the Father, God from God, Light from Light, true God from true God, begotten, not made, one in Being [substance, essence] with the Father" (*Nicene Creed*).

"Christ is, therefore, said to be the 'only-begotten of the Father,' in order to distinguish his origin of the Father from all other kinds of origin. Thus Christ is absolutely unique in proceeding from the Father, in complete contrast to others, like angels and human persons, who are also called sons of God.

"He is of the substance of the Father, which in the original Greek says that he is 'out of the being (*ousia*) of the Father.' This affirms that, unlike mere creatures, who may be said to be *from* God, his only-begotten Son comes literally out of the Father's own being. Creatures come from God, indeed, because he wills them to exist. Not so the Son of God, who cannot not exist. His existence does not depend on the free will of the Creator.

"He is God of God, in the sense that he is as much God as the Father, sharing perfectly in the one and same divine nature. Yet the two are really distinct, because one originates and the other is originated." [25]

"With reference to Christ, the phrase 'the only begotten from the Father,' John 1:14 . . . indicates that as the Son of God He was the sole representative of the Being and character of the One who sent Him. In the original the definite article is omitted both before 'only begotten' and before 'Father,' and its absence in each case serves to lay stress upon the characteristics referred to in

---

[24] Raymond E. Brown, ed. and trans., *The Gospel according to John*, vol. 1, Anchor Bible, vol. 29 (Garden City, N.Y.: Doubleday, 1966), 33–35.

[25] John A. Hardon, *The Catholic Catechism* (Garden City, N.Y.: Doubleday, 1981), 128. For an excellent discussion of the Trinity and the eternal generation of the Son, see Frank J. Sheed, *Theology and Sanity* (San Francisco: Ignatius Press, 1978).

the terms used. The Apostle's object is to demonstrate what sort of glory it was that he and his fellow-Apostles had seen. That he is not merely making a comparison with earthly relationships is indicated by παρα 'from.' The glory was that of a unique relationship and the word 'begotten' does not imply a beginning of His Sonship. It suggests relationship indeed, but must be distinguished from generation as applied to man.

"We can only rightly understand the term 'the only begotten' when used of the Son, in the sense of unoriginated relationship. 'The begetting is not an event of time, however remote, but a fact irrespective of time. The Christ did not become, but necessarily and eternally is the Son. He, a Person, possesses every attribute of pure Godhood. This necessitates eternity, absolute being; in this respect He is not "after" the Father' (Moule)." [26]

28. Notice the parallel between the phrase "full of grace and truth" in v. 14 and the phrase in Exodus 34:6. How is God's glory revealed to Moses on the mountain? Now compare John 1:17 and read CCC 2466. Explain how God's glory is revealed now to the world.

» OLD TESTAMENT BACKGROUND: "The words 'grace and truth' are synonyms of 'goodness and fidelity', two attributes which, in the Old Testament, are constantly applied to Yahweh (cf., e.g., Ex 34:6; Ps 117; Ps 136; Osee [Hosea] 2:16–22): so, grace is the expression of God's love for men, the way he expresses his goodness and mercy. Truth implies permanence, loyalty, constancy, fidelity. Jesus, who is the Word of God made man, that is, God himself, is therefore 'the only Son of the Father, full of grace and truth'; he is the 'merciful and faithful high priest' (Heb 2:17). These two qualities, being good and faithful, are a kind of compendium or summary of Christ's greatness." [27]

29. According to verse 15, what does John the Baptist testify to concerning Jesus (Jn 1:27–30)? Was Jesus born before or after the Baptist (Lk 1:26–31, 36, 56–60)? How is it that John can say that Jesus existed or was "before" him (Jn 1:30)? What is John telling us about Jesus' existence (cf. Jn 8:56–58)?

30. Who contains the fullness of deity (Col 1:19; 2:9; CCC 504)? What does John mean by "grace upon grace" in verse 16? What is "grace", merely God's attitude of favor or an actual imparted or infused gift of God's very life (1 Cor 1:4; 2 Cor 5:17; 8:1; Eph 4:7; CCC 1197, 2787)?

---

[26] W. E. Vine, *An Expository Dictionary of Biblical Words* (Nashville: Thomas Nelson Pub., 1984), 812.
[27] Casciaro, *John*, 49.

How do various Christian traditions differ in their understanding of "grace"?

» WORD STUDY: GRACE: Generally, Evangelical Protestants consider grace to be merely an attitude of divine favor, not an actual quality of soul, a gift of the very life of God. Catholic teaching understands grace as both: God's unmerited attitude of favor toward sinners *and* the gift of his own life—a quality infused into the soul by God. One Evangelical dictionary defines grace as "an objective relation of undeserved favor by a superior to an inferior. . . . The subjective effects of grace may sometimes seem to make God's grace an independent virtue, a 'thing' possessed by the believer (Acts 4:33; 11:23; 13:43; Rom. 5:21), but attention to context reminds us that these are rather references to the operations of the Spirit of grace (Heb. 10:29). Theories that the [Greek] idea of *charis* [grace] as an independent potency is present in NT usage are quite unproven." [28] "Protestant theologians commonly say that the difference between Luther and Rome was that grace, for the latter, was an impersonal substance or medicine while, for the former, it was the attribute of God, his graciousness." [29] Also refer to Henry Thiessen's *Lectures in Systematic Theology*, where he defines grace as simply "the goodness of God manifested toward the ill-deserving".[30] "Grace may be defined as the unmerited or undeserving favor of God to those who are under condemnation." [31] "Grace is the unmerited favor of God. It is an action or disposition of God toward us. Grace is not a substance that can inhabit our souls." [32]

That Catholics understand grace as both a favorable attitude of God toward sinners *and* a "quality of soul" bestowed by God is evident in the *Catechism*, where we read, "Sanctifying grace is the gratuitous gift of his life that God makes to us; it is infused by the Holy Spirit into the soul to heal it of sin and to sanctify it" (CCC 2023).

God infuses this grace into our souls in various ways, for example, through his Spirit and the sacraments (CCC 2003, 1996–97, 2023–24). "The term 'grace' refers generally to any divine assistance given to persons (human or angelic), in order to advance them toward their supernatural destiny of fellowship with God. . . . As a quality transforming the soul in this way, grace is

---

[28] R. Kearsley, "Grace", in *New Dictionary of Theology*, ed. Sinclair B. Ferguson, David F. Wright, and J. I. Packer (Downers Grove, Ill.: InterVarsity Press, 1988), 280.

[29] Van A. Harvey, *A Handbook of Theological Terms* (New York: Macmillan Pub., 1964), 109.

[30] Henry Thiessen, *Lectures in Systematic Theology* (Grand Rapids, Mich.: Eerdmans, 1979), 132.

[31] Paul P. Enns, "Relative Attributes", in *The Moody Handbook of Theology* (Chicago: Moody Press, 1989); published in electronic form, in Logos Library System 2.1e, by Logos Research Systems, 1997.

[32] R. C. Sproul, *Essential Truths of the Christian Faith* (Wheaton, Ill.: Tyndale House Pubs., 1992), 195.

something created. But because the term 'grace' refers also to the very indwelling of God, there is an important sense in which grace is uncreated, identical with God himself." [33] Grace is an undeserved gift—something to which individuals have no right or claim, but which comes simply from the benevolent nature of God.

"[Sanctifying grace:] In order to live the life of heaven, for which man is destined, he needs new powers of knowing and loving in his soul over and above the natural powers of his intellect and will. Therefore a new life-principle, a new principle of operation, must be given to his soul. . . . Sanctifying grace does not provide us with a new soul; it enters into the soul we already have. Nor does it give the soul new faculties but elevates the faculties that are already there, giving intellect and will new powers of operation. . . . The giving of supernatural life by way of sacrament, then, corresponds with the structure of the man." [34]

"This, then, must be our first point: grace is a positive reality superadded to the soul. But what is the nature of this positive reality? Here we are faced by the inability of the human mind to grasp the magnificence of the glorious truth." [35] Other theologians have said that the gift of divine grace penetrates the soul as the glow of the fire enters the iron in a blacksmith's shop, communicating a new quality to the soul by which it is transformed into the image of God.[36] It takes the supernatural grace of God to bring us to holiness and perfection in our Lord Jesus Christ.

31. Has Jesus been identified by name before John 1:17? With whom is Jesus contrasted in verse 17? Where else are they compared to each other (Heb 3:1–6)? How do their "glories" compare (Ex 34:29–35; 2 Cor 3:7; 4:6; CCC 2583)? What caused Moses' glory (Ex 34:29)? Was the Law of Moses devoid of grace, or was it a gift of God's grace (Rom 7:12; Gal 3:19–24; CCC 1963)? What is "glory" (CCC 2809, 294)? What was the source of Christ's glory (Jn 7:16–19; 17:24)? What happened to Isaiah when he saw the Lord's glory (Jn 12:41; Is 6:1–7)?

» HISTORICAL NOTE: "The radiance of Moses' face marks a reflection of the divine glory he has in some way confronted on the mountain. To convey the brilliant rays of light emanating from the countenance of Moses, the MT [Hebrew text] uses the term *qeren*. Because the first meaning of this word is

---

[33] Peter Stravinskas, "Grace", in *Our Sunday Visitor's Catholic Dictionary* (Huntington, Ind.: Our Sunday Visitor Pub., 1991), electronic edition, 449.

[34] Sheed, *Theology and Sanity*, 298, 300–301.

[35] E. Towers, *Sanctifying Grace* (London: Burns, Oates, & Washbourne, 1930), 8.

[36] See Matthias Joseph Scheeben, *The Glories of Divine Grace* (Rockford, Ill.: TAN Books, 1994).

'horn,' St. Jerome translated it as such. Michelangelo was following the [Vulgate] when he adorned his heroic Moses with horns projecting from his forehead." [37] To see St. Paul's treatment of this passage in relation to the New Covenant, see 2 Corinthians 3:7—4:6.

32. How do "law" and "grace" relate to each other (Rom 3:28–31; CCC 1992)? Are Christians freed from the Law of God (CCC 1963–68; Mt 5:17–20; 7:12; Jas 2:24)? Is the Law lessened for us, or are we expected to reach a higher obedience and holiness (Jn 13:34; CCC 2822)?

» THEOLOGICAL NOTE: "Law and Grace": In Fundamentalist circles, St. Paul's words are often taken to imply that we are no longer obligated to obey the Law in any fashion—grace has freed us altogether. Favorite biblical passages that supposedly support this view include "You are not under law but under grace" (Rom 6:14), and "But now we have been released from the Law, having died to that by which we were bound, so that we serve in newness of the Spirit and not in oldness of the letter" (Rom 7:6; NASB).

Martin Luther, in order to help calm a friend's anxieties over sin, wrote him, "Be a sinner, and sin boldly, but believe more boldly still; and rejoice in Christ, Who is the conqueror of sin, death and the world; we must sin as long as we are what we are. . . . Sin shall not drag us away from Him, even should we commit fornication or murder thousands and thousands of times a day. Do you think that the price and the ransom paid for our sins by this sublime Lamb is so insignificant? Pray boldly, for you are in truth a very bold sinner." [38] However, Luther's view is a misunderstanding of St. Paul's words, the meaning of grace, and the teaching of the Bible.

"The Catholic doctrine on this point is in direct opposition to the strange theories of Protestantism. Faced by his failure to control his violent and sensuous character, Luther evolved a theory which is a combination of pessimism and easy optimism. Through the fall of Adam, he maintained, our nature has become essentially evil and must ever remain evil; it is a mass of corruption, and even the redeeming blood of our Saviour does not cleanse or heal it; and he pressed his theory so far as to draw the conclusion that all our actions are sinful, not excluding those which we look upon as virtuous. Here we have the pessimism of the system: but now comes its easy optimism. For Luther taught that if only we will have complete confidence that the merits of Christ are actually applied to us, our sins are ignored, as it were, by God; our souls remain indeed hideous in themselves, but God covers them over with the merits of

---

[37] Brown, Fitzmyer, and Murphy, *Jerome Biblical Commentary*, 1:66.
[38] Luther in a letter to Melanchthon, in Hartmann Grisar, *Luther*, trans. E. M. Lamond (St. Louis, Mo.: B. Herder Book Co., 1919), 3:196.

Christ so that these are looked upon by him as being ours; our sins are not 'imputed' to us, but the merits of Christ are.

"This is the famous doctrine of justification by Faith. For the Lutheran, then, justification does not mean (as it means for a Catholic) an inner change by which the soul becomes a sacred thing, but a mere external non-imputation of sins; and Faith means, not an assent to truths divinely revealed, but a personal persuasion that the merits of Christ have been applied to us. This Faith, in the Lutheran system, is the only thing which counts: good works are of no avail—indeed, they are impossible, since all our actions are made evil by the evil source from which they spring. A further conclusion from Luther's principles is that there can be no such thing as Merit, a point with which we shall deal later on. . . . This is inevitable, for, although our chief concern is with the positive statement of Catholic truth, the official statement of this truth by the Council of Trent was drawn up with direct reference to the errors of the sixteenth century. In the first place, then, the Council lays it down that we become just before God not through a non-imputation of sin but by an interior renovation which blots out sin. This is effected by sanctifying grace, which is explained as a reality poured forth upon us and inhering in us. Beyond any doubt, this is the teaching of Scripture and of the great leaders of Christian thought from the beginning." [39]

Messianic Jew David Stern writes, "Being 'under grace' is a subjection which, because of the nature of grace itself, does not have the usual oppressive characteristics of subjection. God's people are to live *en* ('within the framework of,' 2:12) [the Mosaic Law], but they are not *upo* ('in subjection to,' Gal 3:23) legalism. God's giving the [Mosaic Law] was itself an act of grace which the New Testament compares with his sending Yeshua [Jesus] . . . the people who are in a trust relationship with him, are and always have been under grace and under [the Mosaic Law] (a gracious subjection) but never under legalism (a harsh subjection)." [40]

Grace does not free us from our moral obligations before God; rather, it provides the strength and ability to live righteously before God. Hebrews tells us plainly that living righteously before God is not optional: "Strive for peace with all men, and for the holiness without which no one will see the Lord" (Heb 12:14). This is a practical, real holiness that is infused into our soul by the grace of God and lived daily by his enabling gift. The Law through Moses offered no grace for the soul to obey and was given to only one nation. But, the grace flowing abundantly from Christ, "grace upon grace" enables men to observe the moral precepts of the Law—men of all nations, languages, and ages.[41]

---

[39] Towers, *Sanctifying Grace*, 4–5.
[40] Stern, *Jewish New Testament Commentary*, 374.
[41] See Hardon, *Catholic Catechism*, 288–90, and MacEvilly, *Exposition*, 19.

33. Verse 18 is deep with spiritual mystery and Old Testament allusions. Some ancient manuscripts refer to Jesus as "the only begotten God". What is a basic attribute of God (Sir 43:31; 1 Tim 1:17; 6:16; Col 1:15; CCC 32, 241)? Was Moses able to see the face of God (Ex 33:11, 18–23; Deut 4:12)? Was Elijah able to see God (1 Kings 19:11–13)? When did Moses and Elijah finally see the glory and face of God (Mk 9:2–8)? Has anyone seen the invisible God or had a vision of him (Gen 32:24–32; Ex 24:9–11; Num 12:6–8; Is 6:5; Ezek 1:26–28; 1 Jn 4:12; CCC 42)? What do we see in the "face of Christ" (2 Cor 4:6; CCC 2583)? How does Jesus make God known or "visible" (Jn 10:30–33; 12:44–50; 14:7–10; Col 1:15; 2:9; Heb 1:1–3; CCC 240, 477, 1159)?

» THE INVISIBLE GOD: "To the bodily eye, even in its glorified state, God is absolutely invisible. . . . To enable us to see God, either God would have to appear in a material vesture, or our own [eyes] would have to be capable of attaining by supernatural means to a bodily vision of purely spiritual substances. Both these suppositions are inadmissible. God, being pure spirit, has no material body, and therefore cannot be visible to the human eye." [42]

Regarding Exodus 24:10: "At first sight, this is a contradiction of Exodus 33:20. But it will be remembered that even there Moses was to be allowed to see God's back (33:23). In this verse it is equally stressed that the elders did not dare raise their eyes above His footstool. Naturally, there is deep spiritual truth in these anthropomorphic metaphors, a truth which finds expression in Moses' hiding his own face (Ex 3:6) and Isaiah's cry (Is 6:5). No mortal man can bear to see the full splendour of God; it is only in Christ that we see Him mirrored (Heb 1:3)." [43]

"Despite the assertion that Moses and his special companions saw God, however, the description of what they saw concentrates not on the appearance of God but on the appearance of what lay at his feet. This can be taken to imply that a description of God original to this passage has been respectfully deleted, or, as is more likely, that the group was not given permission to lift their faces toward God and so could describe only what they actually did see, the 'pavement' beneath him, before which they were prostrate in reverential awe. . . . Thus what Moses and his companions experience is a theophany [self-disclosure] of the Presence of God, not a vision of his person, and what they see, bowed before even that awesome reality, is what could be seen from

---

[42] Joseph Pohle, *God: His Knowability, Essence, and Attributes*, adapted and edited by Arthur Preuss (St. Louis, Mo.: B. Herder Book Co., 1925), 82–83.

[43] Alan R. Cole, *Exodus*, Tyndale Old Testament Commentaries (Downers Grove, Ill.: InterVarsity Press, 1973), 186–87.

a position of obeisant prostration, the surface on which his Presence offered itself." [44]

» THEOLOGICAL NOTE: "By this revelation then, the deepest truth about God and the salvation of man is made clear to us in Christ, who is the Mediator and at the same time the fullness of all revelation." [45]

"There is no greater revelation God could make of himself than the Incarnation of his eternal Word. As St. John of the Cross puts it so well: 'In giving to us, as he has done, his Son, who is his only Word, he has spoken to us once and for all by his own and only Word, and has nothing further to reveal' (St. John of the Cross, *Ascent of Mount Carmel*, Book II, chap. 22)." [46]

» OLD TESTAMENT PARALLELS: The Moses/Christ contrast and comparison is a central theme of John's Gospel. Jesus is portrayed as the new Moses, the Prophet who is to come—fulfilling Moses' prophecy in Deuteronomy 18:15, 18. "The Prologue ought to suggest this to us, for in 1:17 we have the statement, 'The law was given through Moses; grace and truth came through Jesus Christ.' Here there is a contrast and a comparison. The very next verse probably continues the thought. Emphasis was often laid by the Jews upon the closeness of Moses' communion with God (Deut. 34:10); there was a sense in which he was granted a vision of the divine (Ex. 33), but this was partial and incomplete, so that it still remained true that 'no man hath seen God at any time' (John 1:18). In contrast with this is the perfect knowledge and revelation of God associated with the only begotten. . . .

"[John] is tacitly drawing attention to the fact that while Moses was a man of vision, the scriptures make it plain that he did not see God. The Son of God, however, has and communicates perfect knowledge of God (1:18b). Cf. 6:46, 'Not that any man hath seen the Father, save he which is from God, he hath seen the Father.' Thus at the outset of the Fourth Gospel we find the coordination of Moses and Christ in comparison and contrast. Mention should also be made of the Torah/Logos theme of the Prologue; for Moses is important not only as a prophet and deliverer but as the embodiment of the Law, as in the phrase 'Moses and the prophets'. Running right through the Prologue is the transference to the Logos of what had been claimed for the Torah." [47]

[44] John I. Durham, *Exodus*, Word Biblical Commentary, vol. 3 (Waco, Tex.: Word Books, 1987), 344.

[45] Vatican II, Dogmatic Constitution on Divine Revelation, *Dei Verbum*, November 18, 1965, no. 2.

[46] Casciaro, *John*, 52.

[47] T. F. Glasson, *Moses in the Fourth Gospel* (Napierville, Ill.: Alec R. Allenson, 1963), 24–26.

JOHN 1 b

JOHN THE BAPTIST; CHOOSING THE DISCIPLES

John 1:19–34
Testimony of John the Baptist

1. St. John uses the words "testify" or "witness" more than forty-six times in his Gospel. Why does he use this word so often (Jn 20:30–31; 21:24)? Why does St. John insert the story of John the Baptist into the narrative at this point? (*Hint*: Notice how John begins and ends this section, Jn 1:19, 34.) In the original Greek, the word for "testimony" is *marturia*, from which we get the English word "martyr". How did the original apostles, John the Baptist, and the early Christians prove to be real witnesses to the gospel of Christ (Mt 14:10–11; Acts 7:59–60; 12:2; CCC 2473)? Why do you think the word "witness" (martyr) took on such a strong meaning in Church history?

» CHURCH FATHERS: In the twentieth century, there were more martyrdoms than in the previous nineteen centuries, and the Church is larger than ever in history—over a billion strong! The early Church understood martyrdom. Tertullian wrote to the persecutors of his age: "But go zealously on, good presidents, you will stand higher with the people if you sacrifice the Christians at their wish, kill us, torture us, condemn us, grind us to dust; your injustice is the proof that we are innocent. . . . Nor does your cruelty, however exquisite, avail you; it is rather a temptation to us. The oftener we are mown down by you, the more in number we grow; *the blood of Christians is seed* [commonly quoted as 'the blood of the martyrs is the seed of the Church']. . . . As the divine and human are ever opposed to each other, when we are condemned by you, we are acquitted by the Highest." [1]

2. Read the Synoptic accounts of John preaching in the wilderness (Mt 3:1–12; 11:2–19; Mk 1:1–8; Lk 3:1–22). How was he dressed, and what

---

[1] Tertullian, *Apology* 50, in ANF 3:55.

did he eat (Mt 3:4; Mk 1:6)? How did John the Baptist respond to the priests' and Levites' question, "Who are you?" (vv. 19–23)? Why did they suspect John might be Elijah (2 Kings 2:11–18; Mal 4:5–6; Mt 11:14)? Why did they suspect he might be "the prophet" (Deut 18:15, 18; cf. Jn 7:40; 4:19, 25, 29; Lk 1:76)? Who, in fact, was John the Baptist (CCC 523)? Why did John the Baptist identify himself as he did in verse 23, and what did he mean (Is 40:3–11, esp. v. 5; Mk 1:1–4; Mal 3:1; CCC 719)? Notice the wording of Isaiah 40:5–8. Why did John come "baptizing in water" (Jn 1:31)?

» HISTORICAL NOTE: "The Jews", as the term is used by St. John, usually refers to leaders of the religious establishment who opposed Jesus. It is not to be interpreted as an anti-Semitic slur against the Jewish race as a whole. This should be obvious, since St. John was himself a Jew, as were Jesus, Mary, and all the first Christians (cf. CCC 575, 597).

The Levites were from the tribe of Jacob's son Levi and were the ministerial priests of Israel, serving the High Priests and distinct from the "priesthood" of all Israelites (Ex 19:6; Num 3:5–13). They were chosen for this honor at Mt. Sinai at the giving of the Law (Ex 32:25–29). Some scholars have held that the Sadducees derive their name from Zadok, the high priest in the days of Solomon, although others dispute this. They were the aristocrats—the ruling class—and thought of themselves as "broad-minded". They denied the resurrection of the dead and did not believe in angels. The scribes were not priests but were esteemed as interpreters of the Law. They formulated a mass of regulations and interpretations that they claimed was the proper application of the Law. The Pharisees, which means "the Separatists", set themselves apart among God's covenant people. They were generally revered and held in the highest esteem by the people. There were about six thousand Pharisees, and they claimed to understand and obey the Mosaic Law and made a public display of their piety. From the very beginning of Jesus' ministry, the Pharisees showed themselves bitter and persistent enemies of our Lord. They could not bear his teaching, and they sought by every means to destroy his influence among the people. St. Paul was originally a Pharisee (cf. Acts 26:5).

3. According to verse 33, what is John the Baptist waiting for—what sign would confirm his discovery? What sign is given to John the Baptist that identifies Jesus as the Messiah (Lk 3:21–22; Jn 1:29–34; CCC 535, 701)? What family relation is John the Baptist to Jesus (Lk 1:36)? At what other times are water and dove/Spirit mentioned together in a work of God (Gen 1:1–2, 8:8–11; CCC 701; Jn 3:3–5; 1 Pet 3:20–21)? What does John mean that Jesus will baptize with the Holy Spirit (Acts 2:1–4; Jn 16:7–15; CCC 1287–89)? How does this baptism or filling of the

Holy Spirit manifest itself in the Church (Acts 4:31; 7:55; 1 Cor 12; CCC 1302–3; 951)?

» Patristic note: St. Theophilus of Antioch (died ca. 185) said, "Those things which were created from the waters were blessed by God [Gen 1], so that this might also be a sign that men would at a future time receive repentance and remission of sins through water and the bath of regeneration." [2]

4. According to verse 28, where was John the Baptist baptizing? How was the Trinity revealed at the baptism of Jesus (cf. Mt 3:16–17; CCC 1224)? At this time, God confirmed Jesus as a priest—anointing him with the Holy Spirit (Acts 10:38; Heb 5:5; CCC 438). Jesus fulfilled the three great offices of Israel: *prophet* (Lk 9:35; cf. Deut 18:15, 18), *priest* (Heb 2:17; 4:14–16; 5:5) and *king* (Jn 12:13, 28). What did Jesus' baptism mean (CCC 536, 1286)? Why did John publicly identify Jesus with the exclamation, "Behold, the Lamb of God, who takes away the sin of the world!" (Ex 12:1–13; Is 53:7; 1 Cor 5:7; Acts 8:32; CCC 608, 613)? The Jewish sacrifice was for the sins of the people of Israel. How effective was the sacrifice of Christ (CCC 614–15)? How would Peter recall this testimony later in his life (1 Pet 1:18–20)? How did Jesus bear the sins of the world (2 Cor 5:21; cf. Lev 16:21)?

» THEOLOGICAL NOTE: "John was affirming we must not look first for a teacher, a giver of moral precepts, or a worker of miracles. First we must look for One Who had been appointed as a sacrifice for the sins of the world. The Passover was approaching, and the highways were filled with people driving or carrying their one-year-old lambs to the temple to be sacrificed. In full view of those lambs, John pointed out the Lamb Who, when sacrificed, would end all sacrifices in the temple, because He would take away the sins of the world.

"John was the parting voice of the Old Testament, in which the lamb played such an important role. In Genesis, we find Abel offering a lamb, the firstling of his flock, in a bloody sacrifice for the expiation of sin. Later on, God asked Abraham to sacrifice his son Isaac—a prophetic symbol of the Heavenly Father sacrificing His own Son. When Isaac asked, 'Where is the lamb?' Abraham said: 'God will provide himself with a young beast for a sacrifice, my son' (Gen 22:8). The answer to the question, 'Where is the lamb of sacrifice?' asked in the beginning of Genesis, was now answered by John the Baptist as he pointed to Christ and said, 'Here is the Lamb of God.' God had at last provided a Lamb. . . .

[2] *To Autolycus* 2, 16, in William A. Jurgens, *The Faith of the Early Fathers*, vol. 1 (Collegeville, Minn.: Liturgical Press, 1970), 75.

"Every family sought to have its own Paschal Lamb; and those who were now taking their lambs to Jerusalem, where the Lamb of God said that He must be sacrificed, knew that the lamb was a symbol of Israel's deliverance from the political slavery of Egypt. John was saying that it was also a symbol of deliverance from the spiritual slavery of sin." [3]

5. How is Jesus, the Lamb of God, presented to the Father for all of eternity (Rev 5:6; CCC 1137)? (See Jan van Eyck's painting *Adoration of the Lamb.*) Is the sacrifice of Christ merely a past event, or is it eternally present to the Father (1 Jn 2:1–2; CCC 519, 1085)? How does the Catholic appropriate this ever-present sacrifice in the Mass (1 Cor 10:16–22; Rev 5:6–14; CCC 1137–39, 1340, 1364–67)? Why is there a golden altar before God's throne (Is 6:6; Rev 8:3)? Why is there a "Table of the Lord" (altar: Mal 1:7–12) in Catholic churches (1 Cor 10:21; Heb 13:10; CCC 1383)? Notice the priestly work of Christ: "Therefore he had to be made like his brethren in every respect, so that he might become a merciful and faithful high priest in the service of God, to make expiation for the sins of the people" (Heb 2:17).

» THEOLOGICAL NOTE: "Yochanan [John] identifies Yeshua [Jesus] with the dominant sacrificial animal used in connection with Temple ritual, and particularly with the sin offerings, since he is *the one who is taking away the sin of the world.* Elsewhere in the New Testament Yeshua the Messiah is equated with the Passover lamb (1 Cor 5:7). The figure of the lamb connects Yeshua with the passage identifying the Messiah as the Suffering Servant in Isaiah 53 (Ac 8:32); and his sacrificial death by execution on a stake is compared with 'that of a lamb without a defect or a spot' (1 Pet 1:19), as required by the Torah (e.g., Exodus 12:5, 29:1; Leviticus 1:3, 10; 9:3; 23:12). In the book of Revelation Yeshua is referred to as the Lamb nearly thirty times. On God's requiring a human sacrifice for sins, see 1 Cor 15:3, Heb 7:26–28, and indeed the entire book of Messianic Jews." [4]

» LITURGICAL NOTE: The exclamation "Behold, the Lamb of God who takes away the sin of the world" is one of the most profound statements in the Bible. It is based on many centuries of Jewish history, rooted in their sacrificial system and the Scriptures. One cannot hear the Gospel more clearly proclaimed. Where do Catholics hear the Gospel every Sunday? Where do they hear these words from the Bible—this wonderful proclamation about the Lamb of God—

---

[3] Fulton Sheen, *Life of Christ* (New York: Image Books/Doubleday, 1990), 71.

[4] David H. Stern, *Jewish New Testament Commentary* (Clarksville, Md.: Jewish New Testament Pubs., 1992), 161–62.

every Sunday? How is it applied to their lives in a real and profound way at each Mass (CCC 1393–94)?

» THE FATHERS: Ignatius of Antioch (ca. 35–ca. 107), a first-century hero of the faith and disciple of the apostles, wrote: "But look at those men who have those perverted notions about the grace of Jesus Christ which has come down to us, and see how contrary to the mind of God they are. . . . They even abstain from the Eucharist and the public [liturgical] prayer, because they will not admit that the Eucharist is the self-same body of our Savior Jesus Christ, which [flesh] suffered for our sins, and which the Father in His goodness raised up again. Consequently, since they reject God's gifts, they are doomed in their disputatiousness. They should have done better to learn charity, if they were ever to know any resurrection. . . . Abjure all factions, for they are the beginning of evils." [5]

6. To what does John bear witness (Jn 1:34; CCC 1286)? Who else proclaims the same thing (Jn 1:49)? What three titles does he attribute to Jesus? Was this a radical statement in the Jewish mind?

John 1:35–51
Jesus Chooses Disciples

7. Read the accounts of how Jesus chose his disciples in the other Gospels (Mt 4:18–22; Mk 1:16–20; Lk 6:12–16). In verses 35 and 40, who were the two disciples of John the Baptist? What did they do when they heard Jesus was the Lamb of God (v. 37)? What does the word "disciple" mean (CCC 2233, 1816)? What does the word "rabbi" mean (Jn 1:38)?

» HISTORICAL NOTE: "The first two [disciples] to move (for probably all the twelve apostles were originally among John's disciples) were Andrew and John the Evangelist: for that the unnamed one was the Evangelist is asserted by the consensus of Church tradition." [6] Throughout the Gospel of John we find phrases such as the disciple "whom Jesus loved" (Jn 13:23; 21:20) and "another disciple" (Jn 18:15), which have since ancient times been understood to refer to St. John the author, the Beloved Disciple.

"At that time the apostle and evangelist John, the one whom Jesus loved, was

[5] Ignatius of Antioch, *Letter to the Smyrnaeans* 7, 8, in *Early Christian Writings*, trans. Maxwell Staniforth (New York: Penguin Books, 1968), 102–3.

[6] G. H. Trench, *A Study of St John's Gospel* (London: John Murray, 1918), 33.

still living in Asia, and governing the churches of that region, having returned after the death of Domitian from his exile on the island. And that he was still alive at that time may be established by the testimony of two witnesses. They should be trustworthy who have maintained the orthodoxy of the Church; and such indeed were Irenaeus [ca. 130–ca. 200] and Clement of Alexandria [ca. 155–ca. 220]. The former in the second book of his work *Against Heresies*, writes as follows: 'And all the elders that associated with John the disciple of the Lord in Asia bear witness that John delivered it to them. For he remained among them until the time of Trajan [reigned 98–117].' And in the third book of the same work he attests the same thing in the following words: 'But the church in Ephesus also, which was founded by Paul, and where John remained until the time of Trajan, is a faithful witness of the apostolic tradition.' " [7]

8. In verses 38 and 39, what do the two disciples ask Jesus, and what does he answer (Jn 1:38–39)? Where does Jesus really dwell (Jn 1:18; 14:1–6, 20)? How might there be a deeper spiritual meaning implied in Jesus' invitation to "Come and see"? In verse 40, we meet Andrew, Simon Peter's brother. What did these brothers do for a living (Mt 4:18–22; Lk 5:9–11)? How is symbolism used here (Mt 4:19)? How might this have been prophesied in advance (Jer 16:14ff.)?

» THEOLOGICAL NOTE: It is interesting that in Matthew's Gospel Peter and Andrew are fishing when Jesus calls them, whereas James and John are mending nets. Is this not how each served the Church? The first two disciples brought people to Jesus and into the Church as fishers of men (cf. Jn 21:11); the second two mended nets, and their apostolate emphasized caring for, mending, and edifying the Church.

9. Andrew is mentioned three times in John's Gospel. What is Andrew doing in each case (Jn 1:40–42; 6:8–9; 12:20–22)? How should we follow Andrew's example? Do we have an obligation to bring people to Jesus (CCC 848)?

10. What type of men did Jesus choose to be his apostles (Acts 2:7; 4:13)? What are possible reasons for such a choice? What kind of people made up the early Church (1 Cor 1:26–29)?

11. There are about seventeen titles for Jesus used in this first chapter of this Gospel—can you find them? How do they each reveal and explain

---

[7] Eusebius, *Church History* [325] 3, 23, 1–4, trans. Arthur Cushman McGiffert, in NPNF2 1:150.

various facets of Jesus' person and mission (Jn 1:1, 4, 9, 14, 17, 18, 29, 30, 34, 38, 41, 45, 49, 51)? How does Andrew identify Jesus (v. 41)? What does this title mean (Dan 9:25–26; Jn 1:41; 4:25; CCC 695, 436)? How has the word "Christ" (*anointed one*) changed from being merely a descriptive adjective into a title and name?

12. In verse 42, Jesus recognizes Simon Peter by divine foresight. The apostolic band is falling into place. It is almost as though he says, "Ah, it's you; my Father chose you before time began to follow me and to be the foundation of my Church. I am going to rename you now, to fit the office I have chosen you to fill." What does the name "Cephas" mean (cf. Mt 16:15–20)? How does Paul acknowledge Peter's unique position (1 Cor 3:22; 9:5; 15:5; Gal 1:18; 2:9)? How does this demonstrate that Jesus spoke Aramaic? Where else does John acknowledge a primacy of Peter—a special office (Jn 21:15–17; CCC 552, 880–82)? Notice how John frames his Gospel in chapters 1 and 21 by informing his readers of the primacy and office of Peter as both Rock and Shepherd.

» WORD STUDY: Cephas is the Greek transliteration of the Aramaic *Kepha*, which means "rock". Jesus tells Peter, "You are Rock, and on this rock I will build my church." Peter and Cephas are not different names, but the same name derived from different languages, Greek and Aramaic respectively. "The first Christians [including St. Paul] regarded this new name as so significant that they used it without translating it (cf. Gal 2:9, 11–14); later its translation 'Peter' (*Petros, Petrus*) became current, pushing the Apostle's old name—Simon—into the background." [8] An argument is sometimes made that Jesus named Simon *Petros* in Matthew 16:18, speaking Greek instead of Aramaic. The name Cephas used here by John (Jn 1:42), which is a transliteration of an Aramaic term, shows that Jesus spoke Aramaic and gives us good reason to believe Matthew 16:18 is a translation of Jesus' words from Aramaic into Greek.

» THEOLOGICAL NOTE: "In the Scriptures, change of name signifies change of role or destiny in the history of salvation (cf. Gn 17:5; 32:28). The significance of the name Cephas ('rock') is explained ecclesiologically by Matthew (Mt 16:16–18). John takes for granted that his readers understand the meaning of the name. In [John] 21:16–19, he will explain the ecclesiological importance of the change of name when he tells how Jesus commissions Peter to be shepherd of his sheep. The two episodes—the change of name in 1 (1:42) and the appointment as shepherd of the sheep in sequence 21 (21:16–19)—are chiastically paralleled. They cannot, therefore, be the work of an ecclesiastical

---

[8] José María Casciaro, *The Navarre Bible: The Gospel of Saint John* (Dublin: Four Courts Press, 1992), 57.

66

redactor, as so many have claimed after Bultmann. Schnackenburg grasps the significance of the little episode when he says, '. . . the Johannine Jesus already has the vision of the later Church before his eyes as he gathers his first disciples around him.' "[9] If we understand this from the beginning, we will perceive throughout the Gospel how Jesus is preparing Peter to fill this role as Rock and Shepherd—the visible head of the visible Church—the vicar shepherd of the Chief Shepherd.

13. In verse 43, what does Jesus command Philip to do? Whom does Jesus command with the same words at the end of the Gospel (Jn 21:22)? What city is Philip from (v. 44)? What other apostles are from the same town? After Jesus "finds" Philip, whom does Philip find (v. 45)? How does Philip identify Jesus (v. 45)?

» HISTORICAL NOTE: "Bethsaida, more than any other New Testament town, can rightly be called the home of the apostles. Specific references in the Gospels link three disciples of Jesus to Bethsaida, namely, Simon Peter, Andrew, and Philip. Later traditions also connect James and John, as well as the other James, to Bethsaida. No other location can make such a claim about the disciples."[10] The name Bethsaida means "house of the fisherman", which is certainly appropriate since Jesus called these disciples to be "fishers of men", as portrayed in the twenty-first chapter of John.

The ancient site of Bethsaida, on the northern tip of the Sea of Galilee, is in ruins today and the location of an archaeological dig. The average fishing families lived in relatively simple homes consisting of only one or two rooms with a small courtyard in front. One particular house unearthed is a structure measuring about twenty-one feet square with walls about two feet thick, leaving a living space of roughly 255 square feet. It was divided into living and sleeping quarters. Light was provided by dim oil lamps. Matting would have provided a surface for sitting and sleeping. Some homes might even have had a second story.[11]

14. In verse 50, what causes Nathanael to believe in Christ? Where does Jesus see Nathanael, and what does this prove to Nathanael? What does Nathanael's faith inspire him to proclaim (v. 49)? Is Jesus surprised that Nathanael believes so easily and with so little proof? How do Nathanael (at the beginning of the Gospel) and Thomas (at the end of the Gospel,

[9] Peter Ellis, *The Genius of John: A Composition-Critical Commentary on the Fourth Gospel* (Collegeville, Minn.: Liturgical Press, 1984), 35.

[10] Fred Strickert, *Bethsaida: Home of the Apostles* (Collegeville, Minn.: Liturgical Press, 1998), 19.

[11] See ibid., 66.

Jn 20:24–28) compare? Again, notice how John frames his Gospel with exclamations of Jesus' deity and lordship. How can we please or, conversely, displease God (Heb 11:6; CCC 161)?

» CULTURAL NOTE: "It was an old custom in Palestine to have a thick-leaved fig tree near one's little house and to enjoy an occasional hour of peace and quiet in its shade (cf. 1 Kings 4:25; Mich. 4:4; Zach. 3:10). In Jesus' time the rabbis sat there to study the Law undisturbed. Hence when Jesus said he had seen Nathanael in that shady retreat he was not announcing an extraordinary discovery from a purely physical point of view. But there must have been something spiritually extraordinary about it to occasion Nathanael's surprise; that is, the thoughts he was pondering within himself in that place must have been related somehow to this imminent meeting. Was he perhaps thinking of the true Messias, having heard the strange rumors spreading through the town about the Jesus who had arrived there? Was he perhaps asking God in his heart for a 'sign' as Zachary had done? We can give no definite answer, but it is clear that Nathanael found the words addressed to him perfectly true. Jesus had truly seen him, not in the shade of the fig tree but within his innermost thoughts. The guileless Israelite was stunned, an impetus of ardor invaded his calm self-possession: 'Rabbi, thou art the Son of God! Thou art King of Israel!' " [12]

15. In verse 47, what does Jesus say about Nathanael? Notice that the word "Israelite" is not common to the New Testament, being used only one other time (Rom 11:1). Whose name did God change to "Israel" (Gen 32:27–28)? What was the character of the man renamed "Israel"— why was he known for his guile and deceit (Gen 25:21–34, esp. 26; Gen 27:1–29)? Using the play on words, one could translate Jesus' pun as "An Israelite in whom there is no Jacob—no guile and cunning". Consider the contrast between Nathanael, a true Israelite, with the children of Israel who rebelled against God in the Old Testament and disbelieved in Jesus in the New.

» WORD STUDY: Nathanael, a name used nowhere else in the New Testament except John 21:2, is probably the same person as Bartholomew, who is not mentioned in the Gospel of St. John. Bartholomew was probably the Jewish patronymic. For more on Bartholomew, see Matthew 10:3; Acts 1:13.[13]

---

[12] Giuseppe Ricciotti, *The Life of Christ*, trans. Alba I. Zizzamia (Milwaukee: Bruce Pub., 1947), 281.

[13] For a full explanation of the names Nathanael and Bartholomew, see John Steinmueller and Kathryn Sullivan, *Catholic Biblical Encyclopedia* (New York: Joseph F. Wagner, 1956), 65.

16. In verse 51, Jesus uses the frequent Johannine phrase "Truly, truly" or "Amen, amen". What does this mean? In response to Nathanael's amazement at such a small thing, Jesus informs Nathanael, "You shall see greater things than these." What will Nathanael see? Why does Jesus say this, and what does he mean (Ezek 1:1; Mt 3:16; Acts 7:56; Rev 4:1; 19:11; Dan 7:13-14)? Does the terminology used by Jesus remind you of an Old Testament story (Gen 28:10-22)? How does this fit into the context of Jesus' conversation with Nathanael?

17. Jacob had a dream of angels ascending and descending into heaven (Gen 28:10-16). Is Jesus drawing attention to Jacob again, and if so, why (CCC 661)? Why does the word "ascending" precede the word "descending"? How does the title "Israelite", the mention of Jacob's vision, the title "Son of man", the presence of God revealed in this first chapter, and Nathanael all fit together? What (or who) is the ladder between heaven and earth? How might this episode illuminate the meaning of John 14:6? How will Jesus be lifted up to bridge the gap between heaven and earth (Jn 12:32-34; Acts 1:9; 1 Tim 2:5; CCC 2795)?

» THEOLOGICAL NOTE: "Here is an Israelite in whom there is no Jacob. You see, although this man is a wisecracker, he is not deceitful or cunning. There is nothing of the old Jacob in him. . . . Our Lord had said to this man, 'Behold, an Israelite in whom there is no Jacob:' Now He follows up on this by referring to the incident in the life of the patriarch Jacob when, as a young man, he had run away from home. In fact, he had to leave home because his brother Esau was after him to murder him. His first night away from home was at Bethel, and there the Lord appeared to him. A ladder was let down from heaven, and on that ladder the angels were ascending and descending. The meaning for Jacob was that God had not lost contact with him. He had thought that when he left home, he had left God back there. He had a limited view of God, of course. At Bethel he learned that God would be with him." [14]

Jacob needed "supernatural" sight to see the spiritual world, which was actually as real as the rock on which he slept. The angels were there, and God was in that place even though Jacob did not know it and could not see it with his natural eyes. Jesus came to the descendants of Jacob, and they did not know that God was in their midst—they were in darkness and did not know him (Jn 1:10-11; see also Mt 4:11; 26:52-53; Mk 1:13). Nathanael recognizes Jesus—God standing in his presence, just as Jacob recognized the presence of God and was also promised a heavenly vision. Jesus has come to start a "New Israel" in a

---

[14] J. Vernon McGee, *Thru the Bible Commentary*, vol. 40: *John Chapters 1-10* (Nashville: Thomas Nelson Publ., 1991), 1:37-38.

sense, with new Israelites from all nations and tongues, and these disciples were the new foundation stones—the new patriarchs (cf. Eph 2:20; Rev 21:14).

» CHURCH FATHERS: St. Augustine wrote: "The Lord said, 'Because I said unto thee, I saw thee when thou wast under the fig-tree, marvellest thou? thou shalt see greater things than these.' What are these greater things? And He said, 'Ye shall see heaven open, and the Angels of God ascending and descending upon the Son of Man.' Let us call to mind the old story written in the sacred Book. I mean in Genesis. When Jacob slept at a certain place, he put a stone at his head; and in his sleep he saw a ladder reaching from earth even unto heaven; and the Lord was resting upon it; and Angels were ascending and descending by it. This did Jacob see. A man's dream would not have been recorded, had not some great mystery been figured in it, had not some great prophecy been to be understood in that vision. Accordingly, Jacob himself, because he understood what he had seen, placed a stone there, and anointed it with oil. Now ye recognise the anointing; recognise The Anointed also. For He is 'the Stone which the builders rejected; He was made the Head of the corner.' He is the Stone of which Himself said, 'Whosoever shall stumble against This Stone shall be shaken; but on whomsoever That Stone shall fall, It will crush him.' It is stumbled against as It lies on the earth; but It will fall on him, when He shall come from on high to judge the quick and dead. Woe to the Jews, for that when Christ lay low in His humility, they stumbled against Him. 'This Man,' say they, 'is not of God, because He breaketh the sabbath day.' 'If He be the Son of God, let Him come down from the cross.' Madman, the Stone lies on the ground, and so thou deridest It. But since thou dost deride It, thou art blind; since thou art blind, thou stumblest; since thou stumblest, thou art shaken; since thou hast been shaken by It as It now lies on the ground, hereafter shalt thou be crushed by It as It falls from above. Therefore Jacob anointed the stone. Did he make an idol of it? He showed a meaning in it, but did not adore it. Now then give ear, attend to this Nathanael, by the occasion of whom the Lord Jesus hath been pleased to explain to us Jacob's vision." [15]

18. Why does Jesus use the title "Son of man" in verse 51? What passage in the Jewish Scriptures would the Jews' think of when hearing this title (Dan 7:13–14)? How is this title used in other places (Mt 9:6; 12:8; Rev 1:13; 14:14)? By using the title "Son of man", what is Jesus telling his disciples about himself (Mt 16:27–28; CCC 440, 664)? How do the Jews respond when Stephen uses this title for Jesus (Acts 7:55–60)? Read Psalm 2 and consider how it might be an explanation of the

---

[15] St. Augustine, *Sermons on New Testament Lessons* 72, 2, in Philip Schaff, ed., *Nicene and Post-Nicene Fathers*, 1st series (hereafter abbreviated NPNF1) (Grand Rapids, Mich.: Wm. B. Eerdmans, 1980), 6:470–71.

title "Son of man". Notice how significant this last statement is, referring to Jesus as the "Son of man", as we embark upon the public
ministry of Jesus.

» FINAL NOTE: "This first chapter of John's Gospel has been lengthy and
extremely important. The prologue presents the incarnation of the Word—He
is God, He became flesh, He reveals the Father. Then He is introduced by
witnesses. John the Baptist testifies that Jesus is the revealer of God. Andrew
testifies that Jesus is the Messiah. Philip testifies that Jesus fulfills the Old
Testament. Nathanael witnesses that Jesus is the Son of God, the King of
Israel." [16]

The musical themes and highlights have been introduced in the "overture"
(Jn 1:1–18) and are already being developed in these initial "movements" in the
life of Christ. As Jesus presents himself to the Jewish people—"his own home",
his own people—will they listen and believe?

---

[16] McGee, *John*, 1:38.

JOHN 2

JESUS, MARY, AND THE WEDDING IN CANA—
CLEANSING THE TEMPLE IN JERUSALEM

» INTRODUCTION OF THE THEME: John does not give us "parables" in the strict sense, such as those recorded in the Synoptic Gospels. Instead, he recounts numerous historical stories in such a way that they serve as parables by inviting us to discover deep spiritual truths in them. Note, I say historical stories. The fact that John points to a deeper spiritual meaning in the events he recounts takes nothing away from their historical reality. They happened. But it is the profound *meaning* of what happened that John wants to stress, in addition to giving us the sheer historical facts.

In John 2, we have two such events: the wedding of Cana and the cleansing of the Temple. Through these two incidents, John masterfully points to the passing away of the Old Covenant and the old order of the Jerusalem Temple based on it. These things have been superseded by the New Covenant and the spiritual Temple of Jesus Christ (CCC 593).

As we have seen, John 1 began with an allusion to Genesis 1, "In the beginning", setting up a contrast with the physical creation. John 2 begins with a reference to "the third day". This seems more than mere chronology, as will be clear shortly. It may, in fact, refer to the beginning of a new creation, a new week of creation. For Jesus was raised "on the third day", and his Resurrection begins the new creation.

John often uses what is called chiastic patterns, in order to emphasize and frame events and truths. Chiasms are parallel phrases escalating to a middle theme to emphasize it.[1] Notice how, in John 2, at the beginning of Jesus'

---

[1] "Chiasm is a development of inclusion. Instead of simply ending and beginning in the same way, chiasm extends the balancing of the first and the last by balancing the second and fourth [thus a-b-c-b-a]. In John's gospel, the author uses the five-member chiasm in every part, sequence, and section. . . . The use of chiasm in the writings of the Old and the New Testaments and in the writings of the Greeks and Romans has been amply documented. Its use by John, as we shall see, is the key to the structure of his Gospel as a whole and to the structure of each individual sequence and section" (Peter Ellis, *The Genius of John: A Composition-Critical Commentary on the Fourth Gospel* [Collegeville, Minn.: Liturgical Press, 1984], 10–11).

ministry, the waters of purification are limited to the people of Israel and are inadequate until turned into wine by Christ (Jn 2:1–10). At the end of his ministry, however, the waters of cleansing flow from the side of Christ, mixed with his blood; and they are adequate for the cleansing of the whole world (Jn 19:34). A few other examples of this "framing" are as follows. Peter's office and authority are emphasized by his placement in the text. He is mentioned as "Cephas" (the Rock) in the first chapter of the Gospel (Jn 1:42), while the last chapter depicts him as the Shepherd (Jn 21:15–17). Similarly, John stresses Mary's importance by placing her at the first moment of Jesus' earthly ministry (Jn 2:1) and at the very last moment (Jn 19:25–26).

John 2:1–5
The Wedding in Cana: Mary and Jesus

1. Cana is mentioned again in John 4:46–54 and 21:2. Look at a map of Israel during the time of Christ and locate Cana in Galilee. Notice its distance from Nazareth. How far do Mary and Jesus travel to attend the wedding? What other journeys have they made together (Lk 2:1ff.; Mt 2:13–14; Lk 2:41ff.)? What transportation do the poor, such as Mary and Jesus, have at their disposal to traverse the dusty, rocky, and hilly terrain? Consider the accommodations along the way. Why do you think "hospitality" was so important in the Jewish and early Christian communities? (See Gen 18:1–15; Mt 25:35; Lk 10:38; Rom 12:13; 1 Tim 5:10; Heb 13:2; 3 Jn 5–8.)

» GEOGRAPHICAL NOTE: Northern Israel is a very rocky and hilly country. "Roads" were little more than rough paths through the hills and deserts. Traveling was dangerous due to thieves (Lk 10:30), wild animals (1 Kings 13:24), hunger and thirst (1 Kings 17:10ff.; Jn 4:5–7), and other hazards. The hillsides were peppered with caves often occupied by wild animals. Prowling animals made the countryside very dangerous at night.

2. Besides keeping track of time, is there another possible significance to the mention of the "third day" in verse 1? What newness came about on another "third day" (cf. Acts 10:40; Rom 6:4; CCC 654)? Jesus' first "sign", given at the wedding, points to his divinity and power. This sign is given on "the third day". What other event is associated with the "third day" that culminates in the final sign (proof) of Jesus' divinity and power (Jn 2:19–22; 1 Cor 15:4)?

» THEOLOGICAL NOTE: "Since in the earlier Christian tradition 'the third day', being that of the Lord's resurrection, was also the day of revelation of His glory, St. John, who wishes the reader to discern the revelation of the Lord's glory— i.e., of His resurrection (cf. 11:25) as well as of His passion—throughout this gospel (cf. 1:14; 2:11), by the use of these words here may be indirectly reminding him to share this interpretation of the Lord's life and work." [2]

3. Some modern scholars assert that the miracle of water transformed into wine is not historical but simply a legend, an exaggeration, or a misunderstanding. Would John agree with their view? What does John relate as an eyewitness, and what does he describe—what do his contemporaries confirm? What effect does this public, visible miracle have on those who see it (Jn 2:9, 11)?

4. As we will see, not only does John relate the historical event but he also communicates its deeper spiritual meaning. What future event do you think the marriage feast in Cana might point forward to—especially since John refers to this event elsewhere (Rev 19:7–9; CCC 1602)? What does the miracle at Cana foretell for the Church (CCC 1612–13, 1244, 2618)?

» CULTURAL NOTE: "[The marriage feast] was usually held at the house of the groom (Mt 22:1–10; Jn 2:9) and often at night (Mt 22:13; 25:6). Many relatives and friends attended; so the wine might well run out (Jn 2:3). A steward or friend supervised the feast (Jn 2:9–10). To refuse an invitation to the wedding feast was an insult (Mt 22:7). The guests were expected to wear festive clothes (Mt 22:11–12). In special circumstances the feast could be held in the bride's home (Gn 29:22; Tobit 8:19). The glorious gathering of Christ and his saints in heaven is figuratively called 'the marriage supper of the Lamb' (Rev. 19:9)." [3]

5. Mary is perhaps a close friend of the bridegroom's family and is probably helping with the wedding and food preparation. Noticing the embarrassment of short supplies, what does Mary do (v. 3)? Do you think, by the way she asks and responds, that she expects a miracle (CCC 2618)? What do the words "intercede" and "mediate" mean? What does Mary do for the master of the house (Jn 2:3–5; CCC 969)? What does Jesus do in response to his Mother's request—her intercession? What is Mary's relationship with Jesus (CCC 964)?

---

[2] R. H. Lightfoot, *St. John's Gospel: A Commentary* (Oxford: Clarendon Press, 1956), 105.

[3] "Marriage", in J. D. Douglas, ed., *New Bible Dictionary* (Downers Grove, Ill.: InterVarsity Press, 1994), 744.

» THEOLOGICAL NOTE: " 'To understand Mary's great goodness, let us remember what the Gospel says. . . . There was a shortage of wine, which naturally worried the married couple. No one asks the blessed Virgin to intervene and request her Son to come to the rescue of the couple. But Mary's heart cannot but take pity on the unfortunate couple . . . it stirs her to act as intercessor and ask her Son for the miracle, even though no one asks her to. . . . If our Lady acted like this without being asked, what would she not have done if they actually asked her to intervene?' (St. Alphonsus, *Sunday Sermons*, 48)." [4]

» MARIAN NOTE: "Jesus' reply seems to indicate that although in principle it was not part of God's plan for him to use his power to solve the problem the wedding-feast had run into, our Lady's request moves him to do precisely that. Also, one could surmise that God's plan envisaged that Jesus should work the miracle at his Mother's request. In any event, God willed that the Revelation of the New Testament should include this important teaching: so influential is our Lady's intercession that God will listen to all petitions made through her; which is why Christian piety, with theological accuracy, has called our Lady 'supplicant omnipotence.' " [5]

"As she [Mary] was the door through which the Son of God passed from heaven to earth, she now introduces him among men." [6] Whereas the other Gospel writers seem primarily to emphasize Mary's role in the Incarnation, John stresses her participation in the manifestation of Jesus' glory.

» PAPAL TEACHING: "What deep understanding existed between Jesus and his mother? How can we probe the mystery of their intimate spiritual union? But the fact speaks for itself. It is certain that that event already quite clearly outlines the new dimension, the new meaning of Mary's motherhood. Her motherhood has a significance which is not exclusively contained in the words of Jesus and in the various episodes reported by the Synoptics (Lk. 11:27–28 and Lk. 8:19–21; Mt. 12:46–50; Mk. 3:31–35). In these texts Jesus means above all to contrast the motherhood resulting from the fact of birth with what this 'motherhood' (and also 'brotherhood') is to be in the dimension of the Kingdom of God, in the salvific radius of God's fatherhood. In John's text on the other hand, the description of the Cana event outlines what is actually manifested as a new kind of motherhood according to the spirit and not just according to the flesh, that is to say Mary's solicitude for human beings, her coming to them in the wide variety of their wants and needs.

"At Cana in Galilee there is shown only one concrete aspect of human need, apparently a small one of little importance ('They have no wine'). But it

---

[4] José María Casciaro, *The Navarre Bible: The Gospel of Saint John* (Dublin: Four Courts Press, 1992), 63.

[5] Ibid., 61.

[6] Louis Bouyer, quoted by Stefano M. Manelli, *All Generations Shall Call Me Blessed* (New Bedford, Mass.: Academy of the Immaculate, 1989), 299.

has a symbolic value: this coming to the aid of human needs means, at the same time, bringing those needs within the radius of Christ's messianic mission and salvific power. Thus there is a mediation: Mary places herself between her Son and mankind in the reality of their wants, needs and sufferings. She puts herself 'in the middle,' that is to say she acts as a mediatrix not as an outsider, but in her position as mother. She knows that as such she can point out to her Son the needs of mankind, and in fact, she 'has the right' to do so. Her mediation is thus in the nature of intercession: Mary 'intercedes' for mankind. And that is not all. As a mother she also wishes the messianic power of her Son to be manifested, that salvific power of his which is meant to help man in his misfortunes, to free him from the evil which in various forms and degrees weighs heavily upon his life. Precisely as the Prophet Isaiah had foretold about the Messiah in the famous passage which Jesus quoted before his fellow townsfolk in Nazareth: 'To preach good news to the poor . . . to proclaim release to the captives and recovering of sight to the blind . . .' (cf. Lk. 4:18).

"Another essential element of Mary's maternal task is found in her words to the servants: 'Do whatever he tells you.' The Mother of Christ presents herself as the spokeswoman of her Son's will, pointing out those things which must be done so that the salvific power of the Messiah may be manifested. At Cana, thanks to the intercession of Mary and the obedience of the servants, Jesus begins 'his hour.' At Cana Mary appears as believing in Jesus. Her faith evokes his first 'sign' and helps to kindle the faith of the disciples. We can therefore say that in this passage of John's Gospel we find as it were a first manifestation of the truth concerning Mary's maternal care." [7]

6. What is the scriptural attitude toward wine (Gen 27:28; Deut 7:13; 14:24–26; Ps 104:14–15; Prov 20:1; 23:29–35; Mt 11:19; Eph 5:18; 1 Tim 3:2–3; 5:23; CCC 1027, 2290, 1852, 1334)? How should we distinguish its use and abuse?

» CULTURAL NOTE: "Nuptial festivities [in Israel] lasted a week and were called in Aramaic *mištîtâ* (drink-festival) with which accords the rabbinical dictum: 'Where there is no wine, there is no joy.'" [8] The lack of wine was not only an embarrassment for the bridegroom, but also a disruption of the feast, and it rendered the family open to a lawsuit.

---

[7] John Paul II, *Mother of the Redeemer* (Boston, Mass.: St. Paul's Books & Media, 1987), 30–31. See also Pope Paul VI, *Devotion to the Blessed Virgin Mary* (Boston, Mass.: St. Paul's Books & Media, 1974), especially sections 16–23.

[8] Dom Bernard Orchard, ed., *A Catholic Commentary on Holy Scripture* (New York: Thomas Nelson Pub., 1953), 983.

7. Mary is never referred to by name in John's Gospel. What does John call the Blessed Virgin in verse 3? How does Jesus address her in verse 4? Except for John 6:42, why do you think Mary is mentioned in John's Gospel only at the very beginning and the very end of Jesus' public ministry—framing John's account of it (Jn 19:26–27; CCC 964)? What is Mary's role with regard to her Son: taking the limelight or retiring into the background? What does she tell the servants—in effect, what does she tell all men—to do? Do Catholics "worship" Mary (CCC 971)?

» HISTORICAL NOTE: In the Old Testament, the kings of Judah (as in other Eastern kingdoms) held their mothers in great esteem. In fact, the king's mother was known as the *gĕbîrah*, the "grand lady" or the "queen mother" (1 Kings 15:13, grandmother in this case; Jer 29:2; 2 Kings 24:15; 10:13; Jer 13:18). Solomon's mother, Bathsheba, was the first Great Lady in Israel. Solomon's first act as king was to rise from his throne, bow to his mother, and place a throne for her at his right hand (1 Kings 2:19). It was not the king's wife who held the position of *gĕbîrah*, rather it was the king's mother. Jesus, as the new king of Israel, seated on the eternal throne of David (Lk 1:32), of whom Solomon was a prefiguring, would most certainly esteem his Mother at least as much as earthly kings had esteemed theirs. Thus, in part based on this scriptural insight, the Church teaches that Mary has been assumed into heaven as the Mother of King Jesus and has been crowned the Queen of Heaven—this is certainly most fitting (CCC 966; Rev 12:1).[9]

» HISTORICAL NOTE: "If there is an Apostle on whom, *à priori*, our eyes would be fixed, as likely to teach us about the Blessed Virgin, it is St. John, to whom she was committed by our Lord on the Cross;—with whom, as tradition goes, she lived at Ephesus till she was taken away. This anticipation is confirmed *à posterior*; for, as I have said above, one of the earliest and fullest of our informants concerning her dignity, as being the Second Eve, is Irenaeus, who came to Lyons from Asia Minor, and had been taught by the immediate disciples of St. John. . . . But if all this be so, if it is really the Blessed Virgin whom Scripture represents as clothed with the sun, crowned with the stars of heaven, and with the moon as her footstool [Rev 12:1ff.], what height of glory may we not attribute to her? and what are we to say of those who, through ignorance, run counter to the voice of Scripture, to the testimony of the Fathers, to the traditions of East and West, and speak and act contemptuously towards her whom her Lord delighteth to honour?"[10]

---

[9] See Roland de Vaux, *Ancient Israel: Its Life and Institutions,* trans. John McHugh (New York: McGraw-Hill, 1961), 117–19.

[10] John Henry Cardinal Newman, *Mary the Second Eve,* comp. Eileen Breen (Rockford, Ill.: TAN Books, 1982), 17, 19.

8. Why would Jesus address his Mother with the unusual and seemingly impersonal title of "Woman" (cf. Jn 19:26)? Why might he use such a title of honor for a Jewish woman, instead of "Mother", a title of intimacy—which he probably used as a son in Nazareth? Does Mary respond to her Son as though he were addressing her with cool disregard or disrespect? Might there be a symbolic and theological reason for referring to his Mother as "Woman" (Gen 3:15; Rev 12:1−6, 17; CCC 2618, 410, 489)? With John's penchant for deeper meanings, what possible themes could he be pointing us to? How are the events of Genesis 3 and Revelation 12 related? Should we possibly view Revelation 12 as the first Marian apparition?

» LANGUAGE NOTE: To understand Jesus' manner of addressing his Mother, we must take into account the idioms of the Semitic languages. "As regards the word 'Woman', it cannot be repeated enough that this 'is an honorific title, equivalent, in antiquity, to that of 'lady'; it is a high and solemn way of expressing oneself." [11] "Among Arabs today the 'mother of X' is an honorable title for a woman who has been fortunate enough to bear a son. John never calls her Mary." [12]

"Greek *gunê* means 'woman,' but saying *Gunê!* to a woman in Greek is not nearly as cold an address as 'Woman!' in English; this is why I have rendered it 'Mother'. . . . Yeshua's comment is meant to aid her in the transition from seeing him as her child to seeing him as her Lord, to keep her from undue pride, and to indicate that he as Lord sovereignly determines when he will intervene in human affairs—he does not perform miracles on demand merely to impress his friends, or even to give *naches* (a Yiddish word that means 'the kind of joy a mother feels') to his mother." [13]

Brown disagrees with translating "Woman" as "Mother". "All of this leads us to suspect that there is symbolic import in the title, 'Woman.' To translate it 'Mother' would both obscure this possibility and cloak the peculiarity of the address." [14] " 'Woman' is a respectful title, rather like 'lady' or 'madam'; it is a formal way of speaking. On the Cross Jesus will use the same word with great affection and veneration." [15] "In Homer [Woman] is the title by which Odysseus addresses Penelope, his well-loved wife. It is the title by which Augustus, the Roman Emperor, addressed Cleopatra, the famous Egyptian

[11] Manelli, *All Generations*, 296.

[12] Raymond E. Brown, ed. and trans., *The Gospel according to John*, vol. 1, Anchor Bible, vol. 29 (Garden City, N.Y.: Doubleday, 1966), 106.

[13] David H. Stern, *Jewish New Testament Commentary* (Clarksville, Md.: Jewish New Testament Pubs., 1992), 163.

[14] Brown, *John*, 1:99.

[15] Casciaro, *John*, 60.

queen. So far from being a rough and discourteous way of address, it was a title of respect." [16]

9. How does Jesus answer his Mother in verse 4? John does not give us the nuances of voice or facial expressions that accompanied the Blessed Virgin's discourse with her Son—which might have helped in interpreting this passage. In verse 4, Jesus responds to his Mother: "O woman, what have you to do with me?" (The Hebrew idiom is, literally, "What to me and thee?") What is Jesus saying? Might the tone of his voice communicate honor, disrespect, frustration, love, respect, severity, aloofness, or veneration? Does his Mother's response give us a hint as to her son's tone and meaning (vv. 4–5)? May he have said it with a gleeful grin, a son's smile, or a heavy sigh of "Oh, is it that time already"? Might she have seen him do miracles before in private?

» LANGUAGE NOTE: All Jews were commanded by God, "Honor your father and your mother" (Ex 20:12). Jesus fulfilled the Law perfectly (Heb 4:15) and thus would never have responded to his Mother with anything but sincere respect and reverence (CCC 532). Yet Jesus also declares the independence of his mission.

"The phrase which gives the impression of brusqueness is rather a very much-used Hebrew idiom, which has no exact equivalent in our western languages, its meaning depending on a gesture, the tone of voice, and the expression of the face: 'Quid mihi et tibi?' In general, it expresses surprise, displeasure, or embarrassment brought on by an unforeseen meeting or unusual turn of events. To translate it, as is often done, by 'What is there in common between thee and me?' is to exaggerate its force and to falsify its meaning. The better translation, and one that is applicable to all cases, would be, 'What wouldst thou of me?' or, better, 'Why ask me that?' As it stands, the answer implies, not a reproach or a reprehension (as several of the Fathers maintain), but a momentary refusal. The expedients thought up by certain exegetes to eliminate this meaning from the phrase seem to us out of place. According to St. John Chrysostom, Jesus wished to show that he was master of his time and yet avoid making his mother blush publicly. Better still, we will say with St. Cyril of Alexandria, 'Christ teaches us here what honor is due to one's parents, since for his mother's sake he did what he would not otherwise have done.' " [17]

---

[16] William Barclay, *The Gospel of John* (Philadelphia: Westminster Press, 1975), 1:98.

[17] Ferdinand Prat, *Jesus Christ: His Life, His Teaching, and His Work*, trans. John J. Heenan (Milwaukee: Bruce Pub. Co., 1950), 1:176–77.

» THEOLOGICAL NOTE: "But if Mary is to have no role during the ministry, she is to receive a role when 'the hour' of his glorification comes, the hour of passion, death, resurrection, and ascension. John thinks of Mary against the background of Gen 3: she is the mother of the Messiah; her role is in the struggle against the satanic serpent, and that struggle comes to its climax in Jesus' hour. Then she will appear at the foot of the cross to be entrusted with offspring whom she must protect in the continuing struggle between Satan and the followers of the Messiah [Rev 12]. Mary is the New Eve, the symbol of the Church; the Church has no role during the ministry of Jesus but only after the hour of his resurrection and ascension." [18]

10. Is Jesus ready to perform his first miracle at this time—pulling back the veil and showing his glory (v. 4)? What does he mean by saying, "My hour has not yet come"? Who seems to have initiated his ministry ("flipped the switch", so to speak), deciding when his "hour" was to begin? The miracle in Cana is the beginning of what, and what is manifested (Jn 2:11; 1:16)?

» THEOLOGICAL NOTE: Throughout John's Gospel the phrase "my hour" refers to the Passion of Christ. In this context, it seems that "my hour" refers to the beginning of Jesus' public ministry, the hour or time when his first public miracle (sign) will start him on the inexorable journey to the Cross. He has lived the quiet life of a son and carpenter for thirty years (Lk 3:23), and now that peaceful life comes to an end and the journey to the Passion begins. In this passage, "His hour is not the hour of His death, nor the time when the want of wine would be fully felt, but the time at which, according to the ordinary providence of God, and prescinding from His Mother' suggestion, His public miracles were to begin." [19]

» MARIAN NOTE: Could Mary have known, as his Mother, when it was time for him to begin his public ministry? Was the Mother "cutting him loose" from her "apron strings", so to speak, so he could now leave to do the will of his Father? Was Mary saying, "It is now time, my Son"? "God himself gave the great 'hour' of Jesus in some way into the hands of Mary. If Mary pleads, then this 'hour' has come. If she does not plead, then the 'hour' has not yet come— it is postponed. Without Mary's plea perhaps no miracle would have taken place at Cana, and the Messianic ministry of Jesus would not have begun at that time. Mary is like the praying Moses [Num 20:10–11], but more believing than Moses. With a plea full of faith and trust she struck the heart of her Son, and the stream of living water began to flow at the first stroke—and it will continue

---

[18] Brown, *John*, 1:109.
[19] Joseph MacRory, *The Gospel of St. John* (Ireland: Browne and Nolan, 1923), 40.

to flow for all time unto life everlasting [1 Cor 10:1–4]. . . . So strong was her plea, so invincible her faith and trust that she was able to make the 'hour' of God strike which would not have struck without her mediation." [20]

11. How do Mary's words, "Do whatever he tells you", demonstrate faith in her Son (CCC 273, 2618)? How does the Church view the "ministry" of Mary—what do her life and example teach us (CCC 494, 2618)?

» THEOLOGICAL NOTE: "Like a good mother, the Virgin Mary knows perfectly well what her son's reply means—though to us it is ambiguous ('What has it to do with you and me?'): she is confident that Jesus will do something to come to the family's rescue. This is why she tells the servants so specifically to do what Jesus tells them. These words of our Lady can be seen as a permanent invitation to each of us: 'in that all Christian holiness consists: for perfect holiness is obeying Christ in all things' (St Thomas Aquinas, *Comm. on St John*, 155)." [21]

12. Has Mary possibly seen tokens of Jesus' power before his public ministry, or has she anticipated miracles based on the angel's words to her at the Annunciation (Lk 1:35)? Does Jesus know his Mother is requesting a miracle? Explain why. Joseph is an Old Testament type of Christ. How do Mary's words echo those of Genesis 41:55?

John 2:6–11
The Wedding in Cana: Water into Wine, Old Transformed into the New

13. John mentions six stone water pots. What were they used for (Jn 2:6; Num 19:9, 17–19; Mk 7:2–5; Mt 23:25–26; Heb 9:9–10; 10:22)? Knowing John's skill with symbolism and allegory, what might the waters of ritual Jewish purification represent (CCC 1215–17; Jn 3:23, 25; Acts 22:16)? What does the new wine represent? (CCC 1335). In Catholic theology—in the theology of the early Church—does one need water (baptism) before he is given "new wine" (Eucharist) (CCC 1003)?

---

[20] Otto Hophan, *Mary, Our Most Blessed Lady*, trans. Berchmans Bittle (Milwaukee: Bruce Pub., 1959), 244.
[21] Casciaro, *John*, 61.

» CULTURAL NOTE: In the Jewish Quarter of the Old City in Jerusalem, archaeologists have discovered the "Burnt House". The house had been burned to the ground by the Romans in A.D. 70. Archaeologists have found large stone jars, such as those mentioned in John 2, and they are on display. Viewing these ancient stone jars used for Jewish purification takes one back in time to relive the miracle of Cana. The stone jars are two to two and one-half feet tall, each cut from a block of stone that could weigh as much as half a ton. They were shaped and finished on a very big lathe, given a pedestal foot and simple decoration. These stone jars could hold up to seventeen gallons of water and were used for washing and kitchen needs. Flat discs of stone served as lids. The jars at Cana may have been similar to these, only larger, holding up to twenty-five gallons each.

14. In this Cana story, how is that which is "old" replaced with that which is "new"? (*Hint*: Jn 1:17.) How is the natural superceded by the spiritual? Since the number six in Scripture can represent imperfection, sin, and man apart from God, why do you think John points out the fact that there were six stone jars? Is the content of the jars changed from within or from without (Ezek 36:25–29; 2 Cor 5:17; CCC 1265)? How does God justify his people? Why are the jars all filled to the brim with water (more than 150 gallons) and then turned into such an overwhelming overabundance of wine (Jn 1:16; Ps 23:5–6)?

» CULTURAL NOTE: "The narrator sets the scene for the following section with an important description of stone jars (v. 6). There are six of them, one short of the perfection of the number 'seven.' This is probably a hint that a former gift is to be perfected (cf. 1:16–17). Later Jewish texts indicate that stone was useful for purificatory purposes because it did not contract uncleanness. They are very large jars, each one containing some twenty-four gallons. There will be a superabundance of wine produced from this water, and the problem raised by the mother is about to be resolved. The water in the jars, used for Jewish purification rituals, will be transformed into a 'sign' (v. 11: *sēmeion*) in and through which the *doxa* [glory] will be revealed." [22]

» THEOLOGICAL NOTE: The story of Cana is framed by two remarkable statements: "They have no wine" (v. 3) and "you have kept the good wine until now" (v. 10). This is a poignant commentary on the bankruptcy and ineffectiveness of Judaism at that time and the arrival of Jesus, the Messiah. (Compare our notes on the crippled man in John 5.) The old wine and old wineskins (Judaism and its spiritual economy) are replaced by the new wine of the Gospel

---

[22] Francis Moloney, *The Gospel of John,* Sacra Pagina, vol. 4 (Collegeville, Minn.: Liturgical Press, 1998), 68.

in the new wineskins of the Church (cf. Mt 9:17). "[The jars'] large size was natural but the sequel suggests that the great quantity they contained reflected the fullness of Christ's grace, in contrast to the limitations of the old covenant (Jn 1:16–17)." [23] Dodd tells us that the stone jars "stand for the entire system of Jewish ceremonial observance. . . . Thus the first of signs already symbolizes the doctrine that [the Law was given through Moses; grace and truth were realized through Jesus Christ] (i. 17)." [24]

"We are talking about 500–700 liters (100–150 gallons) of top quality wine. St. John stresses the magnificence of the gift produced by the miracle—as he also does at the multiplication of the loaves (Jn 6:12–13). One of the signs of the arrival of the Messiah was abundance; here we have the fulfillment of the ancient prophecies: 'the Lord will give what is good, and our land will yield its increase', as Psalm 85:12 proclaims; 'the threshing floors shall be full of grain, the vats shall overflow with wine and oil' (Joel 2:24; cf. Amos 9:13–15). This abundance of material goods is a symbol of the supernatural gifts Christ obtains for us through the Redemption; later on St John highlights our Lord's words: 'I came that they may have life, and have it abundantly (Jn 10:10; cf. Rom 5:20). 'Up to the brim': the evangelist gives us this further piece of information to emphasize the superabundance of the riches of Redemption and also to show how very precisely the servants did what they were told, as if hinting at the importance of docility in fulfilling the will of God, even in small details." [25]

15. Through the Gospel, John portrays Jesus as the new Moses, thus fulfilling Moses' prophecy (Deut 18:15, 18). What was one of Moses' first signs before Pharaoh (Ex 7:20)? What kind of containers of water were all turned to blood (Ex 7:19)? What is Jesus' first "sign" before the world (Jn 2:7–11)? Jesus takes the "bitter water" of purification—water not for drinking—and turns it into something sweet to drink. What did Moses do in the wilderness (Ex 15:23–27)? What was thrown into the water and what was the result (cf. Gal 3:13–14)? On Good Friday in the Catholic Church, what do we venerate and why?

» JESUS, THE NEW MOSES: "The whole of the first chapter of St John is in a sense preparatory. When we come to the second chapter, we may find a point of contact in the first sign of Jesus at the wedding at Cana (2:1ff.). The change of water to wine should remind the reader of the first of the plagues in Egypt, the changing of water to blood. There is a verbal echo of the Exodus story which

---

[23] G. R. Beasley-Murray, *John*, Word Biblical Commentary (Waco, Tex.: Word Books, 1987), 35.

[24] C. H. Dodd, *The Interpretation of the Fourth Gospel* (Cambridge: Cambridge Univ. Press, 1955), 299.

[25] Casciaro, *John*, 61–62.

would confirm that this was in the Evangelist's mind. Ex. 7:19 says that 'there shall be blood throughout all the land of Egypt, both in vessels of wood and in vessels of stone'; cf. John 2:6 with its reference to the 'waterpots of stone'.

"Some words of Archbishop Trench in his book *Notes on the Miracles* may be quoted here: This first miracle of the New Covenant has its inner mystical meaning. The first miracle of Moses was a turning of water into blood (Ex 7:20); and this had its fitness; for the law, which came by Moses, was a ministration of death, and working wrath (II Cor. 3.6–9). But the first miracle of Christ was a turning of water into wine, this too a meet inauguration of all which should follow, for his was a ministration of life. . . . From another angle, the waterpots, 'set there after the Jews' manner of purifying' (2:6), symbolize the religion of the Law, now replaced by the festive wine of the gospel." [26]

16. In verse 11, what does John call this miracle of water into wine—does he call it a miracle? What does a "sign" do—what does it point to? What happens as a result of this miracle? How does this verse prepare the way for the rest of the Gospel?

» THEOLOGICAL NOTE: "While He tabernacled as the Son of Man upon earth it was for the most part hidden. The veil of flesh which He had consented to wear concealed it from the sight of men. But now, in this work of grace and power [in turning water into wine], it burst through the covering which concealed it, revealing itself to the eyes of his disciples; they 'beheld his glory, the glory as of the only begotten of the Father.' And his disciples believed on him." [27]

17. What does John 2 teach us about Jesus' attitude toward marriage (CCC 1613)? What does the Catholic Church teach about marriage (CCC 372, 1603, 1660)? What does marriage teach us about Jesus and his bride, the Church (Eph 5:22–33; CCC 796)?

John 2:12–21
The Temple in Jerusalem, the Resurrection Proclaimed

18. In verse 12, after the miracle—the first sign—of water transformed into wine, where does Jesus go with his Mother, brethren, and disciples?

---

[26] T. F. Glasson, *Moses in the Fourth Gospel* (Napierville, Ill.: Alec R. Allenson, 1963), 26.

[27] Richard C. Trench, *Notes on the Miracles of Our Lord* (Grand Rapids, Mich.: Baker Book House, 1976), 73.

While there, where and with whom does he live (Mk 1:21, 29; 2:1; Lk 4:31, 38)? Why does he leave his hometown of Nazareth (Lk 4:14, 28–31; Mt 13:54–58)? Does Jesus have literal brothers (CCC 499–501)?

» APOLOGETICAL NOTE: Jesus and "his brethren" are mentioned by John (v. 12). In Aramaic and Hebrew there is no word for "cousin" or "stepbrother". Extended family members were kinsmen, or as the Greek text often renders it, "brothers" (for example, Gen 12:5; 14:14; 29:15). Mention of Jesus' brethren (or brothers) within the Jewish context is certainly no proof that Mary had other children. Scripture and tradition refute the idea that Mary had children after Jesus. Even Martin Luther and John Calvin, the leading Protestant Reformers, taught that Mary was ever-virgin.[28]

19. In verse 13, Jesus mentions the Passover of the Jews. What is the Passover (Ex 12:1–51; Mk 14:12–25; CCC 1334, 1340)? Notice other times John mentions the Passover (Jn 5:1; 6:4; 11:55; 12:1). What is the relationship between Jesus and the Passover (Jn 1:29; 1 Cor 5:7; CCC 560)?

20. Look on a map of Israel and locate Jerusalem and Capernaum (vv. 12, 13), which are at least a three-days' journey apart. The Bible contains the phrase "up to Jerusalem" twenty-seven times (for example, 2 Kings 24:10; Ezra 1:3; Acts 11:2; Gal 1:17–18), but never says "down to Jerusalem". Geographically speaking, why does the Scripture say that Jesus went "up" to Jerusalem (*hint*: Gen 22:2, 14; 2 Chron 3:1)? How might this phrase also reflect the importance of Jerusalem?

» GEOGRAPHICAL NOTE: "Jerusalem is located on top of the Judean hills, some 2,500 feet above sea level and higher than most inhabited places in Israel. This particular ascent was being made from Jericho, 900 feet below sea level. But 'going up to Jerusalem' has a spiritual dimension which does not depend on altitude—the earth's spiritual geography is such that from the summit of Mount Everest one still 'goes up' to Jerusalem. Today when Jews come to live in Israel they do not 'immigrate' but 'make *aliyah*' (the word means 'going up'), even if they plan to live on the shore of the Dead Sea, the lowest place on earth."[29]

---

[28] For a comprehensive discussion of the topic, see Karl Keating, *Catholicism and Fundamentalism: The Attack on "Romanism" by "Bible Christians"* (San Francisco: Ignatius Press, 1988); Andrés Fernández, *The Life of Christ*, trans. Paul Barrett (Westminster, Md.: Newman Press, 1959); and especially St. Jerome's treatise on *The Perpetual Virginity of Blessed Mary*, in NPNF2 6:334–46.

[29] Stern, *Jewish New Testament Commentary*, 60.

21. What is the significance of the Temple in Jerusalem (1 Kings 8:1–30)? What existed before the Temple was built (Ex 40:34–38; 2 Chron 1:3–4)? What would someday replace the "Tabernacle" and "Temple" (Jn 1:14; 2:21; Col 2:9; Eph 2:19–22; 1 Cor 3:16–17; CCC 586, 756)? What eventually happened to the Temple in Jerusalem and why (Lk 19:41–44; 21:5–9; CCC 585, 593)? Why were the Jews not prepared for the "Bridegroom's" visit? How should we prepare for his *second* coming (1 Pet 2:11–12; Lk 1:17; 1 Thess 5:1–11; CCC 716)?

» HISTORICAL NOTE: "Despite the fact that the Temple's existence for over a millennium was nearly continuous, it did undergo two major reconstructions, one following the Exile, beginning in 520 B.C., and the other as part of the enormous building projects carried out by King Herod, who reigned in Palestine from 37 to 4 B.C. Because of these two rebuilding projects, it is customary to consider the Jerusalem Temple as having had three distinct stages of existence. The First Temple, also known as Solomon's Temple, is the product of Israel's United Monarchy in the tenth century B.C. The Second Temple was rebuilt on the site of its destroyed predecessor at the end of the sixth century; it is sometimes known as Zerubbabel's Temple because Zerubbabel was the chief political officer in the Persian subprovince of Yehud (Judah) at the time of the restoration of the Temple. The third stage of the Jerusalem Temple is known as Herod's Temple and consisted of Herod's enlargement and embellishment of the Second Temple." [30] Herod began reconstruction of the Temple in 19 B.C., which was finally completed in A.D. 64, six years before its destruction. It was leveled by the Roman Emperor Titus in A.D. 70. This last Temple stood during the life of Jesus. The western wall ("Wailing Wall") is all that remains of the Temple complex today and is the holiest site in the world for Jews.

Herod rebuilt the Temple, which had been built centuries earlier by Zerubbabel. "The most radical change of all, associated with the grandiose building schemes of Herod the Great in the last decades of the 1st century B.C.E., resulted in a temple building that was not technically a renovation: it was an entirely new structure. Consequently, the Herodian Temple constituted in fact a 'Third Temple,' although it is often subsumed under the designation 'Second Temple' since there was no chronological interruption of consequence involved when Herod built a spectacular new edifice to replace the Temple dating back to Zerubbabel." [31] Jews often use the term "Third Temple" to refer to the Temple that will be built in the future.[32]

---

[30] Paul J. Achtemeier, ed., *Harper's Bible Dictionary* (San Francisco: Harper & Row, 1985), 1021.

[31] "Temple, Jerusalem", in David Noel Freedman, ed., *The Anchor Bible Dictionary* (New York: Doubleday, 1996); published in electronic form by Logos Library System.

[32] For more information, see Yisrael Ariel, *The Odyssey of the Third Temple,* trans. Chaim Richman (Jerusalem: G. Israel Pub. & Productions, Temple Institute [1993?]), 75ff.

22. What was required of each Jewish family as they came to the Temple for Passover and other legal obligations (Deut 16:1–2, 5–6; Lev 5:7; Lk 2:21–24)? Why were money changers and merchants filling the outer courts of the Temple? Do you think Joseph and Mary carried their sacrifices during their difficult journey to Jerusalem (Lk 2:24)? Where would they probably purchase the turtledoves for their offering (Jn 2:14)? Where might they have exchanged currency to secure the offering and pay the Temple tax (Jn 2:14)?

» HISTORICAL NOTE: People traveled from great distances to celebrate the Passover in Jerusalem. Instead of dragging sacrificial animals along with them, they usually purchased them in Jerusalem. Many varieties of coin and currency would be brought to Jerusalem for purchasing animals for sacrifice and to pay the Temple tax (Mt 17:24). But only the Temple currency (ancient half-shekel) was allowed. Any currency with the image of a foreign sovereign would defile the Temple. Money changers were there to provide the necessary service of exchanging currency, just as a bank near an airport will exchange foreign currency for the traveler. The outer courts were reserved for non-Jews so they could worship God (Is 56:6–7). The Jews were to be a light to draw the nations to the God of Israel. Instead, they turned the outer courts into a manure-filled, noisy marketplace. Those who were to be drawn to prayer were instead crowded out, pushed away from God.

"Various kinds of sacrificial animals were for sale at the Temple so that the pilgrims would not have the added expense of bringing them from afar. The only money accepted at the Temple was the Tyrian half-shekel: Roman coinage could not be used; hence the money-changers performed a necessary function." [33]

23. In verse 16, what does Jesus think about the Temple, and what is his relationship to this magnificent structure in Jerusalem (Lk 2:45–51; CCC 583–84, 586, 593)?

24. Why does Jesus expel the money changers and "cleanse" the Temple (Mal 3:1ff.; Mt 21:12–13; Mk 11:15–17; Lk 19:45–46)? Are money, business, enterprise, and merchandise evil in God's eyes (Deut 8:18; 2 Thess 3:8–12; 1 Thess 4:11; 1 Tim 5:8; CCC 2426–28)? Are the money changers and merchants wrong for selling, or wrong for the *manner* and *location* of their activity? Does this aggressive and "rude" behavior of Jesus fit the picture often given of the "meek and mild

---

[33] Raymond Brown, Joseph Fitzmyer, and Roland Murphy, eds., *The Jerome Biblical Commentary* (Englewood Cliffs, N.J.: Prentice-Hall, 1968), 2:429.

Jesus"? How does Jesus' cleansing of the Temple apply to the Church and to us as Christians (1 Pet 4:17; 1 Cor 6:13–20, esp. v. 19; Heb 12:4–11, 14; CCC 1695)?

» HISTORICAL NOTE: "The Gospels refer to two types of persons dealing with money: the *trapezitai*, 'bankers' (Matt. 25:27) and the *kollybiston* (Matt. 21:12; Mark 11:15; John 2:15, with *kermatitas* 'coin dealers,' in John 2:14), who were authorized to operate in the Temple precincts. The Mishna, in *Seqalim*, indicates that the changers took a commission. Jesus' action against them was possibly justified by their abuses, especially at the times of the pilgrimages, and by their bribing of the High Priest and Temple officials." [34]

"Besides the money-changers there were also the sellers of oxen and sheep and doves. Frequently a visit to the Temple meant a sacrifice. Many a pilgrim would wish to make thankoffering for a favourable journey to the Holy City; and most acts and events in life had their appropriate sacrifice. It might therefore seem to be a natural and helpful thing that the victims for the sacrifices could be bought in the Temple court. It might well have been so. But the law was that any animal offered in sacrifice must be perfect and unblemished. The Temple authorities had appointed inspectors (*mumcheh*) to examine the victims which were to be offered. The fee for inspection was 1p. If a worshipper bought a victim outside the Temple, it was to all intents and purposes certain that it would be rejected after examination. Again that might not have mattered much, but a pair of doves could cost as little as 4p outside the Temple, and as much as 75p inside. Here again was bare-faced extortion at the expense of poor and humble pilgrims, who were practically blackmailed into buying their victims from the Temple booths if they wished to sacrifice at all— once more a glaring social injustice aggravated by the fact that it was perpetrated in the name of pure religion. It was that which moved Jesus to flaming anger." [35]

"The removal of the sacrificial animals signals the end of temple sacrifice. . . . Theologically, the cleansing of the temple emphasizes the same theme as the miracle at Cana—the theme of replacement. What is new in John's account of the cleansing is the linking of the new dispensation with the death and resurrection of Jesus." [36]

» SPIRITUAL NOTE: " 'He goes to the temple as the only-begotten Son who must ensure that all due decorum is observed in the House of the Father: And from thenceforth Jesus, the Anointed of God, always begins by reforming abuses and purifying from sin; both when he visits his Church [Temple], and

---

[34] John J. Rousseau and Rami Arav, *Jesus and His World: An Archeological and Cultural Dictionary* (Minneapolis, Minn.: Fortress Press, 1995), 58.

[35] Barclay, *John*, 1:110–11.

[36] Ellis, *Genius of John*, 47.

when he visits the Christian soul' (Origen, *Hom. on St John*, 1)." [37] Compare 1 Peter 4:16.

25. When Jesus claims that the Temple is "my Father's house", what do the Jews understand him to mean about his relationship with God (Jn 5:18; 10:29–33; CCC 1027)? What does Jesus do in the Temple (v. 15; CCC 584)? Read similar passages in the Synoptic Gospels (Mt 21:12ff.; Mk 11:15, 17; Lk 19:45–46).

26. The Jews ask for a sign to demonstrate Jesus' authority to perform such a cleansing of the Temple. Is his action a sign in itself, a fulfillment of prophecy (Mal 3:1–3; Zech 14:21)? What should the Jews have understood from his action based on Old Testament clues? Does any other prophet condemn such merchandizing in the Temple (Jer 7:10–11)? At what other time was a sign requested, and how did Jesus respond (Mt 12:38–42)?

» RELIGIOUS NOTE: "What Jesus did is best classified as an act of prophetic symbolism. If he had Zech. 14:21 in his mind when he protested against his Father's house (cf. Luke 2:49) being turned into a supermarket, we may recall that the preceding verses of Zech. 14 tell how all nations will go up to Jerusalem to worship. The only place within the temple precincts which was open to people of 'all nations' (apart from the Israelites) was the outer court (sometimes called the 'court of the Gentiles'); if this area were taken up for trading it could not be used for worship. Jesus' action reinforced his spoken protest." [38] The Jews were to be a light to the nations (Gentiles), but when the Gentiles visited, the only place they could worship was filled with wrangling, beasts, and manure.

27. In verse 17, why does John quote from Psalm 69? Are there other aspects of this psalm that prophesy of Jesus (cf. Ps 69:21 and Jn 19:28–30)? Notice how this psalm is used at the beginning and end of Jesus' public ministry. What or who probably brought Psalm 69 to mind when the disciples later recalled what Jesus had done (Jn 14:26)?

28. What does Jesus mean when he says that he will destroy the Temple and raise it up in three days (Jn 2:21–22; CCC 585–86, 994)? What do the Jews think he means (v. 20)? What *is* he speaking about (v. 21; CCC

---

[37] Casciaro, *John*, 64.

[38] F. F. Bruce, *The Gospel of John* (Grand Rapids, Mich.: William B. Eerdmans, 1983), 75.

593)? Who will raise Jesus' body from the dead (v. 19)? How is this a claim of his deity and his complete control of the situation (Jn 10:18; Acts 3:15)? Why is Jesus so cryptic and mysterious about his death and Resurrection (Jn 2:23–25; Lk 11:29–32; Mt 16:20; CCC 546)?

» Linguistic note: Typical of John's Gospel is the use of words with two meanings. "All the words in this statement [v. 19] are subject to double meanings. 'Destroy' can refer to destruction of a building or to the dissolution of a human life. 'Temple' can refer to a material edifice or to a human body. 'Raise' can refer to rebuilding or resurrection. The Jews take the first meaning in every case; Jesus, as John explains in vv. 21–22, intends the second." [39]

» Chronological note: When did Jesus begin his ministry? "We are, however, given a very important hint quite incidentally when the Jews arguing with Jesus exclaim regarding the Temple of Jerusalem: 'Forty-six years has this temple been in building, and wilt thou raise it up in three days?' (John 2:20.) With his usual careful attention to chronology, the Evangelist has indicated in the context that this statement was made during the Pasch [Passover] of the first year of Jesus' public life (ibid., 2:13, 23). Since we can establish with certainty that Herod the Great began the complete reconstruction of the Temple in 20– 19 B.C., forty-six years later would give us A.D. 27–28 as the first year of Jesus' public ministry." [40]

29. Compare the Temple/Tabernacle allusion and deeper meaning of John 2:21 and John 1:14. What is John telling us about Jesus' person and nature (Jn 1:1, 14; Col 1:19; 2:9)?

» Theological note " 'But he spoke of the temple of his body.' The evangelist clarifies the Jews' misunderstanding by reminding his readers at the end of the first century that Jesus was really talking about his death and resurrection. Implicit in Jesus' words and in the evangelist's clarification of what he meant is the replacement of the temple as God's place of worship by the crucified and risen body of Jesus, which is to become the temple of the new dispensation. In him, as the prologue so succinctly puts this same truth (1:14), the Word 'became flesh and dwelt among us'." [41] Just as one always went "up to Jerusalem", emphasizing its importance, so the Temple was the center of the universe for the Jew—it was a microcosm of the universe. How did Jesus' presence in their midst change this situation? What or who is really the center of the universe?

---

[39] Ellis, *Genius of John*, 47.
[40] Giuseppe Ricciotti, *The Life of Christ*, trans. Alba I. Zizzamia (Milwaukee: Bruce Pub., 1947), 159.
[41] Ellis, *Genius of John*, 48.

» HISTORICAL NOTE: "This is another newness or transformation story. The temple itself will be replaced. Destroyed in A.D. 70 by the soldiers of Titus' Roman army, its place as the center of worship and sacrifice, the site of God's presence and the visible symbol of his fidelity, will be taken by the risen body of Christ. The physical destruction of the temple was a spirit-crushing disaster for Israel. The loss was softened for Jewish Christians by this Johannine theology of the Christ-temple, which, indeed, Paul had already expanded into a doctrine of the Christian-temple (1 Cor 6:19).

"This physical purification of the temple might remind us of the type of symbolic deeds acted out by the prophets; and, indeed, Jesus' approach to the temple on this occasion resembles that of Jeremiah (Jer 7). The action, though not a miracle, is a sign, a double sign. The temple, soon to be destroyed, stood in need of purification. And its function would be replaced by the risen body of Christ." [42]

John 2:22–25
Belief and the Heart of Man

30. After the death and Resurrection of Christ, what did the disciples remember (Jn 2:22; cf. 14:26)? What action followed their remembering (v. 22)? Why did John write this Gospel (Jn 20:30–31; CCC 514)?

31. According to John 2:24–25, what does Jesus know about the inner condition of man (Mt 17:17; Gen 6:5–6; CCC 401)? What kind of "belief" do the people referred to in John 2:23 have (cf. Jas 2:17–26; CCC 150, 1815)? What kind of faith does God require of us (CCC 1814)? Even though they have a superficial belief in him, how does Jesus react to them (v. 24)? How does Jesus know what is inside the people (CCC 473)? How does John 2 flow into John 3 as a seamless narrative?

» THEOLOGICAL NOTE: "Although Jesus does not satisfy the malicious request for a 'sign,' nevertheless during that first Paschal sojourn in Jerusalem, 'many believed in his name, seeing the signs that he was working' (John 2:23). But this was not so much faith from the heart as faith of the intellect, and Jesus wanted the former much more than the latter. That was one reason why he 'did not trust himself to them, in that he knew all men' (John 2:24), while he had trusted himself to the rough but generous disciples from Galilee. Even the faith

---

[42] Neal M. Flanagan, O.S.M., "John", in *The Collegeville Bible Commentary: New Testament*, ed. Robert J. Karris, O.F.M. (Collegeville, Minn.: Liturgical Press, 1992), 984.

of the intellect, however, is a preparation for, and invitation to, faith of the heart, and it is at this point precisely that the 'spiritual' Evangelist presents to us an interview between one who already believed with his mind and Jesus who lifted him into quite another sphere." [43] The story of Nicodemus flows seamlessly from this narrative and gives an example of a man who failed to believe fully and from the heart. He becomes a case study.

---

[43] Ricciotti, *Life of Christ*, 290.

JOHN 3

"YOU MUST BE BORN ANEW"—"FOR GOD SO LOVED THE WORLD"

John 3:1–21

Jesus and Nicodemus

1. The chapter and verse divisions are artificial divisions within the text of the Bible and of recent inclusion. Thus, John wrote his Gospel with no chapter divisions. Without stopping at the chapter break, read the last few verses of John 2 and right into chapter 3, as John wrote them. What strikes you about the flow of the text, and why is the dialogue with Nicodemus included here? (*Hint*: John uses the word "man" [*anthropos* in Greek] twice in John 2:25 and once in John 3:1. How does John use Nicodemus as an example of the kind of man to whom Jesus would not entrust himself?)

» TEXTUAL NOTE: "The different divisions of the material within the NT books are not ancient. The chapter divisions are usually attributed to Cardinal Hugo de San Caro, who in A.D. 1248 used them in preparing a Bible index, but he may have borrowed them from the earlier [Catholic] archbishop of Canterbury, Stephen Langton. The modern verses derive from Robert Estienne (Stephanus), who, according to his son Henry, made the divisions while on a journey on horseback from Paris to Lyons. They were first published in Stephanus' Greek Testament of 1551 and first appeared in an English translation of the NT in William Whittingham's version of 1557. The first complete Bible in English with our verses was the Geneva Bible of 1560." [1]

» BIBLE TRANSLATIONS: The way this passage is translated shows the difference between the various Bible versions. How these translations render the word "man" (*anthropos*) in the current passage is very instructive. The Revised Standard Version uses the word "man" in each instance, whereas the New Revised

---

[1] Paul J. Achtemeier, ed., *Harper's Bible Dictionary* (San Francisco: Harper & Row, 1985), 699.

Standard Version uses the inclusive language of "everyone" or "all people". The New American Standard Bible, the King James Version, and the Rheims New Testament use "man" or "men"; the New American Bible and the New Jerusalem Bible do not use "man" but "them all", "anyone", and "human nature". Literal translations tend to use the word "man", whereas dynamic translations tend to "explain" the meaning of the text—"interpreting" the meaning for the reader. Reading several translations always helps bring to light the various nuances of a text.

» HISTORICAL NOTE: Nicodemus means "victorious or conqueror over the people" (from *nico*, crusher; and *demos*, people). In verse 1, how might this represent the way Nicodemus and the Pharisees ruled the people (Mt 23:1–7, 13ff.)? The Pharisees were an elite group—never more than six thousand—and they entered this exclusive *chabura* (brotherhood) by taking a public pledge to spend their life observing every detail of the Mosaic Law. Nicodemus, in addition to being part of this elite group, was also probably a member of the Sanhedrin, the supreme council of the Jews. The Sanhedrin had seventy members who were responsible for religious decisions concerning every Jew in the world and also, under the Romans, for civil rule as the "Supreme Court".

2. Nicodemus seems to play an important role in John's Gospel since he is mentioned three times. What is Nicodemus' disposition toward Jesus, and how does it progress throughout the Gospel (Jn 3:1–5; 7:50; 19:39)? Are any other members of the Sanhedrin favorably inclined toward Jesus (Jn 19:38; Acts 5:34–39; 15:5; CCC 595)? What well-known Pharisee becomes an apostle (Acts 26:5; Phil 3:5)?

3. What is the practical reason Nicodemus comes to Jesus at night, and what is the symbolic meaning of this action (Jn 9:4; 1:4–5; 3:19; 19:38–39)? How does Nicodemus' greeting in verse 2 differ from those of Andrew (Jn 1:41) and Nathanael (Jn 1:49)? Why does Nicodemus' observation in verse 2 ("God is with him") fall short of the full truth (Jn 1:1, 14)?

» NOTE ON SYMBOLISM: "The Jew [Nicodemus] who comes is thus entirely representative. Not only Christ and Nicodemus, but the Church and Judaism, may be held to meet in this story. Nicodemus comes by night; the evangelist here, as at many points in his narrative, has an eye for the symbolic detail. It is likely enough that a member of the Sanhedrin would have been well advised to visit the new Rabbi by night; but equally, in the mind of the evangelist, Nicodemus would have come to Jesus from that world of darkness in which the true light of God was now pleased to shine. And Judaism had its own particular darkness, because it deemed itself already to be in possession of the light. But

Nicodemus does not come with this as a self-conscious belief; he is a genuine seeker of the truth, hampered only by the religious situation he is already in." [2]

4. Again we come across the word "sign" instead of "miracle". John uses the word "sign" twenty-four times, while never using the word "miracle". What did "miracle" mean to the disciples, and how is the word used differently today? Why does John use "sign"; whereas the other Gospels use the word "miracle"? What is a "sign", and what is its purpose (Jn 2:11; 6:30; CCC 515)? How is John's use of "signs" a significant key to understanding his Gospel (Jn 20:30)?

5. For Jesus' words "Truly, truly"—his double "amen", see the textual note on John 10:1. Why do you think Jesus speaks of being "born anew" or "born from above" in this context? What do Nicodemus and his system represent (Rom 7:5–6; CCC 1963)? Is being born of the seed of Abraham sufficient for real spiritual life (Mt 3:8–9; Jn 8:33–47; Gen 17:15–27)? What is Jesus bringing to mankind, and what does he represent (Ezek 36:25–27; Jer 31:31–34; Lk 22:20; Heb 12:24; 2 Cor 5:17; CCC 1214)? Who is the initiating cause of the new birth from above (Jn 1:12–13; CCC 505, 526)? How does Nicodemus misunderstand Jesus in verse 4? Why do the Jewish leaders turn away (CCC 591)? How might Ezekiel 37:1–10 apply (CCC 715)?

» THEOLOGICAL NOTE: What does "born again" mean in the context of American Evangelicalism? According to the *Dictionary of Christianity in America*, "This term [born again] has acquired a broad and imprecise usage in general American discourse. It has come to mean any Christian who exhibits intensity or overt self-identification or a keen sense of divine presence, or one who attributes causation to God for events in personal life or in the historical and natural processes. In the understanding of American Christians, born again is associated with revivalism or any conversionist form of Protestantism. It describes the direct experience of a person in a notable single event or a specifiable period when that person shifts his or her life focus from any other center to Jesus Christ. It is as if that person had undergone a personal microchronic passage from B.C. to A.D. Whenever used, it bespeaks an earnest, outspoken and transformed Christian and refers to churches that preach that message." [3]

Unfortunately, in the theology of contemporary Evangelicalism, the definition of "born again" has been divorced from its biblical definition. Ironically, it

---

[2] John Marsh, *The Gospel of St John* (Baltimore, Md.: Penguin Books, 1968), 173–74.
[3] Daniel G. Reid, ed., *Dictionary of Christianity in America* (Downers Grove, Ill.: InterVarsity Press, 1990), 177.

is on this point that many Catholics are confronted by "born-again Christians" who claim that they are now "saved the Bible way" and charge that the Catholic Church is somehow "unbiblical". In reality, this popularized view of being "born again" is a rather recent development of Evangelical Protestant doctrine and has come from an experiential, sociological phenomenon, usually accompanied by great emotion, and has little to do with the definition of being "born anew" that Jesus gave Nicodemus. So-called "born again" experiences can be real and meaningful encounters with the risen Christ, but one must ask if the term "born again" is the biblically correct phrase to describe them. Jesus explained this "new birth"—regeneration—as a direct result of "water and the Spirit", with an obvious reference to baptism in water. "Truly, truly, I say to you, unless one is born of water and the Spirit, he cannot enter the kingdom of God" (3:5). We will discuss this more in due course, but keep in mind that it is the Christian who understands that "new birth" is tied to baptism who properly interprets the biblical term "born again".[4]

» TEXTUAL NOTE: "Born again", or "born anew", is the typical rendering of this phrase in verse 3. The word "again" in the Greek is *anothen* (ανωθεν), which can mean "anew", "again", or "from above". In the context of St. John's Gospel, how is the word used elsewhere (Jn 3:7, 31; 19:11; also see Jas 1:17; 3:15, 17)? Peter employs a different Greek word in 1 Peter 1:3, 23, which clearly means "born again" or "given new birth". Why do you think translators use one instead of the other? "The phrase 'of water' is not the only reference to Baptism in this scene, and so its presence cannot be explained as an isolated act of censorship. The Nicodemus discourse is followed immediately by a story in which it is emphasized that both John the Baptist and Jesus were *baptizing*. . . . [O]ne of the most plausible reasons for [the Nicodemus story] having been placed where it now stands is precisely because its baptismal motif matched that of the Nicodemus scene. . . . The theme of 'being born [again]' is a baptismal theme in I Pet i 23 (cf. 'rebirth' in Titus iii 5). The fact that the early versions translated John iii 3 and 5 in terms of being born again means that from the earliest days this passage was thought of in a baptismal context."[5]

6. According to verse 5, what is necessary to "enter the kingdom of God"? In Jesus' words, how is one "born from above" ? What does Jesus mean by "born of water and the Spirit" (Tit 3:5; 1 Pet 3:20–21; CCC 720, 1215, 1225, 1257; see also Acts 2:38; 22:16; Mk 16:16)? Being "born from above" implies a new nature; what nature derives from this regeneration (2 Pet 1:4)? Notice how significant water is in John's

---

[4] For more on this subject, see Stephen K. Ray, *Crossing the Tiber: Evangelical Protestants Discover the Historical Church* (San Francisco: Ignatius Press, 1997), 112–14.

[5] Raymond E. Brown, ed. and trans., *The Gospel according to John,* vol. 1, Anchor Bible, vol. 29 (Garden City, N.Y.: Doubleday, 1966), 143.

Gospel (Jn 1:33; 2:6–9; 3:5; 3:22–26; 4:1ff.; 5:3–7; 7:35–37; 6:19; 13:5; 19:34; 21:1ff.).

» APOLOGETICAL NOTE: Even though this passage on "water and Spirit" has been consistently held to refer to "baptismal regeneration" since the apostolic period, some Protestants still attempt to undermine the Catholic teaching of baptismal regeneration (which is based, in part, on John 3:5) by offering a variety of conflicting interpretations. Some assert that "water" refers to semen, or the watery fluid (amniotic fluid) accompanying natural birth. These ideas are untenable and have no corresponding biblical parallels or precedent in Jewish or early Christian thought. Others contend that "water" and "Spirit" are synonyms, as in "water, even the Spirit" (John Calvin adopted this perspective). These interpretations are novel and recent attempts to avoid the obvious intent of Jesus, as clearly understood by those who heard him and were being baptized, by the Fathers, and by the whole early Church.

"Water" refers to Christian baptism. Baptist commentator George Beasley-Murray, commenting on the attempts to interpret "water and Spirit" as something other than baptism, writes, "Suggestions like these do not do justice to the text and have not commended themselves to scholarly opinion. It would seem that the text relates birth from above to baptism and the Holy Spirit. . . . The need for cleansing and expectation of the renewal of the Spirit, accordingly, was in the air in the period of Jesus and the early Church. . . . In the time of the Church the gifts [baptism and Spirit] are conjoined, since the Lord by his death and resurrection has achieved a once-for-all cleansing and sent the Spirit of the kingdom: he who is baptized in faith in the Son of Man, exalted by his cross to heaven, becomes a new creation by the Spirit, 'sees' the kingdom, and in Christ has life eternal (vv. 14–15)."[6]

Protestant commentator R. V. G. Tasker writes, "In light of the reference to the practice by Jesus of water baptism in verse 22, it is difficult to avoid construing the words 'of water and of the Spirit' conjunctively, and regarding them as a description of Christian baptism, in which cleansing and endowment are both essential elements."[7]

» THEOLOGICAL NOTE: Being "born from above" clearly refers to baptism, given the context and framework of John's text. How does John frame this episode? Jesus' comments about being "born from above" and being "born of water and Spirit" bring to the reader's mind Jesus' own baptism, discussed in John 1:32. In that passage, John the Baptist reports having seen the "Spirit descend as a dove from heaven" (Jn 1:31–37; Lk 3:21–22). This was the model

---

[6] G. R. Beasley-Murray, *John*, Word Biblical Commentary (Waco, Tex.: Word Books, 1987), 48–49.
[7] R. V. G. Tasker, *The Gospel according to St. John*, Tyndale New Testament Commentaries (Grand Rapids, Mich.: Wm. B. Eerdmans, 1977), 71.

of birth "from above"—"*anothen*". At Jesus' baptism, the Spirit again hovers over the water as he did in Genesis 1:1–2 at the first creation. He lights on Jesus, initiating the second and new creation. Here we have two "in the beginnings". So it is with each of us, as we are baptized and become new creations—"born from above".

Immediately following the dialogue with Nicodemus about being born of "water and Spirit", John tells us that Jesus and his disciples went into Judea, where Jesus spent time with them baptizing (Jn 3:22). This makes the baptismal framework of this "born-from-above" passage unmistakable.

» MARTIN LUTHER: Many heirs of the Protestant Reformation are unaware that Martin Luther was much closer to Catholic teaching in many ways than to Evangelical Protestantism. On this passage regarding "water" and the "new birth" Luther wrote, "Here Christ is speaking of Baptism, of real and natural water such as a cow may drink, the Baptism about which you hear in the sermons on this subject. Therefore the word 'water' does not designate afflic-tion here; it means real, natural water, which is connected with God's Word and becomes a very spiritual bath through the Holy Spirit or through the entire Trinity. Here Christ also speaks of the Holy Spirit and teaches us to regard Baptism as a spiritual, yes, a Spirit-filled water, in which the Holy Spirit is present and active; in fact, the entire Holy Trinity is there. And thus the person who has been baptized is said to be born anew. In Titus 3:5 St. Paul terms Baptism 'a washing of regeneration and renewal in the Holy Spirit.' In the last chapter of Mark we read that 'he who believes and is baptized will be saved' (Mk 16:16). And in this passage Christ declares that whoever is not born anew of the water and the Holy Spirit cannot come into the kingdom of God. Therefore God's words dare not be tampered with. Of course, we are well aware that Baptism is natural water. But after the Holy Spirit is added to it, we have more than mere water. It becomes a veritable bath of rejuvenation, a living bath which washes and purges man of sin and death, which cleanses him of all sin." [8]

» CHURCH FATHERS: Without exception the Church Fathers interpreted John 3:5 as referring to regenerative water baptism, necessary for salvation and the means to wash away sin. Four examples will suffice here.[9]

Justin Martyr (ca. 100–ca. 165): "Then they are brought by us where there is water, and are regenerated in the same manner in which we were ourselves regenerated [reborn]. For, in the name of God, the Father and Lord of the universe, and of our Saviour Jesus Christ, and of the Holy Spirit, they then receive the washing with water. For Christ also said, 'Except ye be born again,

---

[8] Martin Luther, *Sermons on the Gospel of St. John Chapters 1–4*, vol. 22 of *Luther's Works*, trans. Martin H. Bertram (St. Louis, Mo.: Concordia Pub. House, 1957), 283.

[9] For a comprehensive collection of patristic quotes and explanations on baptism and the Eucharist, see Ray, *Crossing the Tiber.*

ye shall not enter into the kingdom of heaven'. . . . And for this [rite] we have learned from the apostles this reason." [10]

St. Theophilus of Antioch (died ca. 185), who first coined the word "Trinity", writes: "Those things which were created from the waters [Gen 1] were blessed by God, so that this might also be a sign that men would at a future time receive repentance and remission of sins through water and the bath of regeneration." [11]

Origen (ca. 185–ca. 254): "The Church received from the Apostles the tradition [custom] of giving Baptism even to infants. For the Apostles, to whom were committed the secrets of divine mysteries, knew that there is in everyone the innate stains of sin, which must be washed away through water and the Spirit." [12]

St. Augustine (354–430): "Who is so impious as to wish to exclude infants from the kingdom of heaven, by forbidding them to be baptized and born again in Christ?" [13] "This [infant baptism] the Church always had, always held; this she received from the faith of our ancestors; this she perseveringly guards even to the end." [14]

7. According to verse 6, what two different births does Jesus compare and contrast? Regarding the issue of "birth", why is the Church called our Mother (CCC 507)? Is baptism necessary for salvation (1 Pet 3:21; CCC 846, 1257)? One might ask, "What about the thief on the cross? He was not baptized. How could he be saved, if baptism is necessary for salvation?" (Lk 23:39–43; CCC 1257–60). God ties salvation to the sacraments, but is he bound by them? For more on baptism, see notes on John 9:7.

» A RIDDLE: "Born once, die twice; born twice, die once." Are you able to explain? [15]

8. Nicodemus is puzzled and elicits further explanation from Jesus. How does Jesus respond to Nicodemus' ignorance (vv. 7 and 10)? Why does Jesus use the example of wind in verse 8 (Gen 2:7; Ezek 37:9;

---

[10] Justin Martyr, *The First Apology* 61, in ANF 1:183.

[11] St. Theophilus of Antioch, *To Autolycus* 2, 16, in William A. Jurgens, *The Faith of the Early Fathers*, vol. 1 (Collegeville, Minn.: Liturgical Press, 1970), 75.

[12] Origen, *Commentary on Romans* 5, 9, in Jurgens, *Faith of the Early Fathers*, 1:209.

[13] St. Augustine, *On Original Sin* 2, 20, in NPNF1 5:244.

[14] St. Augustine, *Sermo* 11, *De Verb. Apost.*, quoted in the article on "Baptism", in Charles G. Herbermann, ed., *The Catholic Encyclopedia* (New York: Robert Appleton Company, 1907), 2:270.

[15] If you are born only physically, then you die physically and also spiritually (damnation). If you are born both physically and spiritually (new birth), then you die physically but not spiritually.

Eccles 11:5; Jn 20:22; Acts 2:2; CCC 691)? What Old Testament passage would immediately come to the mind of the Jewish listener (Ezek 36:25–27; 37:1–14; CCC 715, 1287)? If you were hearing these amazing things for the first time, from a man who claimed to be the Son of God, how would you react?

» WORD STUDY: The English words "wind" and "spirit" in the New Testament are the same Greek word—*pneuma*. So, when we read "wind" and "spirit" in this passage, we do so because the translators have made the distinction for us based on the context. The original readers would have read only the one word *pneuma*. Why does Jesus engage in such wordplay with Nicodemus? "The grace of the Spirit is free, and mysterious in its action; but though unseen it is none the less real, and men must believe in its reality. It comes from the unseen God, and leads to things unseen; yet its presence may be inferred from its fruit in the soul of man—charity, joy, peace, patience, benignity, goodness, longanimity, mildness, faith, modesty, continency, chastity (Gal. v. 22, 23)." [16]

» OLD TESTAMENT BACKGROUND: "There is no difference between seeing the kingdom of God and entering into it. . . . Neither is there any difference between being born anew (or born from above) and being born 'of water and Spirit'; but the latter way of putting it echoes OT phraseology and might have been calculated to ring a bell in Nicodemus's mind. If he thought it impossible for one to acquire a new nature in later life, let him recall that God had promised to do this very thing for his people Israel: 'I will sprinkle clean water upon you, and you shall be clean . . . and a new spirit I will put within you' (Ezek. 36:25f.). This 'new spirit' was God's own Spirit: 'I will put my spirit within you' (Ezek. 36:27). The promise to Israel through Ezekiel was amplified in the vision of the valley of dry bones, when the prophet obeyed the divine command: 'Prophesy to the breath, prophesy, son of man, and say to the breath, "Thus says the Lord GOD: Come from the four winds, O breath, and breathe upon these slain, that they may live"' (Ezek. 37:9, RSV). . . . The cleansing with water in Ezek. 36:25 was invoked as biblical authority for the baptism of [Gentile] proselytes. . . . Now the Coming One in person urges Nicodemus to accept the promise in its fullness—the new birth 'of water and Spirit'. The kingdom of God is a spiritual order which can be entered only by spiritual rebirth." [17]

9. Why does the discussion change from the first person ("I") to the second person ("we") in verse 11? (*Possible solution:* Jn 3:26–27, 31–32.)

---

[16] John McIntyre, *The Holy Gospel according to Saint John* (London: Catholic Truth Society, 1899), 33.

[17] F. F. Bruce, *The Gospel of John* (Grand Rapids, Mich.: William B. Eerdmans, 1983), 84.

Is there a point where the dialogue changes into a monologue, and a point in the monologue where Jesus ceases to be the speaker and the apostle takes over?

10. In verse 12, Jesus says that if Nicodemus cannot understand earthly things, which should be easily understood, how much more will he not understand heavenly things. What is Jesus talking about?

» THEOLOGICAL NOTE: "Up to this point, Jesus has been speaking of what should be comparatively easy to understand, at least by analogies. In this sense rebirth and the presence of the Spirit are 'earthly things.' If Nicodemus cannot understand these, if they cannot bring him to faith in Jesus' true character, then he is obviously in no position to receive the revelation of 'heavenly things,' that is, mysteries of which faith alone can provide the basis of understanding. . . . The 'heavenly things' of which Jesus has just spoken cannot be grasped by any man at will. Here the reader may have been reminded of the Gnostic 'mystery' religions that pretended to transfer initiates into a realm of heavenly knowledge. The only one who can speak authoritatively of heavenly things is the only Person who has both come down from heaven and ascended into heaven, the Son of Man." [18] When John was writing in about A.D. 90, he was undoubtedly writing with the Gnostic heretics in mind, as well as Jewish sceptics. His observation that Jesus had come down from heaven and would return to heaven was absolutely contrary to Gnostic thought, according to which spirit and heaven were pure and good, and flesh and earth were evil, and never the twain shall meet.

11. In verse 13, why does Jesus mention ascending and descending from heaven (cf. Deut 30:11–12; Jn 1:51; Wis 9:16–18; Bar 3:28–29)? What is Jesus again claiming for himself with the title "Son of man" (Dan 7:13–14; CCC 423, 440, 661)? Read Proverbs 30; how does the similar wording demonstrate a probable connection to Jesus' words to Nicodemus?

» A LESSON IN INTERPRETATION: How do we understand the New Testament in light of the Old Testament? Old Testament passages quoted or alluded to in the New Testament are always extremely significant, and when "chased down" and studied they can provide nuggets of gold. Having read Proverbs 30:1–4, do you think Jesus might have borrowed the words "ascending" and "descending" from Proverbs 30 (thus drawing Nicodemus' attention to it)? What is the

---

[18] Raymond Brown, Joseph Fitzmyer, and Roland Murphy, eds., *The Jerome Biblical Commentary* (Englewood Cliffs, N.J.: Prentice-Hall, 1968), 2:430.

context of Proverbs 30? Agur wrote Proverbs 30 and, as an author of Proverbs, was also "a teacher of Israel" (contrasted with Nicodemus, "teacher of Israel"). In his musings, Agur ponders "earthly things" (Prov 30:11–33). He also understands his own shortcomings and ignorance in contrast with the inaccessible and superior wisdom of the Holy One who ascends and descends from heaven, where he dwells. Who dwells in heaven and descended to earth (Jn 1:1, 14, 51) and has superior knowledge (Jn 3:34–35; 8:26–27; Mt 11:27)? How did Nicodemus address Jesus (Jn 3:2)?

By alluding to Proverbs 30, especially verse 4, how does Jesus reveal himself—as merely a good teacher with God's blessing (cf. Jn 3:10; Prov 30:4) or something more? Why should Nicodemus have known these things? Would you have understood Jesus had you been standing in the crowd listening? How does the allusion to Proverbs 30:2–3 reprove Nicodemus as "the teacher of Israel", especially the phrase "Surely you know" (Prov 30:4)? What other words in Proverbs 30:1–4 have we seen repeated in the first chapters of John? Notice the use of "water" and "wind" in verse 4. How are they used in Jesus' dialogue with Nicodemus? Who created and gave them power? How, through the sacrament of baptism, will these blessings of God go to the ends of the earth? How does Jesus reveal his deity and humanity in this passage, not to mention his messiahship? In a sense, Nicodemus is queried by Jesus against the background of Proverbs 30: "What is his name, and what is his son's name? Surely you know! Every word of God proves true." What is the Creator's name and what is the name of his Son? Who or what is the Word of God (Jn 1:1, 14) that is proving to be true (cf. Jn 14:6)?

12. Read the next verse, John 3:14, where Jesus refers to Moses and the image of the serpent in the desert. We often forget how important the Old Testament is to understanding our Catholic faith. Imagine for a minute that there were no Old Testament and you were reading John 3:14. How would you understand what John is talking about? What does St. Paul tell us about the Old Testament (1 Cor 10:11; Rom 15:4)?

13. But, of course, the Jews received and carefully preserved the sacred writings of the Old Covenant (cf. Rom 3:1–2). Read Numbers 21:4–9 and Wisdom 16:5–8 to discover the background of Jesus' comment about the serpent. How did God's command to make this bronze serpent—an image—harmonize with his earlier command to "make no graven images" (Ex 20:4; cf. also Ex 25:18–22; CCC 2129–32)? What later happened to the bronze serpent and why (2 Kings 18:4)? Was making a bronze image contrary to the Law of God? Or was the divine Law really about making an image *with the intent of worshipping it as a god?*

14. What does the snakebite represent (Gen 3:1ff.; Jn 8:44; Eph 2:1–6; 1 Cor 15:56; CCC 402)? What is the remedy for the venom of sin (2 Cor 5:21; 1 Jn 3:8; Jn 12:31–33); who is the "ruler of this world" (1 Jn 5:19; Eph 6:11–12)? What does it mean that Christ will "be lifted up" (Is 53:4ff.; Jn 8:28; 12:32–34; Lk 23:33; CCC 662)? Why is Christ likened to a serpent (2 Cor 5:21; Rom 8:3; CCC 603)? How were the sinful Jews saved from the sting of the serpents (Num 21:9)? How was looking at the serpent raised up on a pole in the wilderness *then* like looking up at Christ lifted up on the Cross *today* (Jn 3:15)? Why does Jesus use the story of the bronze serpent at this point in the story?

» OLD TESTAMENT BACKGROUND: "Jesus Christ came to save us by healing us, as the children of Israel that were stung with fiery serpents were cured and lived by looking up to the brazen serpent; we have the story of it, Num. 21:6–9. It was the last miracle that passed through the hand of Moses before his death. Now in this type of Christ we may observe,

"First, The deadly and destructive nature of sin, which is implied here. The guilt of sin is like the pain of the biting of a fiery serpent; the power of corruption is like the venom diffused thereby. The devil is the old serpent, subtle at first (Gen. 3:1), but ever since fiery, and his temptations fiery darts, his assaults terrifying, his victories destroying. Ask awakened consciences, ask damned sinners, and they will tell you, how charming soever the allurements of sin are, at the last it bites like a serpent, Prov. 23:30–32. God's wrath against us for sin is as those fiery serpents which God sent among the people, to punish them for their murmurings. The curses of the law are as fiery serpents, so are all the tokens of divine wrath.

"Secondly, The powerful remedy provided against this fatal malady. The case of poor sinners is deplorable; but is it desperate? Thanks be to God, it is not; there is balm in Gilead. The Son of man is lifted up, as the serpent of brass was by Moses, which cured the stung Israelites. It was a serpent of brass that cured them. Brass is bright; we read of Christ's feet shining like brass, Rev. 1:15. It is durable; Christ is the same. It was made in the shape of a fiery serpent, and yet had no poison, no sting, fitly representing Christ, who was made sin for us and yet knew no sin; was made in the likeness of sinful flesh and yet not sinful; as harmless as a serpent of brass. The serpent was a cursed creature; Christ was made a curse.

"Thirdly, The way of applying this remedy, and that is by believing, which plainly alludes to the Israelites' looking up to the brazen serpent, in order to their being healed by it. If any stung Israelite was either so little sensible of his pain and peril, or had so little confidence in the word of Moses as not to look up to the brazen serpent, justly did he die of his wound; but every one that looked up to it did well, Num. 21:9. If any so far slight either their disease by sin or the method of cure by Christ as not to embrace Christ upon his own terms, their blood is upon their own head. He hath said, Look, and be saved (Isa. 45:22), look and live." [19]

15. John 3:16 is arguably the most well-known and cherished verse in the Bible, summarizing the whole gospel of Christ. Why does John say that God loves the "world" (*cosmos*) instead of just the souls of men (Gen 1:31; 3:17–18; Jn 1:29; 4:42; Rom 8:19–22; CCC 421, 293)? See notes on John 15:18–27 and 19:2.

16. God graciously gave his Son to be the sacrifice for sins, as the Lamb of God. Who else offered an "only [begotten] son" (Heb 11:17; CCC 2572)? How must the Father have felt when he offered up his only Son? Read Genesis 22 for a gripping story of another father offering an only begotten son. On which mountain was that sacrifice to be offered (Gen 22:2)? On which mountain was Jesus offered as a sacrifice by his Father (cf. 2 Chron 3:1; Lk 18:31–33)? We are told God sent his Son from heaven to earth—as a champion to deliver us. Did God send his Son to judge or to save (Jn 3:17; Rom 5:8; CCC 734)? What kind of love is this (Eph 4:2–5; Jn 15:13; CCC 218–21, 604–5)? What is God (1 Jn 4:8)? How was this manifested for us (1 Jn 4:9–10; CCC 457–58)?

» THEOLOGICAL NOTE: In verse 16, we come across the first use of the word "love" in John's Gospel. In Greek, there are four words that correspond to our English word "love". These words refer to four kinds of love: affection, friendship, eros, and charity.[20] In 1 John 4:16, we are told "God is love"; in John 3:16, that God loved the world; and in John 3:35, that God loves the Son (cf. Gen 22:2, 12; CCC 1823). The Greek word used is *agape*, which means the perfect, constant, unconditional love of a perfect Being who is Love. It is love given even when completely undeserved (1 Jn 4:10). This is the love of God (CCC 218–21). As Meir Ben Isaac Nehoral wrote in 1050, "Could we with ink the ocean fill, and were the skies of parchment made; were every stalk on earth a quill, and every man a scribe by trade; to write the love of God above would drain the ocean dry; nor could the scroll contain the whole, though stretched from sky to sky." [21] How can we practice "agape" love? How does it differ from and include the other forms of love?

[19] Matthew Henry, *Matthew Henry's Commentary* (Peabody, Mass.: Hendrickson Pub., 1991), 5:887–89.
[20] C. S. Lewis, *The Four Loves* (London: Collins, 1960).
[21] T. B. Gilbert, *Hymns of Truth and Praise* (Fort Dodge, Iowa: Gospel Perpetuating Pub., 1971), 39.

17. We are told that Jesus is the "only begotten" Son. What does that mean (CCC 242)? (See notes on John 1:14, 18, pp. 52–53, 58.)

» THEOLOGICAL NOTE: Jehovah's Witnesses, Mormons, and similar groups deny the full divinity of Christ and appeal to the title "only begotten Son", asserting that Jesus had a beginning, that he was created. However, the Church has always understood the expression "only begotten Son" to mean that the Son uniquely proceeds eternally from the Father, not as a creature, not with a "beginning", but as the eternal second Person of the Trinity.

The creed of the Council of Nicaea 325 says: "We believe in one God the Father almighty, creator of all things visible and invisible. And in our one Lord Jesus Christ the Son of God, the only begotten born of the Father, that is of the substance of the Father, God of God, light of light, true God of true God, born, not made, of one substance [in Greek, *homousion*] with the Father, by whom all things were made, which are in heaven and on earth, who for our salvation came down, and became incarnate and was made man, and suffered, and arose again on the third day, and ascended into heaven, and will come to judge the living and the dead. And in the Holy Spirit.

"But those who say: 'There was [a time] when he was not,' and, 'Before he was born, he was not,' and 'Because he was made from nonexisting matter, he is either of another substance or essence,' and those who call 'God the Son of God changeable and mutable,' these the Catholic Church anathematizes." [22]

18. In verse 16, we are told "belief" is a criterion for obtaining eternal life. Is believing a "work", something we must do (Jn 6:29; Jas 2:24; CCC 154–55)? If we must believe, as an act of the will, how does that relate to John 1:12–13? John adopts the terms of the great debate between Paul and his Jewish Christian opponents, "faith vs. works", but instead of replacing works by faith, John interprets true work as faith, true faith as work. The word "believe" in verse 16 is in the present, active tense and therefore means "whoever is presently believing" might have eternal life. How does this affect the Calvinist doctrine of "eternal security" (Col 1:22–23; CCC 162)? Do we have to continue in faith in order to obtain eternal life (Col 1:22–23; Jn 15:6; Mt 10:22; 24:13; CCC 161, 1821)?

19. How does belief as a "once-for-all" past event differ from "currently and actively believing" in the present? The opposite of "believe"

---

[22] Heinrich Denzinger, *The Sources of Catholic Dogma*, trans. Roy J. Deferrari (St. Louis, Mo.: B. Herder Book Co., 1957), 26. For one of the finest explanations of the Trinity and the description "the only begotten Son", read Frank Sheed, *Theology and Sanity* (San Francisco: Ignatius Press, 1978), chap. 7.

is not "disbelieve", according to John. What is the opposite of "believe" (Jn 3:36; 1 Pet 4:17; Heb 3:18–19)? Can we say salvation is by "faith alone", apart from obedience (Jas 2:18–26)? What does Paul mean by "the obedience of faith" (Rom 1:5; 16:26)? How does Luke explain the conversion of Jewish priests (Acts 6:7)? Are we saved by any works we do—can we obligate God to save us by obeying the Law (Tit 3:5; Gal 2:16)? How are we saved (Eph 2:8–9)? What were we created for (Eph 2:10)? What is the basis for final judgment (Jn 5:28–29; Rev 20:12–13; Mt 16:27; Rom 2:6–10; CCC 1038)?

20. When a Christian performs good works, do the good works originate from himself alone, or are they the works of God's grace (Jn 3:21; Phil 2:12–13; 1 Cor 15:10; CCC 308)? How do judgment and condemnation relate to the Christian (Jn 3:18; 1 Pet 4:17; Rom 8:1; Rev 20:12; Jn 5:28–29; CCC 679, 1022)? What is the difference between darkness and light, and why does John use these descriptions again in verse 19? How might Jesus be referring to Nicodemus (cf. Jn 3:1–2)? What is the main reason that men turn away from Jesus, the gospel, and the Church (Jn 3:19–20)? Is it generally due to theological or moral reasons? How are we to live (1 Thess 5:4–11)?

» THEOLOGICAL NOTE: In this passage, especially verse 18, it "is proved by a kind of implied dilemma, that God did not send His Son 'to judge the world.' For, either a man believes, in Him, or refuses to do so. If he believes; then, he is not judged; but is rescued and saved by the mercy of God and the superabundant merits of our Saviour, from the general condemnation, in which all men would be involved, and receives abundance of grace.

"If he believes not; then, no further sentence is needed. He remains in the state of damnation, in which all men are involved, as 'children of wrath.' He is condemned by the original decree of God and his own determined obstinacy of will to persevere in his unbelief, 'because he believeth not in the name of the only begotten Son of God,' thus rejecting the only means instituted by God, to save and rescue him from damnation.

"St. Augustine (Tract 12) illustrates this by the example of a physician who comes to cure all the infirm. Such as refuse his ministrations, die; not on account of the physician, as if he came to cause their death; but, on account of the infirmities already contracted by them, which they refuse to have cured by the physician." [23]

---

[23] John MacEvilly, *An Exposition of the Gospel of St. John* (New York: Benziger Bros., 1889), 59–60.

The light has come, but those who hide from the light and wallow in their darkness and sin cannot be saved by the light. They are doomed to temporal and eternal darkness. The one who escapes death and darkness is the one who steps into the light, allows his evil deeds to be washed away, and then practices the truth, showing that his deeds have been "wrought in God". The man does the good deeds, but they have been accomplished by the light and grace of God.

John 3:22–36
John the Baptizer

21. When Jesus finishes speaking to Nicodemus about being "born of water and the Spirit", what does Jesus begin doing (Jn 3:22)? In light of his actions, how might it help John's readers to interpret his words in verse 5? What would his listeners think Jesus meant by "water"? Who else was baptizing in the same region (v. 23)?

» HISTORICAL NOTE: We are told that "John also was baptizing at Aenon near Salim, because there was much water there." An interesting historical note on baptism in the early Church comes from the *Didache*, written perhaps as early as the year 60. It says, "Baptize as follows: after first explaining all these points, baptize in the name of the Father and of the Son and of the Holy Spirit, in running water. But if you have no running water, baptize in other water; and if you cannot in cold, then in warm. But if you have neither, pour water on the head three times in the name of the Father and of the Son and of the Holy Spirit." [24] St. Irenaeus writes of baptism around 180: "And again, giving to the disciples the power of regeneration into God, He said to them, 'Go and teach all nations, baptizing them in the name of the Father, and of the Son, and of the Holy Ghost' ";[25] and, "For He came to save all through means of Himself—all, I say, who through Him are born again to God—infants, and children, and boys, and youths, and old men." [26] Infant baptism was part of the apostolic teaching preserved and practiced in the early Church.

22. What is the difference between the baptism of Jesus and that of John the Baptist (Mt 3:11; Acts 18:25; 19:2–6; CCC 696, 1288)? Having water in common, what was the added "ingredient" of the baptism offered by Jesus (Jn 3:5)?

---

[24] *Didache* 7, 1–3, in Johannes Quasten, *Patrology* (Westminster, Md.: Christian Classics, 1993), 1:31.

[25] Irenaeus, *Against Heresies* 3, 17, 1, in ANF 1:444.

[26] Ibid., 2, 22, 4, in ANF 1:391.

23. When John tells us that the Baptizer was not yet in prison, he is announcing that his narrative covers material earlier than that of the other three Gospels (Mk 1:14–15). Why was John the Baptist "thrown into prison" (Mt 14:3ff.)? Was the Baptizer arrested and beheaded for preaching the "simple gospel" (Mt 14:3–4)? How would you feel, languishing for ten months in the Machaerus prison,[27] knowing the Son of God is nearby and apparently doing nothing to save you (Mt 11:2–6)? His disciples seemed to be jealous of Jesus' popularity (v. 26). How does John the Baptist respond (Jn 3:27–30)? In verse 25, the disciples of John argue about "purification". How does this draw our attention back to John 2:6 and the passing away of the old for the new?

24. In verse 23, we are told that the Baptist is baptizing at "Aenon near Salim". *Aenon* means "fountain", and *Salim* means "peace". Knowing John's penchant for symbolism, how might the mention of these names add to the meaning of the narrative? Compare this with Zechariah 13:1.

25. In verse 31, we again find the use of the Greek word "above", *anothen*, used by John to describe Jesus' descent from heaven. Jesus is from *above*, and is therefore *above all*. Since the same Greek word is used, how might this verse help us understand John 3:3?

26. In verse 32, why is it that John's witness is not received (cf. Jn 5:33–38)? Should men not jump at the opportunity to know more about God, the cosmos, heaven, truth, and so on? Why do they turn away and reject John's witness and Jesus' testimony (Jn 7:7)? How are they following in the footsteps of their fathers (Acts 7:39–41, 51–53)? Do we receive Jesus and his truth with open arms? Are we willing to leave darkness and our favorite sins to walk in the light (1 Jn 1:5–7)—to confess Christ openly and boldly, with our words and our actions?

27. Read verses 33–35. In the Old Testament, the Holy Spirit did not normally indwell God's people but would "come upon them" at certain times to accomplish certain deeds. They received a "measure of the Spirit". Rabbi Acha (fourth century) wrote that the Holy Spirit who rested on the prophets did so "according to the measure" of each prophet's assignment.[28] Jesus, unlike any mere prophet, *is* the Word of

---

[27] Flavius Josephus, *Antiq.* XVIII, 5, in *Josephus: Complete Works*, trans. William Whiston (Grand Rapids, Mich.: Kregel Pubs., 1978), 382.

[28] *Leviticus Rabbah* 15:2, in Bruce, *John*, 99.

God (Jn 1:1; Heb 1:1–4), comes "from above", and gives "the Spirit without measure". (John testifies that he saw the Spirit "descending and remaining" on Jesus in John 1:32–33; CCC 504.) What would this have proved to the Jewish people (Is 11:1–2; 42:1; 61:1; Mt 11:2–6; Lk 4:16–21; Jn 1:34; CCC 1286)? Why should they have listened intently to Jesus?

28. In your own words, summarize the gospel as presented in John 3. Is salvation a one-time event or a process? Is salvation wrought by belief or baptism or the Spirit or all three (CCC 977, 161, 1257)? What choices are we presented with (Jn 3:36; Deut 30:15–20)? What are the temporal and eternal consequences of *our* choices and the choices of those near to us (CCC 161)? Look at several translations and notice what the opposite is of the word "believe" (Jn 3:36). How does this help us better understand the biblical meaning of the word "believe"?

JOHN 4

THE SAMARITAN WOMAN, THE GENTILE OFFICIAL: CONVERSION AND FAITH

John 4:1-42
The Samaritan Woman Is Offered Living Water

1. Cana and Nazareth are in Galilee, in northern Israel; Jerusalem is in Judea, in southern Israel. Galilee is about eighty miles north of Jerusalem and was practically removed from the religious community of the Pharisees. Galilee was populated with Gentiles and Jewish settlers. What had Isaiah prophesied about "Galilee of the nations [gentiles]" (Is 9:1ff.)? Why was Jesus in Judea, and why did he return north to Galilee (Jn 2:13; 4:1, 3)? What was the attitude of Judeans toward the Galileans (Is 9:1; Jn 1:46; 7:51-52; Mt 26:73; Acts 1:11; 4:13)? In which of these areas was Jesus raised?

2. According to verse 1, how many disciples did Jesus have? What is symbolic and sacramental about the fact that "Jesus was making and baptizing more disciples . . . although Jesus himself did not baptize, but only his disciples" (Jn 13:20; CCC 858, 1548)?

» THEOLOGICAL NOTE: The priest in the Catholic Church sacramentally stands "in the place of Christ" (CCC 1142, 1548). The priest shares in the work and priesthood of Christ, without in any way detracting from Christ's unique and singular position as High Priest. As one who prays for another shares in the intercessory work of Christ (Rom 8:34; Heb 7:25; Rom 11:2, which refers to Elijah interceding with God; Eph 6:18; 1 Tim 2:1), so those who are disciples of Christ do things in his name, especially the priest who acts in a special way—*in persona Christi*—in the person of Christ.

3. In verse 1, John refers to Jesus as "the Lord". What had Isaiah prophesied eight hundred years earlier (Is 9:1ff. cf. Is 40:3; Mt 3:3; Jn

1:23)? What do the Baptizer (Jn 1:23) and John the Apostle claim for Jesus by using the title "Lord" (CCC 209, 446)? Why is it significant that in John 4:1 Jesus is called "Lord" by John for the first time; in other words, what is it that John assumes his readers are now becoming convinced of (CCC 449)?

4. Samaria lies directly between Judea in the south and Galilee in the north; therefore, to take the direct route, Jesus "had to pass though Samaria" (v. 4), which was a three-days' journey. Often pilgrims would bypass Samaria by traveling along the Jordan River to the east. Why does John imply a necessity of passing through Samaria when other routes were possible? Was it a *practical* or an *evangelistic* necessity? Why did the Jews avoid Samaria whenever possible (Lk 9:52–54; Mt 10:5–6; Lk 17:11–19; Jn 4:9; Acts 10:28)? What had happened centuries before that caused the great animosity between the Jews and the Samaritans?

» HISTORICAL BACKGROUND: Israel was a united kingdom under David and Solomon (1000–930 B.C.). When Solomon's son Rehoboam succeeded to the throne he raised taxes. In 924 B.C., Jeroboam led the northern tribes in revolt. They "seceded from the union" and became a separate nation called Israel (1 Kings 12:1–24). The southern tribe of Judah (and the half tribe of Benjamin) remained with Rehoboam, and their nation was called Judah (from which we get the word Judaism)—staying loyal to Jerusalem and the Temple. In 721 B.C., the cruel Assyrians captured Israel and exported the ten northern tribes to Assyria (2 Kings 17:1–6). In their place, the Assyrians populated Samaria (Israel) with captured foreigners (2 Kings 17:24–26). The Samaritans were their descendants. Today, there are between five hundred and one thousand descendants of the first-century Samaritans. They are still led by priests, they still live on Mt. Gerazim, and they offer animal sacrifices. They claim to be the rightful heirs of Abraham, Isaac, and Jacob, descendants of the ten tribes of northern Israel, especially the tribe of Joseph (Jn 4:5). Even today you can visit the rock upon which they say Abraham offered Isaac, and when visiting the site one must remove his shoes.

Scholars follow Josephus (A.D. ca. 37–ca. 100) in doubting the Samaritans' claim and have concluded that the Samaritans were actually descendants of the pagan nations (or "half-breeds", through intermarriage with the idolatrous Gentile settlers) who repopulated Israel under the Assyrians. The Samaritans' background led to hatred and suspicion between them and the Jews. The Samaritans were hated more than foreigners because they established the city of Shechem as a rival to the holy city, Jerusalem, claiming true continuity with the patriarchs.

5. In Samaria, Jesus comes to the town Sychar (which means "drunkenness"), about forty-one miles north of Jerusalem. This was probably the ancient city of Shechem (modern name of Nablus). Might there be a symbolic importance to the name "drunkenness"? Think of this in contrast to the events in Cana, where the Son of man also asked someone to fill jars with water (Jn 2:7). What are the similarities and differences? For what is the city of Shechem known (Gen 12:6; 33:18–20; 34:1–31; 37:12–14, read the whole story; Josh 17:1–2; 24:1, 23–32; 1 Kings 12:1, 25–33; Acts 7:15–16)? Shechem means "shoulder" or "slope", since it was on the slope of Mt. Gerazim. (See Gen 48:22, where "slope" or "portion" is the Hebrew word *shechem*.)

» GEOGRAPHICAL NOTE: The location of Jacob's well (v. 6) is still known in Israel, and water can be drawn from it today. It is located at an old crypt beneath the unfinished Greek Orthodox church near Tell Balatah, very near the tomb of Joseph. Its location is identified in the text by the reference to "this mountain" (Jn 4:20), Mt. Gerazim, revered by Samaritans, and, in verse 5, to the field Jacob gave Joseph. Jacob had earlier bought this field in Shechem from the local Canaanites (Gen 33:18–20). Early Christian tradition correctly connected Jacob's well to an area a quarter-mile southeast of ancient Shechem's edge. The well is very deep, exceeding a depth of one hundred feet, and the water is cool and delicious even to this day.

6. We take the abundance and easy access to water and traveling accommodations for granted today. Traveling in Israel today one finds water for sale at every turn, and water must be drunk frequently to avoid dehydration, which can set in quickly. Why were wells and water so important to inhabitants of the Middle East (Ex 17:1ff.)? What does Jesus' weariness in verse 6 tell us about Jesus (Phil 2:7; Jn 1:14; Heb 2:9; see also Mt 4:2; Heb 2:17; 4:15; CCC 544)? On what other occasion does Jesus become thirsty (Jn 19:28)? How does a passage such as this refute the heresies that deny the full humanity of Christ? How can God be weary and thirsty? How is thirst used symbolically in the Bible (Ps 42:2; 63:1; Is 44:3; Mt 5:6; Jn 6:35)?

7. After trudging for hours along a dusty footpath in the rocky, hilly desert, Jesus arrives at noon, "the hour of thirst". Walking at noon in the sun of Israel can make one quite hot and dry. Jesus sits by the well waiting for someone to draw him a drink. Does he know the Samaritan woman will arrive at this odd hour, since water is usually drawn in the cool of the morning and evening? Jews did not talk to *any* Samaritan, *especially* a

female Samaritan, *especially* one living in adultery. It was said that to drink Samaritan water was worse than drinking the blood of a pig. Samaritans were despised more than Gentiles. According to the Jewish laws of purification (cf. Jn 2:6; 3:25), the Samaritans were unclean, and it was unlawful for a Jew to drink from an unclean pitcher (Mk 7:3–5). Why do you think Jesus would disregard the customs of the Jews when speaking with this woman?

» CULTURAL NOTE: "Not only was it unheard of for a rabbi to speak familiarly with a woman in public but also for a Jew to request water of a Samaritan. Jews considered Samaritans, and therefore their utensils for eating and drinking, unclean. Jesus was untroubled by such scruples; the Gospels frequently record his enlightened attitude toward women and also that on occasion he spoke favorably of Samaritans (cf. Lk 10:33; 17:6)." [1]

"That this Samaritan woman comes to the well alone rather than in the company of other women probably indicates that the rest of the women of Sychar did not like her, in this case because of her sexual activities (cf. comment on 4:18). Although Jewish teachers warned against talking much with women in general, they would have especially avoided Samaritan women, who, they declared, were unclean from birth. Other ancient accounts show that even asking water of a woman could be interpreted as flirting with her—especially if she had come alone due to a reputation for looseness. Jesus breaks all the rules of Jewish piety here. In addition, both Isaac (Gen 24:17) and Jacob (Gen 29:10) met their wives at wells; such precedent created the sort of potential ambiguity at this well that religious people wished to avoid altogether." [2]

8. Why might this woman have come alone and not with a group of other women? Was this providentially arranged (CCC 2560)? Do we see "chance meetings" with people in our lives as opportunities provided by God to share the good news? We can see from this carefully described episode, and that of Nicodemus, how Jesus "evangelized" those who crossed his path. What can we learn from Jesus' example? Is Jesus blunt, getting right to the "simple gospel", or does he plant the seed that will bear its fruit later? How does he use the woman's daily experience to bring her to a "knowledge of the truth"?

» THEOLOGICAL NOTE: When Paul addressed the Greeks, he used elements in their religion to find common ground as a basis of discussing the gospel (Acts

---

[1] Raymond Brown, Joseph Fitzmyer, and Roland Murphy, eds., *The Jerome Biblical Commentary* (Englewood Cliffs, N.J.: Prentice-Hall, 1968), 2:431.

[2] Craig Keener, *The IVP Bible Background Commentary: New Testament* (Downers Grove, Ill.: InterVarsity Press, 1993), 272.

17:22ff.). When he addressed the Jews, he started with the Old Testament (Acts 13:16ff.), the common authority he shared with them. Jesus does something similar here. The Jews accepted the full canon of the Old Testament used by Catholics today (Lk 24:44; 24:25). The canon of Scripture for the Samaritans (and the Sadducees), on the other hand, was limited to the first five books of Moses (the Pentateuch). When Jesus conversed with Nicodemus, a Jewish Pharisee, he could refer to the whole Old Testament (for example, Gen 1:2; Ezek 36:25–30; Prov 30:1–4); but with the Samaritans, he draws his metaphors and allusions exclusively from the five books of Moses, for this is what they accepted and were familiar with. What does this teach us about communicating the gospel of Christ with our modern society? How do we discover where to begin with our neighbor? Each person is different. Must we always begin with the Bible, which may not represent common ground, or should we sometimes consider another starting point?

9. Jesus has no way of drawing water from a well—it was over a hundred feet deep. He has to depend on a local villager and drink from someone else's pitcher. What does he say to the Samaritan woman (v. 7)? Of whom is this reminiscent (Gen 24:14)? Who else found a bride by a well (Gen 29:11ff.)?

» THEOLOGICAL NOTE: Jesus came into the world to prepare himself a bride, the Church (Eph 5:25–27; CCC 796), and to love her and to lay down his life for her. The two Jewish patriarchs born in the land promised to Abraham— Isaac and Jacob—found their wives by a well north of their land. Jesus came in the flesh to choose his bride from every tongue and nation (Acts 1:8; Rev 5:9; 21:9–10) and to cleanse her as a spotless bride. Abraham, like the Father in heaven, sent the unnamed servant, like the Holy Spirit, to find a bride for his son (Gen 24:1–4). He found the bride at a well and asked for a drink (Gen 24:15–21), just as Jesus does in verse 7. He brought the bride home for the wedding (Gen 24:61–67). Jacob, too, whom the Samaritans claim as their father (v. 12), found his bride at a well (Gen 29:1ff.). Is this merely coincidence, or does it help us understand the deep, sacramental thinking of St. John? What might John be telling us about the intent of Jesus as he talks with this woman? How do Acts 1:8 and 8:4–40 explain Jesus' long-term goals? What is his eternal perspective? How should we see our interaction with people from God's eternal perspective?

10. In verse 9, how does the Samaritan woman respond to Jesus? How does Jesus answer her? How does she then misunderstand Jesus in verse 11? What does Jesus mean by "living water" (Jn 7:37–39; CCC 694, 1137, 1999)?

» TEXTUAL NOTE: Jesus offers the Samaritan woman "living water". Jesus, as recorded by John, typically uses words that have two meanings—double entendres. Some examples we have seen: *pneuma*, which can mean "wind" and "spirit", and *anothen*, which can mean "above" or "again". Here Jesus does it again to challenge the listener and the reader. Jesus speaks of "living water". The word "living" in Greek is *zōē* (ζωή) and means both "living" and "flowing", as in a spring or river. Jesus uses Old Testament imagery (Jer 2:13; Zech 14:8; Ezek 47:9; Prov 13:14), which signifies divine vitality, revelation, and wisdom. And often in rabbinical thought "living" was applied to the Torah. But the woman misunderstands Jesus and assumes he means running water, as opposed to water from a cistern.

11. How does the Samaritan woman misunderstand the meaning of "living water"? How is she like Nicodemus in this respect (Jn 3:4)? What does Jesus really mean by "living" or "flowing" water (Jn 4:14; 7:37–39; Jer 2:13; Rev 22:1, 17; CCC 694, 1137)? To what gift is he referring (Eph 2:8; Acts 2:38, which, incidentally, refers to water; Heb 6:4; CCC 278, 2020)? Some might ask, why does Jesus "beat around the bush" with this woman instead of just speaking in a forthright manner? How does "water" play into earlier situations in John's Gospel (Jn 1:33; 2:6–9; 3:5, 22–26; 4:1ff.)? How is it going to be significant as we move through the rest of the Gospel (Jn 5:3–7; 7:37; 6:19; 13:5; 19:34; 21:1ff.)?

» THEOLOGICAL NOTE: "Within the scope of Johannine theology there are really two possibilities [as to the meaning of living water]: living water means the revelation which Jesus gives to men, or it means the Spirit which Jesus gives to men. . . . [B]oth these interpretations go back to the 2nd century; and we shall find convincing arguments for both. . . . The rabbis made frequent allegorical use of water to refer to the Law, although only rarely did they allegorize '*living water*'. However, now we have clear Qumran evidence for the use of 'living water' to describe the Law. . . . We may also mention that the expression 'gift of God' that appears in John iv 10 was used in rabbinic Judaism to describe the Law" (Barrett, p. 195).

"For Jesus to refer to his own revelation as 'living water' with this background in mind is perfectly plausible, for in John Jesus is presented as divine wisdom and as the replacement of the Law." [3]

There are many convincing reasons to support the interpretation that "living water" can also refer to the gift of the Spirit. We can conclude that there is no

[3] Raymond E. Brown, ed. and trans., *The Gospel according to John*, vol. 1, Anchor Bible, vol. 29 (Garden City, N.Y.: Doubleday, 1966), 178–79.

need to chose between the two and that Jesus probably meant to reference both. "Johannine symbolism is often ambivalent, especially where two such closely related concepts as revelation and Spirit are involved. After all, the Spirit of truth is the agent who interprets Jesus' revelation or teaching to men (xiv 26, xvi 13)." [4] There may also be baptismal overtones to the idea of "living water", as it is portrayed in the art of the catacombs.

12. Having misunderstood Jesus (v. 11), the woman asks a probing question of him (v. 12). What does she ask Jesus, and what historical figure does she bring up? How is this an attempt by a Samaritan to gain advantage over a Jew? (*Hint*: The Jews took their name from their father Judah.) Whom did the Samaritans claim as their father (v. 12), and what relation was he to Judah (Mt 1:2)? Can Jesus give her better water than the patriarch Jacob could, the father of Judah, who actually received God's blessing (cf. Gen 27:26–29)? Did Jacob provide plenty of water— enough for everyone and even the cattle? To what kind of thirst is Jesus referring?

13. Compare verse 14 with John 6:27 (food) and 7:38 (water). Notice the beautiful play on words: *water, spring, well, life*. What does Jesus mean by "the *water* that I shall give him will become in him a *spring* of *water welling* up to eternal *life*" (Jn 7:37–39)? How does John add to this in another of his writings (Rev 21:6; 22:17)? Do you think the woman is being sarcastic or showing simple faith, in verse 15? Is she beginning to understand that Jesus is not just *another* man?

14. In verse 16, how does Jesus "up the ante"—what does he ask her to do? He knows this woman and her adulterous situation, for he is God and knows the hearts of all men (Jn 2:24–25). How is she both honest and dishonest in her answer (v. 17)? He comments that she has had five husbands and that the man she is now living with is not her husband. Imagine the look on her face. Why would this surprise her; who else experienced something similar with Jesus (Jn 1:48–49)? What was the woman's reaction here? How does it compare with the incident in John 1:48–49?

» Note on Symbolism: There may be a deeper symbolism implied by John. The Samaritan woman has had five husbands. Gods are like husbands to their people. (The true God often revealed himself in this relationship with his

---

[4] Ibid., 179.

people [Is 54:5; Jer 31:32; Hos 2:19–20].) The Samaritans are descendants of the five Gentile nations who colonized Israel (2 Kings 17:24), each of which had a pagan god (2 Kings 17:29), that is, a false husband. Jesus may intend a double meaning: to show that the woman represents the Samaritan people, who have had five pagan gods or "husbands". The true God who is now visiting them—Jesus—is not "the woman's" husband, that is, the Samaritans' "husband". Yet, he intends to wed "the woman", in the sense understood by the term "the Bride of Christ".

Other commentators have seen the "five husbands" as symbolic of the five books of Moses—the Pentateuch—which comprised the entire Samaritan canon. The woman has had five "husbands", which represent the bondage of the Law. But "he whom you now have is not your husband"—she is not wedded to Christ and therefore is still condemned in her sin and blindness. She is a soul that "had" five husbands and is a law unto itself.

Origen wrote, "And what more proper place than Jacob's well, for exposing the unlawful husband, i.e., the perverse law? For the Samaritan woman is meant to figure to us a soul, that has subjected itself to a kind of law of its own [possibly of her 'five senses'], not the divine law. And our Saviour wishes to marry her to the lawful husband, i.e., Himself; the Word of truth which was to rise from the dead, and never again to die." [5]

15. Leaving possible symbolism aside, explain why it seems the Samaritan woman suddenly changes the topic. Why would she want to change the topic? How do we often respond when our sins and weaknesses are suddenly exposed? How do we try to gain the advantage in a discussion or argument by changing the topic?

» THEOLOGICAL NOTE: The fact that the woman perceives that Jesus is "a prophet" is profound indeed for a Samaritan, since Samaritans rejected the prophets, accepting only Moses as "the" prophet. The Jews, on the other hand, accepted many prophets, including those contained in their fuller Jewish canon of Scripture. What does her reaction say about her perception of Jesus? Moses had said that "the LORD your God will raise up for you a prophet [singular] like me from among you, from your brethren—him you shall heed" (Deut 18:15, 18). This was "the" prophet the Samaritans anticipated and looked for, the only one, for they accepted Moses' writings as Scripture, and Moses had prophesied a future prophet like himself.

16. Jesus says that worship will no longer be tied to a geographical location, neither Jerusalem nor Mount Gerazim (cf. CCC 1179). Ancient

---

[5] Origen, *Homily 13 on John*, in St. Thomas Aquinas, *Catena Aurea: St. John* (Albany, N.Y.: Preserving Christian Publications, 1995), 4:146.

peoples believed gods were tied to the land. Therefore, to leave Israel and the Temple was to leave the God of Israel (cf. Ps 137:4). In the future, Jesus tells her, worship will be different. First, it will be universal, over the face of the earth (Is 66:18; Mal 1:11; CCC 1138). Second, it will be no longer exclusive to one people, the Jews, but will include all nations (Mal 1:11; Eph 2:11ff.; Gal 3:27–29; CCC 775). Third, it will be in spirit and truth, for God is spirit. The Holy Spirit will be given, and he will change the interior aspect of worship. It will not be external forms only, but internal communion with the Father through the Spirit (Phil 3:3; Gal 5:18; Eph 2:18; CCC 586).

What is a spirit (Lk 24:39)? Why would worshipping God as "Father" be so surprising to the woman (Gal 4:4–7; Rom 8:15; CCC 2782, 2787)? Was God addressed intimately as a Father—as "Abba"—in the Old Testament (Ex 19:7–25)? Where is the "new temple" of the New Covenant to be located (Eph 2:19–22; CCC 797)? Where will the "pure offering" be offered (Mal 1:11; CCC 1330, 1350)?

17. In verse 22, what does Jesus mean that "salvation is from the Jews" (Is 2:3; Rom 3:1–2; 9:4–5; CCC 839, 528)? From the site of the well, Jesus and the woman could look up and see the ruins of the Samaritan temple on the mountainside. What mountain is the woman talking about (Josh 8:33; Deut 27:12)? Could the Samaritans determine willy-nilly where they would worship (Deut 12:5; 2 Chron 6:4–6; CCC 584)? Can you find any passage in the books of Moses that specify Jerusalem as the holy city, the city set apart for the worship of God?

18. How can Christians justify leaving the "one holy, catholic and apostolic Church" to begin their own "churches"? How many churches did Jesus establish (Mt 16:18; 18:17; Jn 17:11, 20–21; 1 Cor 1:10–17; Eph 4:4–6; CCC 813, 816)? Do we ever see Old Testament prophets encouraging God's covenant people to leave Israel and start a "Reformation Israel"?[6] How is the situation with the Samaritans similar and dissimilar with respect to Protestantism today (CCC 817, 838, 846–47)?

19. In verse 25, how is the woman beginning to understand who Jesus is? What will the Messiah do when he comes? How does Jesus prove himself to this woman (cf. Jn 1:48–49)? Jesus says, "I who speak to you

[6] For more on this point, see Stephen K. Ray, *Crossing the Tiber: Evangelical Protestants Discover the Historical Church* (San Francisco: Ignatius Press, 1997), 43–44.

am he." There is no word "he" in the Greek, simply "I am". What does this remind you of (Ex 3:13–14)? These words used in John 4:26 (εγω ειμι) might possibly allude to Yahweh's pronouncement in Exodus 3:13–14 and Isaiah 52:6. In view of the special significance of the name "I am", what might Jesus be claiming for himself (CCC 590)? Remembering that the Samaritans accepted only the first five books of the Jewish Bible, might Jesus have used the name ("I AM") from the books of Moses so that the Samaritan woman could more easily understand and accept his claim?

» THEOLOGICAL NOTE: "I, the one speaking to you, am he, literally, 'I am, the one speaking to you.' Thus he answers everyone who questions whether Yeshua proclaimed his own Messiahship. The declaration, 'I am,' echoes *Adonai's* self-revelation, 'I am who I am' (Exodus 3:14). Yeshua [Jesus] says this 'I am' nine times in [John's] Gospel (here; 6:20; 8:24, 28, 58; 13:19; 18:5, 6, 8), implying a claim even greater than being the Messiah." [7]

"The woman has already recognized in Jesus a prophet; now she begins to surmise that he might be the prophet of Dt 18:18. . . . Her statement is, again, an implied question. It was probably under this figure that the Samaritans, who accepted only the Pentateuch as inspired Scripture, represented their belief in the coming of a Messiah. Little is known about the messianic belief that the Samaritans shared with the Jews; the Messiah himself they called *Tā'eb*, "he who returns" or "he who restores." Jesus accepts this designation of himself. . . . *I who am speaking to you, I am*: These words reproduce Yahweh's pronouncement in Is 52:6. In view of the special significance of "I am" as Jesus' designation of himself . . . , it is likely that J[oh]n characteristically suggests another level of meaning here in Jesus' affirmation." [8]

20. Where are the disciples during this interesting dialogue (v. 8)? What do they think when they return (v. 27)?

» CULTURAL NOTE: The disciples were amazed that Jesus was speaking with a Samaritan, especially a woman. "For a rabbi to engage in conversation even with a true-born Jewish woman was regarded by many as a waste of time that might have been more profitably spent. The classical comment on this verse is provided by the words of Yose ben Yohanan, a rabbi of the second century AD, 'Prolong not conversation with a woman', together with the editorial remark of whoever was responsible for preserving his words: 'That is to say, even with

---

[7] David H. Stern, *Jewish New Testament Commentary* (Clarksville, Md.: Jewish New Testament Pubs., 1992), 168.

[8] Brown, Fitzmyer, and Murphy, *Jerome Biblical Commentary*, 2:432.

one's own wife; how much more with a neighbour's wife. Hence the wise men say, "He who prolongs conversation with a woman brings evil upon himself, ceases from the words of the law, and at the last inherits Gehanna [hell]." ' " [9] However, the disciples knew from experience that their Master always had good reason for what he did, even when it was strange and unconventional, so none of them asked the woman what she wanted with him or asked him why he was talking to her.

21. In verse 28, why might the Samaritan woman's leaving "her water jar" behind with Jesus represent conversion (cf. Mk 1:20; 1 Tim 6:11)? How might it represent leaving the sinful, unclean life behind? (*Hint*: Was her water pot clean according to the Jews?) How did John know about this dialogue between Jesus and the woman, since he was away at the time?

22. In verses 28–30, after the woman meets Jesus and leaves her unclean water jar behind, how does her enthusiasm and testimony bring others to Christ? Why is it easier for them to believe than it was for Nicodemus? What causes them to believe (Jn 4:39, 42)? How do our words and our enthusiasm (witness) bring others to hear Jesus for themselves (CCC 904–5)? Have we lost the joy and excitement of our salvation? What does Jesus say about losing our first love (Rev 2:4)? If we are not full of a contagious joy in the Lord, what should we do (Ps 51:10–13; CCC 1428–29)? How can the springs of living water and the bread of God incite us to sow the seed of good news for our neighbors?

23. Jesus often does unusual things to present object lessons (for example, Jn 13:5). Why does he refuse to eat when the disciples bring food (vv. 31, 32; cf. Jn 6:27)—is he not hungry and weary? Does Jesus cease eating food while on earth because he does the work of his Father (cf. Lk 5:30; 24:41–43)? What, then, is Jesus' "food" (Mt 4:4; CCC 606)?

24. What is Jesus talking about as he looks out on "the fields" (Jn 4:35–38)? What does Jesus mean by "the fields are already white for harvest" (cf. Lk 10:2ff.)? Who has labored and sown the gospel, but not lived to reap the harvest (Lk 3:18; Mt 14:8–10)? How does this work of evangelism apply to the apostles and those who follow them in the apostolic succession (2 Tim 4:5; CCC 2, 888)? How do the disciples actually reap

---

[9] F. F. Bruce, *The Gospel of John* (Grand Rapids, Mich.: William B. Eerdmans, 1983), 112.

the Samaritan harvest (Acts 8:4–40)? How do evangelism and participation in the gospel apply to the laity—the average Christian (1 Pet 3:15; Phil 1:5; CCC 904, 934)? It is the privilege of his Church and all of his disciples, in all generations and in all lands, to reap the harvest that continues to spring up from the good seed that was sown (and is now white for the harvest).

» CULTURAL NOTE: Barley was harvested in March, and it was barley, not wheat, that made a field look white as it ripened. As the people came out of the village in their white robes and moved toward Jacob's well in small bunches, Jesus told his disciples to look up and see the harvest. He had sown the seed, and it was already bearing fruit to be harvested. If it was with weariness that he approached the woman, it was now with a full stomach and "living water" that he rejoiced in the harvest (Ps 126:5–6). Second, the Jews looked for a "Golden Age" when God would reign upon the earth, when sin would be gone and the earth would yield her crop supernaturally. Amos the prophet said, " 'Days are coming,' declares the LORD, 'When the plowman will overtake the reaper And the treader of grapes him who sows seed; When the mountains will drip sweet wine' " (Amos 9:13, NASB; cf. Lev 26:5). There would be no period of waiting between sowing and harvest.

By sowing and reaping the same day, Jesus is confirming his claim to be the Messiah, God dwelling on earth. The "Golden Age" of the kingdom of God has arrived. Third, Jesus would be sown as the seed (Jn 12:23–24), and through death he would "bear much fruit", which the Church then harvests. Interestingly enough, Pentecost was originally a festival to celebrate the harvest. It was on Pentecost that the first three thousand Jews were "harvested" as a result of Jesus—the grain of wheat that died and bore much fruit. The Samaritans soon followed, and then the Gentiles. Blessed be God forever for a fruitful harvest of which we are a part!

John 4:43–54
Jesus' Second Sign; He Heals a Gentile's Son

25. Jesus continues his journey back to his own "stomping grounds" in Galilee. What does he mean in verse 44 that "a prophet has no honor in his own country"? Here Jesus is probably speaking of Jerusalem, but later this proverb would also be used of his hometown of Nazareth (Mk 6:4). Does he seem to be popular in Galilee, a sort of hometown hero? Why? How would this change (Mt 13:53–58)?

26. We have just seen Jesus present the gospel to the *Jews* (Nicodemus in Jerusalem), then to a *Samaritan* (the woman at the well), and now he reaches out to the *nations* (a Gentile royal official). How does John use this series of confrontations to demonstrate the expansion of the gospel as commanded by Christ (cf. Acts 1:8)?

27. In verse 46, we are introduced to a royal official, probably in the service of Herod Antipas, tetrarch of Galilee, and most likely a Roman. Why would he travel the sixteen miles of rocky ground to find Jesus in Cana? Where was Jesus' first "sign" or miracle performed (Jn 2:11; 4:46)? Where was the second sign performed (Jn 4:54)? Compare Matthew 8:5–13.

» HISTORICAL NOTE: "Long-distance miracles were rare by Old Testament, other Jewish and Greco-Roman standards; people generally believed prophets and Greek magicians more easily if they were present in person. The rare stories of long-distance miracles suggested to ancient readers that these miracle workers had extraordinary power." [10]

28. Why does Jesus mention "signs and wonders" to this official? Notice that "signs and wonders" are performed, especially for Gentiles, so that they may believe (cf. Ex 7:3, 5; Dan 4:1–3; 6:25–27; Acts 15:12; CCC 547–49). These references demonstrate that Gentile kings believed in the God of Israel because of "signs and wonders". Why does John bring up this well-known phrase at this point in the narrative (CCC 1151)?

29. In verse 50, what part does the official's faith play in the healing of his son (Mt 9:29; 13:58; Lk 7:50; 8:48; 17:19; 18:42)? We have another instance of evangelism: Who else believed because of the official's faith (v. 53)? What effect can a parent's faith and choices have on his family (Acts 16:34; CCC 2225–26)? How many "signs" of Jesus have we seen so far (v. 54)?

---

[10] Keener, *IVP Bible Background Commentary*, 275.

JOHN 5

INFIRM MAN HEALED AT THE POOLS OF
BETHESDA—JESUS CALLS FOUR WITNESSES

John 5:1–9
Healing at the Pool on the Sabbath

1. Again Jesus walks for three days south, up to Jerusalem for "a feast". We are not told *which* feast. Why does Jesus go up to Jerusalem so often (CCC 583)? Notice other feasts mentioned by John (Jn 2:13; 7:2; 10:22).

» ARCHAEOLOGICAL NOTE: Since so many sheep were brought into the Temple for sacrifice, a special gate was built in the northwest corner of Jerusalem to get the sheep into the Temple. It was called the Sheep Gate (Neh 3:1; Jn 5:2)— with direct access into the Temple precincts—and nearby the gate was the pool of Bethesda (Jn 5:2). The pool was fed by two springs, which in New Testament times were used, according to some, to bathe the sheep in preparation for sacrifice. It is more likely that the pool was used by men for bathing and purification purposes, thus symbolizing baptism. A twin pool north of the Temple area was discovered in 1856 at St. Anne's Church, and many have since identified it with the story in John 5:2. Remains of magnificent porticoes (covered colonnades) have survived. The name "Bethesda" (RSV and JB: "Bethzatha") was generally thought to mean "house of mercy", though recent finds of a Copper Scroll in Qumran may indicate the correct name might mean "the place of the twin outpourings" because of the two springs. One can still see the impressive ruins and step down into the water today.

2. What language did John use to write his Gospel (*hint*: CCC 436)? What was his native language, and what was one of the daily languages of Jesus (Mt 27:46; Jn 5:2; 19:13, 17, 20; 20:16)?

» CULTURAL NOTE: "One can conclude that Jesus certainly spoke a dialect of Aramaic, one which was somewhat different from any written form that has come down to us. . . . One may also conclude, although without such good evidence as for Aramaic, that Jesus probably knew . . . [Hebrew], and that he had at least a minimal competence in Greek." [1]

» TEXTUAL NOTE: The end of verse 3 and all of verse 4 are later additions and were not included in the original writing of John. They were probably added by a later scribe to clarify the situation for the reader. This addition does not alter the meaning of the text, since the content is substantially repeated in verse 7. The added text tells us the stirring of the water by an angel caused the water to have healing properties that would heal the first one to enter the pool during the angel's visit. There is no doubt it is part of inspired Scripture.

3. In verse 3, we learn of the miserable, sick people who lay around the pool of Bethesda; what must the condition and atmosphere within the porticos have been? Why would Jesus come here (Lk 7:22; 10:9; CCC 1503)? How did it indicate his deity and messiahship (Is 35:4ff.; 61:1; CCC 1505)? He may also have been going through ritual purification before entering the Temple.

Imagine being a man lame for thirty-eight years, lying within inches of being healed yet unable to make it a reality. Since we have already been told that many sick people were present, why does John tell us that "one man was there" (v. 5)? Why might this man be singled out from the rest? Why does Jesus not heal all the people there? How might Jesus know or perceive that the invalid has been "a long time" in that condition?

4. Since the pools stand at the entrance to the Temple, and one has to be purified before entering the House of God, how might the pools represent baptism? The invalid has no one to help him into the water—can one baptize oneself? The Church is the new Temple; what is the door through which one must enter her (CCC 846)? St. Peter's Church in Rome has two huge fountains in front of the basilica to represent the need for cleansing with water before one enters to worship and partake of the Supper of the Lamb. Why might the crippled in the time of Jesus, or those sick in sin today, think they would be healed by the waters of purification? How long has the man been crippled and sick (v. 5)? How long did the people of Israel wander in the wilderness (Deut 2:14)? What might John be telling us?

---

[1] *Dictionary of Jesus and the Gospels*, ed. Joel B. Green and Scot McKnight (Downers Grove, Ill.: InterVarsity Press, 1992), 442–43.

» DEEPER SIGNIFICANCE: The name "Jesus" (Greek: "Yeshua") is the Greek equivalent for the Hebrew name "Joshua" and means "Savior" (Mt 1:21). Joshua led the people out of the wilderness after thirty-eight years of wandering (Deut 2:14) and into the Promised Land. The early Jewish converts understood this episode in John's Gospel as a picture of the salvation of the Jewish people through baptism, freedom from the condemnation of the Law (CCC 430–31).

Why is it mentioned that the man has been an invalid for thirty-eight years? Augustine said that forty is the number of perfection, minus the two commands of charity (God and neighbor), and one is left with thirty-eight: imperfection and infirmity. "If therefore the number forty holds the perfection of the Law and the Law is not fulfilled except in the double commandment of love, why do you wonder that he was sick who had two less than forty?" [2] Consider the thoughts of William Barclay: "Certain scholars think this passage is an allegory. The man stands for the people of Israel. The five porches stand for the five books of the law. In the porches the people lay ill. The law could show a man his sin, but could never mend it; the law could uncover a man's weakness, but could never cure it. The law, like the porches, sheltered the sick soul but could never heal it. The thirty-eight years stand for the thirty-eight years in which the Jews wandered in the desert before they entered the promised land; or for the number of the centuries men had been waiting for the Messiah. The stirring of the waters stands for baptism. In point of fact in early Christian art a man is often depicted as rising from the baptismal waters carrying a bed upon his back." [3]

The number thirty-eight is used only twice in Scripture, here and in Deuteronomy 2:14. Is it coincidental that Moses is mentioned at the end of this chapter (5:45–47) as the one who will accuse and condemn the Jews for clinging to the old system and refusing the "House of Mercy", the double fountains of God's grace: water and Spirit (Jn 3:5)? At the Easter Vigil, the priest stirs the water of the baptismal font with the end of the Easter candle and calls upon the Holy Spirit to prepare the water for the cleansing of souls. At this point in the Church year those sick from sin and under the curse of the Law are born anew by water and Spirit (Jn 3:3, 5).

5. In verse 6, what question does Jesus ask the lame man, the answer to which is seemingly obvious? In verse 7, how does the man answer Jesus? In verse 8, what does Jesus command him to do? Why does John mention in verse 9 that it is the Sabbath? In the eyes of the Pharisees,

---

[2] St. Augustine, *Tractate 17*, in *Tractates on the Gospel of John 11–27*, trans. John W. Rettig, The Fathers of the Church, vol. 79 (Washington, D.C.: Catholic Univ. of America Press, 1993), 115.

[3] William Barclay, *The Gospel of John* (Philadelphia: Westminster Press, 1975), 1:180.

what law did the man violate when he obeyed Jesus' command (v. 10)? What was the basis for the Pharisees' interpretation of the Law (Ex 20:8–11; Neh 13:22; Jer 17:19–27; cf. CCC 582)? Did Jesus violate the Mosaic Law (CCC 2173)? If you were a Jew, how would you have explained Jesus' command to carry the mat? Was carrying the mat a violation of God's Law?

» THEOLOGICAL NOTE: What is the Sabbath? We are told that God created the world in six days and on the seventh day he rested. "And on the seventh day God finished his work which he had done, and he rested on the seventh day from all his work which he had done. So God blessed the seventh day and hallowed it, because on it God rested from all his work which he had done in creation" (Gen 2:2–3). When God gave the Law to Moses at Mount Sinai he commanded the people to "Remember the sabbath day, to keep it holy. Six days you shall labor, and do all your work; but the seventh day is a sabbath to the LORD your God; in it you shall not do any work, you, or your son, or your daughter, your manservant, or your maidservant, or your cattle, or the so-journer who is within your gates" (Ex 20:8–10). When a law is given it must be further defined. For example, someone will ask, What is work? At this point "work" must be defined and given practical boundaries. The Pharisees implemented a vast array of legalistic restrictions and penalties. It was in this situation that Jesus found himself when he healed the crippled man on the Sabbath.

» HISTORICAL NOTE: As soon as the man picks up and carries his mat, the Pharisees stop him and charge him with violating the Sabbath laws. There are a multitude of Sabbatarian laws in the Mishna, *Shabbath* against carrying items, including beds or furniture. One such law says that anyone who carries anything out of a private place to a public place on the Sabbath, or from a public place to a private place, must offer sacrifice for his sin, if it is done unadvisedly. If on the Sabbath he has done this work of carrying presumptuously, he is punished by being cut off from the people and being stoned.[4]

6. Compare the healing of the crippled man in John 5 with the healing in Capernaum (Mk 2:1–12). How are they similar and different? What is the implied cause of the illness in each (Jn 5:14; Mk 2:5, 9; CCC 1502) Can sin or wrong conduct bring sickness or death (1 Cor 11:30; James 5:14–16)? This healing on the Sabbath sets the stage for a major confrontation with the Jewish leaders and an opportunity for Jesus to give witness to who he is.

[4] See J. B. Lightfoot, *Commentary on the New Testament from the Talmud and Hebraica* (Peabody, Mass.: Hendrickson Pub., 1995), 3:296; and Herbert Danby, ed. and trans., *The Mishnah* (New York: Oxford Univ. Press, 1933), 103–8.

John 5:10–18
The Jews React to the "Sabbath Violation"

7. In verse 10, what concerns the Jewish leaders more: the act of healing or the man's carrying of his mat? Were the Jewish leaders glad that one of their people had been healed? Were they concerned more for the man made in God's image or for their own laws? Were the laws made for man, or man for the laws (Mk 2:27; CCC 2173)? What was the Jewish leaders' relationship with Jesus (CCC 575)? Why does God's revelation have priority over the commands of civil rulers (Acts 4:19; 5:29)? Would your loyalties have been torn at this point? If you had been a Pharisee dedicated to the Law of God, how would *you* have felt about this situation? Would Jesus' miracles ("signs") override your conviction that Jesus was a lawbreaker and lead you to conclude that he was actually divine (cf. Jn 12:37)?

8. In verse 12, what do the Pharisees ask of the healed man? Why does he not know who Jesus is? What probably preoccupies his mind? Why has Jesus slipped away as the crowds gathered? Why do you think the man is in the Temple after the healing (cf. Mt 8:1–4; Lev 14:1–32)? Why do you think Jesus looks for the man in the Temple later in the day?

9. In verse 14, what does Jesus tell the man (cf. Jn 8:11; Mk 2:5)? Do we know if the man's malady was caused by sin? Did the Jews believe sin caused disease or death (1 Kings 13:4; Jn 9:2)? Is this always the case, or is sin always the cause of affliction (Jn 9:1–3; also see the story of Job)? Jesus says something worse could happen if he continues to sin (cf. Jn 5:29): What is worse?

After we enter the new Temple (Eph 2:21) through baptism, what happens if we continue to live in sin (Heb 10:26–29; Rev 21:8; CCC 1861)? Of what does Jesus remind *us* once we have been made whole and come into the Temple (Jn 5:14)?

10. Why do you think that the man informs the Jews that it was Jesus who healed him (v. 15)? Is this a form of evangelism, ignorance, or betrayal? Do you think the man expects the Jews to join him in celebration? What was commanded of a leper who was healed (Lev 14:2ff.; Lk 5:12–14)? Would you have told the Pharisees? Why or why not? What would have been the consequences either way?

11. What does verse 16 indicate about why the Jews persecuted Jesus? Were they concerned for truth or the letter of the Law? What were they missing, and why was their approach backwards (Lk 10:21–22; CCC 582)? What could Jesus have done to convince them? What would it take to convince you? Can everyone see the truth and be convinced (Mt 13:10–17; 16:17; 1 Tim 2:4; CCC 153, 1432–33)?

12. Jesus explains why he healed the man on the Sabbath, claiming an intimate relationship with the Father. Did the Jews call God their father (Ex 4:22; Deut 32:6; 1 Chron 29:10; Is 63:16)? How was Jesus' claim of sonship different from theirs (CCC 443, 465, 242)? How is the claim of Jews that God is the father of Israel different from the claim of Christ that God is his *own* Father (CCC 444)?

13. In verse 17, Jesus makes a "blockbuster" comment. What is Jesus actually saying? What does he mean "My Father is working still, and I am working"? In the discussion that follows, Jesus asserts his authority with a battery of witnesses and proofs that should have caused the Jews to revere him.

» THEOLOGICAL NOTE: The Law of Moses established the Sabbath, the seventh day, as a day of rest. Through keeping the Sabbath, the Jews felt they were imitating and obeying God, who "rested" from the work of creation on the seventh day. According to St. Thomas Aquinas, Jesus rejects this strict interpretation of the Jews who "in their desire to imitate God . . . did not do any work on the Sabbath, as if God entirely ceased from work on that day. In fact, although God rested on the Sabbath from producing new creatures, he is working always and continuously even till now, conserving creatures in existence. . . . But according to Augustine, God is the cause of all creatures in such a way as to be the cause of their existing: for if his power were to cease even for a moment, all things in nature would at once cease to be, just as we may say that the air is illuminated only as long as the light of the sun remains in it." [5]

We learn from Colossians 1:17 that Jesus "is before all things, and in him all things hold together". The universe is held together by Jesus; he is at work all the time, like his Father. Jewish women gave birth ("going into labor") even on the Sabbath, and priests circumcised baby boys and performed their ceremonial duties. Even according to the pharisaical regulations, Jews were allowed to rescue a child or animal from danger (Lk 14:5) and to take care of basic necessities of life. Jesus demonstrates that his healing on the Sabbath was no

---

[5] St. Thomas Aquinas, *Commentary on the Gospel of St. John*, vol. 1 (Albany, N.Y.: Magi Books, 1980), 295.

more Sabbath-breaking than the continuous action of his Father in the world. It was one thing for the law to forbid commerce and "life as usual" on the Sabbath (Neh 13:15ff.), but it was another to say that God did nothing altogether, and therefore we should cease even from doing good. God does good on the Sabbath, so does his Son (CCC 582), and so—argues Jesus—should the Jews of his time.

14. Read paragraph 594 in the *Catechism* in preparation for the following questions. In verse 18, for what two reasons did the Jews want to kill Jesus? By healing the invalid (and by implication, forgiving his sins), what does Jesus claim for himself, and how do the Jewish leaders understand the claim (cf. Mt 9:1–8)? By saying that he works like his Father, even on the Sabbath, what is Jesus claiming for himself? What do the Jewish leaders understand Jesus to mean? Are they clear on the implications of Jesus' words (Jn 5:18)? If a man came to *you* and claimed to be God and have the authority to "reinterpret" the Law of Moses, how would you react? What proof would you require? The Jews cite the *Shema*, copies of which they wear in their phylacteries: "Hear O Israel: The LORD our God, the LORD is one" (Deut 6:4, NASB). Why would they fear to accept Jesus as God (CCC 594)? How many Gods are there (Deut 4:39)? With the prophecies of the coming Messiah, the "signs" Jesus performed, and the "witnesses" Jesus calls (as we shall see), should the Jews have accepted him as the Christ?

15. Notice the difference in approach: not *understanding* how it was possible, the Jews refused to *believe* in him; the Church, on the other hand, *believing* in him, progresses toward a full *understanding* of him. As the eleventh-century Christian theologian Anselm put it, "*Credo ut intelligam*" (I believe in order that I may understand).[6]

» THE CHURCH FATHERS: "For we all say to God, 'Our Father which art in heaven'; we read also that the Jews said, 'Seeing Thou art our Father.' Therefore it was not for this they were angry, because He said that God was His Father, but because He said it in quite another way than men do. Behold, the Jews understand what the Arians do not understand. The Arians, in fact, say that the Son is not equal with the Father, and hence it is that the heresy was driven from the Church. Lo, the very blind, the very slayers of Christ, still understood the words of Christ. They did not understand Him to be Christ, nor did they

---

[6] See Peter Kreeft and Ronald K. Tacelli, *Handbook of Christian Apologetics* (Downers Grove, Ill.: InterVarsity Press, 1994), 16.

understand Him to be the Son of God: but they did nevertheless understand that in these words such a Son of God was intimated to them as should be equal with God. Who He was they knew not; still they did acknowledge such a One to be declared, in that 'He said God was His Father, making Himself equal with God.' Was He not therefore equal with God? He did not make Himself equal, but the Father begat Him equal." [7]

John 5:19–47

Jesus Defends and Explains His Equality with God

» INTERPRETIVE NOTE: The phrase "My Father is working still, and I am working" is the key to understanding the rest of this chapter. It is the thesis that Jesus now explains and defends. Understanding this clearly will help with interpreting the remainder of this chapter.

16. In verse 19, how does Jesus "up the ante"? What is the source of Jesus' works—whom do they reflect? How is Jesus claiming a special love from the Father, different from what the Jews would be able to claim individually? (*Note*: "love" in verse 20 is not *agape* (self-sacrificial love), but *philei*, which in Greek means "fond affection"; cf. notes on Jn 3:16)? Why might *philei* be used here? Since it is the Sabbath, and Jesus says the Father shows the Son all the Father himself is currently doing (present tense, active, indicative), what is implied about the Father working on the Sabbath? St. Cyril of Jerusalem said the one divine action of Father and Son is a result of one divine nature.

» THEOLOGICAL NOTE: We continue to see the parallels between Moses and Jesus in John's Gospel. Another interesting parallel shows up here. "The entire conception of a prophet like unto Moses, Deut. 18:15ff., is basic to the understanding of St John and there is no need to emphasize this further here; but at the moment we are thinking of various expressions and phrases associated with it. In Deut. 18 the prophet is to speak in the name of the Lord (v. 19); God's words are put in his mouth and 'he shall speak unto them all that I shall command him' (v. 18). In this connexion we may recall a few Johannine passages: 5:43, 'I am come in my Father's name'; 8:28, 'as the Father taught me, I speak these things'; 7:16, 'My teaching is not mine, but his that sent me'; 12:49, 'For I spake not from myself; but the Father which sent me, he hath

---

[7] St. Augustine, *On the Gospel of John* 17, 16, in NPNF1 7:116.; cf. CCC 464–65.

given me a commandment, what I should say, and what I should speak' (cf. 17:8).

"An interesting parallel may be traced in John 5:19f., where it is said that the Son does (*poieō*) what he sees the Father doing, and the Father shows (*deiknumi*) him all (*panta*) that he does. In Ex. 2:5–9 Moses makes (*poieō*) the Tabernacle according to all (*panta*) that God shows (*deiknuō*) him. Cf Ex. 25:40, quoted in Heb. 8 in a Moses/Christ passage; see also Ex. 26:30; 27:8; Num. 8:4." [8]

17. Jesus now escalates the discussion: What they have just seen is insignificant compared with what he is going to show them. What has he just done (Jn 5:8–9)? If they want proof of his divinity, a "sign" that is thoroughly convincing, he will shortly provide a sign that will cause them to "marvel" (v. 20). Why does he mention the resurrection of the dead at this point (CCC 994)? What is Jesus about to do (Jn 11:1ff.; Lk 8:49–56)? How is this more significant than healing the crippled man? What does the Son have the authority to do (vv. 21–22, 25, 27–29)? How are resurrection and judgment related (CCC 1038)?

» HISTORICAL NOTE: The Jewish sect of the Sadducees did not believe in the resurrection of the dead (Mt 22:23; Acts 23:8), but the Pharisees, the larger of the sects, did (CCC 993). Jesus' statement would immediately bring to mind Ezekiel's prophecy of the dry bones (Ezek 37:1–10). It was God's prerogative alone to raise the dead (1 Sam 2:6; 2 Kings 5:7). "In the great synagogue prayer [of the Jews] called the 'Amidah' or 'Eighteen Benedictions', which may go back to pre-Christian times, the second benediction addresses God as follows: You, O Lord, are mighty forever; you quicken the dead; you are mighty to save. You sustain the living with loving-kindness, you quicken the dead in great mercy, you support the fallen, healest the sick, loosest those who are bound, and keepeth faith with those who sleep in the dust. Who is like thee, O Lord of mighty acts? Who is comparable to thee, O King, who bringest to death and quickenest again, and causest salvation to spring forth? Yea, thou art faithful to quicken the dead. Blessed are thou, who quickenest the dead!' " [9] Jesus fits this description of praise to a tee: He raises the dead, heals, sustains the living (even on the Sabbath!), provides "living water" springing up to eternal life, loosens the bound, and so on. The Jews probably sang this benediction, which sang the praises of Jesus Christ, even though they rejected him. For Jesus to claim such a divine prerogative as the power to raise the dead caused great anger among his enemies.

---

[8] T. F. Glasson, *Moses in the Fourth Gospel* (Napierville, Ill.: Alec R. Allenson, 1963), 80.

[9] F. F. Bruce, *The Gospel of John* (Grand Rapids, Mich.: William B. Eerdmans, 1983), 129.

18. Jesus has been given the power of life, death, and judgment (CCC 679). How does he prove this (Jn 5:8)? If the Jewish leaders honor the Father, how should they honor his perfect image tabernacling among them—God the Son (cf. Jn 1:14, 18)? When they refuse to honor God's Son, what does this reveal about them, and who are they actually rejecting?

19. In verse 24, why does Jesus use the present tense: "he who *hears* my word and *believes . . . has* eternal life"? What happens if we cease to hear and believe and obey (Mt 13:18–23)?

20. Read Luke 20:9–15. How is this an accurate picture of God the Father sending his Son into the world as savior and judge? How do the Jewish leaders "play out" this parable with Jesus, the Son of God? What final proof does God provide to establish the appointment of his Son as Judge (Acts 17:31)? What is the imminent punishment for rejecting the Messiah (Lk 19:43–44)? In 70, forty years after the Jewish leaders rejected their Messiah and assassinated him, the Romans flattened Jerusalem and more than 1.2 million Jews died in the onslaught.

21. What Old Testament basis did the Jews have to believe in a resurrection (2 Kings 4:18–37; Is 26:19; Dan 12:1–4; Ezek 37:1–14; CCC 992, 297)? What is the basis for judgment as described in verses 28–29: faith alone or works? Compare other passages concerning the basis for judgment (Mt 25:31–46; Acts 24:15; Gal 6:8; Rom 2:5–8; Mt 19:29; Jn 3:36; Rev 2:23; 20:12–13; 21:7–8; 22:11–12)? Can you find a biblical passage that declares that the judgment will be based on faith alone? According to these passages, is salvation by "faith alone" biblical doctrine (cf. Jas 2:24)? Who will raise the believer up on the last day (Jn 6:40)? What determines the kind of resurrection a person is raised to (Jn 5:28–29; CCC 1038)? By what power will Christ raise our dead bodies from the grave (Rom 8:11; Phil 3:21; CCC 658, 989–90; 1016)?

22. The Jews have presented two indictments against Jesus: breaking the Sabbath and claiming equality with God. Jesus has made his case that he is doing the work of his Father. His case is strong. But the Law required witnesses. Jesus, therefore, calls four witnesses to substantiate his case. How many witnesses were necessary to substantiate an allegation under Mosaic Law (Num 35:30; Deut 19:15)? If the Jews will not accept Jesus' testimony about himself (Jn 5:31), what four *additional* witnesses does

Jesus present to them as proof (Jn 5:33, 36–37, 39)? Why does Jesus provide these various witnesses to his deity and mission (Jn 5:34)? Why does he call more witnesses than is necessary?

23. Please "call the first witness"! Read John 1:6–8, 15, 19, 32. How did John the Baptist give witness to Jesus? John pleads with them to save themselves, and they refuse to hear and obey. How does this remind you of our current society, and even of ourselves at times?

» CONTEXTUAL NOTE: Notice that the first verses of John give the theme of the whole book—John the Baptist's witness is an example of this (Jn 1:6–8). Here in chapter 5 we see the theme of "bearing witness" repeated and fleshed out, as already expressed in what we called "the overture" of John's Gospel. The "musical themes", so to speak, of the first verses of John continue to be developed throughout the book.

24. Three additional witnesses are "called to the stand". Witness number two: In verse 36, what *works* does God give the Son that testify to his deity (Mt 11:4–6; Mk 2:1–12; CCC 548)? How do the *works* bear witness to the Son (Jn 5:36; 3:2; 9:24–34; 14:11; 15:23–24; Acts 2:22)? Why should the people have believed him (Jn 14:11)?

25. In verse 37, we have witness number three. In what concrete ways does the *Father* himself repeatedly bear witness to Jesus his Son (Jn 5:37; Mt 3:17; 17:5; Jn 12:28; 1 Jn 5:9–10; CCC 444, 536, 554)?

26. In verse 39 we have witness number four: How do the *Scriptures* bear witness to the Son (Jn 5:39; Lk 24:27; Gen 3:15; Num 21:9; Deut 18:15; Is 7:14; 53:1–12; Dan 7:13; Mic 5:2ff.; Zech 9:9, and so on; CCC 156)? Moses might possibly be seen as another "witness", though he may be synonymous with "the scriptures" (Jn 5:45–47). Why do you think Jesus "calls" more than two or three witnesses?

» OTHER WITNESSES: There were many other "witnesses" who testified to the deity and messiahship of Jesus besides his disciples and followers. For example: angels (Lk 1:6ff.); shepherds (Lk 2:8–16; CCC 525); demons (Lk 4:33–34); the Magi (Mt 2:1–2); Simeon (Lk 2:25ff.); Anna (Lk 2:36–38); Zechariah and Elizabeth (Lk 1:16–17); John in the womb (Lk 1:41); a Roman centurion (Mt 27:54); Pilate's wife (Mt 27:19), and many others (CCC 444). His appearance as the Messiah and Son of God was well attested to, and everyone, especially the Jews, was without excuse. Around the year 100, how would this "trial scene" have affected John's readers, who were dealing with heresies that denied the physical reality of God in the flesh dwelling as a man upon the earth? The Gnostics denied his humanity, and, later, the Arians denied his deity.

27. In verse 37, Jesus says that the Jews arguing with him have never seen the Father's form or heard his voice (cf. Ex 33:20; 1 Tim 6:16; Col 1:15; Jn 1:18; 6:46). By saying he has seen and knows God, what is Jesus claiming for himself? How is merely studying the Scriptures different from actually having the word of God "abiding in you" (Jn 5:38–39; 8:31, 37; Bar 4:1–2)? Is the source of eternal life the Scriptures themselves or is it Jesus (Jn 5:39–40)?

» "TRIAL TRANSCRIPTS": Jesus changes roles from "defense attorney" to "prosecutor". This "trial" before the people takes a somewhat traditional form. "Jesus now levels counter-charges against his opponents: Their rejection of him, God's envoy, shows that they do not know God (v. 38); they search the Scriptures for life but will not come to him who alone can give them life. Correct reading of the Scriptures would have led them to him (vv. 39–40); the obstacle to their believing is their self-seeking glory which they exercise in a kind of club; Jesus refuses to join this club (vv. 42–45). Ultimately Moses, on whom they claim to stand (in the Scriptures), will testify against them for their unbelief. The section ends with two rhetorical questions (vv. 44, 47). The first court hearing ends; the court adjourns until a further hearing." [10]

28. In verse 44, what kind of glory do the Pharisees seek (Mt 6:1–2, 5, 16, 23:1–7)? What does it gain them? How are we to practice our faith and good deeds? Do we love the glory of men rather than glory and reward from God (Jn 12:43)? Think of ways we might be like the Pharisees.

29. In verses 45–47, how does Moses become a witness for the prosecution against the Jewish leaders who claim to safeguard the Law of Moses (Jn 5:45–47; Rom 2:17–29; Mic 3:11)? As we asked earlier, according to Moses, how many witnesses were needed to condemn a man (Deut 19:15; Heb 10:28–31; 2 Cor 13:1)? How many witnesses has Christ called to the "witness stand" to testify to his divinity and Sonship in this discourse? How then does Moses condemn these Jewish leaders? Consider the irony as Jesus turns the tables on them—causing their own Law

---

[10] William R. Farmer, ed., *The International Bible Commentary* (Collegeville, Minn.: Liturgical Press, 1998), 1471.

and prophet to condemn them. Compare this with the rich man's dilemma in Luke's Gospel (Lk 16:31). What did Jesus come to do with the Law (Mt 5:17ff.)?

30. Why was it so hard for the Pharisees to accept Jesus, yet so easy for the Samaritans, the Gentiles, and the common folk? How can a man's perceived "adequacy and self-sufficiency" blind him to the good news of Christ?

» PRACTICAL APPLICATION: "The last section of the episode can serve as a warning to scholars and Church leaders. It is possible to be so engrossed in defending traditional orthodoxy [or opposing and resisting it] or in searching the Scriptures (thereby winning honor and prestige among colleagues) that one loses contact with Jesus and misses the life that only he can give. The episode challenges us to ensure that our defense of orthodoxy and assiduous biblical scholarship are rooted in a deep personal relationship with Jesus. The Fathers of the Church studied the Scriptures primarily in order to strengthen their own faith and then that of the people. Verses 39–40 may also serve as a warning to some modern-day charismatics who tend to play down the sacramental life of the Church, especially the Eucharist, in favor of the Bible. The Word/God, Jesus, is bigger than and gives full meaning and life to the word of God in the Scriptures." [11]

» SUMMARY: In this portion of John's Gospel, the theme of Jesus as the Son of man (Dan 7:13) and the Son of God is fleshed out, signs and testimony are given, and the world is called to make a decision that will conclude with each person receiving eternal life or eternal condemnation. No one has an excuse for rejecting the Son of God.

---

[11] Ibid.

JOHN 6 a

MIRACULOUS BREAD TO FEED THE PEOPLE—
JESUS WALKS ON THE WATER

John 6:1–15
Multiplication of Loaves, the Eucharist Foreshadowed

1. We now approach the fourth of seven "signs" recorded by John before the death of our Lord. Of what were the "signs" an indicator and proof (CCC 547–49)? Sometime after leaving the feast in Jerusalem (Jn 5:1), Jesus went to the other side of the Sea of Galilee. The Sea of Galilee is 6.8 miles wide by 13 miles long, 700 feet below sea level and 150 feet deep. What are some of the various names for this small sea (Mk 1:16; Num 34:11; Jn 6:1; Lk 5:1)?

2. John starts out with the words: "after these things". After what things? Remembering again that chapter/verse breaks in our modern Bibles are not in the original text itself, who is the last person Jesus has mentioned (Jn 5:45–47), and how might he fit in with a story of the miraculous supply of bread? The other Gospels provide Jesus' actual institution of the Eucharist; what does John provide (CCC 1338)? This passage is profoundly eucharistic. It is recommended that paragraphs 1322–44 of the *Catechism of the Catholic Church* be read in preparation for studying chapter 6 of John's Gospel.

3. In verse 2, why are the multitudes following Jesus? Are they genuine followers (vv. 26, 66)? What makes a disciple genuine (Mk 8:34–38)? Who else went up on a mountain and fed miraculous "bread" to the people in the wilderness (Ex 16:4–21)? We learn from parallel accounts (Mk 6:34; Mt 5:1ff.) that Jesus taught the people many things. Who else sat among the people to teach and judge them (Ex 18:13ff.)? Might John be drawing parallels so we will understand what is soon to take

place—a reenactment of the provision of manna? Imagine the power of Jesus' voice, which enabled him to teach five thousand men—not counting the women and children who accompanied them—in the open air, while sitting down, no less. What kind of voice must Jesus have had?

» THE JEWISH MISHNAH ON MOSES' SUCCESSORS: The Jews have always maintained that, along with the Law of God written on stone, the oral Law or tradition was also passed down through succession from Moses. The ancient oral tradition of the Jews was codified in the Mishnah, which states, "Moses received the Torah on Sinai, and handed it down to Joshua; Joshua to the elders; the elders to the prophets; and the prophets handed it down to the Men of the Great Assembly. . . . Simon the Just was one of the last survivors of the Great Assembly. He used to say, Upon three things the world is based: upon the Torah, upon Divine service, and upon the practice of charity." [1]

» THEOLOGICAL NOTE: The teachers of Israel sat when they formally taught the people. This is demonstrated by the fact that synagogues contained the "seat of Moses", from which the scribes and Pharisees expounded the law (Mt 23:2).[2] The Pharisees were the "successors of Moses", and they inherited his "seat" or authority among the people to teach them God's Law (Ex 18:13ff.). Moses taught the Old Law; Jesus came to teach the New Law—of grace (Mt 5:17ff.) or, as we call it, the law of Christ. The Gospel writers use the imagery of Moses to portray Christ as the new prophet, who, like Moses, was sent from God (Deut 8:15–18). When Jesus "redefines" the law in the Sermon on the Mount (Mt 5:21–22, 27–28, 31–34, 38–39, 43–44, and so on), notice how the text clearly alludes to Moses: "Seeing the crowds, he went up on the mountain, and when he sat down his disciples came to him. And he opened his mouth and taught them" (Mt 5:1–2).

There is much in Jewish teaching that implies the Messiah will teach the Torah anew. "Raphael Patai has summarized material relating to the Messianic alteration of the Torah in the chapter 'New Worlds and a New Tora,' in *The Messiah Texts* (Avon, 1979). He quotes the 9th-century Alphabet Midrash of Rabbi Akiva: 'In the future the Holy One, blessed be He, . . . will expound to [the pious] the meanings of a new Tora which He will give them through the Messiah' [many more references are given in the text]. . . .

"These texts do not 'prove' that normative Orthodox Judaism necessarily expects a new Torah when the Messiah comes, but they do show that such

---

[1] Rabbi Joseph H. Hertz, trans., *Mishnah: Sayings of the Fathers* (New York: Behrman House, 1945), 13–15.

[2] For more information on the "seat of Moses", see Stephen K. Ray, *Upon This Rock: St. Peter and the Primacy of Rome in Scripture and the Early Church* (San Francisco: Ignatius Press, 1999).

expectations have been accepted within an Orthodox Jewish framework during a period covering at least 1,500 years. If this stream of thought existed in the first century as well, it is not unreasonable to expect Yeshua the Messiah might rightfully 'change the customs handed down to us by Moshe'." [3]

4. In verse 4, why would John mention the Passover being "at hand" (cf. Lk 22:7ff.; CCC 1338)? What is he pointing to in the past (CCC 608) and in the future? The Greek word used is "near". Do the disciples realize at the time how "near" the real Passover is—the sacrifice of the Lamb of God?

» TEXTUAL NOTE: The discussion that takes place in John 6 centers on the theme of the manna and the Eucharist. Protestant theologian Oscar Cullmann writes, "The long speech which Jesus makes in John's Gospel, after the miracle of feeding the multitude, about the meaning of this miracle, has, since ancient times, been considered by most exegetes a discourse on the Eucharist. . . . Here the author makes Jesus himself draw the line from the miracle of feeding with material bread to the miracle of the Sacrament. That to which the miracle of feeding only points, is here expounded in a discourse, while, in most other passages, it is left to the reader to read between the lines the references to the sacraments from scanty but carefully emphasized hints. . . . The evangelist saw, as he was writing down the story, a reference in this miracle to the Eucharist, that he had the Eucharist in mind therefore without actually saying so." [4] Baptist theologian George Beasley-Murray writes, "It is evident that neither the Evangelist nor the Christian readers could have written or read the saying without conscious reference to the Eucharist; to say the least, they would have acknowledged it as supremely fulfilled in the worship event." [5]

5. Alluding to the throngs that followed Moses to the other side of the Red Sea, John tells us that Jesus looked up and saw the multitudes in the fields. Seeing the crowds, what does Jesus ask Philip—a question that should have stirred a recollection of the Exodus story? At what other time did someone ask about bread in the wilderness (Num 11:13; Deut 16:3–4; Ps 78:18–20, 23–25)? How does this again demonstrate that Jesus is the new Moses?

[3] David H. Stern, *Jewish New Testament Commentary* (Clarksville, Md.: Jewish New Testament Pubs., 1992), 242–43.

[4] Oscar Cullmann, *Early Christian Worship,* trans. A. Stewart Todd and James B. Torrance (Philadelphia: Westminster Press, 1953), 93–94.

[5] G. R. Beasley-Murray, *John,* Word Biblical Commentary (Waco, Tex.: Word Books, 1987), 95.

6. In verse 6, why does Jesus ask this question of Philip? Is Jesus unsure of what to do, or is he making a point—even a correlation with the Old Testament? How does Jesus test us in the same manner? Andrew intervenes in verse 8. Again, what does Andrew always do (Jn 1:40–42; 6:8–9; 12:20–22)? How do we bring people to Jesus?

» CULTURAL NOTE: In verse 9, Philip responds that two hundred denarii would not purchase enough to feed them. A Roman denarius was about a day's wage (Mt 20:2). In today's terms, if a day's wage were $100, Philip is suggesting it would cost over $20,000 to buy enough food to feed the crowd, but feed them very poorly.

7. It is interesting to note that, besides the Resurrection, this is the only miracle mentioned by all four Gospels, which obviously signifies its importance. Read the parallel accounts (Mt 14:13–21; Mk 6:33–44; Lk 9:12–17). How many men gathered around Jesus and were fed? How many people in total do you think were fed, including the women and children? With this miracle given as a "sign", is it hard to believe that Jesus can feed the whole world with the new Bread come down from heaven—the Eucharist?

8. In verse 9 an "offering" is made. Among other things, what does this represent (CCC 1333–34)? What is a small boy willing to give Jesus? How is this like the offertory of the Mass (cf. CCC 1350)? Similar to those who try to explain "manna" on the basis of natural occurrences, there are some who try to "demythologize" the Gospels and reduce the miracle of the loaves and fishes to a simple act of sharing. They suggest that the boy shares what he has and that Jesus uses the lad's example to teach others to share. When inspired by such generosity, everyone shares the food he has hidden on his person. Then there is enough to feed everyone—no actual *miracle* is performed. Can you find one shred of evidence, in John or the other Gospels, that the writers or eyewitnesses considered this event anything less than a supernatural act—a miracle? What makes it clear that John is relating the event as an eyewitness to a real miracle (Mt 14:15; Mk 6:36; Lk 9:16; Jn 6:11, 14)? Was the manna supplied by Moses in the wilderness just a simple lesson in sharing or a divine and miraculous provision? Would the crowd want to make Jesus king (v. 15) for simply teaching them to share, or rather for proving that he was the "prophet to come" like Moses by giving them miraculous bread in the wilderness? It is too bad that many pastors today allow the

secular bias against the miraculous to erode their faith in the ability of God to work his wonders in the world of nature, thereby reducing miracles such as these to nonexistent events or events having a natural explanation. It is obvious that John and those witnessing these super-natural events understood them for what they were.

9. There is a theological understanding that "grace does not destroy but builds upon nature." In other words, God uses nature and the works of men's hands to do his work. God is not opposed to material things or the physical world. He uses "natural things"—builds off of them—to bless us. How was this demonstrated in the creation of Adam and Eve (Gen 2:7, 21)? How is this demonstrated in the multiplication of the loaves? How is it demonstrated in the Mass?

» LITURGY OF THE MASS: "Blessed are you, Lord, God of all creation. Through your goodness we have this bread to offer, which earth has given and human hands have made. It will become for us the bread of life." [6]

» CULTURAL NOTE: Barley and wheat were the main staples in Palestine. Barley loaves were the food of the poor, and barley was fed to the livestock. Bread made from barley was less favored than wheat bread; it was also cheaper. The "five loaves" can be seen as the five books of the Law of Moses, a recurring theme in John. The Law is poor in comparison to the grace provided by Jesus in the New Covenant. Jesus takes the old and transforms it into the new, like the water into wine. In both instances, bread and wine, there is an overabundance ("grace upon grace", Jn 1:16). Interestingly, John wrote his Gospel in about the year 100, when, in the early Church, barley bread was used for the Eucharist. This provides a possible link between this miracle and the Eucharist.

» ST. AUGUSTINE ON THE "BARLEY LOAVES": "To run over it briefly: by the five loaves are understood the five books of Moses; and rightly are they not wheaten but barley loaves, because they belong to the Old Testament. And you know that barley is so formed that we get at its pith with difficulty; for the pith is covered in a coating of husk, and the husk itself tenacious and closely adhering, so as to be stripped off with labor. Such is the letter of the Old Testament, invested in a covering of carnal sacraments: but yet, if we get at its pith, it feeds and satisfies us. A certain lad, then, brought five loaves and two fishes. If we inquire who this lad was, perhaps it was the people Israel, which, in a childish sense, carried, not ate. For the things which they carried were a burden while shut up, but when opened afforded nourishment. And as for the two fishes, they appear to us to signify those two sublime persons, in the Old Testament, of priest and of ruler,

---

[6] Liturgy of the Eucharist: preparation of the altar and the gifts.

who were anointed for the sanctifying and governing of the people. And at length Himself in the mystery came, who was signified by those persons: He at length came who was pointed out by the pith of the barley, but concealed by its husk. He came, sustaining in His one person the two characters of priest and ruler: of priest by offering Himself to God as a victim for us; of ruler, because by Him we are governed. And the things that were carried closed are now opened up. Thanks be to Him. He has fulfilled by Himself what was promised in the Old Testament. And He bade the loaves to be broken; in the breaking they are multiplied. Nothing is more true. For when those five books of Moses are expounded, how many books have they made by being broken up, as it were; that is, by being opened and laid out? But because in that barley the ignorance of the first people was veiled, of whom it is said, 'Whilst Moses is read, the veil is upon their hearts;' for the veil was not yet removed, because Christ had not yet come; not yet was the veil of the temple rent, while Christ is hanging on the cross: because, I say, the ignorance of the people was in the law, therefore that proving by the Lord made the ignorance of the disciple manifest." [7]

10. Where else do we find barley loaves multiplied (2 Kings 4:42–44)? Read all of 2 Kings 4 and 5. How do these chapters prefigure the miracles of Jesus and the sacraments of baptism and the Eucharist? What is similar to both miracles? Does this episode have any bearing on our present text? What other miracles are performed by Elisha that are similar to miracles of Jesus (2 Kings 4:18–37; 5:1–19; Lk 4:27)?

11. In verse 11, what does Jesus do before distributing the bread? In Luke's account (Lk 9:16), what four verbs are used to describe the procedure? What four verbs do we see again at the Last Supper (Mt 26:26; Lk 22:19)? How does this language link this event to the Eucharist?

» THEOLOGICAL NOTE: "The word for 'thanks' in Greek is εὐχαριστέω, from which we get the word 'Eucharist'. John deliberately repeats this verb in verse 23, where it should be regarded as a distinct allusion to the eucharistic intent of the passage. This conclusion is especially justified inasmuch as we know that the Gospel was written at the end of the first century, at a time when the Lord's Supper was already technically referred to as the Eucharist, as can be demonstrated by the letters of St. Ignatius of Antioch, a disciple of the Apostle John (e.g., *Philadelphians* 4, *Smyrnaeans* 7–8)." [8]

---

[7] St. Augustine, *Tractate* 24, 5, in *Lectures or Tractates on the Gospel according to St. John*, trans. John Gibb and James Innes, in NPNF1 7:159.

[8] Stephen K. Ray, *Crossing the Tiber: Evangelical Protestants Discover the Historical Church* (San Francisco: Ignatius Press, 1997), 197.

"The Jewish Passover (v. 4) was an unleavened bread feast, so the reference prepares us for the bread miracle that is about to take place. This miracle is the only one narrated by all four evangelists. . . . It must be that the primitive Christian Eucharist made the prefiguring loaves miracle common property in all the Christian communities. And, indeed, what Jesus does with the bread sounds like the rubrics for what the Christian minister continually did in the celebration of the Eucharist. In the accounts of Mark, Matthew, and Luke, Jesus took the bread and blessed and broke and gave. So would the Christian minister. John's description is equally ceremonial, but with one even more Christian peculiarity. In 6:11, Jesus took, gave thanks, and distributed. The Greek for 'give thanks' is *eucharisteo*, which gives us our word for Christian Eucharist. It occurs again in 6:23. This same Eucharistic overtone is heard again in verses 12–13, where the fish have disappeared from the discussion, which speaks exclusively of the bread and the care to be taken of the remaining fragments. The ultimate sign (v. 14) of this miracle points to Jesus as the bread of life, particularly in the Eucharist.

"The reaction in verse 14, 'This is truly the Prophet, the one who is to come into the world,' refers again (as in 1:21, 24) to the prophet like Moses (Deut 18:15, 18) who was expected in the final days. Jesus has just fed the people with bread; Moses did the same with the desert manna.

"One final note of interest is that the two disciples who function in this manifestation of Jesus to the crowd are Philip and Andrew, the same two who in 1:41, 45 acted as apostles to Nathaniel and Simon Peter, and who will later be apostles to the Greeks (12:20–22). Their role in the Fourth Gospel is to reach out." [9]

12. In verse 11, how did Jesus distribute the bread and fish? How do the other Gospels shed light on the actual means of distribution (Mt 14:19; Mk 6:40–41; Lk 9:14–16)? How did Jesus work *through* his apostles (cf. Jn 4:1–2; CCC 1335) as his delegated agents, with the claim that it was done by Christ himself? How does this help us understand the priesthood and the sacraments (cf. Jn 4:1–2; CCC 1548)? How does this help us understand the deeper meanings and sacramental content of St. John's Gospel?

» THEOLOGICAL NOTE: This is the only miracle in which Jesus allows his disciples to participate. Why? What does it symbolize? Compare it with Numbers 11:13ff. Here the appointed leaders participate in the "spirit" with Moses; so with the apostles and their successors with Jesus. This is a beautiful picture of the Catholic Church: "all the people" representing the universal Church,

---

[9] Neal M. Flanagan, O.S.M., "John", in *The Collegeville Bible Commentary: New Testament*, ed. Robert J. Karris, O.F.M. (Collegeville, Minn.: Liturgical Press, 1992), 990.

gathered in "small groups" of fifty to one hundred, representing the local churches, all being fed by Christ, the great High Priest, who provides the miraculous "bread" of the Eucharist to all the people through the hands of his priests, the apostles.[10]

13. In verse 10, Jesus tells the people to sit down (literally "recline") on the green grass before distributing the bread. How might the use of the word "recline" associate this passage with the institution of the Eucharist in the other Gospels? What other time were the disciples reclining while eating bread with Jesus (Mk 14:17–18, 22)? What is signified by the posture of reclining? Does one work to earn God's grace, or is it freely given (Eph 2:8–9)? What does "reclining" tell us about the Eucharist and salvation (CCC 2008, 2169, 1166)? How could this be described as the real Sabbath rest (CCC 624)? How is this different from Numbers 11, where the Jews had to get up early and go out to gather the manna from the ground (Ex 16:14–18)? Under the New Covenant, how is the eating and gathering different from the gathering and eating of the Old Covenant (notice the different sequence of actions)?

» THEOLOGICAL NOTE: The eating and gathering of bread is also tied in with the Sabbath. In the Old Testament, men worked for six days, then rested on the seventh. In the New Testament, we start the week with rest and then work for six days (CCC 2175, 2190). Regarding salvation, this change in the work week is an example of "work" versus "grace" (Jn 1:17; CCC 2025). Works alone will not save a man. We cannot work six days to earn our rest on the seventh day. We must first receive the free gift of God, by resting in Christ by faith, and then go out to serve him and do the good works of charity and sanctification required of us (cf. Eph 2:8–10; Tit 2:14, 3:8). In the Old Testament, the people of Israel worked—gathering with their hands; by contrast, in the New Testament, Christ does the work and then gives bountifully into our hands with basketfuls left over (cf. Jn 16). The people of the Old Israel worked with their hands to gather; whereas the people of the New Israel receive in their hands while resting (reclining). "For by grace you have been saved through faith; and that not of yourselves, it is the gift of God; not as a result of works, so that no one may boast. For we are His workmanship, created in Christ Jesus for good works, which God prepared beforehand so that we would walk in them" (Eph 2:8–10, NASB). Compare Titus 2:14; 3:8; James 2:24.

14. After the people had eaten their fill, Jesus instructed them to collect the leftover fragments. Why? What do the twelve basketfuls represent?

---

[10] See Ray, *Crossing the Tiber*, 198.

(*Hint*: Gen 49:28; Deut 33:4–5; Josh 24:1ff.; Rev 21:12; CCC 191, 765, 1335.) How might it also represent the abundance of God's grace (Jn 1:16; 6:35)? How might it be significant that there was no surplus with the manna in the wilderness (Ex 16:16–21), yet there is an abundant surplus with Jesus' provision? How does the Eucharist help us understand this great generosity of God?

» HISTORICAL NOTE: In the ancient *Didache* ("Teaching of the Twelve"), written ca. 60, we find wording parallel with John's Gospel: "At the Eucharist, offer the eucharistic prayer in this way. . . . Then over the broken bread [the Greek word here means 'fragmented']: 'We give thanks [Gr.: *eucharistein*] to thee, our Father, for the life and knowledge thou hast made known to us through thy servant Jesus.'

"'Glory be to thee, world without end.'

"'As this broken bread, once dispersed over the hills, was brought together [gathered] and became one loaf, so may thy Church be brought together [gathered] from the ends of the earth into thy kingdom.'

"'Thine is the glory and the power, through Jesus Christ,
for ever and ever.'" [11]

15. Why was God angry with the Israelites in Moses' day, after they sat to eat and drink (Ex 32:5–7; 1 Cor 10:1–12)? How are they an example for us (cf. 1 Cor 11:27–32; CCC 1509)? Why was Jesus irritated with those who were fed the miraculous bread (Jn 6:26)? How and why did they mistake the heavenly kingdom of God for an earthly kingdom (Jn 6:14–15; CCC 439, 559)? Why was Jesus angry at those who just came to eat and ignored the spiritual significance of the profound event they had witnessed? In verses 14–15, why did the Jews try to use Christ for their political ends? In verse 14, what were the Jews expecting (Deut 18:15–18)?

16. Why does Jesus go off alone to the mountain, leaving the disciples behind (Lk 5:16; 6:12; 9:18, 28; CCC 2602). If Jesus seeks such times of solitude and prayer, what does it suggest for us?

» THEOLOGICAL NOTE: For Jesus as "the Prophet", see Deuteronomy 18:15, 18; cf. John 1:21; 7:40; Acts 3:22–23; 7:37; Matthew 21:11. During Passover,

---

[11] *Didache* 9, in *Early Christian Writings*, trans. Maxwell Staniforth (New York: Penguin Books, 1968), 194–95 (brackets added).

when the Jews recalled their deliverance from the tyranny of Egypt, their desire for liberation from Rome boiled in their blood. Many false messiahs led people into the wilderness with promises of national independence. "The crowd wanted freedom from Roman rule and peace for Israel, and they thought Yeshua was the man for the hour. But his own view was different: 'My kingship does not derive its authority from this world's order of things' (18:36). Had they succeeded, they would have nullified God's way of making Yeshua the Messiah, which was through his being the Suffering Servant dying for the sins of humanity, being resurrected, ascending to God's right hand and returning in future glory to assume the throne. The hope then as now among traditional non-Messianic Jews was for a conquering hero." [12]

John 6:16–21
Jesus Walks on the Water: The Fifth Sign

17. Why do you suppose this story is sandwiched between the multiplication of loaves (Jn 6:1–15) and the explanation of the miraculous bread (Jn 6:22–71)?

» PROBABLE EXPLANATION: "What role does this miracle play in relation to the multiplication [of loaves] and the rest of the chapter? To a certain extent the evangelist uses it as a corrective of the inadequate reaction of the crowd to the miracle. Impressed by the marvelous character of that sign, they were willing to acclaim him as a political messiah. But he is much more than can be captured by the traditional titles of 'the Prophet' and king; the walking on the water is a sign that he interprets himself, a sign that what he is can only be fully expressed by the divine name 'I am.' " [13]

Jesus was more than "the Prophet" or "the Messiah"; he was the second Person of the Blessed Trinity, God in human flesh, as declared by St. John in the first chapter. Jesus did something Moses never did—walked on water. Jesus tried to get the disciples to understand who and what he was by his works and life among them, but most of their understanding came later, after the Resurrection and the descent of the Holy Spirit. Thus, later in his life, as an aged man of God, John could clearly see and proclaim that the Word was God and became flesh and dwelt among us (Jn 1:1, 14).

» THEOLOGICAL NOTE: "The significance of such a 'nature' miracle, like that of the multiplication of the loaves, neither in J[oh]n nor in the [other Gospels]

---

[12] Stern, *Jewish New Testament Commentary*, 172.

[13] Raymond E. Brown, ed. and trans., *The Gospel according to John*, vol. 1, Anchor Bible, vol. 29 (Garden City, N.Y.: Doubleday, 1966), 255.

is intended to portray Jesus merely as a wonder-worker. The power of God over the sea is a commonplace theme of the O[ld] T[estament] (Gn 1:2, 6ff.; Pss 74:12–15; 93:3f.); more specifically, it was through his control of the sea that the first Israel had emerged in the Exodus (Ex 14:19ff.; 15:1–21; Ps 77:17–21). Just as the miracle of the loaves portrayed Jesus as a new Moses, who will be brought out in the following discourse as one greater than Moses, the present miracle underlines the power of him who was to bring forth the New Israel." [14]

18. Read the other accounts of Jesus walking on the water and compare them (Mt 14:22ff.; Mk 6:45ff.). How are they alike; how do they differ?

19. Throughout history, many commentators have seen a correspondence in this story between the boat and the Church. Read this story carefully, and think about how John might be telling a deeper story by applying this story to the Church. Look for clues in Matthew and Mark's accounts.

» A FEW HINTS: Compare a similar story in John 21:1–14. Where was home port; where were they headed (v. 17)? What time of day was it? How does John again use the theme of night and darkness (cf. Jn 3:2; 11:10; 13:30; 20:1; 21:3)? What was going on with the sea and the wind? What is the "Barque of Peter" (see notes on Jn 21:6)? Do you think they were asking each other where Jesus was, what was taking him so long, and when would he "return"? Matthew tells us that Peter walked on the water. What can this possibly mean? Was Peter able to keep from floundering without the ready and willing help of the Lord Jesus (Mt 14:28ff.)? How are Peter and his successors, the popes, though fallible human beings in the natural order, able to "stay afloat" and infallible in their official capacity as teachers of the faith (CCC 892)?

» THE CHURCH FATHERS: "In meditating on this episode Christian tradition has seen the boat as symbolizing the Church, which will have to cope with many difficulties and which our Lord has promised to help all through the centuries (cf. Mt 28:20); the Church, therefore, will always remain firm. St Thomas Aquinas comments: 'The wind symbolizes the temptations and persecution the Church will suffer due to lack of love. For, as St Augustine says, when love grows cold, the sea becomes rougher and the boat begins to founder. Yet the wind, the storm, the waves and the darkness will fail to put it off course and wreck it' (*Commentary on St John*)." [15]

---

[14] Raymond Brown, Joseph Fitzmyer, and Roland Murphy, eds., *The Jerome Biblical Commentary* (Englewood Cliffs, N.J.: Prentice-Hall, 1968), 2:436.

[15] José María Casciaro, *The Navarre Bible: The Gospel of Saint John* (Dublin: Four Courts Press, 1992), 98.

20. In verse 20, John records that Jesus used the divine name, "I AM". Where did God first reveal himself with these words (Ex 3:14)? We will see Jesus use the divine name frequently in John's Gospel. What is John telling us about Jesus?

» THE CHURCH FATHERS: "He does not say, I am Jesus, but only *I am*. He trusts to their easily recognising a voice, which was so familiar to them, or, as is more probable, He shews that He was the same who said to Moses, *I am that I am*." [16]

» THEOLOGICAL NOTE: "The most plausible explanation is that John treats the scene as a divine epiphany centered on the expression *egō eimi* ["I AM"] in vs. 20. . . . The fourth evangelist has taken the expression, neutral in itself, and made it a leitmotiv of the Gospel as that form of the divine name which the Father has given to Jesus and by which he identifies himself. . . . The majesty of Jesus is that he can bear the divine name." [17]

21. How might "crossing the sea" prepare the reader for the "miraculous bread", the "manna come down from heaven" (CCC 1003, 1212, 1298)? How does Jesus describe himself (Jn 6:35)? What did the Israelites "cross" before manna was provided (Ex 14:16; 1 Cor 10:1–4)?

» CULTURAL NOTE: "Is there also a Passover symbolism in the walking on the sea by way of a reference to the crossing of the Reed Sea at the time of the Exodus? (This would fit the miracle into the general context of ch. vi.) The Passover *Haggadah*, the liturgical narrative recited at the Passover meal, as it is preserved for us from a slightly later period, closely associates the crossing of the sea and the gift of the manna. Since the latter theme appears in vi 31, John may be making the same association. . . . Aileen Guilding . . . points out that one of the synagogue readings (*a haphtarah*) for the Passover cycle was Isa li 6–16 in which there are references to how the redeemed pass over the depths of the sea (vs. 10) and the Lord God stirs up the sea so that its waves roar (15); moreover, vs. 12 is one of the most important *egō eimi* passages in the OT. Perhaps the most complete assemblage of OT parallels to the themes of John vi can be found in Ps cvii: in 4–5 we hear of the people wandering hungry in desert wastes; in 9 we are told that the Lord fills [John's *empimplasthai*] these hungry people with good things; in 23 some go down to the sea in ships; in 25 the Lord raises a stormy wind that lifts up the waves of the sea; in 27–28 they are troubled and cry out to the Lord; in 28–30 He delivers them, calming the sea and bringing them to their haven." [18]

---

[16] St. Bede, Mt 9, in St. Thomas Aquinas, *Catena Aurea: St. John* (Albany, N.Y.: Preserving Christian Publications, 1995), 4:219.

[17] Brown, *John*, 1:254–55.

[18] Ibid., 1:255.

Now we are prepared by our discussion of this "fifth sign" to learn about the great gift of God in the Eucharist, which John treats in the remaining verses of this chapter.

JOHN 6 b

"UNLESS YOU EAT MY FLESH AND DRINK MY BLOOD"—THE EUCHARIST

John 6:22–59
Jesus, the Bread of Life

» INTRODUCTORY COMMENTS: We now embark on one of the most profound and deeply spiritual passages in the whole New Testament. Since we have seen John's expertise at revealing deeper spiritual truths through the vehicle of historical events, dialogues, and stories of Jesus' life, it is our duty here to discover the levels of meaning John has carefully embedded in chapter six. John's is a "spiritual Gospel"[1] and in this chapter he intends to provide readers with the fundamental truths and mysteries of the Eucharist.

The other three Gospels give careful accounts of the institution of the Eucharist (CCC 1334)—John does not. What John does give is the theology behind it, and he recalls the promise that Christ made of the sacred food and drink—his body and blood—the Eucharist, that would be offered by the "nations" (Gentiles) from "east to west", a "pure offering" on the "table of the Lord" (Mal 1:11–12; CCC 1330).

1. The day before this discourse on the Bread of Life, Jesus had just performed two other "signs": feeding up to twenty thousand people with five barley loaves and two fish and then walking on water and instantly causing the boat to reach shore. He then walked across the Sea of Galilee and joined the disciples in their boat on their way back, in the dark, to Capernaum. The crowds stayed on the opposite side of the sea, waiting to see Jesus at daybreak, not knowing he had left for Capernaum. What did they do when they realized Jesus had slipped away in

---

[1] "Last of all, John, perceiving that the external facts [of Christ's life] had been made plain in the Gospel, being urged by his friends, and inspired by the Spirit, composed a spiritual Gospel. This is the account of Clement [c. 150–c. 215]" (Eusebius, *Church History* 6, 14, 7, trans. Arthur Cushman McGiffert, in NPNF2, 1: 261).

the night (Jn 6:24)? Why did they assume Jesus was back in Capernaum (Mk 2:1)? We see the word "sign" used again in verse 26. Were the crowds interested in the signs Jesus was providing (cf. Jn 2:11, 23; 4:53–54; 6:2)? What preoccupied their minds (vv. 24, 26)? Is seeking Jesus always commendable? Do we seek Jesus for *himself* or for what he can *do* for us (CCC 305, 428, 2709)?

2. By the end of the first century (at the time John wrote this Gospel), the "breaking of bread" was already commonly called the Eucharist (for example, St. Ignatius of Antioch, see CCC 1369), which means "blessing" or "thanks". Read verse 23. Considering John's audience, why do you think he uses the word "thanks" (*eucharistia*)? What context do you think he is establishing for the discourse that follows? What would have been the first readers' immediate association?

» TEXTUAL NOTE: As noted, referring to John 6, Baptist theologian George Beasley-Murray writes, "It is evident that neither the Evangelist nor the Christian readers could have written or read the saying without conscious reference to the Eucharist; to say the least, they would have acknowledged it as supremely fulfilled in the worship event." [2] W. Leonard writes, "[John] does use εὐχαρισ-τήσας instead of the εὐλογήσας of the Synoptists. This verb deliberately repeated in 23 should be regarded as a distinct allusion to the Eucharistic significance of the miracle. . . . Let us take St Augustine's advice and not merely look at the outside of the miracle, like a man who admires calligraphy which he cannot read. Mental comprehension, not mere ocular or imaginative apprehension, should be our endeavour, when we read this miracle on *Laetare* Sunday. The same Word, 'by whom are all things', feeds the world from a few grains of corn, and the same also multiplies himself Incarnate on thousands of altars." [3]

3. In verse 25, why does Jesus refuse to give the crowds a simple answer to their question but instead comments on their motives? How and why does he try to point out the real intent—the intent of man's heart (Jn 2:24–25; Mt 9:4; Lk 9:47; Rev 2:23; CCC 473, 1781, 2563, 2715)?

4. In verse 27, what are we to "work" for? The Jews ask literally "What *works* must we *work* to do the *works* of God?" How does Jesus answer? How does this compare with Romans 3:28 and James 2:24? What are the

---

[2] G. R. Beasley-Murray, *John*, Word Biblical Commentary (Waco, Tex.: Word Books, 1987), 95.

[3] Dom Bernard Orchard, ed., *A Catholic Commentary on Holy Scripture* (New York: Thomas Nelson Pub., 1953), 991.

"works" of God (v. 29)? Is "believe" a *verb*, something we "do"—how is it a "work" or action on our part? How does this compare with Martin Luther's theology of "faith alone" (cf. Jn 3:16)? What kind of food were the crowds interested in? What kind of "food" is Jesus concerned with (Is 55:1–3; Jn 4:32–34)? What kind of "doing" or "works" does this "food" involve (cf. Jn 4:31–34)? Contrast the word "perish" in verse 27 with the word "lost" in verse 12 ("lost" and "perish" are the same word in Greek). What does this tell you about the two different "breads" (cf. Lk 12:29–30)? Consider James 2:14–26, especially verse 22.

» THEOLOGICAL NOTE: What does Jesus mean that "believing" is the "work of God"? "The crowd have no conception of 'life' as a gift: it is something that must be worked for. Religion for them is not the living of a divinely given 'life,' but the performance of sundry religious duties. . . . The religious life-relationship depends not on the performance of the law and the consequent acquiring of merit, but on a freely offered faith. It should be noted that in the Greek final construction, 'to believe' 'marks not only the simple fact of believing, but the effort directed to and issuing in this belief' (Westcott). (Cf. 4:34.) There is a sense in which 'to believe' is to perform a work. The influence upon our writer of Paul's doctrine of 'justification by faith' is obvious." [4] "Believe" is a verb, it is something we *do* by the grace of God.

"His answer is direct and to the point (v. 29). John here adopts the terms of the great debate between Paul and his Jewish Christian opponents, faith and works, but, instead of replacing works by faith, interprets true work as faith." [5] "Our Lord marks out one special work, which they must do by the aid of God, who by His all powerful grace, Himself produces this work in them, they at the same time co-operating with His grace and concurring in the work, viz., 'to believe in Him whom He hath sent.' He specially selects faith, as, in the first place, indispensable, because, on it must be founded all the works necessary for securing this food. . . . From His saying, that faith is the chief work, or means, necessary for securing this food, it would seem to follow, that the food itself is not faith, that faith is distinguished from the food, as means from the end, this food being no other than His own adorable body and blood, which is given as the reward of faith; and therefore, distinct from it." [6]

Too often, in some circles, "faith alone" is espoused as the beginning and end of salvation, with no cooperation required from the individual. However,

[4] G. H. C. MacGregor, *The Gospel of John*, Moffatt New Testament Commentary (New York and London: Harper and Brothers Pub., 1928), 141.

[5] "6:25–34, Bread from Heaven", in Paul J. Achtemeier, ed., *Harper's Bible Dictionary* (San Francisco: Harper & Row, 1985), published in electronic form, Logos Bible Software.

[6] John MacEvilly, *An Exposition of the Gospel of St. John* (New York: Benziger Bros., 1889), 19.

faith is believing, and believing is "work"—in the sense that it is something we "do"—it is a verb. In verse 29, Jesus uses the word "believe" in the present tense, which means the act of currently and presently "believing". "The present tense here denotes the continuing attitude, not the once-for-all-decision." [7] St. Paul reminds us, as he opens and closes his epistle to the Romans, that *to believe* inherently includes *obedience* (Rom 1:5; 16:26, cf. also Jn 3:36). We also find other elements that belief and obedience require: baptism (Acts 22:16; Jn 3:5; 1 Pet 3:21), works (Jas 2:24; Rom 2:6–7), repentance (Acts 2:38; 2 Pet 3:9), perseverance (Mt 24:13; Col 1:22–23), confession (Lk 12:8; Rom 10:9), taking up our cross and following Jesus (Lk 9:23ff.), and so on. No one can earn the mercy and grace of God; these can only be received by faith (cf. Eph 2:8–10), but this faith must be worked out in charity (cf. Gal 5:6).

5. According to verse 27, God the Father has placed his "seal" on Jesus. How and when did he do that (Jn 1:32–34; CCC 698, 1296)? Remember the five witnesses who testify to Christ in John 5:31–39?

» ST. THOMAS AQUINAS: St. Thomas Aquinas comments on the Father's seal placed on Jesus the Son. " 'When a seal is impressed on wax, the wax receives the complete form of the seal. So it is that the Son received the entire form of the Father. This occurred in two ways; eternally (eternal generation), which is not referred to here because the seal and the sealed are different in nature from one another; what is referred to here is the other manner, that is, the mystery of the Incarnation, whereby God the Father impressed on human nature the Word, who is the reflection and the very stamp of God's nature, as Hebrews 1:3 says' (*Commentary on St. John*, 358)." [8]

» KEY TO THIS PASSAGE: Deuteronomy 8:3 is a key to understanding this initial portion of Jesus' dialogue. Moses says of the Lord, "And he humbled you and let you hunger and fed you with manna, which you did not know, nor did your fathers know; that he might make you know that man does not live by bread alone, but that man lives by everything that proceeds out of the mouth of the LORD." How do Moses words apply to the crowds following Jesus? The Israelites of Moses' day saw only the physical bread and did not understand the deeper significance. Their descendants in Jesus' time are the same. The first part of this eucharistic section deals with belief in Jesus' word so that he can lead them deeper into the spiritual reality of the second half of the discourse—the truth of the Eucharist, the daily bread.

---

[7] Leon Morris, *The Gospel according to John*, The New International Commentary on the New Testament (Grand Rapids, Mich.: Wm. B. Eerdmans Pub., 1971), 360.

[8] José María Casciaro, *The Navarre Bible: The Gospel of Saint John* (Dublin: Four Courts Press, 1992), 99–100.

6. Having already seen and heard of the signs performed by Jesus and eaten the miraculous bread, what does the crowd ask for now (Jn 6:30–31; cf. CCC 549)? Why should the sign of bread provided in the wilderness (vv. 1–14) have been sufficient? What does the crowd conclude after that sign (v. 14)? How is the bread Jesus fed them on a one-time basis different from the manna Moses gave them (Ex 16:4–21)? How does this set the stage for Jesus to explain the "daily bread" of the Eucharist (Mt 6:11; CCC 1334, 2837)? How does the Eucharist apply to the petition for daily bread in the Our Father (CCC 2861)? The crowd recites a line from Psalm 78:17–33 to challenge Jesus. Read this passage and explain how it actually reproves these Jews who quote it to Jesus, especially verses 18, 19, and 32. How are they acting exactly like their ancestors, and why can they not see that fact?

» MANNA IN THE WILDERNESS: We learn about the Jewish understanding of manna from a Jewish commentary on the Torah: "There is, then, a general resemblance of the biblical manna to what is still found under natural circumstances; this resemblance extends to appearance, color, and taste, and the need to gather it early in the morning and its subsequent melting in the warm sun. There are, at the same time, important differences: the manna we know from experience is relatively sparse and could not become a significant food for large numbers of people; it is dependent on certain weather conditions and is not found regularly; it is not subject to quick putrefaction; and of course it is found on Sabbaths as well as on other days. These differences are decisive. The Bible sees the manna not as a natural phenomenon; rather, it transforms natural occurrences into acts of God, willed by Him in support of Israel. Manna is thus, in the biblical view, literally *lechem shamayim*, the bread of heaven (Ps. 105:40), a gift of God. . . .

"God interrupts the natural order to establish once more the ideal relationship between himself and man, the original and pure relationship between master and servant, in which the former takes total care of the latter. He feeds a portion of His people as He had fed Adam and Eve and continues to do so until the process of this people's creation has been completed." [9] Once again, the miraculous invades space and time. Jesus now claims to be the true bread sent down from heaven—informing the world of God's care and signifying the creation of a new people with a new miraculous and spiritual food. This is the Eucharist, the Body and Blood of Christ.

» THEOLOGICAL NOTE: "Let him give further evidence of being the second Moses (v. 14). If Moses had given their forefathers manna in the wilderness, let

---

[9] Gunther W. Plaut, ed., *The Torah: A Modern Commentary* (New York: Union of American Hebrew Congregations, 1981), 502–3.

the second Moses vindicate his authority in a similar way—not by a once-for-all feeding but on a more lasting basis. . . . In later times the Rabbis taught that the new age would be marked by the restoration of the gift of manna. . . . So the people may have meant: 'In the messianic age the gift of manna will be renewed; give us manna, and we shall know that the messianic age has truly dawned'. . . . The loaves and fishes were a timely provision indeed, but they were earthly food, not bread from heaven. One who could give them bread from heaven would beyond all doubt be the prophet like Moses." [10]

7. In verse 32, who gave the manna to the Israelites (Ex 16:15)? Was manna perishable or imperishable (Ex 16:20)? How does Jesus distinguish the new, "true" bread? How does it give "life to the world"? What does this description of the bread remind you of (cf. Jn 4:14–15)? How does the "overture" in John 1:1–18 set the stage for the bread of God that came down from heaven (Jn 1:1, 14)? Notice the "musical theme" being developed here. It is also interesting to note that "Bethlehem", the small town where Jesus was born, literally means "the house of bread". What does a manger hold? Food for the sheep, does it not? How does this illuminate the reality of Jesus as the true bread (food) for the sheep of God? He is both their shepherd *and* their food, just as he is the priest *and* the sacrifice, the giver of bread *and* the Eucharist itself. Another interesting note about Jesus' birth: Who were the first ones notified of it (Lk 2:8ff.)? Why is it appropriate that they should be the first told of the *Lamb's* birth?

» THEOLOGICAL NOTE: Moses or Jesus, who was greater? The Jews had come to a crossroads. "This is the crux of the question and Jesus faces it squarely: 'Amen, amen I say to you, Moses did not give you the bread from heaven. For the bread of God is that which comes down from heaven and gives life to the world.' The judgment of Jesus' challengers has been reversed. Jesus is greater than Moses as heaven is greater than earth. Jesus, not Moses, 'comes down from heaven and gives life to the world.' " [11] St. Augustine wrote, "But the Lord Jesus declared Himself to be such an one, that He was superior to Moses. For Moses dared not say of Himself that He gave, 'not the meat which perisheth, but that which endureth to eternal life.' Jesus promised something greater than Moses gave. By Moses indeed was promised a kingdom, and a land flowing with milk and honey, temporal peace, abundance of children, health of body, and all other things, temporal goods indeed, yet in figure spiritual; because in the Old

---

[10] F. F. Bruce, *The Gospel of John* (Grand Rapids, Mich.: William B. Eerdmans, 1983), 151.
[11] Giuseppe Ricciotti, *The Life of Christ*, trans. Alba I. Zizzamia (Milwaukee: Bruce Pub., 1947), 390.

Testament they were promised to the old man. They considered therefore the things promised by Moses, and they considered the things promised by Christ. The former promised a full belly on the earth, but of the meat which perisheth; the latter promised, 'not the meat which perisheth, but that which endureth unto eternal life.' " [12]

8. In verse 35, the people do not understand, so what does Jesus tell them plainly? Is Jesus the gift (v. 35), or the giver (v. 27), or both? How does this already relate to the Eucharist (CCC 1410, 1586)? What kind of hunger and thirst is Jesus referring to in verse 35 (cf. Jn 4:13–15; 1 Cor 10:3–4; CCC 2835)? What is the Old Testament basis for this correlation between the bread and the word of God (Deut 8:3)? Did Jesus' listeners or their forefathers understand what God was doing?

» TEXTUAL NOTE: "Christ proclaims that He is the Bread of Life (John vi. 35); no doubt of itself this might refer to the food of His doctrine, or something of that kind, but in the context He is clearly leading up to something more, to His offering of His own Flesh to be the spiritual Food of the soul, an outward sign of inward grace; a nourishing which is to maintain and strengthen the life of grace." [13]

9. According to verses 37–39, what did Jesus come to do? What is the will of God? How did John previously introduce his readers to the Resurrection (Jn 2:18–22, Jn 11, and Jn 20; cf. notes on Jn 5, pp. 131–32)? Look ahead to verses 44, 54. How are "heavenly food" and resurrection related?

10. In verse 40, how is the statement, "every one who sees the Son and believes in him should have eternal life", reminiscent of an earlier dialogue and Old Testament story (Jn 3:14; Num 21:9)? *Who* will raise the believer on the last day (v. 40; Rom 8:11; 1 Cor 6:14)? How do the Persons of the Trinity work together? What do we learn later about Jesus (Jn 11:25–26)?

11. The Jews expected the "new Moses" to reproduce the "daily manna miracle" of the Old Testament. Why would they grumble at Jesus for claiming he was the *eternal* (not just *daily*) bread from heaven?

---

[12] St. Augustine, *Tractate* 25, 12, in *Lectures or Tractates on the Gospel according to St. John*, trans. John Gibb and James Innes, in NPNF1 7:164.

[13] C. Lattey, *Catholic Faith in the Holy Eucharist* (St. Louis, Mo.: B. Herder Book Co., 1923), 14.

Would they think Jesus had dodged their question, or were they blind to the whole situation? Why? Where did Jesus claim to come from (v. 38)? What did the Jews living in Galilee know about Jesus (v. 42)? From the perspective of the neighbors and villagers, where did Jesus come from (v. 42; cf. Jn 7:41–42)? They understood his humanity—what did they fail to comprehend? If *you* had been his neighbor and heard his words, would *you* have recognized him for who he was—God in the flesh?

12. In verse 43, Jesus reproves the people for grumbling. Grumbling is what their forefathers did, and they are following closely on their ancestors' heels. In verse 44 Jesus addresses the subject of the resurrection of the dead for the second time (recall Jn 5:28–29). What does "bread from heaven" have to do with resurrection and eternal life (Jn 6:54, 58)? Jesus offers his listeners heavenly bread, but what do *they* want (Jn 6:26–27)? He performs signs to prove that he is the Messiah, and what is their only response (Jn 6:41–42; cf. Lk 4:22)? Why is it that the people misunderstand Jesus' promise as *either* from heaven *or* from human beings, instead of *both* spirit *and* flesh? They prove that they understand his claim in verse 42, when they question how he can say, "I have come down from heaven." Why do they not believe his words? Would you have believed him if you had lived in Capernaum and had known Jesus from childhood? Would you have had theological clarity and been able to understand his words?

» THEOLOGICAL NOTE: The Jews claimed to know God and his commands. Yet Jesus says that since they do not know him who was sent by the Father, they obviously do not know the Father. They should be taught of God but have failed because they have not listened to God. But there will come a time when all will be taught of God, and those who listen and learn from God will be drawn to Christ. Jewish theology accepted both human choice and God's sovereignty. Jesus here points out that those who know the Father, who are taught by him, will recognize the Son. Remember St. Anselm's words, "*Credo ut intelligam*" (I believe in order that I may understand).

13. How and when will "all" be taught of God (Is 54:13; Jer 31:31–34)? Why does Jesus quote from the prophets here? What is implied by the fact that the Isaiah passage mentioned above follows the prophecy of the Suffering Servant in Isaiah 53? Notice the New Covenant terminology of the passage from Jeremiah. When and how will God teach his people under the New Covenant (Heb 1:1–4; Jn 7:16; 14:26)?

14. In verse 44, what does Jesus mean when he says no one can come to him unless the Father draws him (CCC 259)?

» CHURCH TEACHING: God must grant each person the gift of grace to seek Jesus, for no one can find him through his own efforts. The Magisterium of the Church has told us this in the documents of Vatican II: " 'The obedience of faith' (Rom. 16:26; cf. 1:5; 2 Cor. 10:5–6) must be given to God who reveals, an obedience by which man entrusts his whole self freely to God, offering the 'full submission of intellect and will to God who reveals,' and freely assenting to the truth revealed by Him. If this faith is to be shown, the grace of God and the interior help of the Holy Spirit must precede and assist, moving the heart and turning it to God, opening the eyes of the mind, and giving 'joy and ease to everyone in assenting to the truth and believing it.' To bring about an ever deeper understanding of revelation, the same Holy Spirit constantly brings faith to completion by His gifts." [14]

15. Regarding Jesus' comments that no one but the Son has "seen" God (v. 46), see the discussion on "seeing God" in the notes on John 1:18.

16. In verse 47, Jesus reaffirms that one must believe (have faith) to obtain eternal life. Why is faith necessary (cf. Heb 11:1, 6; CCC 161, 848)? Again, Jesus uses "believe" in the present tense, literally: He who is believing has (or, is having) eternal life. Jesus now escalates the discussion by reaffirming that he is the fulfillment of the manna in the Old Testament. Moses fed the people with doctrine and manna—how does Jesus feed them? Does he claim or imply that he is speaking exclusively in symbolic terms in this section?

» TEXTUAL NOTE: We now close out the first part of the "bread of life" dialogue and begin the second part with the reaffirmation of verse 35, "I am the bread of life" (Jn 6:48). In the first section (Jn 6:35–47), "Jesus presents himself as the Bread of Life, in the sense that faith in him is food for eternal life. In the second part (Jn 6:48–59) Christ reveals the mystery of the Eucharist: he is the Bread of Life who gives himself sacramentally as genuine food." [15] Remembering John's penchant for double meanings and deeper, spiritual realities, read the following passage, starting with John 6:48, with Jesus' eucharistic meaning in mind.

---

[14] Vatican II, Dogmatic Constitution on Divine Revelation, *Dei Verbum*, no. 5, in Walter M. Abbott, *The Documents of Vatican II* (New York: American Press, 1966), 113–14.
[15] Casciaro, *John*, 99.

17. According to verse 49, what happened to those who ate the manna in the wilderness? How is the "bread which comes down from heaven" different from the manna (v. 50)? In verse 50, what does Jesus mean when he says that the man who eats "the living bread which came down from heaven" will not die (Jn 11:21–27; CCC 1052)?

18. In verse 51 Jesus gets right to the heart of the matter and defines what the "bread" actually is. What is the bread, and for what is it given (CCC 1355, 2837)? To whom was the bread ("manna") given after the Exodus (v. 49)? The bread that was once *only* for the Israelites is now provided to whom (Jn 6:33)? How does this help explain the New Covenant (1 Cor 11:23–26), in contrast to the Old Covenant, which was exclusively for the Israelites? At this point, *has* the bread been given, or *will* it be given at a future time (v. 51)? How did Jesus fulfill this promise later (Lk 22:19–20)? How was he recognized after his Resurrection (Lk 24:25–35)?

» HISTORICAL NOTE: "How would the first recipients of John's Gospel perceive these words—remembering that the Gospel of John was probably written between 90 and 100? According to George Beasley-Murray, arguably the most prestigious Baptist exegete in print, 'it is not necessary to interpret the statement exclusively in terms of the body and blood of the Lord's Supper. Nevertheless, it is evident that neither the Evangelist nor the Christian readers could have written or read the saying without conscious reference to the Eucharist; to say the least, they would have acknowledged it as supremely fulfilled in the worship event.'" [16]

19. As Jesus gets more explicit and demanding, notice the progressive resistance of the crowd (vv. 28, 41, 52, 66).

» THEOLOGICAL NOTE: We must remember that John uses words with double meanings and that he records Jesus' words to reveal the multiple layers of meaning within the dialogue. "The Gospel of John indicates in so many places the necessity of a double meaning, that inquiry into the deeper unexpressed sense is to be raised, in this Gospel, to the status of a principle of interpretation." [17] There are many implications to the "Bread of Life" discourse. "Here too we find the writer has in mind at once the historical appearance

---

[16] Stephen K. Ray, *Crossing the Tiber: Evangelical Protestants Discover the Historical Church* (San Francisco: Ignatius Press, 1997), 198, quoting Beasley-Murray, *John*, 95.

[17] Oscar Cullmann, *Early Christian Worship*, trans. A. Stewart Todd and James B. Torrance (Philadelphia: Westminster Press, 1953), 57.

of Jesus in time past and the presence of the risen Christ in the Lord's Supper." [18]

20. In verse 51, there can be no misunderstanding—the "living bread", as Jesus clearly states, is his *flesh*. Notice the dramatic transition: first, God giving the "living bread which has come down from heaven"; then, Jesus giving his flesh for the "life of the world". In verse 52, what did the people dispute about among themselves? Was Jesus talking about cannibalism? (*Cannibalism* was abhorrent to the Jews, but they were reduced to practicing it during extreme famine and military siege. Cannibalism was an extreme sign of God's curse and punishment: Lev 26:27–29; Ezek 5:10.) Why should the Jews have been able to understand the eating of this "flesh", based on their own Scriptures and religious ceremonies (Ex 12:5–8; Is 53:7; Jn 1:29; Lk 22:7–8; 1 Cor 5:7–8; CCC 608)?

» HISTORICAL NOTE: In the early centuries of the Church, Christians were frequently accused of cannibalism because rumors spread widely that they ate human flesh, obviously a reference to the body and blood of Jesus, the Real Presence as taught by the Church Fathers. "Not so long after Pliny [112], Christians were accused of clandestine rites involving promiscuous intercourse and ritual meals in which human flesh was eaten. . . . By the second century such charges had become widespread." [19]

21. In verse 53, we come to the very pinnacle of the discourse. Notice the double "Amen", or, as the RSV translates it, "Truly, truly". Why is that placed in front of this statement? For more on Jesus' "double amen", see the textual note on John 10:1. The double meaning of *belief* and *sacrament* in John 6 is now being revealed to the readers. Why does Jesus call himself the "Son of man" (Dan 7:13)? Why does the discussion change from the "bread from heaven" to eating the flesh of Jesus? Compare verse 53 with the words of Jesus at the institution of the Eucharist (1 Cor 11:23–26; Mk 14:22–25). How are these words similar to and a fulfillment of John 6:53–56? What is required for one to be raised from the dead on the last day?

» NOTE ON "EATING": In this discourse it seem as if Jesus is being overly difficult and desires to scare off his disciples unnecessarily. At this point, he

---

[18] Ibid., 96.

[19] Robert Wilken, *The Christians as the Romans Saw Them* (New Haven: Yale Univ. Press, 1984), 17.

speaks extremely hard words to them, seemingly asking them to become cannibals, and, as a result, most of them turn away in disgust and leave him. The
word translated "eat" (*trōgein*) is not a dignified word used to describe fine
dining, but is the Greek verb for "gnaw" and "munch" and could be translated
"masticating the flesh". The use of *trōgein* certainly emphasizes "the realism of
the eucharistic flesh and blood."[20] "This offense", according to Cullmann,
"belongs now to the Sacrament just as the [offense of the] human body belongs
to the [divine] Logos."[21]

» THE EUCHARIST FORETOLD: "There are two impressive indications that the
Eucharist is in mind. The first indication is the stress on eating (feeding on)
Jesus' flesh and drinking his blood. This cannot possibly be a metaphor for
accepting his revelation. . . . Thus, if Jesus' words in vi 53 are to have a favorable
meaning, they must refer to the Eucharist. They simply reproduce the words
we hear in the Synoptic account of the institution of the Eucharist (Matt xxvi
26–28): 'Take, *eat*; this is *my body*; . . . *drink* . . . this is *my blood.*' The second
indication of the Eucharist is the formula found in vs. 51 [when] . . . John
speaks of 'flesh' while the Synoptic accounts of the Last Supper speak of 'body.'
However, there is no Hebrew or Aramaic word for 'body,' as we understand the
term; and many scholars maintain that at the Last Supper what Jesus actually
said was the Aramaic equivalent of "This is my flesh."[22]

It should be remembered that by all indications, John wrote this Gospel
between 90 and 100, when early documents make it clear that the Eucharist
was being celebrated as the literal flesh and blood of Christ in the Church
across the Roman Empire. If these words were *not* referring to the Eucharist,
would John not have made an explanation in the text to avoid misunderstanding and to clarify Jesus' words (as he was wont to do, for example, Jn 1:42;
21:18–19)? He could have simply told his readers that this discussion of eating
flesh and drinking blood was all symbolic language and did not mean what the
first generation Christians thought it meant—what they practiced in their
liturgies. John wrote a sacramental Gospel and knew exactly what he was
writing, and why. He intended his readers to see in this discourse of Jesus the
explanation and deep mysteries of the Eucharist and the sacrifice of the
Church.[23]

» THE CHURCH FATHERS ON THE REAL PRESENCE: With one voice the Church
Fathers proclaimed the Real Presence of Christ in the Eucharist. If the Fathers
spoke of the bread and wine as being symbols, as they sometimes did, it was not
a negation of their understanding of the Real Presence of Christ in the

---

[20] See Raymond E. Brown, ed. and trans., *The Gospel according to John*, vol. 1, Anchor Bible,
vol. 29 (Garden City, N.Y.: Doubleday, 1966), 283.

[21] Cullmann, *Early Christian Worship*, 100.

[22] Brown, *John*, 1:284–85.

[23] See Ray, *Crossing the Tiber*, 199.

Eucharist and of its sacrificial nature. Speaking of the bread and wine in symbolic terms is in no way contrary to the reality of the Real Presence of Christ in the Eucharist and the Eucharist's sacrificial nature. Approaching the altar to partake of the Eucharist under the appearance of bread and wine provides a sign of our communing with Christ and of sharing the family meal, which is what the sacrament actually accomplishes. The sacraments are signs and realities. The *Catechism of the Catholic Church* informs us that the sacramental elements both signify and confer grace. "Celebrated worthily in faith, the sacraments confer the grace that they signify (cf. Council of Trent [1547]: DS 1605; DS 1606). They are *efficacious* because in them Christ himself is at work: it is he who baptizes, he who acts in his sacraments in order to communicate the grace that each sacrament signifies" (CCC 1127). To drive a wedge between the aspects of "sign" and "reality" is to do a disservice to biblical teaching and historic Christian teaching. A few patristic passages referring to the Real Presence of Christ in the Sacrifice of the Mass are provided as representative of the whole.

St. Ignatius of Antioch (ca. 35–ca. 107), a disciple of St. John and second bishop of Antioch from Peter, wrote, "But look at those men who have those perverted notions about the grace of Jesus Christ which has come down to us, and see how contrary to the mind of God they are. . . . They even abstain from the Eucharist and the public [liturgical] prayer, because they will not admit that the Eucharist is the self-same body of our Savior Jesus Christ, which [flesh] suffered for our sins, and which the Father in his goodness raised up again. Consequently, since they reject God's gifts, they are doomed in their disputatiousness. They should have done better to learn charity, if they were ever to know any resurrection. . . . Abjure all factions, for they are the beginning of evils." [24]

St. Ignatius of Antioch again, "Obey your bishop and clergy with undivided minds. . . . Share in one common breaking of bread [Eucharist]—the medicine of immortality, and the sovereign remedy by which we escape death and live in Jesus Christ for evermore." [25]

St. Basil the Great (ca. 330–79) writes, "It is good and beneficial to communicate every day, and to partake of the holy body and blood of Christ. For He distinctly says, 'He that eateth my flesh and drinketh my blood hath eternal life [Jn 6:54]'. And who doubts that to share frequently in life, is the same thing as to have manifold life. I, indeed, communicate four times a week, on the Lord's day, on Wednesday, on Friday, and on the Sabbath, and on the other days if there is a commemoration of any Saint." [26]

---

[24] St. Ignatius of Antioch, *To the Smyrnaeans* 6, 7, in *Early Christian Writings*, trans. Maxwell Staniforth (New York: Penguin Books, 1968), 102–3.

[25] St. Ignatius of Antioch, *To the Ephesians* 20, in ibid., 66.

[26] St. Basil the Great, *Letter* 93, in NPNF2 8:179.

St. Augustine (354–430), "He took flesh from the flesh of Mary. He walked here in the same flesh, and gave us the same flesh to be eaten unto salvation. But no one eats that flesh unless first he adores it. . . . We do sin by not adoring." [27]

Cyril of Jerusalem (ca. 315–86), "Since then He Himself has declared and said of the bread, 'This is My Body', who shall dare to doubt any longer? And since He has affirmed and said, 'This is My Blood', who shall ever hesitate, saying, that is not His blood? (*Cat. Myst.* 4, 1 LNPF). . . . That what seems bread is not bread, though bread by taste, but the Body of Christ; and that what seems wine is not wine, though the taste will have it so, but the Blood of Christ (*ibid.* 4, 9).

"Contemplate therefore the bread and wine not as bare elements, for they are, according to the Lord's declaration, the Body and Blood of Christ; for though sense suggests this to thee, let faith establish thee. Judge not the matter from taste, but from faith be fully assured without misgiving, that thou hast been vouchsafed the Body and Blood of Christ (*ibid.* 4, 6). . . . He once turned water into wine (μεταβέβληκεν), at Cana in Galilee, at His own will, and shall not we believe Him when He changes (μεταβαλών) wine into blood? (*ibid.* 4, 2)." [28]

22. In verse 54, what happens to those who eat his flesh and drink his blood? What are the two resurrections that will take place (Jn 5:28–29; CCC 1038)? What is the criterion for each resurrection (Rev 20:12–15)? How does that harmonize with John 6? How does it contrast with Protestant theologies of "faith alone" as the sole means of salvation (cf. Jas 2:24)? How might the old adage "You are what you eat" apply to this passage? Of what are we to become partakers (2 Pet 1:4)? In verse 55, how do we abide in Christ (cf. Jn 15:1–10)?

» IS THE MASS A SACRIFICE? Is there an actual *offering* presented on the altars of the Catholic churches? With unanimous consent, the Fathers of the Church taught that Malachi 1:11 referred to the Eucharist. The Fathers of the Church taught that the Eucharist was the fulfillment of Malachi's "pure offering" presented on the table of the Lord from east to west by the "nations", that is, the Gentiles. Malachi uses the technical term "table of the Lord" to signify the altar of sacrifice. Read 1 Corinthians 10:16–21 carefully. St. Paul is comparing three important categories of sacrifices that are all offered on altars (tables): that of the Jews (v. 18), that of the pagans (vv. 19–21; offered to idols), and that of the Christians—the Eucharist. Comparing these three various offerings, Paul confirms the sacrificial nature of the Christian Eucharist. The "table of the Lord" is

---

[27] St. Augustine, *Explanations of the Psalms* 98, 9, in William A. Jurgens, *The Faith of the Early Fathers*, vol. 3 (Collegeville, Minn.: Liturgical Press, 1979), 20.

[28] Cyril of Jerusalem, *Mystagogical Catecheses* 4:1–2, 6, 9, in Johannes Quasten, *Patrology* (Westminster, Md.: Christian Classics, 1993), 3:375.

a common technical term in the Old Testament referring to the altar of sacrifice (Lev 24:6–7; Ezek 41:22; 44:15; Mal 1:7, 12); the correlation would have immediately been made by Paul's readers. The "table of the Lord" in the Church, referred to by Paul and drawn from Old Testament terminology and practice, is now the altar for the *new* offering referred to by Malachi (Mal 1:11). Notice that the "table of the Lord" is mentioned twice in the first chapter of Malachi, before and after God's promise of a future, world-wide sacrifice that will be offered by the Gentiles. The "table of the Lord", or sacrificial altar, will be the place of this offering, which corresponds to the Eucharist offered on the "table of the Lord" in 1 Corinthians 10:21.

The sacrificial parallels used by St. Paul are striking and unmistakable: Malachi twice frames the "pure sacrifice" of the Gentiles with the sacrificial "table of the Lord". Paul uses this same terminology to explain the new sacrifice offered on the "table of the Lord" in the Church. The sacrifice of the Eucharist on the "table of the Lord" is contrasted with the other well-known sacrifices offered on tables or altars. Paul, the brightest student of the brightest Jewish teacher, Gamaliel, is not using this Old Testament terminology lightly— he is a scholar. He knows his readers understand the significance of his sacrificial terminology relating to the Eucharist. It is quite apparent that St. Paul, the brilliant teacher of the Torah, understood the Eucharist in sacrificial terms, offered on the "table of the Lord" as a fulfillment of Malachi 1:11.

"The parallelism that Paul draws between Jewish and pagan participation in their sacrifices through eating the meat of the victims and Christian fellowship with Christ through the Eucharist shows that he considers the eating of the Eucharist a sacrificial repast and implies that the Eucharist itself is a sacrifice." [29]

THREE SACRIFICES COMPARED BY ST. PAUL 1 Corinthians 10:16–21		
ISRAEL	PAGANS	THE CHURCH
Jews in Corinth	*Gentiles in Corinth*	*Christians in Corinth*
"altar"	altar; "cup" and "table of the demons"	Communion table or altar; "table of the Lord"
"eat the sacrifices"	"Gentile sacrifice"	Christian sacrifice
sharers or "partners in the altar"	sharers or "partners with demons"	"participation in the body of Christ"

[29] Raymond Brown, Joseph Fitzmyer, and Roland Murphy, eds., *The Jerome Biblical Commentary* (Englewood Cliffs, N.J.: Prentice-Hall, 1968), 2:269. For more detailed information, read CCC 1382–83 and Ray, *Crossing the Tiber*, 187–276.

23. With what in the Old Testament does Jesus contrast his flesh ("true food") and blood ("true drink") (cf. 1 Cor 10:1–4)? If we eat his flesh and drink his blood, how is it that we abide in him and he abides in us (Jn 6:56)? According to verse 58, how is the manna of the Old Covenant different from and inferior to the body of Christ in the Eucharist—the true bread provided by the Father in the New Covenant (CCC 1094, 1509)? What happens if the flesh and blood of Christ are received unworthily (1 Cor 11:27–30; CCC 1385)? How should we partake of the Eucharist (CCC 1127)?

24. In verse 59, John records that Jesus' words about the bread from heaven were spoken in the synagogue at Capernaum. The crowds did not believe in Jesus or in his signs. What does he say to Capernaum and to any who refuse to believe in him (Mt 11:22ff.)?

» Archaeological note: Extensive archaeological excavations in Capernaum, along the northwestern shore of the sea of Galilee, have unearthed the town in which Jesus lived with Peter (Mt 4:12–13; Mk 2:1). The foundations from the first-century synagogue can still be seen with the ruins of the fourth-century synagogue built on top of the first. It was in this synagogue that Jesus spoke these immortal words, words that ring out through time and eternity. These words are like a huge rock dropped into a pond, and the ripples have spread through all of time and to every corner of the world. Here was the great God of creation, the awesome I AM of the Jews standing in sandals, his voice ringing out with the ineffable words—God speaking to men about his flesh and blood and eternal life.

Capernaum can still give visitors a profound sense of eternity and mystery, as they stand at a cosmic junction of heaven and earth and sense the ambiance of two thousand years ago. The mystery of the Eucharist is still palpable to those who understand and have the eyes and ears of faith. Visitors can experience a sense of the sacred, of standing on holy ground. The same sense of the sacred can be experienced in the sacred liturgy. Indeed, the One who made the ground of Capernaum sacred is himself really present in the Eucharist. The holy *re-presentation* of the flesh and blood of Jesus in the Sacrifice of the Mass, seen by the eyes of the spirit, causes those abiding in Christ to bow their hearts to that mighty Presence and freely and gratefully to receive the words and food of eternal life. In that moment, they, too, are on "sacred ground".

John 6:60–70
Many Disciples Abandon the Words of Eternal Life

25. How did his disciples respond to the prophecy of the Eucharist (Jn 6:60–61, 66)? Did they understand Jesus? What did they do (v. 66)? Did they leave him because they understood and found it hard to accept, or because they did not understand at all (vv. 60–61)? This is a crucial question—if Jesus was only speaking "symbolically" about his flesh and blood, why did he not call his disciples back and explain the symbolism?

» THEOLOGICAL NOTE: "This is the only recorded case of disciples turning away from Christ over doctrinal issues. Why didn't Jesus stop the departing disciples as they scattered in revulsion over the hillsides? He could have easily shouted out to them, 'Wait, don't you understand that I was speaking symbolically? Come back, I was only speaking figuratively'. He didn't do this, and many of his disciples left him. But the Twelve remained: they realized that his words were the words of eternal life." [30] How many other Christian traditions have also, in the last four or five centuries, walked away from this teaching of Jesus that is maintained in the Catholic Church?

26. According to verse 61, what is the result of the peoples' unbelief? What do they begin to do? What does Jesus ask them? (Cf. Ex 16:8ff.; Is 8:9–16; Rom 9:30–33; 1 Pet 2:6–8; Mt 11:6; Mk 6:3; 1 Cor 1:23; where *offense* and *stumbling* are the same Greek word, from which we derive our English word *scandal*.) How are the crowds *scandalized* by Jesus' words about the Eucharist (CCC 1336)? How are some people today scandalized by the Real Presence of Christ in the Eucharist?

27. In verse 62, why does Jesus introduce again the concept of "ascending" (cf. Jn 1:51; 3:13; 20:17)? If the Jews were offended and stumbled because Jesus claimed to "come down from heaven" (Jn 6:42), how would they respond when he ascends to his Father where "he was before" (cf. Jn 1:1)?

» THEOLOGICAL NOTE: "These disciples, who now show themselves as lacking the true characteristics required of those who are to follow Jesus (v. 44f.), cannot bring themselves to believe that Jesus could really be one who has come down from heaven (cf. v. 41); what, then, would they make of the far greater

---

[30] Ray, *Crossing the Tiber*, 199.

mysteries that surround his return to the Father? These mysteries are the subject of the second half of John's Gospel, where their consequences are detailed for the true disciples of the Lord." [31]

28. How should seeing Jesus bodily ascend into heaven help the listeners understand these matters spiritually and not just with the eyes of "the flesh"? How might it help eliminate the perceived scandal of Jesus' words—the scandal of actual cannibalism, of cutting up his body and eating his literal arms and legs right on the spot? In what context might "eating his flesh" be understood spiritually and sacramentally after his ascension (1 Cor 15:42ff.)? If he *ascends* as he descended, how and in what form will this take place (Jn 1:14; Acts 1:9–11, 22)? Does Jesus, after his death and Resurrection, still possess his physical body (Lk 24:39–43; Jn 20:20, 27–29; CCC 659, 999–1001)?

» THEOLOGICAL NOTE: The miracle of the Ascension is brought into the discourse to help the disciples understand the miracle of the Eucharist. The Ascension and bodily existence of Jesus in heaven are important for the Catholic understanding of the Eucharist (see Rev 5:6). "Let them not think of His Flesh *as they see It now.* . . . Suppose they were to see this very Flesh of His not merely risen from the dead but ascending to Heaven, they would find it easier to understand, for they would then realize that this Flesh of His exists not only *as they see It now*, viz. in Its phenomenal or physical mode, but that It exists also in a spiritual mode. And it is in Its spiritual mode that He gives It as Food: but under either mode It is one and the same Flesh." [32]

29. In verse 63, Jesus refers to *"the* flesh" as distinguished from *"my* flesh" throughout this discourse. How many times does Jesus use the phrase "my flesh" in John 6 (cf. Jn 6:51, 54, 55, 56)? How does the clear distinction between *"the* flesh" and *"my* flesh" help us understand the meaning of verse 63 (see Jn 1:13; 8:15)? The *New International Version* translates John 8:15 as "You judge by human standards; I pass judgment on no one"; whereas many other translations render it "You people judge according to the flesh; I am not judging anyone." Is Jesus saying that *his flesh* profits nothing? Against those who use this passage to attack the Real Presence, how does this application prove *too* much (cf. Jn 1:1, 14; Eph 2:15–16; 1 Pet 2:24)? Does the flesh of Christ profit nothing— even in the Incarnation and Redemption? Explain why the statement

---

[31] Brown, Fitzmyer, and Murphy, *Jerome Biblical Commentary*, 2:438.
[32] G. H. Trench, *A Study of St John's Gospel* (London: John Murray, 1918), 170.

"the flesh profits nothing", as used by opponents of the Real Presence of Christ in the Eucharist, proves too much and falls flat.

» TEXTUAL NOTE: "In the Fourth Gospel one must distinguish between the *sarx* [flesh] of Jesus and the *sarx* of human beings. *Sarx* is used thirteen times in the Fourth Gospel, and its use is consistent. The *sarx* of Jesus tells the story of God (1:14, 18), and is essential for life (cf. 6:51, 52, 53, 54, 55, 56). But the *sarx* of human beings is confined to the human sphere, that which is 'below' (1:13; 3:6; cf. 8:23), and is the source of judgment limited by the superficial criteria provided by the physically observable (8:15; cf. 7:24). In 17:2 'all flesh' (*pasēs sarkos*) is used to render a Hebraism that means 'every created thing.' There is no contradiction between the use of *sarx* in vv. 51–58, where Jesus speaks of his own flesh, and v. 63 where he speaks of the superficiality of the limited human expectations the disciples have of Jesus (v. 62): 'the flesh is of no avail.' " [33]

» ST. JOHN CHRYSOSTOM: "[Jesus] tries to remove their difficulties in another way, as follows, 'It is the spirit that quickeneth, the flesh profiteth nothing': that is to say, You ought to understand My words in a spiritual sense: he who understands them carnally is profited nothing. To interpret carnally is to take a proposition in its bare literal meaning, and allow no other. But we should not judge of mysteries in this way; but examine them with the inward eye; i.e., understand them spiritually. It was carnal to doubt how our Lord could give His flesh to eat. What then? Is it not real flesh? Yea, verily. In saying then that the flesh profiteth nothing, He does not speak of His own flesh, but that of the carnal hearer of His word." [34]

30. Who would dare say that the flesh of Jesus avails nothing—this would prove the ultimate insult to the Incarnation. How does John use the word "flesh" in the "overture" (Jn 1:13–14) and with Nicodemus (Jn 3:6–7)? Can a man in his "fleshly", natural mind-set understand the deep things of God (cf. Nicodemus in Jn 3:12; 1 Cor 2:12–14; CCC 152)? Can the fleshly mind or the carnal man understand the spiritual things Jesus is explaining? What is necessary to understand the spiritual meaning and depth of Jesus' words (CCC 687)?

» THEOLOGICAL NOTE: "The flesh profits nothing" is "not a downgrading of the body in some Greek [Gnostic] dualistic sense, but rather a typically Jewish assertion that without the Spirit of God the physical things have no value of

---

[33] Francis Moloney, *The Gospel of John,* Sacra Pagina, vol. 4 (Collegeville, Minn.: Liturgical Press, 1998), 231.

[34] St. John Chrysostom, *Homily on John* 47, 3, in St. Thomas Aquinas, *Catena Aurea: St. John* (Albany, N.Y.: Preserving Christian Publications, 1995), 4:248.

their own." [35] "Such words [as Jesus has spoken] cannot be comprehended by the fleshly, whose horizon is bounded by this earth and its outlook. Only as the life-giving Spirit informs him may a man understand these words. . . . All His teaching presupposes the necessity for a work of the divine Spirit within man." [36] Jesus is simply saying that the "fleshly" mind cannot understand the deep things of God. He is not saying that "his flesh" profits nothing; rather, it is natural understanding, "the flesh" devoid of God's Spirit, that profits and understands nothing. The Father must draw each person into belief. Without the assistance of the Spirit, Jesus' words are not believed (Jn 6:64–65). If these words of Jesus are not believed, the divine life is not participated in, the body and blood of the Lord in the Eucharist are partaken of unworthily, and the person chances the forfeiture of the resurrection of eternal life. Jesus makes this clear.

» Spiritual application: "Those who are shocked have taken his words in the flesh rather than in the spirit. Promptly reminded of their animal sacrifices, they have made no attempt to reach the plane from which understanding would be possible. You are doing the same thing: judging without being in the position to judge. 'It is the spirit that gives life; the flesh profits nothing. The words that I have spoken to you are spirit and life.' The sentence by no means weakens what has gone before. The fact that his words are spirit and life does not mean that they are to be taken as a parable. They are to be taken literally, concretely, but in the spirit; they must be lifted from the coarseness of daily physical life into the realm of sacred mystery, from immediate reality into the sacramental. Understood in the first sense, they must repulse; in the second, they are the holy truth of God, which, accepted in love, brings endless fulfillment.

"Should they have understood? Hardly. It is inconceivable that at that time anyone could have grasped intellectually the meaning of these words. But they should have believed. They should have clung to Christ blindly, wherever he led them. They should have sensed the divine depth behind his words, known that they were being directed toward something unspeakably huge, and simply said: We do not understand; show us what you mean! Instead they judge, and everything closes to them." [37]

Unhappily, many still do not understand the words of Jesus, even though his words have been realized in the Church, through the sacrament of the Eucharist, and his teaching has been clarified. Many still say the "words are too hard, we can't comprehend them", and they walk away. Some have completely

---

[35] David H. Stern, *Jewish New Testament Commentary* (Clarksville, Md.: Jewish New Testament Pubs., 1992), 174.

[36] Leon Morris, *The Gospel according to John*, The New International Commentary on the New Testament (Grand Rapids, Mich.: Wm. B. Eerdmans Pub., 1971), 385.

[37] Romano Guardini, *The Lord* (Washington, D.C.: Regnery Publishing, 1982), 239–40.

rejected the faith, others have tragically reduced Jesus' words to mere parable, thereby emasculating the intent, refusing the Gift, and walking away from the body and blood freely offered unto eternal life.

31. Notice again how the response of the crowd disintegrates (Jn 6:34, 41, 52, 60–61, 66). Were the people following Jesus because the Father drew them or because they had hungry bellies looking for more bread (Jn 6:26)? Compare that with the disposition of the disciples who believed (Jn 6:67–69). What came first, *belief* or *knowing*? Does this mean that the Christian faith is anti-intellectual or irrational (CCC 2500)? What does it mean to be a true disciple (vv. 66, 68; Lk 9:23ff.)?

32. If the words of Jesus had been merely symbolic (that *eating* him was merely a figurative way to say "*believing* in him"), why did Jesus not call the departing disciples back and explain the symbolic meaning of his words (Jn 6:66–67)? Did the crowds understand him to be speaking symbolically or literally? When they questioned the literal meaning of "the bread which came down from heaven" in verses 41–42, what did he tell them that the bread from heaven actually was (Jn 6:51, 53)? If this is merely symbolic language, why does John leave the reader in A.D. 90–100 hanging with a mysterious dilemma? As St. Ignatius of Antioch indicates, the Church at the end of the first century considered the Eucharist to be the actual body of Christ.[38] If the words of Jesus were merely symbolic, why did St. John not take this opportunity to correct the error instead of perpetuating it? Why, if Jesus used only symbolical language for "ingesting the word of God", did John not tell his readers that the literal interpretation of Jesus' words about the Eucharist was incorrect? In fact, John's Gospel reveals the mystery of the sacrament; it does not reduce Jesus' words to mere symbol or metaphor. John's readers were already celebrating the Eucharist as the real body and blood of Christ.

33. Why do Peter and the eleven other disciples stay with Jesus (v. 68; cf. Jn 17:8)? Why does Peter say Jesus has "words of eternal life" (Jn 6:68)? The term "word" used here is not *logos*, but another Greek word meaning "words of instruction" or "the message". Who can come to Jesus (v. 65)? How was this demonstrated with the Twelve (Jn 17:9, 24; 18:9)?

---

[38] See, for example, his *Letter to the Smyrnaeans* 7.

34. Peter acts as the spokesman here—the leader of the band. On whose behalf does Peter speak (vv. 67–69)? What does this show us about the relationship of Peter to the other apostles (cf. Mt 16:15–19; Lk 22:31–32, Jn 21:15–17; CCC 552, 553, 862, 879)? Who speaks on behalf of the Church (Acts 1:15; 2:14; 15:7)? Who speaks the true faith on behalf of the Church?

» THE CHURCH FATHERS: "[Jesus] saith unto him, 'Feed My sheep.'
"And why, having passed by the others, doth He speak with Peter on these matters? He was the chosen one of the Apostles, the mouth of the disciples, the leader of the band; on this account also Paul went up upon a time to enquire of him rather than the others. And at the same time to show him that he must now be of good cheer, since the denial was done away, Jesus putteth into his hands the chief authority among the brethren; and He bringeth not forward the denial, nor reproacheth him with what had taken place, but saith, 'If thou lovest Me, preside over thy brethren.' " [39]

35. Compare the only other places in Scripture that Jesus is called "the Holy One of God" (Mk 1:24; Lk 4:34; cf. Lk 1:35). How might this title be a full recognition of Jesus as the Messiah, the Son of God, and a recognition that Jesus would rise from the dead (Ps 16:10: messianic prophecy; Acts 13:34–39)? How does Peter's confession of faith in verses 68–69 correspond with his confession in Matthew 16:13–20?

36. From what area did Judas Iscariot (*Iscariot* probably means "man of Karioth") probably come (Josh 15:21, 25)? What tribe of Israel was Jesus from (Heb 7:14)? What was the northern homeland of the eleven other disciples (Acts 1:11; 2:7)? Judas may have been the only one of the Twelve who was not a Galilean. If Judas was the only disciple from Jesus' tribe (extended family), what significance might this have in the narrative (Ps 41:9; Jn 13:18, 21; Jn 1:11: "his own people")? Since Jesus knew of, and tolerated, a traitor among his own intimate band of disciples, what does that say of possible "traitors" within the Church today, even those in high places (Mt 13:24–30; CCC 827)? How should Jesus' example instruct us in the Church today?

37. Why does John (and Jesus) decide to place the mention of Judas' betrayal at this location in the narrative (vv. 70–71)? How does John set

---

[39] St. John Chrysostom, *Homilies on the Gospel of St. John* 88, 1, in NPNF1 14:331. See also John 21:15–17.

the stage at the start of the chapter (v. 4)? How does John use this device of "contextual framework" to tell us that this passage is speaking of the Eucharist? Compare John's framework with that of the Synoptic Gospels (Mt 26:19–25; Mk 14:16–21; Lk 22:1ff.).

» CONTEXTUAL NOTE: When one is interpreting a given biblical passage, knowing the immediate and wider context is always very important. There are no dumb questions when studying the Bible. You should ask questions such as, Why is this particular passage placed here instead of somewhere else? By placing this text here, is the author trying to draw your attention to something? In John chapter six it seems obvious contextually that John mentions Judas' betrayal at this point of the narrative to make a specific point. Where else in the Gospels do we discover the betrayal by Judas? The Synoptic Gospels mention Satan entering Judas in the context of the last Supper. They each begin by noting that it was the Passover, and each account of the Last Supper ends with Satan entering Judas—and so it is with John 6. *John uses these two elements (Passover and Judas) as "bookends" in chapter 6 to point the reader to the clear parallel with the Synoptic accounts of the Last Supper—the Eucharist.* The mention of Judas in this location seems to be out of place unless understood within this eucharistic framework of the whole chapter. Remember that John 6 begins by informing us that the time of the Passover was at hand (v. 4).

JOHN 7

JEWISH FEAST OF BOOTHS—TWO DEBATES: WHO IS JESUS? RIVERS OF LIVING WATER

John 7:1–13
Jesus Goes Up to Jerusalem for the Feast of Booths

1. When Jesus refers to "the Jews", to whom in particular is he referring (Jn 7:32, 35; CCC 597)? Why does Jesus remain north in Galilee (v. 1)? Why are the leaders in Judea trying to kill Jesus (cf. Jn 5:18; 7:19; 8:37, 40; 11:53; 19:7)?

2. In verse 2, what is the "feast of Booths" or "Tabernacles" (Lev 23:33ff.; Deut 16:13–17; Num 29:12–40; Zech 14:16–19; Neh 8:14–18)? How many days did this feast last (Neh 8:18)? What was dedicated on this day, and what are the implications (1 Kings 7:51–8:13, 65; here and elsewhere it is simply called "the feast", which indicates its importance)? *It is important to remember that the feast of Booths is the background for the whole of chapters 7 and 8.*

» HISTORICAL NOTE: Like Passover, "the feast" attracted great multitudes to Jerusalem. It was called "Sukkot" or "Sukkoth" and was observed at the end of September (in the Jewish month of Tishri). The Puritans modeled the American holiday of Thanksgiving after Sukkot. Sukkot celebrates the completion of the harvest and commemorates God's goodness to the people during the forty years of desert wanderings and was called by Josephus "the holiest and greatest feast". The name comes from the leafy covered "booths" built as temporary dwellings ("tabernacles"), reenacting the nomadic travel through the wilderness, just as Passover commemorates the great deliverance of God from Egypt. Besides the essential ritual, in Christ's time it featured extensive water libations and the illuminating of the Temple court with magnificent torches. This lighting may not seem very impressive to us, since we have electricity, but it was nevertheless a marvelous event replete with meaning and symbolism. We will see the great implications of Jesus' comments about "water" (Jn 7:37) and "light" (Jn 8:12) during the festival. Not merely pointing to the past, the festival primarily emphasized the truth that Israel's life rested upon redemption, which in its ultimate meaning is the forgiveness of sins.

» THEOLOGICAL NOTE: "The festival is prophetically connected with the fate of the Gentiles [see Zech 14:16–19]. . . . This refers to the Messianic Age, after the whole world has come against Yerushalayim [Jerusalem] and been defeated; in the light of the New Testament it should be understood as taking place after the second coming of Yeshua the Messiah. The Rabbis of the Talmud recognized the connection of this festival with the Gentiles: speaking of the seventy bulls required by Numbers 29:12–34 to be sacrificed during the seven days of the festival, 'Rabbi El'azar said, "To what do these seventy bulls correspond? To the seventy nations"' (Sukkah 55b). In rabbinic tradition, the traditional number of Gentile nations is seventy; the seventy bulls [70 = 7 x 10, the number for completeness] are to make atonement for them." [1]

3. According to verses 3–4, how do Jesus' brothers (brethren) trouble him? Do they believe in him (v. 5)? What must they think of his miraculous signs? Why might his relatives reject Him (Jn 6:66)? How can rejection in our own families unite us more closely to the Lord? How does this rejection again replay the theme in the "overture" (Jn 1:11; cf. Jn 4:44)? How is this situation similar to an Old Testament "type" (prefiguring) of Christ (Gen 37:3ff.)? What eventually happened with some of Jesus' brethren (Acts 1:12–14; 15:13; 21:18; Gal 1:19; 2:9, 12; Jas 1:1; Jude 1)?

» THEOLOGICAL NOTE: In verse 3, Jesus and "his brothers" are again mentioned (cf. Jn 2:12). In Aramaic and Hebrew there are no specific words for "cousin" and "stepbrother". Even though John writes in Greek and in Greek there are words for "cousin" and "stepbrother", Jesus and his disciples spoke in Aramaic, and Aramaic usages frequently carried over into Greek terms used by the early Jewish Church. In other words, sometimes many of the early Jewish Christians wrote in Greek but thought in Aramaic, their native tongue. We see an example of this Aramaic carryover in Paul, who refers to Simon as "Cephas", which is a transliteration of the Aramaic "Kephas" and the equivalent of the Greek word for "Peter". Something similar presumably happened with the phrase "brothers of the Lord"—which, in its Aramaic form, could easily apply to blood brothers, half-brothers, step-brothers, cousins, or close relatives. When Christianity became more Greek-speaking, the Aramaic usage probably carried over, instead of the more precise Greek term for "cousin".

[1] David H. Stern, *Jewish New Testament Commentary* (Clarksville, Md.: Jewish New Testament Pubs., 1992), 175.

Extended family members in Jewish society were all considered "brothers", brethren, or kin (for example, Gen 12:5; 14:14; 29:15). Even the King James Version refers to these "brothers of the Lord" as "brethren". Mention of Jesus' brethren (or brothers) certainly cannot be taken as proof that Mary had other children, though it is possible that Joseph may have had other children by a previous marriage. To assume that "brothers" means Mary had other children, based on current English word usage and opposed to the whole tradition of the Church, is anachronistic and forces modern English usage back into Semitic languages and customs, even though there is plenty of biblical evidence against doing so.

Furthermore, we never read of other "sons of Mary"; only Jesus is called the son of Mary (Mk 6:3). Scripture and tradition do not support the idea of Mary giving birth to other children (some of those listed as Jesus' "brethren" are also listed as the sons of another Mary: Mt 13:55; 27:56). The early Church strongly opposed any idea of Mary as the mother of other sons, calling her "ever-virgin"—not only a virgin *prior* to the birth of Jesus but afterward as well (CCC 499–500). This truth was held not only by the early Church but also by the early Reformers, such as Martin Luther and John Calvin. Much has been written on this matter, and we will not delve into it here.[2]

4. What does Jesus mean by saying "for my time has not yet fully come" (Jn 7:8, 30; 8:20)? Why does he consider it too soon to go up to Jerusalem (Jn 7:1)? When *did* his time come (Jn 12:23; Mt 26:45–46)? Jesus said to them, "My time has not yet come, but your time is always here." What does he mean by this?

5. Imagine the excitement, especially for the children, when the cara-van started off on the three- or four-day journey to Jerusalem. Think of the packing and celebrating. What does Jesus decide (vv. 7–9)? Does Jesus lie to his brethren about *not* going up to the festival (vv. 8, 10)? An ancient writer, Porphyry, accused Jesus of inconstancy or dishonesty. How can this best be understood? In verse 10, how did he eventually go up to Jerusalem? If he was afraid of detection, why did he cry out in John 7:28 and 8:12?

» TEXTUAL NOTE: For purposes of safety, convenience, and comaraderie, the Jews would travel to Jerusalem in caravans for the festivals (for example, Lk

---

[2] For a comprehensive discussion of the topic, see Karl Keating, *Catholicism and Fundamen-talism: The Attack on "Romanism" by "Bible Christians"* (San Francisco: Ignatius Press, 1988); Andrés Fernández, *The Life of Christ*, trans. Paul Barrett (Westminster, Md.: Newman Press, 1959); and especially St. Jerome's letter *On the Perpetual Virginity of Blessed Mary*, which first appeared in 383. This topic will be discussed in more detail in the study of chapter 19.

2:41–44). Jesus decided not to travel with the group, which could have precipitated his arrest prematurely—before God's time—but to go up secretly to avoid detection. It was to be according to God's plan and not based on a human challenge. Many have tried to explain this passage. In fact, some of the Greek New Testament manuscripts appear to have been tampered with to "cover" for Jesus' apparent dishonesty, by adding the word "yet", as in, "I do not go up to the festival yet". That Jesus meant "yet" is one plausible explanation. Another plausible explanation is provided by David Stern, "The Greek present tense, which often has ongoing force, allows this understanding: 'I am not at present in the process of going up,' or, more simply, 'I am not going up now but may do so later—I'm not telling.' " [3]

Others find a deeper, spiritual meaning: "Going up" may have a geographical meaning (since Jerusalem is in the hills) as well as a theological meaning (going back to the Father through death and Resurrection). For Jesus, "going up" often means his death, Resurrection, and Ascension (Jn 20:17, same Greek word; Jn 3:13; 6:62; cf. Lk 9:51), in other words, "I go not up at this feast." He may attend the feast, but he will control the hour of his sacrifice. Others conclude that Jesus' refusal meant that he was not going up on the terms suggested by his brothers. He would go in his own time and way, but would remain in Galilee for the time being.

6. In verse 11, what do the crowds in Jerusalem expect of Jesus—why are they looking for him? What are the people muttering about (vv. 12–13)? Why do some say he is a good man? Why do others believe he leads people astray? What is the punishment for this crime (Deut 13:5)? Would *you* have been leery of believing him or a bit confused, especially since the religious leaders opposed him? How is it that *everyone* seemed to know about him? Why were they muttering but not speaking openly about Jesus (v. 13)? Why were people afraid of the Jewish leaders (Jn 9:22; 12:42; 16:2; 19:38–39; 20:19)? How did the questioning and speculation of the crowds escalate after he spoke publicly (Jn 7:40–43)?

» HISTORICAL NOTE: How could Jesus go up to Jerusalem privately, "in secret"? This raises the question of Jesus' physical appearance: "Greco-Roman biographers often liked to describe their subjects' appearances, flattering or not. That none of the Gospels does so suggests that Jesus' appearance may have been average enough to allow him to pass unnoticed in a crowd: probably curly black hair, brown skin, perhaps a little over five feet in height—unlike the Aryan pictures of him that circulate in some Western churches. . . . Although Diaspora

---

[3] Stern, *Jewish New Testament Commentary*, 176.

Jewish men, like Greek and Roman men, were normally clean-shaven, coins portray Palestinian Jews in this period with full beards and hair down to their shoulders." [4]

Does Isaiah 53:2 describe Jesus' physical appearance? "The earliest descriptions of Jesus in literature are equally ideal and fall into two completely different groups. The characteristics in both cases derive from passages in the Old Testament which refer to the Messias, though these present him under different aspects. One of the prophecies of the 'servant of Yahweh' asserted: 'There is no beauty in him, nor comeliness: and we have seen him, and there was no sightliness, that we should be desirous of him' (Isa. 53:2); on the other hand, a messianic hymn, resembling in form a mystic epithalamium, exclaimed: 'Thou art beautiful above the sons of men; grace is poured [out upon] thy lips' (Ps. 44 [45]:3).

"Unquestionably texts of this kind were not concerned with the physical features of the future Messias; they were simple allegorical expressions foreshadowing, the former his sufferings and the latter his triumphs. However, we do not lack Christian writers who took them literally and claimed them as descriptions of Christ's appearance. Hence he was believed to have been handsome or ugly depending on the quotation favored." [5]

The earliest portrayals of Jesus' face are consistently close to the imprint on the Shroud of Turin. According to the Shroud, Jesus was about five feet nine inches tall and weighed about 150 pounds.

John 7:14–24
Jesus Teaches at the Feast

7. Jesus stood up in the middle of the feast, which would have been about the third or fourth day of the great festival. Since Jerusalem is about a three-day rugged walking journey from Galilee, Jesus must have left Capernaum on the first day of the festival to arrive in the middle of the celebration. What does Jesus boldly begin doing, knowing that the Jewish leaders want to kill him (v. 14; cf. v. 19)? Why do you think he waited until the middle of the feast to arrive?

8. In verse 15, why did the Jewish leaders marvel (cf. Mt 7:28–29)? What did they mean that Jesus had "never studied" (unlearned and

---

[4] Craig Keener, *The IVP Bible Background Commentary: New Testament* (Downers Grove, Ill.: InterVarsity Press, 1993), 281.

[5] Giuseppe Ricciotti, *The Life of Christ*, trans. Alba I. Zizzamia (Milwaukee: Bruce Pub., 1947), 174–75.

ignorant) (cf. Lk 2:41–47; 4:22; Jn 3:10; Acts 4:13)? Why did the leaders not arrest Jesus on the spot (Mt 26:5)?

» CULTURAL NOTE: Jesus may well have been from the class of folks known as "of the land", or not from the centers of learning or culture. Joseph, a carpenter (Greek, *tekton*) and a man "of the land", would probably have been unable to afford formal training in the Law for his son (cf. Acts 22:3). Jesus, according to the customs of the time, would have been trained as a carpenter, a construction worker (cf. Mk 6:3). Those not officially trained in Scripture and the teaching of the rabbis were considered outside the pale of religious life.

Pharisees would not even converse with people "of the land", yet Jesus, even though he comes from such a despised and lowly social class, outspeaks and outwits the learned Rabbis—teaching as one having authority! "In this context the question does not mean (though the words could mean), How is this man able to read? but, How is it that this man who has never been a disciple in the rabbinic schools can carry on a learned disputation? . . . [Jesus] laid no claim to the teaching succession which authorized the utterances of an ordained Rabbi, but he was not a self-taught upstart. If others drew their teaching from a rabbinic lecture room, he brought his from his Father. . . . [H]is authority was not that of a learned, influential, or distinguished man, . . . but the authority of God." [6] A constant theme of John's Gospel is that Jesus is from the Father. He is not of this world, nor is his teaching of this world. The rabbis quote other rabbis—Jesus speaks only what God has given him to say (v. 16).

"Suddenly, when the eight days of the Tabernacles were half over, it became known that Jesus had arrived and had begun to teach in the Temple court. Both admirers and detractors ran to hear him, all recognizing without exception the power of his preaching. But his detractors immediately posed a damaging question. No one could be truly learned and wise if he had not attended the schools of the great Rabbis and Scribes and been trained in their methods: 'How does this man come by learning, since he has not studied?' There was good reason to suspect the self-made teacher who in matters religious dared to deviate from 'tradition'. Jesus answered: 'My teaching is not my own, but his who sent me. If anyone desires to do his will, he will know of the teaching whether it is from God, or whether I speak on my own authority.' " [7]

"Without having studied, that is, without having attended any of the usual *yeshivit*, sitting under the rabbis and *Torah*-teachers who inculcated the Pharisaic oral tradition of *Torah*. The implication is that the speakers regarded Yeshua as an *ha'aretz*, that is, a 'hick' (see v. 49N, Ac 4:13&N; compare Mt 13:54–55, 21:2–7; Mk 6:2; Lk 4:22). Actually, Talmudic tradition reports that 'Yeshu' [Jesus] learned from Rabbi Y'hoshua ben-Perachyah, who was the chief

---

[6] C. K. Barrett, *The Gospel according to St. John* (London: SPCK, 1970), 317–18.
[7] Ricciotti, *Life of Christ*, 425.

teacher of his day (Sanhedrin 107b, Sotah 47a). Although this is historically impossible, since the rabbi lived about a hundred years earlier, we see that Jewish tradition does not regard Yeshua as religiously ignorant. The New Testament reports demonstrate that he had not only wide knowledge of both biblical and traditional materials, but wisdom from God transcending academic credentials." [8]

9. According to verse 16, what is the source of Jesus' teaching (cf. Jn 3:11–13)? How should God's people teach today (CCC 427)? What is the criterion for discerning if Jesus' words are from the Father or from himself (v. 17)? What kind of glory do the Jewish leaders seek, and how does that compare with the glory that Jesus seeks (Jn 5:41–46)? What does Jesus claim for himself (v. 18)? Notice that Moses is also mentioned in this context—why (cf. CCC 578)? Remember how Moses played a crucial role in exposing the Jews in John 5.

10. In verses 21–23, the leaders are still furious about the "one deed" Jesus performed in Jerusalem on a previous visit. What sign was it (Jn 5:1–9)? How does Jesus, in the context of this feast, press the point that they are not without sin (Jn 8:7–9)? Were the Israelites contemporary with and under the authority of Moses without sin—did they keep the Law perfectly (Ex 32:1ff.; CCC 578)? Once again, how are these Jews like their ancestors?

11. The Jewish leaders accused Jesus of breaking the Sabbath when he healed a crippled man (Jn 5:1ff.; CCC 2173; for more on the Sabbath, see notes on John 5). What do the *Jewish leaders* themselves do on the Sabbath (Jn 7:22)? How can they justify this "work" on the Sabbath? Jesus asks if healing is not consistent with their Law and traditions (CCC 582). What inconsistency does Jesus expose (v. 23)? How does Jesus teach and act differently from the Pharisees (CCC 581)?

Notice how Jesus compares and contrasts affecting a small part of the body on the Sabbath through circumcision with affecting the whole body on the Sabbath through healing. Circumcision on the Sabbath sanctified a man by affecting a *small* part of his body—by cutting or wounding it. How then can sanctifying a man by affecting his *whole* body through healing on the Sabbath be wrong? "This is an argument *a minori ad maius* (from the lesser to the greater), quite com-

---

[8] Stern, *Jewish New Testament Commentary*, 176.

mon in Rabbinic logic. Circumcision affects only a part of the body; if that is permitted, an action affecting the good of the whole body should be permitted." [9] Why do the Jewish leaders consider the first one permissible on the Sabbath and not the other? Jesus claimed to have no unrighteousness in himself (v. 18), and none could be pointed out by the Jews, yet what were the leaders seeking to do to him (v. 19)?

» THEOLOGICAL NOTE: "The Torah states that a Jewish male child is to be circumcised on the eighth day of his life (Genesis 17:12, Leviticus 12:3), but it also prohibits work on *Shabbat* [Sabbath] (Exodus 20:9–10, 23:12, 31:14–15, 34:21, 35:2; Leviticus 23:3; Deuteronomy 5:12–14). Therefore, if the eighth day of a boy's life falls on *Shabbat*, is circumcision to be put off till the ninth day, or is *Shabbat* to be broken by doing the work of tool-carrying and cutting needed for the operation? The Judeans (the Jewish religious authorities centered in Judea; see 1:19N) of Yeshua's time had already decided the question, and their decision stands on record in the Talmud." [10] If the eighth day after birth falls on the Sabbath, the priests pick up the tools, carry them, and perform the operation of circumcision. Why should Jesus not, likewise, act on the Sabbath to heal?

12. Knowing the Jewish leaders themselves did not keep the Law perfectly (CCC 578), Jesus asks why they target *him* for death—*they* did circumcision, actually carrying a knife and working with it, cutting a body part; whereas, he *healed* a *whole* man, not by working with his hands, but only with a word! How was killing a righteous man addressed in the Law (Ex 23:7)? What two laws of Moses were the Jews violating, in addition to dishonoring "God in the flesh" (Ex 20:8, 13)? Was Jesus violating the Sabbath laws by healing a man (Jn 5:15–17; Lk 14:5; CCC 581)? What other activities did the Jews allow that suspended the Sabbath observance (cf. Lk 13:15; 14:5).

13. In verse 24, what does the Jewish Law require concerning right or just judgment (Lev 19:15; Zech 7:9–12)? How did the Jewish leaders violate the Law outwardly and in their hearts? Could Jesus read their minds and hearts (Jn 2:24–25)?

---

[9] Raymond E. Brown, ed. and trans., *The Gospel according to John*, vol. 1, Anchor Bible, vol. 29 (Garden City, N.Y.: Doubleday, 1966), 313.

[10] Stern, *Jewish New Testament Commentary*, 177.

John 7:25–44
Is Jesus the Christ?

14. In verses 27, 41–42, the Jews deny that Jesus is the Christ. Where was the Messiah expected to come from (Mt 2:4–6; cf. Mic 5:1–2)? Where was Jesus born (Mt 2:1; Lk 2:4–7)? What is the objection of the Jews—where did they think Jesus was from (Jn 7:41, 52)? Where is Jesus actually from (Jn 1:1, 14; 6:38; 7:28–29)? Should the Jews know that Jesus is the Messiah—that he has come down from heaven (Jn 5:36, 39; 46–47; Lk 3:22; CCC 438–40)?

15. Jesus' opponents try to seize and kill him. Notice other instances when he miraculously avoids capture (Jn 7:44; 10:39; 18:6; Lk 4:29–30), though it is usually understated. Notice Luke 22:53. How do Jesus' signs affect many of the common folks? How do even some of the Pharisees respond (Jn 7:50–51)?

16. In verses 33–34, Jesus again speaks of the spiritual aspect of his death, Resurrection, and Ascension. In what ways do the Jews judge according to "the flesh" here (cf. Jn 6:63; 7:24; 8:15) and again miss the whole point Jesus is making? Compare this passage with John 14:1–4.

17. In verse 37, John tells us that Jesus stood up and "proclaimed" (cried out) "on the last day of the feast, the great day" (cf. Lev 23:36; Num 29:35; Neh 8:18). Imagine the huge Temple courtyards bustling with excited throngs of people. Suddenly a voice rises above the din of the crowd and attracts everyone's attention. What does Jesus proclaim (vv. 37–38)? Where have we already heard this message of being thirsty and coming to Jesus for a drink (Jn 4:13–14)? What does Jesus mean by "drinking" in verse 37? Where do the Scriptures say, "Out of his heart shall flow rivers of living water" as Jesus "quotes" in verse 38 (cf. Is 44:3; 55:1; 58:11, Ezek 47:1ff.)? How does the water flowing from the Temple, in Ezekiel, correspond to what we know about Jesus (Jn 1:14; 2:21; 19:34), the Church (1 Pet 2:5; CCC 1179), and heaven (Rev 22:1, 17)? What other source of water could be alluded to here (1 Cor 10:1–4; Ex 17:4–7; Ps 78:15–16)? Is there any common ground between Exodus 17:6 and John 7:26, 31? Compare the disposition of the Jews in each situation (v. 43). What were they attempting to do with Moses (Ex 17:4) and with Jesus (Jn 7:19)?

» HISTORICAL NOTE: Pouring water out before the Lord was of ancient origin (1 Sam 7:6). How appropriate were Jesus' words (v. 38) on the last day of the feast! "Two distinctive features of this week-long ceremony in September–October have made an impression on the text. Water was brought daily from the pool of Siloam to the temple, where it was poured over the altar as prayers were recited for the all-important winter rain. And the lights in the women's court flamed so brightly that the city was lit up by them. Water and light play a fairly important part in these two chapters [chapters 7 and 8]." [11] The rabbinic literature says, "They have said: 'He that never has seen the joy of the Beth ha-She'ubah [drawing of water during the feast] has never in his life seen joy.' " [12] How much more is so, when the Lord himself, the real Temple, is present among them in the flesh!

"On each of the seven mornings a procession went down to the fountain of Gihon on the southeast side of the temple hill, the fountain which supplied the waters to the pool of Siloam. There a priest filled a golden pitcher with water, as the choir repeated Isa 12:3, 'With joy you will draw water from the wells of salvation.' The procession went up to the Temple through the Water Gate. The accompanying crowds carried the symbols of [the feast of] Tabernacles. . . . They also sang the Hallel Psalms (cxiii–cxviii). Then the priest went up the ramp to the altar to pour the water into a silver funnel whence it flowed into the ground. . . . It was at this solemn moment in the ceremonies on the seventh day that the teacher from Galilee stood up in the Temple court to proclaim solemnly that he was the source of living water. . . . Their prayers for water had been answered in a way they did not expect; the feast that contained within itself the promise of the Messiah had been fulfilled. . . . Now Jesus says that these rivers of living water will flow from his own body, that body which is the new Temple (2:21)." [13]

18. Remember that "living water" can mean either "living" or "running, flowing" water. What is happening at the very moment Jesus speaks to give a living illustration of his words? (See above note.) How has Jesus referred to living water earlier (Jn 4:10–14)?

19. What does Jesus mean by "living water" in verse 38 (Jn 7:39; CCC 728, 1287, 2561)? What is the sequence of events in the giving of the Spirit (Jn 13:31ff.; Acts 1:4–5; 2:33; CCC 244, 690)? Compare this sequence with verses 38–39. How was this promise fulfilled (Acts 2:1–4;

---

[11] Neal M. Flanagan, O.S.M., "John", in *The Collegeville Bible Commentary: New Testament*, ed. Robert J. Karris, O.F.M. (Collegeville, Minn.: Liturgical Press, 1992), 992.

[12] C. K. Barrett, *The New Testament Background* (San Francisco: HarperSanFrancisco, 1987), 201.

[13] Brown, *Gospel according to John*, 1:327.

10:44–47; CCC 730, 729)? How are we appropriating this promised gift in our worship and daily life as Catholics?

» TEXTUAL NOTE: "John 7:38 has always posed difficulties for interpreters. The New International Version makes the believer the one in whom living water is flowing. But the Greek can be punctuated another way: 'if anyone thirsts, let him come to me; and let him drink, who believes in me.' This reading is best. It means that Jesus is the source of the eschatological Tabernacles water. Jesus is the source of the Spirit (v. 39). In 19:34 we may even have a symbol of this flowing when Jesus is glorified (v. 39b)." [14]

"The marginal rendering is less difficult. If it is followed, the statement of v. 38 applies to Jesus: out of his heart (Gk., 'belly') the rivers of living water flow (cf. 19:34), not from the believer, as is otherwise the case. The source of the Scripture reference is unclear." [15]

20. Some in the crowd were saying, "This is really the prophet." Where is the promise given of a singular "prophet" (Deut 18:15, 18; cf. Acts 3:22)? "The prophet" was a key eschatological sign for the Jews. Who had the Jews earlier thought might be "the prophet" (Jn 1:19–21)? What had Moses given the people that the new "prophet-like-Moses" would also give (1 Cor 10:1–4)?

21. Why would some of the people think Jesus was the Messiah (Jn 7:31)? Where do the Scriptures say that "the Christ is descended from David, and comes from Bethlehem, the village where David was" (v. 42), and not from Galilee (cf. Ps 89:3–4; Mic 5:1–2; Mt 2:4–6; Lk 2:4ff.)?

Some may suggest that St. John himself did not know that Jesus was born in Bethlehem since he does not mention it here, but this is quite untenable considering the close relationship John had with Jesus and with his Mother, Mary (cf. Jn 19:26–27), and his awareness that Joseph was his foster father (Jn 6:42). Also, the earliest accounts referring to John's Gospel inform us that John was aware of and gave his approval of the earlier Synoptic Gospels. "The three Gospels already mentioned having come into the hands of all and into [John's] too, they say that he accepted them and bore witness to their truthfulness." [16] (See the intro-

---

[14] Walter A. Elwell, ed., *Evangelical Commentary on the Bible* (Grand Rapids, Mich.: Baker Book House Co., 1989); published in electronic form by Logos Research Systems, 1997.

[15] James L. Mays, *Harper's Bible Commentary* (San Francisco: Harper & Row, 1988); published in electronic form by Logos Research Systems.

[16] Eusebius, *History of the Church* 3, 24, 7, in NPNF2 1:153.

duction for more information.) For more on the earthly origins of Jesus, see John 7:27. It is likely that John is merely being ironic regarding Jesus' origins.

John 7:45-53
Unbelief of Jewish Leaders

22. According to verse 46, why are the court officers afraid to seize Jesus (cf. Mt 26:4–5)? Are the Pharisees concerned with truth or merely with maintaining their positions of authority? How do the Pharisees put pressure on the officers (vv. 46–49)? What attitude do the Pharisees display toward the common people (v. 49)? What attitude does the Lord display toward the average person (Lk 7:36–50)? Do the "rulers" believe in Jesus (Jn 7:48, 50–52; 19:38–39)? Where did we come across Nicodemus earlier (Jn 3:1ff.)?

» HISTORICAL NOTE: The Pharisees called all the other Jews "people of the land", which was a term of disparagement; but even more disparaging was the practical attitude they maintained toward their fellow countrymen.

"On this point, too, both Christian and Jewish sources agree. In the Gospel of St. John (7:49), the Pharisees exclaim, 'But this multitude, that knoweth not the Law are accursed!' (ἐπάρατοι). The word 'multitude' here means the non-Pharisees or 'people of the land,' who are 'ignorant of the Law' and completely 'accursed.' Jewish documents confirm the 'curse.' It is the great Hillel himself who says that 'no rustic (*bur*) fears sin, and the people of the land are not pious' (*Pirqe Aboth*, II, 5), 'rustic' and 'people of the land' here being synonymous. A true Pharisee, therefore, was not to have any contact whatever with the 'people of the land,' but show himself 'Pharisee,' that is, 'separated' from them. That is why one rabbi proclaimed: 'To participate in an assembly of the people of the land brings death' (*ibid.*, III, 10); the celebrated Judah the Holy cried in remorse, 'Alas! I have given bread to one of the people of the land!' (*Baba Bathra*, 8 a); and Rabbi Eleazar adjudged, 'It is lawful to stab one of the people of the land even on a Day of Atonement which falls on the Sabbath' (*Pesahim*, 49 b). Many other passages forbid the Pharisees to sell fruit to one of the people of the land, to offer him hospitality or accept any from him, to become his kin through marriage, etc. (*Demai*, II, 3; etc.). Needless to say, even a wealthy or aristocratic Jew or a member of the high-priesthood could be in the Pharisees' eyes a 'rustic,' one of the 'people of the land.' The standard of judgment was the practice and knowledge of the Law according to Pharisaic principles, and membership in the chosen class of the 'separated.'

"Only rarely did non-Pharisees answer this class pride with scorn or hostility. The common people, especially in the cities and the women among them particularly, were wholeheartedly on the side of the Pharisees and cherished a boundless respect for them. It was possible to say that the Pharisees 'have so much power over the multitude, that even if they say something which is contrary to the king or to the high priest they are immediately believed' (*Antiquities of the Jews*, XIII, 2 and 8). Such popular support was the true strength of these aristocrats of dogma." [17] How does this historical fact explain Jesus' harsh teaching against the Pharisees and their self-righteousness? How did their interpretation of the Law violate the very intent of the Law: love of God and love of neighbor?

23. Nicodemus refers to the Mosaic Law to defend Jesus; what passages does he allude to in Jesus' defense (Ex 23:1; Deut 17:6; 19:15; Prov 18:13)? What does Nicodemus' defense show about his spiritual development (cf. Jn 19:39)? How do the other Pharisees insult him (v. 52)? Do any Pharisees believe in Christ (CCC 595–96)? Why do the Jewish leaders dislike Jesus so much (Jn 3:19; 1 Jn 3:12)? Why are most of the Pharisees unable to understand and believe (Mt 11:25–30; Lk 10:21–24)? The Pharisees sarcastically ask Nicodemus if he is also from Galilee, which is intended as an insult. The Pharisees fail to realize that although Jesus is from Galilee, he was born in Judea. How does their superficial understanding of Scripture condemn them rather than enlighten them?

24. The chapter ends with the observation that "They went each to his own house." Was the festival over at this point? What does Jesus do again the next day (Jn 8:2)?

---

[17] Ricciotti, *Life of Christ*, 38.

JOHN 8

THE ADULTEROUS WOMAN; MORE DEBATES:
WHO IS CHRIST? TRUE "I AM"

John 8:1–13
The Woman Caught in Adultery

1. Take a look at several different Bible translations, and see how they treat John 7:53—8:11.

» SHOULD THIS STORY BE IN THE BIBLE? Many Bible translations place brackets around the story of the woman taken in adultery (the first eleven verses of chapter eight) with marginal notes explaining that these verses may or may not be part of John's original text. Margin notes may say something such as, "The early manuscripts and other ancient witnesses do not have John 7:53–8:11." Since no original writings (autographs) of the apostles are in existence, scholars must reconstruct the original text of the New Testament by comparing the multitude of handwritten copies available from the early centuries.

Even though these initial verses of chapter 8 are not contained in many early Greek manuscripts, they are found in the early Latin texts, including the Vulgate, and are therefore included in the Protestant versions of the New Testament as well as the Catholic. We read nothing of them in the early Greek Fathers, though the story was known in the East and was truly ancient. Papias (ca. 60–130) mentions a story of a woman accused of many sins before the Lord, and he may very well be referring to this story.[1] It is also mentioned in the third-century *Didascalia Apostolorum*, which shows it was known in second-century Syria.

St. Jerome says the story was found in both Latin and Greek; St. Ambrose says it was always famous in the Church; and St. Augustine expounds the story as well. There is no real question that the story constitutes authentic material from the life of Christ.[2]

---

[1] *Fragments of Papias* 6 in ANF 1:54.

[2] For more information, see F. F. Bruce, *The Gospel of John* (Grand Rapids, Mich.: William B. Eerdmans, 1983), 413, and Raymond E. Brown, ed. and trans., *The Gospel according to John*, vol. 1, Anchor Bible, vol. 29 (Garden City, N.Y.: Doubleday, 1966), 335.

Most scholars agree that 7:53—8:11 was not original to John's Gospel, though it authentically records a genuine event in Jesus' life. In some ancient manuscripts, it appears in St. Luke's Gospel. This passage was accepted by the Council of Trent as canonical, and thus it is received by the Catholic Church as inspired Scripture. It was included in the Vulgate, the Bible of the Byzantine (Eastern) Church, and ultimately in the King James Bible, and so the majority of non-Catholic Christians also accept it. For the Catholic, there is no question of inspiration or canonicity involved, since the Catholic Church has the authority to recognize and determine the canon of Scripture, and the Church has always accepted these verses as canonical and authoritative.

2. John 8:1–13 raises the question of who has the authority to determine which texts belong in the Bible. Can the canon be determined by each individual Christian? How do we know which of the hundreds of early texts claiming apostolic authorship are inspired and which are not? What criterion was employed in determining which writings were inspired and therefore to be included in Scripture (CCC 120, 1117; 1 Tim 3:14–15)?

» How were New Testament books determined? "The books were acknowledged because of their content as witnesses to the apostolic gospel; their formal acceptance as canonical scripture was a matter of discussion and decision by gradual consensus among the communities [Catholic Church] of the late second century and afterwards. But the term 'canon' was being used for the standard of authentic teaching given by the baptismal confession of faith well before it came to be used for the list of accepted books. The criterion for admission was not so much that traditions vindicated an apostolic authorship as that the content of the books was in line with the apostolic proclamation received by the second-century churches."[3]

3. "St. Augustine said that the reason doubts were raised about the passage was that it showed Jesus to be so merciful that some rigorists thought it would lead to a relaxation of moral rules—and therefore many copyists suppressed it from their manuscripts (cf. *De coniugiis adulterinis*, 2, 6)."[4] How might this passage be used to relax moral rules? How might it be seen as allowing people to sin with little concern or contrition (cf. Rom 3:8; 6:1, 15)?

---

[3] John McManners, ed., *The Oxford Illustrated History of Christianity* (New York: Oxford Univ. Press, 1992), 29. This is clearly stated in CCC 120 and 1117.

[4] José María Casciaro, *The Navarre Bible: The Gospel of Saint John* (Dublin: Four Courts Press, 1992), 120.

4. What is the geographical setting of this chapter (Jn 7:3, 10, 14)? What is the great feast that provides the backdrop for this chapter (Jn 7:2)? For several days the people have been living in makeshift "booths"; what do we learn from John 7:53? (A full discussion of the feast is contained in the previous chapter.) Many scribes have teaching tents pitched in the outer courts of the Temple where they teach their students. Why does Jesus teach in the Temple?

5. Why do the Pharisees bring a woman caught in adultery to Jesus (Jn 8:6)? What laws governed the sin of adultery, and what was the legitimate penalty this woman should have suffered (Lev 20:10; Deut 22:22ff.)? Does the Mosaic Law apply only to the woman? How might we theorize that she was "caught in adultery", since adultery takes two people (v. 3)? Why do they not also bring the man who committed adultery with her? Are the Pharisees concerned with justice, or with using a poor woman's sin to confound and trap Jesus (v. 6; cf. Lk 11:53–54)? The dilemma had two horns on which to impale Jesus—what were the two options the scribes and Pharisees assume Jesus had? First, what if Jesus commanded her to be stoned (Jn 18:31)? What would the Romans have done? Second, what if Jesus had excused her and thereby failed to follow the mandates of the Mosaic Law? Compare with Luke 20:19–26.

» HISTORICAL NOTE: "Such crimes [as adultery] are often severely punished in the Near East. It was reported a number of years ago, 'Two Muslim pilgrims returning from Mecca, were found guilty of adultery on July 11, 1957, [they] were taken to the judge in Mecca and sentenced to death by stoning. The sentence was executed on July 12, the Mufti himself casting the first stone' (Vatican periodical, *Oriente Moderno* 37, [1957], p. 593)." [5]

6. Verse 6 mentions Jesus writing on the ground with his finger. What might Jesus have written? What had God written with his finger (Ex 31:18)? This is the only account of Jesus writing anything, and what he wrote is a matter of conjecture. How did Jesus respond to the scribes and Pharisees (v. 7)? How did this present *them* with a *four*-horned dilemma—"damned if they do and damned if they don't"? First, what would the man to throw the first stone be claiming (cf. Rom 2:1–29)? Second, if they all failed to throw stones, what were they all admitting? Third, if they stoned her in broad daylight, what might the Romans have done (Jn 18:31)? And fourth, if they failed to stone her, was it Jesus

---

[5] Bruce, *John*, 414.

or they themselves who ignored Moses' clear command? Were they guilt-free (CCC 588)?

» THEOLOGICAL NOTE: "Since He said He was God, the Law of Moses must have come from Him. If He disobeyed that Law, He was negating His own Divinity. Hence their questions, 'Moses in his Law prescribed that such persons should be stoned to death; what of Thee? What is Thy sentence?' It would be a hard question for a mere man to solve, but, He was God as well as man. He Who had already reconciled justice and mercy in His Incarnation now applied it further as He leaned over and wrote something on the ground—it is the only time in the life of Our Blessed Lord that He ever wrote. What He wrote, no man knows. The Gospel simply says: Jesus bent down and wrote with his finger on the ground (John 8:6).

"They had invoked the Law of Moses. So would He! Whence did the Law of Moses come? Who wrote it? Whose finger? The Book of Exodus answers: Moses turned and went down the mountain with the two tablets of the Tokens in his hands, inscribed on both sides, on the front and on the back they were inscribed. The tablets were the handiwork of God, and the writing was God's writing, engraved on the tablets (Ex 32:15–17).

"They reminded Him of the Law! He in turn reminded them that He had written the Law! The same finger, in a symbolical sense, that was now writing in the tablets of stone of the temple floor, also wrote on the tablets of stone on Sinai! Had they eyes to see the Giver of the law of Moses standing before them? But they were so bent on ensnaring Him in His speech that they ignored the writing and kept on hurling questions; so sure were they that they had trapped Him." [6]

7. How many witnesses does it take to condemn someone of breaking the Law (Deut 17:5–7; 19:15)? How many witnesses were left to testify against the woman (vv. 9–11)? In the end, who followed the Law—Jesus or the Jews? Jesus gave the woman a command. What was it (vv. 10–11)? How was this similar to the command given to the man healed at the pool of Bethesda (Jn 5:14)? Can one assume that a personal encounter with Jesus is adequate for salvation, in and of itself, without repentance and good works and a subsequent holy life? To follow Christ, why is it necessary to take up our cross and to sin no more?

8. How is this story a clear picture of the gospel (cf. Rom 8:1–4)? What does the Law pronounce against us (Rom 3:19–20; 4:15; 7:9; CCC 708)? Who accuses us (Rev 12:10)? How does the Law bring us to

---

[6] Fulton Sheen, *Life of Christ* (New York: Image Books/Doubleday, 1990), 184–85.

Christ (Gal 3:24–26; CCC 1982)? What supercedes the condemnation of the Law (Rom 5:20–21; Jn 1:16–17; CCC 1963–64, 1983–85)? How must we live after being forgiven and released from the Law of condemnation and sin (Heb 12:14)? Think about this story as a "parable of salvation". How could one use this story inappropriately, especially by ignoring the last sentence of verse 11 (CCC 162)?

John 8:12–30

Jesus Is the Light of the World

9. According to verse 12, how does Jesus' announcement develop a theme from the "overture" (Jn 1:4–5; CCC 2466)? Why do these words have such significance during this feast of Booths?

» HISTORICAL NOTE: "It is still the Feast of Tabernacles (cf. Jn 7:2); and it was the custom on the first night to fill the court of the women with the bright light of huge lamps which lit up the sky. This brought to mind the bright cloud of God's presence which guided the Israelites through the wilderness during the exodus." [7]

From the rabbinic literature of the Jews, the Mishnah, we read (Sukkah 4, 5): "The flute playing, sometimes five and sometimes six days'—this is the flute-playing at the Beth ha-She'ubah, which overrides neither a Sabbath nor a Festival-day. They have said: He that never has seen the joy of the Beth ha-She'ubah has never in his life seen joy. At the close of the first Festival-day of the Feast they went down to the Court of the Women where they had made a great amendment. There were golden candlesticks there with four golden bowls on the top of them [75 feet high] and four ladders to each candlestick, and four youths of the priestly stock and in their hands jars of oil holding a hundred and twenty logs [9 liters] which they poured into all the bowls. They made wicks from the worn out drawers and girdles of the priests and with them they set the candlesticks alight, and there was not a courtyard in Jerusalem that did not reflect the light of the Beth ha-She'ubah." [8] The next paragraph of the Mishnah 5:4 says, "The pious men and wonder workers would dance before them with flaming torches in their hand, and they would sing before them songs and praises. And the Levites beyond counting played on harps, lyres, cymbals, trumpets, and [other] musical instruments." [9]

---

[7] Casciaro, *John*, 123.

[8] C. K. Barrett, *The New Testament Background* (San Francisco: HarperSanFrancisco, 1987), 200–201.

[9] Jacob Neusner, trans., *The Mishnah: A New Translation* (New Haven & London: Yale Univ. Press, 1988); published in electronic form by Logos Research Systems.

189

10. According to verse 12, after participating in one of the most exciting and meaningful light shows imaginable for a non-technological
society, what does Jesus stand up and announce to the throngs in the
Temple precincts? The lights burning in the great candlesticks are just *a*
light for the *Jews*, but what is Jesus? How is Jesus *the* light of the *world*?
What are the quantitative and qualitative differences? Notice again the
metaphor of darkness or night (cf. CCC 2466). How was this theme
introduced in the "overture" of John's Gospel (Jn 1:4–5, 8–9)? How
does Jesus' claim relate to the Old Testament (Is 9:1–6; cf. Mt 4:15–16; Is
42:6; 49:6; Ps 27:1; Dan 2:19–22; Mal 4:2; Lk 1:76–79; 2:30–32)? Based
on the Old Testament texts, what and who is Jesus claiming to be?

» THEOLOGICAL NOTE: "When one turns on the light, all the rats, the bats, and
the bedbugs crawl away. Light exposes sin, which is the reason the scribes and
the Pharisees had to leave [earlier]. 'I am the light of the world' is the highest
claim that He has made so far in the Gospel of John. One of the definitions of
God is that He is Light (see 1 John 1:5). He is absolute in His holiness and in
His justice. Even physical light is one of the most complicated things as well as
one of the most essential things for us. Who really knows what it is? In some
ways it acts like waves, and in some ways it acts like particles of matter. The
startling thing is that men, acting on both of these definitions or principles,
have been able to make remarkable inventions and discoveries. Some say that
both are true and yet others say both can't be true. Is light the absence of
darkness? Is darkness the absence of light? We say a room is filled with light.
What do we mean? Does it weigh any more when it is filled with light? There
could be no such thing as color without light. The red rose is red because it has
absorbed every other part of light except red. That is the reason we see red in
the red rose.

"We don't understand light, and certainly a child doesn't understand light,
but he does know enough about it to turn on the light switch when he enters
a dark room. Jesus Christ is the Light of the World. Just as the sun is the physical
light of this world, He is spiritual Light. Just as a little child can have enough
sense to come into the presence of light, so any sinner today, though he be 'a
fool and a wayfaring man' (see Isa. 35:8), can come into the presence of the
Lord Jesus Christ." [10]

11. The Pharisees say Jesus is false because he bears witness about
himself. Ostensibly, their claim seems justified, based on Jesus' own
words (Jn 5:31); but who also bears witness to him (Jn 8:18, cf. Jn 5:33,

---

[10] J. Vernon McGee, *Thru the Bible Commentary*, vol. 40: *John Chapters 1–10* (Nashville:
Thomas Nelson Publ., 1991), 1:134–35.

36–37, 39, 46)? Why is his self-witness true anyway (v. 14)? Where does Jesus come from (Jn 5:36–37; 16:28)? Where is he going (Jn 13:1; 16:28)? Why can the Pharisees not understand (Jn 8:15)? What is the basis for their judgment? Is this the same reason they cannot understand his teaching of the Eucharist (Jn 6:63)? What kind of judgment is this?

12. In verse 17, why does Jesus refer to the law as "your law"? Based on their own law, which they have used against him in John 5, there are two who bear witness to Jesus. Who are they (Jn 8:18)? Is Jesus a true witness (Rev 1:5; 3:14)? Do Jesus' opponents understand his identity—that God is his father (v. 19)? Does Jesus mention Joseph as his father? How could they know God the Father (v. 19; cf. Jn 14:8–9)? In verse 20, John mentions the treasury, which was the "financial district" of the Temple. It was in the outer court of women, in which thirteen trumpet-shaped receptacles were placed for financial dues and offerings (cf. Mk 12:41ff.). Even though Jesus teaches publicly in the open court, why can no one seize him? When is his "hour" (Jn 13:1)?

13. In verse 21, what does Jesus tell the scribes and Pharisees (cf. Jn 7:34)? What does he warn them about? What is the result of dying in sin (CCC 1005, 1034)? Have the Jews heard such words before (cf. Num 27:3)? How has Jesus already forced them to admit they are *not* without sin (Jn 8:7–9)? In verse 24, he repeats the warning that they will die in their sins, this time adding an "escape clause": "*unless you believe that I* AM", you will die in your sins (emphasis added). What does Jesus mean by "I AM" (cf. Ex 3:14; CCC 211, 203–4)? What do the Jews think Jesus might do to himself (v. 22)? Though there were no specific laws against suicide in the Old Testament, the Mosaic Law mandated, "You shall not murder." This command forbids suicide, because the commandment does not distinguish between self-murder and the murder of others. What does the Church teach about suicide (CCC 2280–83)? Where is Jesus from and where are his opponents from (v. 23; cf. Jn 3:31–32)? Has someone previously descended from the higher realm to enable others to comprehend and ascend back with him to the heavenly realm (Prov 30:4; Jn 1:51; 3:13)? What must one believe about Jesus to gain forgiveness from sin and the gift of eternal life?

» HISTORICAL NOTE: "The duty of preserving life, including one's own, is one of the paramount injunctions of Judaism. The prohibition of suicide is a natural corollary to this, and yet it is nowhere explicitly forbidden in the Talmud.

However, post-talmudic authorities considered suicide a most heinous sin, even worse than murder. It was thought to be a denial of the doctrines of reward and punishment, the world to come, and the sovereignty of God, and the opinion was expressed that the suicide forfeits his portion in the world to come." [11]

» TEXTUAL NOTE: Various translations provide the pronoun "he" in verse 24 to make the passage read: "Unless you believe I am *he*". However, in the Greek the phrase is simply *ego eimi*—I AM. Only those who recognize him for who he actually is and believe in him with all that the word "believe" means can make the ascent with him to eternal life. So, who is he? The New English Bible renders this "If you do not believe that I am that I am, you will die in your sins." The New American Bible renders this phrase "If you do not believe that I AM, you will die in your sins." When God delivered Israel from Egypt, he revealed himself as I AM WHO I AM. It was by this name that the people of Israel were to know him. Jesus comes to deliver his people from sin and reveals himself, their God and deliverer, as I AM. The name YHWH was derived from the verb "to be", based on Exodus 3:14 (cf. CCC 446, 653).

14. The Jews begin to catch on to what they consider the "outrageous" claim Jesus makes, and they ask, "Who are you?" Does he answer them directly? Why does he not tell them plainly (cf. Mt 13:34-35)? What is the source of his words (v. 26)? Do they understand Jesus (v. 27)?

15. What does Jesus mean here by "lifted up the Son of man" (Jn 3:12-21; cf. Jn 12:32)? Notice the parallels between John 8 and John 3:12-21. When he is "lifted up", how will they know him (cf. Mk 15:38-39; Jn 20:27-28)? What was the result of his words (Jn 8:30; cf. Jn 2:23)?

John 8:31-59
The Truth Will Make You Free

16. According to verse 31, what is required to be a true disciple of Christ? Who truly believes in Jesus (v. 30; cf. Jn 12:11, 42-43)? What does he say to the Jews who *do* believe in him? What is required before we can know the truth? What effect does the truth have on a disciple of Christ? How does one abide in Christ (Jn 15:1ff.)? What does Jesus

---

[11] Louis Isaac Rabinowitz, "Suicide", in Geoffrey Wigoder, *Encyclopedia Judaica Multi-media* (Jerusalem: Judaica Multimedia (Israel), 1997), CD-ROM edition version 1.0.

mean by "freedom", when he says that the truth will set us free (cf. Jn 8:34–36; 15:1–11; Rom 8:2; 2 Cor 3:17; Gal 5:1, 13)?

17. According to verse 33, do Jesus' opponents think they have ever been enslaved? Have they, in fact, ever been enslaved (Ex 1:8–14; 2 Kings 25:1–7)? To what pagan empire were the Jews then subject (Jn 11:47–48; 19:15)? How could they claim to have always been free? What does Jesus mean by "slavery" (v. 34; cf. Rom 6:1–15; 2 Pet 2:19)? After implying that his opponents were slaves, how does Jesus compare their eternal destiny with his own? How are they to become free (v. 36; 1 Tim 2:4; 2 Tim 2:25; CCC 908, 1741)?

» THEOLOGICAL NOTE: This is a poignant and cutting parallel that would certainly recall the story of Abraham in Genesis 21:8–12. Jesus compares his Jewish opponents to the rejected son, Ishmael, thus implying that they are in bondage, but he is the true son who offers freedom. Paul comments in Galatians 4:22–26, "For it is written that Abraham had two sons, one by a slave and one by a free woman. But the son of the slave was born according to the flesh, the son of the free woman through promise. Now this is an allegory: these women are two covenants. One is from Mount Sinai, bearing children for slavery; she is Hagar. Now Hagar is Mount Sinai in Arabia; she corresponds to the present Jerusalem, for she is in slavery with her children. But the Jerusalem above is free, and she is our mother."

These Jews claim to be the sons of Abraham, but because they are proving to be in bondage to sin (and Rome), which son of Abraham are they—the son of Sarah (freedom) or the son of Hagar (bondage)? Jesus is "Isaac"; his opponents descend from Ishmael. There was no more blistering reproof possible—except the one that will be pronounced in verse 44.

During the institution of slavery in the United States, a slave could not free himself, but the son of the master, upon inheriting the estate, could free the slaves. Jesus is the son, and "if the Son makes you free, you will be free indeed."

18. In verse 37, Jesus, after admitting that the Jews are the physical sons of Abraham, recounts the Fatherhood that is *really* important (Rom 9:7–8). In verse 41, the Jews retort, probably with sarcasm, something like " 'We're not illegitimate children, like you' (implied)! Apparently they knew something about the unusual circumstances of Yeshua's birth." [12] Are all "circumcised sons" of Abraham sons of the promise (Gen 16:15; 17:26; 21:10; Rom 9:6–8)? Compare the two sonships. How does one

---

[12] David H. Stern, *Jewish New Testament Commentary* (Clarksville, Md.: Jewish New Testament Pubs., 1992), 138.

know if he is the true son of Abraham? What did Abraham do that earned him favor in God's eyes (Gen 15:6; Heb 11:8; Jas 2:1ff.; CCC 2571)? How did Abraham's response to God in Genesis 18 differ from the response of the Jewish leaders to Jesus—true I AM, God in the flesh? In verse 40, how did Abraham treat the Lord when the Lord visited him and told him the truth (Gen 18:1ff.)? How did the Jews treat Jesus when through the Incarnation he came from heaven, visiting them to proclaim the truth (Jn 1:10–11)? The Jews planned to kill Jesus; therefore they were doing the deeds of whom (Jn 8:44)? Who was their real father, and whom did they really imitate?

» OLD TESTAMENT NOTE: Three strangers approached Abraham in Genesis 18, and he prostrated himself before them. Jewish tradition has struggled to understand who these messengers were because Scripture says that "the Lord" appeared to Abraham, yet they were in a human form. In Christian tradition, some have seen in these three men a manifestation of the three Persons of the Trinity. A famous icon by Andrei Rublev entitled *The Trinity* (ca. 1422–1427) depicts this scene from Abraham's life (Tretiakov Gallery, Moscow).[13] When the Lord visited Abraham at the institution of the vastly important event of the confirmation of the Abrahamic Covenant and the announcement of the son of promise, he appeared in what is called a "theophany" (cf. CCC 706–7). How did Abraham respond to this visit, and what did it foreshadow (Gen 18:1ff.; CCC 2571)? He immediately bowed to the ground and showed warm hospitality. When the Lord (even the Trinity) visits again at the inauguration of the New Covenant (notice the Trinity at Jesus' baptism; Mt 3:16–17), how do the Jews eventually respond? The Jews claim to be the children of Abraham, yet when God visits them, instead of showing the worship and hospitality of their father Abraham, they denounce Jesus as demon-possessed and try to kill him. What does Jesus then mean in verses 39–40, "If you were Abraham's children, you would do what Abraham did, but now you seek to kill me, a man who has told you the truth which I heard from God; this is not what Abraham did"?

19. According to Scripture and history, are the Jews right in claiming God as their Father (Deut 32:6; Is 63:16; 64:8)? How is the relationship of God as the Father of the Jews different from God as the Father of Jesus? Would you have clearly understood Jesus (v. 43; CCC 441)?

20. In verse 44, another "father" is brought into the discussion. Describe the three "fathers". Jesus "drops a bomb" by saying that his

---

[13] Mahmoud Zibawi, *The Icon: Its Meaning and History* (Collegeville, Minn.: Liturgical Press, 1993), 132–33.

opponents' father is whom (cf. 1 Jn 3:8–9, 12–15)? Why does he say the devil is a murderer from the beginning (cf. Gen 3:1ff.; 4:8; Wis 2:24; 1 Jn 3:8, 12; CCC 391–94, 2852)? The word "devil" means *slanderer* or *false witness*. If Jesus speaks the truth and speaks from his Father, how does his enemies' conduct prove they are sons of the devil? The Hebrew "from the beginning" means that Satan was a murderer from the days of the creation. Satan's objective is to slander Jesus, bear false witness as to his identity, and then to kill him. How are the Jews following in his footsteps (Jn 5:18; 7:1)? Can anyone expose falsehood in Jesus' words (vv. 45–46; CCC 578)?

» THEOLOGICAL NOTE: "In claiming to be children of God, the Jews appeal to certain statements in the Old Testament (cf. Ex 4:22; Deut 32:6; Is 63:16; Jer 3:4; 31:9; Mal 1:6). However, the attitude they adopt towards Jesus is in contradiction with this condition of being children of God—for that should lead them to accept Jesus, since he is the One sent by the Father. Because they reject the only-begotten Son they are acting like partisans or sons of God's enemy, the devil. The devil, because he opposes our Lord, who is the Truth, is the father of lies: by lying he seduced our first parents and he deceives all those who yield to his temptations and commit sin." [14]

21. It seems that anyone who disagreed with the Jewish leaders was accused of having a demon. Who else was likewise accused (Mt 11:18; cf. Jn 7:20; 10:20)? Jesus says those who keep his word will not see death. Since Abraham and the prophets were great and they died, what would the Jews think about Jesus' claim? What is death, and how do we explain it (CCC 365–56, 400, 1008)? Would you have believed Jesus or thought he was crazy?

» LANGUAGE DISTINCTION: Jesus uses two different Greek words for "know" in verse 55, when he says "you have not known him; I know him." The first Greek word is from *ginōskō* (γινώσκω), which frequently suggests inception or progress in knowledge, while *oida* (οἶδα) suggests fullness of knowledge. So, this passage could be translated "You have not begun to know him, and do not know him experientially; but I know him fully and perfectly and eternally" (cf. CCC 473).

22. According to verse 53, since Jesus claims to be greater than father Abraham and the prophets, what do the Jews want to know? Up to this

---

[14] Casciaro, *John*, 131.

point, has Jesus specifically stated "who" his father is? How does Jesus finally make it clear whom he claims as his Father (vv. 54–55)?

23. In verse 56, what does Jesus say about Abraham? Contrast Abraham's reception of "Jesus' day" or arrival, with the reception Jesus is granted by his opponents. Abraham lived 1,850 years earlier. How could Abraham have seen Jesus? In John 12:36–41, we are given a similar situation. Compare the two situations. Was Abraham "nonexistent" at the time of Jesus' birth—were Moses and Elijah "dead" or nonexistent (cf. Mt 22:32; 17:3; Lk 16:19–31; CCC 962)? How did Abraham see into the future (Heb 11:8–19, esp. 13; Gen 22:14)? Since John the Baptist was born six months before Jesus, how could John say "[Jesus] was before me" (Jn 1:15; cf. Jn 1:1–2, 14)? How does the "overture" explain this riddle (Jn 1:1, 14)?

» HISTORICAL NOTE: How could Abraham have seen Jesus' day? "Probably the reference is to Gn 17:17, taking Abraham's laughter as a sign of rejoicing, as the Jews commonly did. In the birth of Isaac, the messianic 'day' had its first beginning." [15] "Jewish tradition emphasized that Abraham had been shown the future kingdoms that would oppress Israel and the messianic era beyond them." [16] That Abraham saw the Messiah was not novel for the Jewish leaders, but applying it to Jesus—as in, "Your father Abraham rejoiced that he was to see my day; he saw it and was glad"—was very offensive to them.

» HISTORICAL NOTE: "Some of the Rabbis had a fanciful interpretation of Genesis 24:1. There the Revised Standard Version has it that Abraham was 'well advanced in years.' The margin of the Authorised Version tells us that the Hebrew literally means that Abraham had 'gone into days.' Some of the Rabbis held that to mean that in a vision given by God Abraham had entered into the days which lay ahead, and had seen the whole history of the people and the coming of the Messiah.

"From all this we see clearly that the Jews did believe that somehow Abraham, while he was still alive, had a vision of the history of Israel and the coming of the Messiah. So when Jesus said that Abraham had seen his day, he was making a deliberate claim that he was the Messiah. He was really saying: 'I am the Messiah Abraham saw in his vision.'" [17]

---

[15] Raymond Brown, Joseph Fitzmyer, and Roland Murphy, eds., *The Jerome Biblical Commentary* (Englewood Cliffs, N.J.: Prentice-Hall, 1968), 2:443.

[16] Craig Keener, *The IVP Bible Background Commentary: New Testament* (Downers Grove, Ill.: InterVarsity Press, 1993), 287.

[17] William Barclay, *The Gospel of John* (Philadelphia: Westminster Press, 1975), 2:35.

24. In verse 57, the Jewish leaders say to Jesus "You are not yet fifty"; how old was Jesus when his ministry began (Lk 3:23)? The period between his baptism and his crucifixion is roughly three years.

25. In verse 58, Jesus makes one of the strongest claims of his deity: "Before Abraham *was*, I AM" (cf. Ex 3:14; CCC 590, 446, 2810). According to verse 59, why do the Jews pick up stones to execute Jesus (Jn 10:31–33; Lev 24:15–16; CCC 594)? Do the Jews understand that Jesus is claiming to be YHWH, the God of Israel? Having been created and formed into a nation by YWHW; and, having been led through the wilderness and blessed by YHWH with the water and the light celebrated at this great feast of Tabernacles; and, having listened to and followed him for almost two thousand years, could anything be more singularly critical or momentous as confronting YwHW himself, face to face in the flesh? How does Paul agree with John (Jn 1:1, 14) in his description of Christ (Col 1:19; 2:9)? Would *you* have accepted this young, untrained, average-looking, backwoods Galilean, who was a self-proclaimed rabbi and critic of the current Pharisaical interpretation of the Jewish Law? Would you have recognized him as the person of YHWH himself—the creator of the universe and the God of Israel?

» HISTORICAL NOTE: "Before Avraham came into being, I AM. This and 10:30 are Yeshua's clearest self-pronouncements of his divinity. On 'I AM' see 4:26. It was very clear to the Judeans exactly what Yeshua's claim was, because they immediately took up stones to put him to death (v. 59) for blasphemy. Claiming to be God and, specifically, pronouncing God's name (as Yeshua had just done) were punishable by death (Leviticus 24:15–16 and Mishna Sanhedrin 7:5, 'The blasphemer is not guilty until he pronounces the Name')." [18] The Jews executed anyone blaspheming the Name, and Jesus had actually used I AM in reference to himself.

» THEOLOGICAL NOTE: This verse is devastating to the Jehovah's Witnesses' theology that Jesus is a "created being". So, in their booklet *Reasoning from the Scriptures*,[19] they incorrectly quote a Christian Greek scholar, A. T. Robertson, in order to attempt to undermine the historical, Christian interpretation of the passage. However, in his *Word Pictures in the New Testament*, Robertson himself writes, "I am (*egō eimi*). Undoubtedly here Jesus claims eternal existence with the absolute phrase used of God. The contrast between '*genesthai*' (entrance into

---

[18] Stern, *Jewish New Testament Commentary*, 183.

[19] *Reasoning from the Scriptures* (Brooklyn, N.Y.: Watch Tower Bible and Tract Society, 1985), 417.

existence of Abraham) and *eimi* (timeless being) is complete. See the same contrast between *ēn* [*was* God] in 1:1 and *egeneto* [*became* flesh] in 1:14." [20]

26. How does this situation remind you of the attempted stoning of the woman caught in adultery (Jn 8:1–11; CCC 574)? Were the Jews honestly attempting to carry out the Law of Moses? How do you think Jesus avoided their assassination attempt in verse 59? (The phrase "Jesus hid himself" is passive in the Greek and could be translated "Jesus was hidden.") Compare with John 10:39 and Luke 4:29–30.

» HISTORICAL NOTE: "The implications of this statement are not lost on the Jews, who seek to stone Jesus for his supposed blasphemy. *they picked up stones*: The objection has often been made that the courtyard of the Temple (cf. v. 20) was not a likely place for stones to be found. However, aside from the probable artificial unity of this lengthy passage, of which we have spoken above, the fact that the Temple was still under construction (cf. 2:20) would explain the presence of stones and other debris." [21]

---

[20] A. T. Robertson, *Word Pictures in the New Testament* (Grand Rapids, Mich.: Baker Book House, 1930–1933), 5:158–59.
[21] Brown, Fitzmyer, and Murphy, *Jerome Biblical Commentary*, 2:443.

JOHN 9

THE BLIND MAN SEES—THE SEEING MEN ARE BLIND; MORE DEBATES: WHO IS JESUS?

John 9:1–12
Jesus Heals the Blind Beggar

1. Calling to mind that the chapter breaks are somewhat arbitrary and not part of John's original composition, what do you think is the setting of this chapter and the healing of a blind beggar (Jn 7:2; 10:22)? Before meeting the blind man, Jesus has just escaped death in the Temple: How does this new event keep alive the controversy between the Jewish leaders and Jesus (Jn 9:13–14)? We are now approaching the sixth sign in John's Gospel. Why do you think Jesus heals again on the Sabbath (cf. Jn 5:8–10)?

2. John tells us that Jesus "passed by a man blind from his birth" (Jn 9:1). Who confirmed this fact (v. 20)? Imagine what it would be like to have been born blind, especially in an ancient society.

» CULTURAL NOTE: How would a blind person make a living in ancient times other than by begging or public charity? Begging was best accomplished near the Temple, where people were more inclined to help the poor and invalid (cf. Acts 3:2). Even today beggars gather at holy sites to beg from people as they come to worship God or view Jewish or Christian sites. Under the Jewish economy, anyone who misled or abused a blind person was cursed by the Law (Lev 19:14; Deut 27:18). The Jews have always considered giving to the poor an act of atonement, a good deed done in obedience to God. What does the Church teach about almsgiving (CCC 2447)? Sirach 3:30 informs us, "Water extinguishes a blazing fire: so almsgiving atones for sin." The prophet Daniel tells King Nebuchadnezzar, "Therefore, O king, let my counsel be acceptable to you; break off your sins by practicing righteousness, and your iniquities by showing mercy to the oppressed, that there may perhaps be a lengthening of your tranquillity" (Dan 4:27).

3. The disciples asked Jesus if the man's blindness was due to his sin or the sin of his parents. In the mind of the Jews, what was the cause of the man's deformity or misfortune (Jn 9:34; Acts 28:4; CCC 1502)? Did they have a biblical basis for this assumption—that misfortune was caused by sin (Gen 19:11; Ex 4:11; Deut 28:15–29; 2 Kings 6:18)? How many generations are affected by an ancestor's sin (Ex 34:7)? But how many generations are blessed by one's obedience to God (Deut 7:9)? What does this teach us about the mercy and goodness of God? Does Jesus attribute all calamities to personal sin (Lk 13:1–5)? Why was this man born blind (v. 3; cf. Jn 11:4)?

» HISTORICAL INFORMATION: Some Jews thought that an infant could sin and incur judgment while still in the womb. "It appears from this dispute, whether true or feigned, that the ancient opinion of Jews was, that the infant, from its first quickening, had some stain of sin upon it. And that great doctor R. Judah the Holy, was originally of that opinion himself, but had lightly changed his mind upon so paltry an argument. Nay, they went a little further, not only that the infant might have some stain of sin in the womb, but that it might, in some measure, actually sin, and do that which might render it criminal. To which purpose this passage of the disciples seems to have some relation; 'Did this man sin, that he was born blind?' That is, Did he, when his mother carried him in her womb, do any foul or enormous thing that might deserve this severe stroke upon him, that he should bring this blindness with him into the world?" [1]

4. In verse 4, notice that Jesus uses the plural "we". Whom is Jesus including here? Jesus claims to be the "light of the world" (Jn 8:12)—how does this claim fit in with the overall context of this story? Remember, the festival of Booths had seventy-five-foot oil-burning lamps to celebrate the pillar of fire and smoke that led Israel through the wilderness (Ex 13:21–22). What does Jesus mean by "night" and "day" (Jn 11:9–10; 12:34–36)? How has the "overture" prepared us for the continuing development of this theme (cf. Jn 1:4–5)? How is Jesus, the Word of God and creator of the universe, again going to separate the night from the day (cf. Gen 1:14)?

5. On what day does Jesus heal the blind beggar (Jn 9:14)? Knowing the earlier conflicts, why does Jesus heal on this day? What are the four steps taken by Jesus to heal the beggar's eyes (vv. 6–7)? What is Jesus' contribu-

---

[1] J. B. Lightfoot, *Commentary on the New Testament from the Talmud and Hebraica* (Peabody, Mass.: Hendrickson Pub., 1995), 3:341.

tion to the healing, and what part is played by the blind man? Compare two other healings of a similar nature (Mk 7:33ff.; 8:23ff.). Why would Jesus use such a "vulgar", unsanitary means of healing? What does the Church teach about matter used for spiritual ends (CCC 1151–52)?

» THE USE OF SPITTLE: In Jesus' day, spittle was believed to have healing and miraculous powers. Roman historian Tacitus writes of a man with a diseased hand and a blind man who came to Vespasian and asked him to apply spittle to the eyes: "The hand immediately recovered power; the blind man saw once more. Both facts are attested to this day . . . by those who were present on the occasion." [2]

» NOTE ON SACRAMENTS: What are the sacraments, and how do the sacraments work (CCC 774, 1114–16)? What are sacramentals (CCC 1667–73)? Why did Jesus use material substances to bring about a spiritual effect? Why did he use "earthy" matter such as spit and dirt for matters of faith? Jesus created matter and is both willing and able to use his material creation for spiritual ends. For example, he did not create man from nothing; rather, "The LORD God formed man of dust from the ground" (Gen 2:7). Though he has the power to heal with only a word, he often used his physical creation to facilitate a spiritual end (CCC 1504, 1116). Jesus once walked the earth in his physical body—a body made of earth, matter—and doing so he healed, forgave, and fed the people. Today, he continues to reach out to his people through matter, the Church, and the sacraments, using water, oil, bread, wine, the laying on of hands, and so on. He continues to work through the medium of matter infused with his word and the power to do things that matter alone could never do.

6. How might washing mud from blind eyes represent baptism, as the Church Fathers taught? How might the story of the beggar represent the Jewish people (Lk 1:77–79)? What did King David acknowledge about his birth and, by inference, the birth of all Israelites (Ps 51:5)? What did David desire (Ps 51:2, 6–10)? In the first recorded "gospel message", what did Peter announce was necessary for salvation (Acts 2:38)? What did Ananias command of Paul (Acts 22:16)? Is baptism necessary for salvation (1 Pet 3:21; Jn 3:5; CCC 1257)? For more on baptism, see notes on John 3:5.

» HISTORICAL NOTE: "The Fathers and Doctors of the Church have seen this miracle as symbolizing the sacrament of Baptism in which, through the medium of water, the soul is cleansed and receives the light of faith: 'He sent the

---

[2] Tacitus, *The Histories* 4:81, in Mortimer Adler, ed., *Great Books of the Western World* (Chicago: Encyclopedia Britannica, 1980), 15:292–93.

man to the pool called the pool of Siloam, to be cleansed and to be enlightened, that is, to be baptized and receive in baptism full enlightenment' (St.
Thomas Aquinas, *Commentary on St. John*, 2:87)." [3]

In the first centuries, one of the descriptions of baptism was "illumination"
or "enlightenment". Catechumens read John 9 in preparation for baptism on
the great day of scrutiny. Gregory Nazianzen (329–389) wrote, "The Word
recognizes three Births for us; namely, the natural birth, that of Baptism, and
that of the Resurrection. . . . Let us discourse upon the second, which is now
necessary for us, and which gives its name to the Feast of the Lights. . . . And as
Christ the Giver of it is called by many various names, so too is this Gift. . . .
We call it, the Gift, the Grace, Baptism, Unction, Illumination, the Clothing of
Immortality, the Laver of Regeneration, the Seal, and everything that is
honourable. We call it the Gift, because it is given to us in return for nothing on
our part; Grace, because it is conferred even on debtors; Baptism, because sin is
buried with it in the water; . . . Illumination, because of its splendour; Clothing, because it hides our shame; the Laver, because it washes us; the Seal,
because it preserves us." [4]

7. What material did God use to "form" the first man—the first creation (Gen 2:7; 1 Cor 15:45–47)? What earthly matter does Jesus, true
I AM, use to "form" the new creation (Jn 9:6–7)?

8. Put yourself in the beggar's shoes: Imagine being unable to see, then
having someone you do not know suddenly grab you, spit, and rub mud
all over your face? You gave no one permission to cover your face with
mud! Was it a prank? Now you must stumble more than six hundred
yards through crowded festival streets to the pool for washing. Imagine
the crowds and the jeering; you are causing an embarrassing scene. How
might other sinners look at a repentant sinner seeking baptism today?

9. In verse 7, the name of the pool, Siloam, is explained by John for his
non-Jewish readers. What does the word "sent" mean? Jesus literally
said, "Go to Sent." In view of the deeper spiritual meanings we often
find in John, what might the water of Siloam represent—besides baptism—and what is its source (1 Cor 10:1–4; Jn 4:14; 7:37–39)? Find a
key repeatedly used in John 8:16, 18, 26, 29, 42, and 9:4. How does
sending the man to the pool called Sent give us a hint of where one

---

[3] José María Casciaro, *The Navarre Bible: The Gospel of Saint John* (Dublin: Four Courts
Press, 1992), 137.

[4] Gregory Nazianzen, *Oration 40: Oration on Holy Baptism* 2–4, preached at Constantinople
on January 6, 381, in NPNF2 7:360.

should go for cleansing and regeneration? Who has been referred to repeatedly as "Sent"? Where do we go for cleansing and new sight? Notice other stories that bear a strong resemblance to this one (2 Kings 5:1ff.; Acts 22:6ff.).

» HISTORICAL NOTE: "This cure is done in two stages—Jesus' action on the eyes of the blind man, and the man being told to go and wash in the pool of Siloam. Our Lord also used saliva to cure a man who was deaf and dumb (cf. Mk 7:33) and another blind man (cf. Mk 8:23). The pool of Siloam was a reservoir built by King Hezekiah in the seventh century B.C., to supply Jerusalem with water (cf. 2 Kings 20:20; 2 Chron 32:30); the prophets regarded these waters as a sign of divine favor (cf. Is 8:6; 22:11). St John, using the broader etymology of the word Siloam, applies it to Jesus who is the "One sent" by the Father. Our Lord works through the medium of matter to produce effects, which exceed anything matter can do. Something similar will occur with the sacraments: through his word he will confer on material media the power of spiritually regenerating man."[5] In this pool, the priests practiced ritualistic washings, and this is where they collected the water to pour at the water libation during the festival of Booths.

10. Notice the relationship between the healing of the beggar and Isaiah 35:4–7. When John the Baptist wanted assurance that Jesus was the "sent" one (possibly to help his disciples perceive Jesus as the Messiah), what did Jesus quote to prove he was from God (Mt 11:2–5)? When he healed the lame and blind, how should the Jews have responded? Were they really expecting the Messiah to come and fulfill the promises? Do you really believe he is coming again? Would you recognize him if he came to your hometown?

11. Who noticed the miraculous healing (Jn 9:8–12)? Do you suppose the miracle was performed on the Sabbath for any particular reason? Many debated the situation—list the various speculations, including the beggar's testimony (vv. 8–9)? How did the beggar describe his healing (v. 11)? Did he need theological precision before God could show him mercy? Was he able to bring others to Christ instantaneously (v. 12)?

12. How does the deeper significance of this story echo a theme of the "overture" (cf. Jn 1:3–5, 9)? List ways this story indicates that it was told by an actual eyewitness.

---

[5] Casciaro, *John*, 136.

John 9:13–34
Dispute over the Healed Man

13. We now embark on one of the longest dialogues in the New Testament, which is obviously recorded by an eyewitness. Where did the beggar's neighbors take the beggar (v. 13)? Was this for medical or religious reasons?

14. Why do you think John waited until verse 14 to tell us the healing took place on the Sabbath? Review the earlier passage when Jesus first healed on the Sabbath (Jn 5:1–17). How do these miracles or "signs" compare? Assuming that the readers of John's Gospel were familiar with the other three Gospels, what is John telling us about Jesus with these two miracles (cf. Is 35:5–6; Mt 11:2–5)? What was the Pharisees' motive for questioning the man—were they seeking the truth or trying to ensnare Jesus? Discuss their motives.

15. Notice how John phrases verse 14: "Now it was a sabbath day when Jesus made the clay and opened his eyes." How does the verb show that Jesus "worked"? Compare this with what God did on the sixth day (Gen 2:7) and the seventh day (Gen 2:1–3). Why does Jesus "create" on the seventh day when God rested on the seventh day and made it holy (Jn 5:16–17; CCC 2173)? Could it also be that God created everything good or whole, and then man "uncreated" that perfection by sinning, so that things became corrupt, and now Jesus is recreating, or making a "new creation" (Gal 6:15; Col 3:10; Eph 4:24; 2 Cor 5:17)?

16. What does "opening eyes" represent for the Jews (2 Kings 6:15ff.; Ps 119:17–18; Is 42; Jer 5:20–22; Acts 26:17–18)? *Read the whole chapter of Isaiah 42 carefully.* Notice the messianic reference (cf. Mt 12:18–21). Notice the mention of opening "blind eyes" (Is 42:7) and "light to the nations" (Is 42:6), which is fundamental to the feast of Booths just celebrated (Jn 8:12). What is Jesus trying to do to prepare his people (Is 42:9)? Notice how many times "blindness" and "sight" are used in this chapter to represent, respectively, spiritual blindness and enlightenment (Jn 9:7, 17–20, 39–41; Is 43:8). What should the Jews have known about Jesus based on his "signs" and their knowledge of the Old Testament?

» THEOLOGICAL NOTE: "The ability to see, or the lack of it, is also used symbolically to describe how well God's people understand his purpose. Lack of vision among them is compared with blindness (Deut. 28:28–29). God will also punish his disobedient people by closing their eyes so that they walk like the blind (Isa. 29:10); their refusal to seek justice will result in their groping like the blind (Isa. 59:9–10). Yet God will enable them to regain their insight, to be filled with hope (Isa. 42:18, 43:8), to have their eyes opened (Isa. 35:5), and to enable others to see God's saving purpose in the world. This vision is not only for Israel but also for all the nations (Isa. 42:6–7). The Dead Sea community believed that the Teacher of Righteousness had been sent by God to free his people from their blindness so that they could see and understand God's purpose for them (CD2). As for the physically blind, the Temple Scroll from Qumran excludes the blind from even entering Jerusalem when it is renewed in the new age (45:13–14). But for Philo of Alexandria in the first century C.E., blindness is a figure of speech for the failure of those concerned with wealth and power to see God and his way for his people. In the Gospel of Luke, Jesus is described as quoting from Isaiah 61 to declare that the coming of Messiah will bring recovery of sight by the blind (Luke 4:18)." [6]

17. The Pharisees were struggling to understand how the blind man's sight had been restored. How complicated was the man's explanation (v. 15)? Rejecting the truth, what possible explanations remained for the Pharisees (v. 16)? Does Jesus violate the Sabbath (Jn 7:23)? Who keeps the Sabbath more perfectly, Jesus or the Pharisees, considering the fact that the greatest commands are to love God and our neighbor (CCC 2173)? Remember that "signs" are much more than simply miracles— they are pointers or signposts directing one to deeper truths. (For a review of Jesus' signs, look at John 2:11, 23; 3:2; 4:54; 6:2, 14, 26, 30; 7:31; 9:16; 10:41; 11:47; 12:18, 37; 20:30.)

18. The Pharisees are deadlocked trying to explain the miracle (CCC 595–96) and so they turn to the healed beggar for his evaluation. What do they hope he will say, and how does he actually respond (v. 17)? How does the healed man describe Jesus? Might he be referring to Jesus in light of Deuteronomy 18:15? How has his thinking developed from his earlier perspective in verse 12? What others have come to the same conclusion (Jn 4:19; 6:14; 7:40)? The Pharisees reject the beggar's explanation. Whom do they question next (v. 18)? How do the parents

---

[6] Jacob Neusner, ed., *Dictionary of Judaism in the Biblical Period* (Peabody, Mass.: Hendrickson Pub., 1999), 98–99.

respond in verses 19–23? In the Jewish culture a boy had to be at least thirteen years old to be admitted as a witness in court. According to the indications in the story, how old is the blind beggar? What conclusion are the Jews hoping to avoid? Are the Jews looking for the truth, or have they already made up their minds (v. 22)? Are all Jews included in the rejection of Jesus (Jn 2:23; 7:31; 10:42; 19:38–39; CCC 575)?

» HISTORICAL NOTE: Why were many of the Jewish people afraid to accept Jesus as the Messiah (v. 22)? "It is commonly suggested today that John, writing towards the end of the nineties, was influenced by a decision that had been taken by the reconstituted Sanhedrin a few years before. The Sanhedrin reconstituted with Roman permission in the period after AD 70 consisted exclusively of doctors of the law. One of these, Samuel the Less, reworded one of the blessings recited daily in the synagogues so as to make it impossible for 'Nazarenes' (Jewish Christians) to take part in synagogue worship. This blessing, which traditionally included a curse on the enemies of God ('let all wickedness perish as in a moment'), was revised so that the curse ran: 'let Nazarenes [Christians] and heretics perish as in a moment; let them be blotted out of the book of life and not be enrolled with the righteous.' The revision was approved by the Sanhedrin and adopted in synagogues, so that Nazarenes, being forced to keep silence when the new form of words were recited by the congregation, would give themselves away. John probably does allude to this situation when he reports Jesus as saying to the disciples in the upper room, 'They will put you out of the synagogues' (John 16:2). The same adjective, *aposynagōgos* (meaning 'excluded from the synagogue'), is used there as here in 9:22. . . . It is uncertain whether we are to understand temporary expulsion or permanent excommunication here."[7]

"*Banned from the synagogue*, here, 12:42 and 16:2; in Greek a single word, '*aposunagogos*,' literally, 'de-synagogued.' Judaism has three degrees of excommunication, though none is common today. The lightest, *n'zifah* ('rebuke'), could be declared by one person and normally lasted seven days. The next, *niddui* ('casting out, rejection'), usually required three people to declare and lasted thirty days, and people were required to stay four cubits (six feet) from him. The most severe, *cherem*, was a ban of indefinite duration; and a person under *cherem* was treated like one dead. (In the Talmud see *Mo'ed Katan* 16a–17a, *N'darim* 7b, *Pesachim* 52a.) For a family so poor as to allow their son to beg—begging charity was to be avoided as much as giving charity was to be practiced—being de-synagogued would have been a dreadful disaster. For Messianic Jews today social ostracism by family and/or the Jewish community—that

---

[7] F. F. Bruce, *The Gospel of John* (Grand Rapids, Mich.: William B. Eerdmans, 1983), 215–16.

is, being treated as if under a *cherem*—can be a cost to be counted when committing one's life to Yeshua (see Lk 14:26–33&N)." [8]

19. In verse 24, the Pharisees again bring the beggar into "court". Whom do they command him to glorify? Whom do they condemn? What is wrong with this dichotomy, this distinction (Jn 1:1, 14; 8:58)? On what basis do they call Jesus a sinner (Jn 9:16; CCC 2173)? How impressive is it that a man blind from birth is healed (v. 32)?

20. From verses 24–34, read the dialogue between the self-righteous leaders and the simple disciple of Jesus who has been healed. Who ignores the facts, suppresses the truth, and attempts to discredit Jesus (cf. Jn 12:10)? Notice the beggar's astute theological reasoning and conclusion (vv. 30–33). How does the Old Testament prepare a foundation for the blind man's claim (Ps 66:18; 145:18–20; Is 1:15)? How does the New Testament echo his claim (Jas 5:16; CCC 2582)? How does verse 27 summarize the problem? Are they *really* disciples of Moses (vv. 28–29; Jn 5:45–47)? Why do the leaders put the beggar out of the synagogue (CCC 596)?

» HISTORICAL NOTE: The Jews denounce the beggar in verse 34. "Why, you *mamzer*! (literally, 'In sins you were born, entirely!'). The Hebrew and Yiddish word '*mamzer*' is often rendered 'illegitimate son,' although technically it refers specifically to the offspring of a marriage prohibited in Leviticus 18; according to *halakhah*, a *mamzer* may not marry a legitimate daughter of Israel, only a *mamzeret*. Here the Jewish English term '*mamzer*' is used colloquially (like the English word 'bastard') to convey with precision and force the hot-tempered and insulting valence of the Judeans' response. And they threw him out, carrying out the threat of v. 22." [9]

John 9:35–41
Jesus Reaffirms His Deity

21. The blind man had been excluded from the world of sight and society as a sinner. Now, he receives his sight (physical and spiritual), and

---

[8] David H. Stern, *Jewish New Testament Commentary* (Clarksville, Md.: Jewish New Testament Pubs., 1992), 184.

[9] Ibid., 185.

he is excluded from the synagogue and Jewish life. What does he gain in this great sacrifice (Mt 10:37–39)?

22. In verse 22, what does Jesus do when he learns that the Pharisees have excommunicated the beggar (v. 35)? By what title does Jesus refer to himself (cf. Dan 7:13–14)? In verse 38, how does the beggar respond (cf. Rom 10:14)? How do the beggar and the Pharisees respond differently (v. 36)? Who has faith and good reason? Does the healed man possess "blind faith" (no pun intended) or a faith based upon reason and sufficient evidence? Can you detect the humor or cleverness of Jesus' response in verse 37? How does Jesus' answer play off the man's prior condition? How many men has this blind beggar actually seen in his life—who was one of the first he saw? Can you sense the compassion and gentleness of Christ?

23. In verse 36, what is the man's simple response? How is his faith similar to the faith of Abraham, the father of faith (Gen 15:6)? Who is the *real* son of Abraham? What makes for a true son of Abraham (Jn 8:39; Rom 4:9–17; Gal 3:7–10)? Who finds favor with God, the beggar who believes or the legalist who enforces the letter of the Law at all cost? What is the action that accompanies his belief in verse 38? How did Abraham demonstrate his belief (Gen 12:7)?

24. What is the progression of response from this blind man (Jn 9:11–12, 17, 33, 36, 38)? For whom is worship reserved (Rev 22:8–9)? Is it right to worship the "Son of man" (Dan 7:13–14; cf. Rev 22:8–9)? Does Jesus rebuke the beggar for worshipping him (cf. Jn 20:27–29; CCC 448)?

25. In verse 39, what does Jesus mean when he says that the blind will see and the seeing will be blind? What kind of sight is Jesus referring to (Mt 13:13; 15:14; Rom 2:17–25)? Compare Jeremiah 2:35 with John 9:39–41. Why are the Jewish leaders blind and guilty (Jn 15:23–25; CCC 588, 595, 1791)? What is cultivated in the heart and mind to bring about spiritual darkness, and how does spiritual blindness come to darken one's soul (CCC 2088)? What attitude should we have toward Jesus and the signs he demonstrated?

» THE CHURCH FATHERS: "For there is a twofold vision, and a twofold blindness; viz. That of sense, and that of the understanding. But they were intent only on sensible things, and were ashamed only of sensible blindness: wherefore He shows them that it would be better for them to be blind [physically] than seeing [for] 'If you were blind, you would have not sin, your punishment would be easier.' " [10]

» SUMMARY: "[The scribes and Pharisees] do not deny the material fact [of the miracle]; they only refuse to draw from it the conclusion and to say: 'The finger of God is here!' The symbolic character of the miracle is no less evident. According to the Prophets, the Messias was to restore sight to the blind. This can be understood in a proper and in a figurative sense. In the miracle of the man born blind, Jesus Christ verifies the prophecy in two ways: he gives to the eyes of the body the faculty of sight, and he illuminates the eyes of the soul by a ray of supernatural faith. He does not work either of the two prodigies without the consent and the concurrence of the interested party; and it is here above all that the symbolism is apparent. To be cured, the blind man must carry out a command the reason for which he does not know; to be delivered from spiritual blindness he must confess that Jesus is the Son of God. The lesson is easy to grasp. The Pharisees will not be delivered from their spiritual blindness unless they wish to emerge from it; but since they boast of their clearness of vision, their blindness has no remedy. Better is the condition of those who, being blind, know it and avow it. Such humble and docile people will be the first to be received into the kingdom of God." [11]

---

[10] St. John Chrysostom, *Homily on John 59*, in St. Thomas Aquinas, *Catena Aurea: St. John* (Albany, N.Y.: Preserving Christian Publications, 1995), 4:342.

[11] Ferdinand Prat, *Jesus Christ: His Life, His Teaching, and His Work*, trans. John J. Heenan (Milwaukee: Bruce Pub. Co., 1950), 2:65–66.

JOHN 10

THE GOOD SHEPHERD MAKES HIMSELF OUT
TO BE GOD! WHO IS JESUS?

John 10:1–21
The Bad Shepherds Oppose the Good Shepherd

1. Notice how the argument flows uninterrupted from chapter 9 into chapter 10. To whom does Jesus continue to speak? In chapter 10, how does Jesus change the image he uses for himself (from what he used in Jn 9:39, for instance)? What does Jesus mean by the expression "Truly, truly"?

» TEXTUAL NOTE: Jesus begins this monologue with the words "Truly, truly", or "Amen, amen". This tells us that the words that follow are extremely important. But it tells us other things as well. First, the double "Amen" always seems to refer to something that has already been said, which is now to be expanded upon or restated, but appears never to introduce a new section in the Gospel. Dodd says it is also used "to mark the transition from dialogue to monologue." [1]

Jesus continues and expands his criticism of the Pharisees. He changes the metaphor for himself from "light of the world" to the "Good Shepherd". How do metaphors and images help us understand deeper spiritual meanings?

2. We now turn to one of the most frequently cited passages in the New Testament—the passage about *Jesus, the Good Shepherd*. Before starting, it would be a good idea to read Psalm 23. There is no image woven more consistently into the fabric of Scripture than that of the shepherd and his sheep. This metaphor is used to refer to a variety of people—God, the leaders of both Israel and the Church, and the people of God. Consider the following references to God: Psalm 23; 77:20; 80:1; 95:7; Jeremiah 31:10; Ezekiel 34; CCC 753.

---

[1] C. H. Dodd, *The Interpretation of the Fourth Gospel* (Cambridge: Cambridge Univ. Press, 1955), 358.

Who wrote most of the psalms, and what was his early profession (1 Sam 16:11–13; 2 Sam 23:1)? Where was he born (1 Sam 17:12–15)? In what city would the "shepherd of my people Israel" be born (Mic 5:2)? Where was the new David, the Good Shepherd, born (Mt 2:1)? How is the Messiah foretold (Is 40:11; Mic 5:2–5; 7:14)? Without an understanding of the Old Testament (for example, Ezek 34), the story of the Good Shepherd loses much of the impact that it had for the Jewish listener.

3. In verse 1, who are the thieves and robbers Jesus refers to (cf. v. 10; Jer 2:8; 10:21; 23:1–4; Ezek 34:2ff.)? Did his listeners know that Jesus was using the analogy to refer to *them* (Jn 10:6)? How is the shepherd/sheep analogy used to describe the Pharisees' dealing with the blind man in chapter 9? Who is among the "sheep", and how did he hear the shepherd's voice (Jn 9:37–38)? How do the Pharisees treat the "sheep" who believe in the True Shepherd (Jn 10:27–29)? Why would the Pharisees consider Jesus' statement "*I* am the Good Shepherd" a slap in the face? How does the true Shepherd call his sheep (v. 3)? Why do the sheep follow him? Read Numbers 27:15–20 and look for parallels, especially the reference to "coming in" and "going out". Since "Jesus" is a Greek name corresponding to "Joshua" in Hebrew, how does this passage look forward to the Good Shepherd who is to come? Remember that John the Baptist, who "anointed Jesus", was a direct descendant (through both of his parents) of Aaron the high priest.

» THEOLOGICAL NOTE: "The 'going out and coming in' of John 10 may be compared with the similar expressions in Num. 27:17; it will be observed that the shepherd imagery occurs in both passages. A successor to Moses is being sought 'which may go out before them, and which may come in before them, and which may lead them out and which may bring them in; that the congregation of the Lord be not as sheep which have no shepherd'; cf. 27:21, 'at his word shall they go out, and at his word they shall come in.' Here there are several ideas and expressions comparable with John 10. The whole passage Num. 27:15–23 is an important one and will come up again in later chapters. We shall see that the thought of Moses as a shepherd was later amplified; and we shall suggest, too, that the action of Moses in 'putting his honour upon Joshua', or 'giving him his glory', is not unrelated to the action of Jesus [the New Moses] in giving his glory to his disciples (John 17:22)." [2]

---

[2] T. F. Glasson, *Moses in the Fourth Gospel* (Napierville, Ill.: Alec R. Allenson, 1963), 80–81. See C. K. Barrett, *The Gospel according to St. John* (London: SPCK, 1970), 306.

» BACKGROUND INFORMATION: "[Jesus] compares his work to that of a good shepherd and the society he has founded to a sheepfold. The sheepfold in modern Palestine (and it was more or less the same twenty centuries ago) is nothing more than an enclosure within a little low wall of stone where the sheep of one or more flocks pasturing in the vicinity are gathered in the evening. The animals go in and out one by one through a low, narrow door in the wall which makes it easy to count them both times. At night one shepherd stands guard alone to protect the fold against thieves and wild beasts; and toward dawn, it is he who opens the little door to the shepherds coming to claim their flocks. Each shepherd gives his own particular call and his sheep come crowding to the door and trot out one by one to follow him all day long over the heath. The other sheep wait until they hear the special cry of their own shepherd; only his voice, which is to guide them throughout the day, brings them to the entrance. Thus, flock by flock, the sheep go out by the little gate in obedience to the cries of the shepherds, who sometimes even call their favorite sheep by name: 'Hey! Whitie!' 'Come on, Beautiful!' That little door, then, is the mainspring of the fold and it alone inspires confidence. Whoever does not pass through it but climbs over the wall proclaims himself an enemy—a thief or a wild beast." [3]

4. In verse 3, who hears Jesus' voice, and who gives the sheep to the Good Shepherd (Jn 6:37–39; 8:47; 10:27–29; 17:24; 18:37)? How does God know each of us (CCC 2157–58)? Who enters by the door (v. 2)? To whom is Jesus referring as "strangers"?

» CULTURAL NOTE: "The relationship between sheep and shepherd is quite different in Palestine. In Britain the sheep are largely kept for killing, but in Palestine largely for their wool. It thus happens that in Palestine the sheep are often with the shepherd for years and often they have names by which the shepherd calls them. . . . It is strictly true that the sheep know and understand the eastern shepherd's voice; and that they will never answer to the voice of a stranger. . . . 'The shepherd calls sharply from time to time, to remind them of his presence. They know his voice, and follow on; but, if a stranger call, they stop short, lift up their heads in alarm, and if it is repeated, they turn and flee, because they know not the voice of a stranger. I have made the experiment repeatedly'. . . . Every detail of the shepherd's life lights up the picture of the Good Shepherd whose sheep hear his voice and whose constant care is for his flock." [4]

---

[3] Giuseppe Ricciotti, *The Life of Christ*, trans. Alba I. Zizzamia (Milwaukee: Bruce Pub., 1947), 437.

[4] William Barclay, *The Gospel of John* (Philadelphia: Westminster Press, 1975), 2:56–57.

5. According to verse 6, do the Jews understand Jesus (cf. Mk 4:33–34)? In verse 7, Jesus explains the metaphor to the Pharisees. John says, "So Jesus again said to them. . . ." John does not use the parables of Jesus in his Gospel as the other evangelists do. Jesus' teaching about the Good Shepherd is as close as we come to a parable in John. In the story of the Good Shepherd, Jesus speaks figuratively to teach truth through a story or common cultural analogy, which is much like what he does with his parables.

Jesus explains the teaching in two ways, with himself functioning as two separate metaphors in the image. How does he describe himself first (vv. 7, 9)? What is the second metaphor he uses for himself (vv. 11, 14)? What does the sheepfold represent (CCC 753–54, 857)? How is Jesus the door (Jn 14:6; cf. Jn 1:51)? Who or what is the flock (CCC 764–65)?

There exists an ancient rock drawing of shepherds driving their flock into a fortified sheepfold erected to protect the sheep from carnivores or marauders. Extended walls shield the narrow entrance. This Safaite rock drawing found in the desert east of Amman, Jordan, shows a sheep fence with a shepherd guarding the gate. It can be seen that the shepherd is acting as the gate, inviting the sheep in and standing between the sheep and any outside danger.

» THEOLOGICAL NOTE: "A pastoral practice exists in the Near East . . . wherein the shepherd is the door. He lies down across the door-space and is thus both shepherd and door." [5]

» HISTORICAL NOTE: The issue of "Jesus as the door" came up again about thirty years later, in 61, when the early believers were questioned about Jesus. "So the Scribes and Pharisees made James stand on the Sanctuary parapet and shouted to him: 'Righteous one, whose word we are all obliged to accept, the people are going astray after Jesus who was crucified; so tell us what is meant by "the door of Jesus".' He replied as loudly as he could: 'Why do you question me about the Son of Man? I tell you, He is sitting in heaven at the right hand of the Great Power, and He will come on the clouds of heaven' [Mt 26:64; Acts 7:56].

"Many were convinced, and gloried in James's testimony, crying: 'Hosanna to the Son of David!' . . . [The Scribes and Pharisees] went up and threw down the Righteous one. Then they said to each other 'Let us stone James the

[5] Francis Moloney, *The Gospel of John*, Sacra Pagina, vol. 4 (Collegeville, Minn.: Liturgical Press, 1998), 309. For a dialogue with an Arab shepherd regarding this subject, see Leon Morris, *The Gospel according to John*, The New International Commentary on the New Testament (Grand Rapids, Mich.: Wm. B. Eerdmans Pub., 1971), 507.

Righteous', and began to stone him, as in spite of his fall he was still alive. But he turned and knelt, uttering the words: 'I beseech Thee, Lord God and Father, forgive them; they do not know what they are doing' (Lk 23:34). . . . Then one of them, a fuller, took the club which he used to beat out the clothes, and brought it down on the head of the Righteous one. Such was his martyrdom. He was buried on the spot, by the Sanctuary, and his headstone is still there by the Sanctuary. He became a true witness, to Jews and Greeks alike, that Jesus is the Christ." [6]

6. In verse 8, who might the "thieves" and "robbers" be that Jesus refers to (Mt 7:15; 23:1–4, 13ff.; Acts 20:28–31)? Why does the robber enter the sheepfold (v. 10)? What does Jesus come to do (vv. 10–11; Jn 5:40; 1:4–5; Rev 7:17)? How is Jesus the Good Shepherd (Is 40:11; Ezek 34:11–16, 23; Heb 13:20; 1 Pet 5:4)? How does Jesus care for his sheep (Lk 15:3–7)? How does the *owner* of the sheep compare to a *hired* shepherd (vv. 11–13)?

7. Read how David risked his life for his sheep in 1 Samuel 17:34–35. How is Jesus the new David? What lion does Jesus destroy (1 Pet 5:8; cf. 1 Jn 3:8)? What characterizes true love (Jn 15:13; 1 Jn 3:16; Rom 5:8)? Who are the "hirelings"? How did Jesus lay down his life for the sheep (Mt 26:31–32; CCC 609)? In verse 12, who scatters the sheep? Who or what is the wolf (cf. Mt 7:15; Acts 20:29; CCC 2285)?

8. In verse 16, Jesus says he has "other sheep that are not of this fold". Who are the "other sheep" (Is 56:6–8; 66:18–21; Eph 2:11–22; 3:6; CCC 60)? How are they included (CCC 60, 781, 755)? How is this "other flock" to be found and evangelized (Mt 28:19–20; Lk 24:46–49; Acts 1:8; CCC 2–3)? How will the new "unified" flock worship (Mal 1:11)? How will the flock be shepherded after Jesus' Ascension (Jn 21:15–17; Eph 4:11; 1 Pet 5:1–4; CCC 874, 816)? How might the primacy of Peter be implied? How is the Chief Shepherd related to "pastors" (in Greek the word "pastor" is *poimen* [ποιμήν] and means shepherd)? Do all of the Jews accept this new hierarchy (Acts 15)? Does a "pastor" usurp or diminish Christ's unique position as Chief Shepherd?

9. In verse 16, how many "flocks" or "churches" are in Jesus' plan? How many "churches", denominations, and sects are there today? What

---

[6] Hegesippus, quoted in Eusebius, *The History of the Church from Christ to Constantine* 2, 23, trans. G. A. Williamson, Penguin Classics (London: Penguin Books, 1989), 60.

does God think of disunited and competing Christian groups (1 Cor 1:10–13, 18; 3:3–4; 11:18; 12:25; Gal 5:20, "factions"; Jude 19)? How does the Nicene Creed describe the four characteristics of Christ's Church (CCC 811, 813–14)? How does the Catholic Church understand this oneness (CCC 817–20, 2089)? How is this unity to be visibly maintained (Mt 16:18–19; 18:15–18; 2 Thess 3:14; Heb 13:17; Acts 20:28–31; CCC 838, 880–82)?

» CULTURAL NOTE: "As of 1980 David B. Barrett identified over 20,800 Christian denominations worldwide and classified them into seven major blocs and 156 ecclesiastical traditions." [7] However, the new *World Christian Encyclopedia* notifies us that by the year 2000 the number had increased to 33,820 denominations. How many are there if we include all those who consider themselves "non-denominational"? [8]

» CHURCH TEACHING: "The unity of the Church is to be found under one visible head, for 'it was to the apostolic college alone, of which Peter is the head, that we believe that Our Lord entrusted all the blessings of the New Covenant, in order to establish on earth the one Body of Christ into which all those should be fully incorporated who belong in any way to the people of God' (Vatican II, *Unitatis redintegratio*, 3). It is a Catholic's constant yearning that everyone should come to the true Church, 'God's only flock, which like a standard lifted high for the nations to see, ministers the Gospel of peace to all mankind, as it makes its pilgrim way in hope towards its goal, the fatherland above' (ibid., 2)." [9]

10. In verses 17–18, why does the Good Shepherd lay down his life—is he murdered against his will (vv. 17–18; CCC 609)? Who raises Jesus from the dead (cf. Jn 2:19–21; CCC 649)?

11. In verse 19, after Jesus announces his desire for unity and one flock, what ironically happens among the Jews when they consider his words? How are the Jews divided in their assessment of Jesus (vv. 20–21)? How does this remind you of an earlier passage (Jn 9:16, 29–33)?

---

[7] Daniel G. Reid, ed., *Dictionary of Christianity in America* (Downers Grove, Ill.: InterVarsity Press, 1990), 351.

[8] For more, see *World Census of Religious Activities* (New York: U.N. Information Center, 1989); David B. Barrett, ed., *World Christian Encyclopedia* (New York: Oxford Univ. Press, 1982), 15–18; David B. Barrett, ed., *World Christian Encyclopedia* (New York: Oxford Univ. Press, 2001), 1:10.

[9] José María Casciaro, *The Navarre Bible: The Gospel of Saint John* (Dublin: Four Courts Press, 1992), 146.

» Textual note: Jesus has seen the blindness and stubborn resistance of the Jewish leaders. They oppose him on every front, searching for something to accuse him of that will allow them to kill him. But because it is not yet his "hour", their nefarious intention fails to materialize. "In 10:1–21 we saw the Pharisees compared with thieves, bandits, and hirelings; now we are told that they are not among the sheep given to Jesus by the Father. . . . To hear the voice of Jesus one must be 'of God' (8:47), 'of the truth' (18:37). . . . In Matt 16:16–17 what enables Peter to recognize Jesus as Messiah and Son of God (the two titles involved in John 10:22–23) is the revelation Peter has from the Father. In Johannine terminology Peter and the other members of the Twelve are sheep given to Jesus by the Father, and so they hear his voice and know who he is (see also Matt 11:25). Those in John who do not hear are like those in the Synoptics who hear the parables but do not understand." [10]

John 10:22–42
The Feast of Dedication: Are You the Messiah? Are You God?

12. Notice how John includes two questions—one posed by the Jews and one by Jesus—that give us the framework for this section of dialogue (Jn 10:24, 34–36). The questions are highly focused, as Jesus approaches the end of his public ministry. Read the passages following each question to see how Jesus answers each. How do the Jews respond to his answers/explanations?

13. The setting for John 7–8 is autumn, with the feast of Booths (Tabernacles, which has been the backdrop up to this point (see notes on Jn 7:1). Where do we now find ourselves in the time line (vv. 22–23)?

» Jewish cultural note—Feast of Dedication: "The Feast of the Dedication of the Temple (Hanukkah) sets the scene for the last of Jesus' lengthy discourses before the people of Jerusalem. It provides a fitting conclusion to the theme of Jesus the Light, and in v. 28 there is an introduction to the next theme of Jesus the Life. . . . This feast, which usually falls in mid-December, commemorates the rededication of the Temple in 165 bc during the Maccabean wars (cf. 1 Mc 4:36–59; 2 Mc 1:18). It was known as 'the Feast of Lights,' not so much because of the customary lighting of the lampstands but because of its

---

[10] Raymond E. Brown, ed. and trans., *The Gospel according to John*, vol. 1, Anchor Bible, vol. 29 (Garden City, N.Y.: Doubleday, 1966), 406–7.

significance of the light of liberty, according to Josephus (*Ant.* 12.7, 7 § 325). Its observance bore a marked resemblance to that of Tabernacles, and it was sometimes even called by the name of Tabernacles (cf. 2 Mc 1:9; 10:6)." [11]

"The Feast of Dedication, in which Jews since 164 B.C.E. have celebrated the victory of *Makkabim* over Antiochus IV, king of Syria. This is the earliest mention of the holiday in all literature and the only mention of it in the Bible. . . . Antiochus, recently defeated in Egypt, expressed his frustration by attacking Judea, ruthlessly slaughtering men, women and children, and invading the Temple. There he carried off the golden altar, menorahs and vessels; and to show his contempt for the God of Israel he sacrificed there a pig to Zeus. He forbade circumcision, observing *Shabbat* [Sabbath] and keeping *kosher*, and commanded that only pigs be sacrificed in the Temple; he himself cooked a pig in the Temple and poured its broth on the holy *Torah* scrolls and on the altar.

"Syrian officers were dispatched to enforce these cruel and blasphemous decrees. . . . After Mattityahu's death his son Y'hudah (Judas Maccabeus, about whom Handel wrote his oratorio so named) assembled a number of courageous Jews and led them to victory over the Syrians, first in guerilla warfare, then later in open battle. On the 25th of Kislev they rededicated the Temple and consecrated a new altar. The *ner tamid* ('eternal light') was relit, but there was only enough consecrated olive oil to keep it burning for one day, and it would take a week to prepare more. By a miracle of God reported in the book of 2 Maccabees the light burned for eight days, by which time a new supply had been prepared. For this reason Jews celebrate *Chanukkah* [Hanukkah, the Festival of Lights]." [12]

14. It is extremely interesting that Ezekiel 34, the passage regarding sheep and shepherds, was read during the Hanukkah celebrations.[13] How does that fit with Jesus' teaching in this chapter? What was Moses' profession before "shepherding" the people of Israel (Ex 3:1)? How is Jesus again presented as the "new Moses"—the Shepherd of God's people?

15. Where was Jesus when he was teaching (v. 23)? Where else is the portico of Solomon mentioned in the New Testament, and where did the Jewish believers meet for worship in the first years of the Church (Acts 3:11; 5:12)?

---

[11] Raymond Brown, Joseph Fitzmyer, and Roland Murphy, eds., *The Jerome Biblical Commentary* (Englewood Cliffs, N.J.: Prentice-Hall, 1968), 2:445.

[12] David H. Stern, *Jewish New Testament Commentary* (Clarksville, Md.: Jewish New Testament Pubs., 1992), 186.

[13] See Brown, *John*, 1:389, 405.

» HISTORICAL NOTE: "The Court of the Gentiles [in the Temple] was enclosed on the east and the south by two famous porticos. The one on the east, which overlooked the Cedron, was commonly called Solomon's Porch. . . . This was a truly remarkable construction, worthy to stand beside the most famous porticoes of Athens and Rome. . . . It was composed of one hundred and sixty-two huge columns with most exquisite Corinthian capitals, arranged in four rows to form a triple nave. The Court of the Gentiles was the great meeting place for all who lived in Jerusalem or were passing through the city. The pagans went there to transact business just as they would have gone to the forum in their own cities. The Jews frequented it to hear the famous doctors of the Law teaching there surrounded by their disciples or disputing some question among themselves; and finally everyone was drawn to it by the thousand and one curiosities typical of so crowded a place and the news of all kinds that could be gathered there." [14]

"At this winter season when the winds sweep in from the east across the great desert, we find Jesus in the east portico of the Temple, the only one of the porticoes whose closed side would protect it from the east wind." [15] Jesus may have been in the portico to avoid the chill and winter rains. The reference to "winter" may also speak symbolically of the spiritual climate of Judea, with the cold hearts and chilly reception of the Jewish Messiah.

16. During the festival of Lights (Hanukkah), it seems that the Jewish leaders were fully preoccupied with Jesus and the challenge he presented. Are these Jews earnestly searching for the truth (vv. 24ff.)? When others were humble and wanted to know the truth, how did Jesus respond (Jn 1:49–50; 4:26; 9:37)? Why did Jesus treat the Pharisees differently from the common man (Mt 11:25; CCC 153, 544)? How does God relate to the humble sinner and the proud Pharisee (Lk 18:9–14)?

17. Does Jesus tell them "plainly" who he is (CCC 439)? Jesus has repeatedly revealed his identity and even presented four witnesses (Jn 5:32–39). What does he conclude about those who do not believe (v. 26)? St. John Chrysostom explains why they do not follow Jesus: "For I on My part have fulfilled all that it behooved a Shepherd to do, and if ye follow Me not, it is not because I am not a Shepherd, but because ye are not My sheep." [16]

How were Jesus' words and signs received, and how did they affect the people (CCC 548)? Were the Jews limited *only* to the seven "signs"

[14] Ricciotti, *Life of Christ*, 46.
[15] Brown, *John*, 1:405.
[16] St. John Chrysostom, *Homilies on the Gospel of St. John* 61, 2, in NPNF1 14:223.

presented by John in his Gospel as proof of Jesus' identity (Jn 20:30; 12:37; 21:25; Mt 4:23–25; 8:16)? Why did the Jewish leaders not accept him (Jn 11:47–48)?

18. Do verses 27–29 give absolute assurance of salvation—eternal security? What are the conditions (Mt 10:32–33, 38; Col 1:22–23; Heb 12:14; CCC 161)? What happens to the one who is incorporated into Christ, yet fails to abide in Christ (Jn 15:2–6). What state of mind and soul belongs to those who hear and follow the Good Shepherd—are they in a state of safety, peace, and eternal life (cf. Jn 3:16, remembering that "believe" is in the present, not the past tense)? What is necessary for eternal life (CCC 161)?

» THEOLOGICAL NOTE: This passage has often been used by certain Evangelical Protestants as a "proof" of their doctrine of the so-called "eternal security of the believer", or final perseverance. But B. F. Westcott, the Protestant New Testament scholar, explains the weakness of such an argument in light of this passage: "The doctrine of 'final perseverance' has been found in this passage. But we must carefully distinguish between the certainty of God's promises and His infinite power on the one hand, and the weakness and variableness of man's will on the other. If man falls at any stage in his spiritual life, it is not from want of divine grace, nor from the overwhelming power of adversaries, but from his neglect to use that which he may or may not use. We cannot be protected against ourselves in spite of ourselves. He who ceases to hear and to follow is thereby shewn to be no true believer, 1 John ii. 19. The difficulty in this case is only one form of the difficulty involved in the relation of an infinite to a finite being. The sense of the divine protection is at any moment sufficient to inspire confidence but not to render effort unnecessary." [17]

In Romans 8:35 and 39, St. Paul says that nothing can separate us from the love of God. But what does he list as those things unable to pry us from our Lord? Does he list idolatry, murder, lying, adultery, stealing, denial of Christ, or other sins? No, he lists physical and spiritual powers. No power in heaven or on earth, physical or spiritual, can separate us from the love and protection of God. But we can defy God with deliberate and willful sin and thereby bring about the death of our souls and separation from the holiness and presence of God.

St. Paul writes, "And you, who once were estranged and hostile in mind, doing evil deeds, he has now reconciled in his body of flesh by his death, in order to present you holy and blameless and irreproachable before him, *provided* [or, *if indeed*: Greek conditional, ει γε] that you continue in the faith, stable and steadfast, not shifting from the hope of the gospel which you heard" (Col 1:21–

---

[17] B. F. Westcott, *The Gospel according to St. John* (London: John Murray, 1903), 158.

23, emphasis added). Notice what a *big* word the little word *"if"* really is. St. Paul lays down a condition. What is the condition of our being presented holy and blameless before Christ?

Challenging the idea of "eternal security" or "once saved, always saved", a Baptist theologian and pastor comments: "Jesus said, 'My sheep hear my voice . . . and they follow me.' No man who is not listening to His voice and following Him has warrant for assuming that he is one of Christ's sheep. No man who is not deliberately persevering in the way of faith has warrant for assuming that he has eternal life in Christ. No man who is not living in obedient faith has warrant for entertaining the hope of everlasting salvation." [18] Read CCC 161. What does the Church teach in this regard, and what is necessary for salvation?

19. In verse 30, what does Jesus mean when he says that he and the Father are one (CCC 590)? How does this explain the unity of the Trinity without confusing the individual Persons? In whose hand are the sheep protected (vv. 28–29), and how does this help explain verse 30? How does Jesus later refer to a similar oneness in respect to believers (Jn 17:21ff.)? What do the Jews understand him to mean by "one" with God (v. 33; cf. Deut 6:4)? Why do they attempt to stone Jesus (vv. 31–33; Lev 24:16; CCC 574)? What was Jesus' "state" prior to taking on human form (Jn 1:1, 14; Phil 2:5–8)? Did the Jews understand Jesus correctly? John's readers in the first century would have retorted, "This is not a man making himself God; on the contrary, he who is God has made himself man!"

» THEOLOGICAL NOTE: This statement, "I and the Father are one", is the pinnacle of the tenth chapter of John and probably alludes to the great Shema of the Jews in Deuteronomy 6:4 "Hear, O Israel: The LORD our God is one LORD." Here Jesus affirms the unique Persons of Father and Son, confounding those who would confuse their unique identities by saying the Godhead has only one person (the heresy of Sabellianism). It also assumes a unique unity in Trinity and Trinity in unity. The Jehovah's Witnesses claim this means only a unity of purpose, not of substance. The heretics of the first centuries, especially the Arians, also denied the unity of substance between the Father and the Son. The Nicene Creed was the answer to this heresy: "true God from true God, begotten, not made, one in Being with the Father". Though there is some discussion whether this passage intends to teach the deity of Christ and the nature of God, or whether it merely emphasizes their unity of purpose, it

---

[18] Robert Shank, *Life in the Son: A Study of the Doctrine of Perseverance* (Minneapolis, Minn.: Bethany House Pub., 1989), 300.

certainly gives us a glimpse into the metaphysical depth contained within the being of God and the relationship between Jesus and the Father.[19]

Augustine said the word "one" refuted the Arians, who denied Jesus' divinity. St. Chrysostom wrote that if "their [the Father and the Son's] power is the same, so is their substance". Notice in verses 28–29 that the same power is claimed for the Father's hand and the Son's hand. Such strong statements as verse 30 laid the groundwork for the early Church in her formulation of the Trinity, defining the doctrine of one divine nature in the Trinity.

"There are no gradations in deity. It is impossible to become God or to be God up to a certain degree. Consequently the Jews wanted to stone Jesus for blasphemy when he claimed to be one with the Father (Jn 10:30–31). This statement implies that everything was created and lives through Christ (I Cor 8:6). The identification of the man Jesus with God is indeed the only way to maintain both the unity of God and justification through Christ. Two gods are impossible, and a mere human being is unable to bring salvation. The man Jesus is the ultimate revelation of God's eternal nature. The resurrection confirms that Jesus' words and deeds are in unison with God's will. The glory that belongs to the only God (I Tim 1:17) is given to Jesus (Phil 2:9–11)."[20] Therefore, Jesus is God and man and one, not only in purpose, but also in being, with the Father—unity in Trinity and Trinity in unity—one God.

20. Read Psalm 82, especially verse 6. Notice terms such as "judgment" and "darkness"; how do these relate to themes in the Gospel of John?[21] Find other parallels. Why does Jesus appeal to this scriptural passage— what is its broader context? In what way were *men* referred to as "gods" and "sons of the Most High"? Why were they called "gods", according to Jesus (v. 35)? What is Moses called (Ex 7:1)? Why should the Jewish leaders resent Jesus for asserting that he is the Son of God, when the Psalms referred to mere men as gods? If the Old Testament can refer to men as "gods" and it is not counted blasphemy, why do they consider Jesus' words blasphemy when he claims to be the Son of God? Jesus is using rabbinical argumentation and a rather overly literal tactic. What is meant by the title "Son of God" (CCC 441–44)?

» THEOLOGICAL NOTE: "If the argument 'from the lesser to the greater' were worked out in full detail, it might run thus: if it is permissible to call men gods because they were vehicles of the word of God, how much more permissible is

---

[19] See G. R. Beasley-Murray, *John*, Word Biblical Commentary (Waco, Tex.: Word Books, 1987), 174.

[20] Leland Ryken, James C. Wilhoit, and Tremper Longman III, eds. *Dictionary of Biblical Imagery* (Downers Grove, Ill.: InterVarsity Press, 1998), 606.

[21] For a good discussion of this in more detail, see Brown, *John*, 1:405–8.

it to use 'God' of him who is the Word of God. This gives us the interesting possibility (but no more) of a foreshadowing of the title 'Word' that became so prominent in the Johannine hymn that serves as the Prologue ['overture']." [22]

21. In verse 36, what has the Father done regarding his Son? Compare this with John 6:69. Both terms derive from the same Greek word meaning "holy" (*hagios*). What does this tell us about Jesus? As the Catholic Church has a methodical cycle of readings for the Mass, so the Jews had a cycle of readings for the Sabbath and feasts. Numbers 7 was read in the synagogues during the feast of Dedication, the feast that was being celebrated in Jerusalem as Jesus spoke. Read Numbers 7:1, and notice the word "consecrated". What was being consecrated? When was Jesus anointed (Acts 10:38; Jn 1:32–33; CCC 438)?

» Theological note: Again Jesus picks the most profound backdrop to make a most poignant statement. Standing in the midst of the Temple courtyard he declares that he has been "consecrated" by God (v. 36). Priests were consecrated, set apart for the priesthood (for example, Ex 29:43–46; 2 Chron 26:18). Is John alluding to Christ as the priest par excellence? Here he prepares the readers for the high priestly prayer in John 17. But even more than this, this is language associated with the Temple. The readings in the synagogue at the time of the feast were about the Temple and its consecration—the feast of Dedication was a celebration of the Temple's reconsecration after defilement by the Gentiles. "In the context of the feast of the Dedication, the word 'consecrated' (*hegiasen*) suggests that Jesus is the new temple that will replace the temple in Jerusalem. Jesus had intimated as much in 2:19: 'Destroy this temple [meaning his body], and in three days I will raise it up.' The feast of the Dedication recalled not only the consecration of the temple that had been desecrated by Antiochus Epiphanes in 168–165 B.C. but all the consecrations of the temple from the time of the temple of Solomon (ca. 940 B.C.) to the time of the temple of Zerubbabel (ca. 519 B.C.). John is renewing the Christian claim that Jesus is the new tabernacle (cf. 1:14) and the new temple (cf. 2:21 and 4:21–24)." [23]

22. In verses 37–38, how does Jesus reaffirm his claim of a singular oneness with the Father, and what proof does he again use (cf. Jn 14:11)? What is the response (v. 39)? Are the Jews Jesus addresses doing the works of their father Abraham (cf. Jn 8:39–40; Gen 18:1–2)? How are Jesus' works unique, and what should the works ("signs") have accom-

---

[22] Ibid., 1:410.

[23] Peter Ellis, *The Genius of John: A Composition-Critical Commentary on the Fourth Gospel* (Collegeville, Minn.: Liturgical Press, 1984), 174–75.

plished in the hearts and minds of the people (CCC 548, 582)? What do they actually accomplish (Jn 15:22–25)? How do you think Jesus was able to elude their grasp (cf. Lk 4:29–30; see note on Jn 18:4)? How does the "overture" prepare us for the "themes" we have found in this chapter (Jn 1:11, 18)?

23. According to verse 40, where did Jesus go after "escaping" from Jerusalem (cf. Jn 1:28)? There were two towns named Bethany. The Bethany mentioned here is the Bethany beyond the Jordan, which was about twenty miles east of Jerusalem.

24. According to verse 41, were John the Baptist's words foretelling the arrival of Jesus remembered by the Jews (cf. Jn 1:26–34; 3:22–36)? What does Jesus do that John did not do (v. 41)? What *did* John do to lead the people to believe that Jesus was the Christ—what did his words relay (v. 41)? Why should the fulfilled "words" of John and the "signs" performed by Jesus have been enough to convince the Jews (CCC 547)? How did the words of John and the words and works of Jesus affect his listeners in verse 42 (cf. Jn 2:23; 7:31; 8:30; 11:45; 12:11)?

25. List John's seven signs (Jn 2:1–11; 4:48–54; 5:1–9; 6:1–14, 16–21; 9:1–16; 11:1–47)? Why seven signs (see notes on Jn 11)? In the next chapter, we will consider the most impressive "pre-crucifixion" sign performed by Jesus. The marvel of this sign should have caused even the most sceptical to believe.

JOHN 11

LAZARUS RAISED FROM THE DEAD:
"I AM THE RESURRECTION AND THE LIFE"

John 11:1–16
The Setting for the Seventh Sign

1. So far, John has presented six miraculous signs. Now he prepares to present the seventh and final sign before Jesus' crucifixion. What is significant about this final sign? How is it a pinnacle? Considering John's emphasis on the deity of Christ (Jn 1:1) and the perfection of the new Covenant, why might it be significant that John limits the number of signs to seven? How might it demonstrate the divinity of Christ and his work?

» THEOLOGICAL NOTE: "Some numbers in biblical usage had symbolic meaning. Seven probably represented completeness and perfection, as seen in the seven days of creation and the corresponding seven-day week, climaxing with the Sabbath (Gen. 1:1—2:4)." [1]

Church Father St. Gregory Nazianzen wrote, "The children of the Hebrews do honour to the number Seven, according to the legislation of Moses. . . . I cannot say by what rules of analogy, or in consequence of what power of this number; anyhow they do honour to it." [2]

"Seven" is the number of God and divine perfection. Think of the seven sayings of Christ from the Cross (CCC 2605); the seven days of the week—God's prefect creation (Gen 2:2–3); the seven sacraments of the Church (CCC 1210); the seven gifts of the Holy Spirit (CCC 1831); the seven weeks of Easter (CCC 731); and the seven petitions in the Our Father (CCC 2759), not to mention the many other symbolic usages of the number seven in Scripture. Even the Hebrew word for oath, used by God and man for ratifying covenants,

---

[1] Paul J. Achtemeier, ed., *Harper's Bible Dictionary* (San Francisco: Harper & Row, 1985), 711.

[2] Gregory Nazianzen, *Oration* 41, 2, in NPNF2 7:379.

comes from the number seven. To swear an oath the Jew would literally "seven himself".

2. In verse 1 we are introduced to a man named Lazarus. What is Jesus' relation to this man (Jn 11:3, 5, 11, 36)? What has Jesus' relationship been with this family from Bethany in the past (Mt 21:17; Mk 11:11–12; Lk 10:38ff.)? What do we know about Lazarus' sisters Martha and Mary (Jn 11:21–27; 12:1–7; Lk 10:38ff.)? How does Mary express her devotion to Jesus (see notes on John 12) (v. 2; cf. Jn 12:1–7)? Look on a map and find the city of Bethany, which is located about two miles east of Jerusalem. Today Bethany is known by the Arabic name El 'Azariyeh, a name derived from "Lazarus".

» GEOGRAPHICAL NOTE: The city of Bethany is across the Kidron Valley to the east, up the side and around the top of the Mount of Olives. It is about two miles from St. Stephen's Gate, easily walked in about an hour. The tomb of Lazarus is still preserved. "This village may justifiably be called the Judean home of Jesus, as He appears to have preferred to lodge there rather than in Jerusalem itself (Matthew 21:17; Mark 11:11). Here occurred the incident of the raising of Lazarus (John 11) and the feast at the house of Simon (Matthew 26:1–13; Mark 14:3–9; Luke 7:36–50; John 1; 2:1–8). The Ascension as recorded in Luke 24:50–51 is thus described: 'He led them out until they were over against Bethany: and he lifted up his hands, and blessed them. And it came to pass, while he blessed them, he parted from them, and was carried up into heaven.' [Today] it is a miserably untidy and tumble-down village facing East on the Southeast slope of the Mount of Olives, upon the carriage road to Jericho. A fair number of fig, almond and olive trees surround the houses. The traditional tomb of Lazarus is shown and there are some remains of medieval buildings, besides rock-cut tombs of much earlier date." [3]

3. Why did Martha and Mary call Jesus to Bethany from Bethany-across-the-Jordan (Jn 10:40; 11:1, 18)? What was the physical condition of Lazarus (vv. 2–3)? How did Jesus respond to their polite request (v. 6)? What would you think if Jesus answered *you* by failing to arrive in time? Do you ever think he neglects to answer your prayers the way you think he should? Jesus said Lazarus was sick for what purpose (v. 4; cf. Jn 9:3; 11:40)? In the disciples' minds, why did Jesus fail to go up to Bethany (v. 8)? Imagine your sentiments if Jesus had refused to come to your aid in such a crisis situation. Was Jesus required to inform his associates what

---

[3] James Orr, *The International Standard Bible Encyclopedia* (Albany, Ore.: Ages Software, 1999), s.v. "Bethany".

he intended to do moment by moment? How does the "overture's" theme of darkness and night reemerge in this story (vv. 9–10; cf. Jn 3:1 and notes)?

4. In verses 11–13, in biblical terminology, what does Jesus mean that Lazarus has "fallen asleep" (Mt 27:52; Mk 5:39; Acts 7:60; 1 Thess 4:13–15; CCC 991)? How do the disciples misunderstand Jesus (v. 13)? Why is Jesus glad he did not arrive before Lazarus died (vv. 14–15)? Why do you think it may be significant that Thomas is mentioned here as a witness to Lazarus' resurrection (v. 16; cf. Jn 20:24–28)? Is Thomas' statement of agreement to go to Jerusalem with Jesus an act of pessimism or courage?

» THEOLOGICAL NOTE: Death is but a kind of sleep. It is a separation of spirit from body as sleep is a temporary cessation or separation of the rational, alert mind from the normal consciousness of the wakened state. Jesus modestly refers to the exercise of his almighty power, which he is soon to display in the raising of Lazarus. Jesus is not concerned; he knows his power, and he knows he can impart new life. What is more difficult: to raise the dead or to give a sinner eternal life and to imbue his mortal body with immortality?

"Lazarus was said, on account of the resurrection so soon to follow, to be asleep. 'To his sisters he was dead, to the Lord he was asleep. He was dead to men, who could not raise him again; but the Lord aroused him with as great ease from the tomb as one arouseth a sleeper from his bed. Hence it was in reference to His own power that He spoke of him as sleeping: for others also, who are dead, are frequently spoken of in Scripture (e.g., Matt. 9:24, 27:52; 1 Cor. 15:6, 18, 20; 1 Thess. 4:13) as sleeping' (St. Aug., Tract xlix. c. 9)."[4]

In the catacombs of the early Church, burial was referred to as "depositing". We do not bury or lose our money in the bank; rather, we deposit it there for later withdrawal. Such is the case with the "deposit" of God's people who have been "sealed", as St. Paul writes: "In him you also, who have heard the word of truth, the gospel of your salvation, and have believed in him, were sealed [until the day of our redemption or resurrection; Eph 4:30] with the promised Holy Spirit, who is the guarantee of our inheritance until we acquire possession of it, to the praise of his glory" (Eph 1:13–14).

---

[4] John McIntyre, *The Holy Gospel according to Saint John* (London: Catholic Truth Society, 1899), 124.

John 11:17–33
Jesus Goes to Bethany

5. In verse 4, how does Jesus view the death of Lazarus—was it out of Jesus' control (vv. 11–15; Lk 7:14; 8:49–56; CCC 994, 997)? Is there any precedent for Jesus healing the sick or raising the dead (Jn 4:46ff., 5:8–9; 9:1–7; Lk 7:11–17)? Why was he in no hurry to heal Lazarus (vv. 14–15)? What was Lazarus' condition when Jesus arrived (v. 17)? How many days had Lazarus been dead? After his crucifixion, why was it important that Jesus be in the grave only *three* days, whereas it was necessary for Lazarus to be dead *four* days (CCC 627)? What condition would a corpse be in, without formaldehyde, after four days in the heat of Israel?

» CULTURAL NOTE: "This detail [that Lazarus had been dead for four days] is mentioned to make it clear that Lazarus was truly dead [CCC 627]. There was an opinion among the rabbis that the soul hovered near the body for three days but after that there was no hope of resuscitation." [5]

"Before medicine could distinguish between being comatose and being dead people were occasionally buried alive. Jewish burial practices attempted to eliminate this grisly possibility. According to a post-Talmudic tractate compiled in the eighth century, 'We go out to the cemetery to examine the dead . . . for a period of three days. . . . Once a man who had been buried was examined and found to be alive'. . . . Marta's [Martha's] remark confirms, then, that she has given up all hope that her brother is still alive—the three-day period has passed: It has been four days." [6]

» BURIAL CUSTOMS: "The dead man therefore had a right to a ceremonial treatment that was laid down by the texts and by custom. As soon as he was dead, his eyes were to be closed—this appears as early as Genesis (46:4)—he was to be kissed with love and washed; aromatics and scents being used for the purpose. The tractate Shabbath said that it was allowable, on the day of rest [Sabbath], to do 'everything that is needed for the dead, to wash them and to anoint them with perfumes.'. . . Nard was the most usual of these scents: it was nard that Mary Magdalene used to anoint Christ. . . . The body was wrapped in a shroud, the face veiled with a *soudarion*, and the feet and hands tied with linen strips. The dead man would then be carried to the 'upper chamber' of the house, where his relatives and neighbors could come and say good-bye for the

---

[5] Raymond E. Brown, ed. and trans., *The Gospel according to John*, vol. 1, Anchor Bible, vol. 29 (Garden City, N.Y.: Doubleday, 1966), 424.

[6] David H. Stern, *Jewish New Testament Commentary* (Clarksville, Md.: Jewish New Testament Pubs., 1992), 190.

last time. He would not be left there for long. The burial usually followed eight hours after the death: in a hot climate it cannot be delayed. Coffins were rarely used. . . . Generally the dead man was carried to his grave on a kind of litter, an open bier, and all the passers-by could see him. . . .

"When the funeral procession set out, the women would go in front of the bier. 'Because,' they said, 'as Eve, a woman, brought death into the world, women should lead death's victims to the grave.' Whether there was a great deal of sorrow or not, the demonstration of it was always noisy—ritually noisy. It would have been indecent not to cry out very loud, not to throw dust upon one's hair: people even hired professional mourners [cf. Mt. 9:23]. . . . Unlike the Romans, the Israelites did not cremate their dead. . . . The dead were therefore buried. . . . The only official cemeteries were for the indigent and for strangers. A man had to be very poor indeed not to make himself a tomb: the wealthy bought a well-chosen place, or had their graves on their own land." [7]

6. Jerusalem is just over two miles away from Bethany, and many Jews come to Bethany to mourn with Mary and Martha. Why does Martha go out to meet Jesus while Mary sits in the house (v. 20)? What do they tell Jesus in verse 3? St. Augustine put it beautifully this way: "They did not dare to say, Come and heal. They did not dare to say, Order there and it will happen here. . . . These women said none of these things, but only, 'Lord, behold the one you love is sick.' It is enough that you know for you do not love and abandon." [8]

» CULTURAL NOTE: "Many of the Judeans had come . . . to comfort them at the loss of their brother. . . . Miryam [Mary] continued sitting *shiv'ah* in the house. The word '*shiv'ah*' means 'seven,' and the phrase, 'Sitting *shiv'ah*,' refers to the Jewish custom of sitting in mourning for seven days following the death of a deceased parent, spouse, sibling or child. The Greek here says only 'sitting,' which is an unusual word if all that is meant is that Miryam [Mary] stayed in the house when Marta [Martha] went out. Because it is so clear from the context that Miryam [Mary] was mourning her brother I have added '*shiv'ah*' in the text to show that her 'sitting' was in fact specifically 'mourning.' The Orthodox Jewish mourner sits unshod on the floor or on a low stool in the home of the deceased or his near relative and abstains from all ordinary work and diversions and even from required synagogue prayers, while friends visit him to comfort

[7] Henri Daniel-Rops, *Daily Life in the Time of Jesus*, trans. Patrick O'Brian (New York: Hawthorn Books, 1962), 372–75.

[8] St. Augustine, *Tractate 49*, 5, in *Tractates on the Gospel of John 28–54*, trans. John W. Rettig, The Fathers of the Church, vol. 88 (Washington, D.C.: Catholic Univ. of America Press, 1993), 242–43.

and pray with him. Both sisters observed the practice, which was not significantly different then from now; but Marta [Martha], who evidently had di-
gested Yeshua's [Jesus'] counsel at Lk 10:41 42, was now the one willing to set
custom aside and leave the house in order to meet him." [9]

7. According to verses 21–22, how confident is Martha that Jesus could
have healed her brother? Who else has the same sentiments (vv. 32, 37)?
What does Martha believe about Jesus (v. 22; cf. Jn 9:31)? After Jesus
assures her that her brother will rise again, what is her response (v. 24)?
What do many Jews believe about the resurrection of the dead (CCC
993)? What Old Testament basis was there for belief in resurrection
(Ezek 37:1–14; Dan 12:2; 2 Mac 7:22–23, 27; CCC 297; and probably
Job 19:25–27)? What has Jesus taught prior to this event (for example, Jn
3:16; 5:28–29; 6:54; 10:28)?

» HISTORICAL NOTE: The Sadducees, a powerful Jewish sect, did not believe in
the resurrection (Mt 22:23; Acts 23:8), but the Pharisees did (Acts 23:8; CCC
993). Jesus' statement would immediately bring to mind Ezekiel's prophecy of
the dry bones (Ezek 37:1–10). It was God's prerogative alone to raise the dead (1
Sam 2:6; 2 Kings 5:7), and Martha believed in the resurrection on the last day.
"In the great synagogue prayer [of the Jews] called the Amidah or 'Eighteen
Benedictions', which may go back to pre-Christian times, the second benediction addresses God as follows: 'You, O Lord, are mighty forever; you quicken
the dead; you are mighty to save. You sustain the living with loving-kindness,
you quicken the dead in great mercy, you support the fallen, heal the sick, loose
those who are bound, and keep faith with those who sleep in the dust. Who is
like thee, O Lord of mighty acts? Who is comparable to thee, O King, who
bring to death and quicken again, and cause salvation to spring forth? Yea, who
quickens the dead!'" [10] For more on the resurrection, see notes on John 20.

8. In verse 25, Jesus makes the startling and cosmically profound statement "I am the resurrection and the life." What does Jesus mean that he
is the "resurrection" (Jn 6:39–40; Rev 1:18; CCC 994, 999)? How do
physical and spiritual death differ (Mt 10:28; Rev 21:8)? How can Jesus
say we will never die when even Abraham, Moses, and the prophets
died? Notice the development of a theme earlier announced in the
"overture" (Jn 1:3–4, 10, 12–13). Who originally gave life to inanimate
earth, material matter (Gen 2:7)?

[9] Stern, *Jewish New Testament Commentary*, 190.
[10] F. F. Bruce, *The Gospel of John* (Grand Rapids, Mich.: William B. Eerdmans, 1983), 129.

» THEOLOGICAL NOTE: This is an all-comprehensive statement of resurrection and life. "Whether the gift of eternal life is conceived as a present and continuing possession ('he who is alive and has faith in me will never die'), or as a recovery of life after death of the body and the end of this world ('even if he dies he will come to life'), the thing that matters is that life is the gift of Christ—and Christ's gift to men, we know, is Himself (vi. 51). Thus He is alike the life by which men live now and always, and the resurrection which is the final triumph over death. The terms [resurrection] and [life] are correlative with the statements in verses 25b and 26a respectively, as follows: I am the resurrection: he who has faith in me, even if he dies, will live again. I am the life: he who is alive and has faith in me will never die." [11]

9. In verse 27, what does Martha confess about Jesus (cf. Mt 16:16; Jn 1:34, 49; 4:42; 6:14; CCC 439)? Why does Jesus remain a distance from the house (vv. 28–30)? How might it be significant (even symbolic) that Jesus calls Mary away from mourning—away from the weeping Jews— to come out to himself, the resurrection and the life? How does Mary respond to Jesus' call (v. 29)? What do the Jews do (v. 31)? How might it be symbolic that the Jews follow her to Jesus? Some of the Jews weep now, but what do some Jews plot to do later (Jn 12:10)?

» ACT OF FAITH: As Mary made a statement of faith in the presence of death and the impossible, so we are continually to speak and act a life of faith in Christ. The Church has provided such marvelous prayers for the faithful. Prayed around the world, the following Act of Faith affirms our trust in Christ, the Trinity, the Incarnation, the Resurrection, and God's saving power: "O my God, I firmly believe that you are one God in three divine Persons, Father, Son, and Holy Spirit. I believe that your divine Son became man, and died for our sins and that He will come to judge the living and the dead. I believe these and all the truths which the Holy Catholic Church teaches because you have revealed them, who can neither deceive nor be deceived." [12]

10. In verse 33, why was Jesus "deeply moved in spirit" at Lazarus' tomb? Why was he troubled if he knew what he was about to do? Notice that verse 35 is made up of only two small words—it is the shortest verse in the Bible—but these two words plumb the depths of God's compassion and love for men and his wrath against sin and

---

[11] C. H. Dodd, *The Interpretation of the Fourth Gospel* (Cambridge: Cambridge Univ. Press, 1955), 364–65.

[12] James Watkins, ed., *Manual of Prayers* (Rome: Pontifical North American College, 1998), 74.

death. When else did Jesus weep (Lk 19:41ff.)? What will happen at the end of time (Rev 21:4)? How does Revelation 21:3–6 repeat themes mentioned in this Gospel? Is there any correlation between Lazarus in John's Gospel and the story of Lazarus in Luke (Lk 16:19ff., esp. v. 31)?

» LANGUAGE INSIGHT: "Although direct references are infrequent (Mk. 1:43; 3:5; Mt. 9:30; Jn. 11:33, 38), wrath is an integral characteristic of Jesus himself. His anger displays his humanity and yet its objects point to his deity. He is angry at forces that oppose God.... By word and act Jesus manifests God's eschatological wrath."[13] "And Jesus wept loses some of its original force by the addition of 'and' to John's asyndetic manner, and loses something in accuracy by use of the same verb as that which denotes the weeping or crying of Mary and the Jews. [In John 11:35] the Greek word (εδάκρυσεν) means that Jesus broke into silent tears. This sign of friendship moves some, and excited criticism in others, who asked if Jesus could not have prevented his friend's death. Again giving expression to his feelings of compassion (the verb seems to suggest that Jesus felt angry with Death or the Prince of Death), he ordered the tomb to be opened."[14]

» THEOLOGICAL NOTE: "To me, what Jesus did at the tomb of Lazarus sets the world on fire—it becomes a great shout into the morass of the twentieth century. Jesus came to the tomb of Lazarus. The One who claims to be God stood before the tomb, and the Greek language makes it very plain that he had two emotions. The first was tears for Lazarus, but the second emotion was anger. He was furious; and he could be furious at the abnormality of death without being furious with Himself as God. This is tremendous in the context of the twentieth century. When I look at evil—the cruelty which is abnormal to that which God made—my reaction should be the same. I am able not only to cry over the evil, but I can be angry at the evil—as long as I am careful that egoism does not enter into my reaction. I have a basis to fight the thing which is abnormal to what God originally made. The Christian should be in the front line, fighting the results of man's cruelty, for we know that it is not what God has made. We are able to be angry at the results of man's cruelty [and the abnormal world resulting from sin] without being angry at God or being angry at what is normal."[15]

---

[13] *Theological Dictionary of the New Testament*, ed. Gerhard Kittel and Gerhard Friedrich, trans. Geoffrey W. Bromiley; abridged in one volume by Geoffrey W. Bromiley (Grand Rapids, Mich.: William B. Eerdmans Pub., 1985), 723.

[14] Dom Bernard Orchard, ed., *A Catholic Commentary on Holy Scripture* (New York: Thomas Nelson Pub., 1953), 1002.

[15] Francis A. Schaeffer, *He Is There and He Is Not Silent*, in *The Complete Works of Francis A. Schaeffer* (Westchester, Ill.: Crossway Books, 1982), 1:301–2.

John 11:34–44
Jesus Raises Lazarus

11. In verses 36–37, how do the Jews react to Jesus' anger and tears? Why is the healing of the man born blind such a benchmark (Jn 9:32)? The blind man is mentioned by the Jews (v. 37). What are the parallels between the blind man and Lazarus in relation to the "overture" (Jn 1:4)? Does anyone have any idea what Jesus is going to do with Lazarus (v. 39)? What emotion does Jesus experience again as he approaches the tomb (v. 38)? How does this demonstrate God's view of death, sin, and the creation deformed by Adam's Fall?

» ARCHAEOLOGICAL NOTE: What was the tomb like, and do we know where it exists today? The tomb is still in Bethany (El 'Azariyeh). For a rotting corpse to ascend from the depths of this tomb would be a marvelous feat indeed. "Like most Jewish tombs of old, that of Lazarus was composed of a vestibule and a burial chamber. Quarried out of soft rock, the tomb was most likely faced [facade provided] during the Byzantine period with stone or marble-work. In its present state, however, with the exception of the entrance, the tomb shows traces of changes and additions made during the Middle Ages. . . . A flight of 24 steps leads down to the vestibule. . . . Three steps connect the vestibule with the inner chamber which is a little more than two meters in size. It contains three funerary niches [for Lazarus, Mary, and Martha?]. . . . According to pilgrims of old, it was in this vestibule that Jesus was standing when he called Lazarus from the grave." [16]

As to the location of the tomb: "The memories left by Jesus in the village of Bethany attracted the faithful from the early days of Christianity. Eusebius (265–340) mentions the crypt of Lazarus and St. Jerome in 390 tells us that the tomb had a church erected over it. From then on till the time of the Crusades its authenticity can be guaranteed by documentary evidence." [17]

» SPIRITUAL NOTE: "Let us take to ourselves these comfortable thoughts, both in the contemplation of our own death, or upon the death of our friends. Wherever faith in Christ is, there is Christ Himself. He said to Martha, 'Believest thou this?' Wherever there is a heart to answer, 'Lord, I believe,' there Christ is present. There our Lord vouchsafes to stand, though unseen—whether over the bed of death or over the grave; whether we ourselves are sinking or those who are dear to us. Blessed be His name! nothing can rob us of this

---

[16] Albert Storme, *Bethany*, trans. Gerard Bushell (Jerusalem: Franciscan Printing Press, 1992), 62.

[17] Eugene Hoade, *Guide to the Holy Land* (Jerusalem: Franciscan Printing Press, n.d.), 465.

consolation: we will be as certain, through His grace, that He is standing over us in love, as though we saw Him. We will not, after our experience of Lazarus's history, doubt an instant that He is thoughtful about us. He knows the beginnings of our illness, though He keeps at a distance. He knows when to remain away and when to draw near. He notes down the advances of it, and the stages. He tells truly when His friend Lazarus is sick and when he sleeps. We all have experience of this in the narrative before us, and henceforth, so be it! will never complain at the course of His providence. Only, we will beg of Him an increase of faith;—a more lively perception of the curse under which the world lies, and of our own personal demerits, a more understanding view of the mystery of His Cross, a more devout and implicit reliance on the virtue of it, and a more confident persuasion that He will never put upon us more than we can bear, never afflict His brethren with any woe except for their own highest benefit." [18]

12. In verse 39, Jesus commands the stone to be moved from the mouth of the tomb. Why does Mary object? What does she think Jesus is going to do? In what condition would a dead body be after four days in a warm climate with no embalming or preservation (v. 39)? Since these tombs had several chambers for additional bodies to be added at a later date, the Jews would have been aware of the stench and unpleasant conditions in a tomb subsequent to the rotting of the first body. Was there any Old Testament precedent for raising a dead body (1 Kings 17:17ff.; 2 Kings 4:32ff.; 13:21)? Was there any precedent during the life of Christ (Lk 7:12ff.; 8:49ff.)?

13. What is manifested by Jesus (Jn 2:11; 11:40)? Why and how does Jesus pray (cf. Jn 12:28; CCC 2604)? Are his eyes open or closed (Jn 17:1)? How does rolling the stone away prefigure a future event (Mt 27:60; 28:2; Jn 20:1; CCC 640)? What does Lazarus hear (Jn 5:28–29)? How is this a glimpse into the future (1 Thess 4:16; CCC 1001)? How is Lazarus able to "come forth", though bound in linen wrappings—a stinking corpse restored? Imagine the scene: a tightly wrapped body moving up twenty-four steep steps, wide-eyed onlookers, the incredulity as he is slowly unwrapped, the wrinkled brows of witnesses puzzled over what has just happened and furtively glancing at each other. How is this event symbolic of spiritual reality: dead, bound, eyes wrapped, in the bowels of the earth—raised, restored, freed, eyes opened, many observers disbelieving (cf. Jn 1:4–5)?

---

[18] John Henry Cardinal Newman, "Tears of Christ at the Grave of Lazarus", in *Parochial and Plain Sermons*, bk. 3, no. 10 (San Francisco: Ignatius Press, 1987), 571.

John 11:45–57

The Sanhedrin Condemns Jesus

14. In verses 45–46, the Jews witnessing the event have two reactions. What are they (CCC 596)? Why do the Jews rush to inform the Pharisees: to evangelize them or to "squeal" on Jesus (vv. 53–54)? As a faithful Jew, what would you have done under these unusual circumstances? What more spectacular work could Jesus have performed to convince the Pharisees to believe and obey him (CCC 547–48)? Were the Pharisees determined to eliminate Jesus because they disagreed with him or because they feared the results of believing in him (v. 48)? Of what were the Pharisees fearful? Considering the fact that the Romans eventually did destroy Jerusalem and the Temple in 70, were the fears of the Pharisees justified, and were the means they would use against Jesus justifiable to save the nation (CCC 1753)? How did the Jews regard the "signs" of Jesus (v. 47)? How had Jesus predicted the fall of Jerusalem (Lk 19:41–44)? Consider the irony: What did the Jews *fear* would destroy their city and Temple (v. 48), and why was it *actually* destroyed (Lk 19:44)?

» HISTORICAL NOTE: The Romans did not tolerate political or social disruption in their provinces, and Judea was already teeming with discontent, ready to explode at any time. The Romans were prepared to squelch any sign of revolt. If Jesus had rallied the crowds around himself claiming to be their new king, the Romans would have acted decisively. They would have destroyed the Jews' Temple and even the city (Jn 11:48) and might even have decimated and deported the Jews, which the Babylonians had done centuries before. In A.D. 70, this is exactly what happened after the Jews revolted from Rome. Killing Jesus, then, did not prevent the Roman destruction of Jerusalem. In fact, in the long run, it was the cause of the catastrophe, since the Jewish nation had rejected their salvation, their deliverer, their king, and their Messiah.

15. In verse 49, we are introduced to Caiaphas, the high priest. Where else do we find Caiaphas (Mt 26:3–5; 57ff.; Jn 18:13–14)? Knowing that Caiaphas was a Sadducee and therefore did not believe in the resurrection of the dead, how do you think he perceived the news of Jesus' "signs", especially that of the raising of Lazarus? With all the eyewitness accounts, was Caiaphas able to deny the reality of Lazarus' being restored to life? Why did Caiaphas think it was all right to eliminate Jesus, even if he was innocent (v. 50)? Was Caiaphas more concerned with

justice or political expediency? How did John (and thus the Holy Spirit) understand the words of Caiaphas (v. 51)? What did Caiaphas mean to say? How did the prophecy correspond with the Good Shepherd's task (v. 52; cf. Jn 10:16)? Was the Israel of the Pharisees the same as the "Israel of God" (cf. Gal 6:15–16; CCC 60)? How is it that God can prophesy through a man who is diametrically opposed to his will and plan? How can God speak and protect his word even through a fallible man? Why is Caiaphas' office (of high priest) mentioned? What correlation might this incident have with the infallibility of the pope?

» THE CHURCH FATHERS: St. Macarius of Egypt (ca. 300–ca. 390) wrote, "For of old Moses and Aaron, when this priesthood was theirs, suffered much; and Caiphas [Caiaphas], when he had their chair, persecuted and condemned the Lord. . . . Afterwards Moses was succeeded by Peter, who had committed to his hands the new Church of Christ, and the true priesthood." [19]

16. In verse 54, John mentions the city of Ephraim just north of Jerusalem and Jericho. Why did Jesus go to Ephraim? Earlier the Jews had wanted to kill Jesus (Jn 7:1); how has that desire intensified with great resolve (vv. 53, 57)? How would Caiaphas and others be reminded of all this later (Acts 4:5ff.)?

17. In verse 55, John informs us how close we are to the crucifixion of Jesus (cf. Jn 12:12–15; 13:1–2; 18:1–3, 12). We must remember that from this point on the events described occur in the last few days before Jesus' crucifixion. Notice how John marks the years of Jesus' earthly ministry of three years (Jn 2:13; 6:4; and now 11:55). What earlier incident and teaching might John be reminding us of by mentioning again "Now the Passover of the Jews was at hand" (Jn 6:4, 39, 52–58)? How is John 6 related to the Passover (Ex 12; Jn 1:29; 1 Cor 5:7)? What was to be eaten at the Passover? What was to be eaten in John 6?

» HISTORICAL NOTE: If the first of the three Passovers mentioned by John fell in A.D. 28, "forty-six years" after Herod began the rebuilding of the Jerusalem Temple (2:20), this third Passover (Jn 11:55) would have been in the year of A.D. 30.

---

[19] St. Macarius of Egypt, *Homily* 26, in Joseph Berington and John Kirk, comps., *The Faith of Catholics*, ed. T. J. Capel (New York: F. Pustet & Co., 1885), 2:22. For more on this, see Stephen K. Ray, *Upon This Rock: St. Peter and the Primacy of Rome in Scripture and the Early Church* (San Francisco: Ignatius Press, 1999), 204, 293.

18. Jesus could not die until "his hour" had arrived and he had transformed the Passover into the eucharistic meal, finishing the work ordained from the foundation of the world (Jn 13:1–4; Lk 22:14ff.). In
keeping with his established pattern of changing the *old* into the *new* (for
example, reinterpreting the Law of Moses in the Sermon on the Mount,
reinterpreting the "bread from heaven" from manna to himself, changing the water into wine), how was this transformation of the Passover
anticipated in the "overture" (Jn 1:11, 17)?

» HISTORICAL NOTE: "From this moment the death of the Son of God is
decreed by the chief Council of the Jews. They will choose a suitable time and
make show of legal forms, but the matter is decided. His hour was not to sound
till the Pasch [Passover] of which he was to be the Lamb. He therefore retired
from Jerusalem to spend the remaining weeks away from hostile maneuvers.
The city of Ephrem to which he went is probably the present village of Et-
Tayibeh, about 12 miles NE. of Jerusalem on the edge of the wilderness of
Bethaven. Early pilgrims to the Pasch were already beginning to move [toward
Jerusalem for Passover]. There was much talk about Jesus, especially because the
chief priests and Pharisees had given orders that his whereabouts should be
reported in view of having him arrested."[20]

» NOTE ON PURIFICATION: Defilement disqualified a man from keeping the
Passover (Lev 7:21; Num 9:6), and the purification rites would frequently take
up to a week to perform. The need for purification reminds one of the need for
sacramental confession prior to partaking of the eucharistic sacrifice, for those
who have unconfessed grave sins. Confession is simpler and more effective than
Jewish ritual cleansing. In the *Didache* (ca. 60–100), one of the earliest Christian
documents, we read, "Assemble on the Lord's Day, and break bread and offer
the Eucharist; but first make confession of your faults, so that your sacrifice may
be a pure one. Anyone who has a difference with his fellow is not to take part
with you until they have been reconciled, so as to avoid any profanation of your
sacrifice."[21] Again, we see the continuity between the Jewish covenant and the
new and eternal covenant in the Catholic Church.

The Jews were looking around for Jesus as "they stood in the temple", having
arrived in Jerusalem early to "purify themselves". "The necessity of ceremonial
purification (e.g. after contact with a corpse) before keeping the Passover is laid
down in Num. 9:6ff. Josephus confirms that pilgrims came up about a week
before Passover [*Jewish War*, 6.290] and indicates that they spent the days in

---

[20] Orchard, *Catholic Commentary*, 1002.

[21] *Didache* 14, in *Early Christian Writings*, trans. Maxwell Staniforth (New York: Penguin
Books, 1968), 197.

Jerusalem before the feast undergoing the appropriate purificatory rites (*Jewish War*, 1.229)." [22]

19. Consider the great dilemma the average Jewish person faced (CCC 596): the ruling council of the Sanhedrin gave orders—binding upon the people—to turn Jesus in to the authorities; yet, many believed Jesus was the Prophet, the Messiah (v. 57)! What would you have done? How do we summarize John 11 (see CCC 994)?

---

[22] Bruce, *John*, 253.

JOHN 12

ANOINTING JESUS—THE TRIUMPHAL ENTRY INTO JERUSALEM

John 12:1–11
Jesus Anointed at Bethany

1. We must again remember that John's Gospel did not originally have chapter/verse breaks; it was one continuous narration. In the original language, the Greek word ουν ("therefore") is used in John 12:1. When we see the word "therefore", we must ask ourselves what it is "there for". In verse 1, why did Jesus "then" or "therefore" go to Bethany again (Jn 10:39–40; 11:53–54)?

2. According to verse 2, what was Lazarus' condition after having been raised from the dead? How do you think Jesus was received in the surrounding area after raising Lazarus from the dead? Imagine the stories Lazarus could tell. Why are these "stories from beyond" not included in the Bible? What other experiences from "beyond" are not recounted (cf. 2 Cor 12:1–5)?

3. Read verse 3 and visualize the situation in your mind: Jesus arrives after many miles of walking on dusty, manure-strewn footpaths, presumably with very dirty feet. Mary approaches Jesus and kneels down at his feet. She pours perfume on his feet, and then *she wipes his feet with her hair*. This act was all the more striking since a Jewish woman never let her hair down in public, which was taken to be a sign of loose morals (cf. Num 5:12, 18). Imagine if someone did this at a dinner party today! Would a man feel uncomfortable or embarrassed by such an act of affection today? Would you consider the woman a little strange? Do we have this kind of regard for our Lord? Read the other stories about this or similar events (Mt 26:6ff.; Mk 14:3ff.; Lk 7:36ff.).

» THE CHURCH FATHERS: "That she did this on another occasion in Bethany is not mentioned in Luke's Gospel, but is in the other three. Matthew and Mark say that the ointment was poured on the head, John says, on the feet. Why not suppose that it was poured both on the head, and the feet? Matthew and Mark introduce the supper and the ointment out of place in the order of time. When they are some way farther on in their narration, they go back to the sixth day before the Passover."[1]

4. Notice the earlier mention of Mary (Jn 11:2). How were the sisters Mary and Martha alike and different (Lk 10:38ff.)? What is really important in life? What is the difference between *good, better,* and *best* when dealing with spiritual matters?

» HISTORICAL NOTE: The perfumed oil that Mary used to wash Jesus' feet was very costly and precious. "But the New Testament *nardo pistikē,* 'precious (spike)nard' (Mk. 14:3; Jn. 12:3), is probably the *Nardostachys jatamansi* of India (Himalayas), a very expensive import for Roman Palestine."[2] The pure nard was a fragrant oil prepared from the roots and stems of an aromatic herb from northern India. It was an expensive perfume, imported in sealed alabaster boxes or flasks that were opened only on special occasions. Mary's lavish gift (a pint) expressed her love and thanks to Jesus for himself and for restoring Lazarus to life. The cost of the pure nard can be calculated this way: A Roman denarius is roughly equivalent to a day's wage (Mt 20:2); so, if an average wage is $100 a day, the cost of Mary's perfume would be $30,000. Perfume was often used as a financial investment due to size, easy transportability, and storage. It was in great demand and easily negotiated in the marketplace. This spikenard perfume may have represented Mary's life savings. The word used to describe the nard, "pure", is from the Greek word *pistis,* which is the word for "faith".

5. What virtue is demonstrated by Mary's extravagance (1 Cor 13:3, 13; Mt 10:37–39; Mk 10:29–31)? What do you own worth almost a year's salary? Would you be willing to pour it out or give it away for love of Jesus? If you were on trial for being a Christian and loving Jesus, would there be enough evidence to convict you? Read Matthew 19:16–26. How would one demonstrate that he loves the Lord his God with all his heart, soul, mind, and strength? Does this mean literally that we must give everything away or that we are to be detached from worldly possessions and not hoard treasures on earth (Mt 6:19–21; 1 Thess 4:11–12;

[1] St. Augustine, *De Con. Evang.* 2, 79, in St. Thomas Aquinas, *Catena Aurea: St. John* (Albany, N.Y.: Preserving Christian Publications, 1995), 4:396.

[2] J. D. Douglas, ed., *New Bible Dictionary* (Downers Grove, Ill.: InterVarsity Press, 1994), 236.

CCC 2424)? What is the "root" of all evil, and where should our love really be placed (1 Tim 6:8–10; CCC 2536, 2544–45)?

6. In verse 2, what was Jesus doing when Mary anointed him; what position had he taken at the supper table?

» CULTURAL NOTE: "In describing meals that Jesus participated in, the Gospels state that he reclined (at table). This expression indicates that in the Palestine of Jesus' day the Greco-Roman custom of reclining at formal meals had become widespread. . . . On couches placed around a large table (or three tables placed to form an open-ended rectangle), guests and host reclined on the left elbow and ate with the right hand, body diagonal to the couch and feet extending off the back. Usually three persons reclined on one couch. The reclining posture at table explains how Luke could describe the woman with the ointment as standing behind Jesus while anointing his feet (Luke 7:36–38). It also explains how, in the Gospel of John, Jesus could wash the disciples' feet as they ate (13:5) and how the beloved disciple could recline on Jesus' breast (13:23)."[3]

7. In the Song of Solomon the bride recalls, "While the king was at his table, my perfume gave forth its fragrance" (1:12, NASB). The Greek words used by St. John are almost identical to those used in the Septuagint, the Greek translation of the Old Testament. Knowing John's use of the Old Testament to reveal who Jesus is, why might he have used the language from the Song of Solomon 1:12 to tell us about Mary's action and the identity of Jesus (cf. Lk 1:30–33; Jn 12:13)?

8. What was the significance of perfumed oil, and for what was it used (Ex 30:22ff.; 1 Sam 16:12; Ps 89:20; Mk 14:8; 16:1; CCC 1241, 783)? What does "Messiah" mean (CCC 436, 695; Jn 1:41)? What might Mary be indicating about Jesus by her extravagance? Does she recognize Jesus in all his kingly glory, though now veiled? Jesus is about to enter the city of David riding on a donkey (Zech 9:9). Is a king usually anointed as king before or after coming into his kingdom?

» THEOLOGICAL NOTE: John continues to draw on Old Testament parallels to explain creatively who Jesus is. We have seen him portrayed as the new Moses—the prophet. In this chapter, Jesus is depicted as the new David—the king. He is the Good Shepherd, as young David was, and is spoken of in kingly terms at his anointing. And he is called the king of Israel as he enters Jerusalem.

---

[3] Paul J. Achtemeier, ed., *Harper's Bible Dictionary* (San Francisco: Harper & Row, 1985), 617.

Later in the Gospel he will be portrayed as the new high priest, wearing a seamless robe and spreading his arms to his Father in the high priestly prayer. Thus, he fulfills the three great offices of the Old Covenant economy: prophet, priest, and king (CCC 783).

Jesus filled the three authoritative offices of prophet, priest, and king. (See section on John 12:20–36, p. 246). David, as an Old Testament type or prefigurement of Christ, had been a prototype of one man filling all three offices. David was the king of Israel (2 Sam 5:4; cf. Lk 3:23); he was a prophet (2 Sam 23:2–7; Acts 2:29–30); and he performed the tasks of the priest (he blessed, offered, sacrificed, and so on) dressed in priestly garb (2 Sam 6:12–19; notice what he was wearing in v. 14, cf. 1 Sam 2:18, 28). Jesus is the final and complete fulfillment of the sacred offices of prophet, priest, and king, as John reveals throughout his Gospel.

9. Regarding "feet," note Isaiah 52:6–7 ("How beautiful upon the mountains are the feet of him who brings good tidings"). What is John telling us about Jesus by the mention of Mary's treatment of his feet—he who has come to bring good tidings? What did the Old Testament say about the existence of the poor (Deut 15:11; CCC 2449)? What does Jesus say about Mary's gift of love (Mt 26:12; Mk 14:6–9; Jn 12:7)?

10. In Jesus' eyes the extravagant love poured out in utter abandon was a rare and precious thing—more precious than the nard itself. In verses 4–5, which disciple objects to the extravagant display of love and devotion? Is he interested in the poor people or something else (v. 6; Mt 26:15)? Notice another place where Judas is described as the treasurer for Jesus and the disciples (Jn 13:29). What does Jesus say about the masters that men serve (Lk 16:13; CCC 2424)? Consider: Mary gave up great wealth for Jesus; Judas gave up Jesus for a little wealth. By refusing to give our best and all to Jesus, how do we join ranks with Judas? A wise man once said, "A man is no fool to give up what he cannot keep, to gain that which he cannot lose."

The phrase "not . . . concerned about the poor" (v. 6, NASB) is the same phrase used in John 10:13 (NASB), where the *hireling* is "not concerned about the sheep". What does this tell us about Judas? A successor had to be found to fill what office (Acts 1:15–26)?

» THEOLOGICAL NOTE: In verses 7–8, Jesus contrasts the extravagance in view of his burial and the giving of alms to the poor. The contrast between giving to Jesus and giving to the poor "fits in well with rabbinic theology. There are two classifications of 'good works': those that pertain to mercy, e.g., burial; those that pertain to justice, e.g., almsgiving. The former were looked upon as more perfect than the latter."[4] Therefore, anointing Jesus for burial was more perfect than selling the nard to give alms to the poor. Judas chose the lesser of the two, for he was unaware, whereas Mary seemed to know, of Jesus' impending death.

» CONTEXTUAL STUDY: Notice another foot-washing story in the next chapter, in which Jesus humbles himself to wash the feet of the disciples (Jn 13:5–17). "The repetition of 'feet' may be a way of stressing Mary's willing acceptance of the lowliest place. R. H. Lightfoot reminds us that Jesus' words to Peter in connection with the feet washing imply that the washing of the feet 'is equivalent to a complete washing' (13:9f.). He adds, 'possibly the same principle may hold good here. If so, the reader is invited to see in Mary's action a symbolical embalming of his body for burial, as though he were already dead."[5]

11. In verse 1, why do the crowds leave Jerusalem and travel almost two miles to Bethany? Why are there great crowds in Jerusalem (cf. Deut 16:1; Lk 2:41–43)? John's seventh and greatest sign of Jesus' divinity is the raising of Lazarus from the dead. What do the chief priests want to do with the evidence of Lazarus' restoration to life (v. 10)? With all their professed concern about the Law of God, what are they really concerned about: (1) the truth (Jn 8:45); (2) obedience to God's Law (for example, Ex 20:13); (3) the prophesies and proof of the Messiah present among them (Jn 12:37); or (4) their own selfish interests (Jn 11:48; 12:10–11)? What is their real motivation (v. 11; Mt 27:18; Jn 11:48)? How are many of the Jews responding to Jesus (v. 11)? How do their actions potentially affect the Jewish leaders and Temple worship?

John 12:12–19
Triumphal Entry into Jerusalem

12. Standing at Dominus Flavit (Latin for "Jesus wept") on the western slope of the Mount of Olives, looking out over Jerusalem, one can image that it was here while riding on the ass acquired at Bethphage that Jesus wept over Jerusalem (Lk 19:28–44). Read the parallel passages in

---

[4] Raymond E. Brown, ed. and trans., *The Gospel according to John*, vol. 1, Anchor Bible, vol. 29 (Garden City, N.Y.: Doubleday, 1966), 449.

[5] Leon Morris, *The Gospel according to John*, The New International Commentary on the New Testament (Grand Rapids, Mich.: Wm. B. Eerdmans Pub., 1971), 577.

the other Gospels (Mt 21:1ff.; Mk 11:1ff.; Lk 19:28ff.). The cry went up that Jesus, who had raised Lazarus from the dead, was coming to Jerusalem. What does the crowd do (v. 13)? Why do they cry out to honor Jesus and glorify God (Lk 19:37)? Do they expect a suffering servant (Is 53:1–12) or a triumphant king to release them from Roman oppression (Jn 6:15; 18:35–36)? What reaction do the Jewish leaders have (v. 19)? Why does Jesus weep over Jerusalem (Lk 19:41–44)?

» HISTORICAL NOTE: "Passover, Pentecost and Tabernacles were the three compulsory festivals of the Jews. To the Passover in Jerusalem Jews came from the ends of the earth. . . . At such a time Jerusalem and the villages round about were crowded. On one occasion a census was taken of the lambs slain at the Passover Feast. The number was given as 256,000. There had to be a minimum of ten people per lamb; and if that estimate is correct it means that there must have been as many as 2,700,000 people at that Passover Feast. Even if that figure is exaggerated, it remains true that the numbers must have been immense." [6] John tells us that "a great crowd who had come to the feast" gathered palm branches and "went out to meet [Jesus]". Imagine such a large throng of people marching into Jerusalem with Jesus.

13. What other festival utilized palm branches (Lev 23:40; Jn 7:2)? To what future event might the use of palms look forward (Rev 7:9–10)? What does the triumphal entry into Jerusalem represent, and how is it celebrated each year in the Church today (CCC 560, 570)?

» BIOLOGICAL NOTE: "The Date Palm is one of the Holy Land's most ancient fruit trees. Its significance in the cultural and agricultural life of the Bible can be measured by the numerous times its fruit is mentioned, and the people and places that bear its Hebrew name *tamar*—unquestionably identified with date palm. In Judges (4:5) Deborah sat under the palm tree, which served in poetry as a symbol of upright stature, justice and righteousness. Its leaves are among the 'four species' for the Feast of Tabernacles (Nehemiah 8:15), and it continues to symbolize holiness and resurrection in Christian worship. . . . The Maccabees (second century BC) used the palm as the emblem of victory on their coins, while Roman coins of the first century AD depicted a woman seated under a palm as an image for the captured Judea." [7] "From the time of the Maccabees palms or palm-branches had been used as a national symbol. Palm-branches figured in the procession which celebrated the rededication of the temple in 164 BC (2 Macc. 10:7). . . . On this occasion, then, palm-branches

---

[6] William Barclay, *The Gospel of John* (Philadelphia: Westminster Press, 1975), 2:115.
[7] Michael Zohary, *Plants of the Bible* (New York: Cambridge Univ. Press, 1982), 60.

may have signified the people's expectation of imminent national liberation, and this is supported by the words with which they greeted our Lord."[8] The palm branch was used during the festival of Tabernacles or Booths (Lev 23:19ff.; Jn 7:2; see comments on Tabernacles in the section on John 7).

14. Psalm 118 was part of the Great Hallel hymns, Psalms 113–18, which were memorized and sung at the Jewish festivals (cf. Mt 26:30). Psalm 118 was on the mind and lips of the Jews at this time. Read Psalm 118:19–29 and notice the messianic themes: cornerstone (1 Pet 2:4–10), entering through the gates (Rev 22:14; Jn 10:7–9), light (Jn 8:12), festival sacrifice on the altar (Jn 1:29; 1 Cor 5:7). Israel was ruled by the Romans and awaited a Messiah—a national deliverer. Read Psalm 118:10–14. Why did the Jews see Jesus as a political liberator from the Romans rather than a spiritual savior from sin? Since Moses had delivered Israel from Egypt, what was the new Moses expected to do (Ps 24:2–10; Jn 6:15)? How might the mention of Jesus as the "King of Israel" have been anticipated and predicted by John 12:2–3 (cf. Song 1:12)? Who proclaimed this from the start (Jn 1:49), and how had the secular authorities responded then (Mt. 2:1–21)? ("Hosanna" means "Lord, save" or "Give victory now" and became an exclamation of praise, cf. Ps 118:25.) On what other occasion did the people speak of Jesus as the king (Jn 6:15)?

15. In verses 17–18, why do the crowds swarm to Jesus, and who witnesses his signs and miracles? How do the Pharisees respond (Jn 12:19; cf. Jn 12:10–11)?

16. Why did Jesus ride into Jerusalem on a donkey's colt, and what prophecy did this fulfill (Zech 9:9; Mt 21:1–7)? In keeping with the theme of royalty in chapter 12, how does John's citing of Zechariah tell us who and what Jesus is? When did the disciples figure out that Jesus' entry into Jerusalem was a fulfillment of prophecy (v. 16; Jn 7:39; 14:26)? What kind of colt did Jesus ride (Mk 11:2)? An old farmer once commented on this verse, "Jesus must have been quite a man. I once climbed upon a donkey 'on which no man had ever sat', and when I hit the ground a moment later, it was *still* a donkey on which no man had ever sat!"

---

[8] F. F. Bruce, *The Gospel of John* (Grand Rapids, Mich.: William B. Eerdmans, 1983), 259.

John 12:20–36
Greeks Seek Jesus; His Death Foretold

17. According to John 12:20, did only Jews come to Jerusalem to worship (Acts 8:27; Is 56:7)? Whenever we encounter Andrew in St. John's Gospel, what is he doing (vv. 20–22; Jn 1:40–42; 6:8)? How does this seem like a sign or turning point for Jesus (v. 23)? Jesus has often said his hour, or the "appointed time", has not yet come (2:4; 7:30; 8:20). What does he say now (vv. 23, 27; 13:1; 17:1)? What will soon happen (Jn 19:18)? How did the Greeks fulfill the words of the Jewish leaders (v. 19)? Jesus had been visited by an envoy of Gentiles at his birth (Mt 2:1–12), and now another group of Gentiles approaches him days before his death. How might this be significant (Is 42:1)? It seems these Gentiles are proselytes to Judaism, since they come to worship at the feast (v. 20). Contrast the Greeks' response to Jesus with that of the Jewish leaders. Would you have sought Jesus out?

18. What happens to a grain of wheat when it falls into the ground and is buried? What is required of those who hope to achieve eternal life (Mk 8:34ff.; Lk 9:23ff.; Mt 10:38–39; Rom 2:5–7; Phil 3:10–14; CCC 161)? How does this passage reflect our prayer life (CCC 2731)?

» THEOLOGICAL NOTE: Jesus foretells that he will be the grain of wheat that must die to produce fruit. When the wheat dies in the ground, mysteriously life is released from its shell and it produces thousands of other grains containing its same nature. Through the death, burial, and Resurrection of Jesus many sons are born unto God, inheriting eternal life and participating in the divine nature (2 Pet 1:4).

» JEWISH BACKGROUND: An interesting area of study is the history of the feast of Pentecost in the Old Testament. This feast, though now a celebration of the anniversary of the giving of the Law on Mount Sinai, was originally a harvest celebration—rejoicing in the first fruits of the harvest (Ex 23:16; Lev 23:10). This festival was to take place on the fiftieth day after Passover (Pentecost meaning "fiftieth day"). Jesus now refers to himself as the grain of wheat that must fall into the ground and bear much fruit. Corresponding to the feast of the Harvest (Pentecost), Jesus was killed and buried at Passover, and fifty days later at Pentecost, as the Jews were celebrating the feast of the Harvest, a great harvest was reaped by the Holy Spirit. We read in Acts 2:1, "When the day of Pentecost had come, they were all together in one place." The Holy Spirit fell upon the 120 in the upper room, and shortly after Peter preached the Gospel and "those who received his word were baptized, and there were added that day about three thousand souls" (Acts 2:41). Interestingly enough, three thousand were executed on the first Pentecost at Mount Sinai (Ex 32:28). On the new Pentecost three thousand would be added. The first fruits of the harvest were reaped on Pentecost as the feast of the Harvest was celebrated in Jerusalem. Jesus died as a "grain of wheat", and then, fifty days later, the great harvest began.

19. What does verse 27 tell us about the time frame of these events and its relation to the Passion? How do the other Gospels portray Jesus' "troubled soul" (cf. Mt 26:36–46; Mk 14:32–42; Lk 22:40–46)? Did Jesus know he was going to die—and willingly choose to do so—or was he an unwilling victim of a plan gone awry (Jn 2:19–22; 10:17–18; CCC 536, 606)? Is he going to the Cross as a victim or as a conquering hero? How does the Father respond to Jesus' willingness to lay down his life (v. 28; CCC 434; cf. Mt 3:17; 17:5)? We are told that God is love (1 Jn 4:8). How does the sacrificial love of God manifest itself in Jesus' willingness to give up his life for sinners (Rom 5:8; CCC 1825)? Why did the Father speak in verse 28 (cf. v. 30)?

» THEOLOGICAL NOTE: The rabbis were convinced that the Spirit of prophecy had been withdrawn from Israel and that now they could receive only the "daughter of a voice", or an echo of God's voice, which was inferior to prophecy. God no longer spoke to men. However, in the Gospels we hear, not just the voice of a prophet, but the direct voice of God from heaven (Mt 3:17; 17:5), as Moses and the people of Israel had at Mount Sinai (Ex 19:18ff.; Deut 5:22–24). Now God speaks to Israel with his own voice from heaven and in his Son—the Word (Heb 1:1–2; Jn 1:1, 14).[9]

» PROPHET, PRIEST, AND KING: We have already seen Jesus portrayed as filling the Jewish offices of prophet, priest, and king. We now see this again through the audible voice of the Father from heaven. In the New Testament the Father speaks audibly from heaven three times to confirm the Son. Each occurrence is a witness to the divine Person and commission of Jesus. The Jews expected the Messiah to fulfill all the three great offices of prophet (Deut 18:18), priest (Ps 110:4; Heb 5:1–10), and king (Zech 6:13; Is 9:6–7). The Father confirmed his Son in all three offices. First, the voice at his baptism (Mt 3:17) established the Son as an honored priest anointed by John the Baptist, who was appropriately a descendant of Aaron the high priest. Second, on the Mount of Transfiguration the Son is confirmed as a prophet with the Father's words "Listen to him" (Mt

---

[9] See Morris, *John*, 596.

17:5; Deut 18:15). And third, in our present passage, Jesus is shown to be the new King David (cf. the Good Shepherd of John 10) and enters Jerusalem as the king of Israel in John 12; he is confirmed as the king of Israel in glory with the palms of victory waving (vv. 15, 28).[10]

20. In verse 31, we learn that the "ruler of this world" shall be cast out. Who is the "ruler of this world" (2 Cor 4:4; Eph 2:1–2; 6:10ff.; 1 Pet 5:8; CCC 550, 2851–53)? What will Jesus' death bring about (1 Jn 3:8; CCC 394)? What does Jesus mean in verses 32–33 when he says that he will be "lifted up" and "draw all men" to himself (Is 52:13–14; 53:1–12; Jn 3:14; 8:28; Num 21:9; CCC 662, 786, 2795)? Jesus explains what all of this anticipates (v. 33).

» OLD TESTAMENT FOUNDATION: "Behold, my servant shall prosper, he shall be exalted and lifted up, and shall be very high. As many were astonished at him—his appearance was so marred, beyond human semblance, and his form beyond that of the sons of men" (Is 52:13). The similarity of language and structure makes it clear that Jesus is referring to Isaiah 52:13, when he speaks of being "lifted up" on the cross. This, along with Isaiah 53, is clearly a reference to the crucifixion. Jesus accepted this ignominious death and, through it, glorified the Father. To Jesus, this was not a defeat but the ultimate act of love and victory. He was no vanquished foe. He was the honored and victorious Son of God, conquering the enemy and destroying "the god of this world".

21. How is it that a "conquering king" could die on the cross and consider it a victory? In verse 34, the crowd challenges Jesus: "We have heard from the law that the Christ remains for ever. How can you say that the Son of man must be lifted up?" (cf. Ps 110; Is 9:6–7; Ezek 37:25). Then they ask: "Who is this Son of man?" Where in the Old Testament could they have found the answer (Dan 7:13–14)? Should they have known who the Son of man was? Jesus first refers to himself as the "Son of man" in John 1:51. Notice how the wooden cross is the ladder of ascent, in that a ladder is raised to gain access to a higher place (Jn 1:51). How is the wooden cross raised up for us (Eph 2:16–18; CCC 2795)? Where would we be without it? In verses 35–36, notice the motif of "the light" and compare it with the "overture" (Jn 1:1–18, esp. vv. 4–5, 8–11; CCC 2466). Also refer to 1 John 1:5ff. and John 8:12, where Jesus is portrayed as "the light of the world".

---

[10] Cf. J. B. Lightfoot, *Commentary on the New Testament from the Talmud and Hebraica* (Peabody, Mass.: Hendrickson Pub., 1995), 3:383.

John 12:37–50

The Disbelief of the Jews

22. According to verse 37, did the Jews have good reason for their disbelief, or did they disbelieve in the "teeth of the evidence" (cf. Jn 5:33, 36–37, 39; CCC 548, 582)? How were the Jewish leaders following in the footsteps of their rebellious ancestors, and what was the question both they and their ancestors asked (Ex 17:1–7; Deut 6:16–19; Ps 95:6–11)? God punished the disbelieving generation for forty years and destroyed them in the wilderness. How might it be significant that he "hid himself from them"? Did they still have the light? What happens when people habitually shun the light (Rom 1:21; 10:10ff.; Eph 2:1–3; CCC 401)?

» HISTORICAL NOTE: The generation of Israelites who refused to believe in God after the Passover and deliverance from Egypt was destroyed after forty years in the wilderness (Ps 95:6–11; Num 14:26–35). The generation that rejected Jesus in the year 30 was decimated exactly forty years later, in the year 70, when Jerusalem was destroyed and 1.2 million Jews were massacred by the Romans (cf. Lk 19:43–44).

23. Read Isaiah 52:5—53:12. Why does John use the passage from Isaiah 53 in verse 38 to explain the people's unbelief? How does John use the full context of Isaiah 53 to explain what was taking place? Of whom and of what does Isaiah 53 prophesy (Acts 8:29–36)?

24. Read Isaiah 6:1–10. Why does John refer to this passage in order to chastise unbelieving Jews? To whom does the word "Lord" refer in Isaiah 6:1 and John 12:41 (CCC 712)? To what were the Jews blinded, which John and Isaiah had seen (cf. Jn 1:14–18 and 12:41)? How should the Jews have responded to Jesus (Isaiah's response: Is 6:5; John's response: Rev 1:17)? How does verse 40 relate to the theme of light and seeing (cf. Jn 9:5, 25–27, 39–41)? Who else in the Old Testament had "seen" Jesus and what was his response (Jn 8:56)?

» THEOLOGICAL NOTE: "They could not believe, not because of what [Isaiah] had said, nor because there was a Divine purpose that they should not, but because of the state of their hearts. Their inability to believe was moral, not physical—a crime, not a misfortune. It grew out of the self-contracted blindness of mind referred to in the verses." [11]

"God offers everyone the opportunity to 'believe' or 'trust' him. . . . But if they reject him, he may eventually make belief impossible: he hardens hearts (Rom 9:18). In this case God blinded them (vv. 40–41), just as he hardened Pharaoh's heart (Ex 9:12, 11:10) after Pharaoh hardened his own heart (Ex 8:32), so that it became impossible for Pharaoh to trust in God. . . . We know that God wants everyone to repent (Rom 2:4; 2 Pet 3:9), but we also know that at death God confirms the unbeliever in the way he chose when alive" [12] (3:16–21; 5:21–30; Rom 2:5–8; Rev 20:13–15).

It seems that God allows people who reject him to continue to reject him and to solidify their will into a permanent state of the soul. This permanent rejection can be understood as "hardening of the heart", and we can attribute it to God insofar as God sovereignly and freely allows it and in that sense wills it. But if the language of God's hardening men's hearts is pressed too far, it contradicts the universal salvific will—God's desire that all men be saved and God's gift of sufficient grace for all to be saved. For it would then mean that God hardens the hearts of men who would otherwise repent, which is contrary to his desire that sinners repent.

25. According to verse 42, how did some of the Jewish rulers respond to the words of Jesus (CCC 595–96)? Why were they afraid (Jn 9:22, 34)? Why did they refuse to confess their belief (v. 43)? Who else had been afraid and why (Jn 9:22)? What happens to those who refuse to confess Christ before men (Mt 10:32–33; CCC 1816, 2145)?

26. How can "seeing" Christ be understood as "seeing" God (Jn 1:1; 14:7–11; Phil 2:5ff., Col 1:19; 2:9; 2 Cor 5:19; Heb 1:1ff.; CCC 515–16)? How many times in verses 44–49 does Jesus refer to the Father as the One "who sent me"? Why is it important to know that hearing Jesus is hearing the Father and rejecting Jesus is rejecting the Father? To whom else must we listen (Jn 13:20; CCC 858–62)?

27. According to verse 48, how will Jesus' listeners be judged on the last day (cf. Jn 5:28–29; CCC 679, 1021–22)? How will you be judged? How does Jesus conclude his "public" ministry in verses 44–50? How had his own people received him (cf. Jn 1:11)? He now turns from the

[11] David Thomas, *The Genius of the Fourth Gospel* (R. D. Dickenson, 1885; electronic edition: Oak Harbor: Logos Research Systems, 1997), 367.

[12] David H. Stern, *Jewish New Testament Commentary* (Clarksville, Md.: Jewish New Testament Pubs., 1992), 193–94.

fickle and unbelieving public to those he has chosen and who have believed in him.

John divides his Gospel into two large sections: chapters 1–12 cover Jesus' public ministry, in which he is rejected by his own people, and chapters 13–21 cover Jesus' private ministry to his disciples, those who have received him.

» TEXTUAL NOTE: Up to this point in the Gospel of St. John, Jesus has spent his time speaking and ministering publicly and performing persuasive signs for the people of Israel. This could be considered the "Book of Signs", which now comes to an end. From this point on, Jesus deals privately with his disciples. The first twelve chapters take up about three years, whereas the next eight chapters take up only about three days. His final words (vv. 44–50) are the last warning to the people of Israel before his death. "This paragraph, then, which summarizes the message of Jesus delivered in many discourses in the earlier part of the Gospel, forms an appropriate transition to the following division of the Gospel, in which Jesus turns from the unbelieving 'world' to reveal the Father's love to the inner circle of those who open their hearts to him and his revelation." [13] Notice how this division is reflected in the "overture": "He came to his own home, and his own people received him not. But to all who received him, who believed in his name, he gave power to become children of God" (Jn 1:11–12).

---

[13] Bruce, *John*, 276.

JOHN 13

THE HUMBLE, COMPASSIONATE KING;
THE FOOLISH, TREACHEROUS SERVANT

John 13:1–17
Maundy Thursday: Jesus Washes Feet

1. St. John wrote his Gospel in two parts. Our examination of the first part of the Gospel, often called the *Book of Signs* (chaps. 1–12), is now complete. We begin the second section of the Gospel, which could be entitled *The Book of the Passion*.[1] How does John 1:11 of the "overture" encapsulate the first twelve chapters of the Gospel? How does John 1:12 encapsulate the final nine chapters? The first twelve chapters cover several years; how much time is involved with the next eight chapters (Jn 13:1; 18:1–3; 19:14–18; 20:1; see also Acts 1:3)?

» THEOLOGICAL NOTE: One theme of St. John's Gospel is Jesus the new Moses, the new prophet (Deut 18:15, 18). Notice how the book of Exodus is like the Gospel of St. John. We are told in Exodus 11:10, "Moses and Aaron did all these wonders before Pharaoh; and the LORD hardened Pharaoh's heart, and he did not let the people of Israel go out of his land." Notice that the Pharisees also hardened their hearts against Jesus, even though he performed the signs and wonders of God before them, and that the Pharisees would not "let the people go" to follow Jesus.

Jesus, like Moses, performed many signs and wonders (Jn 12:37–40), but the leaders hardened their hearts and killed Jesus. The greatest sign performed in Egypt was the Passover. After Jesus had performed his seven signs before the final Passover, as recorded by John, at Passover Jesus, like Moses, also performed his greatest sign, the sign of Jonah (Lk 11:29–32), three days and nights, burial and resurrection "from the belly of the fish" (cf. Jon 1:17), that is, from the dead. Jesus' seven signs represent perfection and divinity, since seven is the perfect number in the Bible. The Resurrection, the greatest sign, took place on

---

[1] Ronald Knox, *A Commentary on the Gospels* (New York: Sheed & Ward, 1952–1956), 250.

the first day of the week to signify a new beginning. The seven signs correspond to the seven days of God's original creation; the eighth and final sign on "the eighth day" signifies the beginning of the new creation, as Passover (after the powerful signs demonstrated in Egypt) was the great miracle that brought about the new freedom of the Israelites.

"The eighth day: But for us a new day has dawned: the day of Christ's Resurrection. The seventh day completes the first creation. The eighth day begins the new creation. Thus, the work of creation culminates in the greater work of redemption. The first creation finds its meaning and its summit in the new creation in Christ, the splendor of which surpasses that of the first creation (cf. *Roman Missal*, Easter Vigil 24, prayer after the first reading)."[2]

2. John does not provide us with the account of the Eucharist's institution at the Last Supper, as the other Gospels do. Where *does* John relate the importance and centrality of the Eucharist (CCC 1338; Jn 6:26–71)? Remember that John frames the context of chapter 6 much as he did that of chapter 13. What Jewish feast is about to be celebrated (Jn 6:4)? Why does each chapter conclude with the mention of Judas (cf. Jn 6:70– 71)? Why do you think John frames these chapters by mentioning the Passover and ending with Satan entering Judas? Notice how the Passover meal is framed the same way in the other Gospels, using the heading of the Passover and later mentioning the devil entering Judas (cf. Mt 26:19ff.). In chapter 13, what meal are they eating when Jesus washes their feet (CCC 1337)?

» TEXTUAL NOTE: The context of a passage is just as important for understanding a biblical text as it is for understanding any other piece of literature. St. John gives us the necessary information to understand that chapters 6 and 13 both refer to the Passover meal and the Eucharist. In chapter 6, he gives us the theological underpinnings for the sacrament, and in chapter 13 he supplements the information provided by the other three Gospels. In each, the narrative begins by mentioning the context of the Passover celebration and ends by notifying us that Satan was entering Judas.

3. Previously, Jesus referred to his disciples as "my brethren", "my sheep", and even "my friends". How does he refer to them now (v. 1)?

4. In verses 3–4, Jesus amazes his disciples by disrobing to perform the task of a slave. What was the source of Christ's quiet composure of mind? How can we appropriate the same peace and composure when

---

[2] CCC 349.

called upon for some difficult or painful task (cf. Phil 2:3–5)? Who was Jesus, and where had he come from (cf. John 8:42; CCC 423)? How can we explain the seeming paradox that the Father had given all things into Jesus' hand and yet Jesus was about to be cruelly murdered (Jn 3:35–36; Mt 11:27)?

» WASHING FEET: One has only to walk around the dirt footpaths or shorelines of Israel in sandals to understand the basic need to wash one's feet after a long, and dusty (or muddy) trek from one village to the next or even from one stone house to another. "It was an act of courtesy of the host to give water to his guests to wash their feet, and to omit this was an act of disrespect [Gen 24:32; 43:24]. The lowest slaves usually performed the actual washing, and even Jewish slaves could not be obliged to render this service. But Paul urged the consecrated widows to perform the humble task of washing the feet of the saints (1 Tim 5:10). Christ stooped to this menial service of washing the feet of the Apostles at the Last Supper. . . . According to tradition, this washing of feet was not a sacrament."[3]

» THEOLOGICAL NOTE: Fundamentalist Protestants usually practice two ordinances: baptism and the Lord's Supper. They avoid the word "sacrament" because it is a Catholic word and implies more than the Fundamentalist is willing to accept. They have settled on the word "ordinance" because it is an order or command from Christ himself. According to Baptist theologian Henry Thiessen, "In order to avoid giving any encouragement to sacramentarianism [such as Roman Catholicism] we prefer the word ordinances [over sacraments]. We may define an ordinance as an outward rite appointed by Christ to be administered in the Church as a visible sign of the saving truth of the Christian faith. It is a sacrament only in the sense of a vow of allegiance to Christ. The New Testament prescribes two ordinances: Baptism and the Lord's Supper."[4]

One of the fundamental reasons an "ordinance" is considered to be instituted for the churches in these groups is that it is considered a direct command of Christ, clearly ordained in the Bible. Christ commanded us to baptize and to celebrate the Lord's Supper; but is the command to wash each others' feet not just as strong a command? Jesus says, "If I then, your Lord and Teacher, have washed your feet, you also ought to wash one another's feet. For I have given you an example, that you also should do as I have done" (Jn 13:14–15). Why do Fundamentalists not practice footwashing as an ordinance in their churches? Actually, some groups, such as the Church of Christ, do have such an ordinance, but the vast majority of Fundamentalists do not. Why? I think the

[3] John Steinmueller and Kathryn Sullivan, *Catholic Biblical Encyclopedia* (New York: Joseph F. Wagner, 1956), 2:662.

[4] Henry Clarence Thiessen, *Lectures in Systematic Theology* (Grand Rapids: Eerdmans, 1979), 422.

answer is simple: The Catholic Church established the tradition that footwashing was not a sacrament, and the Fundamentalist practice follows the long-standing teaching of the Church, often without knowing it.

How do we know what and how many sacraments exist as means of grace in the Church? The *Catechism* says, "As she has done for the canon of Sacred Scripture and for the doctrine of the faith, the Church, by the power of the Spirit who guides her 'into all truth,' has gradually recognized this treasure received from Christ and, as the faithful steward of God's mysteries, has determined its 'dispensation' (*Jn* 16:13; cf. *Mt* 13:52; *1 Cor* 4:1). Thus the Church has discerned over the centuries that among liturgical celebrations there are seven that are, in the strict sense of the term, sacraments instituted by the Lord" (CCC 1117). The Catholic Church still practices the "washing of feet" as commanded by her Lord, both in spirit, by caring for the poor and lost, and liturgically, by actually washing the feet of twelve men each Maundy Thursday.

5. Where else in Scripture do we read of washing feet (Gen 18:1–4 [did Abraham wash God's feet?]; 1 Sam 25:41; 1 Tim 5:10 [is this meant literally?])? Think of all the times "feet" are mentioned as we work through this series of chapters in John. What had happened the day before, and who had already been an example of humility for the disciples (Jn 12:2–3)? What were the disciples discussing among themselves at this time (Lk 22:24–27)? Consider how contrary to the mind of God we often are. Do we try to climb to the top of the heap, or do we serve our fellowman? How might Jesus' actions have graphically illustrated what it means to be the greatest?

6. In verses 4–5, notice how the details suggest the writings of an eyewitness and how John describes the procedure of Jesus as he prepares to wash their feet. What preparations were taken in the foot-washing process? Ponder how this might parallel the Incarnation and ministry of Jesus (cf. Phil 2:6–8).

» THEOLOGICAL NOTE: "The scene was a summary of [Jesus'] Incarnation. Rising up from the Heavenly Banquet in intimate union of nature with the Father, He laid aside the garments of His glory, wrapped about His divinity the towel of human nature which He took from Mary; poured the laver of regeneration which is in His Blood shed on the Cross to redeem men, and began washing the souls of His disciples and followers through the merits of His death, Resurrection and Ascension."[5] Compare John 13:3–5, 12, with Philippians 2:3–10. See if you can discover the parallels.

---

[5] Fulton Sheen, *Life of Christ* (New York: Image Books/Doubleday, 1990), 283.

7. Does Jesus know in advance that Judas is going to betray him (Jn 6:70–71)? What emotion does Jesus experience regarding Judas (CCC 1851)? Does Jesus wash Judas' feet? Jesus gives Judas a last warning—he is not clean, he is not in the state of grace, and his soul is in great jeopardy. How does Jesus' example prepare us for such betrayal—how are we to respond to our enemies even if they are in the Church or are our trusted friends (Jn 15:20; Lk 6:27–29)? Does this provide an example of how we are to treat members of the Church, especially her leaders? What does Judas do with the grace of Christ and the cleansing offered? How does our sin affect Jesus Christ today (CCC 598; Heb 6:4–6)?

8. Imagine your shock if you had been eating with Jesus and he stood up, undressed, and began doing what only a slave would do—washing your dirty feet! What would you have done? Have you had your feet washed by the priest on Maundy Thursday? If not, ask someone who has and get his reaction. How does Peter respond when Jesus kneels at his feet (v. 6)? Why does Peter have this reaction? Was it proper for the Master to wash the disciples' feet? What does Peter freely admit (Lk 5:8)?

» PERSONAL NOTE: In my second year as a Catholic, I was chosen to participate in the foot-washing ceremony on Maundy Thursday. I immediately felt like protesting, much as Peter did. It was a very strange sensation to allow a priest in alb and stole, respected and loved by all and a personal friend, to kneel in front of my bare feet and begin washing. After the washing, he stooped low to kiss my feet. I pictured Christ, in the person of the priest, washing my feet, and, through tears of humility and emotion, I was carried back in spirit to the year 30 and sensed the great continuity with the apostolic Church and with Jesus himself. It was a most profound experience.

9. What is more foul, the road dust on the disciples' feet or the corruption of sin in the souls of men? Is it more shocking that the Creator would stoop to wash dirty feet or that he would step down from heaven to suffer the trauma of death to cleanse evil, sinful souls? What did Jesus mean when he said that Peter would understand afterward (v. 7; cf. Jn 14:26)?

» CONTEXTUAL NOTE: "*'He cometh therefore to Simon Peter.'* Most Catholic commentators are agreed that our Lord knelt *first* before Peter, whom He had chosen to be His Vicar upon earth. Many non-Catholic writers hold this view likewise. Thus Westcott writes: 'It is more natural to suppose that our Lord began with St. Peter'; and Lightfoot remarks: 'If he did observe any order, He began with Peter' " [6]

10. Remembering that chapter/verse divisions were added much later to the text, and that St. John never quotes from the Old Testament without carefully considering its wider context, how might Isaiah 52:7 apply to this passage, since John just quoted from Isaiah 53:1? What does Isaiah say about feet? Jesus has been persecuted for preaching the good news; how might the disciples be treated for doing the same (Jn 15:20)? Do you think Jesus is commissioning them and prophesying their end? Why does St. Paul quote these two verses together in Romans 10:15–16? How do Paul's words relate to John 13 and the washing of the disciples' feet?

11. In verse 10, two separate Greek words are used, and each has a distinct meaning. *Bathe* means to cleanse the whole body; *wash* means to cleanse one part of the body, such as hands or feet. What does Jesus mean by *bathe* and *wash* (Tit 3:5; 1 Pet 3:20–21; Jn 3:5; Acts 22:16, literally *bathed away*; 1 Cor 6:11, literally *bathed*; CCC 537, 1216, 1228)? Does this imply that the disciples had all been previously baptized?

12. Even though a man might be clean after a bath, what would happen as he walked over dusty footpaths to another village? As the sandaled feet of a freshly bathed man come in contact with the soil of the earth, so the soul of a baptized man comes in contact with the corruption of the world. If baptism is the bath whereby we are cleansed from all sin, how might the *foot-washing* represent confession (1 Jn 1:9; CCC 1847)? Compare Song of Solomon 5:3.

» ST. AUGUSTINE: "The whole of a man is washed in baptism, not excepting his feet; but living in the world afterwards, we tread upon the earth. Those human affections then, without which we cannot live in this world, are, as it were, our feet, which connect us with human things, so that if we say we have no sin, we deceive ourselves. But if we confess our sins, He who washed the disciples' feet, forgives us our sins even down to our feet, wherewith we hold our converse with earth." [7]

---

[6] Madame Cecilia, *St. John*, Catholic Scripture Manuals (London: Burns, Oates, & Washbourne, 1923), 257.

[7] Quoted in St. Thomas Aquinas, *Catena Aurea: St. John* (Albany, N.Y.: Preserving Christian Publications, 1995), 4:427.

» THEOLOGICAL NOTE: Baptism is the bath of regeneration and cleansing from sin, whereas the washing of feet probably represents cleansing from subsequent sins. "In all likelihood, John expects the Christian reader also to relate Jesus' words to his own life and to be reminded of the function of baptism. This interpretation was commonly put on this passage by the Fathers. . . . Having their share in Christ, they have all that is needful. By his choice of [Greek] words, John probably again suggests baptism to the Christian reader ("bathe," *louō*, was a word used for religious washings, and in 1 Cor 6:11; Eph 5:26; Ti 3:5; Heb 10:22 various forms of it are used to signify baptism). . . . In this case, the foot washing would appear to signify the necessity of the Christian to purify himself of his postbaptismal sins. . . . Jesus has just pronounced that the disciples as a group are clean, even as the symbol of washing signified. Yet one was not clean, despite the fact that he, too, had been washed. Not even the sacraments can purify when the inmost dispositions are impure." [8]

» JEWISH RITUAL: "Compare Exodus 30:20: 'Aaron and his sons are to wash their hands and feet . . . when they come near the altar to minister . . . , so that they will not die.' The [priests] were already cleansed from impurity, but even so they had to wash their hands and feet. Once sins of the past have been forgiven we need not have them forgiven again; the initial confession and immersion that washes away past sin need not be repeated. But there is continual need to repent of newly committed sins, make reparation for them and seek forgiveness for them." [9]

13. Since the disciples had just been arguing about which of them was the greatest, how do you think they felt after Jesus' demonstration and command? Since Jesus demonstrates forgiveness and service, how should we treat those who offend us (Eph 4:32), as Judas was about to offend Jesus? The disciples admit that Jesus is Lord and a slave is not above his master, therefore, how should they treat others (Mt 22:39; 1 Jn 3:16; CCC 1269)? How does Peter exhort his fellow bishops (1 Pet 5:3)?

John 13:18–38
The Betrayal and Glory

14. Since we have been dealing a lot with feet in the last chapters, think about the metaphor used of Judas in John 13:18. In verses 18–19 Jesus

---

[8] Raymond Brown, Joseph Fitzmyer, and Roland Murphy, eds., *The Jerome Biblical Commentary* (Englewood Cliffs, N.J.: Prentice-Hall, 1968), 2:451.

[9] David H. Stern, *Jewish New Testament Commentary* (Clarksville, Md.: Jewish New Testament Pubs., 1992), 194–95.

speaks about Judas and quotes Psalm 41:9. Read the whole psalm and notice the fuller context. Why do you think Jesus chose this verse and wider context of the psalm at this point? Notice the parallels between Psalm 41 and Judas' betrayal. What do they both say about concern and sacrifice for others and about being *blessed*? How does the psalmist's experience reflect the death and Resurrection of Jesus? What about the enemy's words and actions? What about the final state of the afflicted psalmist? Would the Jews understand the wider context and why Jesus quotes this psalm of the treacherous friend?

» HISTORICAL NOTE: A certain situation in David's life may be the background for Psalm 41, from which Jesus quotes. King David's friend and trusted councilor conspired with Absalom against David. As David was betrayed by his trusted advisor and table companion Ahithophel, who then hanged himself (2 Sam 16:20—17:3, 23), so Judas, Jesus' close companion, betrayed his Lord and then hanged himself. A further "coincidence" needs to be mentioned. After Ahithophel's treachery, King David left Jerusalem and "went up the ascent of the Mount of Olives, weeping as he went, barefoot and with his head covered" (2 Sam 15:30). Jesus likewise went up the Mount of Olives after the treachery of Judas.

15. In verse 19, why does Jesus explain in advance that Judas will betray him? Was Judas a puppet in this drama, or did he make the free choice to betray Jesus? What was probably going on in the soul of Judas (cf. 2 Cor 4:4)? Was Jesus a victim of Judas' treachery, or was Jesus' arrest and crucifixion planned by God in advance (Jn 10:17; 14:29)? Again we see Jesus refer to himself as I AM. To what does I AM refer (Ex 3:14; Jn 8:24, 58–59; CCC 590)?

16. In verse 20, what does Jesus mean by saying "he who receives any one whom I send receives me; and he who receives me receives him who sent me" (Jn 20:21; CCC 858–62)? The word *apostle* means "one who is sent". Who is the primary apostle (cf. Heb 3:1)? Who is Jesus speaking about—all people or those whom Jesus has invested with his authority (CCC 1087)? To whom is Jesus speaking at this time?

17. In verse 21, while reclining at the table, Jesus became troubled. Take a few minutes to picture this, and share the moment with Jesus. Imagine the betrayal of a friend, the weight of sin soon to be placed on him, the agony of humiliation and torture (Rom 8:17; CCC 609–10). How did the disciples respond to Jesus' declaration that one of them was going to

betray him (vv. 21–26)? What happened to Judas (vv. 27, 30)? Even a slave ate the bread of the master, but in the East, it was a special honor for the host to hand a choice morsel of food personally to a guest. It was a gesture of deep friendship. Judas was given, and accepted, this gesture from Jesus (vv. 26, 30).

» RECLINING AT TABLE (13:23): This was the customary position for the Passover meals: "The usual arrangement at a meal was to have a series of couches each for three persons arranged in a U round the table. The host, or the most important person reclined in the centre of the chief couch placed at the junction of the two arms of the U. The guests reclined with their heads towards the table and their feet stretched out obliquely away from it. They leaned on the left elbow, which meant that the right hand was free to secure food. The place of honor was to the left of, and thus slightly behind the principal person. The second place was to his right, and the guest there would have his head on the breast of the host. Plainly this was the position occupied by the beloved disciple. . . .

"We have no means of knowing how seating would be arranged in the apostolic band. But Peter was somewhere where he could be observed by the beloved disciple and he made signs indicating that he would like to know who it was [that would betray Christ]. It seems not unlikely that Judas was in the chief place. From Matthew's account it seems clear that Jesus could speak to Judas without being overheard by the others (Mt 26:25). His position as treasurer (Jn 12:6; 13:29) would give him a certain status in the little group, and thus make the seat of honor not inappropriate. It is also possible that the giving to Judas of this place was part of Jesus' last appeal to the traitor." [10]

We might have thought that Peter would have the place of honor. But Peter seems to have been too far from Jesus to whisper a question himself (13:24), and he could scarcely have motioned to John if he were behind Jesus, who was behind John. Judas was near enough to Jesus to receive a piece of food from him (13:26), so Judas may have had the place of honor at this meal. Jesus may have been making a subtle last appeal to him to repent of his betrayal.

We are told that Jesus and the disciples reclined at the table for the Passover meal. However, what was the posture commanded in the Exodus for eating the Passover meal (Ex 12:11)? "After the Captivity [in Babylon], even the Paschal Supper was eaten reclining, though originally the Jews were commanded to partake of it standing." [11]

---

[10] Leon Morris, *The Gospel according to John*, The New International Commentary on the New Testament (Grand Rapids, Mich.: Wm. B. Eerdmans Pub., 1971), 625–26.

[11] Madame Cecilia, *John*, 262.

18. In verse 30, when does Judas go out to perform his nefarious task? Why do you think John mentions *the time of day* Judas went out to plot against Jesus? What does it represent (CCC 1851; see Lk 22:53; Jn 3:2, 19; 11:10; 12:35)? What two effects can eating "the morsel" of eucharistic bread have on a person, depending on the state of his soul before God (Jn 6:53–54; 1 Cor 11:28–30)?

19. Jesus again refers to himself as the *Son of man* and says it is now time for him to be glorified. How does this fulfill the prophecy of the Messiah and the coming kingdom (Dan 7:13–14; cf. Mt 26:64; Rev 14:14)? Notice how Daniel and Jesus both use the word *glory* (Dan 7:14; Jn 13:31–32). Knowing there are other forces in the spiritual world where Christ has been glorified, what else is taking place in the heavens (Eph 1:20–22; 2:2; 6:10–17)? What does Satan think he is going to accomplish in this cosmic battle through the betrayal of Judas (1 Cor 2:8)? Who is actually conquering every step of the way? Consider the imagery of a victorious conqueror returning from war with the booty of battle and the enemy humiliated in chains bowing before the conquering Lord (cf. Col 2:15).

» HISTORICAL NOTE: In Ancient Rome the conquering general would return home triumphantly with great pomp and circumstance. Leading the procession before the emperor would be the defeated enemy, the royal family, and the booty and riches from the vanquished country. The humiliated enemy would be forced to bow to the emperor, acknowledging the power and glory of Rome. King Jesus' victory procession before the Throne of God is implied in Colossians 2:15. "In 2:8 Paul used a word that could mean 'take as a prisoner of war'; here the cosmic powers themselves are shown off as captives in Christ's triumphal procession, an image familiar to Romans and presumably known to others throughout the Empire. . . . In Roman triumphs, the general dressed as the chief god Jupiter and led behind him humiliated captives, stripped of their possessions; prominent captives were the most impressive. Here Christ displays his triumph over the most prominent captives possible." [12]

"One other great picture flashes on the screen of Paul's mind. Jesus has stripped the powers and authorities and made them his captives. As we have seen, the ancient world believed in all kinds of angels and in all kinds of elemental spirits. Many of these spirits were out to ruin men. It was they who were responsible for demon-possession and the like. They were hostile to men. Jesus conquered them for ever. He stripped them; the word used is the word

---

[12] Craig Keener, *The IVP Bible Background Commentary: New Testament* (Downers Grove, Ill.: InterVarsity Press, 1993), 576.

for stripping the weapons and the armour from a defeated foe. Once and for all Jesus broke their power. He put them to open shame and led them captive in his triumphant train. The picture is that of the triumph of a Roman general. When a Roman general had won a really notable victory, he was allowed to march his victorious armies through the streets of Rome and behind him followed the kings and the leaders and the peoples he had vanquished. They were openly branded as his spoils. Paul thinks of Jesus as a conqueror enjoying a kind of cosmic triumph, and in his triumphal procession are the powers of evil, beaten for ever, for every one to see. In these vivid pictures Paul sets out the total adequacy of the work of Christ. Sin is forgiven and evil is conquered; what more is necessary? There is nothing that Gnostic knowledge and Gnostic intermediaries can do for men—Christ has done it all already." [13]

» THEOLOGICAL NOTE: The world, or age, refers to the world under the reign of Satan and his minions. Satan had just entered into Judas (Jn 13:27) with the goal of destroying Jesus, yet he did not realize he was working God's plan. How Satan must have shrieked in despair when he learned that not only had he not destroyed the Christ but had actually helped to effect salvation for the world! Referring to 1 Corinthians 2:8 and the word "age" or "world", we read, "This *aiōn* [world, age] is the world that has not yet been transformed by the redemptive power of Christ and that lies in subjection to Satan and the wicked spirits until the final act of the drama of redemption, the parousia of the Lord. . . . *the rulers of this world*: The wicked spirits who, since Adam's sin, hold this world in slavery (Col 2:15; Eph 6:12; 2 Cor 4:4). *the wisdom of this world*: The philosophy of the pagans who, blinded by sin, failed to recognize and worship God the Creator (Rom 1:19–20), and Jewish interpretations of Scripture, which failed to see in Jesus the promised Messiah. Both Jew and Gentile are enslaved by the elements of the world, the wicked spirits who rule this *aiōn* (Gal 4:3, 8–9; Col 2:20). . . . Had the wicked spirits known the mystery of Christ, they would never have incited men to crucify him. His death and resurrection are the world's redemption and the destruction of their power and empire." [14] The greatest cosmic battle is being fought and the heavenly forces—the kingdom of God—have outsmarted and outmaneuvered the kingdom of evil!

20. According to verse 34, what is the new commandment that Jesus gives the disciples? Compare Leviticus 19:18 and John 13:34. What is *new* about the "new command" in John 13:34? How does Jesus "up the ante"? How has Jesus just vividly illustrated sacrificial love (vv. 12–15),

---

[13] William Barclay, *The Letters to the Philippians, Colossians, and Thessalonians* (Philadelphia: Westminster Press, 1975), 143.

[14] Brown, Fitzmyer, and Murphy, *Jerome Biblical Commentary*, 2:258.

and how will he illustrate it further (cf. 1 Jn 3:16)? What will be the result if they obey his commandment (v. 35)? Are love among the brethren and unity of the Body of Christ important (Jn 17:22–23; CCC 1823)? How will all people know that these twelve men, and all those who believe through their word, are disciples of Jesus (vv. 34–35)? What is *our* strongest and most effective witness to the reality of Christ and his Church? How is it ironic that Jesus gave this new commandment, knowing what Judas and Peter were about to do?

» THEOLOGICAL NOTE: "Why is this a new commandment? Doesn't Leviticus 19:18 already say, 'Love your neighbor as yourself'? The difference is this: Leviticus says, 'as yourself'; Yeshua [Jesus] says, 'In the same way that I have loved you,' which presupposes that God's way of loving can be ours. Humanly this is impossible. But Yeshua gives us a new nature, a new spirit, in fulfillment of [Old Testament] promises (Ezekiel 36:26, 37:14; Jeremiah 31:32–33), God's Spirit the Holy Spirit. This is how we can love as God loves; God makes it possible." [15] Under the grace of Christ, we are not released from the obligations of the moral law in the Old Testament; rather, we are held to a higher standard now that the Holy Spirit of God enables us to obey more completely. (Notice Mt 5:17–20; CCC 2054–55.)

» EARLY CHURCH WRITINGS: Tertullian writing to the heathen, in a celebrated passage of his *Apologeticus* (39), says, "But it is mainly the deeds of a love so noble that lead many to put a brand upon us. *See*, they say, *how they love one another*, for they themselves are animated by mutual hatred; how they are ready even to die for one another, for they themselves will sooner put to death. And they are wroth with us, too, because we call each other brethren; for no other reason, as I think, than because among themselves names of consanguinity are assumed in mere pretence of affection. But we are your brethren as well, by the law of our common mother nature, though you are hardly men, because brothers so unkind. At the same time, how much more fittingly they are called and counted brothers who have been led to the knowledge of God as their common Father, who have drunk in one spirit of holiness, who from the same womb of a common ignorance have agonized into the same light of truth! But on this very account, perhaps, we are regarded as having less claim to be held true brothers, that no tragedy makes a noise about our brotherhood, or that the family possessions, which generally destroy brotherhood among you, create fraternal bonds among us. One in mind and soul, we do not hesitate to share our earthly goods with one another." [16]

---

[15] Stern, *Jewish New Testament Commentary*, 196.

[16] Tertullian, *Apology* 39, trans. S. Thelwall, in ANF 3:46.

21. What does Jesus tell the Jews about where he is going (Jn 7:33–36)? Do the disciples understand Jesus any better than the Jewish leaders had (Jn 13:36)? While Jesus, as the new Moses, is giving them his new commandment to love, what preoccupies Peter (v. 36)? How does Jesus pull back the "curtain of eternity" and explain where he is going later (Jn 14:2–4; CCC 2795)? What do the disciples later watch with their own eyes (Acts 1:9–11; CCC 665)?

22. Peter rashly declares that he will lay down his life for Jesus. In the comfortable setting of the upper room, such boisterous courage is easy. What does Jesus prophesy about Peter (Jn 13:38)? What actually happens (Jn 18:17, 25–27)? How are the betrayals of Judas and Peter similar (Mk 14:43–46; Jn 18:25–27) and different (Mt 27:5; 26:75 CCC 1429)? Compare them in light of Paul's teaching (2 Cor 7:10). How do we handle sorrow over our sins and betrayals? Are we a Judas or a Peter? Does Peter eventually lay down his life for Jesus (Jn 21:18–19)?

» HISTORICAL NOTE: "But, to leave the examples of antiquity, let us come to the athletes who are closest to our own time. Consider the noble examples of our own generation. Through jealousy and envy the greatest and most righteous pillars [of our church in Rome] were persecuted, and they persevered even to death. Let us set before our eyes the good Apostles: Peter, who through unwarranted jealousy suffered not one or two but many toils, and having thus given testimony went to the place of glory that was his due." [17]

"Meanwhile the holy apostles and disciples of our Saviour were dispersed throughout the world. Parthia, according to tradition, was allotted to Thomas as his field of labor, Scythia to Andrew, and Asia to John, who, after he had lived some time there, died at Ephesus. Peter appears to have preached in Pontus, Galatia, Bithynia, Cappadocia, and Asia to the Jews of the dispersion. And at last, having come to Rome, he was crucified head-downwards; for he had requested that he might suffer in this way. What do we need to say concerning Paul, who preached the Gospel of Christ from Jerusalem to Illyricum, and afterwards suffered martyrdom in Rome under Nero? These facts are related by Origen in the third volume of his Commentary on Genesis." [18]

23. In verse 33, why does Jesus call the disciples "little children" (cf. Lk 13:34; 1 Jn 2:1, 12, 28; 3:7, 18; 4:4; 5:21)?

---

[17] St. Clement of Rome, *Letter to the Corinthians* 5, 1–6, written ca. 96, in William A. Jurgens, *The Faith of the Early Fathers*, vol. 1 (Collegeville, Minn.: Liturgical Press, 1970), 7–8.

[18] Eusebius, *Church History*, trans. Arthur Cushman McGiffert, in NPNF2, 1:132–33.

24. Judas has now left to conspire with the Jewish leaders against Jesus. Therefore, Jesus has only a short time left to impart his last instructions to his disciples and to pray to the Father. How much space does John allocate in his Gospel for Jesus' last discourse, prayer, and instruction (notice when the discourse ends, Jn 18:1–3)? How would you summarize chapter 13 (CCC 1337)?

JOHN 14

THE WAY TO HEAVEN—THE GIFT
OF THE HOLY SPIRIT

John 14:1–14
Heaven and the Way to Get There

» HISTORICAL NOTE: Jesus now gives his farewell address to those who have received him, specifically his twelve disciples. "In the body of Jesus' last discourse (chaps. 14–17) he speaks to 'his own' as he contemplates his departure. This Discourse is a unique composition, comparable to [Matthew's] Sermon on the Mount or to Luke's collection of Jesus' words spoken on the way from Galilee to Jerusalem. John's Discourse presents as one final message diverse material found in the Synoptics not only at the Last Supper but also scattered through the public ministry. Poised between heaven and earth and already in the ascent to glory, the Johannine Jesus speaks both as still in the world and as no longer in it (16:5; 17:11). This atemporal, nonspatial character gives the Discourse an abiding value as a message from Jesus to those of all time who would believe (17:20). In terms of form and content it resembles a 'testament' or farewell speech [cf. Jacob to his twelve sons (Gen 49); Moses to Israel (Deut 33); Joshua to Israel (Josh 23–24) and David (2 Sam:1–7; 1 Chron 28–29)] where a speaker (sometimes a father to his children) announces the imminence of his departure (see John 13:33; 14:2–3; 16:16), often producing sorrow (14:1, 27; 16:6, 22); he recalls his past life, words, and deeds (13:33; 14:10; 15:3, 20; 17:4–8), urging the addressees to emulate and even surpass these (14:12), to keep the commandments (14:15, 21, 23; 15:10, 14), and to keep unity among themselves (17:11, 21–23). He may wish the addressees peace and joy (14:27; 16:22, 33), pray for them (17:9), predict that they will be persecuted (15:18, 20; 16:2–3), and pick a successor (Paraclete passages)." [1] The Paraclete is the successor who will indwell them in the place of Jesus himself; whereas Peter has been chosen the visible successor of the kingdom (Mt 16:18–19 and Jn 21:15–17).

---

[1] Raymond E. Brown, *An Introduction to the New Testament* (New York: Doubleday, 1997), 352.

1. Why does Jesus begin this chapter with these comforting words? Why might the disciples be confused and troubled—even afraid? What has just happened in chapter 13? What did Jesus predict (Jn 13:21, 33, 34, 36, 38)? Compare John 16:22. Why should the disciples *not* "be troubled", or what do they need in order to be calm and confident (v. 1; Heb 11:1, 6; CCC 151)? Does Jesus have a legitimate reason to be "troubled" (Jn 12:27; 13:21)? Who is he thinking about instead of himself (Jn 14:1)?

2. How did Moses speak to the people of Israel just before he was to die, when they were to enter and conquer the Promised Land without him? Read Moses' farewell speech to the Israelites, especially Deuteronomy 31:7–8. What parallels can you discover between Jesus and Moses? The same Greek word for "troubled" is used by both Moses and Jesus (Jn 14:27).

» THEOLOGICAL NOTE: The parallels between Moses and Jesus continue to demonstrate that John is portraying Jesus as the New Moses (Deut 18:15, 18). "It is in the charge [commission] to Joshua in Deut. 31:7–8 that we find the words 'fear not, neither be dismayed'. And so the final charge of Jesus to his disciples includes the injunction, 'Let not your heart be troubled, neither let it be fearful' (14:27, cf. 14:1). . . . According to Deut. 34:9, Moses apparently imparted the Spirit to Joshua and ordained him to his responsible office: 'And Joshua the son of Nun was full of the spirit of wisdom; for Moses had laid his hands upon him: and the children of Israel hearkened unto him, and did as the Lord commanded Moses.' The Rabbis regarded this incident as vital for the whole idea of succession. All ordinations looked back to this one. . . . Just as Moses when leaving the world appointed Joshua as shepherd (Num. 27:16–18) so Jesus appoints Peter as shepherd (Jn 21). According to Aboth R. Nathan 17, Moses said to Joshua, 'This people which I commit to you, I commit to you only as kids and lambs, as frail children.' Similarly Jesus says to Peter, 'Feed my lambs' (21:15). Eusebius in the course of an extended comparison of Christ and Moses regards Peter as answering to Joshua: 'Moses changed the name of Nave to Jesus, and likewise the Saviour changed that of Simon to Peter.' "[2] (For more on the succession of Moses' teaching authority, see notes on John 6:3, pp. 137–38).

3. Where does Jesus tell the disciples he is going—a place to which they can follow him later (Jn 7:33–36; 8:21; 13:3, 33)? What does he disclose to his disciples? What does he promise them that he withholds from the Jews (Jn 13:36; 14:2–4)? Where is Jesus going (Jn 16:28; Acts 1:9–11;

---

[2] T. F. Glasson, *Moses in the Fourth Gospel* (Napierville, Ill.: Alec R. Allenson, 1963), 83–85.

Dan 7:13–14)? When will he keep his promise and return (1 Thess 5:2; Lk 21:34–35; 2 Pet 3:10–13; Rev 16:15; Mt 24:33–34; 1 Cor 15:50–52; CCC 672–77, 1001)? How will his Second Coming take place (cf. Mt 24:30–31; Acts 1:9–11; 1 Cor 15:50–57; 1 Thess 4:13–18; CCC 673–77)? What will happen when we die or Christ returns, whichever comes first (1 Thess 4:13–18; CCC 1012)?

» THE SECOND COMING OF CHRIST: The Catholic Church does not teach an interim, "halfway" return of Christ prior to the Second Coming, as taught by the Secret Rapture theology of some conservative Protestant groups. There are many variations and permutations on that newly developed doctrine. According to this theory, Jesus will come in secret (the Rapture) for his true followers shortly before he comes publicly in judgment on the world (the revelation). Those left behind on earth will experience the Great Tribulation and God's judgment on evil.

The doctrine of the Secret Rapture was first proposed in the late 1700s or early 1800s. Some have argued that the Secret Rapture doctrine originated among the Plymouth Brethren in Scotland. Another possible origin is a "prophecy" of a young woman, Margaret MacDonald, who was part of a Bible prophecy, end-times movement in Scotland connected with the preacher Edward Irving. Others point to J. N. Darby, one of the progenitors of Dispensationalist theology, as the originator of the Secret Rapture doctrine. Still others think it was a late eighteenth-century Baptist minister, Morgan Edwards.

"In any case, the doctrine was introduced to America in the mid–19th century and was spread through the *Scofield Reference Bible*, which incorporated the doctrine into its study notes. More recently, it has been popularized by authors such as Hal Lindsey (in his best-selling *Late Great Planet Earth*) and Tim LaHaye and Jerry Jenkins in their *Left Behind* novels. Many Evangelical scholars acknowledge that the doctrine is not ancient. As an example, Evangelical commentator Craig Keener writes, 'The idea of a rapture before the tribulation first explicitly appears in history around 1830, as a corollary of dispensationalism.' " [3]

Professor of Systematic Theology and director of the Institute of Protestant Theology at the University of Regensburg, Germany, Hans Schwarz writes, "As the many and often conflicting ideas concerning rapture and millennialism indicate, these are highly controversial topics, even in 'conservative' Christian circles where one or the other variety is advocated. We could simply discard these theories as 'undue speculation over highly symbolic teachings.' Indeed, most of these speculations do not stand up to historically informed exegesis of the biblical texts, and, as we have seen with [Hal] Lindsey, they often rest on dangerous theological presuppositions. Even dispensationalists agree that they

---

[3] Craig Keener, *The IVP Bible Background Commentary: New Testament* (Downers Grove, Ill.: InterVarsity Press, 1993), 602.

'must protect themselves and their churches from speculations and sensational-
ism which do not build up the body of Christ, but lead to delusion, resentment,
and faithlessness when would-be prophecies under the guise of interpretation
fail. . . . Interpreters of the Bible who identify specific current events as the
future tribulational fulfillment of the Day of the Lord or the mysterious visions
of biblical apocalyptic are overstepping their boundaries."[4]

   Rapture advocates disagree about the details on the end times. But their
conflicting teachings are neither expounded in the Bible nor taught by Christians prior to the eighteenth or nineteenth century. How ironic this is, since
some proponents of the Secret Rapture have accused Catholics of "inventing"
new doctrines. (For a thorough treatment, see Paul Thigpen, *The Rapture Trap*
[West Chester, Penn.: Ascension Press, 2001].)

4. Read verses 1–3 and consider what heaven is like (cf. Rev 4:1ff.;
CCC 1024–25). What does Moses refer to as our dwelling place (Deut
33:27; Ps 90:1)? Where else does Jesus refer to "my Father's house" (Lk
2:49; Jn 2:16)? Where did God dwell upon the earth (2 Chron 6:13–7:3,
especially 7:1–3; Acts 7:46–47)? Where did the fullness of God dwell on
earth during Christ's lifetime (Col 2:9; Jn 1:14; CCC 484, 594)? What is
now being built as a dwelling place for God (Eph 2:22; CCC 756)?
Where is the new Temple (House) of God (Rev 7:14–17; 11:19; 21:3,
22)? Where will the believer go to "dwell" (Jn 14:2)? Where do Jesus
and the Father come to "dwell" (Jn 14:23, same Greek word as 14:2;
CCC 260)?

5. Consider John 14:1–6 in the light of marriage festivities in the time
of Jesus. How might Jesus' leaving his disciples and later returning to
receive them represent the marriage formalities in Israel? Should the
betrothed bride be sad or troubled when the groom is going to prepare
a home for her? In Jesus' time, the groom left his betrothed with her
parents at her house to prepare a home for her in his own city. He would
prepare the home and feast for his bride, and then come, usually at night
(Mt 25:6; consider the repeated phrase "as a thief in the night": Mt
24:43; 1 Thess 5:2) to escort his bride to the wedding at his house. How
does the Jewish cultural background help us understand John 14:3? How
might the *bathing* and *washing* mentioned in John 13 apply to this
wedding imagery?

» CULTURAL NOTE: "The bride was literally adorned like a queen (see Revelation 21:2). She was bathed, and her hair braided with as many precious stones as

---

[4] Hans Schwarz, *Eschatology* (Grand Rapids, Mich.: William B. Eerdmans Pub., 2000), 335.

the family possessed or could borrow (Psalm 45:14–15; Isaiah 61:10; Ezekiel 16:11–12). The girls who had dressed her accompanied her as 'companions.' The bridegroom too was dressed in finery and jewelry (Isaiah 61:10) and was accompanied by the 'friend of the bridegroom' (John 3:29). The dressing up for the wedding was so important that it was unforgettable (Jeremiah 2:32). The bride and groom looked like and acted like a king and queen.

"Another important element of the wedding was the procession at the end of the day. The bridegroom set out from his home to fetch his bride from her parents' home. At this point the bride was wearing a veil. At some point the veil was taken off and laid on the shoulder of the bridegroom, and the declaration was made, 'The government shall be upon his shoulder.' A procession then set out from the bride's home to the couple's new home, and the dark roadway would be lit with oil lamps held by wedding guests. In the story told by Jesus, the bride and groom were later than expected so the oil in the lamps began to run low. Only those who had brought a reserve flask of oil were able to refill their lamps and welcome the bride and groom (see Matthew 25:1–13, esp. vv. 8–9). There was singing and music along the way (Jeremiah 16:9), and sometimes the bride herself would join in the dance (Song of Songs 6:13)."[5]

Ephesians speaks of "having cleansed her [the Church and Bride] by the washing of water with the word" (Eph 5:26). Joseph A. Grassi comments, "The image is derived from the ceremonial bath of the bride before marriage. The only other place in the N[ew] T[estament] where the word *loutron* (bath, washing) occurs is in Ti 3:5 where 'the bath of regeneration and renewal by the Holy Spirit' refers to baptism. The phrase 'by the word' may allude to either the baptismal formula or the confession of faith. *so that he might present the Church to himself.* This completes the image of the presentation of the bride to her husband. The Christian counterpart is the presentation of the cleansed, newly clothed candidates to Christ. However, the word 'present' . . . is at times used by Paul in reference to the presentation of men at the Second Coming (2 Cor 4:14; Rom 14:10; cf. Col 1:27–28). This would parallel the presentation of the chaste virgin to Christ in 2 Cor 11:2. According to Jewish custom, there was a lapse of time between the contract or espousal and the presentation of the bride to her husband. This could parallel the time interval between the contract at baptism and the final presentation of the bride to Christ at the Second Coming."[6]

6. Thomas is confused and frightened. What does he ask (Jn 14:5)? Each time "doubting" Thomas asks questions, what is the result (cf. Jn

---

[5] Ralph Gower, *The New Manners and Customs of Bible Times* (Chicago: Moody Press, 1987), 66.

[6] Raymond Brown, Joseph Fitzmyer, and Roland Murphy, eds., *The Jerome Biblical Commentary* (Englewood Cliffs, N.J.: Prentice-Hall, 1968), 2:349.

14:6; 20:24–28)? Does Jesus respect those who have *honest* questions and doubts? What are the two kinds of doubt (CCC 2088)? How do faith and doubt relate (CCC 157)? What is the way to heaven (Jn 14:6; 1:51)? What does the image of Jacob's ladder teach about the way to heaven (cf. Jn 1:51; CCC 661)? How do we arrive at our Father's house (CCC 2795–96)? It is significant in the Greek that each of the three nouns (*way*, *truth*, and *life*) has a definite article. How is Jesus *the* Way (Jn 6:68; 10:9; Rom 5:1–2; Eph 2:17–22; Heb 10:19–22; CCC 459–60)? How is Jesus *the* Truth (Jn 1:14, 17; CCC 2466)? How is Jesus *the* Life (Jn 1:1–5; 5:26, 29; 6:51, 68)? Is there any other way to be saved than Jesus (Acts 4:12; 1 Tim 2:5; CCC 432)?

7. In verse 8, what does Philip ask of Jesus? What do the Scriptures say about *seeing* God (Ex 33:18–23; Is 6:1–7; 1 Tim 6:14–16)? How does Jesus reveal or unveil the Father (Jn 1:18; 10:30–33; Col 1:15, 19; 2:9; Heb 1:1–3; CCC 151)? Refer back to the "overture" (Jn 1:1–18); what simple formula does John use to explain God's "unveiling" of himself (Jn 1:1, 14, 18)? How can knowing Jesus show us the Father (CCC 65, 516)? Remember when the Jews asked the same kinds of questions and Jesus had already answered them (Jn 5:36–40; 10:37–38)? What should the works, the signs, the words, and the sinless life of Jesus have proved (Jn 14:11; 5:36; CCC 548)? How do the Jews respond as their fathers responded (Ps 95:6–11)?

» THE CHURCH FATHERS: "And therefore the Lord answered Philip thus;— *Have I been so long time with you, and ye have not known Me, Philip?* He rebukes the Apostle for defective knowledge of Himself; for previously He had said that when He was known the Father was known also. But what is the meaning of this complaint that for so long they had not known Him? It means this; that if they had known Him, they must have recognised in Him the Godhead which belongs to His Father's nature. For His works were the peculiar works of God. He walked upon the waves, commanded the winds, manifestly, though none could tell how, changed the water into wine and multiplied the loaves, put devils to flight, healed diseases, restored injured limbs and repaired the defects of nature, forgave sins and raised the dead to life. And all this He did while wearing flesh; and He accompanied the works with the assertion that He was the Son of God. Hence it is that He justly complains that they did not recognise in His mysterious human birth and life the action of the nature of God, performing these deeds through the Manhood which He had assumed."[7]

---

[7] St. Hilary of Poitiers, *De Trinitate* 7, 36, in NPNF2 9:133.

» CHURCH TEACHING: "Obviously the sight of the Father which Jesus refers to in this passage is a vision through faith, for no one has ever seen God as he is (cf. Jn 1:18; 6:46). All manifestations of God, or 'theophanies', have been through some medium, they are only a reflection of God's greatness. The highest expression which we have of God our Father is in Christ Jesus, the Son of God sent among men. 'He did this by the total fact of his presence and self-manifestation—by words and works, signs and miracles, but above all by his death and glorious resurrection from the dead, and finally by sending the Spirit of truth. He revealed that God was with us, to deliver us from the darkness of sin and death, and to raise us up to eternal life' (Vatican II, Dei Verbum, 4)."[8]

» THE NICENE CREED: "We believe in one Lord, Jesus Christ, the only Son of God eternally begotten of the Father, God from God, Light from Light, true God from true God, begotten, not made, one in Being with the Father. Through him all things were made." The illustration of "light from light" helps us understand the unity of Father and Son. The Son is in the Father, as light is in that light out of which it flows, without separation; the Father is in the Son as the light in the light which it causes and does not leave.

8. In verse 12, what does Jesus mean when he says that a believer will do greater works than he himself did? Is Jesus speaking of greater in *quality* or *quantity*? Upon what basis or why will the apostles be able to do greater works?

» THEOLOGICAL NOTE: Jesus himself is the sacrament (or mystery) of God, and the sacraments of the Church are simply the work and power of Christ continuing to flow to mankind through the Church, his mystical Body (CCC 774). Jesus was localized in Israel for a few short years in the first century. Power flowed from him to forgive, heal, sanctify, and so on. Those powers and mysteries are no longer localized in his fleshly body but are now available world-wide through the sacraments still flowing from his mystical Body, the Church.
"[John 14:12] does not refer primarily to miracles, though these too will continue (cf. Acts 5:12–16), but to the far greater scope, geographically and numerically, within which the Church will exercise its salvific power; the nature of these greater deeds has already been suggested by such texts as 4:35–38; 10:16f.; 11:52; 12:20f. . . . The condition of this activity is Christ's glorification and the giving of the Spirit."[9] "The disciples knew that in themselves they were quite incapable of any such achievement, but he went on to tell them

[8] José María Casciaro, *The Navarre Bible: The Gospel of Saint John* (Dublin: Four Courts Press, 1992), 186.
[9] Brown, Fitzmyer, and Murphy, *Jerome Biblical Commentary*, 2:453.

of the coming of the Paraclete [Holy Spirit], who would empower them and make their witness effective. The 'greater works' of which he now spoke to them would still be his own works, accomplished no longer by his visible presence among them but by his Spirit within them. And it was only by his going to the Father that the Paraclete would come to them (Jn 16:7)." [10]

9. How many times does Jesus use the phrase "in my name" in John 14? What does this mean (cf. Jn 15:16; 16:23–24; CCC 2614, 2633, 2666)?

John 14:15–31
Jesus Promises the Holy Spirit

10. In verse 15, Jesus declares that if his disciples love him, they will keep his commandments. What are his commandments (2 Jn 5–6; Mt 5:17–20; Lk 10:25ff.; Jn 13:34; CCC 1823, 1965)? Does salvation by grace mean we no longer have to obey the laws of God and Christ (1 Jn 2:1–11)?

» THEOLOGICAL NOTE ON THE LAW: "The Law of the Gospel 'fulfills,' refines, surpasses, and leads the Old Law to its perfection (cf. Mt 5:17–19)" (CCC 1967). The negative prohibitions of the Old Covenant are now restated in a positive form in the New Covenant. For example, it is not enough to avoid murder; one must love one's enemies. In this way, the Old Law is made new in Christ. The core of the Law has not changed. The "coin" has only been "flipped" from the "letter-side" to the "spirit-side" of the Law. Each of the Ten Commandments now has a positive counterpart for us to achieve. We must still observe the prohibitive laws, of course, but by the grace of Christ and the indwelling of the Holy Spirit we can obey the more demanding law of Christ.

If we love God, live the fruits of the Spirit, and love our brother *and* our enemy (the whole Law encapsulated), we have already entered into the fullness of the positive side of the Law. By loving our neighbor (internal, positive, with power from the Spirit to obey), we not only meet the negative, external commands of the Law, we surpass them (Gal 5:22–23). The spirit of the Law—the law of grace—exceeds the letter of the Law. In this way the whole Law is fulfilled (cf. Rom 8:2–4; 13:8–10; Mt 7:12; 22:40; Gal 6:2; CCC 2196). Jesus came to fulfill the Law, to give it to us in its fullness and to provide the grace to live the Law. He did not come to take it away or abolish it (Mt 5:17–19).

God's character does not change. He requires us to conform to his holiness (Heb 12:14). He wants his people to be *like* him, to have his same righteousness

---

[10] F. F. Bruce, *The Gospel of John* (Grand Rapids, Mich.: William B. Eerdmans, 1983), 300.

actually in their souls and in their lives. Martin Luther alleged that we were so corrupt that we could not attain such holiness and that one was simply "declared" righteous—righteous in a forensic, judicial sense—not infused with the real and practical righteousness of Christ. The Catholic Church, conforming to Scripture, teaches that we must become holy (CCC 1474, 2013). We exceed the requirements of the Law when, by the Spirit, we live out the spirit of the Law, doing the good works spoken of so often in the Scriptures. Therefore Paul says in Galatians 5:23, after reciting the fruits of the Spirit, "Against such there is no law." If the fruits of the Spirit are being manifested in our lives, we are not only obeying the Law, we are exceeding it, and against such persons and behavior there is no law. See Romans 13:8–11 and CCC 1824, 2196.

11. According to verse 16, what is Jesus going to ask the Father to give the disciples? Who is the "Counselor" that the Father will give them forever (Jn 14:26; 15:26; 16:7, 13; CCC 685, 692, 729)? How will this Counselor "take the place" of Jesus (CCC 729)? How is the Holy Spirit related to Jesus and the Father (CCC 253–56, 689)? How will the Counselor be with the disciples and in them (Acts 2:1–4, 33, 38; 4:31; 5:32; Eph 1:13–14; CCC 260, 687, 2671)?

» THEOLOGICAL NOTE: "Here and in v. 26 the Spirit is said to be sent by the Father in the name of Christ; in 15:26 Christ sends him from the Father; Christian tradition has spoken of the procession of the Holy Spirit both as from the Father through the Son and as from the Father and the Son. The Spirit is 'another' Paraclete because the Son himself has been the first (cf. 1 Jn 2:1). 'Paraclete' is a legal term that had been taken into Jewish use, signifying 'advocate,' 'helper,' 'mediator.' (The role of the Paraclete is explained in greater detail in v. 26; 15:26; 16:7–14). . . . *to be with you forever*: The age of the Church is the era of the Spirit (cf. Acts, 'the Gospel of the Spirit') to whom is attributed the divine presence in sanctification and testimony throughout the Church's life. [Verse] 17: *the Spirit of truth*: This term (used also in 15:26; 16:13) partially defines the role of the Paraclete, to guide the Church in truth; truth is his characteristic as it has been that of the first Paraclete (1:14; 14:6). *the world cannot accept him*: Neither could the world . . . accept the Son, refusing to see in him the revelation of the Father. *because it neither sees nor recognizes him*: The presence of the Spirit will be visible, as was the true nature of Christ, only to the eye of faith. *he remains with you . . . within you*: The Holy Spirit will be both in the Church and in every Christian (cf. the similar language in 1 Cor 3:16f.; 6:19)." [11]

» HOLY SPIRIT, BOND OF LOVE: "The Spirit, according to [St. Augustine], is the bond of love who binds the Father and the Son together and is the full

---

[11] Brown, Fitzmyer, and Murphy, *Jerome Biblical Commentary*, 2:453.

expression of the love which flows between the Lover and the Beloved. The disciples, already loved by the Father and by the Son, now have the same Spirit imparted to them and, being introduced by him into the circle of the divine love, are enabled not only to reciprocate that love but also to manifest it to one another and to all mankind (cf. Rom 5:5; 15:30; Col. 1:8)." [12]

12. In verse 18, notice that Jesus promises not to leave the disciples as orphans (desolate). In the Old Testament "orphans" had no father to defend or protect them, and they were powerless—without a legal defender. Disciples who lost their rabbi were frequently called orphans. [13] What does Jesus mean "I will not leave you desolate" (Rom 8:15; Gal 4:5–7; 2 Cor 6:16–18; CCC 788)? How will Jesus come to them? Are we orphans (Rom 8:15, 23; Eph 1:5; CCC 1265, 1996–97, 2021, 2782)? Has the Church been left desolate or orphaned for the last two thousand years (Mt 28:18–20; CCC 860–62)? How will the world fail to see Jesus even though the disciples will be able to see him? Notice the union that is to exist among the believers, the Son, and the Father in verse 20.

13. Does verse 21 imply that one can be right with God by "faith alone"? What is the relationship between *belief* and *obedience* (Jn 3:36: "He who believes in the Son has eternal life; he who does not obey the Son shall not see life, but the wrath of God rests upon him")? What sequence follows from having and obeying Christ's commands (v. 21; cf. 1 Jn 4:16)? Compare Proverbs 8:17. What does Jesus promise to do in the disciples who love and obey him (v. 23; 2 Cor 6:16–18; 1 Jn 2:24; Rev 3:20; 21:3)? The words for *home* or *dwelling* are the same in both John 14:2 and 14:23. Compare them and their relationship.

14. In verse 22, why does Judas (not Iscariot) ask Jesus why he is going to disclose himself privately to the disciples, but not to the world? What do the disciples (and the Jews) expect Jesus to do immediately (Lk 19:11; Jn 6:15; 18:36)?

15. In verse 26, how does John identify the Person of the Paraclete? The name or title "Holy Spirit" is mentioned three times in John (Jn

---

[12] Bruce, *John*, 304.

[13] See Walter A. Elwell, ed., *Evangelical Commentary on the Bible* (Grand Rapids, Mich.: Baker Book House Co., 1989); published in electronic form, as Logos Software 2.1, by Logos Research Systems, 1997.

1:33; 14:26; 20:22). Compare the three instances. In verse 26, what will the Holy Spirit do? Who assumes the role of teaching and leading the disciples? In the context, to whom is Jesus speaking, his disciples or all believers (Jn 13:5, 12)? Does the Holy Spirit bring to "your remembrance" all that he said to his disciples, or was he speaking specifically to the apostles? How do more than thirty thousand competing denominations demonstrate the anarchy caused when each believer presumes to be individually led by the Holy Spirit *apart from* the apostolic leadership established by Jesus in his Church?

16. What does the Bible warn about "private interpretation" of Scripture (2 Pet 1:20; CCC 119)? Who is responsible for providing a definitive teaching and interpretation of the Bible (CCC 84–85, 95)? Who has the authority to protect and interpret the Bible (CCC 119; Acts 20:27–31; Tit 1:7–9)? What is the "pillar and bulwark of the truth" (1 Tim 3:14–15)? Who or what has judicial authority over a believer (Mt 18:17)? How are the faithful to respond to the teaching authority of the Church (CCC 87–88).

17. What does Jesus mean when he says that the Holy Spirit will bring to their "remembrance" all that he has said to them (cf. Lk 24:8; Jn 2:22; 12:16; Acts 11:16; CCC 729)? Read CCC 1099 and 2625 and think about the Holy Spirit, tradition, the Magisterium, the liturgy, and the memory of the Church, in light of Jesus' promise (Jn 14:26; CCC 91–93). How, and by whom, is the fullness of Christ manifested in the Church (CCC 2623–25)?

» ARTISTIC NOTE: The Holy Spirit of God is the "soul of the Church". In St. Peter's Basilica in Vatican City, the Holy Spirit is given a prominent place in the architecture of the church. Behind the high altar is a luminescent alabaster window, which on a sunny day floods the front of the basilica with golden light. The window is circular and divided into twelve radiating sections, which represent the twelve apostles. The gospel never changes because represented in the center of the window is the dove hovering through the centuries—the Holy Spirit who pours the Light of Christ out to the world through the apostles and the Church. Jesus sent his Paraclete to teach and remind the apostles of all that he told them. Angels intermingle with the golden rays of light surrounding the window. Under the window there is displayed a magnificent bronze chair that contains an ancient chair of acacia wood inlaid with ivory said to be the remains of the episcopal chair in which, according to ancient tradition, St. Peter sat and taught Roman Christians. This beautiful chair represents the authority of Peter and the continuity of pure doctrine. On either side of the chair are two Doctors of the Church: two from the West, St. Augustine and St. Ambrose, and two from the East, St. Athanasius and St. John Chrysostom. The significance of the Fathers flanking the chair is quite profound—the Doctors of the Church are in harmony with the teaching of Peter and his successors as they teach the faith. The Fathers flank the chair but are not holding up the chair, since Peter's authority is not from flesh and blood but from God. This breathtaking structure was the creation of Gian Bernini, who designed and built it between 1658 and 1666.[14]

» THEOLOGICAL NOTE: "He will . . . bring to your remembrance all that I have said to you." What do these words mean? "Following the glorification of Christ, it will be the function of the Spirit to complete the revelation of Christ by enlightening the Church concerning the true and full meaning of what Jesus had done and said (cf. 2:22; 12:16; Acts 11:15f.). J[oh]n's Gospel itself is the result of the fulfillment of this promise."[15]

A priest once asked the congregation, "If you had the choice of either a video of Christ's entire life or the four existing Gospels, which would you prefer?" The people all thought, "The video, of course!" The priest explained his preference by saying, "I would take the Gospels. Those who lived during the time of Christ and watched him on a daily basis did not understand him or his teaching, including his own disciples. Thus a video may be interesting but would do little to enlighten us. On the other hand, the Gospels are not just a 'video' of the life of Christ. The Gospels are the life of Christ as interpreted and explained by the Holy Spirit as he instructed and brought to the memory of the apostles all that Jesus had taught them according to his promise in John 14:26. It is through the ministry of the Holy Spirit that we understand Christ and his life." This priest understood the nature of the Gospel, the ministry of the Holy Spirit, and the fullness of the Catholic Church.

"The word translated here as 'bring to your remembrance' also includes the idea of 'suggesting': the Holy Spirit will recall to the Apostles' memory what they had already heard Jesus say—and he will give them light to enable them to discover the depth and richness of everything they have seen and heard. Thus, 'the Apostles handed on to their hearers what he had said and done, but with that fuller understanding which they, instructed by the glorious events of Christ and enlightened by the Spirit of truth, now enjoyed' (Vatican II, *Dei Verbum*, 19). . . . 'This same Spirit guides the successors of the Apostles, your bishops, united with the Bishop of Rome, to whom it was entrusted to preserve the faith and to "preach the Gospel to the whole creation." Listen to their voices,

---

[14] For more information, see Giovanni Giuliani, *Guide to Saint Peter's Basilica* (Rome: ATS Italia, 1995), and Nicolo Suffi, *St. Peter's Guide to the Square and the Basilica,* trans. Kate Marcelin-Rice (Vatican City: Libreria Editrice Vaticana, 1999).

[15] Brown, Fitzmyer, and Murphy, *Jerome Biblical Commentary*, 2:454.

for they bring you the word of the Lord' (John Paul II, Homily at Knock Shrine, Sept. 30, 1979)."[16]

18. What is Jesus going to leave his disciples (v. 27)? How will it be different from what the world offers (v. 27; cf. Jn 16:33)? How does the encouragement of Jesus (the new Moses) just before his departure resemble the words of Moses just before his departure (Deut 31:8; same Greek word for "troubled")?

19. Why does Jesus tell his disciples in advance that he is leaving (v. 29; cf. Jn 13:19; 16:4)? What will they believe when they see these things take place?

20. In verse 30, Jesus says he has very limited time to give the final instructions to his disciples (actually less than twenty-four hours). Satan is on his way and has conspired to put Jesus to death. This will apparently destroy the Son of God and foil his plan of redemption. But Satan will actually fulfill the plan of God and destroy himself (cf. 1 Jn 3:8; CCC 395, 1851). Why does Jesus submit to the evil plot of Satan (v. 31; Jn 12:31–32; CCC 606–7, 2853)? What does Jesus mean that Satan has "no power over me", or, as in some translations, "nothing in me" (Heb 4:15; 7:26; 2 Cor 5:21; CCC 612)? Verse 31 contains the only instance in the New Testament where Jesus states that he loves the Father; how is that love demonstrated? How is our love of Jesus concretely demonstrated?

21. In preparation for the next study, consider the idea of abiding, dwelling, rooms (especially, Jn 14:3, 10, 23, 25) and compare this with the word "abide" in John 15. The word is translated "remain" in the NAB, NJB, and the NIV. (The Greek word that is translated as "rooms" or "dwellings" derives from μενω—"remain" or "abide".)

---

[16] Casciaro, *John*, 190–91.

JOHN 15

THE VINE AND BRANCHES—IN THE WORLD,
BUT NOT OF THE WORLD

John 15:1–17
Abide Fruitfully in Christ or Burn

1. In the last phrase of chapter 14, Jesus interrupts his four-chapter dialogue with the Twelve and says, "Rise, let us go hence." What location are they leaving (Jn 13:1–4; Mk 14:13–16)? To what site are they headed (Jn 18:1–3)? Jesus often uses the physical surroundings to illustrate his teaching (cf. Mk 11:20–21; Mt 4:18–19). How might he have used the environs around Jerusalem to demonstrate his teaching on the vine and the branches?

» HISTORICAL NOTE: "It has been the belief of many expositors that our Lord gave this chapter in a discourse down in the Valley of Kidron or on the side of the Mount of Olives, because we know that at that time there was a vineyard in that area which covered that valley. We also know that it was full moon because it was the time of the Passover. He may well have spoken these words as they walked through the vineyard. It would have been an appropriate place.

"Another suggestion has been made . . . that that night He went by the temple, following the Law as He so meticulously did. The gates would have been open during the Passover nights. Those beautiful gates of the temple were actually a tourist attraction. They had been forged in Greece, floated across the Hellespont, then brought to Jerusalem, and placed in Herod's temple there. The gates were made of bronze and wrought into them was a golden vine. That the vine symbolizes the nation Israel is apparent from the following verses: 'Thou hast brought a vine out of Egypt: thou hast cast out the heathen, and planted it. Thou preparedst room for it, and didst cause it to take deep root, and it filled the land' (Ps. 80:8–9)."[1]

---

[1] J. Vernon McGee, *Thru the Bible Commentary*, vol. 41: *John Chapters 11–21* (Nashville: Thomas Nelson Pub., 1991), 89.

278

» HISTORICAL NOTE, VINES ON THE TEMPLE GATES: "[The holy Temple's] first gate was seventy cubits [eighty-two feet] high, and twenty-five cubits [thirty feet] broad; but this gate had no doors; for it represented the universal visibility of heaven, and that it cannot be excluded from any place. Its front was covered with gold all over. . . . That gate which was at this end of the first part of the house was, as we have already observed, all over covered with gold, as was its whole wall about it; it had also golden vines above it, from which clusters of grapes hung as tall as a man's height." [2] "The vine was of great importance in the religion of Israel. It was used as a symbol of the religious life of Israel itself, and a carving of a bunch of grapes often adorned the front exterior of the synagogue. The symbolism was based upon passages such as Psalm 80 and Isaiah 5:1–5 where Israel is God's vine." [3]

2. Since it was not out of the way to pass by the Temple on the way to the Kidron Valley, why might Jesus have stopped at the Temple to illustrate his parable? Imagine the scene in the moonlight, the magnificent Temple glistening with gold. What does gold represent? [4] What was the "old vine", and who is the "new vine" (Jn 15:1)? Who is the new Temple (Jn 1:14; 2:21; Col 2:9; Eph 2:19–22; 1 Cor 3:16–17; CCC 586, 756)? Who is the gate (Jn 10:7–9)? Who is the new high priest (Heb 9:11)?

3. Union with Jesus means participation in the new Israel, the people of God—Jesus marks the beginning of the new Israel. Who is the new sacrifice (Jn 1:29)? Who is the genuine vine (Jn 15:1; CCC 755)? Who is the vinedresser, the farmer (v. 1)? Who are the branches (Jn 15:1–2)? What is the fruit of the vine (v. 1)? What happens to the branches that bear fruit (vv. 2, 7–8)? What happens to the branches that do not abide in the vine or bear much fruit (vv. 2, 6)?

4. In the Old Testament, Israel is often referred to as the vine, and God as the vinedresser (cf. Is 5:1–7; Ezek 19:10). Read Psalm 80, and consider the parallels with John 15. Notice the use of the word *son* (Ps 80:15,

---

[2] Flavius Josephus (ca. 37–ca. 100), *Wars of the Jews* 5, 5, 4, in *Josephus: Complete Works*, trans. William Whiston (Grand Rapids, Mich.: Kregel Pubs., 1978), 555.

[3] Ralph Gower, *The New Manners and Customs of Bible Times* (Chicago: Moody Press, 1987), 111.

[4] "The mysticism of St. Bernard [of Clairvaux] centers in Christ. Christ is the pure lily of the valley whose brightness illuminates the mind. As the yellow pollen of the lily shines through the white petals, so [with Jesus] the gold of his divinity shines through his humanity" (Philip Schaff, *History of the Christian Church* [Grand Rapids, Mich.: Wm. B. Eerdmans Pub., 1907], 5:642–43).

NIV), and the phrases "the man at your right hand" and "the son of man you have raised up for yourself" (Ps 80:17, NIV). How might this terminology have been understood by the early Christians (Dan 7:13; Jn 1:51; 6:53; 12:23)?

» St. Augustine on Psalm 80: "'Look from heaven and see, and visit this vineyard.' 'And perfect Thou her whom Thy right hand hath planted' (ver. 15). No other plant Thou, but this [plant] make Thou perfect. For she is the very seed of Abraham, she is the very seed in whom all nations shall be blessed: there is the root where is borne the grafted wild olive. 'Perfect Thou this vineyard which Thy right hand hath planted.' But wherein doth He perfect? 'And upon the Son of man, whom Thou hast strengthened to Thyself.' What can be more evident? Why do ye still expect, that we should still explain to you in discourse, and should we not rather cry out with you in admiration, 'Perfect Thou this vineyard which Thy right hand hath planted, and upon the Son of man' perfect her? What Son of man? Him 'whom Thou hast strengthened to Thyself.' A mighty stronghold: build as much as thou art able. 'For other foundation no one is able to lay, except that which is laid, which is Christ Jesus.'"[5]

5. How does Isaiah 4:2–4 shed light on this passage about the vine (cf. CCC 64)?

6. In his conversation with his twelve disciples, which carries over from chapter 14, Jesus has told them that they would be "in" him (Jn 14:20) and that he will be "in" them (Jn 14:20, 23). How does the image of the vine and branches explain this relationship (CCC 755)? How does St. Paul describe this relationship in other words (Gal 2:20; Phil 4:13)?

7. Since in the Old Testament the vine was Israel, and now is Jesus, how are the Gentiles able to partake of the vine and become fruitful branches (Rom 11:17–24; CCC 60)?

8. What use is a branch that produces no fruit? What are the alternative uses for unfruitful branches (Ezek 15:1–5)?

» Theological note: "Dead, fruitless branches of vines are obviously of no use for carpentry; their only possible value is for fuel. Jewish teachers believed that God had awful punishments in store for apostates, because those who had known the truth and then rejected it had no excuse."[6]

---

[5] St. Augustine, *On the Psalms* 80, 9, in NPNF1 8:389.
[6] Craig Keener, *The IVP Bible Background Commentary: New Testament* (Downers Grove, Ill.: InterVarsity Press, 1993), 301.

» THEOLOGICAL NOTE: Jesus frequently uses words with double meanings to emphasize his point (for example, "wind" and "spirit", born "again" and born from "above"). John uses such a double meaning here in 15:2, where the word "prune" means both to prune or trim back a vine and to cleanse or purify. Where has Jesus just referred to cleansing (Jn 13:8–10)? "In Jn 15.2 the verb [prune] involves a play on two different meanings. The one meaning involves pruning of a plant, while the other meaning involves a cleansing process."[7] Notice how Jesus ties the pruning of the fruitful branches to our moral conduct and practice. God cleanses his people through baptism and confession, as we have seen in John 3 and 13. God also cleanses his Church by pruning unfruitful vines. How are "pruning" and "cleansing" similar and different?

9. What is the difference between *pruning* in verse 2 and *throwing away* in verse 6? Some adherents of the "eternal security" doctrine ("once-saved, always-saved") attempt to avoid the obvious import of this text by claiming the burned branches are not *actual* branches but only *professing* branches that actually are *not* branches at all. Does Jesus say he will cut off a branch or a non-branch? If one fails or ceases to bear much fruit, how certain can he be of his "eternal security" (Mt 10:22; Jn 15:6; Col 1:22–23; Heb 10:26–27; Rom 11:21–22; CCC 162)? Can one live without good works and still be assured of salvation (Rom 2:6; Jas 2:20–26; CCC 1033)? Where else does Jesus refer to *fire* in a similar context (Mt 7:15–23; 13:40–43; 18:8; 25:41–46)? What happens to the unfruitful tree (Mt 3:10)? What are the things that can cause us to be cut off (Rom 6:16; CCC 1033, 2089)? What is the Church's teaching on hell (CCC 1033–37)?

» THEOLOGICAL NOTE: Many commentators argue that the burned branches were never actually authentic branches. However, "This passage assumes that the person who falls away was already 'in' Christ, that is, as a genuine branch of the vine, not a pseudo-branch or branch that was never connected to the vine. Rather, Jesus pictures a branch, once a healthy part of the vine, that subsequently withered. Once withered, it falls off the vine and is thrown in the fire."[8]

"Our Lord does not mention the possibility of repentance. The soul can, by

---

[7] Καθαίρω, in Johannes P. Louw and Eugene A. Nida, eds., *Greek-English Lexicon of the New Testament,* 2d ed. (New York: United Bible Societies, 1989); published in electronic form, as Logos Software 2.1, by Logos Research Systems, 1996; cf. CCC 1839.

[8] Robert A. Sungenis, *Not by Faith Alone: The Biblical Evidence for the Catholic Doctrine of Justification* (Santa Barbara, Calif.: Queenship Pub., 1997), 278.

mortal sin, cut itself off from the vine-stock; but there is always hope for it till death decides its fate." [9]

10. What does Jesus mean by "pruning" the branches? How does God prune the branches? What does it indicate if God refuses to prune the branches (Is 5:6, and preceding verses)? How should we perceive and receive the pruning and discipline of God (Prov 3:11–12; 1 Cor 11:32; Heb 12:7–11)?

11. In the first section, John 15:1–8, how many times is the word "abide" or "remain" used? In the second, John 15:9–17, how many times is the word "love" used? How are they summarized in John 15:16–17? With these key thoughts, how would you summarize the theme of this section? Read the first epistle of St. John and notice how frequently John uses the words *abide* and *love* throughout the book.

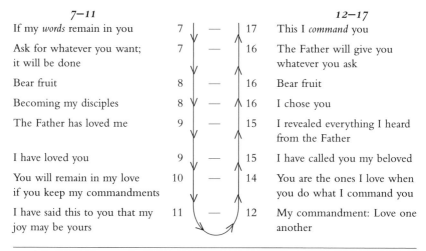

	7–11				*12–17*
If my *words* remain in you	7		17	This I *command* you
Ask for whatever you want; it will be done	7		16	The Father will give you whatever you ask
Bear fruit	8		16	Bear fruit
Becoming my disciples	8		16	I chose you
The Father has loved me	9		15	I revealed everything I heard from the Father
I have loved you	9		15	I have called you my beloved
You will remain in my love if you keep my commandments	10		14	You are the ones I love when you do what I command you
I have said this to you that my joy may be yours	11		12	My commandment: Love one another

Based on a chart in *The Gospel according to John*, vol. 1, Anchor Bible, vol. 29 (Garden City, N.Y.: Doubleday, 1996); used with permission.

12. The chart above shows the interesting structure of the first section of John 15. Brown comments, "It is always difficult to be sure that the discovery of such an elaborate chiastic structure does not reflect more of the ingenuity of the investigator than of the intention of the Johannine writer. . . . Nevertheless, here there are too many correspondences to be

---

[9] C. C. Martindale, *The Gospel according to Saint John*, Stonyhurst Scripture Manuals (Westminster, Md.: Newman Press, 1957), 123–24.

coincidental." [10] Notice the inverted and parallel themes of the chiastic structure with the pinnacle being verse twelve—Jesus' new commandment that we love one another. [11]

13. In an earlier instance, how has Jesus instructed us to abide in him (Jn 6:56: CCC 787)? How does he continue to love and communicate his grace (life) to us today (CCC 1380, 1406)? How does prayer enable us to abide in Christ (CCC 2615, 2711–14)? Why is the presence and relationship with Christ more intense now than it was when he walked the earth (Jn 14:16–19; CCC 788)?

» THE CHURCH FATHERS: "Having said that they were clean through the word which He had spoken unto them, He now teaches them that they must do their part.... Then he shews what it is to abide in Him, 'If ye abide in Me, and My words abide in you, ye shall ask what ye will, and it shall be done unto you.' It is to be shewn by their works." [12]

14. A new commandment is given: to love one another (Jn 13:34). How are we to love (Jn 15:13; 1 Jn 3:16; CCC 1823)? To what extent are we to show charity (CCC 1825)? How is the greatest love demonstrated (v. 13)? Does this love proceed from ourselves as a source (Jn 15:4–5, 10)? If we do not love our brother and lay down our life for others, can we claim to have the love of God abiding in us (1 Jn 3:16–17)? How can we show this love in practical ways (CCC 2447)?

15. Later, in his first epistle, John restates Jesus' teaching about *abiding in Christ*. Read 1 John 3:13–24. This passage helps us understand the

---

[10] Raymond E. Brown, ed. and trans., *The Gospel according to John,* vol. 2, Anchor Bible, vol. 29A (Garden City, N.Y.: Doubleday, 1970), 668.

[11] Chiasm is a clever and effective means of emphasis in writing. It is a structure within the text designed for emphasis and highlighting. Hebrews wrote poetry using parallelism of thought, not by using rhyming words properly placed. Chiastic writing is a means of using parallel thoughts or statements to point to the main idea or emphasis at the very center of the progressively ascending or descending thoughts. As discussed in the commentary on John 2, "Chiasm is a development of inclusion. Instead of simply ending and beginning in the same way, chiasm extends the balancing of the first and the last by balancing the second and the fourth (thus, *abcb'a'*, or *ab-b'a'*). In John's Gospel, the author uses the five-member chiasm in every part, sequence, and section.... The use of chiasm in the writings of the Old and the New Testaments and in the writings of the Greeks and Romans has been amply documented" (Peter Ellis, *The Genius of John: A Composition-Critical Commentary on the Fourth Gospel* [Collegeville, Minn.: Liturgical Press, 1984], 10–11).

[12] St. John Chrysostom, *Homilies on John,* Homily 76, in St. Thomas Aquinas, *Catena Aurea: St. John* (Albany, N.Y.: Preserving Christian Publications, 1995), 4:479–80.

importance of the teaching after the apostle had reflected upon it for many decades, under the guidance and mentoring of the Paraclete.

16. What is the difference between a slave and a friend (Jn 15:15–16; Gal 4:5–7; CCC 1972)? Enoch and Noah "walked with God" (Gen 5:24; 6:9), but who is the first and only Old Testament character to be called the "friend of God" (2 Chron 20:7; Is 41:8; Jas 2:23)? What does it benefit us to be God's friends (CCC 142, 1972)? What prerequisite is required to be considered a friend of God (v. 14; cf. Mt 12:50)?

» HISTORICAL NOTE: "The idea of being the friend of God has also a background. Abraham was the friend of God (Isaiah 41:8). In Wisdom 7:27 Wisdom is said to make men the friends of God. But this phrase is lit up by a custom which obtained both at the courts of the Roman Emperors and of the eastern kings [e.g., 2 Sam 15:37; 1 Ch 27:32–34]. At these courts there was a very select group of men called the friends of the king, or the friends of the Emperor. At all times they had access to the king: they had even the right to come to his bedchamber at the beginning of the day. He talked to them before he talked to his generals, his rulers, and his statesmen. The friends of the king were those who had the closest and the most intimate connection with him.

"Jesus called us to be his friends and the friends of God. That is a tremendous offer. It means that no longer do we need to gaze longingly at God from afar off; we are not like slaves who have no right whatever to enter into the presence of the master; we are not like a crowd whose only glimpse of the king is in the passing on some state occasion. Jesus gave us this intimacy with God, so that he is no longer a distant stranger, but our close friend." [13]

17. According to verse 16, how were the Twelve chosen (Jn 1:35–51; 6:70; Lk 6:12–16)? Do these words spoken intimately to the chosen Twelve automatically apply to all believers? Is there a sense in which what Jesus says to the Twelve here applies only to them and a sense in which his words apply to all disciples of Jesus (cf. Jn 6:70; CCC 737–38)? Do the Twelve hold a unique position (cf. Lk 22:28–30; Rev 21:14; CCC 857, 869)? What does Jesus mean that we can ask and receive (CCC 2745)? In whose name do we ask of the Father (v. 16; 16:23–24; Eph 2:18)?

---

[13] William Barclay, *The Gospel of John* (Philadelphia: Westminster Press, 1975), 2:178.

John 15:18–27
In the World, but Not of the World

18. How are the disciples *in* the world but not *of* the world (Jn 13:1–2; 17:14–17; CCC 2850)? Can we be friends with the world (Jas 4:4; CCC 2737)? What does "world" mean in this context (Jn 3:19; 8:23; 16:28; CCC 408–9)? How is the word "world" used with various meanings (cf. CCC 341)? How might the use of "world" in John 3:16 differ from the use of "world" in our current passage? How did the "overture" prepare us for the world's rejection of Jesus (Jn 1:10)? What can the disciples expect (Mt 10:16–23; 24:9–14)? How should the Christian respond to persecution and suffering (Rom 12:14; 1 Pet 4:15–16; CCC 2636)?

» THEOLOGICAL NOTE: "1. It is true that the world, so designated, remains fundamentally the *excellent creature* which God made in the beginning (Ac 17,24) by the agency of His Word (Jn 1,3,10; cf He 1,2; Col 1,16). This world continues to bear witness to God (Ac 14,17; R 1,19f). Moreover, it would be wrong to prize the world too highly, for man far surpasses it in real worth: what will it profit him to gain the whole world if he loses his own soul (Mt 16,26)?

"2. But there is more yet: in its present state, this world, closely linked as it is with sinful man's condition, is, in fact, *under the power of Satan*. Sin entered the world at the beginning of history, and with sin, death (R 5,12). Hence, it has become a debtor to divine justice (3,19), for it is intimately bound up with the mystery of evil which is at work here below. Its most apparent element is made up of those rebellious men who set their will in opposition to God and to His Christ (Jn 3,18f; 7,7; 15,18f; 17,9 [and] 14 . . .). Behind them stands the invisible leader, Satan, prince of this world (12,31; 14,30; 16,11), the god of the present age (2 Co 4,4). Established as chief of this world by his creator's will, Adam has given to Satan's hands his person and his dominion; since then the world has lain in the power of the evil one (1 Jn 5,19), who communicates power and glory to whomever he will (Lk 4,6).

"This world of darkness is ruled by evil spirits (E 6,12); it is a deceiving world whose constitutive elements weigh man down and enslave him, even in the ancient economy itself (G 4, 3.9; Col 2,8.10). The spirit of this world, since it is incapable of tasting the secrets and gifts of God (1 Co 2,12), is opposed to the Spirit of God, just as is the spirit of Antichrist which is at work in the world (1 Jn 4,3). The wisdom of this world, because it relies on the speculations of human thought cut off from God, is convicted of folly by God (1 Co 1,20). The peace which this world gives, comprised as it is of material prosperity and false security, is only a shadow of the true peace which only Christ can give (Jn

14,27): the final effect of this false peace is a sadness which brings death (2 Co 7,10)." [14]

» THE WORLD: "John makes clear that the world's hatred of the Christian is not a passing phenomenon; hate is just as much of the essence of the world as love is of the essence of the Christian. The world is opposed to God and His revelation; it can never have anything but hate for those who recognize that revelation in His Son. In a series of four conditional sentences it is repeated that the world's hatred for Christians is basically a refusal of Jesus himself. Love of Jesus has made the true Christian so much like Jesus that he is treated in the same manner as Jesus. We may remember that by the time the Fourth Gospel was in its final form, persecution by the Romans and the expulsion of Jewish Christians from synagogues were already accomplished facts and no longer morose forebodings." [15]

19. Why does the world hate Jesus (Jn 7:7; 3:19–20)? Why does the world hate the Christian (vv. 19–21; Jn 17:14; 1 Pet 2:3–4; Rev 12:17)?

» HISTORICAL NOTE: "It was not only that the government persecuted the Christians; the mob hated them. Why? It was because the mob believed certain slanderous things about the Christians. There is no doubt that the Jews were at least to some extent responsible for these slanders. It so happened that they had the ear of the government. To take but two examples, Nero's favorite actor Aliturus, and his harlot empress Poppaea, were both adherents of the Jewish faith. The Jews whispered their slanders to the government, slanders which they must have well known to be untrue, and four slanderous reports were spread about the Christians. (i) They were said to be insurrectionaries. . . . (ii) They were said to be cannibals. This charge came from the words of the sacrament. 'This is my body which is for you.' 'This cup is the new covenant in my blood.' On the basis of these words, it was not difficult to disseminate amongst ignorant people, prepared to believe the worst, the story that the Christians' private meal was based on cannibalism. The charge stuck, and it is little wonder that the mob looked on the Christians with loathing. (iii) They were said to practice the most flagrant immorality. . . . It was not difficult to spread abroad the report that the Love Feast was an orgy of sexual indulgence, of which the kiss of peace was the symbol and the sign.

"They were said to be incendiaries. . . . In the reign of Nero came the disastrous fire which devastated Rome and it was easy to connect it with people who preached of the consuming fire which would destroy the world. . . . (v) There was actually another charge brought and for this fifth charge there were understandable grounds. It was that the Christians 'tampered with family

---

[14] Xavier Léon-Dufour, ed., *Dictionary of Biblical Theology*, trans. P. Joseph Cahill (New York: Desclée Co., 1967), 597.

[15] Brown, *John*, 2:695.

relationships,' divided families, split up homes and broke up marriages. In a way that was true. Christianity did bring not peace but a sword.

"The world acutely dislikes people whose lives are a condemnation of it. It is in fact dangerous to be good. The classic instance is the fate which befell Aristides in Athens. He was called Aristides the Just; and yet he was banished. When one of the citizens was asked why he had voted for his banishment, he answered: 'Because I am tired of hearing him always called the Just.' That was why men killed Socrates; they called him the human gadfly. He was always compelling men to think and to examine themselves, and men hated that and killed him. It is dangerous to practice a higher standard than the standard of the world. Nowadays a man can be persecuted even for working too hard or too long.

"To put it at its widest—the world always suspects nonconformity. It likes a pattern; it likes to be able to label a person and to put him in a pigeon-hole. Anyone who does not conform to the pattern will certainly meet trouble. It is even said that if a hen with different markings is put among hens that are all alike, the others will peck her to death. The basic demand on the Christian is the demand that he should have the courage to be different. To be different will be dangerous, but no man can be a Christian unless he accepts that risk, for there must be a difference between the man of the world and the man of Christ." [16]

20. What does Jesus mean when he says that the Jews (and the world) would be without sin if he had not come and revealed himself (Jn 9:41; Jas 4:17; Rom 7:7–11)? How are the works of Jesus a witness against them (Jn 5:36; 10:37–38; CCC 548)? In the face of the evidence, what do the Jews try to do with the evidence (Jn 12:9–11)? How does God treat those who reject him even though works and signs are provided (cf. Ps 95:6–11)? Why are the Jewish leaders afraid of people believing in Jesus (Jn 11:48; CCC 596)? Do the Jews reject Jesus out of ignorance and pure motives, or out of selfishness, jealousy, and disobedience? Would you have received and worshipped a "man" who claimed to be God? Read Psalm 95:6–11. How does it parallel the Jews of old with the Jews of Jesus' time? How were the Jewish leaders of Jesus' time hardening their hearts even though he showed them signs and wonders?

21. John quotes the words about those "who hate me without cause". Read Psalm 69, especially verse 4. How should this psalm have illuminated the Jews as to Jesus and his mission? Compare Psalm 69:9 with John 2:17 (cf. CCC 584). Also, compare Psalm 69:21 with John 19:28–30. What do we learn about Jesus from this psalm? Revelation 3:5, 13:8,

---

[16] Barclay, *John*, 2:183–86.

16:1, and 17:8 also refer to this psalm. Psalm 35 is another, possible source for this quote, though less likely. Notice especially verse 19. How is *this* psalm of David also related to Jesus and his rejection?

22. Who and what is the *Helper, Counselor,* or *Paraclete* (cf. CCC 263, 691–92;)? See John 14. Where else does John mention this *Paraclete* (Jn 14:16; 16:7; 1:32)? Who else is a *Paraclete* (1 Jn 2:1)? How does Jesus reveal the Spirit to his followers (cf. CCC 728)? When would this *Helper* be given (Jn 7:39; CCC 729)? Who actually sends the Holy Spirit (Jn 14:16; 15:26; 16:7; CCC 244, 248, 264)? How should we ask for the *Helper* (CCC 2671)? What does the Nicene Creed, recited each Sunday at Mass, explain about the Holy Spirit? How will the Holy Spirit bear witness to Jesus (Jn 16:8–15; Acts 4:31, 33; CCC 1433)?

23. Moments before he ascended into heaven, what commission did Jesus give his apostles (Acts 1:6–8)? What were the twelve apostles required to have witnessed (Acts 1:21–22; 2:32)? How will the apostles "bear witness" to Jesus (Mt 28:18–20; Acts 2:14–36; 4:31–33; 5:32; 10:34–43)? What and who have already borne witness to Jesus (Jn 5:33, 36–37, 39)? How will the Spirit assist the apostles (Mt 10:16–20; Acts 6:10; 13:2; 15:28)?

» PRACTICAL NOTE: "Every Christian should be a living witness to Jesus, and the Church as a whole is a permanent testimony to him: 'The mission of the Church is carried out by means of that activity through which, in obedience to Christ's command and moved by the grace and love of the Holy Spirit, the Church makes itself fully present to all men and peoples in order to lead them to the faith, freedom and peace of Christ by the example of its life and teaching, by the sacraments and other means of grace' (Vatican II, *Ad gentes,* 5)."[17]

The dialogue flows without interruption into the next chapter.

---

[17] José María Casciaro, *The Navarre Bible: The Gospel of Saint John* (Dublin: Four Courts Press, 1992), 200.

JESUS PREPARES TO LEAVE AND RETURN;
THE ACTION OF THE HOLY SPIRIT

John 16:1–6

Christians and Persecution

1. Notice the uninterrupted flow of dialogue between chapters 15 and 16. What is going to happen to Jesus in only a few of hours (Jn 18:1–3)? How long does Jesus have to impart his last instructions and consolations to his close friends—his disciples? What disturbing news does Jesus give them (Jn 13:21, 33, 37–38; Jn 15:19–20)? Why does Jesus explain these things in advance (Jn 16:1; 13:19; 14:29)? Of what does Jesus warn (Jn 16:2)? Is Jesus the kind of king and messiah they are expecting (Jn 12:13; Acts 1:6)? Why has Jesus not told them this unsettling news earlier (Jn 16:4–6)?

2. In verse 1, the Greek word for "falling away" or "stumbling" (σκαν-δαλίζω) means "to lay a snare or something to catch or trip the feet". Notice that the only other place John uses this word is in John 6:61. What causes many of the disciples to stumble (Jn 6:52–58)? How do many Christians today continue to stumble at this point? What else would cause some disciples to stumble (Jn 6:62)? Corresponding to that, what does Jesus tell his disciples he is going to do (Jn 16:5)?

3. Jesus warns of severe persecution on account of him. What did it mean for a Jew to be "put out of the synagogue"—an outcast from the corporate worship of Israel (Jn 9:22; 12:42; CCC 596)? Who was the first believer to be excommunicated—put out of the synagogue (Jn 9:24, 34)? What motivation will those who kill the disciples claim (Jn 16:2)? What is the cause (v. 3; 15:21; Acts 3:17)? What does God say about such misdirected zeal (Is 66:5)? Who was the first Christian martyr (Acts 7:54–60)? Which of the Twelve was the first to die for the faith as

a witness (Acts 12:2; the Greek word for "witness" is *marturia*, from which we get the word martyr)? How did one Jewish leader persecute Christians (Acts 26:9–11)?

» HISTORICAL NOTE: An example of Jewish persecution of the early believers in Jesus is provided by the first-century Jewish historian Josephus. "When, therefore, Ananus was of this disposition, he thought he had now a proper opportunity [to exercise his authority]. Festus was now dead, and Albinus was but upon the road; so he assembled the sanhedrin of judges, and brought before them the brother of Jesus, who was called Christ, whose name was James, and some others, [or, some of his companions]; and when he had formed an accusation against them as breakers of the law, he delivered them to be stoned."[1]

"Christians in John's day were being expelled from many local synagogues, perhaps under the influence of Palestinian Pharisaic propaganda. Hostile Jewish non-Christians in Asia Minor do not appear to have killed Christians directly; but their participation in Christians' deaths was no less significant. By betraying Jewish Christians to the Roman authorities and claiming that Christians were non-Jewish, they left Christians with no legal exemption from worshiping the emperor. Worried that Christians were a messianic and apocalyptic movement that could get them in trouble with Rome, many synagogue leaders may have thought their betrayal of Christians would protect the rest of their community (cf. 11:50)."[2]

» THEOLOGICAL NOTE: Those who opposed the Jewish leaders and their rules would often be put out or banned from the synagogue. Being excommunicated or "de-synagogued" caused those so excommunicated to be treated as dead by those still "in the synagogue". Even their immediate family shunned them. For more details, see chapter nine, number 18.

4. According to verse 5, where is Jesus going (Jn 7:33)? What does Jesus say has filled his heart with sorrow? Who else would have sorrow (Jn 16:22)? Why does Jesus say, "None of you asks me, 'Where are you going?'" when the disciples have asked that question twice in the last few hours (Jn 13:36; 14:5)?

» TEXTUAL NOTE: "St. Peter (13:36) had asked this very question, and St. Thomas (14:5) had questioned on the subject. But, from the context, we learn

---

[1] Josephus, *Antiquities of the Jews* 17, 1, in *Josephus: Complete Works*, trans. William Whiston (Grand Rapids, Mich.: Kregel Pubs., 1978), 423.

[2] Keener, *The IVP Bible Background Commentary: New Testament* (Downers Grove, Ill.: InterVarsity Press, 1993), 302–3.

that the disciples had questioned Jesus from their point of view. Saddened at the thought of the impending separation, they did not ask what benefits would accrue to our Lord from His return to the Father." [3]

John 16:7–15
The Action of the Holy Spirit

5. According to verse 7, why is it to the apostles' advantage for their Master and Friend to leave (Jn 7:37–39; 14:26; CCC 689–90)? Do the apostles understand what Jesus is teaching them, and do they have courage (Mt 16:9; Jn 10:6; 20:9; 20:19)? In how many places at one time could Jesus be in his human form (Phil 2:6–7; CCC 461, 476)? How was Jesus limited by his human body? In contrast, how many places could the *Paraclete* inhabit at any one time (CCC 2671)? How did Jesus reside with the disciples while a man? How will Jesus, through the Spirit, reside with them after his Ascension (Jn 14:17; Col 1:27; CCC 2, 813)? Who will send the Spirit to indwell believers and the Church (CCC 730–31)? Who is the Trinity (CCC 202)?

6. In their book *Reasoning from the Scriptures*, the Jehovah's Witnesses conclude, "The holy spirit is the active force of God. It is not a person but is a powerful force that God causes to emanate from himself to accomplish his holy will." [4] How do we know that the Holy Spirit is not simply a *force*, but a *Person*—God, the third Person of the Trinity (Acts 5:3–4; 13:2–4; 21:10–11; Eph 4:30; CCC 243, 252–55; 258–59)? According to John 16:13, the Spirit of truth "speaks" only what he "hears". Does an impersonal, "active force" *speak* and *hear*? Does a force have the personal ability to *show* things to others? Are these verbs associated with impersonal forces or persons?

» THEOLOGICAL NOTE: The Church has defined, based upon Holy Scripture and the apostolic tradition, that "the Holy Ghost is a real Person. . . . He is a Person distinct from the Father and the Son; and . . . He is a truly Divine Person, or God Himself. Once these three points are established from Holy Scripture, no further proof will be needed to show the existence of a Third

---

[3] Madame Cecilia, *St. John*, Catholic Scripture Manuals (London: Burns, Oates, & Washbourne, 1923), 295.

[4] *Reasoning from the Scriptures* (Brooklyn, N.Y.: Watch Tower Bible and Tract Society, 1985), 381.

Person in the Godhead. . . . An impersonal being could not 'teach all truth,' 'give testimony,' 'bring all things to [the Apostles'] mind,' remind them of what Christ had told them, and so forth. There are many other texts of Sacred Scripture in which the Holy Spirit is described as possessing all the marks of a real personality." [5]

» THE ATHANASIAN CREED: "Whoever wishes to be saved must, above all, keep the Catholic faith. For unless a person keeps this faith whole and entire, he will undoubtedly be lost forever. This is what the Catholic faith teaches: we worship one God in the Trinity and the Trinity in unity. We distinguish among the Persons, but we do not divide the substance. For the Father is a distinct Person; the Son is a distinct Person; and the Holy Spirit is a distinct Person. Still, the Father and the Son and the Holy Spirit have one divinity, equal glory, and coeternal majesty. What the Father is, the Son is, and the Holy Spirit is." [6]

7. In John 14:17 Jesus tells us the Counselor will reside in us (Jn 14:17). Compare this with the action of the Holy Spirit with the believers in the Old Testament (Num 11:17; Judg 3:10; 1 Sam 16:13; Ezek 11:5). Very few times in the Old Testament are we told that the Holy Spirit was actually "in" a person (for example, Ex 31:3 and Num 27:18).

8. What will the Holy Spirit do when Jesus sends him (Jn 16:8–15; CCC 729)? How will he convict the world of sin (Jn 16:9; Acts 2:37; CCC 388, 1433)? How will he convict the world of righteousness (Jn 16:10; Acts 7:52)? How will he convict the world of judgment (Jn 16:11; 12:31; CCC 550)?

» THEOLOGICAL NOTE: "The idea [of this passage] is that, in a reversal of the trial of Jesus, the world is found guilty of sin in that it has not acknowledged the justice of God in the glorified Jesus, and this very conviction is a judgment on the Prince of this world who accused Jesus and put him to death. . . . Commentators have not found the detailed exposition of [verses] 8–11 easy. Augustine avoided the passage as very difficult; Thomas Aquinas cited opinions but gave none of his own; Maldonatus found it among the most obscure in the Gospel. [7]

---

[5] Joseph Pohle, *God: His Knowability, Essence, and Attributes*, adapted and edited by Arthur Preuss (St. Louis, Mo.: B. Herder Book Co., 1925), 96, 100; for more information on the Person and divinity of the Holy Spirit, see Yves Congar, *I Believe in the Holy Spirit*, trans. David Smith (New York: Crossroad Pub. Co., 1983), and Frank J. Sheed, *Theology and Sanity* (San Francisco: Ignatius Press, 1978), 88–123.

[6] James Socías, ed., *Handbook of Prayers* (Princeton, N.J.: Scepter Pub., 1995), 345.

[7] Raymond E. Brown, ed. and trans., *The Gospel according to John*, vol. 2, Anchor Bible, vol. 29A (Garden City, N.Y.: Doubleday, 1970), 2:705, 711.

"The first element (vs. 9) in the Paraclete's forensic activity is to prove to the disciples that the world is guilty of sin—the basic sin which consists in refusing to believe in Jesus. . . . The second element (vs. 10) in the Paraclete's forensic activity is to prove the world wrong about justice by showing that Jesus, whom it adjudged guilty, was really innocent and just. . . . The last element (vs. 11) is the Paraclete's forensic activity, namely, to prove that in condemning Jesus the world itself was judged. In Jesus' death on the cross the trial that endured throughout this ministry seemed to end with the victory of his enemies. But in the Paraclete Jesus is still present after his death, and so the trial had a surprising outcome." [8]

"The Spirit is the 'advocate' or helper of those who believe in Jesus, their counsel for the defense. But in relation to unbelievers, to the godless world, he acts as counsel for the prosecution. In both respects he duplicates the work of Jesus: Jesus had been his disciples' helper while he was with them, and at the same time his presence and witness in the world had served as an indictment of those who closed their minds to his message. The Spirit's prosecuting ministry is here expressed by the verb 'elenchō', meaning (according to the context) expose, refute, convince or convict. His very presence will be a demonstration to the world which condemned Jesus that he was in the right and they were in the wrong. In the paraphrastic wording of the [New English Bible], he will 'show where wrong and right and judgement lie' and thus, 'confute the world'. . . . The Spirit bears witness to the world . . . that Jesus, rejected, condemned and put to death by the world, has been vindicated and exalted by God. His rejection, condemnation and execution expressed in violent clarity the world's refusal to believe in him; that unbelief is now exposed as sin. His condemnation, promulgated after due process of law, is now shown to have been utterly unrighteous; his return to the Father is the demonstration of his righteousness—and at the same time the vindication of the Father's righteousness." [9]

9. According to verse 12, was Jesus able to impart to his disciples everything he wanted them to know? How will his teaching develop in the future (Jn 16:13; 14:26; Acts 4:8; Acts 15:22, 28; 1 Jn 2:20, 27; CCC 78, 85, 91, 113, 171, 2421)? Does Jesus indicate that the sum total of his teaching will be in the "Bible only"? Jesus says the Holy Spirit "will declare to you the things that are to come". Examine three incidents where this "foretelling" took place (Rev 1:1; Acts 11:27–28; 21:10–11).

10. How does the "Spirit of Truth" differ from the *other* spirit who attempts to influence and indwell mankind (Jn 8:44; 13:26–27; CCC

---

[8] Ibid., 712–14.

[9] F. F. Bruce, *The Gospel of John* (Grand Rapids, Mich.: William B. Eerdmans, 1983), 318–19.

392, 2482)? What kind of activity takes place in the Christian life of which the Christian must be aware and for which he must be prepared (Eph 6:10–18; 2 Cor 10:3–4)? Does Satan always show his evil face (2 Cor 11:14–15)? What are we told of false prophets (Mt 7:15)?

11. What is the basis and source of the Holy Spirit's "speaking" (Jn 16:13)? How is the Holy Spirit like Jesus (Jn 8:28, 38; 12:49–50; 14:10; CCC 687)? Is the Holy Spirit, practically speaking, "another" Jesus (Jn 14:16)? What does he do besides convict the world of sin? How does he teach the apostles "all things" and bring to their remembrance all that Jesus has taught them? Do we have a personal relationship with the Holy Spirit?

» DOCTRINAL NOTE: While reading the following Church document, notice the work and ministry of the Holy Spirit. "This Tradition which comes from the apostles develops in the Church with the help of the Holy Spirit. For there is a growth in the understanding of the realities and the words which have been handed down. This happens through the contemplation and study made by believers, who treasure these things in their hearts (cf. Lk. 2:19, 51), through the intimate understanding of spiritual things they experience, and through the preaching of those who have received through episcopal succession the sure gift of truth. For as the centuries succeed one another, the Church constantly moves forward toward the fullness of divine truth until the words of God reach their complete fulfillment in her.

"The words of the holy Fathers witness to the living presence of this tradition, whose wealth is poured into the practice and life of the believing and praying Church. Through the same tradition the Church's full canon of the sacred books is known, and the sacred writings themselves are more profoundly understood and unceasingly made active in her; and thus God, who spoke of old, uninterruptedly converses with the Bride of His beloved Son; and the Holy Spirit, through whom the living voice of the gospel resounds in the Church, and through her, in the world, leads unto all truth those who believe and makes the word of Christ dwell abundantly in them (cf. Col. 3, 16).

"Hence, there exist a close connection and communication between sacred tradition and sacred Scripture. For both of them, flowing from the same divine wellspring, in a certain way merge into a unity and tend toward the same end. For sacred Scripture is the word of God inasmuch as it is consigned to writing under the inspiration of the divine Spirit. To the successors of the apostles, sacred tradition hands on in its full purity God's word, which was entrusted to the apostles by Christ the Lord and the Holy Spirit. Thus, led by the light of the Spirit of truth, these successors can in their preaching preserve this word of God faithfully, explain it, and make it more widely known. Consequently, it is not from sacred Scripture alone that the Church draws her certainty about everything which has been revealed. Therefore both sacred tradition and sacred Scripture are to be accepted and venerated with the same sense of devotion and reverence.

"Sacred tradition and sacred Scripture form one sacred deposit of the word of God, which is committed to the Church. Holding fast to this deposit, the entire holy people united with their shepherds remain always steadfast in the teaching of the apostles, in the common life, in the breaking of the bread and in prayers (cf. Acts 2, 42, Greek text), so that holding to, practicing and professing the heritage of the faith, there results on the part of the bishops and faithful a remarkable common effort.

"The task of authentically interpreting the word of God, whether written or handed on, has been entrusted exclusively to the living teaching office of the Church, whose authority is exercised in the name of Jesus Christ. This teaching office is not above the word of God, but serves it, teaching only what has been handed on, listening to it devoutly, guarding it scrupulously and explaining it faithfully by divine commission and with the help of the Holy Spirit; it draws from this one deposit of faith everything which it presents for belief as divinely revealed.

"It is clear, therefore, that sacred tradition, sacred Scripture and the teaching authority of the Church, in accord with God's most wise design, are so linked and joined together that one cannot stand without the others, and that all together and each in its own way under the action of the one Holy Spirit contribute effectively to the salvation of souls." [10]

12. How else does the Holy Spirit work within the Church (1 Cor 2:10–13; 12:4–13; Acts 15:28; Eph 4:30; CCC 737, 739, 768, 799–801, 2003)?

John 16:16–24
Jesus' Crucifixion and Resurrection Foretold

13. What does Jesus mean (v. 16) that he will leave, and then in a short time they will see him again (Jn 20:19–20; Acts 1:9–11)? In verses 17–19, the Twelve do not have a clue what Jesus means. Who else failed to understand (Jn 7:32–36)? When will the disciples weep and lament (Mk 16:10; Lk 23:27)? When will the mourning be turned to joy (Jn 20:20)? How does this "weeping turned to joy" also apply to the future (Rev 7:17; 21:4)? Would Mary also experience sorrow (Lk 2:35; Jn 19:25)?

---

[10] Vatican II, Dogmatic Constitution on Divine Revelation, *Dei Verbum*, November 18, 1965, nos. 8–10.

14. How is the joy of the world different from the joy of the Lord? Why is it that no one can take away the joy Christ gives (CCC 769–70)? How is "hope" related to "joy" (CCC 1820)? (The word "joy" is used in St. John only seven times in the Revised Standard Version translation, four of which are in chapter 16; one each in chapters 3, 15, and 17.) Notice the use of "joy" and "mourning" in Jeremiah 31:9–15. Who is the Shepherd who brings this joy to Israel (Jn 10:14)? How did the disciples experience this joy (Acts 13:52; Rom 15:13; 2 Cor 7:4; Gal 5:22; 1 Thess 1:6)? What do all these references to joy have in common, or *whom* do they all have in common (CCC 2819)?

15. How should we pray, and for what (Jn 16:23–24; Rom 8:26; CCC 2615, 2683, 2750)? How does the Paraclete help us to pray (Rom 8:26–27; CCC 2766)? To whom was this promise of answered prayer given? Have you received *everything* you have asked for? What conditions do Peter, James, and John give us for "asking" (1 Jn 5:14–15; 1 Pet 3:12; Jas 5:16; CCC 2737)?

John 16:25–33
Jesus' Last Consolations

16. In verse 25, what does Jesus mean when he says he has spoken to the disciples in "figures" or "parables"? The disciples have learned that Jesus loves them; who else loves them (v. 27)? What is the new relationship between the disciples and the Father, and how can we now address God the Father (Rom 8:15–17; Gal 4:6–7; CCC 2777)? What does the "overture" tell us about our new relationship (Jn 1:12; CCC 1692)?

» CULTURAL NOTE: To this day, young children in Israel called their fathers "Abba". The term "Abba" is and was a title of affection and love. " 'Abba' is the Aramaic word for 'Papa,' a term of great intimacy and affectionate respect. It was normally the first word a child would utter, but adults could use it for their fathers as well, and students sometimes used it of their teachers. Perhaps because it implied such intimacy, Jewish people never used it of God (though they did call him a heavenly father) except in an occasional parable by a charismatic teacher." [11]

---

[11] Keener, *IVP Bible Background Commentary*, 176.

17. According to verse 27, why does the Father love Jesus' disciples (Jn 14:21, 23)? How does verse 28 summarize the whole Gospel of St. John? Was Jesus "of this world" (Jn 8:23; 18:36)? Think about the Creator of the universe actually becoming human and thus becoming part of his own creation. How, in a sense, is Jesus a cosmic visitor to our planet?

» POETIC MYSTERY AND THEOLOGY: St. Augustine wrote, "My mouth will utter the praise of the Lord,/ of the Lord through whom all things have been made,/ And who has been made [man] amidst all things;/ Who is the Revealer of His Father, Creator of His mother;/ who is the Son of God from His Father without a mother,/ The Son of Man through His mother without a father. / He is as great as the Day of the Angels,/ and as small as a day in the life of men;/ He is the Word of God before all ages,/ and the Word made flesh at the destined time./ Maker of the sun, He is made [man] beneath the sun./ Disposing all the ages from the bosom of the Father,/ He consecrates this very day in the womb of His mother./ In His Father He abides; from His mother He goes forth./ Creator of heaven and earth,/ under the heavens He was born upon earth./ Wise beyond all speech, as a speechless child He is wise./ Filling the whole world, He lies in a manger./ Ruling the stars, He nurses at His mother's breast./ He is great in the form of God/ and small in the form of a servant,/ So much so that His greatness/ is not diminished by His smallness./ Nor His smallness concealed by His greatness./ For when He assumed a human body,/ He did not forsake divine works./ He did not cease to be concerned mightily/ from one end of the universe to the other,/ And to order all things delightfully, when,/ having clothed Himself in the fragility of the flesh,/ He was received into, not confined in,/ the Virgin's womb./ So that, while the food of wisdom/ was not taken away from the angels,/ We were to taste how sweet is the Lord." [12]

18. What does Jesus mean by saying that he goes to the Father (Lk 22:69; Acts 1:9–11; Eph 1:19–23; Col 3:1)? How are we also "raised" with Christ into "heavenly places" (CCC 1002)?

19. In verses 31–32, how does Jesus respond to the disciples' claim that they finally believe in him? What are the disciples about to do (Jn 18:17; Mt 26:31; Mk 14:50)? Do they all abandon Jesus (Jn 19:25–27)? Will the Father leave Jesus in his hour of trial (v. 32)? What then does Jesus mean when he cries out from the Cross "My God, my God, why have you forsaken me?" (Mt 27:46; Ps 22; CCC 603)? Is Psalm 22 a cry of despair

---

[12] St. Augustine, *Sermo in Natale Domini IV* [a poetic version], in Johann Moser, ed., *O Holy Night: Masterworks of Christmas Poetry* (Manchester, N.H.: Sophia Institute Press, 1995), 96–97.

or a psalm of victory (Ps 22:22ff.)? Was the eternal Trinity divided, or did the Father just remove the outward, external, and physical protection that would have prevented the crucifixion (see the notes on John 19:28–37)? Why does the Father never leave Jesus (Jn 8:29; CCC 2824)? How can we imitate Christ in this matter (CCC 2825)?

20. What virtue is required for us to be of courage while persecuted in the world (CCC 1808)? What reality gives us the confidence of victory (v. 33; Rom 8:31–39; CCC 2853)? How do we overcome the world in Christ (2 Cor 4:7ff.; Rev 12:11; 1 Jn 5:4–5)? Will God allow his people to be tested beyond their ability (CCC 2848)? Who will partake of heaven and the promises (Rev 21:7; CCC 2788)? What happens to those who succumb to sin and fail to overcome (2 Pet 2:20–22; Heb 6:4–8; Rev 21:8)? Can one who has failed to be steadfast in the faith be certain of eternal life (Col 1:22–23)?

21. Why does Jesus explain all these things (chapters 13–16) to his twelve disciples (Jn 16:1; 33)? Notice that these are the *last* words of Jesus to his disciples before his arrest and crucifixion! How are these words very appropriate?

» PAPAL TEACHING: "The mission of the Church, like that of Jesus, is God's work or, as Luke often puts it, the work of the Spirit. After the resurrection and ascension of Jesus, the apostles have a powerful experience which completely transforms them: the experience of Pentecost. The coming of the Holy Spirit makes them witnesses and prophets (cf. Acts 1:8; 2:17–18). It fills them with a serene courage which impels them to pass on to others their experience of Jesus and the hope which motivates them. The Spirit gives them the ability to bear witness to Jesus with 'boldness'. When the first evangelizers go down from Jerusalem, the Spirit becomes even more of a 'guide,' helping them to choose both those to whom they are to go and the places to which their missionary journey is to take them. The working of the Spirit is manifested particularly in the impetus given to the mission which, in accordance with Christ's words, spreads out from Jerusalem to all of Judea and Samaria, and to the farthest ends of the earth." [13]

» SECOND VATICAN COUNCIL: "As for the rest, the Lord Jesus, Who said: 'Take courage, I have overcome the world' (Jn. 16:33), did not by these words promise His Church a perfect victory in this world.

---

[13] John Paul II, *Mission of the Redeemer* (Boston, Mass.: St. Paul's Books and Media, 1990), no. 36.

"This holy Synod rejoices that the earth has been sown with the seed of the Gospel which now bears fruit in many places, under the influence of the Lord's Spirit. He it is who fills the whole earth and has stirred up a true missionary spirit in the hearts of many priests and faithful. For all of these blessings, this most holy Synod gives most loving thanks to all the priests of the world.

" 'Now to him who is able to accomplish all things in a measure far beyond what we ask or conceive, in keeping with the power that is at work in us—to him be glory in the Church and in Christ Jesus' (Eph. 3:20–21)."[14]

---

[14] Vatican II, Decree on the Ministry and Life of Priests, *Presyterorum ordinis*, December 7, 1965, no. 22.

JOHN 17

OUR HIGH PRIEST PRAYS—THE VISIBLE UNITY
OF THE CHURCH

John 17:1–5
Jesus Prays for Himself

1. With chapter 17, we move into a new section, which is a unique chapter in all the New Testament. Jesus was speaking with his disciples but now shifts his attention elsewhere. With whom does he converse throughout the chapter (Jn 17:1)? Why does Jesus raise his eyes (Ps 123:1)? When else does he do this (Jn 11:41)?

2. Read this chapter aloud with the emotion and intensity you would expect Jesus had moments before he was arrested. As you read, try to find the three distinct sections of this chapter.

3. Often the Our Father is called the "Lord's Prayer". In what sense might John 17 be rightly referred to as *The Lord's Prayer*? What is this prayer called in the *Catechism*, and how is it described (CCC 2758)? This is the longest prayer recorded in the Gospels. Where else in John do we see Jesus praying in similar terms (Jn 12:27–28)? According to Jesus, what has finally come (v. 1)? Where else has Jesus referred to "the hour", and what does he mean (Jn 2:4; 7:30; 8:20; 12:23, 27; 13:1; CCC 730, 1085)? What does Jesus desire more than anything else (v. 1)?

» ELUCIDATION: "Jesus has unfolded to His disciples the meaning of His approaching departure; and with this He concludes His ministry of teaching. His priestly ministry, however, is not yet ended; and He moves steadily toward its completion in the atmosphere of prayer. He turns His gaze from earth to heaven, from His disciples to His Father, and utters the prayer which can perhaps best be described as the prayer of the great High Priest. It is the only long, continuous prayer of Jesus recorded in the Gospels. In it He prays for

Himself, for the welfare of His disciples after His departure, and for all who will become believers through their ministry." [1]

"Of all the grand and touching passages that make up this, the grandest of all books, the Bible, this chapter stands pro-eminent [sic], so simple in language, that a child can interpret it; so sublime in ideas and sympathies as to surpass the grasp of an angel's intellect. It reveals the heart of Christ as it points up to the Infinite Father, and looks down through all the scenes and ages of the race. It is a prayer for Himself, the Apostles, and for the universal Church. '*And lifted* (R.V. LIFTING) *up His eyes to heaven.*' The words ought not to be taken to imply that He looked up to the sky, and must therefore have been in the open air. The upward look is naturally expressive of feeling, and irrespective of place." [2]

» HISTORICAL NOTE: "In this prayer of Jesus, our High Priest, for His disciples we have 'the noblest and purest pearl of devotion of the N.T.' The most profound mysteries are expressed in the simplest terms. As the Jewish high priest, on the Day of Atonement, prayed publicly for himself and the people, when he entered the Holy of Holies, and sprinkled the Propitiatory with the blood of the victims, so St Cyril (fifth century) compares our Lord's prayer on this occasion to that sacerdotal prayer of the Jewish Pontiff, and many ancient and still more modern writers refer to this prayer as the Prayer of Jesus, our High Priest. Thus St Cyril writes: 'This great High Priest is Himself the Propitiator and the Propitiation, the Priest and the Victim.'

"St. Rupertus refers to our Lord as 'the Reconciler and the Mediator, the truly great and most holy Pontiff who sacrificed His Life for us and appeased His Father by His intercession.'

"These citations prove that, as early as the fifth century, exegetes saw the similarity between this prayer of Jesus for His disciples and the prayer of the Jewish high priest. (Some Protestant writers, P. Schaff *inter alia*, wrongly give to Chytræus, a Lutheran pastor [sixteenth century], the honour of having first given the title 'Sacerdotal Prayer of Jesus' to St John xvii." [3]

4. Read CCC 2746–51. What place does Jesus' prayer have in the work of salvation? What is its enduring force, and what can we learn from it (CCC 2604)? How does this prayer reveal Jesus as our Paraclete? Notice how Jesus, the "new Moses", prays for the apostles before going up the hill of Golgotha to die, just as Moses of old prayed for the twelve tribes of Israel before going up Mount Nebo to die (Deut 32:48—33:29).

---

[1] R. V. G. Tasker, *The Gospel according to St. John*, Tyndale New Testament Commentaries (Grand Rapids, Mich.: Wm. B. Eerdmans, 1977), 188.

[2] David Thomas, *The Genius of the Fourth Gospel* (R. D. Dickenson, 1885; electronic edition: Oak Harbor: Logos Research Systems, 1997), 70.

[3] Madame Cecilia, *St. John*, Catholic Scripture Manuals (London: Burns, Oates, & Washbourne, 1923), 304.

5. What is a main task of the Jewish high priest and the priesthood (Ex 28:29; 2 Chron 30:27)? What does Jesus constantly do for his people (Heb 7:27; 1 Jn 2:1–2)? Who is the new and eternal High Priest (Heb 2:9, 17; 4:14; CCC 1137)? How does our new High Priest, Jesus Christ, fulfill this priestly office (Heb 7:25; Rom 8:34; 1 Tim 2:5; CCC 2747, 2749, 1348, 1410)? In the Old Testament, priesthood had three levels: (1) high priest (Neh 3:1), (2) Levitical/ministerial priesthood (Num 3:32), and (3) the universal priesthood (Ex 19:6; 1 Pet 2.9). Does Jesus' high priesthood eliminate the need or possibility of the ministerial priesthood under the New Covenant (1 Pet 2:9; CCC 1141–42)? What does the Church teach about the priesthood and ordination (CCC 1590–96)? Who is the High Priest and how do Catholic priests work in conjunction with him (CCC 1384, 1410)? Are all the baptized also a holy priesthood (Rev 1:6; CCC 784, 1546)?

6. The priestly line in Israel came through the line of Aaron. Was Jesus of the line of Aaron (Heb 7:14)? Hebrews is the only book in the New Testament that refers to Jesus as a priest. How was Jesus' priesthood established (Heb 7:11–26)?

» THEOLOGICAL NOTE: "When the priest delivered an oracle, he was passing on an answer from God; when he gave an instruction, a 'torah', and later when he explained the Law, the Torah, he was passing on and interpreting teaching that came from God; when he took the blood and flesh of victims to the altar, or burned incense upon the altar, he was presenting to God the prayers and petitions of the faithful. In the first two roles he represented God before men, and in the third he represented men before God; but he is always an intermediary. What the Epistle to the Hebrews says of the high priest is true of every priest: 'Every high priest who is taken from among men is appointed to intervene on behalf of men with God' (He 5:1). The priest was a mediator, like the king and the prophet. But kings and prophets were mediators by reason of a personal charisma, because they were individually chosen by God; the priest was 'ipso facto' a mediator, for the priesthood is an institution for mediation. This essential feature will reappear in the priesthood of the New Law, as a sharing in the priesthood of Christ the Mediator, Man and God, perfect victim and unique Priest." [4]

» TEMPLE CONTEXT: The dialogue Jesus has with his disciples in John 13–16 is a great picture of Jesus' priestly ministry against the backdrop of the Jewish

---

[4] Roland de Vaux, *Ancient Israel: Its Life and Institutions,* trans. John McHugh (New York: McGraw-Hill, 1961), 357.

Temple. One enters the Temple, approaches first the laver for washing (Jesus washes the feet in John 13), and ends with the High Priest in the Holy of Holies (Jn 17) interceding for the people.

7. According to verse 2, what was Jesus given (Jn 3:35–36; 5:26–27; CCC 2749)? To whom is eternal life given (v. 2; Jn 10:26–29)? What is eternal life (v. 3; Mt 16:27; cf. Wis 16:13)? By implication, what is the most egregious (and stupid) sin (Jn 3:35–36)? What does it mean to know God and Jesus Christ (Phil 3:8–14; Eph 4:11–16; CCC 217, 1721, 1996, 2045, 2751)? How is the Trinity revealed (CCC 684)? What two qualities are attributed to the Father (v. 3; cf. 1 Thess 1:9)? Is John making a distinction between the Son and the Father; or, knowing that the apostles were soon to be sent out to the Gentile nations (cf. "all flesh" in v. 2; Mt 28:18–20), might he be making a distinction between the one true God and the idolatry and pagan worship of false gods and idols, in which even the Jews were known at times to participate?

» LANGUAGE NOTE: In the phrase "And this is eternal life, that they may know Thee", the word "know" is a present subjunctive, which implies that the knowledge is a present, growing knowledge, flowering into a full and experiential knowledge of God, and therefore eternal life. It is not merely something that we intellectually perceive, nor is it merely a one-time event; rather, this is an existential, on-going, deepening relationship with God. Just as "believe" means a continuing and habitual believing in John 3:16, so this "knowing" implies a knowledge advancing beyond the intellect to include and become communion and relationship, a fellowship with and in the very life of the Trinity.

"It is not that abstract knowledge that books, or the teaching of a master, suffice to give, and which an intelligent man, even one of no moral worth, can acquire and possess, and which he could communicate fully to a being as intelligent as himself. It is a personal, interior, experimental knowledge, and in its depths incommunicable. Every man must acquire it for himself, for it is not the knowledge of an idea which other men have made to themselves of God, but the knowledge of God Himself, of God within the soul, speaking to the conscience, forming the soul to obey His voice, and according to the measure of its obedience stripping it of egoism, sensuality, pride; revealing to it ever a more splendid ideal, teaching it in such sort that till then it seems to have known nothing. Oh! this converse with God! inspiring an ever more ardent desire to grow in purity, in love at once effective and generous, and in a more and more courageous effort to become of one spirit with Him, melting our will in His." [5]

---

[5] Abbé Nouvelle, *Our Lord's Last Discourses: Meditations on Chapters XIII–XVIII of the Gospel of St. John*, trans. M. E. M. (London: Burns, Oates, & Washbourne, 1921), 142.

"Eternal life is not merely survival after death, which everyone shares (3:16, 5:29&N; Daniel 12:2), but having intimate 'knowledge' of the Father and the Son. The Hebrew word for 'knowledge,' '*da'at*,' denotes not only the comprehending of the acts and circumstances of the world, but also the most intimate experiencing of the object of knowledge (hence its use in Hebrew to mean sexual intercourse in such expressions as, 'And Adam knew Chavah [Eve] his wife' (Genesis 4:1). Here the word 'know' is used exactly as in Jeremiah 31:33(34), in the passage promising Israel a new covenant: 'And no longer will each one teach his neighbor and his brother, "Know *Adonai*," for they will all know me.'"[6]

"The means of attaining to eternal life *is* the knowledge of God. Note the present tense *is*, because he who possesses sanctifying grace has even now a pledge of eternal life. *that they may know. i.e.*, 'may come to know' (γινώσκω), as in verse 23, 10:38, etc. We grow in the knowledge of God. *To know God* thus unto salvation includes practicing faith, hope, and charity, for man is not saved by faith alone as some Protestant sects assert."[7]

» THEOLOGICAL NOTE: "*This is life everlasting*; that is, the way to life everlasting, *that they may know thee, the only true God, and Jesus Christ, whom thou hast sent.* The Arians, from these words pretended that the Father only is the true God. [St. Augustine] and divers others answer, that the sense and construction is, *that they may know thee, and also Jesus Christ thy Son, whom thou hast sent to be the only true God.* We may also expound them with [St. Chrysostom] and others, so that the Father is here called the only *true God*, not to exclude the Son, and the Holy Ghost, who are the same one true God with the Father; but only to exclude the false gods of the Gentiles."[8]

St. Augustine writes, "The Holy Spirit too is understood because he is the Spirit of the Father and the Son, as the substantial and consubstantial love of both. For there are not two gods, Father and Son, nor three gods, Father and Son and Holy Spirit, but the Trinity itself is the one, sole, true God. Yet neither is the Father the same one who the Son is, nor is the Son the same one who the Father is, nor is the Holy Spirit the same one who the Father and the Son are, because they are three, Father and Son and Holy Spirit, but the Trinity itself is the one God."[9]

[6] David H. Stern, *Jewish New Testament Commentary* (Clarksville, Md.: Jewish New Testament Pubs., 1992), 203.

[7] Madame Cecilia, *John*, 305.

[8] George Leo Haydock, comp., *The Douay-Rheims New Testament with Catholic Commentary* (Monrovia, Calif.: Catholic Treasures, 1991), 1425.

[9] St. Augustine, *Tractates on the Gospel of John 55–111*, trans. John W. Rettig, The Fathers of the Church, vol. 90 (Washington, D.C.: Catholic Univ. of America Press, 1994), 258–59.

» AN INTERESTING NOTE: In verse 3 we find the only recorded instance, any-where in the Gospels, that Jesus refers to himself as "Jesus Christ". Here he refers to himself by his name as a man and by his messianic title.

8. How did Jesus glorify the Father on the earth (v. 4; Jn 4:34; 5:36; 15:10; CCC 2750)? How is the work of Christ continued in the Church today (CCC 1069, 2045)? What glory did Jesus share with the Father "before the world was" (Gen 1:26; Jn 1:2; 17:24; Phil 2:5–7; CCC 241, 266, 468)? Jesus asks to be glorified with God. Can God share his glory with another (Is 42:8; 48:11)? If Jesus shares God's glory, what does this say about Jesus? Jesus shares the Father's glory—it is a clear claim of deity.

Interestingly enough, the Arians of old and the Jehovah's Witnesses and similar groups today erroneously use John 17:3 against the divinity of Jesus, arguing that Jesus claims that the Father is the only true God. This supposedly implies that the Son cannot also be the only true God. But of course that is fallacious: just because the Father is the only true God does not mean that only the Father is the true God. In order to keep their error consistent, they have to deny the correct rendering of John 1:1 and claim that the Word was not "God" but "a god". (See notes on Jn 1:1, 14; 5:18; 8:58; 10:30, 13:19–20; and 20:28 for issues relating to the deity of Christ and the Trinity.)

» HISTORICAL NOTE: "The Old Testament declared that God would not give his glory to another (Is 42:8; 48:11); Jesus' sharing the Father's glory in this sense is a claim that he is divine. Judaism did have a category in which to understand Jesus' divine claim here: God's Wisdom was related to and in some sense identified with his glory (Wisdom of Solomon 7:25–29). John's Jewish Christian readers may have understood Jesus' identity in analogous (albeit superior) terms." [10]

9. According to verse 5, how would Jesus be glorified? How did Moses display the glory of God (Ex 33:18–23; 34:29–35)? How was Jesus glorified before the world was made (Jn 1:1–3; 17:24)?

» HISTORICAL NOTE: We must remember that John's Gospel frequently uses words with double meanings (for instance, "born again" and "born from above" (Jn 3:3), "wind" or "spirit"). "Glory" here has a double meaning. Moses only reflected God's glory in Exodus 33–34, but Jesus is actually to be

---

[10] Craig Keener, *The IVP Bible Background Commentary: New Testament* (Downers Grove, Ill.: InterVarsity Press, 1993), 304–5.

"glorified" in the same sense as the Father, with his preexistent glory (17:5). In this way, Jesus claims divinity.[11]

Jesus has glorified God by accomplishing the work he was given to do—the proof being the disciples at his side and his imminent sacrifice for these friends. Now Jesus asks that God, in return, glorify him again in heaven with the glory he had with the Father before the worlds began. Accomplishing "the work" is possibly what Jesus refers to in John 19:30 when he says, "It is finished" (cf. Jn 4:34).

» THEOLOGICAL NOTE: "In [John 17:5] the glory that Jesus requests is identified with the glory that Jesus had with the Father before the world existed. Later in [John 17:24] this glory will be said to stem from the love that the Father had for Jesus before the creation of the world. . . . [W]e suggest the same background that we suggested for the Logos, namely Jewish speculation about personified Wisdom. Wisdom *existed before the earth was created* (Prov viii 23); during creation she was *with God* who took *delight* in her (viii 30); she was a pure effusion of His *glory* (Wis vii 25). Jesus who speaks as divine Wisdom had the same origins. The relation that xvii 5 established between the ultimate glory of Jesus and his pre-creational glory helps to explain why the first action of the glorified Jesus is that of a new creation in imitation of Genesis." [12]

John 17:6–19

Jesus Prays for His Disciples

10. According to verse 6, how did Jesus manifest or reveal the Father to the disciples (Col 1:15; 2:9; Jn 14:8ff.; CCC 516)? How have the disciples kept Jesus' word? Jesus says, "Now they know that everything that thou hast given me is from thee." Where do the disciples acknowledge that they are finally understanding the words of Jesus (Jn 16:29–30)? How are the disciples partakers of Christ's words (Jn 15:15)? What is revealed to them through Jesus' priestly prayer (CCC 2751)?

11. In verse 8, what does the Logos, the Word (Jn 1:1, 14), give to the disciples? What three things are mentioned about the disciples in verse 8? Notice the procedure for living the word of God in our lives: receive it, know (understand) it, and believe (obey) it.

---

[11] See ibid.

[12] Raymond E. Brown, ed. and trans., *The Gospel according to John*, vol. 2, Anchor Bible, vol. 29A (Garden City, N.Y.: Doubleday, 1970), 753–54.

12. In verse 9, for whom does Jesus now pray? Why does Jesus not pray for the world? Likewise, why does Jesus pray only for Peter and not the other disciples (cf. Lk 22:31–32)? How *does* Jesus pray for the world (Jn 17:21, 23)? Through whom and what would Jesus' prayers for the world be realized? What would be the basis for the world to understand that the Father sent the Son?

13. In verse 11, Jesus says he is no longer in the world; why does he say this (Jn 13:1)? How are the disciples still "in the world" (Jn 13:1; 15:19)? How does Jesus address the Father (v. 11)? How does this emphasize his "nearness" and his "transcendence"? How else does Jesus address his Father in this prayer (Jn 17:25)?

14. In verse 11, what does Jesus pray for his disciples? What is the goal he desires them to achieve and maintain? Is the "oneness" of the disciples to be a visible or invisible unity? Is it to be an organizational or simply a theoretical unity? Is it to be an organic, family unity, or is it competing sects maintaining their own identities? Are there to be distinctions between believers (Gal 3:28; Acts 20:28; 1 Cor 1:11–13; yes, no, or both)? How are Jesus and the Father "one" (Jn 10:30; CCC 590)? How many "bodies" of Christ are there (Eph 4:4; 1 Cor 12:12; CCC 172–75)? Did Jesus intend to establish a *kingdom* or a *democracy* (Mt 16:18–19)?

15. Who was the "son of perdition" or the "one to be lost" (Jn 6:70–71; 13:2)? How were his betrayal and perdition prophesied in Scripture (Ps 41:9; Jn 13:18)? If John had not informed us of the fact, would you have known Psalm 41 was a prophetic statement about Judas? Jesus chose twelve apostles (Mt 10:2–4), and one was a betrayer and an apostate. Did Jesus fail because he had an apostate among his apostles? Did this dissident apostle invalidate or corrupt the Church Jesus was founding? Did a "bad bishop" disprove or negate the ministry of Jesus or his Church? Do "renegade" bishops today nullify the Church's authenticity or mission? What are we told about the Church, the kingdom of God (Mt 13:24–29)? Should we expect traitors within the Church and within her leadership (Acts 20:28–31)? Did Jesus continue to love Judas and treat him with respect, hoping he would choose life?

16. Why are the disciples no longer of the world (Jn 3:3, 5; 17:16; Phil 3:20; Eph 4:17–24; 1 Jn 3:1; 1 Pet 4:3–6; CCC 1003, 2796)? Jesus will

soon be leaving the world. Are the disciples also going to leave the world (v. 15; Jn 14:1–3)? From what does Jesus ask they be protected (v. 15; 2 Thess 3:3; CCC 2851–52)? Why (1 Pet 5:8; CCC 409, 2849)? What *other* "Lord's Prayer" includes a similar petition (Mt 6:13)?

17. What does Jesus mean by "sanctify [consecrate] them in the truth; thy word is truth"? Is God's word limited to the "Bible alone" (Heb 1:1–2; 1 Thess 2:13; 2 Thess 2:15; CCC 80–82)? Who sanctifies (Heb 2:11)? How are we sanctified (CCC 1989, 1995, 1999, 2813)? Is the "truth" a concept or a Person or both (Jn 14:6; CCC 65)? How was the Word communicated to the world (Jn 1:1, 14, 18; CCC 73)? What effect did Jesus' words have on the disciples (Jn 15:3)? What does the word "sanctify" mean? How necessary is sanctification (holiness) (Heb 12:14; Rev 21:27)? Is a one-time "faith alone" decision for Christ and the forgiveness of past sins adequate to achieve this holiness and sanctification, without which we will not see the Lord (cf. Heb 12:14)?

» DEFINITIONS: The English word "sanctify" comes from the Latin word *sanctus*, which means sacred. "Consecrate" comes from two Latin words, *com* + *sacrare*, meaning "to make sacred" or "to set apart for a sacred purpose". In Greek, the word "sanctification" is *hagiasmos*, which is also the Greek word for holiness. The opposite of the word "sacred" is "profane", which comes from two Latin words meaning "outside the Temple". Therefore "sacred" means "set apart for God", or "cleansed and consecrated for service inside the Temple". Since all holiness derives from God and since it is primarily the attribute of God, what is "sanctified" is transferred from "profane" or "secular" use and is reserved exclusively to the Lord.

18. How is God's word "truth" in verse 17 (Jn 1:1, 14; 14:6; Rev 19:13; CCC 65, 241)? How and why does Jesus "sanctify himself" in verse 19 (CCC 2812)? What is the result of the sanctification of the apostles (CCC 611)? Jesus says that he was *sent* by the Father, and now he *sends* his apostles (v. 18). The Greek word for "apostle" (ἀπόστολος) means "one who is sent". How does this definition of "apostle" explain verse 18 and the commission of the Twelve (Heb 3:1; Lk 6:13; Mk 3:14; CCC 858)?

John 17:20–26

Jesus Prays for the Church—Those Believing the Apostles' Word

19. In verse 20, for whom does Jesus pray? When you read Jesus' words in verse 20, did you realize that Jesus had just prayed for *you*? How effective is this prayer, and how long lasting (CCC 2749)? How will future believers come to believe in Christ (CCC 76, 857)? How does Christ demonstrate his ministry of high priest for the whole people of God (v. 20; 1 Jn 2:1–3; Heb 5:1ff.)? How does the Church demonstrate that the prayers of Christ have been answered? How long has the Catholic Church maintained her visible unity (CCC 820)? How do the pope and the bishops help maintain the visible unity of the Church and protect the true word of the apostles (CCC 877)? Is an organizational unity sufficient to fulfill Jesus' prayer (Eph 4:1–3; Col 3:12–17)? Is sanctification found only in the visible bounds of the Catholic Church (CCC 819)? Have the gates of hell prevailed against the Church to destroy her (Mt 16:18; 28:18–19)?

20. According to verse 21, what is to characterize those who believe in Christ? What will the world conclude based on this characteristic? What may the world conclude if the believers *fail* to achieve Christ's wishes? How does denominationalism give a poor witness to the reality of God and his kingdom? How are the Trinity and the unity of the apostles to be our model (Acts 2:41–47; CCC 877)?

» APOSTOLIC FATHERS ON JOHN 17 AND VISIBLE UNITY: "[L]et me urge on you the need for godly unanimity in everything you do. Let the bishop preside in the place of God, and his clergy in place of the Apostolic conclave, and let my special friends the deacons be entrusted with the service of Jesus Christ, who was with the Father from all eternity and in these last days has been made manifest. Everyone should observe the closest conformity with God; you must show every consideration for one another, never letting your attitude to a neighbour be affected by your human feelings, but simply loving each other consistently in the spirit of Jesus Christ. Allow nothing whatever to exist among you that could give rise to any divisions; maintain absolute unity with your bishop and leaders, as an example to others and a lesson in the avoidance of corruption.

"In the same way as the Lord was wholly one with the Father, and never acted independently of Him, either in person or through the Apostles, so you yourselves must never act independently of your bishop and clergy [presbyters].

309

On no account persuade yourselves that it is right and proper to follow your own private judgement; have a single service of prayer which everybody attends; one united supplication, one mind, one hope, in love and innocent joyfulness, which is Jesus Christ, than whom nothing is better. All of you together, as though you were approaching the only existing temple of God and the only altar, speed to the one and only Jesus Christ—who came down from the one and only Father, is eternally with that One, and to that One is now returned." [13]

21. How many "churches" exist (Mt 18:17; Eph 4:4; 1 Cor 10:32; CCC 866, 172–75)? How does the Church manifest herself in local areas (Rev 1:20; 1 Cor 7:17; 1 Thess 2:14; CCC 832–33)? How are the local "churches" part of the "Church" (CCC 834–35, 886)? Are the local "churches" of the New Testament era different sects, denominations, competing and disagreeing among themselves (1 Cor 1:10; 11:16; CCC 172–75)? Where do we find the word "denomination" in the Bible; or rather, *do* we find it? Does a *theoretical* "spiritual unity" in an "invisible Church" adequately demonstrate the visible unity that Jesus wants his Church to manifest to the watching world? How did the visible unity of the early Church turn the world upside down?

22. How does the Church teach us to think about the unity of the Church (CCC 775, 820)? How and why is the Eucharist so essential to unity (1 Cor 10:17: CCC 1369, 1396)? How should we think about Protestant and Orthodox believers (CCC 817–19)? What is necessary to restore the desired unity among Christians (CCC 837–38)? Why should we work toward true ecumenism (CCC 816)? Not neglecting efforts to love, teach the truth, and foster unity under Peter's successor, how will *true ecumenism* be achieved (CCC 822)? How will the world know that the Father sent the Son (v. 23)?

» THE CHURCH AND ECUMENISM: "This solicitude will serve as a motivation and stimulus for a renewed commitment to ecumenism. The relationship between ecumenical activity and missionary activity makes it necessary to consider two closely associated factors. On the one hand, we must recognize that 'the division among Christians damages the holy work of preaching the Gospel to every creature and is a barrier for many in their approach to the faith.' The fact that the Good News of reconciliation is preached by Christians who are divided among themselves weakens their witness. It is thus urgent to work for

---

[13] St. Ignatius of Antioch, *To the Magnesians* 6–7, wirtten about 106, quoted in *Early Christian Writings*, trans. Maxwell Staniforth (New York: Penguin Books, 1968), 72.

the unity of Christians, so that missionary activity can be more effective. At the same time we must not forget that efforts toward unity are themselves a sign of the work of reconciliation which God is bringing about in our midst.

"On the other hand, it is true that some kind of communion, though imperfect, exists among all those who have received Baptism in Christ. On this basis the Council established the principle that 'while all appearance of indifferentism and confusion is ruled out, as well as any appearance of unhealthy rivalry, Catholics should collaborate in a spirit of fellowship with their separated brothers and sisters in accordance with the norms of the Decree on Ecumenism: by a common profession of faith in God and in Jesus Christ before the nations—to the extent that this is possible—and by their cooperation in social and technical as well as in cultural and religious matters.'

"Ecumenical activity and harmonious witness to Jesus Christ by Christians who belong to different churches and ecclesial communities has already borne abundant fruit. But it is ever more urgent that they work and bear witness together at this time when Christian and para-Christian sects are sowing confusion by their activity. The expansion of these sects represents a threat for the Catholic Church and for all the ecclesial communities with which she is engaged in dialogue. Wherever possible, and in the light of local circumstances, the response of Christians can itself be an ecumenical one."[14]

"The Church also has a lively solicitude for the Christians who are not in full communion with her. While preparing with them the unity willed by Christ, and precisely in order to realize unity in truth, she has the consciousness that she would be gravely lacking in her duty if she did not give witness before them of the fullness of the revelation whose deposit she guards."[15]

23. When a wonderful thing happens to us, what is the first thing we do? Share it with those we love, right? What did Jesus want to share with his disciples and friends (v. 24)? What else happened before the "foundation of the world" (Rev 13:8, RSV, NIV, KJV, Douay-Rheims, Knox)? Where was Jesus before the "foundation of the world" (Jn 1:1–2, 17:5)? In referring to his relationship with the Father (v. 21), Jesus uses the pronoun "us". Where do we first find, possibly, an allusion to this divine "plurality" in the Scriptures (Gen 1:26; 3:22; 11:7)?

24. According to verse 24, why does Jesus want to have the disciples in heaven with him? Do they not already see his glory (Jn 2:11)? What glory does Jesus now have in mind? Notice Jesus' last words before his

---

[14] John Paul II, *Mission of the Redeemer* (Boston, Mass.: St. Paul's Books & Media, 1990), no. 50.

[15] Paul VI, *On Evangelism in the Modern World* (Boston, Mass.: St. Paul's Books & Media, 1990), no. 54.

arrest and crucifixion (v. 26). What is so important to Jesus? What takes place next (Jn 18:1ff.)?

» THEOLOGICAL NOTE: The unity that Jesus desires us to have with him, with the Father, and with each other is brought about by the Holy Spirit. "St. John Chrysostom explains that this union is effected thus: The soul is united to Christ and to the Father by the indwelling of the Spirit, and even the body of the Christian is united to that of Christ by the worthy reception of the Holy Eucharist. This twofold union presupposes the existence in the soul of faith and charity, and that submission to the authority of the Church which our Lord required of the faithful." [16]

---

[16] Madame Cecilia, *John*, 313.

JOHN 18

THE BETRAYAL, ARREST, AND TRIALS OF JESUS—
"KING OF THE JEWS?"

John 18:1–11
Jesus Is Betrayed and Arrested

1. Jesus and his disciples leave the upper room (called the *cenacle*) at the end of John 14. The Temple lies between the cenacle and the Kidron Valley. Where is Jesus now headed (Jn 18:1)? Jesus has just completed his high priestly prayer. How do the other Gospels describe the beginning of Jesus' Passion immediately following the Passover meal, his walk to Gethsemane, and his prayer in the Garden (Mt 26:30–46)?

» GEOGRAPHICAL NOTE: Even with the modern layout of Jerusalem, the distance between the upper room and the Garden of Gethsemane can still be walked in about a half-hour. Nowadays, one walks past the Muslim Dome of the Rock instead of the Jewish Temple. The Wailing Wall is the last remnant of Herod's Temple complex. With a bit of imagination, however, one can still travel through Jerusalem with Jesus on the emotional last night with his disciples. The Kidron Valley lies to the east of the city of Jerusalem, between the city and the Mount of Olives. The valley is dry except for a few occasions of the year—during the rainy season. The name "Gethsemane" comes from a Hebrew word meaning "oil presses". The Golden Gate has been walled in, but standing in the olive grove in Gethsemane, one can see the probable route taken by Jesus on this fateful night. The traditional site of the sorrowful prayer of Jesus in the Garden of Gethsemane is preserved within the Church of All Nations. This garden was mentioned in the fourth century as a place of prayer, and some allege that a few of the ancient olive trees still standing are from the time of Christ. The walk from the Garden to the center of the Old City of Jerusalem is less than a mile.

2. In verse 1 we are told that Jesus enters a garden. Remembering that St. John often alludes to the Old Testament, how might it be significant

here that he mentions the "garden" where Satan (who "inhabits" Judas) approaches Jesus (cf. Gen 2:15; 3:1–7)? Notice also that Jesus was crucified, buried, and resurrected in a garden (Jn 19:41). How might Adam and Eve, in the *original* garden, be a "type" or "figure" of Jesus in *this* garden? How are Jesus and Adam related (1 Cor 15:45–47; CCC 411, 504)? How might the two gardens explain something of the relationship between the Fall in Genesis and the redemption in the Gospels? What is Jesus unraveling or undoing, so to speak (Rom 5:18–21)? How are Jesus' choices and actions in a garden overturning or unraveling the disastrous effects of choices made in a previous garden? What does the word "redeem" mean?

» THEOLOGICAL NOTE: "Early Christians conceived of [the garden of] Gethsemane as analogous to the garden of Eden in the divine plan for human redemption. The sinful actions of the first Adam are contrasted with the prayerful obedience of the second Adam—Jesus Christ." [1]

The early Christians understood that the redemption in Christ was an undoing of the sin in the Garden. Paul states, "For as by one man's disobedience many were made sinners, so by one man's obedience many will be made righteous" (Rom 5:19). As we have said, St. Irenaeus wrote, "The knot of Eve's disobedience was loosed by the obedience of Mary. For what the virgin Eve had bound fast through unbelief, this did the virgin Mary set free through faith." [2] Tertullian wrote, "God recovered His own image and likeness, of which He had been robbed by the devil. For it was while Eve was yet a virgin, that the ensnaring word had crept into her ear which was to build the edifice of death. Into a virgin's soul, in like manner, must be introduced that Word of God which was to raise the fabric of life; so that what had been reduced to ruin by this sex, might by the selfsame sex be recovered to salvation. As Eve had believed the serpent, so Mary believed the angel. The delinquency which the one occasioned by believing, the other by believing effaced." [3]

» THEOLOGICAL NOTE: "John's account plunges directly into the action of Jesus' violent nighttime arrest. This opening scene immediately introduces the reader to the tone of paradox that runs throughout John's Passion story. On one level of the story we have the ominous rituals of violence and apparent defeat: betrayal by a friend; the threatening presence of armed soldiers; a nighttime arrest of an innocent man; summary interrogation, trial and torture; finally, a public execution and a hasty burial. The genius of John's Passion narrative is

---

[1] David Noel Freedman, ed., *The Anchor Bible Dictionary* (New York: Doubleday, 1996); published in electronic form by Logos Library System, s.v. "Gethsemane".

[2] St. Irenaeus, *Against Heresies* 3, 22, 4, in ANF 1:455.

[3] Tertullian, *On the Flesh of Christ* 17, in ANF 3:536.

that these gruesome realities of seeming defeat and death do not dominate the story. Woven in and through the account of Jesus' suffering and death is another, more dominant mood: Jesus, God's powerful Word, is triumphant over death. He is not a victim from whom life is violently taken, but one who gives his life freely as an act of love for the world. We can trace this blend of death and triumph in almost every element of this opening scene."[4]

3. How did Judas know where to find Jesus (Lk 21:37)? What two distinct groups came out to arrest Jesus (v. 3)? For further insight into the betrayal, read Matthew 26:47ff. and Mark 14:43ff. Why did they bring so many armed men (Jn 18:36)?

» HISTORICAL NOTE: A legion was the main division within the Roman army. "The legions numbered about six thousand men, under a legate (ex-senator) in New Testament times. There were ten divisions (cohorts) of about six hundred men under military tribunes (see Acts 22:24–29). Each division was divided into three maniples (or units), which were themselves divided into two centuries, each under command of a centurion. Four legions (the third, sixth, tenth, and twelfth) were based in this area. The centurions were always chosen from among Romans who were stable and reliable and who had demonstrated their courage and maturity. There were fifty-nine centurions to a legion and they seem to have been respected by New Testament writers (see Matthew 8:8–9; Acts 10:1; 27:43). In addition to the infantry units, specialist troops were appointed to each legion: engineers, bowmen, cavalry, medical officers. Each century had its own trumpeter, orderly, and standard bearer."[5] Therefore, according to St. John, roughly four hundred or more Roman soldiers came out to arrest Jesus, at least enough soldiers to require the presence of the chiliarch— commander of a thousand (cf. Jn 18:12).[6]

"Meanwhile, Judas had been active, and had gathered a sizeable company of men to arrest Jesus. Some were Roman soldiers, and some officers and men of the Temple Guard, so that from the beginning 'Church and State' moved together against Jesus. It was the season of the Passover full moon, yet Judas' company went out provided with torches and lanterns: as John had said in reporting Judas' exit from the Last Supper: 'it was night', and in that night nothing but the light of the world could bring effective light to bear on what was taking place. No torch or lantern, not even the light of the moon which so

[4] Donald Senior, *The Passion of Jesus in the Gospel of John* (Collegeville, Minn.: Order of St. Benedict, 1991), 46–47.

[5] Ralph Gower, *The New Manners and Customs of Bible Times* (Chicago: Moody Press, 1987), 296–98.

[6] James Orr, ed., *The International Standard Bible Encyclopedia* (1915; Albany, Ore.: Ages Software, 1999), published in electronic form by Logos Library System.

clearly lit up the landscape, could suffice to relieve the utter darkness of the time when men extinguished the light of the world." [7]

4. According to verse 4, does Jesus run and hide (Jn 14:30–31; CCC 609)? Is he surprised by the betrayal and arrest (v. 4; Jn 6:64; 13:1, 11; CCC 557)? For whom do they say they are looking, and what do they mean by "the Nazarene" (Mt 2:19–23; Lk 24:19; Acts 22:8; Jn 1:45; CCC 423)? Where did Jesus spend his childhood (Jn 1:45)? What happens to the disciples (Jn 18:8–9; 16:32; Mt 26:56)?

5. In response to their question, Jesus answers "I AM". What does he mean by "I AM" (Ex 3:14; Jn 8:58; CCC 207)? What happens to the cohort of Roman soldiers (v. 6)? Jesus steps forward, and the Romans draw back and fall down. What would you have done at this point if you had been one of Jesus' adversaries? Why does John mention that Judas was "standing with them"? How did Judas betray Jesus (Lk 22:48; Mt 26:48–49)? The approaching troops are stunned; what does Jesus ask again? Why does he release his disciples before the arrest, and what *word* is he fulfilling (v. 9; Jn 17:12)?

» THEOLOGICAL NOTE: "[T]he reaction of falling back in confusion at Jesus' answer is not simply spontaneous astonishment. The adversaries of Jesus are prostrate on their face before his majesty, and so there can be little doubt that John intends 'I AM' as a divine name. Falling down is a reaction to divine revelation in Dan 2:46, 8:18; Rev 1:17. Perhaps Ps 56:9 may have entered the formation of the scene: 'My enemies will be turned back . . . behold I know that you are my God.' Even better background would have been available if the legend was already in circulation that when Moses uttered before Pharaoh the secret name of God, Pharaoh fell speechless to the ground. . . . The Johannine scene illustrates that Jesus has God's power over the forces of darkness because he has the divine name. It reinforces the impression that Jesus could not have been arrested unless he permitted it. The attitude will be put into words before Pilate in 19:11: 'You would have no power over me at all were it not given to you from above'. But this time Jesus does not choose to leave his enemies powerless. In the agony scene in the Synoptics it is clear that Jesus does not wish to resist his Father's will; so in John, Jesus permits himself to be arrested provided that his followers are not harmed. Jesus does not use the protection of the divine name for himself but for those whom he loves." [8]

---

[7] John Marsh, *The Gospel of St John* (Baltimore, Md.: Penguin Books, 1968), 582.

[8] Raymond E. Brown, ed. and trans., *The Gospel according to John*, vol. 2, Anchor Bible, vol. 29A (Garden City, N.Y.: Doubleday, 1970), 818.

» THEOLOGICAL NOTE: "Christ's foreknowledge is pointed out, both to prove His Divinity, and to show His readiness to suffer. For, though aware of the sufferings He was to endure, He did not seek to escape from them. He who had before withdrawn from His enemies (8:59; 12:36), now that His hour was come, went forth (from the enclosure of the garden) to meet them. We learn from St. Luke (12:47) that Judas preceded the soldiers, and gave the traitor's kiss to Jesus, thus marking Him out as the person to be arrested. We learn too from St. Matthew (26:50), that Jesus addressed the traitor, even in this hour of infamy as His friend. . . . After meekly receiving the kiss from the wretched Apostle, Jesus addressed the crowd." [9]

6. According to verse 10, how does Simon Peter respond to the arrest of Jesus? What had Jesus said earlier about swords (Lk 22:35–38)? What does Jesus do with Malchus' ear (Lk 22:50–51)? John is the only Gospel writer who mentions the name of the high priest's servant; what might this tell us (cf. Jn 18:15; this "disciple" is understood to be St. John)? Why does Jesus not want his disciples to fight (Mt 26:52–54; Jn 18:36)? Why does Jesus give himself into the hands of his enemies (Mk 14:36; Jn 10:17; 15:13; CCC 606–7)?

John 18:12–23
Trial before Annas

7. The Roman *cohort* is mentioned again along with the *commander*, which in Greek is "chiliarch", the "commander of a thousand men". Where else are the "court officers" mentioned (Jn 7:32, 44–48)? What two actions are taken against Jesus as his suffering begins (v. 12)? Notice the sequence of trials mentioned by John (Jn 18:13; 24; 28–29). Which trial does John *not* mention and which is mentioned only by St. Luke (Lk 23:6–12)? For more detail on Jesus' trial before the high priest and the Jewish Council, read St. Matthew's account (Mt 26:57–27:32) and St. Luke's account (Lk 22:66–23:25). What made the high priest tear his robe and charge Jesus with blasphemy (Mt 26:63–65)? Where have we seen Jesus described as the "Son of man" (Dan 7:13–14; Jn 1:51; 6:62; Acts 7:56; Rev 14:14)?

» HISTORICAL NOTE: "Annas had been high priest from 6 to 15 A.D., when he was deposed by the Roman procurator Gratus. Since such a [Roman]

---

[9] Joseph MacRory, *The Gospel of St. John* (Ireland: Browne and Nolan, 1923), 297–98.

deposition would have no validity for the Jews, it is likely that Annas was still considered a true high priest. If this deduction is correct, there can be no objection to a preliminary hearing before Annas such as that described in John 18:13ff. This was followed by a second hearing before Caiaphas." [10] "Josephus (*Antiquities of the Jews*, XX, 198) pictures [Annas] as a 'most happy man' for two reasons: he himself had been high priest for a very long time, and then he had been succeeded in office by five of his sons [and his son-in-law, Caiaphas], which brings out even more clearly the actual monopoly of the high-priest-hood exercised by the influential families. . . . Annas still had very great author-ity even after he was removed from office, for he secretly or openly controlled the pontificates of his five sons and his son-in-law." [11]

8. When are Annas, Caiaphas, and Jesus' other "judges" first mentioned in the Gospels (Lk 3:1–3)? Notice another trial with some of the same men involved (Acts 4:5ff.). What had Caiaphas advised the Jews earlier (v. 14; Jn 11:47–53; CCC 596)? How is this ironic? What did Jesus' death accomplish (Rom 5:12–21)? The Jews feared the Romans; how did this fear of the Romans help to bring about the death of Jesus (Jn 11:47–53)? What other elements played into his death (Mt 27:18; Jn 10:33; Mt 26:65; Acts 2:23; CCC 600)? The title "high priest" is used seven times in chapter 18. How might this be intended to set up a contrast with the true High Priest (Heb 2:17–3:2; remember the "high-priestly Prayer" of John 17)?

» THEOLOGICAL NOTE: "The reminder that Caiaphas had counseled that it 'was expedient that one man should die for the people' is a reference back to Jn 11:50, where John, with the subtlest of irony, pointed out how Caiaphas unwittingly had spoken the truth about Jesus even though he meant his words in a completely different sense. In 11:50, Caiaphas counseled Jesus' death in order to save the people from the Romans. Jesus, as John knew, would indeed be put to death, but to save the Jewish people from sin and not to save them from the Romans. Thus, the high priest Caiaphas was proved a false prophet, whereas, as John will demonstrate . . . Jesus, the true high priest, had shown himself to be a true prophet by foretelling accurately Peter's threefold denial before cockcrow (cf. 13:38). It is this theme rather than the trial theme that dominates the account." [12]

---

[10] Peter Ellis, *The Genius of John: A Composition-Critical Commentary on the Fourth Gospel* (Collegeville, Minn.: Liturgical Press, 1984), 255.

[11] Giuseppe Ricciotti, *The Life of Christ*, trans. Alba I. Zizzamia (Milwaukee: Bruce Pub., 1947), 49.

[12] Ellis, *Genius of John*, 256.

» HISTORICAL NOTE: The steps leading up to Caiaphas' house, and the dungeon beneath in which Jesus was imprisoned Thursday night, are still existent in Jerusalem at the Church of St. Peter in Gallicantu. "On the eastern slope of Mount Zion stands the Church of St. Peter in Gallicantu (the Cock's Crow), and next to it the Monastery of the Assumptionists. As early as 1888, excavations were carried out in this area. North of the church, the archaeologists discovered steps that are believed to date from the time of Jesus. Byzantine mosaics were found as well, and a deep cistern, with crosses engraved into the neck which seem to come from an early period. This cistern is known as 'Christ's Prison'. Recently (1994/95), more mosaic parts have been found. This supports the assumption that this place was venerated by the early Christians as the site of the high priest's palace, where Jesus stood before Caiaphas and where he was kept prisoner.... The earliest reports of pilgrims and other early Christian sources are consistent with the location of the high priest's palace in the region of Gallicantu." [13]

9. Is it proper to charge all Jews with Jesus' mistreatment and death (CCC 597–98)?

10. Tradition has always concluded that the other "disciple" with Peter (v. 15), who actually entered the "court of the high priest", was the apostle John. How would this explain his detailed account of this first interrogation (Jn 18:19–24)? How did Peter gain access to the courtyard of the high priest (v. 16)? Why do you think John twice mentions that he was "known to the high priest"? Compare the other Gospel accounts of Peter's denial (Mt 26:69–75; Mk 14:66–72; Lk 22:54–62; what does Jesus do in Luke's account?). What did complicity with the devil eventually produce for Judas (Mt 27:5; Acts 1:18)?

11. In verse 18, why do you think John makes the point that it was *cold* (Mt 24:12), as he has already made the point that it was *night* (Jn 13:30; CCC 1851)? Notice the sinner's use of artificial light and heat, when the *true light* and comfort are in their presence (Jn 18:3, 18). How does Peter answer three questions in front of the "charcoal fire" in the high priest's courtyard (Jn 18:17–18, 25–27)? When is the only other time St. John mentions a "charcoal fire" (Jn 21:9)? How does Peter answer three questions in front of the *second* charcoal fire? What is St. John trying to teach us about Peter? About Jesus? About forgiveness, repentance, redemption, and restoration? About the way he writes his Gospel with

---

[13] Bargil Pixner, *With Jesus in Jerusalem* (Rosh Pina, Israel: Corazin Pub., 1996), 102.

deeper meanings, and how he expects us to analyze and interpret the Gospel?

» THEOLOGICAL NOTE: Pope Gregory the Great wrote: "The fire of love was smothered in Peter's breast, and he was warming himself before the coals of the persecutors, i. e. with the love of this present life, whereby his weakness was increased." [14]

"Their attachment to Him [Jesus] was not yet sufficiently supernatural; discouragement has displaced bravery and loyalty—and will soon lead to Peter's triple denial. However noble his feelings, a Christian will be unable to live up to the demands of his faith unless his life has a basis of deep piety." [15]

12. In John 18:15, we learn that Peter was "following Jesus", but at a *distance*. What happened to Peter's bold claim that he would lay down his life for Jesus (Jn 13:36–38)? Was Peter following Jesus in the way Jesus intended his disciples to follow him (Jn 21:18, 22; Mt 16:24–26)? What does it mean truly to follow Jesus (Lk 9:23; CCC 226, 618)? Does Peter eventually follow Jesus to the point of laying down his own life for Jesus and the sheep entrusted to him (Jn 21:18–19)?

» CHURCH FATHERS: "The apostolic Churches in which the very thrones of the Apostles remain still in place, in which their authentic writings are read, giving sound to the voice and recalling the faces of each. . . . If you are near to Italy, you have Rome, whence also our authority derives. How happy is that Church, on which Apostles poured out their whole doctrine along with their blood, where Peter endured a passion like that of the Lord [crucifixion], and where Paul was crowned in a death like John's [the Baptist: beheaded], where the Apostle John, after being immersed in boiling oil and suffering no hurt, was exiled to an island." [16] See also the quotation from Clement, section 22, John 13, above.

13. In verse 17, Peter not only denies the Lord Jesus. Which of the commandments does he blatantly break (Lev 19:11; Eph 4:25; CCC 2482)? On what other occasion was Peter recognized by a slave girl at the door (Acts 12:13)?

---

[14] St. Thomas Aquinas, *Catena Aurea: St. John* (Albany, N.Y.: Preserving Christian Publications, 1995), 4:554.

[15] José María Casciaro, *The Navarre Bible: The Gospel of Saint John* (Dublin: Four Courts Press, 1992), 219.

[16] Tertullian, *The Demurrer against the Heretics* 36, 1–3, written ca. 200, in William A. Jurgens, *The Faith of the Early Fathers*, vol. 1 (Collegeville, Minn.: Liturgical Press, 1970), 122.

» CHURCH FATHERS: "Therefore did Divine Providence permit Peter first to fall, in order that he might be less severe to sinners from the remembrance of his own fall. Peter, the teacher and master of the whole world, sinned, and obtained pardon, that judges might thereafter have that rule to go by in dispensing pardon. For this reason I suppose the priesthood was not given to Angels; because, being without sin themselves, they would punish sinners without pity. Passible man is placed over man, in order that remembering his own weakness, he may be merciful to others." [17]

14. The eyewitness account of St. John continues with the questioning of Jesus. What two things does Annas question Jesus about (v. 19)? How does Jesus respond? Had he done anything in private that a subversive might be inclined to do (vv. 20–21; CCC 586)? Where are evil acts performed (Jn 3:19–21)? Where had Jesus done his teaching and works (v. 20)? What was the real intention of the high priest and his supporters (Mt 26:59)?

» HISTORICAL NOTE: "Although rabbis offered particular special teachings only to small groups of disciples (e.g., teachings on creation and on God's throne-chariot), they had a tradition that one must teach the law openly, in contrast to false prophets, who taught 'in secret.' " [18] Jesus has spoken freely and out in the open, not like the false prophets who taught in seclusion. The leaders of Israel have heard Jesus speak to the crowds in the Temple and in the synagogues (for example, Jn 7:14–15, 28; 8:2, 20) and know quite well what Jesus taught and his holy manner of conduct.

15. Why does Jesus ask why *he* is being questioned instead of having *witnesses* called to testify against him (Deut 17:6; 19:15; Mt 18:16)? Remember how John's Gospel deals so much with testifying and witnesses (Jn 1:7, 15, 19; 5:31–39; 19:35). Are witnesses brought forth (Mt 26:59–68; Mk 14:55–65; Lk 22:63–71)? What does one of the officers do to Jesus (v. 22)? Even though striking Jesus was against the Law, what Old Testament passage might they have twisted to justify striking Jesus (Ex 22:28; Deut 13:1–6; 18:20; Acts 23:5)? Annas' reason for interrogation may have been to find out if Jesus was teaching his disciples to be subversive or if he was instigating a political insurrection. Why would Annas be concerned about a Jewish rebellion against Rome (Jn 11:48; CCC 596)?

---

[17] St. John Chrysostom, *Serm. de Petro et Elia*, in St. Thomas Aquinas, *Catena Aurea*, 4:554.
[18] Craig Keener, *The IVP Bible Background Commentary: New Testament* (Downers Grove, Ill.: InterVarsity Press, 1993), 307.

» HISTORICAL NOTE: "According to what we know of Jewish law, interrogators were not supposed to force the accused to try to convict himself. But if this law is in effect in Jesus' day, the priestly aristocracy, upheld by Rome and acting on what they believe to be right for the people, does not concern itself with it."[19] "Yeshua [Jesus] was not answering disrespectfully but pointing out that even though this late night meeting was most irregular, normal legal procedure requires the obtaining of independent witnesses. Yeshua was willing to trust public reports of his public behavior, as is clear from v. 23. 'These things . . . didn't happen in some back alley' (Ac 26:26). Compare Ac 22:30—23:10."[20]

"The examination before Annas was a mockery of justice. It was an essential regulation of the Jewish law that a prisoner must be asked no question which would incriminate him. Maimonides, the great Jewish medieval scholar, lays it down: 'Our true law does not inflict the penalty of death upon a sinner by his own confession.' Annas violated the principles of Jewish justice when he questioned Jesus. It was precisely of this that Jesus reminded him. Jesus said: 'Don't ask me questions. Ask those who heard me.' He was, in effect, saying: 'Take your evidence about me in the proper and legal way. Examine your witnesses, which you have every right to do; stop examining me, which you have no right to do'. When Jesus said that, one of the officers hit him a slap across the face. He said, in effect, 'Are you trying to teach the High Priest how to conduct a trial?' Jesus' answer was: 'If I have said or taught anything illegal, witnesses should be called. I have only stated the law. Why hit me for that?'

"Jesus never had any hope of justice. The self-interest of Annas and his colleagues had been touched; and Jesus was condemned before he was tried. When a man is engaged on an evil way, his only desire is to eliminate anyone who opposes him. If he cannot do it by fair means, he is compelled to resort to foul."[21]

16. Is Annas known for having his defendants struck in violation of the Law (Acts 23:2–5)? Does Jesus strike back in anger (Mt 5:39)? What is the significance of the facial blow given by one of the officers?

» NOTE ON SYMBOLISM: The slapping of our Lord has deeper significance than simply an angry officer striking out maliciously. "What is its function in the structure of the whole scene? In other words, what does it symbolize? The answer to this question will enable us to grasp how everything is significant and coherent, and conveys a profound spiritual meaning. . . . So in the scene of the interrogation of Jesus by the high priest, Annas, the brutal reality of the

---

[19] Ibid.

[20] David H. Stern, *Jewish New Testament Commentary* (Clarksville, Md.: Jewish New Testament Pubs., 1992), 206.

[21] William Barclay, *The Gospel of John* (Philadelphia: Westminster Press, 1975), 2:227.

humiliating blow becomes a sign and a symbol of the refusal of a whole category of men, of whom the high priest and his servant, both Jews, are the personification: 'The Jews' have said 'No' to the revealing word of Jesus! If that is true, if the whole scene should be read in that light, then it is clear that it contains a theological significance. Furthermore, what is true of the symbolic sign of the blow is also true of its parallel which took place outside, Peter's denials." [22]

» THEOLOGICAL NOTE: "We see Jesus' serenity; he is master of the situation, as he is throughout his passion. To the unjust accusation made by this servant, our Lord replies meekly, but he does defend his conduct and points to the injustice with which he is being treated. This is how we should behave if people mistreat us in any way. Well-argued defense of one's rights is compatible with meekness and humility (cf. Acts 22:25)." [23] How did Paul conduct himself in a similar situation (Acts 23:1–5)?

John 18:24–27
Trial before Caiaphas

17. According to verse 24, where is Jesus sent after undergoing Annas' interrogation? Who is Caiaphas (Jn 18:13–14)? What are we told about the trial before Caiaphas? Recall the other Gospel writers' narratives of the trials of Jesus. Imagine the prospect of Caiaphas falling at the feet of Jesus and proclaiming for all Israel to hear, as Thomas will proclaim later, "My Lord and my God! "

» HISTORICAL NOTE: After Annas concludes Jesus is getting the best of the situation, he gives up trying to get Jesus to incriminate himself. We are told nothing by John of the trial of Jesus before the Sanhedrin and the high priest, Caiaphas. John appears to have been absent from the scene, though he was present during the preliminary trial before Annas. The other three Gospel writers relate that the court was unable to solicit consistent testimony from the false witnesses. (Which law were the witnesses breaking? Cf. Ex 20:16.) After the Sanhedrin fails to find adequate testimony against him, it concludes that he has committed blasphemy and sends him on to the secular government, the Roman governor Pontius Pilate, to be tried on political charges. [24]

---

[22] Ignace de la Potterie, *The Hour of Jesus: The Passion and the Resurrection of Jesus according to John*, trans. Gregory Murray (New York: Alba House, 1989), 50, 52.

[23] Casciaro, *John*, 220.

[24] Karen Lee-Thorp, ed., *John*, Lifechange Series (Colorado Springs, Col.: Navpress, 1987), 173.

18. In verse 25, what does Peter do for the second time? Then, what does he do a third time (vv. 26–27)? How is Jesus' prophecy *immediately* fulfilled (Jn 13:38; 18:27)? What does Jesus do (Lk 22:60–62)? How does Peter respond? Take a few minutes and put yourself in Peter's shoes. Imagine his grief and remorse. How do you think sin and disobedience affect our friendship with Jesus today? Did Peter have an opportunity to apologize to Jesus before the crucifixion?

John 18:28–40

Trial before Pilate

19. We are given some interesting information in verse 28. Jesus is now taken from the religious authorities and given over to the secular Roman government (cf. CCC 596). Where is Jesus taken?

» HISTORICAL NOTE: "For the Romans the *praetorium* was the place where the *praetor* [Roman magistrate] discharged the duties of his office.... The function of the praetorium had originally been of a military nature and it never lost its austere military simplicity. It had two principal accessories, the 'tribunal,' and the curule chair. The 'tribunal' (βῆμα) was a kind of semicircular platform, quite high and wide but easily transported and set up wherever necessary. The curule chair was the old conventional chair of the Roman magistrates; it was set in the center of the platform, and from it the praetor officially administered justice. The defendants and plaintiffs, the witnesses and advocates presented themselves before the 'tribunal,' and the praetor, when he had heard the whole case and consulted his advisers or assistants seated on either side of him, pronounced sentence sitting in the curule chair." [25]

The site of the praetorium was probably the Antonia fortress, named in honor of Mark Antony, which was linked to the Temple by the steps (cf. Acts 21:35, 40). This gave the Roman troops easy access in case of public disruption, especially during Jewish festivals. "On the site of part of this fortress the Convent of Our Lady of Zion now stands. This is the traditional location of Pilate's praetorium; here, at the Ecce Homo arch ['Behold, the man'; Jn 19:5], the Via Dolorosa begins its course which ends in the Church of the Holy Sepulchre." [26]

---

[25] Ricciotti, *Life of Christ*, 610–11.
[26] F. F. Bruce, *The Gospel of John* (Grand Rapids, Mich.: William B. Eerdmans, 1983), 349.

20. Who now questions Jesus and requires information from the Jews (v. 29)? Who is Pontius Pilate (Lk 3:1; CCC 423)?

» HISTORICAL NOTE: It has been popular in earlier times to deny the historical existence of Pontius Pilate. However, a recent discovery in 1961, in Caesarea Maritima, has dispelled any doubts and once again proved the historical reliability of the sacred Scriptures. An important piece of archaeological evidence was uncovered. It was a dedication inscription on a stone slab, found in Caesarea, the Roman capital of Judea, in which Pilate is given the title of prefect (not procurator). Part of his name can be read on the second line of the stone. We also have confirmation in the historical writings of Philo Judaeus and Flavius Josephus:

"The best known of the prefects of Judea was Pontius Pilatus (Lk 3:1). . . . Appointed to office by Sejanus, Tiberius' anti-Jewish adviser, Pilate was a high-handed and stern ruler, who never went out of his way to ingratiate himself with the Jews. Writing to the Emperor Caligula, Herod Agrippa I described Pilate as a man 'inflexible by nature and cruel because of stubbornness.' He accused him of 'graft, insults, robberies, assaults, wanton abuse, constant executions without trial, unending grievous cruelty'. . . . This high-handed attitude of Pilate toward the people of the province was, however, his undoing. In AD 35 he attacked, imprisoned, and slaughtered some credulous Samaritans who had gathered on Mt. Gerizim to witness the 'discovery' of sacred vessels, allegedly buried by Moses on their holy mountain. The Samaritans, who had made their pilgrimage to Mt. Gerizim without any revolutionary intent, complained of his attack to the legate of Syria, L. Vitellius. He eventually sent Pilate back to Rome to account for his deeds before the emperor (*Ant.* 18.4, 1–2 § 85–89). What happened to Pilate after this is unknown; later legends tell of his suicide under Caligula (Eusebius, *HE* 2.7), or of his execution under Nero (John of Antioch, in *Fragm. hist. graec.* 4.574). Tertullian (*Apol.* 21.24) believed that at heart he was a Christian." [27]

21. Imperial Rome had well-established legal procedures requiring evidence against a defendant from witnesses. What is Pilate's first question to the Jews (v. 29)? Does the crowd provide Pilate with credible witnesses or substantial charges against Jesus (v. 30)? What does Pilate tell them to do with their petty religious issues (v. 31)? Pilate knows the Jews and has no desire to become embroiled in their religious squabbles. How does he prod them to discover their real motives? Why do the Jewish leaders *really* bring Jesus to Pilate (v. 31)?

---

[27] Raymond Brown, Joseph Fitzmyer, and Roland Murphy, eds., *The Jerome Biblical Commentary* (Englewood Cliffs, N.J.: Prentice-Hall, 1968), 2:698.

» LEGAL NOTE: Pilate's directive that the Jews try Jesus according to their own laws "obviously did not mean that the accusers could do what they wanted with the prisoner, including putting him to death: it was merely a suggestion that they apply the laws of their nation, exclusive, of course, of capital punishment. But this was the very crux of the matter, and the accusers indirectly called it to Pilate's attention: 'It is not lawful for us to put anyone to death.' This answer revealed their true purpose and also indicated what had taken place that night. If the Sanhedrin appealed to Rome's representative, it was not for permission to impose a fine or a sentence of excommunication or the thirty-nine legal stripes, all punishments which they could lawfully inflict without the procurator's approval. The accusers wanted permission to carry out the death sentence which the Sanhedrin had passed that night, but which they were still powerless to execute. Pilate, therefore, understood that the accusers wanted the prisoner put to death."[28]

22. What charge against Jesus do the Jewish leaders present to Pilate, and how do you think they hope Pilate will respond (Lk 23:2)? How do the Jewish leaders try to manipulate Pilate (CCC 596)? Even though they oppose Jesus for perceived *blasphemy*, notice how they trump up charges of *treason* and *sedition*. Anyone who claimed to be king in a Roman province implicitly denied the sovereignty of Caesar; therefore the claimant was guilty of sedition against the true king.

23. In verse 32, what does John mean that the words of Jesus might "fulfil the word which Jesus had spoken to show by what death he was to die"? How did *Jews* inflict capital punishment (Deut 13:10–11; Jn 10:31; Acts 7:59; CCC 574)? How did Romans inflict capital punishment (Mt 27:38; Jn 19:15–16)? When had Jesus predicted what kind of death he would suffer (Jn 3:14; 8:28; 12:32; Mt 20:19; 26:2)?

24. Since the Jews could not enter Gentile buildings, such as Pilate's praetorium, lest they become ritually defiled and unable to celebrate the Passover the following day, what does Pilate have to keep doing (Jn 18:28–29, 33, 38)? For a discussion of the day of Jesus' crucifixion, see page 337. What does Pilate ask Jesus (v. 33)? Why would this concern Pilate, and why had it concerned Herod earlier (Mt 2:1ff.)? How does Jesus question Pilate's motive and information (v. 34)? The Jews had been taken captive to Babylon in 586 B.C., and they had only a few periods of independence and self-rule. How long had it been since the

---

[28] Ricciotti, *Life of Christ*, 613.

Jews had had a king of their own, sitting on the throne of David? What had God promised David and Solomon (2 Sam 7:12–13; 1 Kings 9:4–5)? What had the angel Gabriel promised Mary (Lk 1:31–33)? How would this promise eventually be fulfilled (compare Acts 1:9–11 and Dan 7:13–14; CCC 664)? What did Nathanael recognize when he first met Jesus (Jn 1:49)?

» THEOLOGICAL NOTE: "The 'inside'—'outside' deployment of the trial scene begins when the Jewish leaders refuse to enter the praetorium because they fear 'defilement' which would prevent them from celebrating the Passover meal that evening. Presumably such defilement or cultic impurity would be due to contact with Gentiles. The irony of the leaders' decision stands out from the page. They are concerned about the proper disposition for celebrating the Passover at the very moment they deliver up to death Jesus, the 'Lamb of God'!"[29]

25. In verse 36, what do we learn about Jesus' kingdom—is he competing for Caesar's throne (Jn 6:15; Phil 3:20; Rom 14:17; Dan 7:13–14; CCC 549)? Is Jesus' kingdom an earthly kingdom (Jn 3:3–5; Col 1:13–14; CCC 541–42)? How do many of his disciples misunderstand (Jn 6:15)? If Jesus' kingdom were "of this world", what would his servants do (v. 36)? What resources are at Jesus' disposal (Mt 26:53)? How does Pilate respond to Jesus' claim of kingship of another realm (v. 37)? Jesus acknowledges that he is a king, but how does he explain his mission (v. 37; CCC 559)? What does Jesus mean, "I have come into the world, to bear witness to the truth" (Jn 1:9, 14, 17; 8:40; 14:6)? (*Note:* the words *true* and *truth* occur forty-six times in John's Gospel in the RSV.) Remember that "bearing witness" is a main theme of St. John's Gospel. How are we to live in and witness to his kingdom (CCC 2471–72)? Who are those who have a claim on Jesus' kingdom (Mt 5:3; CCC 559)?

» THEOLOGICAL NOTE: "All during Our Lord's life He had spoken of Himself as coming into this world; this was the only time that He ever spoke of being born. Being born of a woman is one fact, coming into the world is another. But He immediately followed up this reference to His human birth with the reaffirmation that He had come into the world. When He said that He was born, He was acknowledging His human temporal origin as the Son of Man; when He said He came into the world, He affirmed His Divinity. Furthermore, He Who came from heaven, came to bear witness, which meant to die for the

---

[29] Senior, *Passion of Jesus*, 77.

truth. He laid down the moral condition of discovering truth and affirmed that it was not only an intellectual quest; what one discovered depended in part on one's moral behavior. It was in this sense, Our Lord said once, that His sheep heard His voice. Pilate evidently caught the idea that moral conduct had something to do with the discovery of truth, so he resorted to pragmatism and utilitarianism, and sneered the question: 'What is truth?' . . . He who was in the robe of the high priest [religious judge] called upon God to repudiate the things that are God's; he who was in the Roman toga [secular judge] just professed a skepticism and doubt." [30]

26. In verse 38, notice Pilate's sarcastic, rhetorical question. What tone of voice do you think he used? How does he "brush Jesus off" and refuse to consider truth and the reality of God's universe and Law? How does he resemble our own relativistic, sceptical, and amoral society? What is standing right in front of Pilate (Jn 14:6; CCC 2466)?

» MORAL NOTE: "Pilate's lame reply, 'What is truth?' serves two purposes for John. First, it prepares the way for the judgment of Pilate the judge (cf. 19:11), who, despite his belief in Jesus' innocence, goes on to condemn him (cf. 18:38b; 19:4, 6, 16). Second, it alerts John's readers to the massive irony of Pilate's asking 'What is truth?' with Jesus, 'the way, the truth, and the life,' standing directly in front of him. Outside, Pilate declares, 'I find no crime in him.' " [31]

"The question 'jesting Pilate' asks by way of reply, typical of the cynical skepticism of the Roman mind, is sufficient to show that he belongs to the world that rejects the light. Pilate expects no answer because he thinks none is possible; indifference to the truth is equivalent to rejecting it. Nevertheless, Pilate has understood sufficiently to know that Jesus' teaching offers no threat to imperial security. . . . At the same time, what follows shows how indifference is, in fact, rejection. Here John condenses severely the account found in much greater detail in the Syn[optic] parallels. Were Pilate a man of truth, he would have freed Jesus without further ado; instead, he begins the series of compromises that leads to his execution of the Savior." [32]

"Here it is the incarnate Logos who is speaking, the embodiment of eternal truth, now revealed on earth at a particular time and place. Roman law took many situations within its purview, but not the nature of eternal truth. Pilate knew his business, and to discuss the nature of truth formed no part of it. So he broke off the interrogation with the curt dismissal 'What is truth?' Whatever [Jesus] might have said or done, he constituted no threat to imperial author-

---

[30] Fulton Sheen, *Life of Christ* (New York: Image Books/Doubleday, 1990), 344–45.
[31] Ellis, *Genius of John*, 263.
[32] Brown, Fitzmyer, and Murphy, *Jerome Biblical Commentary*, 2:459.

ity.... Jesus' words may be lost on Pilate, but John hopes and believes that many of his readers will take them to heart, and come to know him who is not only 'a witness to the truth' but the truth in person—the truth that makes men and women free." [33]

27. According to verse 38, does Pilate find in Jesus anything worthy of a death sentence, according to Roman law? How do the Jewish leaders respond to Pilate's pronouncement of Jesus' innocence (Lk 23:4–5, 13–25; Jn 19:4–7; Mt 27:25)? How might Pilate's pronouncement about Jesus' innocence be an ironic reflection of Exodus 12:1–11, especially verses 5 and 11? What has Jesus become (1 Cor 5:7; Jn 1:29)? How has Pilate judged rightly about Jesus (Heb 4:15; 1 Pet 2:22)?

28. According to verse 39, what custom have the Jews established with the Romans (Mt 27:15–17; Lk 23:15–19)? Who is accused of the same crime as Jesus (CCC 596)? Why do you think the crowd chooses Barabbas instead of Jesus for release (Mt 27:15–23)? It appears that Barabbas had been involved in a political insurrection against Rome (Mk 15:7). What is less odious to the Jews, someone imprisoned for aggressively trying to overthrow the Romans or someone practicing military nonresistance and "blaspheming" by using I AM, the divine Name? Why is it stunningly ironic that the name "Barabbas" means "Son of Abba" or "son of a father"? Which "son of the father" do the Jews choose? Who was the true "son of the Father" (CCC 503)? Barabbas *was* a robber (Jn 18:40); how did they come to arrest Jesus (Mt 26:55)?

» TEXTUAL NOTE: "An interesting variant occurs in Matt 27:16–7, where he [Barabbas] is called 'Jesus Barabbas.' While extant manuscript evidence is weak, Origen implies that most manuscripts in his day (ca. A.D. 240) included the full name. Many scholars today accept the full name in Matthew as original and suggest that it was probably omitted by later scribes because of the repugnance of having Jesus Christ's name being shared by Barabbas (TCGNT 67–8). It is not improbable for Barabbas to have the very common name Jesus. Matthew's text reads more dramatically with two holders of the same name: 'Which Jesus do you want; the son of Abba, or the self-styled Messiah' (cf. Albright and Mann Matthew AB, 343–4). There is some evidence that the full name 'Jesus Barabbas' also originally appeared in Mark's gospel (Mann Mark AB, 637).... The absence of extra-biblical historical verification for the paschal pardon

---

[33] Bruce, *John*, 354.

custom remains a problem. Some scholars have attempted to resolve the difficulty by suggesting that the entire incident, including Barabbas himself, is an apologetic creation of the evangelists (e.g., Rigg 1945; Maccoby 1970; Davies 1980). But recent studies have produced evidence of widespread customs of prisoner releases at festivals in the ancient world (e.g., Merritt 1985:53–68). The gospel account of a custom of reprieve of a prisoner at the Passover echoes the practice of the ancient world." [34]

» HISTORICAL NOTE: "Pilate is judicious in replying that Jesus had done nothing wrong, and that there was no reason to suspect Him of aiming at [an earthly] kingdom. For they might be sure that if He set Himself up as a King, and a rival of the Roman empire, a Roman prefect would not release Him. When then He says, 'Will ye that I release onto you the King of the Jews?' [Pilate] clears Jesus of all guilt, and mocks the Jews, as if to say, 'Him whom ye accuse of thinking Himself a King, the same I bid you release: He does no such thing.'" [35]

29. The narrative flows without interruption into chapter 19. We will continue the study of the Passion in the next chapter.

[34] Freedman, *Anchor Bible Dictionary*, 1:607.
[35] Theophylact, in St. Thomas Aquinas, *Catena Aurea*, 2:568.

JOHN 19 a

JESUS CONDEMNED—THE PAIN OF
THE CRUCIFIXION

John 19:1–16
Jesus Abused before Pilate

1. Notice the uninterrupted flow of the narrative between chapters 18 and 19. To prepare for this chapter, read Isaiah 52:13—53:12.

2. After the betrayal, binding, unjust treatment, judicial corruption, and a blow to the face, what is the next step in the torture and humiliation inflicted upon Jesus (v. 1)? How was St. Paul punished (2 Cor 11:24)? Was this treatment prophesied in the Old Testament (Is 53:3–6)? How are we affected by Christ's ill-treatment (1 Pet 2:24; CCC 612–17)?

» HISTORICAL NOTE ON SCOURGING: "Our Lord's scourging probably took place in public, before the crowd, in the courtyard in which Pilate pronounced  sentence a short while later.... Punishment by scourging was in use both among the Romans and the Jews, but the [Romans] applied it much more cruelly than the [Jews]. The Jews limited the number of lashes to forty, and furthermore, to avoid exceeding this amount inadvertently, they used to give only thirty-nine strokes of the whip.... The Jewish flagellum or whip was made of three plain strips of leather. But among the Romans there was no set amount of lashes, the number of strokes being left to the judgment of the executioners, who increased or diminished them according to their sadistic pleasure or their powers of endurance. Nor was the Roman scourge made of plain strips of leather but of hard thongs studded with fragments of bone, little balls of lead, and sometimes sharp iron points. This instrument of torture was called the *flagrum*, and Horace could with justice describe it as fearsome.

"The Romans tied the victim to a low column in such a way that he was bent forward and his shoulders fully exposed to the thongs of the whip, which could then also curl around his abdomen, his chest and even his very face. The effects of such a scourging can be imagined—the torn body, the gashed veins, the entrails laid bare, the flesh on the limbs lacerated or even hanging in shreds. No wonder many died under the lash. . . . The scourging was savagely cruel. Because of the hatred and contempt which the Roman soldiers felt for the Jews, the executioners undoubtedly vented their fury on the Divine Victim and swung the whips until sheer fatigue compelled them to stop." [1]

Why is the Christ of the Crucifix often portrayed so clean and undamaged, when in actuality he was mangled and broken, possibly beyond recognition?

3. According to verse 2, what cruelty followed the treacherous flogging (v. 2)? Notice when thorns are first mentioned in the Bible (Gen 3:17–18)? What was the result of the Fall, and how were thorns involved (cf. Rom 8:18–22)? How might Jesus be bearing the curse on the earth by bearing its penalty? How might he be bearing the penalty for Israel's disobedience (Josh 23:12–13)? How is he removing the curse from men (Gal 3:13)? Jesus is the "substitutionary" sacrifice—how is his sacred head "caught in the thicket" (cf. Gen 22:13; Jn 19:2)? What do "purple" robes represent (Dan 5:29)? Read the other Gospel accounts (Mt 27:27–31; Mk 15:16–19).

» HISTORICAL NOTE ON THE THORNS: We know that the "crown of thorns" was more like a cap that covered and punctured the whole head, not just a ring around the head as usually depicted in art. The Shroud of Turin seems to confirm this conclusion. "St. Vincent of Lerins [died before 450] (*Sermo in Parasceve*) was to write . . . 'They placed on His head a crown of thorns; it was, in fact, in the shape of a pileus [cap], so that it touched and covered His head in every part.'" [2] This type of crown/cap would be very painful. "The scalp bleeds very easily and very vigorously, and as this cap was driven against the head by blows with the stick, the wounds must have caused much [pain and] loss of blood." [3] "In a crypt of the Cemetery of Praetextatus, which dates from the middle of the second century, our Lord is depicted wearing a crown of thorns that apparently covers the whole head like a close-fitting cap or helmet." [4]

» THEOLOGICAL NOTE ON THE THORNS: "This [crown of thorns] was to carry on the humour of making him a mock-king; yet, had they intended it only for a reproach, they might have platted a crown of straw, or rushes, but they

[1] Andrés Fernández, *The Life of Christ*, trans. Paul Barrett (Westminster, Md.: Newman Press, 1959), 709–10.
[2] Pierre Barbet, *A Doctor at Calvary* (Harrison, N.Y.: Roman Catholic Books, 1953), 84.
[3] Ibid., 85.
[4] Fernández, *Life of Christ*, 717.

designed it to be painful to him, and to be literally, what crowns are said to be
figuratively, lined with thorns; he that invented the abuse, it is likely, valued
himself upon the wit of it. Thorns came in with sin, and were part of the curse
that was the product of sin, Gen. 3:18. Therefore Christ, being made a curse for
us, and dying to remove the curse from us, felt the pain and smart of those
thorns, nay, and binds them as a crown to him (Job 31:36); for his sufferings for
us were his glory. Now he answered to the type of Abraham's ram that was
caught in the thicket, and so offered up instead of Isaac, Gen. 22:13.... Christ
was crowned with thorns, to show that his kingdom was not of this world, nor
the glory of it worldly glory, but is attended here with bonds and afflictions,
while the glory of it is to be revealed." [5]

4. In verse 3, with what title do the "mockers" jeer at Jesus? Does Jesus
fit this description (Dan 7:13–14; Is 9:5–7; Mt 2:2; Lk 1:30–33)? Knowing John's love of irony, how does the Roman mockery backfire—how
does Jesus stand out from the mob with "royal composure"? Consider
how the Roman magistrate and military look foolish, while the convict
rises above them all with integrity and dignity? Pilate is really on trial
before Jesus, against whom he really has no power. What did they do to
his face (Is 50:6; Mt 26:67–68; 27:30; Mk 14:65; 15:19; Lk 22:63)? Have
you ever been hit in the face? If so, what was your reaction? How does
Jesus practice what he preaches (Mt 5:39)? Imagine the disgust and
revulsion of having Roman soldiers spitting in your face when your
hands are tied behind your back, being unable to protect yourself or
wipe the spittle off your face!

5. According to verse 4, does Pilate find any guilt in Jesus worthy of
death (Jn 18:38; Is 53:9)? How does Pilate violate the laws of God
(CCC 2258, 2237)? Is Jesus a threat to the secular throne (Jn 18:36)?

6. Why do you think Pilate brings Jesus back out for the people to see,
mangled and bloody? How would you respond to a man so mistreated,
mutilated, and disfigured? Would you desire to extend him pity and
wish to help him—or would you spitefully desire to increase his misery?
Why do the people not take pity and consider Jesus' merciless flogging
sufficient punishment? After the wicked flogging and mocking, Pilate
says more than he realizes. How does Pilate present Jesus to the crowd
(Jn 19:5)? How is Adam referred to when placed in the Garden (Gen

[5] Matthew Henry, *Matthew Henry's Commentary* (Peabody, Mass.: Hendrickson Pub.,
1991), 5:422.

1:26; 2:15)? How might John be making a point about Jesus as the "new man" (1 Cor 15:45–47)? How is Mary referred to in St. John's Gospel (Jn 2:4; 19:26)?

» HISTORICAL NOTE: "The procurator's cowardice was to subject the Prisoner to untold torture and deepest humiliation. Both his plans for releasing Jesus had failed; yet, not being able to bring himself to pronounce sentence of death against the Man whom he had publicly declared innocent, he made a last desperate attempt to save Him. He decided to appeal to the compassion of the crowd, to have the Prisoner scourged and reduced to such a pitiable state that no heart, no matter how savage and evil it was, could fail to be touched with pity at the sight. The fury of the crowd would vanish when they saw their Victim bleeding and humbled. With this last hope, Pilate ordered Jesus to be scourged." [6]

"The Prisoner's flesh was so torn and His countenance so disfigured that He looked scarcely human. So pitiful did He appear that Pilate did not for an instant doubt that the sight would move the crowd to compassion. Accordingly he again went out on the balcony and pointing to Jesus, who now came into view in His crown of thorns and the purple cloak he cried, 'Behold the man.'" [7] St. John Chrysostom wrote, "That the Jews might cease from their fury, seeing Him thus insulted, Pilate brought out Jesus before them crowned." [8]

7. In verse 6, what form of execution do the Jews demand for Jesus? Does their Law prescribe crucifixion for capital crimes (Deut 13:6–11; 17:5)? How do the Jews reveal their real reason for despising Jesus—do they consider him simply a common evildoer (Jn 18:30) or a blasphemer of their God (v. 7)? Why do they really want to kill Jesus (Jn 5:18; 10:33; CCC 596)? Of what crime is Jesus accused (Lev 24:16; Mt 26:63–66)? Has Jesus "made himself the Son of God" or *is* he the Son of God— what is the difference? Would *you* have recognized this nondescript Jewish man, Jesus, as the eternal Son of God? How does Pilate react when learning of Jesus' claim to be the Son of God (v. 8)? What does Pilate's wife say (Mt 27:19)?

» HISTORICAL NOTE: "It appeared to Jesus' accusers that their attempt to have him convicted and sentenced by Pilate on a charge of sedition was going to be unsuccessful. They therefore tried to gain their end by another route. The

---

[6] Fernández, *Life of Christ*, 708–9.

[7] Ibid., 712.

[8] St. John Chrysostom, *Homily* 84, in St. Thomas Aquinas, *Catena Aurea: St. John* (Albany, N.Y.: Preserving Christian Publications, 1995), 4:570.

governors of Judaea not only had the duty of enforcing Roman law in the province; they also undertook the responsibility of respecting and (where necessary) enforcing Jewish religious law. The claim to be king of the Jews was a capital offence against Roman law; the claim to be Son of God was a capital offence against Jewish law. But if the governor would not grant a capital conviction in respect of the former offence, he might be persuaded to permit the execution of the capital sentence required by Jewish law in respect of the latter offence." [9]

8. According to verse 10, what authority does Pilate have over Jesus from a practical, political standpoint? What authority does Pilate have over Jesus from a cosmic, eternal standpoint (v. 11)? Does Pilate want to crucify Jesus? What does Pilate know of the Jewish leaders' real motivation (Mt 27:18)? How do the Jewish leaders finally "twist the arm" of Pilate to coerce the conviction of Jesus (v. 12; CCC 596)? How adamant are they (Mt 27:22–25)? Can all Jews be blamed for the death of Jesus (CCC 597–98)?

» POLITICAL NOTE: John's real interest in this passage is theological. John uses the Jewish leaders' decision as a dramatic demonstration of the Jewish rejection of the sacred Davidic covenant. While the Jews attempt to condemn Jesus, the heir of David's throne, they condemn themselves by rejecting their Messiah-King and by pledging loyalty to no king but Caesar. This was in blatant defiance of the God and laws of Israel. Their words are nothing less than a blasphemous denial of the kingship of God over their nation.

"[The Jews] renew their political blackmail by implicitly raising again the threat of denouncing [Pilate] to Rome. . . . [Earlier we saw] Pilate's terrified reaction to the implication that he was open to blame for not respecting local Jewish customs; now his loyalty to the Emperor is pointedly questioned. If those are right who suggest that Pilate bore the privileged title 'Friend of Caesar,' then 'the Jews' may be hinting that his title will be taken away from him. This would entail severe punishment, for the Emperor was harsh in dealing with the disloyalty of those whom he had favored. It would be understandable that Pilate might feel his position as 'Friend of Caesar' jeopardized. . . . Pilate remains convinced that Jesus is harmless, but 'the Jews' are forcing his hand. The prefect who had just boasted to Jesus that he had the power to release and the power to crucify is now deprived of a truly free exercise of that power. If a charge of lese majesty is filed in Rome against Pilate for having released a king who is a potential threat to the Emperor, Pilate will be thoroughly examined, and all his shortcomings as governor will come to

---

[9] F. F. Bruce, *The Gospel of John* (Grand Rapids, Mich.: William B. Eerdmans, 1983), 360.

light. Possible disgrace is too great a price [for Pilate] to pay for defending the truth. Pilate yields to the Jews. . . .

"Pilate shows Jesus to 'the Jews' as their king. When they persist in demanding crucifixion, Pilate takes his revenge by humbling their nationalistic spirit. In their quest to have Jesus condemned, 'the Jews' have shown a touching loyalty to the Emperor—does this mean that they have given up their hope in the expected king? No price is too great to pay in the world's struggle against the truth: 'the Jews' utter the fateful words: 'We have no king other than the Emperor.' The real trial is over, for in the presence of Jesus 'the Jews' have judged themselves; they have spoken their own sentence." [10] Pilate does not seem to hate the truth as the accusers of Jesus do; he seems ambivalent about truth and does not appear to despise Jesus as the Jewish leaders do. Pilate reveals a pragmatic and self-preserving stance, therefore his guilt in this matter may be less than theirs.

» POLITICAL NOTE: "Pilate finally goads the chief priests who want Jesus' death at any cost into repudiating their proudest religious and national heritage (cf. Jgs 8:23; 1 Sm 8:7; Zeph 3:15; see also 8:33, 41). Their reply is doubly ironical, since by John's time these same Jews had seen their autonomy destroyed as the result of their rebellion against Caesar." [11]

9. According to verses 13–16, after hearing the blackmail and political arm-twisting, what does Pilate do? How is the culpability and guilt of these men real even though God's sovereign plan was being carried out (CCC 600)? Where does Pilate sit?

» ARCHAEOLOGICAL NOTE: "Taking his place on the judgment seat (which was always public and out of doors) [Pilate] prepares to render the judgment of death. *the Stone Pavement*: J[oh]n uses this term (*Lithostrōtos*) as a proper name, the [Greek] equivalent (not a translation) of the Aram[aic] place name *Gabbathā*, which means 'elevated place.' This site, mentioned only in J[oh]n, appears to have been connected with the *praetorium*. The *praetorium* of Jesus' trial has been identified both with the Fortress Antonia [north] of the Temple area on the eastern side of the city . . . and with the Palace of Herod on the western side. . . . Excavations beneath the site of the Antonia seem to confirm the view that this was the *praetorium* of the passion . . . , revealing a topography and a large stone pavement that accord with the description given in [John]. Rough carvings in the pavement [used for games and] made by the Roman soldiers have also suggested further correspondences with the Gospel narrative.

---

[10] Raymond E. Brown, ed. and trans., *The Gospel according to John*, vol. 2, Anchor Bible, vol. 29A (Garden City, N.Y.: Doubleday, 1970), 893–94.

[11] Raymond Brown, Joseph Fitzmyer, and Roland Murphy, eds., *The Jerome Biblical Commentary* (Englewood Cliffs, N.J.: Prentice-Hall, 1968), 2:460.

In particular, the Roman 'game of the king' may have been connected with the treatment accorded Jesus in vv. 1–3."[12] This pavement can be seen today and is the starting point for pilgrims tracing the steps of Jesus' crucifixion along the Via Dolorosa through Jerusalem.

» DATES AND TIMES: In verse 14 we are told, "Now it was the day of Preparation of the Passover; it was about the sixth hour", and in verse 16, "Then he handed him over to them to be crucified." (For discussion of the *day* of the crucifixion, see below under v. 17.) What timeline of the crucifixion does Mark provide (Mk 15:1, 25, 33–34)? How do John and Mark's account relate? It seems on the surface that there is a discrepancy, but it is quite likely the matter is simply explained with the manner of reckoning time in the first century. Without wristwatches and on cloudy days when the sun was not easily visible, they just took an educated guess as to the time. Discovering the "exact time", as we know the exact time today, would have been impossible in the first century. Mark says, "It was about the third hour." On top of that, it seems they viewed the days in four sections: early morning, the third hour, the sixth hour, and the ninth hour. After that the day was finished and it was time for bed. Anything from 6 A.M. to 9 A.M. was "early morning"; anything from 9 A.M. to noon was "the third hour", anything from noon to 3 P.M. was considered "the sixth hour", and so on. Understanding it this way puts Mark within range of John and minimizes or eliminates the seeming contradiction.

Mark says Jesus was crucified in the third hour, which could mean, by his estimation of the time, that the crucifixion took place sometime in the late morning, leading up to noon. John says Jesus was tried by Pilate at about the sixth hour (or a bit earlier since he did not have a precise means of ascertaining the exact time) and was straightaway crucified. This puts Mark and John very close, even overlapping. So, Jesus was on the Cross from possibly late morning or almost noon until the ninth hour, or about 3 P.M.[13]

John 19:17–24
The Crucifixion Begins

10. Knowing that the Passover lambs were being slaughtered in the Temple (see historical note below), how is it significant that Jesus is being tried and given over for crucifixion at the very same time (Jn 1:29; 1 Cor 5:7; CCC 613)? What other Lamb is being prepared for

---

[12] Ibid.

[13] For a more thorough discussion, see Robert H. Stein, *Difficult Passages in the New Testament* (Grand Rapids, Mich.: Baker Book House, 1990).

sacrifice (cf. 1 Cor 5:7)? What kind of lamb was prescribed for Passover (Deut 15:19–23)? Did Pilate find any blemish (or sin) in Jesus (Jn 19:4)? Notice other parallels: consecrated to the Lord, firstborn lamb, blood running into the ground, flesh must be eaten, and so on. Do you think the timing is more than mere coincidence? How does Pilate present Jesus—probably out of disdain for the Jews (v. 14)? How does John show the "real" King, using irony to expose the blindness of the Jews (CCC 440)? What does Pilate finally do (v. 16; Mt 27:26; Mk 15:15; Lk 23:25)?

» HISTORICAL NOTE: The Synoptic Gospels and John's Gospel seem to portray the Passover meal and crucifixion on different days. It is a conundrum; however, there are many satisfactory explanations correlating the two seemingly opposed time frames. "All the Gospels state that Jesus ate the Last Supper the day before his crucifixion (Mt 26:20; Mk 14:17; Lk 22:14; Jn 13:2; cf. also 1 Cor 11:23). The Synoptic Gospels (Mt 26:17; Mk 14:12; Lk 22:7–8) portray the Last Supper as the Passover meal celebrated on Thursday evening Nisan 14, with Jesus crucified the following day, namely, Friday Nisan 15. On the other hand, John states that the Jews who took Jesus to the praetorium did not enter it "in order that they might not be defiled but might eat the Passover" (Jn 18:28) and that Jesus' trial was on the "day of preparation for the Passover" and not after eating the Passover (Jn 19:14). This means that Jesus' Last Supper (which occurred on Thursday night, Nisan 13) was not a Passover and that Jesus was tried and crucified on Friday, Nisan 14, just before the Jews ate their Passover.

"Several theories have been proposed in the attempt to reconcile the Synoptics and John. Some think that the Last Supper was not a Passover meal but a meal the night before the Passover (Jn 13:1, 29). However, the Synoptics explicitly state that the Last Supper was a Passover (Mt 26:2, 17–19; Mk 14:1, 12, 14, 16; Lk 22:1, 7–8, 13, 15). In trying to harmonize the accounts some have proposed that Jesus and his disciples had a private Passover. However, the Passover lamb had to be slaughtered within the Temple precincts and the priests would not have allowed the slaughter of the Paschal lamb for a private Passover. Others think that they celebrated it according to the Qumran calendar, but there is no evidence that Jesus and his disciples followed the Qumran calendar. Some think it was celebrated on two consecutive days because it would have been impossible to slay all the Passover lambs on one day. Finally, it may be that different calendars were in use during the period. On the one hand, the Synoptic Gospels followed the method of the Galileans and the Pharisees. By this reckoning the day was measured from sunrise to sunrise, with Jesus and his disciples having their Paschal lamb slaughtered in the late afternoon of Thursday, Nisan 14, and eating the Passover with unleavened bread later that evening. On the other hand, John's Gospel followed the method of the Judeans in reckoning the day from sunset to sunset. Thus, the Judean Jews had the Paschal lamb slaughtered in the late afternoon of Friday Nisan 14, and ate the Passover with the unleavened bread that night, which by then had become Nisan 15. Thus, Jesus had eaten the Passover meal when his enemies, who had not yet celebrated the Passover, arrested him." [14]

11. According to verse 17, where is Jesus taken for crucifixion? Why is it significant that Jesus—the sacrifice of God—is crucified outside the city walls (Heb 13:11–13; Ex 29:14; Lev 16:8–10, 27; Num 15:35)? According to John, who carried the Cross (v. 17)? In the Synoptic Gospels, who helped carried the Cross (Mk 15:21)? John writes from a different perspective from the Synoptic writers: he emphasizes how from the Garden, to the trial, to the crucifixion, Jesus was in complete control, even to the point of carrying his own Cross.

How does Jesus view these events (Jn 13:31–32)? How is the future death of Peter described—what would it accomplish (Jn 21:19)? He is no reluctant victim, he is in charge, this has been planned from eternity, this is the ultimate act of God's love for man—and Jesus is completely in control of himself and the situation. What does Jesus mean that *we* must take up our cross daily and follow him (Lk 9:23)?

» TEXTUAL NOTE: John specifies that Jesus carried his own Cross; whereas the Synoptics inform us that Simon of Cyrene was pressed by the Romans to carry the Cross for Jesus. The harmonization of the two seemingly contradictory accounts can be visualized in the Stations of the Cross in which Jesus carries the Cross until utterly exhausted. At that point, at Station Five, Simon of Cyrene is seized to carry the Cross for Jesus.

12. Let us look back to the Old Testament to see the crucifixion foreshadowed. What other father offered up his only son (Gen 22)? Who else carried the wood for his execution on his own back (Gen 22:6–8)?

---

[14] *Dictionary of Jesus and the Gospels*, ed. Joel B. Green and Scot McKnight (Downers Grove, Ill.: InterVarsity Press,1992), 120–21. This is a larger matter than we are able to address completely here. For further reading on this matter, see John Steinmueller and Kathryn Sullivan, *Catholic Biblical Encyclopedia* (New York: Joseph F. Wagner, 1956); Stein, *Difficult Passages*; John Marsh, *The Gospel of St John* (Baltimore, Md.: Penguin Books, 1968); Gleason L. Archer, *Encyclopedia of Bible Difficulties* (Grand Rapids, Mich.: Zondervan Pub. House, 1982); Giuseppe Ricciotti, *The Life of Christ*, trans. Alba I. Zizzamia (Milwaukee: Bruce Pub., 1947); Fernández, *Life of Christ*; D. A. Carson, *The Gospel according to John* (Grand Rapids, Mich.: W. B. Eerdmans, 1991); among many others. For a summary of the teachings of the Fathers on this matter, consult Constant Fouard, *The Christ: The Son of God,* trans. George F. X. Griffith (New York: Longmans, Green, and Co., 1903), vol. 2.

How many men accompanied Abraham and Isaac to Mt. Moriah (Gen 22:3)? How many men were on either side of Jesus on the Cross? On what mountain did Abraham offer up Isaac as a sacrifice (Gen 22:1–2; 2 Chron 3:1)? How does the mountain of Abraham's sacrifice correspond, 1,800 years later, with the location of Jesus' sacrifice? Compare these two events (cf. CCC 2572). What was provided in Isaac's place (Gen 22:13–14)? What did Abraham name the place, and what would be provided?

» THEOLOGICAL NOTE: "First, then, Isaac, when he was given up by his father as an offering, himself carried the wood for his own death. By this act he even then was setting forth the death of Christ, who was destined by His Father as a sacrifice, and carried the cross whereon He suffered." [15]

» ARCHAEOLOGICAL NOTE: "The verb 'went out' may mean that he went out from the precincts of Pilate's praetorium or that he went out of the city through one of the gates in the wall (cf. Heb. 13:12). 'Golgotha' is 'gulgolta', the Aramaic word for 'the skull'. . . . The familiar designation 'Calvary' is derived from Latin calvaria ('skull') and has come into Western European languages from the use of the Latin word in the [Catholic] Vulgate text of all four passion narratives. The origin of the name 'Skull-place' remains a matter of conjecture. As for its actual location, it lay outside the city wall. . . . If the praetorium of the trial narrative is to be identified with the Antonia fortress, then the present Via Dolorosa probably marks the route to the cross with substantial accuracy, although it runs several feet above the first-century level. Until a few years ago it was uncertain whether the traditional site of Golgotha, covered by the Church of the Holy Sepulchre, was outside the line of the second north wall or not; that it actually was outside was indicated by excavations conducted in 1963." [16]

» HISTORICAL NOTE: In 1885, General Gordon "discovered" a rock resembling a skull with an eighth-century B.C. tomb nearby. He also mistakenly claimed that the traditional Catholic site of the crucifixion was within the city walls, which has been proven to be false. Since then, some Protestants claim the "Garden Tomb" of General Gordon as the true site of Golgotha. Archaeologists and historians, Protestant, Catholic, and secular alike, overwhelmingly accept the traditional site under the Church of the Holy Sepulchre and reject this alternate site as an unfounded, unhistorical theory. The historical site within the Church of the Holy Sepulchre in Old Jerusalem has been a pilgrimage site for two thousand years. For more on this topic, refer to our discussion of John 19:41.

---

[15] Tertullian, *The Five Books against Marcion* 3, 18, in ANF 3:336.
[16] Bruce, *John*, 367.

13. In verse 18, what do they do to Jesus? What is Jesus' perspective on being "lifted up" on the Cross (Jn 3:14; 8:28; 12:32; CCC 440)? Read and compare the crucifixion accounts in the other three Gospels (Mt 27:33-44; Mk 15:22-32; Lk 23:33-43). Why do you think John mentions that Jesus was "in between" the two criminals (cf. Is 53:12; Ps 22:16; Mk 15:28)? Read the account of Joshua's battle with the Amalekites (Ex 17:8-13). How might John be alluding to this historical battle to illustrate the current spiritual battle going on in the unseen world? Moses goes up a hill and holds up his arms with a man on each side to support the arms. John seems to bring out the parallels between the crucifixion and the battle with the Amalekites, which were understood by the Fathers.

» THEOLOGICAL NOTE: We again see John alluding to the Old Testament, something early Christian writers and the Church Fathers readily picked up on. Justin Martyr writes, "For it was not without design that the prophet Moses, when Hur and Aaron upheld his hands, remained in this form until evening. For indeed the Lord remained upon the tree almost until evening, and they buried Him at eventide; then on the third day He rose again." [17]

St. Cyprian (martyred 258) wrote, "By this sign of the cross also Amalek was conquered by Jesus [Joshua] through Moses. . . . And it came to pass, when Moses lifted up his hands, Israel prevailed; but when Moses had let down his hands, Amalek waxed strong. But the hands of Moses were heavy; and they took a stone, and placed it under him, and he sat upon it; and Aaron and Hur held up his hands, on the one side and on the other side; and the hands of Moses were made steady even to the setting of the sun. . . . That in this sign of the Cross is salvation for all people who are marked on their foreheads." [18]

Others of the Fathers (for example, Barnabas 12) saw Moses' raised hands as a type of the crucifixion. As Boismard writes, "The three Synoptics indicate that Jesus was crucified between two thieves (Matt 27: 38; Mark 15: 27; Luke 23: 33). All three use almost the same formula 'one at (his) right and one at (his) left'. But the Johannine text is very different. First, it suppresses the indication that the two other condemned men were thieves, and to indicate the respective position of the crucified, it has this formula: '. . . one on either side, and Jesus between them'. . . . To support Moses, the two men who accompanied him stood 'one on either side'. . . . Why does John differ here from the synoptic tradition? Why does he insist on the fact that Jesus was 'in the middle'? Why above all does he here use a Semitic formula in a passage which contains no other? Probably because, for a reader used to the Jesus/Moses parallel, which

---

[17] Justin Martyr, *Dialogue with Trypho* 97, in ANF 1:247.
[18] St. Cyprian, *Treatise* 12, bk. 3, *Testimonies* 21-22, in ANF 5:524-25.

runs throughout the gospel, he wants to insinuate that Jesus, arms outstretched on the cross, has overcome Satan just as Moses, his arms outstretched and supported by Hur and Aaron, overcame the Amalekites.

"Let us add two details which connect the two events. In the Exodus account, Moses climbs to the top of a hill; in the same way, Jesus will be crucified at the place of the skull, which was a little rise of ground. In Aramaic, the same word means 'head' and 'top' or 'summit'. Moreover, Jesus, like Moses, remained with his arms extended until sunset (Exod 17: 12; cf. John 19:31ff)."[19]

14. What does Pilate's inscription proclaim (v. 19)? How do the Jews respond to this inscription (v. 21)? How does John use irony with Pilate's words, "King of the Jews", realizing the Jews are claiming Caesar as their only king (cf. Jn 19:15)? Why might Pilate put such an inscription on the Cross? What are the three main languages of the inscription (v. 20)?

» HISTORICAL NOTE: "Condemned criminals normally carried their own cross (the horizontal beam, the 'patibulum', not the upright stake) to the site of the execution; the victim was usually stripped naked for the procession and execution as well, although this full nakedness must have offended some Jewish sensibilities in Palestine. . . . Several stakes, at most about ten feet high, stood in Golgotha ready to be reused whenever executions occurred. On the top of the stake or slightly below the top was a groove into which the horizontal beam of the cross would be inserted after the prisoner had been fastened to it with ropes or nails. According to Jewish tradition dating from the second century or earlier, Passover lambs would be hung up on iron hooks and flayed."[20]

"In Cicero's opinion no Roman citizen could legally be crucified. He exclaims in horror: 'For a Roman citizen to be bound, is a misdemeanor; for him to be struck is a crime; for him to be killed is almost parricide; what must I say then when he is hung on the cross? There is no epithet whatever which may fittingly describe a thing so infamous' (In Verrem, II, 5, 66)."[21] Which of these things happened to Jesus, and in what order?

15. Why was Jesus crucified (Col 2:13–15; Eph 1:7; 2:11–19; Rom 5:9–10; Heb 2:14–15; 9:22)? Did Satan understand what was going on (1 Cor 2:6–9)? Was there a tree in the Garden of Eden (Gen 2:9; 3:22–24)? What did Jews think about one hanging from a "tree" (Deut 21:23; Gal

---

[19] Marie-Emile Boismard, *Moses or Jesus: An Essay in Johannine Christology*, trans. B. T. Vivian (Minneapolis, Minn.: Fortress Press, 1993), 19–20.

[20] Craig Keener, *The IVP Bible Background Commentary: New Testament* (Downers Grove, Ill.: InterVarsity Press, 1993), 312.

[21] Ricciotti, *Life of Christ*, 627.

3:10–13)? The first Adam ate from the Tree of Life in the garden; Jesus, the last Adam, was hung on a "tree" of death in this garden—a death that restored lost life. Justin Martyr (martyred in 165) said, "Our Lord reigns from a tree."[22] What has Jesus now opened to mankind (Rev 2:7; 22:2, 14)? How does this again show Jesus rewinding history to bring redemption?

» NOTE ON THE CRUCIFIXION: "The unnatural position and violent tension of the body, which cause a painful sensation from the least movement.... The nails, being driven through parts of the hands and feet which are full of nerves and tendons (and yet at a distance from the heart) create the most exquisite anguish.... The exposure of so many wounds and lacerations brings on inflammation, which tends to become gangrene, and every movement increases the poignancy of suffering.... In the distended parts of the body, more blood flows through the arteries than can be carried back into the veins: hence too much blood finds its way from the aorta into the head and stomach, and the blood vessels of the head become pressed and swollen. The general obstruction of circulation which ensues causes an intense excitement, exertion, and anxiety more intolerable than death itself.... The inexpressible misery of gradually increasing and lingering anguish.... Burning and raging thirst."[23]

16. According to verse 23, how many Roman soldiers crucify Jesus (cf. Acts 12:4), and what do they do after their gory work? How many items of clothing do they distribute? Taking a clue from verse 26, how do you think John knew what the soldiers did and said? Josephus (A.D. 37–ca. 100) mentions that the Jewish high priest wore a seamless robe;[24] how might this common knowledge of the time be used by John to emphasize Jesus' priesthood at this Pascal Sacrifice? Could the high priest's robe be torn (Ex 28:32; Lev 21:10)?

» THEOLOGICAL NOTE: "All the Gospels mention the distribution of Jesus' garments. The clothing of the executed person belonged to the executioners by right. Probably, too, all the Evangelists (who say nothing of the distribution of the garments of the other two who were crucified) see in this fact the fulfillment of the typically messianic Ps 22:19, which John notes explicitly.... Only John notes that there were four soldiers, which was probably the number detailed regularly for such purposes (cf. Acts 12:4). Only John speaks of the 'tunic

---

[22] *Dialogue with Trypho*, 73.

[23] Dale M. Foreman, *Crucify Him: A Lawyer Looks at the Trial of Jesus* (Grand Rapids, Mich.: Zondervan, 1990), 139. Published in electronic form by Logos Library System.

[24] *Antiq. of the Jews* 3, 7.

without seam' worn by Jesus. The robe of the high priest is described in similar terms by Josephus (*Ant.* 3.7, 4 § 161), and rabbinic tradition also associates seamless robes with Moses (cf. Str-B 2, 573) and Adam; it is possible that John insinuates Christ's priestly character in the crucifixion, since it was forbidden to tear the high priest's garment (Lv 21:10). He may also be thinking of the tunic of Joseph (Gn 37:3), a type of Christ as one betrayed by his brothers and yet their Savior (cf. Acts 7:9–11; in Jn 2:5 the "woman" again to be introduced in vv. 25–27 alludes to Jesus in the character of Joseph). The Fathers who saw in the seamless robe a symbol of the unity of the Church, the heritage of Christ, contrasting with the division his coming had meant for the Jews (7:43; 9:16; 10:19), may also have correctly perceived John's meaning." [25]

17. According to verse 23, what do the soldiers do with the outer garment? What do they do with the undergarment—the tunic? Even though Roman law allowed soldiers to take the convicted man's property, from a prophetic viewpoint, why do the soldiers divvy out the clothing as they do (vv. 24–25)? Where else in this episode does John demonstrate the fulfillment of Old Testament prophecy (Jn 19:28, 36, 37)?

18. Read all of Psalm 22 and find the amazing correlations with the life and Passion of Christ. (Cf. Ps 22:1 with Mt 27:46; Ps 22:8 with Mt 27:43; Ps 22:18 with Mt 27:35; Ps 22:17 with Lk 23:35; Ps 22:22 with Heb 2:12; Ps 22:24 with Heb 5:7.) Why do we see Christ in this psalm (CCC 112)? How is the action of the soldiers a fulfillment of Psalm 22:18? How might the *visible unity* prayed for in John 17:20–23 be reflected in the seamless robe of Christ?

» THEOLOGICAL NOTE: "The word 'schism' used in 1 Corinthians 1:10 is the same word, *rent*, used to describe the tearing of cloth. The Fathers understood the seamless robe of Christ (Jn 19:23–25) as a type of the visible unity of the Church—the Body of Christ clothed with the seamless white robe of holiness and unity. The seamless robe has now been rent and torn, not by Roman centurions, but by those who bear the name of the Christ himself." [26]

» FATHERS OF THE CHURCH: "Since the East, shattered as it is by the long-standing feuds, subsisting between its peoples, is bit by bit tearing into shreds the seamless vest of the Lord, 'woven from the top throughout', . . . I think it

---

[25] Brown, Fitzmyer, and Murphy, *Jerome Biblical Commentary*, 2:461–62.

[26] Stephen K. Ray, *Crossing the Tiber: Evangelical Protestants Discover the Historical Church* (San Francisco: Ignatius Press, 1997), 64.

my duty to consult the chair of Peter, and to turn to a church [i.e., the Roman Church] whose faith has been praised by Paul. . . . My words are spoken to the successor of the fisherman, to the disciple of the cross. As I follow no leader save Christ, so I communicate with none but your blessedness, that is with the chair of Peter. For this, I know, is the rock on which the church is built! This is the house where alone the paschal lamb can be rightly eaten. This is the ark of Noah, and he who is not found in it shall perish when the flood prevails." [27]

» ST. CYPRIAN ON UNITY: "This sacrament of unity, this bond of a concord inseparably cohering, is set forth where in the Gospel the coat of the Lord Jesus Christ is not at all divided nor cut, but is received as an entire garment, and is possessed as an uninjured and undivided robe by those who cast lots concerning Christ's garment. . . . That coat bore with it an unity that came down from the top, that is, that came from heaven and the Father, which was not to be at all rent by the receiver and the possessor, but without separation we obtain a whole and substantial entireness. He cannot possess the garment of Christ who parts and divides the Church of Christ. . . . Who, then, is so wicked and faithless, who is so insane with the madness of discord, that either he should believe that the unity of God can be divided, or should dare to rend it—the garment of the Lord—the Church of Christ? . . . Also, the sacrament of the passover contains nothing else in the law of the Exodus than that the lamb which is slain in the figure of Christ should be eaten in one house. God speaks, saying, 'In one house shall ye eat it; ye shall not send its flesh abroad from the house.' The flesh of Christ, and the holy of the Lord, cannot be sent abroad, nor is there any other home to believers but the one Church." [28]

---

[27] St. Jerome, *Letter* 15 to Pope Damasus, written in 376 or 377, in NPNF2 6:18.
[28] St. Cyprian, martyred in 258, *Treatise* 1, *On the Unity of the Church*, 7–8, in ANF 5:423–24.

JOHN 19 b

THE CRUCIFIXION AND BURIAL OF JESUS—
THE BIRTH OF THE CHURCH

John 19:25–27
Mary and John at the Cross

1. Please read Isaiah 52:13—53:12 again to prepare for this chapter. The soldiers have just nailed Jesus to the Cross and divided his clothes among themselves. After "the soldiers did this", who now takes center stage (v. 25)? Who is standing near the Cross? There has been much discussion on how many women were near the Cross (Jn 19:25; Mt 27:55–56; Mk 15:40–41; Lk 23:49). Do the other Gospels mention the Blessed Virgin? Why might John contrast four believing women with four unbelieving soldiers (v. 23)? Where did all the male followers of Jesus go (Jn 16:32; 20:19)?

» DIGNITY OF WOMEN: "Whereas the Apostles, with the exception of St John, abandon Jesus in the hour of his humiliation, these pious women, who had followed him during his public life (cf. Lk 8:2–3), now stay with their Master as he dies on the Cross (cf. note on Mt 27:55–56).

"Pope John Paul II explains that our Lady's faithfulness was shown in four ways: first, in her generous desire to do all that God wanted of her (cf. Lk 1:34); second, in her total acceptance of God's Will (cf. Lk 1:38); third, in the consistency between her life and the commitment of faith which she made; and, finally, in her withstanding this test. 'And only a consistency that lasts throughout the whole of life can be called faithfulness. Mary's "fiat" in the Annunciation finds its fulness in the silent "fiat" that she repeats at the foot of the Cross' (*Homily in Mexico Cathedral*, 26 January 1979).

"The Church has always recognized the dignity of women and their important role in salvation history. It is enough to recall the veneration which from the earliest times the Christian people have had for the Mother of Christ, the Woman *par excellence* and the most sublime and most privileged creature ever to come from the hands of God. Addressing a special message to women, the

Second Vatican Council said, among other things: 'Women in trial, who stand upright at the foot of the cross like Mary, you who so often in history have given to men the strength to battle unto the very end and to give witness to the point of martyrdom, aid them now still once more to retain courage in their great undertakings, while at the same time maintaining patience and an esteem for humble beginnings' (Vatican II, *Message to Women*, 8 December 1965)."[1]

2. John never refers to the Blessed Virgin by her name, "Mary". How *does* John refer to her (Jn 2:1, 3; 6:42; 19:25–26)? How does Jesus refer to his Mother (Jn 2:4; 19:26)? As regards the eternal kingdom given to Jesus (Dan 7:13–14), what position is Jesus to inherit (Lk 1:30–33; Jn 12:13)? What position was held by the *mother of the king* in Israel and Judah (1 Kings 2:19; 2 Kings 10:13; Jer 29:2)? With John's penchant for Old Testament symbolism, why might he refer to Mary merely as the "mother of Jesus"? Would it be surprising if King Jesus followed Jewish custom and honored his Mother with the throne of the Queen Mother (CCC 966)? What "apparition" or vision does John see well after the Passion of Christ (Rev 12:1–5; CCC 1138)? Who is the Woman?

» THEOLOGICAL NOTE: In the Old Testament, the kings of Israel and Judah held their mothers in great esteem; in fact, the mother of the king was also the queen. A king could have many wives (for example, how many wives did Solomon have? 1 Kings 11:1–3), but he could have only one mother. No matter how much esteem a king had for a given wife, it was not enough to give the wife official rank and title. A wife wanted a son, and the wife wanted her son to be the next king. Then she would be known as the *gĕbîrah*, the "grand lady" or the "queen mother" (1 Kings 15:13, grandmother in this case; Jer 29:2; 2 Kings 24:15; 10:13; Jer 13:18; 1 Kings 2:19; 15:13). The term *gĕbîrah* corresponds to the word "lord". Solomon's mother, Bathsheba, was the first "Great Lady" in Israel. Solomon's very first recorded act as king was to bow to his mother and enthrone her at his right hand on a specially placed throne (1 Kings 2:19). Jesus, as the eternal king of the New Israel, on the eternal throne of his father, David, of whom Solomon was a prefiguring, would most certainly esteem his Mother at *least* as much as the earthly kings had esteemed their own mothers. Thus, one understands the Jewish and biblical basis for the Church's teaching on the Assumption and Queenship of Mary.[2]

"As a rule the queen mother was much more powerful and influential than the king's wives. Polygamy naturally lessened the influence of the king's wives,

---

[1] José María Casciaro, *The Navarre Bible: The Gospel of Saint John* (Dublin: Four Courts Press, 1992), 232.

[2] See Roland de Vaux, *Ancient Israel: Its Life and Institutions*, trans. John McHugh (New York: McGraw-Hill, 1961), 117–19.

whose hold on his affection was shared by others and was at best precarious. But the queen mother shared a fixed position of dignity; she took rank almost with the king. . . . The political importance of the dowager queens is illustrated by the fact that in the book of Kings, with two exceptions, the names of the Heb. kings are recorded together with those of their mothers."[3]

» JOHN PAUL II: "Together with John, the Apostle and Evangelist, we turn the gaze of our soul *towards* that '*woman clothed with the sun*', who appears on the eschatological horizon of the Church and the world in the Book of Revelation (cf. 12:1ff.). It is not difficult to recognize in her the same figure who, at the beginning of human history, after original sin, was foretold as the Mother of the Redeemer (cf. Gen 3:15). In the Book of Revelation we see her, on the one hand, as the exalted woman in the midst of visible creation, and on the other, as the one who continues to *take part in the spiritual battle for the victory of good over evil*. This is the combat waged by the Church in union with the Mother of God, her 'model', 'against the world rulers of this present darkness, against the spiritual hosts of wickedness', as we read in the Letter to the Ephesians (6:12)."[4]

3. What two people are singled out in verse 26? Who is "the disciple whom [Jesus] loved" (Jn 13:23; 20:2; 21:7, 20–24)? What disciple is frequently mentioned with Peter (Acts 3:1; 4:13; 8:14)?

4. Why would Jesus address his Mother with the seemingly impersonal title of "Woman" (see also Jn 2:4), a title of honor for a Jewish woman, instead of "Mother", a title of intimacy he probably used as a son in Nazareth? What might Jesus be alluding to when he calls his mother "Woman" (Gen 3:15; Rev 12:1–6, 17; CCC 726)? How is John a "type" or representative instance of *believers* and Mary a "type" or representative instance of the *Church* (CCC 963)? How is the Church, the new Jerusalem, our Mother (Gal 4:26; CCC 757)? How are the events of Genesis 3 and Revelation 12 related (CCC 2853)? If Jesus is the "Last Adam" (1 Cor 15:45) what is Mary (CCC 411, 494, 511)? How did Mary help "give birth" to the Church at Pentecost (CCC 726, 2617)?

» THEOLOGICAL NOTE: "Something similar must be said of the figure of 'the mother of Jesus,' as she appears in J[oh]n. Mary is represented not merely in her historical character but in the function that has been reserved to her in salvation

---

[3] Charles F. Pfeiffer, *The Wycliffe Bible Encyclopedia* (Chicago, Ill.: Moody Press, 1975); published in electronic form by Logos Research Systems, s.v. "Queen".

[4] John Paul II, *Letter of the Holy Father John Paul II to Priests for Holy Thursday 1988* (Boston, Mass.: St. Paul's Books & Media, 1988), no. 7.

history. If John has seen a new history of creation unfold in the preceding 'seven days,' he has also reserved a special place in this history for her who has been addressed as 'woman.' The woman of the first creation was called Life (LXX: Zōē = 'Eve'), because she was 'mother of all the living' (Gn 3:20). Mary is mother of the new life, not only of the Word become flesh, but also of all those who live with his life (14:19f.). She is, in other words, a figure of the Church, the new Eve, as the Fathers called her." [5]

» CHURCH FATHERS: "In accordance with this design, Mary the Virgin is found obedient, saying, 'Behold the handmaid of the Lord; be it unto me according to thy word.' But Eve was disobedient; for she did not obey when as yet she was a virgin. And even as she, having indeed a husband, Adam, but being nevertheless as yet a virgin . . . having become disobedient, was made the cause of death, both to herself and to the entire human race; so also did Mary, having a man betrothed [to her], and being nevertheless a virgin, by yielding obedience, become the cause of salvation, both to herself and the whole human race. . . . [And so] the knot of Eve's disobedience was loosed by the obedience of Mary. For what the virgin Eve had bound fast through unbelief, this did the virgin Mary set free through faith." [6]

"For just as the former was led astray by the word of an angel, so that she fled from God when she had transgressed His word; so did the latter, by an angelic communication, receive the glad tidings that she should sustain (*portaret*) God, being obedient to His word. And if the former did disobey God, yet the latter was persuaded to be obedient to God, in order that the Virgin Mary might become the patroness (*advocata*) of the virgin Eve. And thus, as the human race fell into bondage to death by means of a virgin, so is it rescued by a virgin; virginal disobedience having been balanced in the opposite scale by virginal obedience." [7] See also the quotation from Tertullian given above in section 2, John 18.

5. With the exception of John 6:42, Mary is mentioned by John only twice. Each occurrence is strategically placed, one at the very beginning of Jesus' ministry (Jn 2:1–12), the other, at the very end (Jn 19:26). Knowing John's compositional technique of "framing" the context for emphasis, why do you think Mary "surrounds" the whole life of Christ in this Gospel? What is Mary's role regarding her Son: taking the limelight or retiring into the background (CCC 487)? Is it not true that the doctrines about Mary were not developed fully in the Church until

---

[5] Raymond Brown, Joseph Fitzmyer, and Roland Murphy, eds., *The Jerome Biblical Commentary* (Englewood Cliffs, N.J.: Prentice-Hall, 1968), 2:428.

[6] St. Irenaeus, *Against Heresies* 3, 22, 4, in ANF 1:455.

[7] Ibid., 5, 19, 1, in ANF 1:547. See also Justin Martyr, *Dialogue with Trypho* 100, in ANF 1:248–49.

the doctrines of her Son Jesus had first been hammered out in the early centuries? How are Mary's faith and suffering at the Cross examples to us (CCC 149, 273)? How was Mary affected, as a mother, by Jesus' agony and death (Lk 2:35; CCC 964)? How might this demonstrate some participation in the work of redemption (CCC 618, 964; Col 1:24)? How is the Church with Mary at the Cross (CCC 1370)?

» TYPOLOGICAL NOTE: Two Eves—two sinless virgins—from the sides of two Adams, approached by two angels, struggle in two gardens under two trees, experience the labor of two births, bringing about two humanities in two creations, with two sinless Adams "born" directly from God who experience two deaths because of one sin.

» THEOLOGICAL NOTE: "Fundamentalists think Catholics put Mary on a par with her Son. After all, what is the word mediatrix but the feminine of mediator? Do not Catholics go even further, calling Mary the Mediatrix of all graces? Does this not deny Christ's role as the one Mediator?

"The contradiction here is illusory. As Thomas Aquinas said in reference to 2 Corinthians 5:19, 'Christ alone is the perfect mediator of God and men, inasmuch as, by his death, he reconciled the human race to God. . . . However, nothing hinders certain others from being called mediators, in some respect, between God and man, forasmuch as they cooperate in uniting men to God, dispositively or ministerially (*Summa theologiae* III, 26, 1).' After all, we mediate for others when we pray to God on their behalf, which, of course, is something fundamentalists themselves do. This does not argue against Christ being the sole Mediator, because our modest efforts are entirely dependent on him. In a far more perfect way, Mary shares in his mediation. Her status as Mediatrix of all graces exists in a double sense.

"First, she gave the world its Redeemer, the source of all graces, and in this sense she is the channel of all graces. She freely cooperated with God's plan (Lk 1:38: 'Be it done to me according to thy word'), and, as St. Thomas wrote, at the Annunciation, at the key moment for our race, she represented the whole of humanity (*Summa theologiae* III, 30, 1). The Fathers of the Church contrast Mary's obedience, which was perfectly free, with Eve's disobedience.

"Second, Mary is the Mediatrix of all graces because of her intercession for us in heaven. . . . Fundamentalists, always looking for a biblical citation, can see no reason to accept a belief in Mary as Mediatrix of all graces, but they can, if they take the effort, come to see that there is, at least, nothing in the doctrine that contradicts Christ's role as the one Mediator. His role as Mediator is not lessened because she has been allowed to assist him."[8]

---

[8] Karl Keating, *Catholicism and Fundamentalism: The Attack on "Romanism" by "Bible Christians"* (San Francisco: Ignatius Press, 1988), 278–79.

6. How was a Jewish son to treat his mother (Lev 19:3; Ezek 22:6–7; Mt 15:4; CCC 2196–97)? Why would Jesus put Mary under the protective care of John if Mary had other sons? According to Jewish custom and law, who should take the widow into their homes? What happens if the only son dies? How does this support the view that Mary was ever-virgin and had no sons except Jesus?

» HISTORICAL NOTE: "In Israel, a childless widow either returned to her father (Gn 38:11; Lv 22:13; Ruth 1:8), or remained a member of her husband's family by a levirate marriage. If a widow had grownup children, they provided for her support. If the children were still young, she may have managed the property left to them as their trustee." [9] If Mary had given birth to other sons, the second-born would have been responsible to care for Mary. Jesus would have been acting contrary to Jewish custom in assigning Mary to John.

If a widow had sons, they took care of her, starting with the firstborn. If she was childless, or had small children to support, she was in a piteous condition. In this dismal situation, they were "protected by religious law and commended to the charity of the people, together with orphans and resident aliens—all those, in fact, who no longer had a family to assist them." [10]

"The firstborn became head of the family and thus succeeded to the charge of the family property, becoming responsible for the maintenance of the younger sons, the widow or widows, and the unmarried daughters. He also, as head, succeeded to a considerable amount of authority over the other members. Further, he generally received the blessing, which placed him in close and favored covenant-relationship with Yahweh." [11] As Mary's "firstborn", Jesus was responsible by Mosaic law to care for his mother. Upon his death, a younger brother, if there was one, should have been assigned the care of Mary. Jesus gave Mary into the care of his young disciple John, implying that there were no other sons to take care of Mary.

» THEOLOGICAL NOTE: Many Church Fathers (for example, Epiphanius, Hilary) interpreted this passage as a biblical argument to support Mary's perpetual virginity: if she had had other sons, Jesus would not have entrusted her to John, son of Zebedee, the Beloved Disciple, but to the "second-born", according to Jewish custom. On the hillside of Panaya Kapulu in modern Turkey, some five miles from Selcuk (Ephesus), is a site that, according to tradition, is where Mary resided with John when he moved to Ephesus, in a house that he had built for

---

[9] De Vaux, *Ancient Israel*, 54.

[10] Ibid., 40.

[11] James Orr, ed., *The International Standard Bible Encyclopedia* (1915; Albany, Ore.: Ages Software, 1999), s.v. "Birthright".

her—called today *Meryemana*. Popes Paul VI and John Paul II visited the site and the rebuilt house, and it is now a pilgrimage location.[12]

St. Basil remarks, "The friends of Christ do not tolerate hearing that the Mother of God ever ceased to be a virgin."[13]

7. When else does John discuss Mary as the "Woman" and "Mother" with other "offspring" (Rev 12:1, 13, 17; CCC 501)? How are all believers in Christ the children of Mary? How is Mary a "type" of the Church and the Mother of the Church (CCC 963)? For a summary of the Church's teaching on Mary's relationship to the Church, read the *Catechism*, paragraphs 963–72.

» THE FATHERS ON MARY: "There is little doubt that in Johannine thought the Beloved Disciple can symbolize the Christian; Origen [ca. 185–ca. 254] is a witness to the antiquity of this interpretation. The real problem concerns the symbolic value of Jesus' mother. There is evidence in the 4th century that Mary at the foot of the cross was taken as a figure of the Church. Ephraem the Syrian states that, just as Moses appointed Joshua in his stead to take care of the people, so Jesus appointed John in his stead to take care of Mary, the Church. In the West, about the same time, Ambrose maintained that in Mary we have the mystery of the Church and that to each Christian Jesus may say in reference to the Church: 'Here is your mother'—in seeing Christ victorious on the cross, the Christian becomes a son of the Church. This 4th-century interpretation of Mary at the foot of the cross as the Church may be related to the 2nd-century (and earlier) understanding of Mary as the New Eve.... By way of summary, then, we may say that the Johannine picture of Jesus' mother becoming the mother of the Beloved Disciple seems to evoke the OT themes of Lady Zion's giving birth to a new people in the messianic age, and of Eve and her offspring. This imagery flows over into the imagery of the Church who brings forth children modeled after Jesus, and the relationship of loving care that must bind the children to their mother. We do not wish to press the details of this symbolism or to pretend that it is without obscurity. But there are enough confirmations to give reasonable assurance that we are on the right track."[14]

---

[12] See George B. Quatman, *House of Our Lady: The Story of the Virgin Mary's Last Years,* rev. Joseph B. Quatman (Lima, Ohio: American Society of Ephesus, 1991); Raymond E. Brown, ed. and trans., *The Gospel according to John,* vol. 2, Anchor Bible, vol. 29A (Garden City, N.Y.: Doubleday, 1970), 923; Stefano M. Manelli, *All Generations Shall Call Me Blessed* (New Bedford, Mass.: Academy of the Immaculate, 1989); Donald Carroll, *Mary's House* (London: Veritas Books, 2000); Ludwig Ott, *Fundamentals of Catholic Dogma,* trans. Patrick Lynch, ed. James Canon Bastible (Rockford, Ill.: TAN Books, 1960).
[13] St. Basil the Great, *Hom. In S. Christi generationem* 5, in Ott, *Fundamentals,* 207.
[14] Brown, *John,* 2:924, 926.

» MARY THE NEW EVE: "John thinks of Mary against the background of Gen iii: she is the mother of the Messiah; her role is in the struggle against the satanic serpent, and that struggle comes to its climax in Jesus' hour. Then she will appear at the foot of the cross to be entrusted with offspring whom she must protect in the continuing struggle between Satan and the followers of the Messiah. Mary is the New Eve, the symbol of the Church; the Church has no role during the ministry of Jesus but only after the hour of his resurrection and ascension." [15]

8. What are the seven last "words" of Christ from the Cross (CCC 2605)? Which of these last "words" belong to John's Gospel (Jn 19:26–27; 28, 29–30)?

John 19:28–37

Jesus Dies on the Cross

9. Starting in verse 28, John tells us that, "After this Jesus, knowing that all was now finished, said (to fulfil the scripture)...." What does John mean "after that"—after what? How does Jesus demonstrate his control of the situation (CCC 607)? Why does Jesus say he is thirsty? How can Jesus promise "living water" to the Samaritan women so *she* would never thirst again (Jn 4:10–15), but now *he* is thirsty (CCC 2560–61)? What will soon flow from his side (Jn 19:34)? Where does the Old Testament prophesy about Jesus being thirsty—"I am thirsty" (Ps 22:15; 69:21)? How does John use this to prove Jesus is the Messiah, the Son of God? Read the parallel passages in the Synoptic Gospels (Mt 27:34, 48; Mk 15:23, 36; Lk 23:36). We know that John is the Book of Signs. How do these fulfilled prophecies also provide *further* signs of the person and work of Jesus the Messiah?

» THEOLOGICAL NOTE: "When John was writing his gospel, round about A.D. 100, a certain tendency had arisen in religious and philosophical thought, called Gnosticism. One of its great tenets was that spirit was altogether good and matter altogether evil. Certain conclusions followed. One was that God, who was pure spirit, could never take upon himself a body, because that was matter, and matter was evil. They therefore taught that Jesus never had a real body. They said that he was only a phantom. They said, for instance, that when Jesus

---

[15] Raymond E. Brown, ed. and trans., *The Gospel according to John*, vol. 1, Anchor Bible, vol. 29 (Garden City, N.Y.: Doubleday, 1966), 109.

walked, his feet left no prints on the ground, because he was pure spirit in a phantom body.

"They went on to argue that God could never really suffer, and that therefore Jesus never really suffered but went through the whole experience of the Cross without any real pain. When the Gnostics thought like that, they believed they were honouring God and honouring Jesus; but they were really destroying Jesus. If he was ever to redeem man, he must become man. He had to become what we are in order to make us what he is. That is why John stresses the fact that Jesus felt thirst; he wished to show that he was really human and really underwent the agony of the Cross. John goes out of his way to stress the real humanity and the real suffering of Jesus." [16]

10. How does burning thirst represent hell? How does it demonstrate that Jesus bears the eternal penalty for our sins (Lk 16:19ff.)? How does John's mention of Jesus' burning thirst indicate that Jesus bore the eternal penalty of mankind's cumulative sins—the penalty that we deserved (CCC 615)?

» THEOLOGICAL NOTE: "It was not at all strange that he was thirsty; we find him *thirsty* in a journey (ch. 4:6, 7), and now thirsty when he was just at his journey's end. Well might he thirst after all the toil and hurry which he had undergone, and being now in the agonies of death, ready to expire purely by the loss of blood and extremity of pain. The torments of hell are represented by a violent thirst in the complaint of the rich man that begged for a *drop of water to cool his tongue* [Lk 16:19ff.). To that everlasting thirst we had been condemned, had not Christ suffered for us.... When they scourged him, and crowned him with thorns, he did not cry, O my head! or, My back! But now he cried, *I thirst*. For, He would thus express *the travail of his soul*, Isa. 53:11. He thirsted after the glorifying of God, and the accomplishment of the work of our redemption, and the happy issue of his undertaking. He would thus take care to see the scripture fulfilled.... Samson, an eminent type of Christ, when he was laying *the Philistines heaps upon heaps*, was himself *sore athirst* (Jdg. 15:18); so was Christ, when he was upon the cross, spoiling principalities and powers." [17]

11. According to verse 29, what is Jesus given to drink? Contrast this with the drink *Jesus* gave his people when they thirsted (Jn 2:6–11)? Notice the parallels with the earlier event: a request to provide drink, the title "Woman", mention of "my hour", jars of wine, redemption,

[16] William Barclay, *The Gospel of John* (Philadelphia: Westminster Press, 1975), 257–58.

[17] Matthew Henry, *Matthew Henry's Commentary* (Peabody, Mass.: Hendrickson Pub., 1991), 5:1200.

the presence of Jesus and his Mother—the Woman. How is the "Woman" intimately involved in both of these events (Jn 2:1; 19:25)? How might this bitter drink express the bitterness of Jesus' experience and the bitterness of sin (cf. 2 Cor 5:21)?

» HISTORICAL NOTE: "The Hebrew word is rendered vinegar in Ps. 69:21, a prophecy fulfilled in the history of the crucifixion (Matt. 27:34). This was the common sour wine (posea) daily made use of by the Roman soldiers. They gave it to Christ, not in derision, but from compassion, to assuage his thirst." [18]

12. In verse 29, notice the plant used to extend the sponge of sour wine to Jesus' mouth. Where else is "hyssop" mentioned in the Bible, and what significance does it have (Ex 12:21–22; Lev 14:4; Ps 51:7; Heb 9:19–22)? What had Jesus "become" for us (2 Cor 5:21)? Why would John draw our attention to the hyssop at this point in the narrative?

» CULTURAL NOTE: "The word *ezov* [hyssop] refers in the Bible to a plant tied into bunches and used as a brush to sprinkle blood on the doorposts and lintels when the house was cleansed against leprosy (Leviticus 14:4), as well as for purposes of worship (Numbers 19:6). . . . The Arabs call it 'zaatar' and use it in tea and in cooked and baked food. It is sold in the markets and is a popular Arab spice. . . . Because of its association with cleaning, the hyssop plant was thought to possess powers of spiritual purification (Psa 51:7)." [19] "[Hyssop is] a small, aromatic plant, growing on or near walls (1 Kings 4:33); burned with the red heifer (Num. 19:6) and used in other purification rituals. Early rabbinic authorities enumerated a number of different types of hyssop (M. Negaim 14:6) and detailed the correct use of this plant in ritual purification (M. Parah 11–12)." [20]

» THEOLOGICAL NOTE: "The reporting of it reflects John's eye for the symbolic again. Hyssop is not a very useful implement for holding a sponge. . . . Hyssop is manifestly the original reading, and while somewhat inappropriate for the purpose of carrying a sponge, it is worth remembering that it did not have to raise the sponge very high (the heads of the crucified were not greatly above ordinary level), and that it is eminently suitable for association with the Passover, perhaps especially with the death of him who was called at the very beginning of the gospel 'the lamb of God', and who is now dying on the cross at the very time that the Passover lambs are being slain in the temple, not very far away. Once again it is important to remember that for John,

---

[18] M. G. Easton, *Illustrated Bible Dictionary*, 3d ed. (Nashville: Thomas Nelson, 1897); published in electronic form by Logos Research Systems, 1996, s.v. "Vinegar".

[19] Michael Zohary, *Plants of the Bible* (New York: Cambridge Univ. Press, 1982), 96.

[20] Jacob Neusner, ed., *Dictionary of Judaism in the Biblical Period* (Peabody, Mass.: Hendrickson Pub., 1999), 304.

history is written in order to indicate the theological meaning he was convinced it really had." [21]

13. According to verse 30, what does Jesus say immediately before dying (CCC 607)? What might Jesus mean (cf. Jn 17:4; 1 Pet 1:18–19; CCC 607)? What other time was Jesus thirsty when he mentions accomplishing or finishing the work of his Father (Jn 4:34)? What does Matthew tell us happened when Jesus gave up his spirit (Mt 27:50–51)? Why is the tearing of the very thick curtain "from top to bottom" significant? Do you think this implies we are given access to the holy of holies, or that God was leaving the Temple? What can we now do (Heb 4:14–16)? What did the centurion say (Mk 15:39)?

» HISTORICAL NOTE: "Then he bowed his head. He was dead. At that moment strange things took place in the darkened city. Two great embroidered curtains hung within the Temple: one (*masak*) between the vestibule and the 'holy place,' and one (*paroketh*) between the 'holy place' and the 'holy of holies' (§ 47), to remind the devout of the inaccessibility and invisibility of God, who dwelt in the 'holy of holies.' About the ninth hour, as Jesus was dying, one of these curtains (probably the inner one) split in two from top to bottom, almost as if to signify that it no longer had any function for the invisible God was no longer inaccessible. There were earthquake tremors also: 'and the rocks were rent, and the tombs were opened, and many bodies of the saints who had fallen asleep arose; and coming forth out of the tombs after his resurrection, they came into the holy city, and appeared to many' (Mt 27:51–53)." [22]

» THEOLOGICAL NOTE: Given John's ability to find deeper meanings and use words and stories at various levels of meaning, we should ask what Jesus means by "It is finished." Perhaps "It is finished" refers to Jesus' work of dying for the sins of man. That *is* finished at the Cross. Earlier, in anticipation of his Passion, Jesus prayed "I glorified thee on earth, having accomplished the work which thou gavest me to do" (Jn 17:4). The "work" the Father gave Jesus to do was to reveal the Father (Jn 1:18; cf. Jn 17:6–8) and to give himself for the life of the world (Jn 5:36; 6:51).

Scott Hahn has suggested that "It is finished" might refer to the institution of the new Christian Passover—the Eucharist. To understand this explanation, we need to know something about the Passover liturgy. During the Passover meal, the Jews drink four cups of wine as part of the "Haggadah" ceremony. They do not leave the table until all four cups have been drunk. According to Galen

---

[21] John Marsh, *The Gospel of St John* (Baltimore, Md.: Penguin Books, 1968), 618.

[22] Giuseppe Ricciotti, *The Life of Christ*, trans. Alba I. Zizzamia (Milwaukee: Bruce Pub., 1947), 641–42.

Peterson, the first cup of the Passover "Haggadah" is the cup of sanctification; the second cup, the cup of deliverance, and the third cup is the cup of Redemption.[23] This third cup was probably the one used by Jesus for the Lord's Supper—the Eucharist (Mt 26:27). With the pouring of the third cup, the Jews declare that God is one and he is the Tree of Life. What better way to explain Jesus, true I AM, dying on a Cross (tree) to bring life to his people.

After the third cup, the Jews sing the great Hallel (a hymn; see Mt 26:30) before blessing and drinking the fourth cup—the Cup of Acceptance. The fourth cup is poured while the Jews pray for final redemption and sing "God is Mighty! May He soon rebuild His Temple."[24] According to the Synoptic Gospels, Jesus apparently leaves the meal after drinking the third cup and singing the Hallel (Mt 26:26–30).

For a Jew to leave the Haggadah service before the final cup would be quite unthinkable. If Jesus did so, he probably would have meant something by his action. Perhaps he was pointing to another "cup" that would complete his new Passover liturgy, the "cup" of his suffering on the Cross. If so, then "It is finished" might refer to his institution of the new Passover liturgy, the Eucharist, even as his death brought about the New Passover.

This is speculation, of course. Jesus may have refrained from drinking the fourth cup for another reason. After drinking the third cup, Jesus pledged not to drink of "the fruit of the vine" until he drank it again in the kingdom (Lk 22:18). Likewise, he pledged not to eat the Passover again until the kingdom (Lk 22:16). These pledges of abstinence may refer to Jesus' looking forward to the fulfillment of the Passover liturgy in the kingdom, at the messianic banquet. In other words, perhaps he deliberately cut short the Passover liturgy in order to complete it, not on the Cross so much as in the fullness of the kingdom to come. Of course, the Eucharist is an earthly anticipation and participation of the heavenly banquet in the fullness of the kingdom to come, so in that sense Jesus' words may be understood as referring to the Eucharist as well.

In any case, Jesus did drink a "cup" on the cross, whether or not it was intended as the fourth cup of the Passover liturgy from the night before. It was the bitter cup of suffering that he had prayed for his Father to remove (Mt 26:39). Perhaps this is the "cup of God's wrath" (cf. Jer 25:15; Rev 14:10; 16:19), poured out on sin, which Jesus had "become" for our sake (2 Cor 5:21). Perhaps that is what is "finished" on the Cross.

14. Consider other instances, at the very beginning and end of time, when God declares it is finished or accomplished (Gen 2:1; Rev 21:6). How might this reflect or parallel the work of Christ in our current

---

[23] Galen Peterson, *Handbook of Bible Festivals* (Cincinnati, Ohio: Standard Pub. Co., 1997), 13ff.

[24] See Moshe Braun, *The Jewish Holy Days: Their Spiritual Significance* (Northvale, N.J.: Jason Aronson, 1996), 323.

chapter? Notice that Revelation 21:6 also mentions thirst and living water! What did Jesus' thirst merit for us?

15. In verse 30, what does John mean that Jesus "gave up his spirit" (Lk 8:49–56; CCC 1005)? How does Luke record this event (Lk 23:46; Ps 31:5)? Where did his spirit go (1 Pet 3:19; CCC 632)?

» HISTORICAL NOTE: "These words from Psalm 31:5 have for centuries formed part of the evening prayer of pious Jews, and may well have been prayed nightly by Jesus. If, then, he was accustomed to repeat these words before going to sleep, so he repeated them now for the last time." [25]

16. Jesus is now dead; it is about 3 P.M. What day is it (Jn 19:14, 31, 42), and what is now on the mind of every Jewish pilgrim in Jerusalem (Jn 19:31)? Why do the Jews want the crucified men to die quickly (Deut 21:22–23; Josh 10:26–27)? Why do they not break Jesus' legs? What does Pilate think of Jesus' speedy demise (Mk 15:14)? What Scripture passage is fulfilled when Jesus' bones are unbroken (Jn 19:36; Ps 34:20)? Considering what Jesus *is* (Jn 1:29; 1 Cor 5:7; CCC 608), why is it important and significant that *his* legs are not broken (Ex 12:43–47; Num 9:12; 1 Pet 1:18–19)? What is John proving with these "signs" (v. 35)?

» HISTORICAL NOTE: "John has yet another 'sign' connected with Jesus' death to relate, an event not mentioned by the Synoptics. . . . It is from J[oh]n that we learn of the coincidence of the Sabbath with Passover the year of Jesus' death (see 13:1), though the Syn[optics] also tell us that the Sabbath was coming and, therefore, that Jesus' crucifixion occurred on a Friday. The law of D[eu]t[eronomy] 21:22f. forbade the body of an executed criminal exposed to public obloquy to remain beyond sunset. It was especially important that the bodies be removed and buried before the coming of the Sabbath, when such work could not be done. The Roman custom was to leave bodies of criminals exposed indefinitely, and in any case a crucified person might linger for several days before death overtook him (according to Mk 15:44, Pilate was surprised at the suddenness of Jesus' death). Here Pilate accedes to the Jewish custom, doubtless as anxious as were the Jews that nothing untoward should affect the coming Passover, when Roman-Jewish trouble might always be expected. . . . The legs were smashed with a mallet, a brutal yet merciful way of hastening the slow death of crucifixion." [26]

---

[25] F. F. Bruce, *The Gospel of John* (Grand Rapids, Mich.: William B. Eerdmans, 1983), 374.

[26] Brown, Fitzmyer, and Murphy, *Jerome Biblical Commentary*, 2:462.

17. According to verse 34, what did a soldier do when he discovered Jesus was already dead (cf. Is 53:5)? What happened as a result of the soldier's evil deed? How do *water* and *blood* represent sacraments of the Church—the body of Christ (CCC 1225)? Where else in John's Gospel does he mention "blood" (Jn 6:53–56) and "water" (Jn 3:5)? Notice the correlation with baptism and the Eucharist, the queen of the sacraments. How are the blood and water witnesses or signs (1 Jn 5:5–8)? Notice that "testimony", "spirit", "water", and "blood" are in both passages (cf. Jn 5:5–8 and Jn 19:30, 34–35). Why is it important that John prove Jesus actually and truly died and was not simply swooning or in a coma (cf. 1 Cor 15:12–19)?

18. How was the piercing of Jesus' side an Old Testament prophecy (Zech 12:10; Is 53:5)? How did Jesus predict the water from his side (Jn 7:38–39)? What does Paul say (1 Cor 10:4; Num 20:11)?

» THEOLOGICAL NOTE: "Finally there follows a strange incident. When the soldiers saw that Jesus was already dead they did not break his limbs with the mallet; but one of them—it must have been to make doubly sure that Jesus was dead—thrust a spear into his side. And there flowed out water and blood. John attaches special importance to that. He sees in it a fulfilment of the prophecy in *Zechariah* 12:10: 'They look on him whom they have pierced.' And he goes out of his way to say that this is an eye-witness account of what actually happened, and that he personally guarantees that it is true.

"First of all, let us ask what actually happened. We cannot be sure but it may well be that Jesus died literally of a broken heart. Normally, of course, the body of a dead man will not bleed. It is suggested that what happened was that Jesus' experiences, physical and emotional, were so terrible that his heart was rup-tured. When that happened the blood of the heart mingled with the fluid of the pericardium which surrounds the heart. The spear of the soldier pierced the pericardium and the mingled fluid [water] and blood came forth. It would be a poignant thing to believe that Jesus, in the literal sense of the term, died of a broken heart." [27]

» A HYMN BY AUGUSTUS TOPLADY: George Rutler says of this hymn: "In three verses are summed up the content of mystical devotion to the Side of Christ, which the Catholic understands to be also a prophecy of the Birth of the Church."

---

[27] Barclay, *John*, 2:261.

Rock of ages, cleft for me,
Let me hide myself in thee;
Let the water and the blood
From thy side, a healing flood,
Be of sin the double cure,
Cleanse me from its guilt and power.

Should my tears for ever flow,
Should my zeal no languor know,
All for sin could not atone:
Thou must save, and thou alone;
In my hand no price I bring,
Simply to thy cross I cling.

While I draw this fleeting breath,
When mine eyelids close in death,
When I rise to worlds unknown
And behold thee on thy throne,
Rock of ages, cleft for me,
Let me hide myself in thee.[28]

19. Was anyone else "put to sleep" before his bride was taken from his side (Gen 2:21–23; CCC 766)? How might this event prefigure the birth of a new creation—the Church—born through the sacraments flowing from Jesus' side?

» CHURCH FATHERS: "If you desire further proof of the power of this blood, remember where it came from, how it ran down from the cross, flowing from the Master's side. The gospel records that when Christ was dead, but still hung on the cross, a soldier came and pierced his side with a lance and immediately there poured out water and blood. Now the water was a symbol of baptism and the blood, of the holy eucharist. The soldier pierced the Lord's side, he breached the wall of the sacred temple, and I have found the treasure and made it my own. So also with the lamb: the Jews sacrificed the victim and I have been saved by it.

"*There flowed from his side water and blood.* Beloved, do not pass over this mystery without thought; it has yet another hidden meaning, which I will explain to you. I said that water and blood symbolized baptism and the holy eucharist. From these two sacraments the Church is born: from baptism, *the cleansing water that gives rebirth and renewal through the Holy Spirit,* and from the

---

[28] George William Rutler, *Brightest and Best: Stories of Hymns* (San Francisco: Ignatius Press, 1998), 142–43.

holy eucharist. Since the symbols of baptism and the eucharist flowed from his side, it was from his side that Christ fashioned the Church, as he had fashioned Eve from the side of Adam. Moses gives a hint of this when he tells the story of the first man and makes him exclaim: *Bone from my bones and flesh from my flesh!* As God then took a rib from Adam's side to fashion a woman, so Christ has given us blood and water from his side to fashion the Church. God took the rib when Adam was in a deep sleep, and in the same way Christ gave us the blood and the water after his own death.

"Do you understand, then, how Christ has united his bride to himself and what food he gives us all to eat? By one and the same food we are both brought into being and nourished. As a woman nourishes her child with her own blood and milk, so does Christ unceasingly nourish with his own blood those to whom he himself has given life." [29]

20. According to verse 35, why does John tell these unique details? How do we know John gives accurate information (1 Jn 1:1–3; Jn 15:27; 21:24)? What is his purpose in writing the Gospel and telling us these things (Jn 20:30–31; CCC 514)?

John 19:38–42
The Burial of Jesus

21. Who is Joseph of Arimathea (Mt 27:57–61; Mk 15:42–47; Lk 23:50–56; CCC 595)? What did he do (v. 38)? Why was Joseph a "secret disciple" (Jn 7:13; 9:22; 12:42)? Are you a *secret* or *public* disciple of Jesus? How do you openly testify to your faith in Christ and obedience to his Church? What virtue helped Joseph step forward to claim the body of a convicted criminal (Mk 15:43)? Was it easy for him? What was a possible result of his action (Jn 9:22; 12:42)? Notice that Jesus came into the world in a borrowed "cave" through a man named Joseph and goes out of this world in a borrowed "cave" through a man named Joseph.

22. In verse 39, who is Nicodemus (Jn 3:1–2; 7:50)? What does he have in common with Joseph of Arimathea (CCC 595–96)? Nicodemus is mentioned three times in John's Gospel. Is there progress in Nicodemus' spiritual life? Why is it significant that Nicodemus originally came to

---

[29] St. John Chrysostom, *Catechesis* 3, 13–19, in *The Liturgy of the Hours according to the Roman Rite*, Office of Readings for Good Friday (Boston, Mass.: Daughters of St. Paul, 1983), p. 480.

Jesus at *night* (Jn 3:2; 11:10), but now comes to care for Jesus' body in the *evening*, before nightfall (Mk 15:42)? What might John be saying to the "secret believers" in the synagogues of his own time (90–100; cf. Rev 3:7–13)? What did the *death* of Jesus accomplish in these men's lives that Jesus' *life* and miracles had not done? Nicodemus was told that new birth comes from *water* and *Spirit* (Jn 3:5). How does he now understand this new life from Jesus' side?

23. According to verse 39, how many pounds of spice were brought to embalm Jesus? What spices were used? At what earlier event was Jesus given myrrh (Mt 2:11)? How might it be significant that the spice of kings and funerals is associated with Jesus' birth and death? What was a key ingredient of the *holy oil* with which priests and kings were anointed in ancient Israel (Ex 30:22–33)? How does this demonstrate the priestly office of Christ? Notice how these spices are mentioned in Psalm 45:8, right after the psalmist prophesies about the "garments" of Christ (quoted in Heb 1:8–9). How were the dead wrapped (Jn 11:44; 20:7)? Does this give credence to the Shroud of Turin?

» THEOLOGICAL NOTE: "The second possible symbolism is a continuation of the theme that Jesus is king. The large outlay of spices may be meant to suggest that Jesus was given a royal burial, for we know of such an outlay on behalf of kings. Josephus, *Ant.* XVII.viii.3:# 199 tells us that at the burial of Herod the Great five hundred servants carried the aromatic oils or spices (aroma). There is a tradition preserved in a 'minor tractate' of the Talmud (TalBab, *Ebel Rabbathi* or *Shemhoth*, 8:6—a medieval work but containing older materials) that at the death of Rabbi Gamaliel the Elder (probably ca. A.D. 50) the proselyte Onkelos burned more than eighty pounds of spices. When asked why, he cited Jer xxxiv 5 as an instance where spices were burned at the death of kings and affirmed that Gamaliel was better than one hundred kings. The mention of a garden may point in the same direction, for the Old Testament references to burial in a garden concern the entombment of the kings of Judah (II Kings xxi 18, 26). From the LXX [Septuagint] of Neh iii 16 we learn that the popular tomb of David (see Acts ii 29) was in a garden. Obviously the evidence is far from probative, and we confess uncertainty about its value; but the theme that Jesus was buried as a king would fittingly conclude a Passion Narrative wherein Jesus is crowned and hailed as king during his trial and enthroned and publicly proclaimed as king on the cross. . . . Thus, if there is a theological theme hidden symbolically in the narrative, it should be the terminal stage of a theme, such as kingship, that played a prominent part in the crucifixion." [30]

---

[30] Brown, *John*, 2:960.

24. How many days was Lazarus in the tomb (Jn 11:17)? Why was that important (see chap. 11 above; CCC 627)? How many days was Jesus in the tomb (1 Cor 15:4)? Why was this time period important (see chap. 11, p. 227; Acts 2:24, 27; CCC 627)?

25. Who else brought spices to anoint Jesus (Mk 16:1; CCC 641)? Where was Jesus' body laid (vv. 41–42)? How did this fulfill Old Testament prophecy (Is 53:9; Mt 27:57–60)? How did Christ experience death for three days (CCC 624)? Why is it significant that Jesus was crucified and buried in a garden (Jn 18:1; 19:41; see notes on John 18, pp. 313–14)? How is *this* garden a reversal of Eden, in which redemption in a garden reverses the Fall of Adam in the Garden of Eden? Find other parallels. Who wrapped Jesus in swaddling clothes at his birth (Lk 2:7,) and who probably wrapped him at his death?

» MARY AND THE SHROUD: Practically the whole of the imprint on the Shroud shows the care taken in arranging the sheet over all parts of the body— not over the whole surface of course—particularly where there were wounds, swellings, and blood-marks. Since the Mother of Jesus was present in the tomb, who else could be responsible for this intentional arrangement? Without this motherly attention we would not have had such an imprint, so eloquent in its details. "[This careful wrapping] is an action mothers perform when swaddling their babies—how many times must the Virgin Mother have done it joyfully to the infant Jesus! Now she repeated the action, in sorrow, on those limbs marked by the whips and fixed in death." [31]

» POETIC THEOLOGY: "The word 'garden' hinted at Eden and the fall of man, as it also suggested through its flowers in the springtime the Resurrection from the dead. In that garden was the tomb in which 'no man had ever been buried.' Born of a virgin womb, He was buried in a virgin tomb, and as Crashaw said: 'And a Joseph did betroth them both.' Nothing seems more repelling than to have a Crucifixion in a garden, and yet there would be compensation, for the garden would have its Resurrection. Born in a stranger's cave, buried in a stranger's grave, both human birth and death were strangers to His Divinity. Stranger's grave too, because since sin was foreign to Him, so too was death. Dying for others, He was placed in another's grave. His grave was borrowed, for He would give it back on Easter, as He gave back the beast that He rode on Palm Sunday, and the Upper Room which He used for the Last Supper. Burying is only a planting [or, as the early Christians in the Catacombs taught, 'a deposit']. Paul would later on draw from the fact that He was buried in a

---

[31] Giulio Ricci, *The Holy Shroud* (Rome: Centro Romano di Sindonologia, 1981), 262.

garden the law that if we are planted in the likeness of His death, we shall rise with Him in the glory of His Resurrection." [32]

» THEOLOGICAL NOTE: "Many of the Fathers have probed the mystic meaning of the garden—usually to point out that Christ, who was arrested in the Garden of Olives and buried in another garden, has redeemed us superabundantly from that first sin which was committed also in a garden, the Garden of Paradise. They comment that Jesus' being the only one to be buried in this new tomb meant that there would be no doubt that it was he and not another that rose from the dead. St Augustine also observes that 'just as in the womb of the Virgin Mary none was conceived before him, none after him, so in this tomb none before him, none after was buried' (*Joann. Evang.*, 120, 5)." [33]

26. According to verse 41, what characterized Jesus' tomb; how old was it? Read the other accounts of Jesus' burial (Mt 27:57ff.; Mk 15:42ff.; Lk 23:50ff.). Do you think that Jesus' followers would remember where he had been buried as the years passed by?

» WHERE WAS JESUS REALLY BURIED? There are two sites that claim to be the authentic burial place of Jesus: the *Garden Tomb* and the *Church of the Holy Sepulchre*. The Garden Tomb has been advocated as Jesus' burial place only since the nineteenth century. A few Protestant groups accept it, while all Christians before the nineteenth century accepted the Church of the Holy Sepulchre. Its claims go back to the earliest centuries of Christianity.

"Gabriel Barkay, who teaches at Tel Aviv University and the American Institute of Holy Land Studies, has made a new study of the case for the Garden Tomb and has concluded that it was first hewn in the Iron Age II period, during the eighth to the sixth centuries B.C., and was not used again for burial purposes until the Byzantine period. So it is not the tomb in which Jesus was buried." [34]

Regarding the Garden Tomb, we read, "There is no possibility that it is in fact the place where Christ was buried. . . . The first visitor to popularize this site as Golgotha was General Charles Gordon in 1883; he thought he recognized the shape of a skull in the hill behind the tomb." [35] Archaeologists claim the skull-like appearance of the cliff is probably not more than a few centuries old and the result of recent quarrying. Referring to "Protestants desirous of

---

[32] Fulton Sheen, *Life of Christ* (New York: Image Books/Doubleday, 1990), 401.

[33] Casciaro, *John*, 238.

[34] Joseph P. Free, *Archaeology and Bible History*, revised by Howard F. Vos (Grand Rapids, Mich.: Zondervan Pub. House, 1992), 254. See also W. Harold Mare, *Archaeology of the Jerusalem Area* (Grand Rapids, Mich.: Baker Book House, 1987), 185–89, 232–33.

[35] Jerome Murphy-O'Connor, *The Holy Land*, 4th ed. (New York: Oxford Univ. Press, 1998), 141.

having a holy place of their very own", Murphy-O'Connor states, "Despite the protestations of those best qualified to judge, the Anglican Church committed itself to the identification, and what had been known scornfully as 'Gordon's Tomb' suddenly became the 'Garden Tomb'. Sanity eventually prevailed, and the Anglican Church withdrew its formal support, but in Jerusalem the prudence of reason has little chance against the certitude of piety. . . . [The] configuration is typical of tombs C9–C7 BC. . . . From a strictly archaeological point of view, therefore, it certainly was not a new tomb in the C1 AD." [36]

"Doubt of the authenticity of the traditional site of the Holy Sepulchre seems natural. When an unprejudiced person sees a church in the centre of a very crowded city, professing to mark the site of the events recorded to have taken place outside the walls, he must ask questions. Scepticism can be justified, but when one suggests arbitrarily a rival site out of mere prejudice, one forfeits all claim to serious attention. Further, to misconstrue original texts and 'plant' remains are acts unworthy of honest men. If we reject tradition in this regard, then we know not where these events took place. Some people faced with what they have called 'Superstitious mummery, lying, and idle mummeries, formalism, trafficking, hateful and despicable rivalries', persuaded themselves that the Church of the Holy Sepulchre could not be the site, and sought another." [37]

---

[36] Ibid.

[37] Eugene Hoade, *Guide to the Holy Land* (Jerusalem: Franciscan Printing Press, n.d.), 322.

JOHN 20

DEATH COULD NOT HOLD HIM—
"MY LORD AND MY GOD"

John 20:1–10
The Empty Tomb

1. To understand the various perspectives of the Resurrection, read the four Gospel accounts and the account of St. Paul (Jn 20:1–8; Mt 28:1–8; Mk 16:1–8; Lk 24:1–10; 1 Cor 15:1–8).

» Textual note: "The confusion that we find in the accounts of Easter morning as given by the four Evangelists is due to the concise brevity of the three Synoptists. Not one of them imagined he was proving the resurrection for his readers, any more than that he had proved the birth, or life, or public ministry, or the humanity, or the divinity of our Lord. Faith, in the readers, depended not so much on the written word as on the oral teaching of the divinely constituted society called the Church, complemented by the co-operation of the Holy Spirit enlightening the minds of the hearers. . . . Only John has described [Mary Magdalene's] visit at any length: he does so because he saw that the synoptic accounts were imperfect and easily misleading."[1]

2. Did any person actually witness Christ rising from the dead? What do we know of Mary Magdalene (Lk 8:2; Mk 15:40; CCC 641)? What time was it when Mary Magdalene arrived at the tomb (v. 1)? Could the mention of "darkness" be symbolic, and if so, what would it symbolize? On what day did she arrive at the tomb (Jn 20:19; CCC 2174)? Why does the Church refer to this as the "eighth day" (CCC 2174, 1166)?

» Tradition of the early Church: "The Gospel tells us nothing of this apparition [Jesus' appearance to his Mother], but Christian tradition takes it for

---

[1] G. H. Trench, *A Study of St John's Gospel* (London: John Murray, 1918), 418–19.

granted: the Doctors in general and the body of the faithful have always believed that after His Resurrection our Lord appeared first to His Mother. And indeed, was it not just that she who had shared most in His Passion should have been the first to participate in His glory? Would He who was so generous to Mary Magdalene have been less so to His own Mother? As Suárez says, we should believe without any shadow of doubt that after His Resurrection Christ appeared first to His Mother, for such is the almost unanimous opinion of all the faithful and the Doctors of the Church, as well as the teaching of every Catholic writer who dealt with the subject." [2]

» HISTORICAL NOTE: "The Hebrews began their day with sunset (Lev. 23, 32; Ps. 54 [55], 18) and reckoned their day from evening to evening (Ex 12, 18; Lev. 23, 32). . . . In [New Testament] times the Jews followed the Roman method of four watches of three hours each: evening, midnight, cock-crow and morning watches." [3] "Sabbath is, of course, our Saturday, so it was on Sunday morning that Mary came to the tomb. She came very early. The word used for *early* is *prōi* which was the technical word for the last of the four watches into which the night was divided, that which ran from 3 a.m. to 6 a.m. It was still dark when Mary came, because she could no longer stay away." [4]

3. According to the Apostles' and the Nicene Creeds, how long was Jesus dead and his body in the tomb (Jn 2:18–22; Acts 10:40; CCC 994)? What did Jesus do for those three days while in the tomb (1 Pet 3:19; 4:6; CCC 631–33)? What Old Testament situation is used as the type or example of Christ's entombment (Jon 1:17, 2:10; Mt 12:40; CCC 994)? Had the disciples been told in advance that Jesus would rise from the dead (Mt 16:21; 27:63)?

» CULTURAL NOTE: "Should the expression 'three days and three nights' be interpreted literally? Three arguments indicate that it should not. First, it appears that this expression is another way of stating 'on the third day' or 'in three days.' This can be illustrated from 1 Samuel 30:12–13. The same Greek expression is found in 1 Samuel 30:12 in the Greek translation of the Old Testament (the LXX) as in Matthew 12:40. Verse 13 refers to this three-day and three-night period as 'three days ago' or, as the LXX literally states, 'the third day today.' If 'three days and three nights' can mean 'on the third day,' there is no major problem in our passage. By Jewish reckoning Jesus could have been

---

[2] Andrés Fernández, *The Life of Christ*, trans. Paul Barrett (Westminster, Md.: Newman Press, 1959), 757; see also Trench, *Study*, 411f.

[3] John Steinmueller and Kathryn Sullivan, *Catholic Biblical Encyclopedia* (New York: Joseph F. Wagner, 1956), s.v. "Time", p. 1082.

[4] William Barclay, *The Gospel of John* (Philadelphia: Westminster Press, 1975), 2:265.

crucified on Friday and raised on Sunday, the third day. Friday afternoon = day one; Friday 6 P.M. to Saturday 6 P.M. = day two; Saturday 6 P.M. to Sunday 6 P.M. = day three. . . .

"For [Matthew], as well as for the other Evangelists, expressions such as 'three days and three nights,' 'after three days,' and 'on the third day' could be used interchangeably. Finally, it should be pointed out that the main point of Jesus' analogy in Matthew 12:40 does not involve the temporal designation but the sign of the resurrection. . . . Understood in the context of biblical Judaism, the designation 'three days and three nights' poses no problem with the Friday crucifixion and Sunday resurrection scheme described in the passion narratives. It is only if a twentieth-century reckoning of time is imposed or if the idiomatic nature of this temporal designation is not understood that a problem appears." [5]

4. Considering Jewish ideas on death and corruption, why did Jesus remain only three days in the tomb and not four days (CCC 627; Ps 16:10; Acts 13:33–37)? Why was it therefore essential that Lazarus be in the tomb four days (CCC 627)? For more on this aspect of Jesus' burial, see the discussion of John 11, page 227.

» CULTURAL NOTE: "It was the custom in Palestine to visit the tomb of a loved one for three days after the body had been laid to rest. It was believed that for three days the spirit of the dead person hovered round the tomb; but then it departed because the body had become unrecognizable through decay. Jesus' friends could not come to the tomb on the Sabbath, because to make the journey then would have been to break the law." [6]

5. According to verse 1, when Mary Magdalene arrived at the tomb after the Passover, what did she find (Mt 28:2; Mk 16:4; CCC 641)? Did she look inside? How had the stone moved from the mouth of the tomb (Mt 28:2)? How was the tomb secured, and why were the Jews careful to guard and seal the tomb (Mt 27:62–66)? What was the penalty imposed on guards who failed their duty (Acts 12:18–19)? What did Mary assume had happened (v. 2)? How did the disciples respond to Mary's report (Lk 24:11)? What happened to the stone and to the guards (Mt 28:2, 11–15)?

» ARCHAEOLOGY: "The mouth of the tomb was sealed either with a disc-shaped stone that ran in an inclined groove in front of the cave or with a

[5] Robert H. Stein, *Difficult Passages in the New Testament* (Grand Rapids, Mich.: Baker Book House, 1990), 120–21. See also Walter C. Kaiser, Jr., et al., editors. *Hard Sayings of the Bible* (Downers Grove, Ill.: InterVarsity Press, 1996), 380–81.

[6] Barclay, *John*, 2:265.

boulder that fell into the access hole beneath it. Either way, the stone was extremely difficult to move once it was in place." [7]

6. According to verses 3–4, who ran to the tomb? Why do you think Mary went to tell Peter instead of someone else (Mt 10:2; 16:18; Mk 16:7)? Who was the first person to look inside the tomb? Tradition informs us that "the other disciple" was the Apostle John. Why do you think they ran? Notice their posture as they approached the tomb (Jn 20:5, 11), and why was this posture appropriate? What did they find (vv. 5–7; CCC 640, 657)? How does Paul later describe the situation (1 Cor 15:1–8; CCC 639)? How was Jesus' corpse tightly bound (Jn 19:40; CCC 515)? Who else had been so bound (Jn 11:44)? How does the wording of John 20:7 give credence to the Shroud of Turin? Would the first believers have treasured and preserved mementos and relics of Christ?

» THE SHROUD OF TURIN: "John mentions the Jewish custom; Jewish people did not burn dead heroes, as Greeks and Romans did, or mutilate them for embalming, as Egyptians did. Bodies were wrapped in shrouds, sometimes expensive ones, especially prepared for burials." [8]

"God's most challenging message to mankind is a message of love: man's eternal salvation through the redemptive work of the Son of God, incarnate, dead and risen. The credibility of this message, entrusted orally to the prophets and, in the fullness of time, to the Messiah Himself, by Him to the Apostles and through them to the Church, is based on the very authority of God Who revealed it. The oral message was written down by the authors of the Old and New Testaments and by the Magisterium, which ensures it is authentically transmitted and taught. I consider it to be quite legitimate to place the Holy Shroud on a par with this tradition written in pen and ink. The Shroud is truly a page of paleography in a unique, unrepeatable edition. Here we read God's love, written in letters of blood." [9]

"According to all that has been said above, *we must conclude that the Man of the Shroud is that Jesus of whom the Gospels speak.* . . . All these data exclude the possibility that this might be any other crucified man; in the light of present research, the possibility of the findings referring to anyone else are so remote that it is bordering on the ridiculous even to suggest it." [10]

---

[7] Ralph Gower, *The New Manners and Customs of Bible Times* (Chicago: Moody Press, 1987), 72–73.

[8] Craig Keener, *The IVP Bible Background Commentary: New Testament* (Downers Grove, Ill.: InterVarsity Press, 1993), 315.

[9] Giulio Ricci, *Guide to the Photographic Exhibit of the Holy Shroud* (Milwaukee: Center for the Study of the Passion of Christ and the Holy Shroud, 1982), ix.

[10] Giulio Ricci, *The Holy Shroud* (Rome: Centro Romano di Sindonologia, 1981), 299.

» SPIRITUAL SYMBOLISM: "Observe the posture in which he found things in the sepulchre. Christ had left his grave-clothes behind him there; what clothes he appeared in to his disciples we are not told, but he never appeared in his grave-clothes, as ghosts are supposed to do; no, he laid them aside, *First*, because he arose to die no more; death was to have no more dominion over him, Rom. 6:9. Lazarus came out with his grave-clothes on, for he was to use them again; but Christ, rising to an immortal life, came out free from those encumbrances. *Secondly*, because he was going to be clothed with the robes of glory, therefore he lays aside these rags; in the heavenly paradise there will be no more occasion for clothes than there was in the earthly. The ascending prophet dropped his mantle. *Thirdly*, when we arise from the death of sin to the life of righteousness, we must leave our grave-clothes behind us, must put off all our corruptions. *Fourthly*, Christ left those in the grave, as it were, for our use if the grave be a bed to the saints, thus he hath sheeted that bed, and made it ready for them; and the napkin by itself is of use for the mourning survivors to *wipe away their tears*. The grave-clothes were found in very good order, which serves for an evidence that his body was not stolen away while men slept. Robbers of tombs have been known to take away the clothes and leave the body; but none [prior to the practices of modern resurrectionists] ever took away the body and left the clothes, especially when it was fine linen and new, Mk. 15:46. Any one would rather choose to carry a dead body in its clothes than naked. Or, if those that were supposed to have stolen it would have left the grave-clothes behind, yet it cannot be supposed they should find leisure to fold up the linen." [11]

7. In verse 9, what did the disciples initially fail to understand (CCC 644)? Did the disciples eventually believe in the Resurrection of Jesus (Jn 2:22)? What was John's response (v. 8)? How should we respond to the empty tomb? Why did John preach the message (Jn 19:35; 17:20; 1 Jn 5:13)? How does Jesus' own Resurrection differ from that of those *he* had raised from the dead (CCC 645)? What did Peter and the disciples do after finding the tomb empty (v. 10; Lk 24:12; CCC 643)?

John 20:11–18
Jesus Appears to Mary Magdalene

8. According to verse 11, who remained at the tomb after the men left? Why was she weeping (v. 15)? Why did she love Jesus so much (Lk 7:46–

---

[11] Matthew Henry, *Matthew Henry's Commentary* (Peabody, Mass.: Hendrickson Pub., 1991), 5:1209–10.

47)? What did she see while she was stooping to look into the tomb (v. 12)?

» HISTORICAL NOTE: Grave-robbing was a problem. Thus, Emperor Claudius (reigned A.D. 41–54) made it a capital offense to disturb a tomb. To insure that no one would rob the grave and proclaim Christ a risen Messiah, Roman guards were stationed at Jesus' tomb with the penalty of death for failure to fulfill their duty. This itself leaves no doubt that a miracle took place (cf. Acts 12:5–19). "Ordinance of Caesar. It is my pleasure that graves and tombs remain undisturbed in perpetuity for those who have made them of the cult of their ancestors or children or members of their house. If however any man lay information that another has either demolished [a grave], or has in any other way extracted the buried, or has maliciously transferred them to other places in order to wrong them, or has displaced the sealing or other stones, against such a one I order that a trial be instituted. . . . Let it be absolutely forbidden for any one to disturb them. In case of contravention I desire that the offender be sentenced to capital punishment on charge of violation of sepulture." [12]

9. Why do you think *Mary* saw the angels but the two apostles did *not*? Did Mary Magdalene's past problems (Mk 16:9) cause Jesus to treat her as a second-class citizen? Did he treat women in a condescending manner? According to verse 14, whom did Mary see when she turned around? What did the angels and Jesus ask (vv. 13, 15)? Imagine Jesus' facial expression: Was he serious, humorous, questioning, compassionate, pedagogical, and so forth? For whom did Mary mistake Jesus (v. 15; CCC 645)? Who was the first "gardener" (Gen 2:15)? How does this again demonstrate Jesus as the "gardener" (new Adam) of the new creation in the new garden? Who were the first and last Adams (CCC 359)?

10. Do others recognize Jesus immediately (Lk 24:15–16)? Do Mary's tears possibly blur her vision? How does Mary Magdalene demonstrate her love for Jesus? What one word from Jesus opens the eyes of Mary? What is her response? According to St. John, who is the first to see the resurrected Christ (CCC 641)? According to St. Paul, who is the first to see the resurrected Christ (1 Cor 15:5)?

11. In verse 17, why does Jesus restrain Mary from clinging to him (CCC 660)?

---

[12] C. K. Barrett, *The New Testament Background* (San Francisco: HarperSanFrancisco, 1987), 15.

» THEOLOGICAL NOTE: Commentators have struggled to understand the injunction against Mary clinging to Jesus. "Mary had evidently thrown herself at Jesus' feet and was attempting to demonstrate her love by throwing her arms about his knees. Jesus must tell her, however, that the old relationships are no more, and he must not be hindered in completing the drama of his glorification. Now he must return to the Father, thus accomplishing the destiny that has been the goal of his entire earthly life." [13]

"It is suggested that the Greek is really a mistranslation of an Aramaic original. Jesus of course would speak in Aramaic, and not in Greek; and what John gives us is a translation into Greek of what Jesus said. It is suggested that what Jesus really said was: 'Hold me not; but before I ascend to my Father go to my brethren and say to them. . . .' It would be as if Jesus said: 'Do not spend so long in worshipping me in the joy of your new discovery. Go and tell the good news to the rest of the disciples.' It may well be that here we have the explanation. The Greek imperative is a present imperative, and strictly speaking ought to mean: 'Stop touching me.' It may be that Jesus was saying to Mary: 'Don't go on clutching me selfishly to yourself. In a short time I am going back to my Father. I want to meet my disciples as often as possible before then. Go and tell them the good news that none of the time that we and they should have together may be wasted.' That would make excellent sense, and that in fact is what Mary did." [14]

12. According to verse 17, what is Mary to tell Jesus' "brethren"? Why are they called "brethren" (Rom 8:29; Gal 4:6–7; Heb 2:11; Jn 1:12; CCC 654)? How might this fulfill Old Testament prophecy (Ps 22:22; cf. Heb 2:11–12; Ruth 1:16)? Since they have been called servants, how is this new disclosure revolutionary? When does Jesus "ascend to the Father" (Jn 16:28; Acts 1:9–11; Mk 16:19; CCC 659)?

13. According to verse 18, what did Mary announce to the disciples (Mk 16:9–11; Lk 24:9–11, 22–24)? How did the disciples respond (CCC 643)? Read John 20:14, 19–20, 26–29; 21:4; Lk 24:36–43. What do these passages tell us about the physical body of the resurrected Christ (1 Cor 15:42–44; CCC 645)? Was the Resurrection of Christ a real historical resurrection (1 Cor 15:3–8; CCC 647)? What would have been the result if the Resurrection had not occurred (1 Cor 15:12–22)? What does the Resurrection prove (CCC 651–53)?

---

[13] Raymond Brown, Joseph Fitzmyer, and Roland Murphy, eds., *The Jerome Biblical Commentary* (Englewood Cliffs, N.J.: Prentice-Hall, 1968), 2:463.

[14] Barclay, *John*, 2:271.

» THEOLOGICAL NOTE: "The existential consequences of the resurrection are incomparable. It is the concrete, factual, empirical proof that: life has hope and meaning; 'love is stronger than death'; goodness and power are ultimately allies, not enemies; life wins in the end; God has touched us right here where we are and has defeated our last enemy; we are not cosmic orphans, as our modern secular worldview would make us. And these existential consequences of the resurrection can be seen by comparing the disciples before and after. Before, they ran away, denied their Master and huddled behind locked doors in fear and confusion. After, they were transformed from scared rabbits into confident saints, world-changing missionaries, courageous martyrs and joy-filled touring ambassadors for Christ.

"The greatest importance of the resurrection is not in the past—'Christ rose'—but in the present—'Christ is risen.' The angel at the tomb asked the women, 'Why do you seek the living among the dead?' (Lk 24:5). The same question could be asked today to mere historians and scholars. If only we did not keep Christ mummified in a casket labeled 'history' or 'apologetics,' he would set our lives and world afire as powerfully as he did two millennia ago; and our new pagan empire would sit up, take notice, rub its eyes, wonder and convert a second time. That is the existential import of the resurrection." [15]

» APOLOGETICAL NOTE: After many pages of superb arguments and proofs for the historical and bodily Resurrection of Jesus Christ, Kreeft and Tacelli conclude, "The historical evidence is massive enough to convince the open-minded inquirer. By analogy with any other historical event, the resurrection has eminently credible evidence behind it. To disbelieve it, you must deliberately make an exception to the rules you use everywhere else in history. Now why would someone want to do that? Ask yourself that question if you dare, and take an honest look into your heart before you answer." [16]

John 20:19–31
Jesus Appears to the Disciples

14. At dawn the disciples had seen the empty tomb and heard from Mary Magdalene that she had "seen the Lord". What did the disciples do the rest of the day and into the evening (v. 19)? What were they afraid of (Jn 7:13; 9:22)? Would you have been afraid? Imagine yourself in their sandals: You have just witnessed the gory death of your rabbi,

---

[15] Peter Kreeft and Ronald K. Tacelli, *Handbook of Christian Apologetics* (Downers Grove, Ill.: InterVarsity Press, 1994), 177.
[16] Ibid., 197.

and you assume the authorities will not be satisfied with the death of only the *leader*. How would you react?

15. According to verse 19, who appeared in the midst of the disciples? John says that the doors were closed. How did Jesus come and stand in their midst (Lk 24:36)? What did Jesus say to them? Why is this repeated three times (Jn 20:19, 21, 26; cf. Jn 14:27; Phil 4:7)? Imagine yourself seeing the Lord appear risen and alive in the room. When did he promise to "come to them again" (Jn 14:18, 28)? Was this a fulfillment of that promise, or was the fulfillment still to come, or both?

» HISTORICAL NOTE: "The disciples would remain inside to mourn; the Feast of Unleavened Bread is also still going on, so none of them would have left Jerusalem for Galilee yet anyway. Proper residences were equipped with bolts and locks. Bolted doors would prevent anyone from entering (a heavy bolt could be slid through rings attached to the door and its frame), unless one could walk through closed doors. Jesus' appearance in the locked room suggests a resurrection body whose nature is superior to that normally envisioned in ancient Jewish literature." [17]

16. According to verse 20, what did Jesus show the disciples (Lk 24:39)? Did he still possess the wounds of the crucifixion—his sacrifice—after the Resurrection (Rev 5:6; CCC 1137; 1 Jn 2:1–2)? How did the disciples respond? Was the Resurrection of Christ a resurrection of his actual physical body (Lk 24:38–45; Acts 2:24, 32; CCC 643, 645, 999)?

17. According to verse 21, Jesus told his disciples, "As the Father has sent me, even so I send you." The word "apostle" means "sent one". What did Jesus mean here? How did Paul refer to Jesus (Heb 3:1)? How did Jesus commission his disciples (CCC 730, 858)? How did the disciples choose and send their successors (CCC 857, 861, 935, 1087, 1594; 2 Tim 2:2)? What if someone refuses to hear Jesus' apostles and their successors, the bishops (Lk 10:16)? How does the Church hierarchy "mediate" Christ (CCC 553, 1444–45; Mt 18:17–18; Acts 20:28; 2 Cor 5:20; Heb 13:17; 1 Pet 5:2)?

» CLEMENT OF ROME (A.D. 96; personally acquainted with Peter and Paul): "Our Apostles, too, were given to understand by our Lord Jesus Christ that the office of the bishop would give rise to intrigues. For this reason, equipped as

---

[17] Keener, *IVP Bible Background Commentary*, 317.

they were with perfect foreknowledge, they appointed the men mentioned before, and afterwards laid down a rule once for all to this effect: when these men die, other approved men shall succeed to their sacred ministry. Consequently, we deem it an injustice to eject from the sacred ministry the persons who were appointed either by them, or later, with the consent of the whole Church, by other men in high repute and have ministered to the flock of Christ faultlessly, humbly, quietly and unselfishly, and have moreover, over a long period of time, earned the esteem of all. Indeed, it will be no small sin for us if we oust men who have irreproachably and piously offered the sacrifices proper to the episcopate." [18]

"Christ sent the apostles as he himself had been sent by the Father, and then through the apostles made their successors, the bishops, sharers in his consecration and mission.

"The function of the bishops' ministry was handed over in a subordinate degree to priests so that they might be appointed in the order of the priesthood and be co-workers of the episcopal order for the proper fulfilment of the apostolic mission that had been entrusted to it by Christ." [19]

18. According to verse 22, what "sacramental action" did Jesus perform on the apostles (the "sent ones") (CCC 1087)? What did Jesus impart by his action? Where else do we find a similar reference (Jn 3:3–8; Acts 2:1–4; Ezek 37:4–10; CCC 703, 715, 730)? From the classic "new life" passage in Ezekiel (Ezek 37:4–10), list other key words used also by St. John. How was the impartation of the Spirit a fulfillment of the Old Testament (Ezek 36:24–27; CCC 1286–87)?

19. Compare Genesis 2:7 with John 20:22. List the similarities between the first, *physical* creation and the second, *spiritual* creation.

» SPIRITUAL APPLICATION: "Then Our Lord breathed on them as He conferred some power of the Holy Spirit. When love is deep, it is always speechless or wordless; God's love is so deep that it can be expressed humanly by a sigh or a breath. Now that the Apostles had learned to lisp the alphabet of Redemption, He breathed on them as a sign and an earnest of what was to come. It was but a cloud that would precede the plenteous rain; better still, it was the breath of the Spirit's influence and a foretelling of the rushing wind of Pentecost. As

---

[18] Clement of Rome, *To the Corinthians* 44, in *The Epistles of St. Clement of Rome and St. Ignatius of Antioch*, trans James A. Kleist, Ancient Christian Writers, no. 1 (New York: Newman Press, 1946), 36.

[19] Vatican II, Decree on the Ministry and Life of Priests, *Presbyterorum ordinis*, December 7, 1965, no. 2, in Austin Flannery, ed., *Vatican Council II: The Conciliar and Post Conciliar Documents*, new rev. ed. (Collegeville, Minn.: Liturgical Press, 1992), 864.

He had breathed into Adam the breath of natural life, so now He breathed into His Apostles, the foundation of His Church, the breath of spiritual life. As man became the image of God in virtue of the soul that was breathed into him, so now they became the image of Christ as the power of the Spirit was breathed into them. The Greek word used to express His breathing on them is employed nowhere else in the New Testament; but it is the very word which the Greek translators of the Hebrew used to describe God's breathing a living soul into Adam. Thus there was a new creation as the first fruit of the Redemption. . . .

"Three times the Holy Spirit is mentioned with some external sign; as a dove at Christ's baptism betokening His innocence and Divine Sonship; as fiery tongues on the day of Pentecost as a sign of the Spirit's power to convert the world; and as the breath of the Risen Christ with all of its regenerative power." [20]

» THEOLOGICAL NOTE: A physical body needs a soul, as does the Body of Christ. The Holy Spirit is the "Soul of the Church". "The Fathers attest the intimate connection of the Holy Ghost with the Church. St. Irenaeus says: 'Where the Church is, there is also the Spirit of God; and where the Spirit of God is, there is the Church and all grace' (*Adv. Haer.* III, 24, 1). St. Augustine compares the working of the Holy Ghost in the Church to the working of the soul in the body: 'What the soul is for the body of man that the Holy Ghost is for the body of Christ, that is, the Church. The Holy Ghost operates in the whole Church that which the soul operates in the members of the one body.' As the soul quickens every member of the body and bestows a definite function on each, so the Holy Ghost, by His grace, quickens every member of the Church, and allocates to each a definite activity in the service of the whole. . . . As the soul does not follow the member that is cut off from the body, so also the Holy Ghost does not dwell in the member who separates itself from the body of the Church." [21]

20. What gift or authority was bestowed on the apostles as a result of the reception of the Holy Spirit (v. 23)? Was this authority given to everyone—to whom was Jesus actually speaking (vv. 19–24; CCC 1461– 67)? Where else do we find authority delegated to the apostles in similar words (Mt 16:17–19, cf. Is 22:22; Mt 18:17–18)? Notice other passages that speak of absolution of sins (Jas 5:14–15; 2 Sam 12:13–14). What does it mean for men to have the authority to *forgive* and *retain* sins? In light of some traditions that teach one must go to God alone to be forgiven, without the absolution of a priest, how would sins be retained?

---

[20] Fulton Sheen, *Life of Christ* (New York: Image Books/Doubleday, 1990), 420.

[21] Ludwig Ott, *Fundamentals of Catholic Dogma,* trans. Patrick Lynch, ed. James Canon Bastible (Rockford, Ill.: TAN Books, 1960), 295.

» THEOLOGICAL NOTE: "By the symbolic gesture of breathing upon them he signified that he was communicating the Holy Spirit—a partial anticipation of the gift of Pentecost. The words: 'Receive ye the Holy Ghost' made the meaning quite clear. The power of remitting and retaining sins, clearly supposes judicial authority exercised over sins in a tribunal. Accordingly the Church has perpetually understood this act of the Saviour as the institution of the sacrament of Penance (Trent, Sess. 14). Thus the sacrament of pardon was instituted under a double sign of the Saviour's peace, on the most joyful day of the world's history. It should be noted that in the intention of Christ who gave this power to the members of an apostolic college, Thomas, who was absent, also received it." [22]

» DOCTRINAL NOTE: "The Council of Trent defined against Luther. . . . Christ promised the power of absolution to the Apostles only (Mt. 18:18) and transferred this power to them only (John 20:23). The power passed from the Apostles to their successors in the priesthood, the bishops and the presbyters. The hierarchical constitution of the Church demands that the judicial power of absolution cannot belong to all the faithful indiscriminately, but only to the members of the hierarchy.

"According to the testimony of Tradition, the direction of all matters connected with Penance was, in the Primitive Christian era, in the hands of the bishops and the presbyters. According to St. Cyprian [died 256], the forgiveness of sins and the giving of the peace of the Church took place 'through the priests' (per sacerdotes: De lapsis 29). St. Basil decrees that the sins must be confessed to those to whom the ministration of the mysteries of God are entrusted (Regulae brevius tractatae, reg. 288). St. Ambrose says: 'This right is given to the priests only (solis sacerdotibus)' (De poen. I. 2, 7). St. Leo I remarks that the forgiveness of sins in the Sacrament of Penance can only be achieved by the prayers of the priests (supplicationibus sacerdotum). (Ep. 108, 2; D 146)." [23]

The abandonment of the teaching and practice of sacramental reconciliation through the office of the priesthood is a deviation from historic Christianity and a rejection of the teaching of Scripture and the early Church.

21. What is the sacrament of Reconciliation (CCC 1440–49, 1461)? How should the Christian appropriate and practice this merciful gift of God—confession (CCC 1450–58)? What is "penance" (CCC 1459–60)? What is the effect of the sacrament (CCC 1468–70)?

---

[22] Dom Bernard Orchard, ed., *A Catholic Commentary on Holy Scripture* (New York: Thomas Nelson Pub., 1953), 1016.

[23] Ott, *Fundamentals*, 439.

» CHURCH TEACHING: "The Church has always understood—and has in fact defined—that Jesus Christ here conferred on the Apostles authority to forgive sins, a power which is exercised in the sacrament of Penance. 'The Lord then especially instituted the sacrament of Penance when, after being risen from the dead, he breathed upon his disciples and said: "Receive the Holy Spirit. . . ." The consensus of all the Fathers has always acknowledged that by this action so sublime and words so clear the power of forgiving and retaining sins was given to the Apostles and their lawful successors for reconciling the faithful who have fallen after Baptism' (Council of Trent, *De Paenitentia*, chap. 1).

"The sacrament of Penance is the most sublime expression of God's love and mercy towards men, described so vividly in Jesus' parable of the prodigal son (cf. Lk 15: 11–32). The Lord always awaits us, with his arms wide open, waiting for us to repent—and then he will forgive us and restore us to the dignity of being his sons.

"The Popes have consistently recommended Christians to have regular recourse to this sacrament: 'For a constant and speedy advancement in the path of virtue we highly recommend the pious practice of frequent confession, introduced by the Church under the guidance of the Holy Spirit; for by this means we grow in a true knowledge of ourselves and in Christian humility, bad habits are uprooted, spiritual negligence and apathy are prevented, the conscience is purified and the will strengthened, salutary spiritual direction is obtained, and grace is increased by the efficacy of the sacrament itself' (Pius XII, *Mystici Corporis*)." [24]

» THEOLOGICAL NOTE: "As the Jewish priest pronounced who were clean and who were unclean among the lepers, so now Christ conferred the power of forgiving and withholding forgiveness on sinners. Only God can forgive sins; but God in the form of man forgave the sins of Magdalen, of the penitent thief, of the dishonest tax collector, and of others. The same law of the Incarnation would now hold; God would continue to forgive sins through man. His appointed ministers were to be the instruments of His forgiveness, as His own human nature was the instrument of His Divinity in purchasing forgiveness. These solemn words of the Risen Savior meant that sins were to be forgiven through a judicial power authorized to examine the state of a soul and to grant or refuse forgiveness as the case demanded. From that day on, the remedy for human sin and guilt was to be a humble confession to one having authority to forgive. To be humble on one's knees confessing to one to whom Christ gave the power to forgive (rather than prostrate on a couch to hear guilt explained away)—that was one of the greatest joys given to the burdened soul of man." [25]

---

[24] José María Casciaro, *The Navarre Bible: The Gospel of Saint John* (Dublin: Four Courts Press, 1992), 244.
[25] Sheen, *Life of Christ*, 421.

John 20:24–31
Jesus and "Doubting Thomas"

22. Who of the Twelve were missing when Jesus appeared to the disciples the first time (Jn 20:24, Mt 27:3–5)? How does the wording "one of the Twelve" help us determine the disciples to whom Jesus appeared? Why did Thomas not learn his lesson the first time when he witnessed a "resurrection" in John 11? What did the other disciples tell Thomas when he returned (v. 25)? What was Thomas' response? How do you think we got the expression "Doubting Thomas"?

23. When are doubt and honest questions healthy and helpful, and when are doubt and questions harmful and damning? How might the attitude behind each be significant? What is the difference between *voluntary* and *involuntary* doubt (CCC 2088)? What is the difference between *difficulties* and *doubts* (CCC 157)? Are we expected to believe "blindly", against facts or reason (CCC 156; Jn 20:30–31)? Was the Resurrection "invented" or produced by the *faith* of the apostles (CCC 644)?

24. According to verse 26, when did Jesus again appear to the disciples? Why is it significant that he appeared on the "first day of the week" (Rev 1:10; Acts 20:7; CCC 2174–77)? Where were the disciples *again* this time? Notice what day Jesus again chose to appear—why did he always appear on this day? How did Jesus get into the room?

25. How did Jesus greet the disciples? "Peace" in Hebrew is *shalom*. *Shalom* means more than an absence of war or conflict. It means the fullness of peace, joy, and prosperity, which one finds in the midst of a joyous and prosperous family. This is still the greeting among Jews in Israel today.

26. According to verse 27, what did Jesus command Thomas to do as he approached him? Do we know if Thomas actually put his finger in Jesus' side? What has the Church taught on the physical nature of the Resurrection (CCC 645)? How are people centuries later, like us, to believe in Christ if we are unable to see the physical proof for ourselves (Jn 20:28–31)?

» JEHOVAH'S WITNESSES AND THE RESURRECTION: The Jehovah's Witnesses teach that Jesus was resurrected as a "spirit being" or an "invisible spirit creature", rather than in an incorruptible, physical, glorified bodily form. They teach that God disposed of Jesus' physical body. But this view of the Resurrection is contrary to what Scripture teaches. Jesus points to the marks of his Passion and crucifixion on his resurrected body, which implies that it is the same body, albeit transformed by the power of God, that suffered and died, not a "spirit body".

27. Will we be raised from the dead in our physical bodies or only as spirits (Job 19:25–27; Jn 5:28–29; Acts 2:31; 2 Cor 4:14; 1 Thess 4:13–18; CCC 1015–17)?

» CREEDS OF CHRISTENDOM: "I believe in . . . the resurrection of the body and the life everlasting" (*Apostles' Creed*). "We look for the resurrection of the dead, and the life of the world to come" (*Nicene Creed*). "On his coming all men with their bodies must rise" (*Athanasian Creed*). As the early Christians were burying their dead in the catacombs of Rome, they did not use the word "bury". Rather, they referred to the burial as a "deposit". The body was "deposited" awaiting the final bodily "withdrawal" at the end of time at the Second Coming of Christ.

28. According to verse 28, the Apostle Thomas burst forth with the most amazing exclamation—an exclamation worthy of the final crescendo of John's Gospel. What did "Doubting Thomas", rising above the rest, say to Jesus (CCC 448–49)? Jehovah's Witnesses, who deny the divinity of Jesus, sometimes claim that this was "just an expression of amazement", like saying, "Oh, my God". Really? Can you imagine a devout Jew using the Lord's Name in vain so flagrantly? Where might Thomas have heard these words before (Ps 35:23)? How did Thomas—the disciple famous for his doubting—end up making this theologically profound exclamation?

29. Notice how the whole Gospel has been written to prove the deity and unique human and divine natures of Jesus, and now "Doubting Thomas" has finally fathomed the ultimate truth. How is Thomas' statement of belief more profound than that of the other disciples? Did they provide such an insightful exclamation? How does Thomas' statement explain and personalize the first verse of John's Gospel (Jn 1:1)? How does the first verse (Jn 1:1, 14) anticipate Thomas' exclamation? Notice again how John *frames* his Gospel: beginning with God taking on flesh and ending with "flesh" being recognized as God.

» SPIRITUAL NOTE: "There was no halfway house about Thomas. He was not airing his doubts just for the sake of mental acrobatics; he doubted in order to become sure; and when he did, his surrender to certainty was complete. And when a man fights his way through his doubts to the conviction that Jesus Christ is Lord, he has attained to a certainty that the man who unthinkingly accepts things can never reach." [26]

Tradition informs us that Thomas, after some misgivings, went to India and the Far East, preaching the Gospel and establishing the Catholic Church, where he is still honored as the founder of the Church there. He was killed by stab wounds in the year 72 after a remarkable apostolate.[27]

» THEOLOGICAL NOTE: "This, then, is the supreme christological pronouncement of the Fourth Gospel. In [chapter] 1 the first disciples gave many titles to Jesus, and we have heard still others throughout the ministry: Rabbi, Messiah, Prophet, King of Israel, Son of God. In the post-resurrectional appearances Jesus has been hailed as the Lord by Magdalene and by the disciples as a group. But it is Thomas who makes clear that one may address Jesus in the same language in which Israel addressed Yahweh. Now is fulfilled the will of the Father '. . . that all men may honor the Son just as they honor the Father' (John v 23). What Jesus predicted has come to pass: 'When you lift up the Son of Man, then you will realize that I AM' (viii 28). . . . It is no wonder that Thomas' confession constitutes the last words spoken by a disciple in the Fourth Gospel (as it was originally conceived, before the addition of ch. xxi)—nothing more profound could be said about Jesus." [28]

30. According to verse 29, how did Jesus respond to Thomas' exclamation of belief? How will future generations come to believe in Christ (cf. Jn 20:31; 1 Jn 1:1–4; Rom 10:14; CCC 425)?

» THEOLOGICAL NOTE: "When John wrote the Church was composed of men who had seen no such resurrection appearance as Thomas had seen, and yet had converted (had come to believe). . . . The disciples of the first generation had the unique distinction of standing as a link between Jesus and the Church; John indicates in this saying that their successors equally may believe, and that their faith places them on the same level of blessedness with the eye-witnesses, or even above it. The following rabbinic passage is often quoted, and indeed it appears to illustrate John's thought; but it is fairly late (ca. A.D. 250), and lays no

[26] Barclay, *John*, 2:277.

[27] For more information on Thomas and the lives of the other apostles after the Resurrection, read C. Bernard Ruffin, *The Twelve: The Lives of the Apostles after Calvary* (Huntington, Ind.: Our Sunday Visitor, 1984); William Steuart McBirnie, *The Search for the Twelve Apostles* (Wheaton, Ill.: Tyndale House Pub., 1973); and Otto Hophan, *The Apostles*, trans. L. Edward Wasserman (Westminster, Md.: Newman Press, 1962).

[28] Raymond E. Brown, ed. and trans., *The Gospel according to John*, vol. 2, Anchor Bible, vol. 29A (Garden City, N.Y.: Doubleday, 1970), 1047–48.

stress on the thought, vital for John, of a generation which beheld and mediated the faith to the next: R. Simeon b. Laqish said: The proselyte is dearer to God than all the Israelites who stood by Mount Sinai. For if all the Israelites had not seen the thunder and the flames and the lightnings and the quaking mountain and the sound of the trumpet they would not have accepted the law and taken upon themselves the kingdom of God. Yet this man has seen none of all these things yet comes and gives himself to God and takes on himself the yoke of the kingdom of God. Is there any who is dearer than this man? (Tanhuma, לֶךְ לְךָ, §6 (32a))." [29]

31. How will others, especially future generations, hear about the death, burial, and Resurrection of Jesus (Jn 17:20; Rom 10:13–15; CCC 75–77)? How will future believers be "blessed" (1 Pet 1:8–9)? Is our belief in Christ's Resurrection simply blind faith without good and sufficient reasons, or is it based on trustworthy historical accounts—good and sufficient reasons for faith? Does the Gospel of John contain *all* the words and works of Christ (v. 30; Jn 21:25)? How does John use the word "sign" again (Jn 2:11; CCC 515, 542)?

32. According to verse 31, why did John write the Gospel (Jn 19:35; CCC 514)? What was his goal in pointing to the "signs" (Jn 2:11, 23; 7:31; CCC 442)? Notice John's use of the word "sign" throughout his Gospel (for instance, Jn 2:23; 3:2; 4:54; 6:2, 14, 26, 30; 7:31; 9:16; 10:41; 11:47; 12:18, 37; 20:30). What is the goal and result of believing (v. 31; Jn 3:15)? Notice how the Gospel seems to end here and the following chapter seems to be something of an appendix or addendum.

---

[29] C. K. Barrett, *The Gospel according to St. John* (London: SPCK, 1970), 477–78.

JOHN 21

THE GRAND FINALE: JESUS MEETS THE APOSTLES—
THE POPE AND THE CHURCH

Appendix
St. John's Grand "Finale"!

1. John packs this last section with deep spiritual insights. The whole "finale" is pregnant with meaning. We must read carefully, think deeply, and move slowly to plumb the depths of this marvelous chapter. We referred to the first eighteen verses of John's Gospel as the "overture". They serve as an introduction and provide all the "musical"—theological—themes developed in St. John's *magnum opus*. Look up the word "finale" in a dictionary, and explain why we refer to this last chapter as the musical finale.

2. Read the last four verses in chapter 20. How might these verses be understood to suggest that the earliest edition of the Gospel may have ended without chapter 21?

» TEXTUAL NOTE: Endless discussion has surrounded chapter 21. Was it written by John or another; part of the original Gospel or a later epilogue? It is included in all the earliest manuscripts. St. Augustine wrote, "The preceding words of the Evangelist seem to indicate the end of the book; but he goes on farther to give an account of our Lord's appearance by the sea of Tiberias."[1] "The mixture of first plural with first singular in these final words seems to justify the view that St John dictated them surrounded by the presbyters of Ephesus, but cf. 1 Jn 1–2. These, according to the Muratorian canon [late second century] had requested him to write the Gospel, and are now giving testimony of its veracity together with him."[2]

---

[1] St. Augustine, *Tractate* 122, in St. Thomas Aquinas, *Catena Aurea: St. John* (Albany, N.Y.: Preserving Christian Publications, 1995), 4:615.

[2] Dom Bernard Orchard, ed., *A Catholic Commentary on Holy Scripture* (New York: Thomas Nelson Pub., 1953), 1017.

» TEXTUAL NOTE: "This twenty-first chapter forms the Epilogue to the Fourth Gospel and is the counterpart to the Prologue ["Overture"]. It is part of the original Gospel, and no afterthought of St John; nor is it the work of another hand, as some Rationalists assert. Grotius, in 1645, was the first to question its authenticity. The Church has declared it to be genuine, and therefore all Catholics are bound to receive it as such. As St Augustine says, though verses 30, 31 of ch. xx. 'seem to indicate the end of the book, St John continues his narrative by giving an account of our Lord's apparition at the Sea of Tiberias' (Trad. cxxii.). The Evangelist, having so far chiefly confined himself to relating our Lord's Judean Ministry, in this section relates two incidents of Jesus' Risen Life that occurred, in Galilee, which no other Evangelist has recorded—incidents which pre-eminently showed forth our Lord's Glory. The Epilogue sets forth the work of the Church in the world, and the introductory incident—the miraculous draught of fishes—is both a miracle and a parable in action, which serves as a prelude to the Great Commission—to feed the lambs and the sheep—bestowed upon St Peter and his successors by our Blessed Lord." [3]

John 21:1–14
Jesus Appears in Galilee

3. Why did the disciples leave Jerusalem and travel north to Galilee (Mt 28:5–10, 16)? What is another name for the Sea of Tiberias (Jn 6:1)? Who were the disciples who were together in Galilee (v. 2; cf. Lk 5:10)? Why only seven disciples in the boat? Who is clearly the leader (v. 3)? What is known about Peter's earlier career (Mt 4:18–22; Lk 5:2–11)? What name did Jesus give to Peter (Jn 1:42)? What do *Cephas* and *Peter* mean (cf. Mt 16:18)?

» ARCHAEOLOGICAL NOTE: In mid-January 1986, when the water level was low, a first-century fishing boat was discovered in the mud along the shore of Galilee south of Capernaum. The boat was about 41 1/2 feet long and is carefully preserved at Kibbutz Nof Ginosar. Could this have been Peter's fishing boat? The possibility is remote, of course. But interesting to speculate about, nonetheless. In any case, the fishing boats from Jesus' time are very similar to the ones currently used, though fiberglass is now the building material of preference. [4]

---

[3] Madame Cecilia, *St. John*, Catholic Scripture Manuals (London: Burns, Oates, & Washbourne, 1923), 366.

[4] See Shelley Wachsmann, *The Sea of Galilee Boat: An Extraordinary 2000-Year-Old Discovery* (New York: Plenum Press, 1995).

4. According to verse 3, why did Peter decide to go fishing? Might the disciples have been "killing time", earning money, having fun, or reverting to their old life? What time of day did they go out to fish, and how might this be significant (cf. Jn 3:2, 19–21; 9:4; 11:10; 13:30; 20:1)? How did St. Paul earn his living while serving God as an apostle (Acts 18:3; 2 Thess 3:8)?

» CULTURAL NOTE: Fishing is done at night on the Sea of Galilee. The fish go deep in the center of the lake during the day and come up to the surface, along the shore, during the night hours. They are attracted to the warm springs in the Capernaum area. The sea contains the Amnun fish that are affectionately called "St. Peter's fish", which is the main species. Attempts to transplant them in other natural waters have failed. "St. Peter's fish" are delicious and served in all the local restaurants and kibbutzim.

» THEOLOGICAL NOTES: Pope Gregory wrote, "It may be asked, why Peter, who was a fisherman before his conversion, returned to fishing, when it is said, 'No man putting his hand to the plough, and looking back, is fit for the kingdom of God.'" St. Augustine on the other hand said, "If the disciples had done this after the death of Jesus, and before His resurrection, we should have imagined that they did it in despair. But now after that He has risen from the grave, after seeing the marks of His wounds, after receiving, by means of His breathing, the Holy Ghost, all at once they become what they were before, fishers, not of men, but of fishes. We must remember then that they were not forbidden by their apostleship from earning their livelihood by a lawful craft, provided they had no other means of living." [5]

There are many opinions as to why the apostles resorted to fishing. It is impossible to imagine any of this taking place in Acts, after Pentecost. The Resurrection of Jesus is still sinking in. They are probably pondering, "What does it all mean? What should we do now?" But this is certainly not the portrait of men who have received the promised Paraclete. There is neither the joy nor the assurance, not to mention the sense of mission and the spirit of unity, that characterize the Church when freshly endowed with the spirit of unity. But, as Beasley-Murray says, "Even though Jesus be crucified and risen from the dead, the disciples must eat!" [6] Brown comments, "The scene is rather one of aimless activity undertaken in desperation." [7]

"Although there is evidence that the night was considered best for fishing on

---

[5] Pope St. Gregory and St. Augustine, *Tractate* 122, both quoted in St. Thomas Aquinas, *Catena Aurea*, 4:615.

[6] G. R. Beasley-Murray, *John*, Word Biblical Commentary (Waco, Tex.: Word Books, 1987), 399.

[7] Raymond E. Brown, ed. and trans., *The Gospel according to John*, vol. 2, Anchor Bible, vol. 29A (Garden City, N.Y.: Doubleday, 1970), 1096.

Galilee, one wonders if the Evangelist is not still employing one of his favorite symbols [darkness and night, 3:2, 19–21; 13:30; 20:1]. They are coming to grips with the resurrection, but they still have not learned the profound truth that apart from Christ they can do nothing (15:5), and so 'that night they caught nothing.'"[8] Fishermen still fish at night on Galilee with lights attached to their boats. They unload and sell their fish to buyers as the sun crests the horizon. They still form partnerships with friends and family (cf. Lk 5:9–1). Veteran fishermen say they can earn up to five hundred dollars on a good night.

5. How many days was Jesus with the disciples between his Resurrection and his Ascension (Acts 1:3; CCC 659)? What did Jesus do during this time (Acts 1:1–11; Mt 28:16–20; Mk 16:12–20; Lk 24:36–51; 1 Cor 15:3–8)? Luke provides us with a singularly touching story of Jesus' last days. How did he reveal himself and instruct two particular men (Lk 24:13–35)? What time of day does Jesus appear to his disciples on the shore (v. 4)? How might appearing at that time be significant? Why did the disciples not recognize Jesus on the shore? Was it a spiritual matter or just the hour of the day? When previously had they failed to recognize Jesus on the sea, and what was the result of embracing him (Jn 6:16–21)? Why might they have not recognized Jesus (CCC 645; 1 Cor 15:42–44; Lk 24:16)? Who else had failed to recognize him (Jn 20:1, 11–16)? What time of day did the latter encounter take place?

6. In verse 5, why did Jesus call his disciples *children*, and how did he know they had no fish? What did they answer? What did Jesus command them to do? Why should fishermen have listened to a stranger on the shore when *they* were the experts? When they obeyed Jesus, what was the result (v. 6)? What might the fish on the "right side" of the boat represent (Mt 25:31–34)?[9] Compare this instance with a similar situation that happened earlier (Lk 5:1–11). What do you think was their immediate recollection?

» A MIRACLE OR A PRACTICAL MATTER: There is some discussion whether the large catch of fish was a miracle or not. It would seem the great number of fish caught, and the immediate recognition of Jesus on the shore as a result of the exceedingly large catch, implies that St. John considered this a miracle. Barclay disagrees, seeing the situation as merely a normal fishing event. He writes,

---

[8] D. A. Carson, *The Gospel according to John* (Grand Rapids, Mich.: W. B. Eerdmans, 1991), 670.
[9] Cf. St. Augustine, *Homilies on the Gospel of John* 122, 7, in NPNF1 7:441–42.

"The catch here is not described as a miracle, and it is not meant to be taken as one. The description is of something which still frequently happens on the lake. Remember that the boat was only about a hundred yards from land. H. V. Morton describes how he saw two men fishing on the shores of the lake. One had waded out from the shore and was casting a bell net into the water. 'But time after time the net came up empty. It was a beautiful sight to see him casting. . . . While he was waiting for another cast, Abdul shouted to him from the bank to fling to the left, which he instantly did. This time he was success-ful. . . . It happens very often that the man with the hand-net must rely on the advice of someone on shore, who tells him to cast either to the left or the right, because in the clear water he can often see a shoal of fish invisible to the man in the water.' Jesus was acting as guide to his fishermen friends, just as people still do today." [10] Ricciotti agrees with Barclay on this point. [11]

Pope St. Gregory, on the other hand, sees the obvious spiritual workings of Christ in the situation. He said, "The fishing was made to be very unlucky, in order to raise their astonishment at the miracle after." [12] Brown concurs, "The fishing expedition is unsuccessful, for without Jesus, they can do nothing (xv 5). It is at this nadir that Jesus comes to reveal himself. The marvelous catch of fish causes recognition—who else but Jesus could work such a sign? The import of the catch may have been more obvious than we suspect, for *Testament of Zebulun* vi 6 implies that an abundant catch of fish was known as a sign of God's favor." [13]

7. The apostles failed dismally at their first return to fishing. How might this have prepared them for Jesus' visit and commission? Knowing John's method of burying deep meanings below the story surface, consider this story carefully and find the spiritual teachings. What might the large number of fish in verse 6 represent? A barque is a small sailing ship; have you heard the title "The Barque of Peter"? Understanding Peter as being the visible head of the Church, what might Peter's boat represent? From what did Jesus teach (Lk 5:3)? Where does he teach today? What might the sea represent? What might the shore represent? Compare this with our study on John 6:16–21.

8. According to verse 7, who recognized Jesus first? Why did he call Jesus "the Lord" (CCC 448)? What did Peter do? Notice their charac-teristic roles: John was the first to recognize; Peter was the first to act.

---

[10] William Barclay, *The Gospel of John* (Philadelphia: Westminster Press, 1975), 2:281.

[11] See Giuseppe Ricciotti, *The Life of Christ*, trans. Alba I. Zizzamia (Milwaukee: Bruce Pub., 1947), 663.

[12] St. Gregory, *Homily* 84, in St. Thomas Aquinas, *Catena Aurea*, 4:616.

[13] Brown, *John*, 2:1096.

Why did Peter dress and jump into the water? Some see Peter's nakedness as his spiritual state after denying Jesus; putting on clothes as his
conversion, plunging into the water as his purification, and his swim-
ming as a return to Jesus."[14]

9. In verse 8, after Peter threw on his outer cloak and jumped into the
sea, what did the other disciples do? What did they find as they stepped
on the beach? Where do you think the cooking fish and bread came
from? Where is the only other place in the New Testament where we
find a "charcoal fire" (Jn 18:18)? What did Peter do three times in the
warmth of the charcoal fire in the courtyard? Hold that thought! It is
important when we get to the next section. What did Jesus ask them to
do (v. 10)?

10. In verse 8, the narrative now comes back to Peter. What had the
other disciples brought to the shore? What did Peter do by himself (v.
11)? What do we know about Peter if he could haul in 153 fish by
himself? What do you make of the fact that John knows exactly how
many fish are in the net? Who do you think counted them, and why is
this statistic provided? How might these fish represent the Church or the
kingdom of God (Mt 13:47-50)? How might the sheer number of fish
demonstrate Christ's blessings (Jn 1:16)? What did Jesus teach about the
prerequisites to "bearing much fruit" (Jn 15:5)? What is demonstrated
by the nighttime of failure and the successful morning?

» THEOLOGICAL NOTE: Much discussion has gone into the possible symbolism
behind the 153 fish dragged ashore by Peter. Every conceivable combination of
numbers and symbols has been tried. Barclay writes, "In the Fourth Gospel
everything is meaningful, and it is therefore hardly possible that John gives the
definite number one hundred and fifty-three for the fishes without meaning
something by it. It has indeed been suggested that the fishes were counted
simply because the catch had to be shared out between the various partners and
the crew of the boat [which is the first thing done even today], and that the
number was recorded simply because it was so exceptionally large. But when
we remember John's way of putting hidden meanings in his gospel for those
who have eyes to see, we must think that there is more to it than that.

"Many ingenious suggestions have been made. . . . The simplest of the explanations is that given by Jerome. He said that in the sea there are 153 different
kinds of fishes; and that the catch is one which includes every kind of fish; and

---

[14] See ibid.

that therefore the number symbolizes the fact that some day all men of all nations will be gathered together to Jesus Christ [Rev 7:9; 14:6].

"Here John is telling us in his own vivid yet subtle way of the universality of the Church. There is no kind of exclusiveness in her, no kind of colour bar or selectiveness. The embrace of the Church is as universal as the love of God in Jesus Christ. It will lead us on to the next great reason why this chapter was added to the gospel if we note that it was Peter who drew the net to land (John 21: 11)."[15] In any case, we must agree with St. Augustine that it is a great mystery.[16] Transcending all the numerical speculation, it is certain that the large number of fish represents the apostolic ministry, which will bring in a miraculous catch of fish—men, since the apostles had been commissioned as "fishers of men" (Mt 4:19). "The unbroken state of the net means than the Christian community is not rent by schism, despite the great numbers and different kinds of men brought into it. . . . The basic symbolism of the catch of fish thus far discussed is widely accepted by scholars."[17]

11. Why is it significant that Peter brought the net full of fish to Jesus on the shore? How did the fishing net hold up under the strain? The fact that John mentions it did *not* tear seems to imply that it should have. Did it tear on a previous occasion (Lk 5:6)? The Greek word for tear is σχίζω (*schizō*), from which we get our English word "schism". Notice the use of the word "schism" in the New Testament (Jn 19:24; 1 Cor 1:10; 12:25). What is a schism (CCC 2089, 817)? What did Peter bring to Jesus without a "schizō"? What is John teaching us about the Church? (See notes on the *seamless robe* in John 19a, pp. 343–44.)

» THEOLOGICAL NOTE: "We may note a further point. This great catch of fishes was gathered into the net, and the net held them all and was not broken. The net stands for the Church; and there is room in the Church for all men of all nations. Even if they all come in, she is big enough to hold them all."[18]

St. Augustine wrote, "This is a great mystery in the great Gospel of John; and to commend it the more forcibly to our attention, the last chapter has been made its place of record. . . . When the morning was come, Jesus stood on the shore; for the shore likewise is the limit of the sea, and signifies therefore the end of the world. The same end of the world is shown also by the act of Peter, in drawing the net to land, that is, to the shore. Which the Lord has Himself elucidated, when in a certain other place He drew His similitude from a fishing net let down into the sea: 'And they drew it,' He said, 'to the shore.' And in

[15] Barclay, *John*, 2:283–84.
[16] See St. Augustine, *Homilies on the Gospel of John* 122, 6, in NPNF1 7:441.
[17] Brown, *John*, 2:1097.
[18] Barclay, *John*, 2:284.

explanation of what that shore was, He added, 'So will it be in the end of the world.'" [19]

This passage has been interpreted by the Fathers and Doctors of the Church as revealing the mystical meaning of this appearance of Jesus: the boat is the Church, the Church's unity is symbolized by the net which is not torn; the sea is the world, Peter in the boat represents the supreme authority of the Church, and the number of fish signifies the number of the elect.[20]

12. According to verse 12, what did Jesus invite the disciples to do? How might we have here a picture of the sacraments of confession and the Eucharist? Jesus washed the disciples' feet in chapter 13 and feeds them in chapter 21. How does this recall a future meal, which Jesus will provide (Rev 19:9)? Notice how the *Catechism* uses this verse in CCC 1166. What did Jesus confirm and prove to the disciples (CCC 645)? Were the disciples again convinced and reassured (v. 12)? What is John proving to his readers? How did two other disciples recognize Jesus (Lk 24:30–31, 35)?

» THEOLOGICAL NOTE: "There are good arguments for finding eucharistic symbolism in the meal of John xxi. . . . The fact that the scenes in [John 6] and [John 21] are the only ones in the Fourth Gospel to occur by the Sea of Tiberias naturally helps the reader to make a connection between the two meals. . . . [I]n John's account of the multiplication meal there were several peculiar details evocative of the Eucharist. We doubt, then, that a meal so similar to the multiplication meal could be described in John xxi without reminding the Johannine community of the Eucharist. Moreover, we have already called attention to the resemblance between the meal in John xxi and the meal that Luke xxiv 30–31, 35 describes in the account of the appearance of Jesus to the two disciples on the road to Emmaus. Luke's insistence that the disciples recognized Jesus in the breaking of the bread is often taken as eucharistic teaching meant to instruct the community that they too could find the risen Jesus in their eucharistic breaking of the bread.

"Some external support for the eucharistic interpretation of John xxi is found in Cullmann's contention [*Early Christian Worship*, pp. 15–17] that the early communities made a direct connection between their eucharistic meals and the meals eaten by the risen Jesus with his disciples. Certainly in primitive iconography, meals of bread and fish (rather than of bread and wine) were the standard pictorial symbols of the Eucharist. . . .

---

[19] St. Augustine, *Homilies on the Gospel of John* 122, 6, in NPNF1 7:441.
[20] Cf. St. Thomas Aquinas, *Commentary on the Gospel of St. John*, vol. 2 (Petersham, Mass.: St. Bede's Pub., n.d.), 625–38.

"If we accept the plausibility of the proposed eucharistic symbolism, then the risen Jesus in xxi plays somewhat the same role he played in ch. xx. In xx 19–23 he was the dispenser of gifts, especially of the Spirit, the source of eternal life. Here too the risen Jesus dispenses life: 'The bread that I shall give is my own flesh for the life of the world' (vi 51)." [21]

13. Within the Gospel of St. John, how many times had Jesus manifested himself to his disciples after he was raised from the dead (v. 14)? When were the previous times (Jn 20:19, 26)? Why do you suppose he manifested himself as many times as he did?

John 21:15–17
Peter Appointed as Shepherd

» GEOGRAPHICAL NOTE: Ancient tradition locates this incident on the western shore of Galilee between Capernaum and Tiberias—the place where the disciples lived and fished. Early Christians built a church over a large rock ("Mensa Christi"—Table of the Lord) in the fourth century. This location is believed, with good reason, to be the location where Jesus served the breakfast. The Franciscans built "The Church of the Primacy" over the ruins of the ancient site. The Church is to honor Peter's appointment as shepherd of God's flock.

14. Let us think about the charcoal fire again. A "charcoal fire" is mentioned only twice in the New Testament, and both times it is in John's Gospel. What did Peter do three times in front of the first charcoal fire (Jn 18:17–18, 25–27)? What does Peter *now* do three times in front of the second charcoal fire (Jn 21:9, 15–17)? How might St. John use the charcoal fire to draw our attention to—and to compare and contrast—these two events? Has Peter had a chance to discuss his betrayal with Jesus since the crucifixion? How did this threefold declaration of love correspond to and overcome his earlier threefold denial (CCC 1429)? How did this action of Jesus demonstrate God's abundant mercy, forgiveness, and restoration?

15. Why do you think Jesus called Peter "Simon, son of John" instead of "Peter"? What did Jesus ask Peter three times (Jn 21:15–17)? What

---

[21] Brown, *John*, 2:1099, 1100.

did Jesus mean, "Do you love me *more than these*"? Did Jesus mean: (1) more than these fish and your old way of life? (2) more than you love the other disciples? or (3) more than the other disciples love me? Should we love anything more than we love Jesus? Much has been made of the fact that Jesus used two different Greek words for "love": *agapaō* and *phileō*. How was Peter's earlier "brash outspokenness" seemingly tempered? Peter had often stated boldly that he would follow Christ even if all others left him (Mt 26:33). Why might Jesus now have asked, after Peter's denial, if he loved him more than the other disciples who did not deny him? How had Jesus already "reproved" Peter for his denial (Lk 22:61–62)?

» PERSONAL NOTE: The words of Jesus "Do you love me more than these" are very ambiguous. "Some say that Christ points to the fishes, or the boats, nets, etc., that is, his worldly calling; others, which is more probable, to the disciples, who were present. Peter had said, in a somewhat boastful spirit: 'Though all men shall be offended because of Thee, yet will I never be offended' (Matt. 26:33). Our Lord might here imply the question, 'Art thou of the same opinion now, Peter? Dost thou love Me more than these other disciples'! '*He saith unto Him, Yea, Lord; Thou knowest that I love Thee.*' That is, with the love of affection and tenderness." [22] If this is the case, Peter has been humbled by his prior denial, and is now toned down, not ready to blurt out his "superior love" and untested loyalty. He is now a meeker and humbled man (cf. Num 12:3).

» WORD STUDY: "The risen Lord uses *agapaō* in his first two questions and *phileō* in the third; Peter uses *phileō* in all three replies. But those who see a difference in force between the two verbs here are not agreed on the nature of the difference. According to R. C. Trench, Peter finds the word on his Lord's lips (*agapaō*) 'far too cold' at a time when 'all the pulses in the heart of the now penitent Apostle are beating with a passionate affection' towards him. He himself uses a word (*phileō*) which more adequately conveys the warmth of that affection, and triumphs when on the third occasion the Lord consents to use that word [Trench, *Synonyms of the New Testament*, 42]. B. F. Westcott, on the other hand, takes *agapaō*, the word used by the Lord in his first two questions, to denote 'that higher love which was to be the spring of the Christian life', whereas Peter, by using *phileō*, affirms only the natural love of personal attachment. When, on the third occasion, the Lord uses *phileō*, Peter is the more hurt because the Lord now seems to be questioning even 'that modified love which he had professed' [Westcott, *The Gospel according to St. John*, 303]. When two such distinguished Greek scholars . . . see the significance of the synonyms so

[22] David Thomas, *The Genius of the Fourth Gospel* (R. D. Dickenson, 1885; electronic edition: Oak Harbor: Logos Research Systems, 1997), 198.

differently, we may wonder if indeed we are intended to see such distinct significance.... It is precarious, then, to press a distinction between the two synonyms here.

"What is important is that Peter reaffirms his love for the Lord, and is rehabilitated and recommissioned. The commission is a pastoral one." [23]

16. When Jesus first promised a special commission to Peter (Mt 16:18–19), did he use the past, present, or future tense? How might that promise in this moment have been fulfilled (vv. 15–17)? What was Jesus doing by appointing Peter to tend and feed his sheep and lambs (CCC 552–53)? How is this office of shepherd "fleshed out" in John 10 and Ezekiel 34? How could Peter have now demonstrated his love for Jesus (CCC 1551)? Did Peter abrogate the authority and priesthood of Christ by becoming the shepherd of Christ's sheep (CCC 1548)?

» THEOLOGICAL NOTE: "Feed my lambs. With these words, repeated three times with variations on the word for 'lambs,' Jesus commissions Peter as vicar-shepherd of his flock, the Church. What this means and what this calls for is explained in 10:1–21, where Jesus speaks of himself as the good shepherd who lays down his life for his sheep (10:15) and has 'other sheep . . . not of this fold' that must be brought into the fold so that 'there will be one flock, one shepherd' (10:16). For the full import of Peter's commission as vicar-shepherd, the reader should study carefully Ez 34, which provides the background in the Old Testament for the shepherd parable in Jn 10:1–21." [24]

17. Earlier Simon was promised a special role when Jesus used the future tense, saying, "You are Peter, and on this rock I *will* build my church", and when he promised, "I will give you the keys of the kingdom of heaven" (Mt 16:18–19; emphasis added). What office did Jesus bestow on Peter (CCC 880–83)? Now, on the shore of Galilee, the "future tense" is made "present active", and Peter is commissioned and appointed as the shepherd of God's flock.

» HISTORICAL NOTE: In the Old Testament, kings appointed a royal steward to fill an office similar to that of a governor (cf. Joseph, Gen 41:38–45). In Israel, the steward was "over the house" of the king and carried the keys of the kingdom. Read Isaiah 22:15–25 for a description of a royal steward. If a steward was deposed or died, another would succeed to the office. So long as there was

---

[23] Bruce, *John*, 404–5.
[24] Peter Ellis, *The Genius of John: A Composition-Critical Commentary on the Fourth Gospel* (Collegeville, Minn.: Liturgical Press, 1984), 305.

a kingdom, the office of steward was filled by successors. When all the Jews were exiled to Babylon in 586 B.C., the Davidic kingdom ceased, as did the office of royal steward.

When Gabriel appeared to Mary, he promised her "you will conceive in your womb and bear a son, and you shall call his name Jesus. He will be great, and will be called the Son of the Most High; and the Lord God will give to him the throne of his father David" (Lk 1:31-32). After five hundred years, the throne of David was restored in the new kingdom of God, and King Jesus appointed Peter to the office of his royal steward.[25]

Notice that the wording of Matthew 16 is taken from Isaiah 22 and that Jesus appointed Peter as the royal steward over Jesus' house, his Church. Keys represent "exclusive dominion", and Peter alone was given the keys of the kingdom—keys that would be passed on to those who succeeded him in the office. On the shore of Galilee, Jesus conferred on Peter the office of shepherd of the flock, steward of the kingdom.

18. What does Jesus mean by "Feed my lambs", "Tend my sheep", and "Feed my sheep"? (CCC 754; 1 Pet 5:1-4)? Who are the "sheep" (cf. Lk 22:32)? Who are the "lambs"? What authority and responsibility was delegated to Peter (CCC 553)? Was Peter chosen as the vicar of Christ because he was perfect? Did Jesus establish a *kingdom* or a *democracy*? Should a sheep live independent of the shepherd's "tending"? What should be our attitude toward St. Peter and his successors? In the Old Testament, how was the shepherd a metaphor for kingly rule (2 Sam 5:2)?

» THEOLOGICAL NOTE: "The word *feed* is βόσκω and means literally 'to feed' and figuratively to teach and promote in every way the spiritual welfare of the members of the Church. The second word, *tend*, is ποιμαίνω and means literally to tend or shepherd the sheep, and figuratively to govern or rule. Jesus appoints Peter the universal shepherd of his whole flock. Protestant scholar Joachim Jeremias writes, 'Only in Jn. 21:15-17, which describes the appointment of Peter as a shepherd by the risen Lord, does the whole Church seem to have been in view as the sphere of activity' (*Theological Dictionary of the New Testament*, 6:498). The Good Shepherd appoints Peter to participate in his own authority as shepherd, to exercise delegated authority and leadership over the flock. What is this but a veritable primacy of jurisdiction? There are two sides to every coin: *When Jesus commands Peter to govern his sheep, he implicitly commands*

---

[25] For a full history of the Old Testament basis for the papacy, see Stephen K. Ray, *Upon This Rock: St. Peter and the Primacy of Rome in Scripture and the Early Church* (San Francisco: Ignatius Press, 1999), 263-97.

the sheep to submit to and obey the universal shepherd—Peter. St. Augustine writes, 'In the Catholic Church, there are many other things which most justly keep me in her bosom. . . . The succession of priests keeps me, beginning from the very seat of the Apostle Peter, to whom the Lord, after His resurrection, gave it in charge to feed His sheep, down to the present episcopate [bishop].' " [26]

» THE CHURCH FATHERS: "The Lord says to Peter: 'I say to you,' He says, 'that you are Peter, and upon this rock I will build my Church, and the gates of hell will not overcome it. And to you I will give the keys of the kingdom of heaven: and whatever things you bind on earth shall be bound also in heaven, and whatever you loose on earth, they shall be loosed also in heaven.' And again He says to him after His resurrection: 'Feed my sheep.' On him He builds the Church, and to him He gives the command to feed the sheep; and although He assigns a like power to all the Apostles, yet He founded a single chair, and He established by His own authority a source and an intrinsic reason for that unity. Indeed, the others were that also which Peter was; but a primacy is given to Peter, whereby it is made clear that there is but one Church and one chair. So too, all are shepherds, and the flock is shown to be one, fed by all the Apostles in single-minded accord. If someone does not hold fast to this unity of Peter, can he imagine that he still holds the faith? If he desert the chair of Peter upon whom the Church was built, can he still be confident that he is in the Church?" [27]

"And why, having passed by the others, doth He speak with Peter on these matters? He was the chosen one of the Apostles, the mouth of the disciples, the leader of the band; on this account also Paul went up upon a time to enquire of him rather than the others. And at the same time to show him that he must now be of good cheer, since the denial was done away, *Jesus putteth into his hands the chief authority among the brethren*; and He bringeth not forward the denial, nor reproacheth him with what had taken place, but saith, 'If thou lovest Me, *preside over thy brethren*, and the warm love which thou didst ever manifest, and in which thou didst rejoice, show thou now; and the life, which thou saidst thou wouldest lay down for Me, now give for My sheep'. . . . [See notes on John 6:68, p. 170.]

"Here again He alludeth to his tender carefulness, and to his being very closely attached to Himself. And if any should say, 'How then did James receive the chair at Jerusalem?' I would make this reply, that He appointed Peter teacher, not of the chair, but of the world." [28]

» CHURCH TEACHING ON PETER'S PRIMACY: Is Catholic teaching on the pri-

---

[26] Ibid., 49–50, quoting St. Augustine, *Against the Epistle of Manichaeus* 4, 5, in NPNF 1 4:130.

[27] St. Cyprian, died 258, *The Unity of the Catholic Church* 4, in William A. Jurgens, *The Faith of the Early Fathers*, vol. 1 (Collegeville, Minn.: Liturgical Press, 1970), 220–21.

[28] St. John Chrysostom, *Homiles on St. John* 88, in NPNF1 14:331–32; emphasis added.

macy of Peter as the pastor of the universal Church biblically implausible? Even D. A. Carson, professor of New Testament at Trinity Evangelical Divinity School and prominent Evangelical Protestant commentator writes, "When John 21:15–17 is tied to the common Roman Catholic exegesis of Matthew 16:16–19, the argument gains a certain plausibility."[29] The Navarre Bible informs us further that "Jesus Christ had promised Peter that he would be the primate of the Church (cf. Mt 16:16–19). . . . Despite his three denials during our Lord's passion, Christ now confers on him the primacy he promised. . . . The primacy was given to Peter directly and immediately. So the Church has always understood—and so Vatican I defined: 'We therefore teach and declare that, according to the testimony of the Gospel, the primacy of jurisdiction over the universal Church of God was immediately and directly promised and given to Blessed Peter the Apostle by Christ our Lord. . . . And it was upon Simon Peter alone that Jesus after his resurrection bestowed the jurisdiction of chief pastor and ruler over all his fold in the words: "Feed my lambs; feed my sheep"'" (*Pastor aeternus*, chap. 1).

"The primacy is a grace conferred on Peter and his successors, the popes; it is one of the basic elements in the Church, designed to guard and protect its unity: 'In order that the episcopate also might be one and undivided, and that [. . .] the multitude of the faithful might be kept secure in the oneness of faith and communion, he set Blessed Peter over the rest of the Apostles, and fixed in him the abiding principle of this twofold unity, and its visible foundation' (*Pastor aeternus*, Dz-Sch 3051; cf. Vatican II, *Lumen gentium*, 18). Therefore, the primacy of Peter is perpetuated in each of his successors: this is something which Christ disposed; it is not based on human legislation or custom. By virtue of the primacy, Peter, and each of his successors, is the shepherd of the whole Church and vicar of Christ on earth, because he exercises vicariously Christ's own authority. Love for the Pope, whom St Catherine of Siena used to call 'the sweet Christ on earth', should express itself in prayer, sacrifice and obedience."[30]

» TEXTUAL NOTE: Read John 1:42 again. What did Jesus tell Simon, the son of John? What does "Cephas" mean (see note on Jn 1:42)? Notice again how John is "framing" his Gospel to demonstrate the importance of this special calling of Peter. The Gospel both begins and ends with the teaching that Peter held a special office, just as Jesus' earthly ministry begins (Jn 2:1) and ends (Jn 19:26) with his Mother, the Blessed Virgin Mary. John is always careful to use such contextual structure to relay important and crucial information.

---

[29] Carson, *John*, 678.
[30] José María Casciaro, *The Navarre Bible: The Gospel of Saint John* (Dublin: Four Courts Press, 1992), 250.

John 21:18–23
The Future of Peter and John

19. Jesus discussed Peter and John's future. What did Jesus say to Peter after appointing him shepherd (v. 18)? Did Peter recognize that he would be a martyr (2 Pet 1:14)? What kind of death involved "stretching out the hands" (Jn 19:18)? What was Peter's death to bring to God (v. 19)?

» HISTORICAL NOTE: The crucifixion of Christ was still clearly etched in the apostles' minds when Jesus spoke these words several days after his Resurrection on the shores of the Sea of Galilee. And, St. John had no doubt what Jesus had meant as he wrote his Gospel, especially since John was writing well after the actual martyrdom of Peter. "Despite scholarly squabbles over the exact nature of the way this might be applied to crucifixion there can be little doubt that by the time this episode was written Peter had already stretched out his hands, an executioner had girded him with the cross, and he had laid down his life for the flock of Jesus." [31]

Recalling the significance of Jesus' prophecy foretelling Peter's death greatly reinforces the unchallenged early accounts that Peter was crucified in Rome, about A.D. 64–67, under Emperor Nero. Jesus knew Peter would be in Rome and die the martyr's death. The common practice of crucifixion in the Roman Empire was to spread a man's arms out on the cross-beams of the cross, attaching him with ropes or nails, and then forcing the condemned man to drag his cross to the site of execution where the cross would then be hoisted vertically into place. This crucifixion procedure is graphically depicted by the words of Jesus. [32]

Several sources, including Eusebius' *History of the Church* 3, 1, refer to Peter's head-down crucifixion. We are told that Peter requested an "inverted" crucifixion since he did not consider himself worthy to die in the same manner as his Lord. The Roman moralist Seneca is an independent witness to the Roman practice of inverted crucifixion in his *Consolation to Marcia* 20.

» THE CHURCH FATHERS: "And if a heretic wants a faith backed by public record, let the archives of the empire speak, as would the stones of Jerusalem. We read the lives of the Caesars. In Rome Nero was the first to stain with blood the rising faith. Peter was gird about by another [Jn 21:18], when he was made fast to the cross." [33]

---

[31] Francis Moloney, *The Gospel of John*, Sacra Pagina, vol. 4 (Collegeville, Minn.: Liturgical Press, 1998), 556.

[32] See Carson, *John*, 679–80.

[33] Tertullian, *Antidote against the Scorpion* 15, 3, in Jurgens, *Faith of the Early Fathers*, 1:152.

20. After appointing Peter as steward of the kingdom (Mt 16:18–19), what future event did Jesus tell Peter about (Mt 16:21–23)? What did Jesus then tell Peter to do (Mt 16:24–28)? How does this sequence parallel that in John 21:15–23? What are we *all* told to do (Lk 9:23)? How is our "daily crucifixion" participation with Christ (CCC 618, 2100; Rom 8:16–18; Phil 3:8–11; Col 1:24; 1 Pet 2:21–24; 4:12ff.)?

21. What does Jesus command Peter to do (v. 19)? How is this to remind Peter of his earlier words (Jn 13:36–37)? What are all the disciples to do (Mt 28:16–20; Acts 1:1–8)? What does Jesus say about James and John (Mt 20:20–23; cf. Mt 26:39)? What cup would they also "drink"? What is the last that the disciples see of their risen Lord (Acts 1:9–11)? Does he keep his promise to send the Paraclete—the Holy Spirit (Acts 2:1–4; cf. Jn 15:26; 16:7)?

» Scriptural note: With the exhortation "Follow me", Jesus commands Peter to imitate his Lord, not only in life, but also in death, even to death on a cross. Peter therefore fulfilled his impetuous words to his Lord when he said, "I will lay down my life for you" (Jn 13:37). Jesus was the Chief Shepherd and was crucified for the sheep; Peter, commissioned by the Chief Shepherd to tend the flock, was also crucified for faithfully tending the sheep. Peter and Jesus had discussed this matter earlier, just before he was taken away by the Roman soldiers: "Simon Peter said to him, 'Lord, where are you going?' Jesus answered, 'Where I am going you cannot follow me now; but you shall follow afterward.' Peter said to him, 'Lord, why cannot I follow you now? I will lay down my life for you'" (Jn 13:36–37). "Since being a shepherd involves laying down one's life for the sheep (Jn 10:11), the command to Simon to feed Jesus' sheep leads into the next section of the scene (21:18–23) where Peter's death is predicted in terms suggestive of martyrdom. . . . Simon's martyrdom is a witness consonant with his shepherd's duty of laying down his life." [34]

22. It seems that Jesus took Peter aside and walked along the shore with him. Why Peter? Would it not be marvelous to know what else they discussed? Who followed them (v. 20)? The one "whom Jesus loved" was St. John. What did Peter ask Jesus (v. 21)? Was this Peter's business (CCC 878)? How did Jesus deflect the question and gently rebuke Peter for worrying about others? What *should* Peter worry about (v. 22)? What rumor was spread, and how were Jesus' words misunderstood (v. 23)? What actually happened to St. John?

---

[34] Raymond E. Brown, Karl P. Donfried, and John Reumann, *Peter in the New Testament* (Minneapolis, Minn.: Augsburg Pub. and New York: Paulist Press, 1973), 145–46.

» HISTORICAL NOTE: As previously mentioned, Eusebius wrote, "At that time the apostle and evangelist John, the one whom Jesus loved, was still living in Asia, and governing the churches of that region, having returned after the death of Domitian from his exile on the island. And that he was still alive at that time may be established by the testimony of two witnesses. They should be trustworthy who have maintained the orthodoxy of the Church; and such indeed were Irenaeus and Clement of Alexandria. The former in the second book of his work Against Heresies, writes as follows: 'And all the elders that associated with John the disciple of the Lord in Asia bear witness that John delivered it to them. For he remained among them until the time of Trajan.' And in the third book of the same work he attests the same thing in the following words: "But the church in Ephesus also, which was founded by Paul, and where John remained until the time of Trajan, is a faithful witness of the apostolic tradition." [35] According to early accounts, John was the only apostle who died a natural death—a death of old age in Ephesus around the year 100.

23. Why did John write this Gospel (Jn 20:30–31; 21:24–25; CCC 515)? John gives us only seven miracles in the first portion of the book—"The Book of Signs" (Jn 1–12). In the last major section, "The Book of the Passion" (Jn 13–20), he reveals the ultimate miracle, the Resurrection, and in the "finale", the epilogue (Jn 21), he tells us of two more miracles, reflecting the future of the Church: the miraculous catch of fish and the miraculous meal. But does John claim to have given us a comprehensive catalogue of everything Jesus did (v. 25)? How and when was the Gospel of John written?

» HISTORICAL NOTE: "Clement [ca. 150–ca. 215] gives the tradition of the earliest presbyters, as to the order of the Gospels, in the following manner: The Gospels containing the genealogies, he says, were written first. The Gospel according to Mark had this occasion. As Peter had preached the Word publicly at Rome, and declared the Gospel by the Spirit, many who were present requested that Mark, who had followed him for a long time and remembered his sayings, should write them out. And having composed the Gospel he gave it to those who had requested it. When Peter learned of this, he neither directly forbade nor encouraged it. But, last of all, John, perceiving that the external facts had been made plain in the Gospel, being urged by his friends, and inspired by the Spirit, composed a spiritual Gospel. This is the account of Clement." [36]

---

[35] Eusebius, *Church History* 3, 23, 1–4, trans. Arthur Cushman McGiffert, in NPNF2 1:150.

[36] Ibid., 6, 14, 5–7, in NPNF2 1:261.

"For Matthew, who had at first preached to the Hebrews, when he was about to go to other peoples, committed his Gospel to writing in his native tongue, and thus compensated those whom he was obliged to leave for the loss of his presence. And when Mark and Luke had already published their Gospels, they say that John, who had employed all his time in proclaiming the Gospel orally, finally proceeded to write for the following reason. The three Gospels already mentioned having come into the hands of all and into his own too, they say that he accepted them and bore witness to their truthfulness; but that there was lacking in them an account of the deeds done by Christ at the beginning of his ministry. . . . They say, therefore, that the apostle John, being asked to do it for this reason, gave in his Gospel an account of the period which had been omitted by the earlier evangelists, and of the deeds done by the Saviour during that period; that is, of those which were done before the imprisonment of the Baptist." [37]

» POPE PAUL VI: "Once one begins to be interested in Christ, one's interest can never cease. There is always something more to be known, to be said— infinitely more. St John the Evangelist ends his Gospel making this very point (Jn 21:25). Everything to do with Christ is so rich, there are such depths for us to explore; such light, strength, joy, desire have their source in him. . . . His coming to the world, his presence in history and culture and . . . his vital relationship with our conscience: everything suggests that it is unseemly, unscientific and irreverent ever to think that we need not and cannot advance further in contemplation of Jesus Christ." [38]

---

[37] Ibid., 3, 24, 6–7, 11, in NPNF2 1:152–53.
[38] Paul VI, General Audience, February 20, 1974.

CONCLUDING THOUGHTS

We have come to the end of the Gospel of St. John, but certainly not to the end of the gospel. The gospel once proclaimed—the Incarnation, life, death, and Resurrection of Jesus Christ—begins its actual work in the lives of those who believe. The gospel is alive; it is not just a book. The "good news" is still thundering around the globe, two thousand years after it was first lived, uttered, and written. We are not reading a story of "the past" but experiencing a living account of a living Lord and his living Church. He was not simply a famous figure of the past; he is also a living Person today. John's eyewitness account of the Christ who suffered once and for all and rose again gives us the assurance that this risen Christ is alive and active in the our lives, our world, and the Church. Alleluia!

It is good to go back and meditate on the "overture", the prologue of John's Gospel (Jn 1:1–18). Remember that an overture contains all the musical themes later developed in the symphony and summarized grandly in the "finale". Meditate on the themes presented in the prologue, and thrill at the way they were made manifest in the life of Christ as so beautifully portrayed by the Beloved Disciple. Take a little time sitting under a tree or in the quiet of a eucharistic chapel and slowly read and ponder again this marvelous, living, breathing document. Allow it to saturate your soul.

For all our study, for all the grasping of the text, the spiritual application, and the intellectual challenge, none of this will be profitable to save our souls unless we willingly and humbly bow our knee to Jesus Christ as Thomas did. We must from the heart confess Jesus Christ our Lord and God. And in so confessing we must live our lives righteously before him. To believe alone is insufficient (cf. Jas 2:17–25). We must allow the grace of God, administered through the Paraclete and the Church—the Barque of Peter—to make us believing and righteous.

In John, Jesus tells us, "Do not marvel at this; for the hour is coming when all who are in the tombs will hear his voice and come forth, those who have done good, to the resurrection of life, and those who have done evil, to the resurrection of judgment" (Jn 5:28–29). We will not be judged on our faith only, but on the way we allowed the grace of God, through faith, to work the righteousness of God out in our lives—putting to death the deeds of the flesh if we are to live (Rom 8:13).

St. Paul lived out the heart of the gospel of Christ. He laid down his life and labored to be like Christ. He told the Philippians that he desired to "gain Christ and be found in him, not having a righteousness of my own, based on law, but that which is through faith in Christ, the righteousness from God that depends on faith; that I may know him and the power of his resurrection, and may share his sufferings, becoming like him in his death, that if possible I may attain the resurrection from the dead" (Phil 3:8–11).

St. John lived such a life and died an aged man. We can assume that in his life as in his writings, he continually reminded his friends and family in Christ to love one another. To love one another fulfills all the law of God (Rom 13:8–10) and puts into practice the new commandment given by Christ (Jn 13:34).

BIBLIOGRAPHY

Abbott, Walter M. *The Documents of Vatican II*. New York: American Press, 1966.

Achtemeier, Paul J., ed. *Harper's Bible Dictionary*. San Francisco: Harper & Row, 1985.

Adler, Mortimer, ed. *Great Books of the Western World*. 54 vols. Chicago: Encyclopedia Britannica, 1980.

Apel, Willi, and Ralph T. Daniel. *The Harvard Brief Dictionary of Music*. New York: Pocket Books, 1960.

Archer, Gleason L. *Encyclopedia of Bible Difficulties*. Grand Rapids, Mich.: Zondervan Pub. House, 1982.

Ariel, Yisrael. *The Odyssey of the Third Temple*. Translated by Chaim Richman. Jerusalem: G. Israel Pub. & Productions, Temple Institute [1993?].

Augustine, St. *Homilies on the Gospel of John*. In NPNF1 7.

———. *Tractates on the Gospel of John 28–54*. Translated by John W. Rettig. The Fathers of the Church, vol. 88. Washington, D.C.: Catholic Univ. of America Press, 1993.

———. *Tractates on the Gospel of John 55–111*. Translated by John W. Rettig. The Fathers of the Church, vol. 90. Washington, D.C.: Catholic Univ. of America Press, 1994.

Baker, Kenneth. *Inside the Bible: An Introduction to Each Book of the Bible*. San Francisco: Ignatius Press, 1998.

Barbet, Pierre. *A Doctor at Calvary*. Harrison, N.Y.: Roman Catholic Books, 1953.

Barclay, William. *The Gospel of John*. 2 vols. Philadelphia: Westminster Press, 1975.

———. *The Letters to the Philippians, Colossians, and Thessalonians*. Philadelphia: Westminster Press, 1975.

Barrett, C. K. *The Gospel according to St. John*. London: SPCK, 1970.

———. *The New Testament Background*. San Francisco: HarperSanFrancisco, 1987.

Barrett, David B., ed. *World Christian Encyclopedia*. New York: Oxford Univ. Press, 1982.

————, ed. *World Christian Encyclopedia*. 2d ed. 2 vols. New York: Oxford Univ. Press, 2001.

Beasley-Murray, G. R. *John*. Word Biblical Commentary. Waco, Tex.: Word Books, 1987.

Berington, Joseph, and John Kirk, comps. *The Faith of Catholics*. Edited by T. J. Capel. New York: F. Pustet & Co., 1885.

Bernard, J. H. *A Critical and Exegetical Commentary on the Gospel according to St. John*. Edited by A. H. McNeile. New York: Charles Scribner's Sons, 1929.

Boismard, Marie-Emile. *Moses or Jesus: An Essay in Johannine Christology*. Translated by B. T. Vivian. Minneapolis, Minn.: Fortress Press, 1993.

Braun, Moshe. *The Jewish Holy Days: Their Spiritual Significance*. Northvale, N.J.: Jason Aronson, 1996.

Brown, Raymond E. *The Community of the Beloved Disciple*. Mahwah, N.J.: Paulist Press, 1979.

————, ed. and trans. *The Gospel according to John*. Anchor Bible, vols. 29 and 29A. Garden City, N.Y.: Doubleday, 1966–1970.

————. *An Introduction to the New Testament*. New York: Doubleday, 1997.

————, Karl P. Donfried, and John Reumann. *Peter in the New Testament*. Minneapolis, Minn.: Augsburg Pub. and New York: Paulist Press, 1973.

————, Joseph Fitzmyer, and Roland Murphy, eds. *The Jerome Biblical Commentary*. Englewood Cliffs, N.J.: Prentice-Hall, 1968.

Bruce, F. F. *The Gospel of John*. Grand Rapids, Mich.: William B. Eerdmans, 1983.

Carr, Arthur. *St John the Revised Version*. Cambridge: Cambridge Univ. Press, 1905.

Carroll, Donald. *Mary's House*. London: Veritas Books, 2000.

Carson, D. A. *The Gospel according to John*. Grand Rapids, Mich.: W. B. Eerdmans, 1991.

Casciaro, José María. *The Navarre Bible: The Gospel of Saint John*. 2d ed. Dublin: Four Courts Press, 1992.

Castelot, John J. *Meet the Bible! New Testament*. Baltimore, Md.: Helicon Press, 1963.

Catechism of the Catholic Church. 2d ed. Vatican City: Libreria Editrice Vaticana, 2000.

Cecilia, Madame. *St. John*. Catholic Scripture Manuals. London: Burns, Oates, & Washbourne, 1923.

Charnwood, Godfrey, Lord. *According to Saint John*. Boston: Little, Brown, and Company, 1925.

Charpentier, Etienne. *How to Read the New Testament*. Translated by John Bowden. New York: Crossroad Pub., 1992.

————. *How to Read the Old Testament*. Translated by John Bowden. New York: Crossroad Pub., 1992.

Clement of Rome. *The Epistles of St. Clement of Rome and St. Ignatius of Antioch*. Translated by James A. Kleist. Ancient Christian Writers, no. 1. New York: Newman Press, 1946.

Cole, Alan R. *Exodus*. Tyndale Old Testament Commentaries. Downers Grove, Ill.: InterVarsity Press, 1973 .

Congar, Yves. *I Believe in the Holy Spirit*. Translated by David Smith. New York: Crossroad Pub. Co., 1983.

Crehan, Joseph. *The Theology of St. John*. New York: Sheed and Ward, 1965.

Cross, F. L., ed. *Studies in the Fourth Gospel*. London: A. R. Mowbray & Co., 1957.

Cullmann, Oscar. *Early Christian Worship*. Translated by A. Stewart Todd and James B. Torrance. Philadelphia: Westminster Press, 1953.

Currie, David. *Born Fundamentalist, Born Again Catholic*. San Francisco, Ignatius Press, 1996.

Danby, Herbert, ed. and trans. *The Mishnah*. New York: Oxford Univ. Press, 1933.

Daniel-Rops, Henri. *Daily Life in the Time of Jesus*. Translated by Patrick O'Brian. New York: Hawthorn Books, 1962.

Denzinger, Heinrich. *The Sources of Catholic Dogma*. Translated by Roy J. Deferrari. St. Louis, Mo.: B. Herder Book Co., 1957.

Derbent, Sümer, trans. *Virgin Mary*. Istanbul, Turkey: Kartpostal Sanayi Ve Ticaret, STI, 2000.

De Vaux, Roland. *Ancient Israel: Its Life and Institutions*. Translated by John McHugh. New York: McGraw-Hill, 1961.

Dodd, C. H. *The Interpretation of the Fourth Gospel*. Cambridge: Cambridge Univ. Press, 1953.

Douglas, J. D., ed. *New Bible Dictionary*. Downers Grove, Ill.: InterVarsity Press, 1994.

Duggan, Michael. *The Consuming Fire: A Christian Introduction to the Old Testament*. San Francisco: Ignatius Press, 1991.

Durand, Alfred, Albert Valensin, and Joseph Huby. *The Word of Salvation: A Commentary on the Gospels*. Translated by John J. Heenan. Milwaukee, Bruce Pub. Company, 1957.

Durham, John I. *Exodus*. Word Biblical Commentary, vol. 3. Waco, Tex.: Word Books, 1987.

Early Christian Writings. Translated by Maxwell Staniforth. New York: Penguin Books, 1968.

Easton, M. G. *Illustrated Bible Dictionary*. 3d ed. Nashville: Thomas Nelson, 1897. Published in electronic form by Logos Research Systems, 1996.

Ellis, Peter. *The Genius of John: A Composition-Critical Commentary on the Fourth Gospel*. Collegeville, Minn.: Liturgical Press, 1984.

Elwell, Walter A., ed. *Evangelical Commentary on the Bible*. Grand Rapids, Mich.: Baker Book House Co., 1989. Published in electronic form, as Logos Software 2.1, by Logos Research Systems, 1997.

Enns, Paul P. "Relative Attributes". In *The Moody Handbook of Theology*. Chicago: Moody Press, 1989. Published in electronic form by Logos Research Systems, 1997.

Eusebius. *Church History*. Translated by Arthur Cushman McGiffert. In NPNF2 1.

―――. *The History of the Church from Christ to Constantine*. Translated by G. A. Williamson. Penguin Classics. London: Penguin Books, 1989.

Farmer, William R., ed. *The International Bible Commentary*. Collegeville, Minn.: Liturgical Press, 1998.

Fernández, Andrés. *The Life of Christ*. Translated by Paul Barrett. Westminster, Md.: Newman Press, 1959.

Fitzmyer, Joseph. *The Biblical Commission's Document "The Interpretation of the Bible in the Church"*. Subsidia biblica, 18. Rome: Pontificio Istituto Biblico, 1995.

Flannery, Austin, ed. *Vatican Council II: The Conciliar and Post Conciliar Documents*. New rev. ed. Collegeville, Minn.: Liturgical Press, 1992.

Foreman, Dale M. *Crucify Him: A Lawyer Looks at the Trial of Jesus*. Grand Rapids, Mich.: Zondervan, 1990. Published in electronic form by Logos Library System.

Fouard, Constant. *The Christ: The Son of God*. Translated by George F. X. Griffith. 2 vols. New York: Longmans, Green, and Co., 1903.

Free, Joseph P. *Archaeology and Bible History*. Revised by Howard F. Vos. Grand Rapids, Mich.: Zondervan Pub. House, 1992.

Freedman, David Noel, ed. *The Anchor Bible Dictionary*. New York: Doubleday, 1996. Published in electronic form by Logos Library System.

Fuentes, A. *Book by Book: A Guide to the Bible.* Dublin: Four Courts Press, 1993.

Fuller, Reginald, ed. *A New Catholic Commentary on Holy Scripture.* Nashville, Tenn.: Thomas Nelson Pub., 1984.

Gilbert, T. B. *Hymns of Truth and Praise.* Fort Dodge, Iowa: Gospel Perpetuating Pub., 1971.

Giuliani, Giovanni. *Guide to Saint Peter's Basilica.* Rome: ATS Italia, 1995.

Glasson, T. F. *Moses in the Fourth Gospel.* Napierville, Ill.: Alec R. Allenson, 1963.

Gower, Ralph. *The New Manners and Customs of Bible Times.* Chicago: Moody Press, 1987.

Graham, Henry G. *Where We Got the Bible: Our Debt to the Catholic Church.* San Diego, Calif.: Catholic Answers, 1997.

Green, Joel B., and Scot McKnight. *Dictionary of Jesus and the Gospels.* Downers Grove, Ill.: InterVarsity Press, 1992.

Grisar, Hartmann. *Luther.* Translated by E. M. Lamond. 6 vols. St. Louis, Mo.: B. Herder Book Co., 1919.

Guardini, Romano. *The Lord.* Washington, D.C.: Regnery Publishing, 1982.

Guthrie, Donald. *New Testament Introduction.* 3d rev. ed. Downers Grove, Ill.: InterVarsity Press, 1970.

Hardon, John A. *The Catholic Catechism.* Garden City, N.Y.: Doubleday, 1981.

Harvey, Van A. *A Handbook of Theological Terms.* New York: Macmillan Pub., 1964.

Haydock, George Leo, comp. *The Douay-Rheims New Testament with Catholic Commentary.* Monrovia, Calif.: Catholic Treasures, 1991.

Hayes, John H., and Carl R. Holladay. *Biblical Exegesis: A Beginner's Handbook.* London: SCM Press, 1997.

Hendriksen, William. *New Testament Commentary.* Vol. 1: *Exposition of the Gospel according to John.* Grand Rapids, Mich.: Baker Book, 1953.

Herbermann, Charles G., ed. *The Catholic Encyclopedia.* 15 vols. New York: Robert Appleton Company, 1907.

Hertz, Rabbi Joseph H., trans. *Mishnah: Sayings of the Fathers.* New York: Behrman House, 1945.

Hoade, Eugene. *Guide to the Holy Land.* Jerusalem: Franciscan Printing Press, n.d.

Hophan, Otto. *The Apostles.* Translated by L. Edward Wasserman. Westminster, Md.: Newman Press, 1962.

————. *Mary, Our Most Blessed Lady*. Translated by Berchmans Bittle. Milwaukee: Bruce Pub., 1959.

John Chrysostom, St. *Homilies on the Gospel of St. John*. Translated by G. T. Stupart. In NPNF1 14.

John Paul II. *Letter of the Holy Father John Paul II to Priests for Holy Thursday 1988*. Boston, Mass.: St. Paul's Books & Media.

————. *Mission of the Redeemer*. Boston, Mass.: St. Paul's Books & Media, 1990.

————. *Mother of the Redeemer*. Boston, Mass.: St. Paul's Books & Media, 1987.

Josephus, Flavius. *Josephus: Complete Works*. Translated by William Whiston. Grand Rapids, Mich.: Kregel Pubs., 1978.

Jurgens, William A. *The Faith of the Early Fathers*. 3 vols. Collegeville, Minn.: Liturgical Press, 1970–1979.

Kaiser, Walter C., Jr., et al., eds. *Hard Sayings of the Bible*. Downers Grove, Ill.: InterVarsity Press, 1996.

Karris, Robert J., ed. *The Collegeville Bible Commentary: New Testament*. Collegeville, Minn.: Liturgical Press, 1992.

————. *A Symphony of New Testament Hymns*. Collegeville, Minn.: Liturgical Press, 1996.

Kavanaugh, Patrick. *Music of the Great Composers*. Grand Rapids, Mich.: Zondervan Pub. House, 1996.

Keating, Karl. *Catholicism and Fundamentalism: The Attack on "Romanism" by "Bible Christians"*. San Francisco: Ignatius Press, 1988.

Keener, Craig. *The IVP Bible Background Commentary: New Testament*. Downers Grove, Ill.: InterVarsity Press, 1993.

Knecht, Frederick Justus. *A Practical Commentary on Holy Scripture*. St. Louis, Mo.: B. Herder, 1930.

Knox, Ronald. *A Commentary on the Gospels*. New York: Sheed & Ward, 1952–1956.

Köstenberger, Andreas J. *Encountering John*. Grand Rapids, Mich.: Baker Books, 1999.

Kreeft, Peter, and Ronald K. Tacelli. *Handbook of Christian Apologetics*. Downers Grove, Ill.: InterVarsity Press, 1994.

La Potterie, Ignace de. *The Hour of Jesus: The Passion and the Resurrection of Jesus according to John*. Translated by Gregory Murray. New York: Alba House, 1989.

Lattey, C. *Catholic Faith in the Holy Eucharist*. St. Louis, Mo.: B. Herder Book Co., 1923.

Laux, John. *Introduction to the Bible*. Rockford, Ill.: TAN Books, 1990.

Lee-Thorp, Karen, ed. *John*. Lifechange Series. Colorado Springs, Col.: Navpress, 1987.

Légasse, Simon. *The Trial of Jesus*. Translated by John Bowden. London: SCM Press, 1997.

Léon-Dufour, Xavier, ed. *Dictionary of Biblical Theology*. Translated by P. Joseph Cahill. New York: Desclée Co., 1967.

Lewis, C. S. *The Four Loves*. London: Collins, 1960.

Lightfoot, J. B. *Commentary on the New Testament from the Talmud and Hebraica*. 4 vols. Peabody, Mass.: Hendrickson Pub., 1995.

Lightfoot, R. H. *St. John's Gospel: A Commentary*. Oxford: Clarendon Press, 1956.

Louw, Johannes P., and Eugene A. Nida, eds. *Greek-English Lexicon of the New Testament*. 2d ed. New York: United Bible Societies, 1989. Published in electronic form by Logos Research Systems, 1996.

Lukefahr, Oscar. *A Catholic Guide to the Bible*. Liguori, Mo.: Liguori, 1992.

Luther, Martin. *Sermons on the Gospel of St. John Chapters 1–4*. Vol. 22 of *Luther's Works*, translated by Martin H. Bertram. St. Louis, Mo.: Concordia Pub. House, 1957.

MacEvilly, John. *An Exposition of the Gospel of St. John*. New York: Benzinger Bros., 1889.

MacGregor, G. H. C. *Moffit New Testament Commentary: The Gospel of John*. New York and London: Harper and Brothers Pub., 1928.

MacRory, Joseph. *The Gospel of St. John*. Ireland: Browne and Nolan, 1923.

Manelli, Stephano M. *All Generations Shall Call Me Blessed*. New Bedford, Mass.: Academy of the Immaculate, 1989.

Mare, W. Harold. *The Archaeology of the Jerusalem Area*. Grand Rapids, Mich.: Baker Book House, 1987.

Marrow, Stanley B. *The Gospel of John: A Reading*. Mahwah, N.J.: Paulist Press, 1995.

Marsh, John. *The Gospel of St John*. Baltimore, Md.: Penguin Books, 1968.

Martin, Walter R. *The Kingdom of the Cults*. Minneapolis, Minn.: Bethany House Pubs., 1982.

Martindale, C. C. *The Gospel According to Saint John*. Stonyhurst Scripture Manuals. Westminster, Md.: Newman Press, 1957.

Mays, James L. *Harper's Bible Commentary* San Francisco: Harper & Row, 1988. Published in electronic form by Logos Research Systems.

McBirnie, William Steuart. *The Search for the Twelve Apostles*. Wheaton, Ill.: Tyndale House Pub., 1973.

McBride, Alfred. *The Divine Presence of Jesus: Meditation and Commentary on the Gospel of John*. Huntington, Ind.: Our Sunday Visitor, 1992.

McGee, J. Vernon. *Thru the Bible Commentary*. Vol. 41: *John Chapters 1–10*. Nashville, Tenn.: Thomas Nelson Pub., 1991.

————. *Thru the Bible Commentary*. Vol. 41: *John Chapters 11–21*. Nashville, Tenn.: Thomas Nelson Pub., 1991.

McIntyre, John. *The Holy Gospel according to Saint John*. London: Catholic Truth Society, 1899).

McKenzie, John L. *Dictionary of the Bible*. New York: Touchstone Books, 1995.

McManners, John, ed. *The Oxford Illustrated History of Christianity*. New York: Oxford Univ. Press, 1992.

Moloney, Francis. *The Gospel of John*. Sacra Pagina, vol. 4. Collegeville, Minn.: Liturgical Press, 1998.

Morris, Leon. *The Gospel according to John*. The New International Commentary on the New Testament. Grand Rapids, Mich.: Wm. B. Eerdmans Pub., 1971).

————. *Jesus is the Christ: Studies in the Theology of John*. Grand Rapids, Mich.: William B. Eerdmans, 1989.

Moser, Johann, ed., *O Holy Night: Masterworks of Christmas Poetry*. Manchester, N.H.: Sophia Institute Press, 1995.

Most, William G. *Free from All Error*. Libertyville, Ill.: Marytown Press, 1990.

Murphy-O'Connor, Jerome. *The Holy Land*. 4th ed. New York: Oxford Univ. Press, 1998.

Murray, Daniel, ed. *Every Catholic's Guide to the Sacred Scriptures*. Nashville, Tenn.: Thomas Nelson Pub., 1990.

Neuner, J., and Jacques Dupuis, eds. *The Christian Faith in the Doctrinal Documents of the Catholic Church*. New York: Alba House, 1996.

Neuser, Jacob, ed. *Dictionary of Judaism in the Biblical Period*. Peabody, Mass.: Hendrickson Pub., 1999.

————, trans. *The Mishnah: A New Translation*. New Haven & London: Yale Univ. Press, 1988. Published in electronic form by Logos Research Systems.

New Dictionary of Theology. Edited by Sinclair B. Ferguson, David F. Wright, and J. I. Packer. Downers Grove, Ill.: InterVarsity Press, 1988.

Newman, John Henry Cardinal. *Favorite Newman Sermons*. Compiled by Daniel M. O'Connell. New York: Spiritual Book Assoc., 1940.

———. *Mary the Second Eve*. Compiled by Eileen Breen. Rockford, Ill.: TAN Books, 1982.

———. *Parochial and Plain Sermons*. San Francisco: Ignatius Press, 1987.

New World Bible Translation Committee. *The Kingdom Interlinear Translation of the Greek Scriptures*. Brooklyn, N.Y.: Watchtower Bible and Tract Society, 1969.

New World Dictionary-Concordance to the New American Bible World. New York: World Pub., 1970.

Nouvelle, Abbé. *Our Lord's Last Discourses: Meditations on Chapters XIII–XVIII of the Gospel of St. John*. Translated by M. E. M. London: Burns Oates & Washbourne, 1921.

Office of Readings according to the Roman Rite. Boston, Mass.: Daughters of St. Paul, 1983.

O'Grady, John F. *According to John, the Witness of the Beloved Disciple*. Mahwah, N.J.: Paulist Press, 1999.

O'Hare, Patrick. *The Facts about Luther*. Rockford, Ill.: TAN Books, 1987.

Orchard, Dom Bernard, ed. *A Catholic Commentary on Holy Scripture*. New York: Thomas Nelson Pub., 1953.

Orr, James, ed. *The International Standard Bible Encyclopedia*. 1915. Albany, Ore.: Ages Software, 1999.

Ott, Ludwig. *Fundamentals of Catholic Dogma*. Translated by Patrick Lynch. Edited by James Canon Bastible. Rockford, Ill.: TAN Books, 1960.

Paul VI. *Devotion to the Blessed Virgin Mary*. Boston, Mass.: St. Paul's Books & Media, 1974.

———. *On Evangelism in the Modern World*. Boston, Mass.: St. Paul's Books & Media, n.d.

Peterson, Galen. *Handbook of Bible Festivals*. Cincinnati, Ohio: Standard Pub. Co., 1997.

Pfeiffer, Charles F. *The Wycliffe Bible Encyclopedia*. Chicago, Ill.: Moody Press, 1975. Published in electronic form by Logos Research Systems.

Pixner, Bargil. *With Jesus in Jerusalem*. Rosh Pina, Israel: Corazin Pub., 1996.

Plaut, Gunther W., ed. *The Torah: A Modern Commentary*. New York: Union of American Hebrew Congregations, 1981.

Pohle, Joseph. *The Divine Trinity*. St. Louis, Mo.: B. Herder Book Co., 1925.

————. *God: His Knowability, Essence, and Attributes*. Adapted and edited by Arthur Preuss. St. Louis, Mo.: B. Herder Book Co., 1925.

Poulin, P. Eugene. *The Holy Virgin's House*. Istanbul, Turkey: Arikan Yayainlari, 1999.

Prat, Ferdinand. *Jesus Christ: His Life, His Teaching, and His Work*. Translated by John J. Heenan. Milwaukee: Bruce Pub. Co., 1950.

Quasten, Johannes. *Patrology*. 4 vols. Westminster, Md.: Christian Classics, 1993.

Quatman, George B. *House of Our Lady: The Story of the Virgin Mary's Last Years*. Revised by Joseph B. Quatman. Lima, Ohio: American Society of Ephesus, 1991.

Ray, Stephen K. *Crossing the Tiber: Evangelical Protestants Discover the Historical Church*. San Francisco: Ignatius Press, 1997.

————. *Upon This Rock: St. Peter and the Primacy of Rome in Scripture and the Early Church*. San Francisco: Ignatius Press, 1999.

Reid, Daniel G., ed. *Dictionary of Christianity in America*. Downers Grove, Ill.: InterVarsity Press, 1990.

Ricci, Giulio. *Guide to the Photographic Exhibit of the Holy Shroud*. Milwaukee: Center for the Study of the Passion of Christ and the Holy Shroud, 1982.

————. *The Holy Shroud*. Rome: Centro Romano di Sindonologia, 1981.

————. *The Way of the Cross in the Light of the Holy Shroud*. Rome: Centro Romano di Sindonologia, 1975.

Ricciotti, Giuseppe. *The Life of Christ*. Translated by Alba I. Zizzamia. Milwaukee: Bruce Pub., 1947.

Ripley, Francis. *The Last Gospel: Doctrinal and Spiritual Conferences on the Opening Verses of St. John's Gospel*. New York: Sheed & Ward, 1961.

Robert, A., and A. Tricot. *Guide to the Bible*. Translated by Edward P. Arbez and Martin R. P. McGuire. 2 vols. New York: Desclèe Co., 1960.

Roberts, Alexander, and James Donaldson, eds. *The Ante-Nicene Fathers*. 10 vols. Grand Rapids, Mich.: Wm. B. Eerdmans, 1985.

Robertson, A. T. *Word Pictures in the New Testament*. 6 vols. Grand Rapids, Mich.: Baker Book House, 1930–1933.

Rousseau, John J., and Rami Arav. *Jesus and His World: An Archeological and Cultural Dictionary*. Minneapolis, Minn.: Fortress Press, 1995.

Ruffin, C. Bernard. *The Twelve: The Lives of the Apostles after Calvary.* Huntington, Ind.: Our Sunday Visitor, 1984.

Rutler, George William. *Brightest and Best: Stories of Hymns.* San Francisco: Ignatius Press, 1998.

Ryken, Leland, James C. Wilhoit, and Tremper Longman III, eds. *Dictionary of Biblical Imagery.* Downers Grove, Ill.: InterVarsity Press, 1998.

Schaeffer, Francis A. *He Is There and He Is Not Silent.* In *The Complete Works of Francis A. Schaeffer.* Westchester, Ill.: Crossway Books, 1982.

Schaff, Philip. *History of the Christian Church.* 8 vols. Grand Rapids, Mich.: Wm. B. Eerdmans Pub., 1907.

―――, ed. *Nicene and Post-Nicene Fathers.* 1st series. 14 vols. Grand Rapids, Mich.: Wm. B. Eerdmans, 1980.

――― and Henry Wace. *Nicene and Post-Nicene Fathers.* 2d series. 14 vols. Grand Rapids, Mich.: Wm. B. Eerdmans, 1982.

Schmiedel, Paul W. *The Johannine Writings.* Translated by Maurice A. Canney. London: Adam and Charles Black, 1908.

Schuster, Ignatius. *Bible History.* Ft. Collins, Co.: Roman Catholic Books, 1956.

Schwarz, Hans. *Eschatology.* Grand Rapids, Mich.: William B. Eerdmans Pub., 2000.

Second Vatican Council. *Dei Verbum* (Constitution on Divine Revelation). Washington, D.C.: United States Catholic Conference, 1965.

Senior, Donald. *The Passion of Jesus in the Gospel of John.* Collegeville, Minn.: Order of St. Benedict, 1991.

Shank, Robert. *Life in the Son: A Study of the Doctrine of Perseverance.* Minneapolis, Minn.: Bethany House Pub., 1989.

Shea, Mark. *By What Authority? An Evangelical Discovers Catholic Tradition.* Huntington, Ind.: Our Sunday Visitor, 1996.

Sheed, Frank J. *Theology and Sanity.* San Francisco: Ignatius Press, 1978.

Sheen, Fulton. *Life of Christ.* New York: Image Books/Doubleday, 1990.

Socías, James, ed. *Handbook of Prayers.* Princeton, N.J.: Scepter Pub., 1995.

Sproul, R. C. *Essential Truths of the Christian Faith.* Wheaton, Ill.: Tyndale House Pubs., 1992.

Stein, Robert H. *Difficult Passages in the New Testament.* Grand Rapids, Mich.: Baker Book House, 1990.

Steinmueller, John E. *A Companion to Scripture Studies*. New York: Joseph F. Wagner, 1946.

————, and Kathryn Sullivan. *Catholic Biblical Encyclopedia*. New York: Joseph F. Wagner, 1956.

Stern, David H. *Jewish New Testament Commentary*. Clarksville, Md.: Jewish New Testament Pubs., 1992.

Storme, Albert. *Bethany*. Translated by Gerard Bushell. Jerusalem: Franciscan Printing Press, 1992.

Stravinskas, Peter. *The Catholic Church and the Bible*. San Francisco: Ignatius Press, 1987.

————. "Grace". In *Our Sunday Visitor's Catholic Dictionary*. Huntington, Ind.: Our Sunday Visitor Pub., 1991. Electronic edition.

Strickert, Fred. *Bethsaida: Home of the Apostles*. Collegeville, Minn.: Liturgical Press, 1998.

Suffi, Nicolo. *St. Peter's Guide to the Square and the Basilica*. Translated by Kate Marcelin-Rice. Vatican City: Libreria Editrice Vaticana, 1999.

Sungenis, Robert A. *Not by Faith Alone: The Biblical Evidence for the Catholic Doctrine of Justification*. Santa Barbara, Calif.: Queenship Pub., 1997.

————. *Not by Scripture Alone: A Catholic Critique of the Protestant Doctrine of Sola Scriptura*. Santa Barbara, Calif.: Queenship Pub., 1997.

Tasker, R. V. G. *The Gospel According to St. John*. Tyndale New Testament Commentaries. Grand Rapids, Mich: Wm. B. Eerdmans, 1977.

Temple, William. *Readings in St John's Gospel*. London: Macmillan & Co., 1961.

Tenney, Merrill C. *John*. Vol. 9 of *Expositor's Bible Commentary*, edited by Frank E. Gaebelein. Grand Rapids, Mich.: Zondervan Pub., 1981.

Theological Dictionary of the New Testament. Edited by Gerhard Kittel and Gerhard Friedrich. Translated by Geoffrey W. Bromiley. Abridged in one volume by Geoffrey W. Bromiley. Grand Rapids, Mich.: William B. Eerdmans Pub., 1985.

Thierry, Elie Remy. *The Mystery of Mother Mary's House in Ephesus*. (No publishing information available; publication purchased in Ephesus at Mary's House.)

Thiessen, Henry Clarence. *Introductory Lectures in Systematic Theology*. Grand Rapids, Mich.: William B. Eerdmans Pub., 1949.

Thomas, David. *The Genius of the Fourth Gospel*. R. D. Dickenson, 1885. Electronic edition: Oak Harbor: Logos Research Systems, 1997.

Thomas Aquinas, St. *Catena Aurea: St. John.* Vols. 1 and 2. Albany, N.Y.:
    Preserving Christian Publications, 1995.
————. *Commentary on the Gospel of St. John.* Vol. 1. Albany, N.Y.: Magi
    Books, 1980.
————. *Commentary on the Gospel of St. John.* Vol. 2. Petersham, Mass.:
    St. Bede's Pub., n.d.
Towers, E. *Sanctifying Grace.* London: Burns Oates & Washbourne, 1930.
Trench, G. H. *A Study of St John's Gospel.* London: John Murray, 1918.
Trench, Richard, C. *Notes on the Miracles of our Lord.* Grand Rapids,
    Mich.: Baker Book House, 1976.
————. *Synonyms of the New Testament.* Grand Rapids, Mich.: Wm. B.
    Eerdmans Pub., 1973.
Vatican Documents on CD ROM, Church Documents. 6th ed. Boston:
    Mass.: Pauline Books & Media, 1999.
Vine, W. E. *An Expository Dictionary of Biblical Words.* Nashville, Tenn.:
    Thomas Nelson Pub., 1984.
von Speyr, Adrienne. *John.* Vol. 1: *The Word Becomes Flesh: Meditations on
    John 1–5.* Translated by Sr. Lucia Wiedenhöver, O.C.D. and
    Alexander Dru. San Francisco, Ignatius Press, 1994.
————. *John.* Vol. 2: *The Discourses of Controversy: Meditations on John
    6–12.* Translated by Brian McNeil, C.R.V. San Francisco, Ignatius
    Press, 1993.
————. *John.* Vol. 3: *The Farewell Discourses: Meditations on John 13–17.*
    Translated by E. A. Nelson. San Francisco, Ignatius Press, 1987.
————. *John.* Vol. 4: *The Birth of the Church: Meditations on John 18–21.*
    Translated by David Kipp. San Francisco: Ignatius Press, 1991.
Vos, Howard. *Effective Bible Study: A Guide to Sixteen Methods.* Grand
    Rapids, Mich.: Zondervan, 1975.
Wachsmann, Shelley. *The Sea of Galilee Boat: An Extraordinary 2000-Year-
    Old Discovery.* New York: Plenum Press, 1995.
Watkins, H. W. *The Gospel According to St. John.* New York: Cassell & Co.
    [1880?].
Watkins, James, ed. *Manual of Prayers.* Rome: Pontifical North Ameri-
    can College, 1998.
Westcott, B. F. *The Gospel According to St. John.* London: John Murray,
    1903.
Wigoder, Geoffrey. *Encyclopedia Judaica Multimedia.* Jerusalem: Judaica
    Multimedia (Israel), 1997. CD-ROM edition version 1.0.
Wilken, Robert. *The Christians as the Romans Saw Them.* New Haven:
    Yale Univ. Press, 1984.

Zibawi, Mahmoud, *The Icon: Its Meaning and History.* Collegeville, Minn.: Liturgical Press, 1993.

Zohary, Michael. *Plants of the Bible.* New York: Cambridge Univ. Press, 1982.

AKNOWLEDGMENTS

The author and publisher express their appreciation for permissions to reprint passages from the following publications:

Quotations from the *Catena Aurea* of St. Thomas Aquinas are taken from the edition published by Preserving Christian Publications, Inc., P.O. Box 6129, Albany, New York 12206. First published 1842 by John Henry Parker, London. First printing 1993, 2nd printing 1995, 3rd printing 1998, 4th printing 2000.

Quotations from *The Gospel According to John and the Johannine Epistles*, by Neal M. Flanagan, O.S.M., *The Collegeville Bible Commentary: New Testament*, volume 4, copyright © 1992 by the Order of St. Benedict, Inc. Published by The Liturgical Press, Collegeville, Minnesota. Used with permission. All rights reserved.

Quotations from *The Gospel According to John I–XII, XIII–XXI (Anchor Bible)*, by Raymond E. Brown, copyright © 1966, 1970 by Doubleday, a division of Bantam, Doubleday, Dell Publishing Group, Inc. Used by permission of Doubleday, a division of Random House, Inc. All rights reserved.

Quotations from F. F. Bruce, *The Gospel of John*, © 1983 by F. F. Bruce, published in the United States by Wm. B. Eerdmans Publishing Company, Grand Rapids, Michigan. Reprinted by permission of the publisher. All rights reserved.

Quotations from *IVP Bible Background Commentary: New Testament*, by Craig Keener, © 1993 by Craig Keener. Used by permission of InterVarsity Press, P.O. Box 1400, Downers Grove, Illinois, 60515.

Quotations taken from the *Jewish New Testament Commentary*, copyright 1992 by David H. Stern and used with permission of Jewish New Testament Publications, Inc., P.O. Box 615, Clarksville, Maryland 21029. All rights reserved. Available through Messianic Jewish Resources. www.messianicjewish.net.

Quotations from the *Navarre Bible, Saint John*, are reproduced with kind permission of Four Courts Press, Dublin. All rights reserved. First edition 1987. Second impression (with corrections) 1992. Second edition 1992.

INDEX OF SCRIPTURE

INDEX OF TOPICS